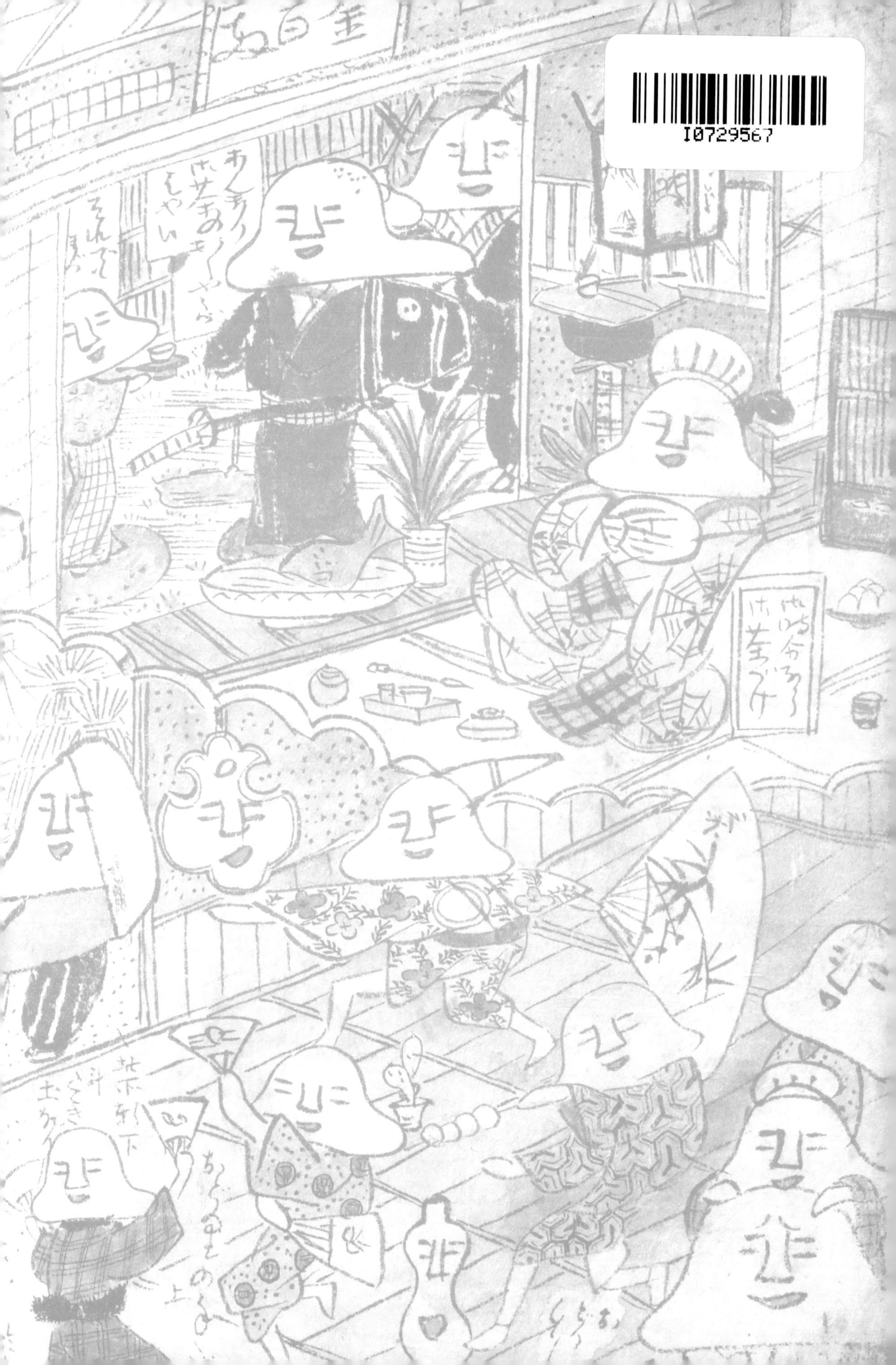
I0729567

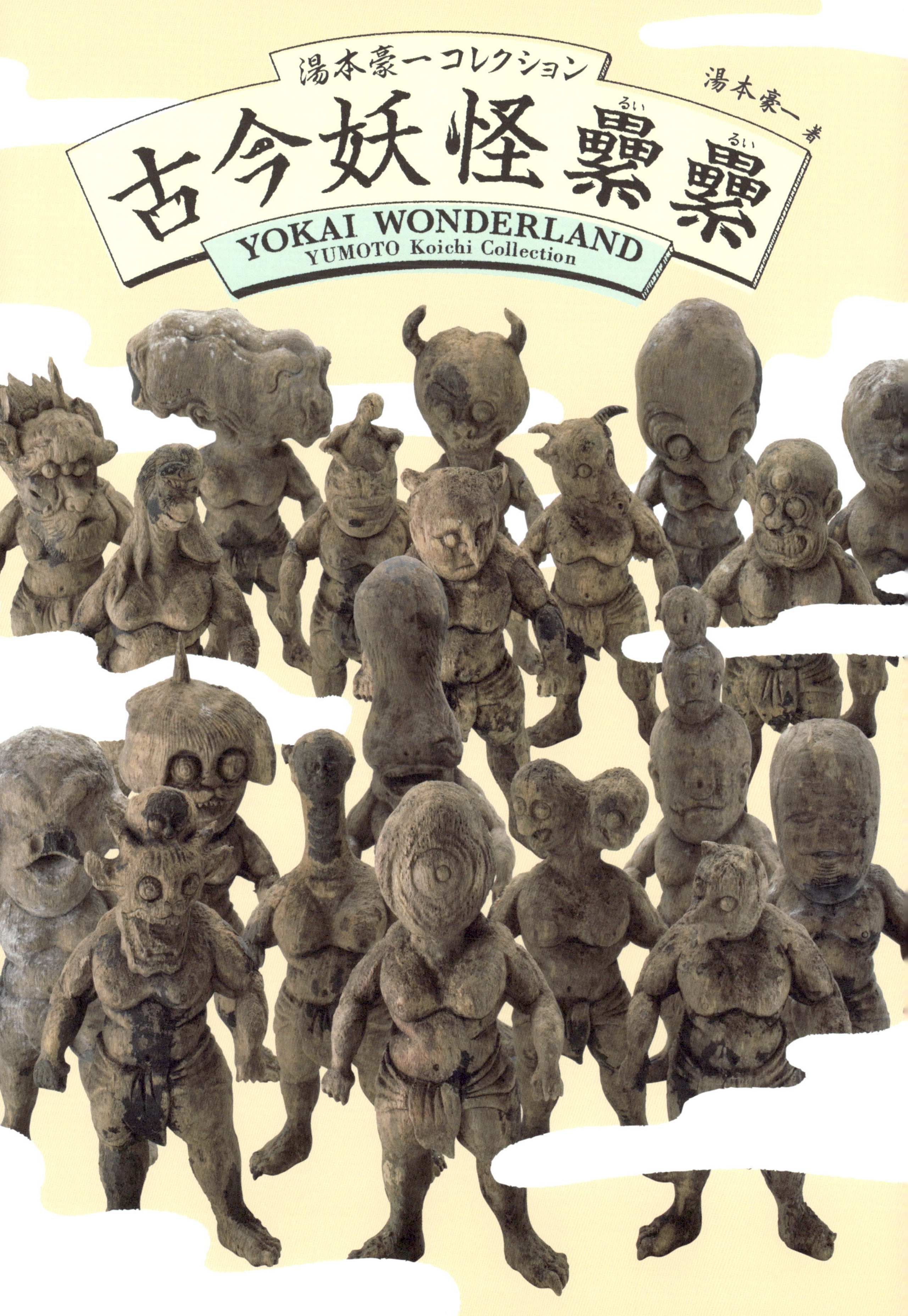

湯本豪一コレクション
湯本豪一 著
古今妖怪纍纍
るい　るい
YOKAI WONDERLAND
YUMOTO Koichi Collection

はじめに Introduction

　2013 年 7 月、『今昔妖怪大鑑 — 湯本豪一コレクション』を刊行して多種多様な妖怪資料を紹介し、妖怪文化が時代を越えていかに広く伝えられて来たかを俯瞰した。その方法として絵巻、本、錦絵といった分類に加えて「妖怪遊び」「生活のなかにひそむ妖怪」「祈りと妖怪」といった視点からも立項して日常の暮らしのなかに妖怪文化が深く浸透していたことをみてきた。しかし、紙幅が限られていたこともあり幾多の妖怪資料の一部を掲載したに過ぎなかったことに鑑み、さらに様々な資料を提示して『今昔妖怪大鑑 — 湯本豪一コレクション』と併せて見ていただくことで "紙上妖怪博物館" 的役割を果たせればと思っている。

　本書の章立ては、絵巻をはじめとした肉筆を収録した「妖怪絵の世界」、江戸時代の木版絵を中心に収録した「印刷の妖怪たち」、紙に描かれた作品以外の数々の資料を収録した「あらゆるモノになる妖怪」に大別している。

第 1 章「妖怪絵の世界」

　肉筆は 1 点 1 点描くことから同じ画題でも同一のものは存在しない。連綿と描き継がれていた百鬼夜行絵巻でも妖怪の順番が入れ替わっていたり、新たな妖怪が挿入されたりと千差万別といった観がある。彩色の指定を添え書きした下絵など、作品として完成するまでのプロセスを確認できる資料も散見できる。また、肉筆のなかには類例のない作品も存在しており、妖怪絵の世界は多くの見どころを有している。絵巻一つとっても著名な絵師の筆による作品から素人が描いたようなものまで確認できて、その幅広さに驚かされるほどで、

My first book *Yokai Museum: The Art of Japanese Supernatural Beings from Yumoto Koichi Collection* was published in July 2013, and showcased a diverse array of materials featuring yokai (demonic creatures), illustrating how the culture of yokai has transcended time and spread widely. In that book, the saturation of yokai culture throughout daily life is explored under the chapter headings of "Yokai Games", "Yokai Lurking in Everyday Life", and "Yokai and Prayer", in addition to the categories of scrolls, books, and *nishiki-e* (multicolored woodblock prints). However, as space was limited, it was only possible to fit a tiny fraction of the multitude of materials into the first book, and so this book serves alongside the first as a "paper museum" presenting a broader spectrum of works.

　The contents of this book are as follows:
- "Chapter 1: The World of Yokai Art" is a collection of original works, including picture scrolls.
As each work is hand drawn line by line, no two are the same even if the same subject has been chosen. With such seemingly infinite variations, even the picture scroll of the Night Parade of One Hundred Demons (*Hyakki Yagyō*), which has been continually recreated for generations, has changed its lineup and gained fresh faces. Also of interest are works in progress where the process towards completion can be seen, such as sketches with color-coding directions written on them. In addition, among these originals are many highlights of the world of yokai art, works so unique they exist in a class of their own. The appeal of original works

肉筆の魅力を発散している。

第2章「印刷の妖怪たち」
　いっぽうで江戸時代を中心に木版印刷による妖怪絵も多数世に送り出された。木版印刷は同じものを同時に多くの人が見ることを可能にした。これによって妖怪文化は飛躍的な広がりを持つようになり、情報の統一という新しい状況を生み出していった。おもちゃ絵、双六などの遊びのなかに妖怪が登場するのもこうした広がりのなかでのことだ。妖怪たちは木版印刷を糧として棲息地を劇的に広げていったのだ。

第3章「あらゆるモノになる妖怪」
　そのしたたかな生命力は絵巻や錦絵といった紙の世界にとどまることなく、人々の身近な品々にも足跡を刻んでいった。着物、帯、印籠、根付といった身につけるものから鍔や小柄といった武具さえも彼らの営巣地となっていったのだ。かくて妖怪は心の不安や自然に対する畏怖の象徴にとどまらず、人々の身近にあって親しまれる存在へと変身を遂げたのだ。その千変万化する姿はまるで万華鏡のなかで展開される妖しく不思議な世界を覗くような観さえある。

　本書ではこのように変化を繰り返しながら輝き続ける妖怪たちの軌跡を俯瞰しようとするものである。そのなかには初めて紹介される資料も多々含まれているので楽しんで見ていただけると思う。初公開となる100体の坐像、36体の立像、20体の件像などの木彫群は一堂に会すると不気味な威圧感さえ感じさせるほどだ。いっぽうで、『人面草紙』なる"奇書"も初めて公開するべく一部を収録した。直接的には妖怪とはいえないかもしれないが、シュールなキャラクターが細密に描かれた想像を絶する画面からは、妖怪という姿を生み出した驚くほどの想像力と相通じるものが脈々と息づいているようであり、そんなことから

is evident in the many different versions of a single picture scroll, which cover a surprising range from masterpieces by famous artists to recreations by amateurs.

- "Chapter 2: Yokai of Prints" is a collection centered on woodblock prints of the Edo period.
In the Edo period, yokai art was sent out into the world in the form of woodblock prints. These prints made it possible for a large audience to view the same image simultaneously. Yokai culture spread exponentially through this medium and a new uniformity of content was produced. Riding high on their newfound popularity, yokai appeared in *omocha-e* (lit. "toy pictures") and *sugoroku* (board games). Yokai flourished in these habitats, nourished by the new mediums.

- "Chapter 3: Yokai of Things" is a collection of materials which use media other than paper. The vital force of the yokai in the previous chapter grew so strong that they burst from the confines of the world of paper, scrolls and woodblock prints, and made their marks on the items closest to people's hearts. From items worn on one's person such as kimono, *obi* sashes, *inrō* (cases for small objects worn suspended from *obi*), *netsuke* (miniature carvings used as fasteners) to sword guards, *kozuka* (knives) and armor; all of these became their nesting places. In this way yokai moved beyond the boundaries of the dark shadows of the heart or the personification of wonder in nature, and developed a new familiarity with people. These ever-changing figures are glimpsed as if peering into a kaleidoscope at a bewitching world of mystery.

　This book aims to give an overview of the path the yokai have taken, constantly evolving as they continue to intrigue us. In this book are many works which have not been

あえて収録している。妖怪絵の周辺にも光を当てる提言になればとの想いだ。

　以上、本書はいくつかの試みをも含めて構成されており、一風変わった妖怪本になっているかもしれないが、ご寛恕をお願いしたい。

湯本豪一

previously revealed to the public, which we are happy to present for the first time. In Chapter 3 are statues carved out of wood (100 seated, 36 standing, and 20 of human-faced bovine *kudan*), which when seen together have an intimidating, powerful presence. As a special premiere, the unique book *Jinmen Zōshi* (*The Book of Faces*) is also presented for the first time. While perhaps not directly classifiable as yokai, one can imagine a similar force is strongly alive in the finely-drawn scenes of surreal characters beyond one's wildest imaginings, with an amazing creativity such as that which gave rise to the figures of yokai. This collection been collated around these points. The context of yokai images offers us an illuminating perspective.

　In conclusion, please recognize that this book may be a very different sort of book to my first, and contains a number of experimental works.

Yumoto Koichi

凡例
・作品解説中に登場する参考書籍『今昔妖怪大鑑』（パイ インターナショナル刊）は、湯本豪一コレクションを紹介したシリーズ第1作の書籍です。
・一部の作品解説は、巻末に収録しました。
・作品寸法の単位は、センチメートルです。
・絵巻は紙面の制約から部分図を掲載しました。
・絵巻は画面の右から左へと展開するものです。

Please note:
· The book Yokai Museum which is referenced in the descriptions of works is the first volume of the Yumoto Koichi Collection series (published by PIE International).
· Some descriptions of works appear at the end of this book.
· All dimensions are given in centimeters.
· Due to page constraints, picture scrolls are only shown in part.
· Picture scrolls read from right to left on the page.

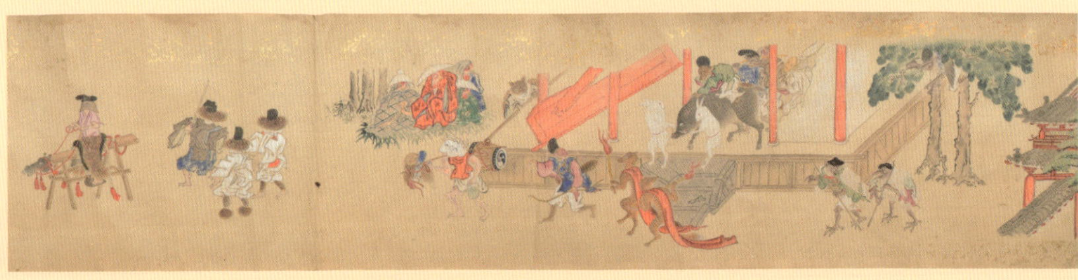

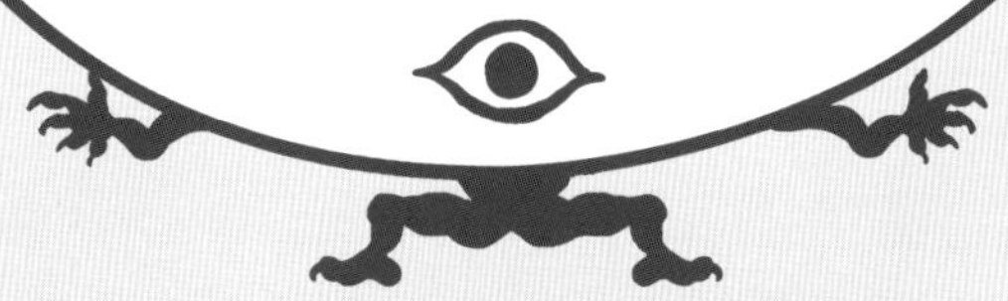

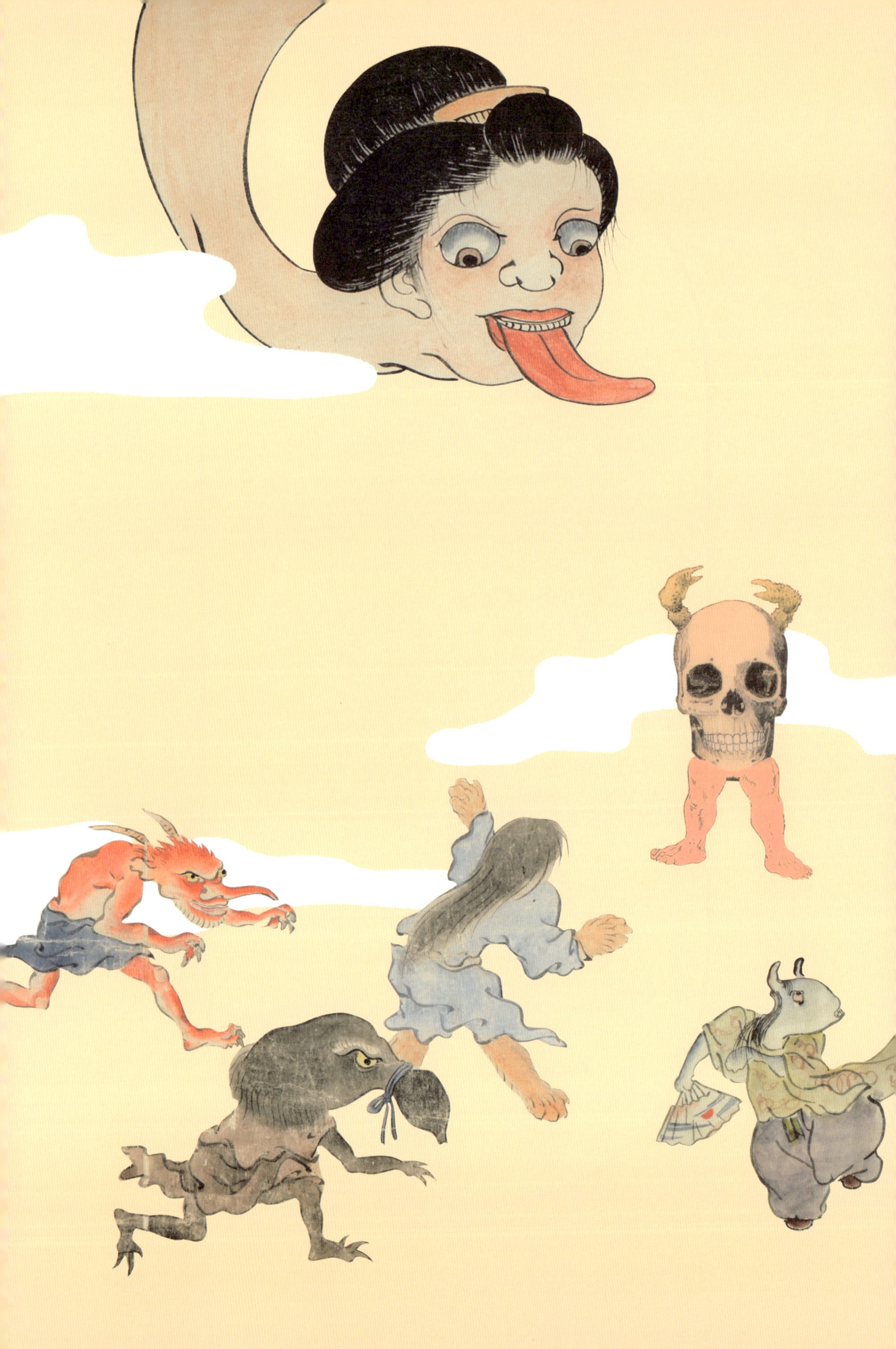

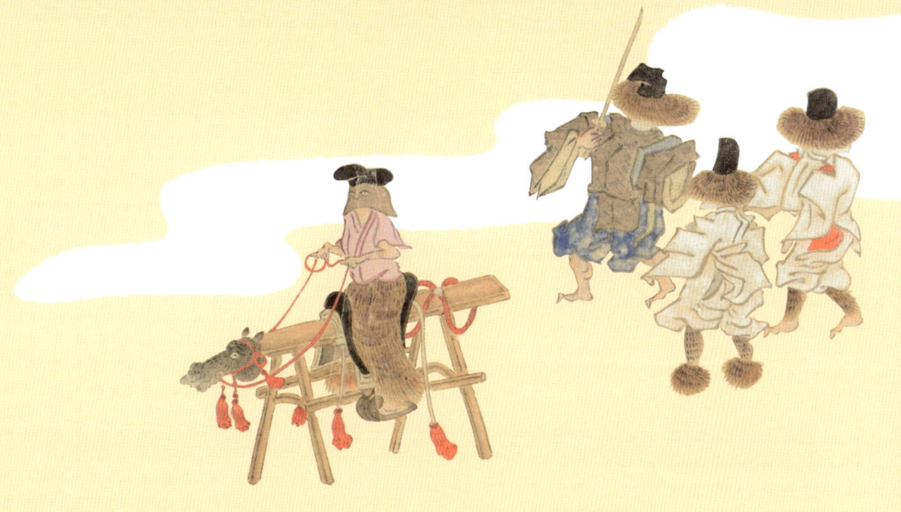

1

妖怪絵の世界

The World of Yokai Art

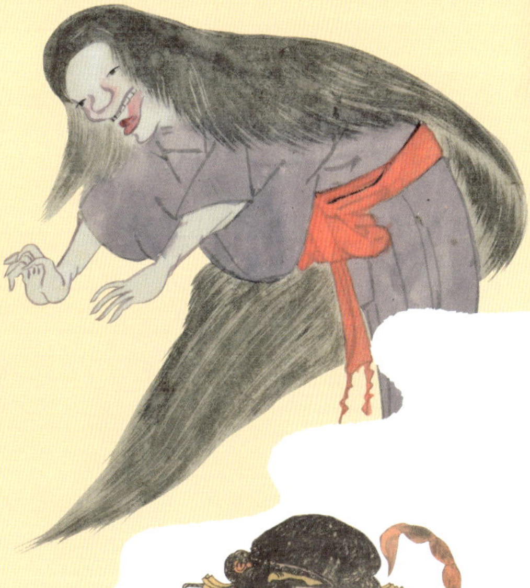

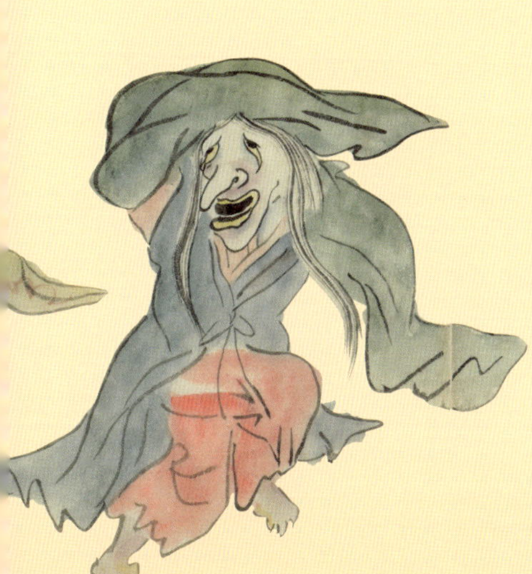

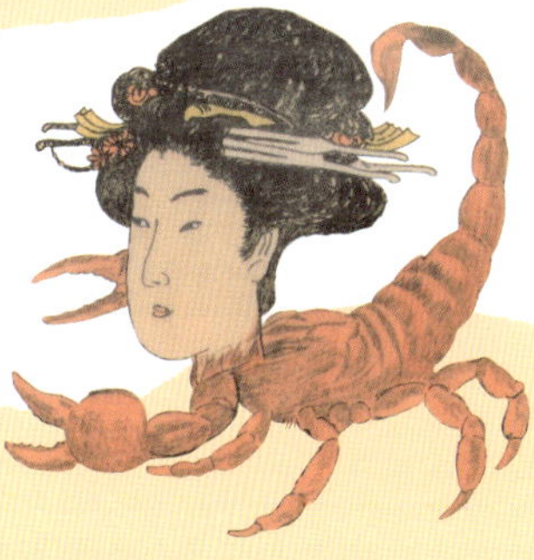

百鬼夜行絵巻
ひゃっきやぎょうえまき

The Night Parade of One Hundred Demons Picture Scroll

青白斉春山　江戸時代　縦 31.5　長 635.5　Seihakusai Shunzan, Edo period, Height 31.5, Length 635.5

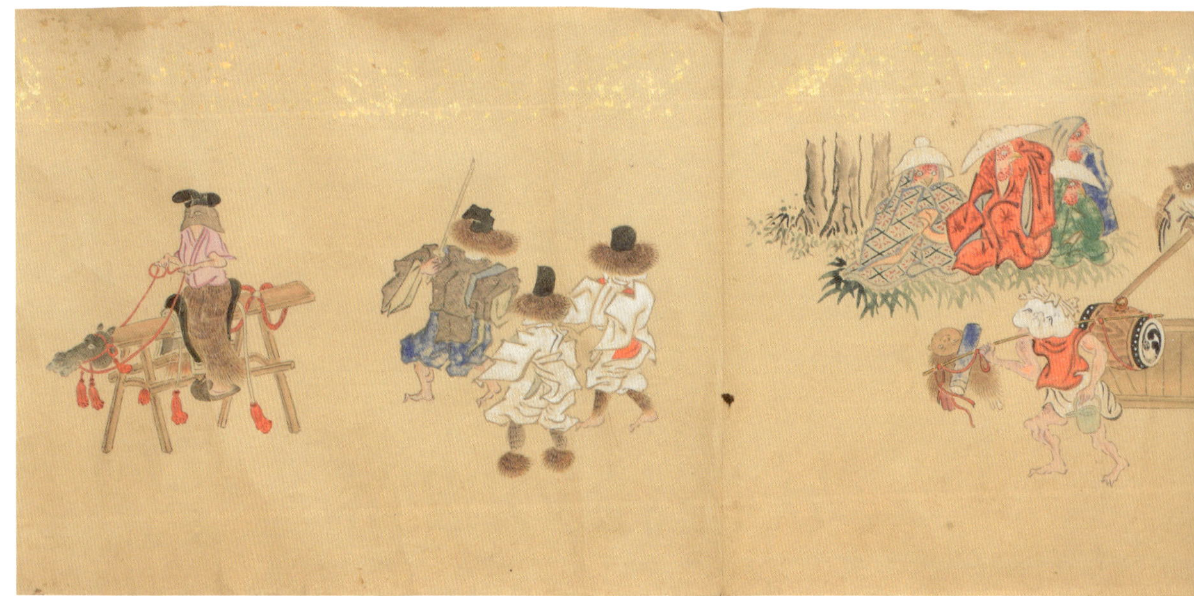

木馬に跨る妖怪と従者と思しき妖怪たち。
A yokai on a wooden horse and its attendants.

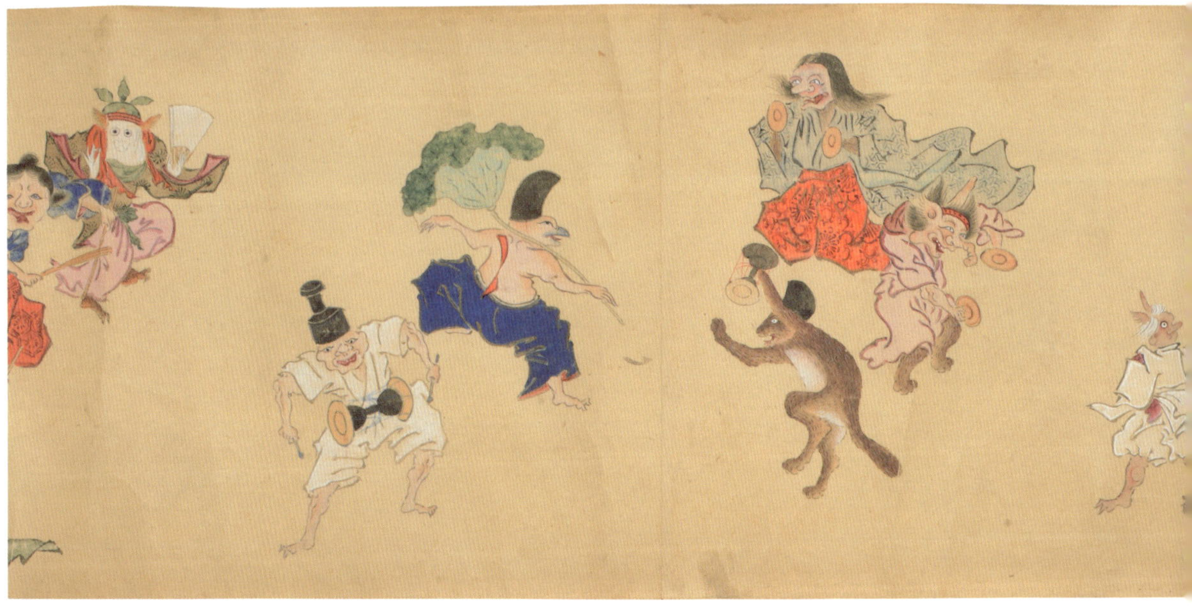

踊りに興ずる妖怪たち。
Dancing yokai.

百鬼夜行絵巻のもっともポピュラーなタイプは真珠庵系のものだが、それとはまったく違う内容のものも何種類か存在する。この作品もその一つで、朽ち果てた建物から出る動物と妖怪たちからスタートして跳梁する妖怪たちが描かれている。同じタイプのものが京都市立芸術大学や東京国立博物館にあるが、この資料は中間に唐櫃の場面など、いくつかの真珠庵系百鬼夜行絵巻の妖怪が登場するスタイルで、その位置づけは今後の研究が必要といえる。巻末に「土佐大蔵少輔藤原行秀筆　青白斉春山画」とある。

The Shinjuan style is the most popular type of Night Parade of One Hundred Demons picture scrolls, but there are many variations with entirely different content. This work begins with beasts and yokai emerging from dilapidated buildings and running rampant. The same type of work is held in the Kyoto City University of Arts and the Tokyo National Museum, but in this one quite a few of the Shinjuan-style yokai also appear, including a depiction of the Chinese-style *karabitsu* chest halfway through; further research on the positioning is required. At the end of the scroll is written "Tosa Junior Assistant Minister of Finance Fujiwara no Yukihide: Illustrated by Seihakusai Shunzan".

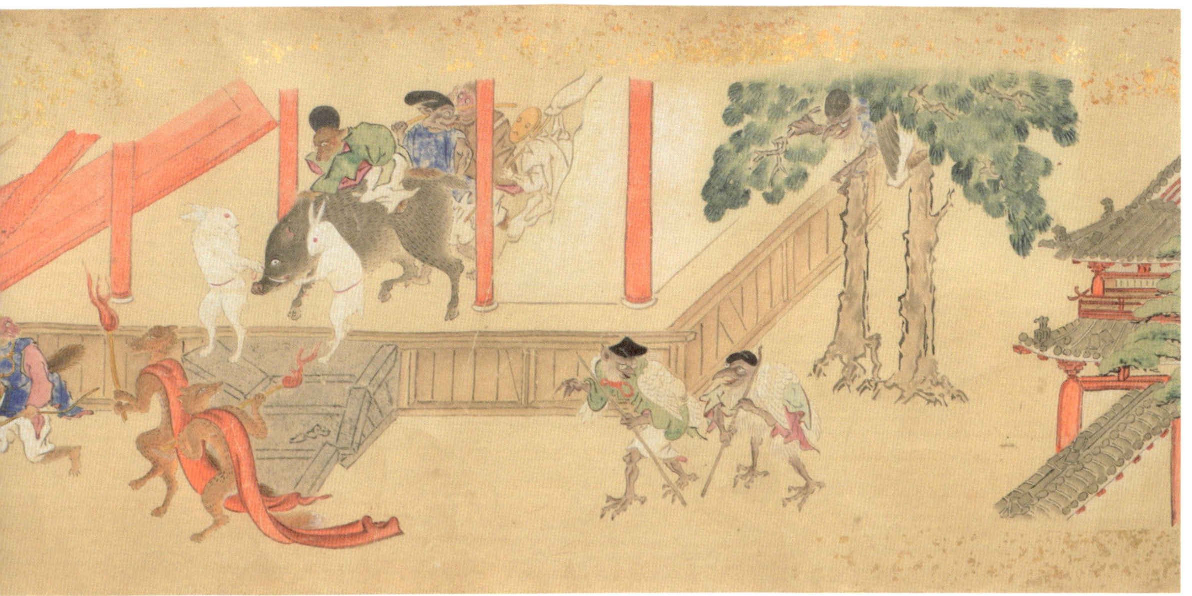

太鼓を担いだ妖怪、巻子を抱えた妖怪などが先導しているようだ。
A yokai carrying a *taiko* drum and another hugging a scroll lead the way.

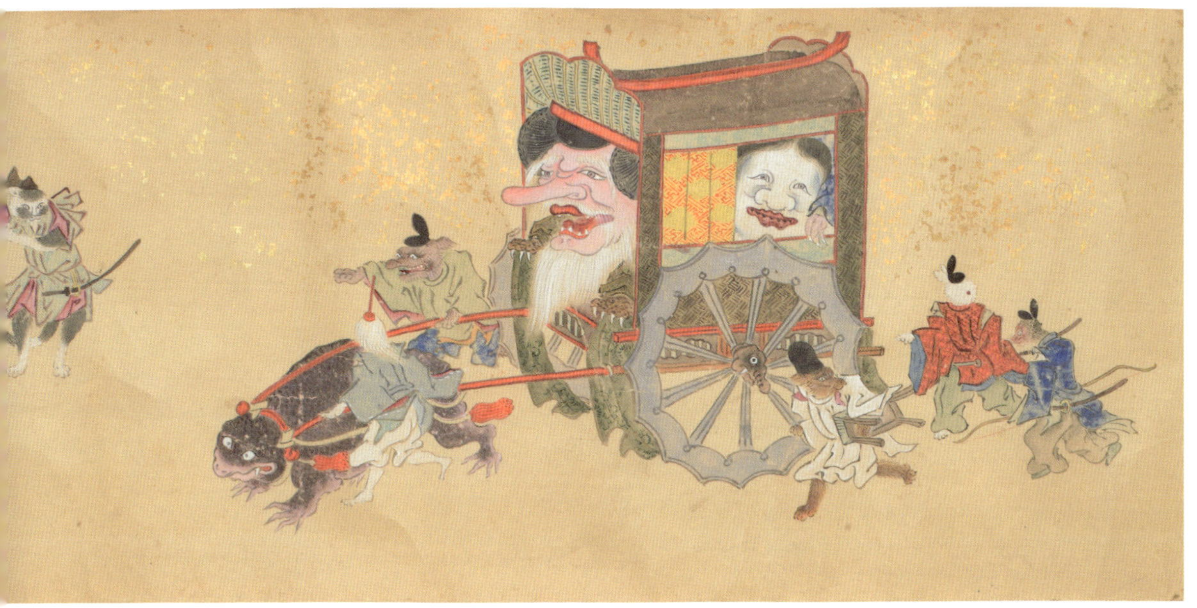

蝦蟇の引く牛車には巨大な天狗と女官が乗っており、従者の妖怪たちも描かれている。
A huge *tengu* goblin and lady-in-waiting ride in an oxcart pulled by a toad; their entourage is also depicted.

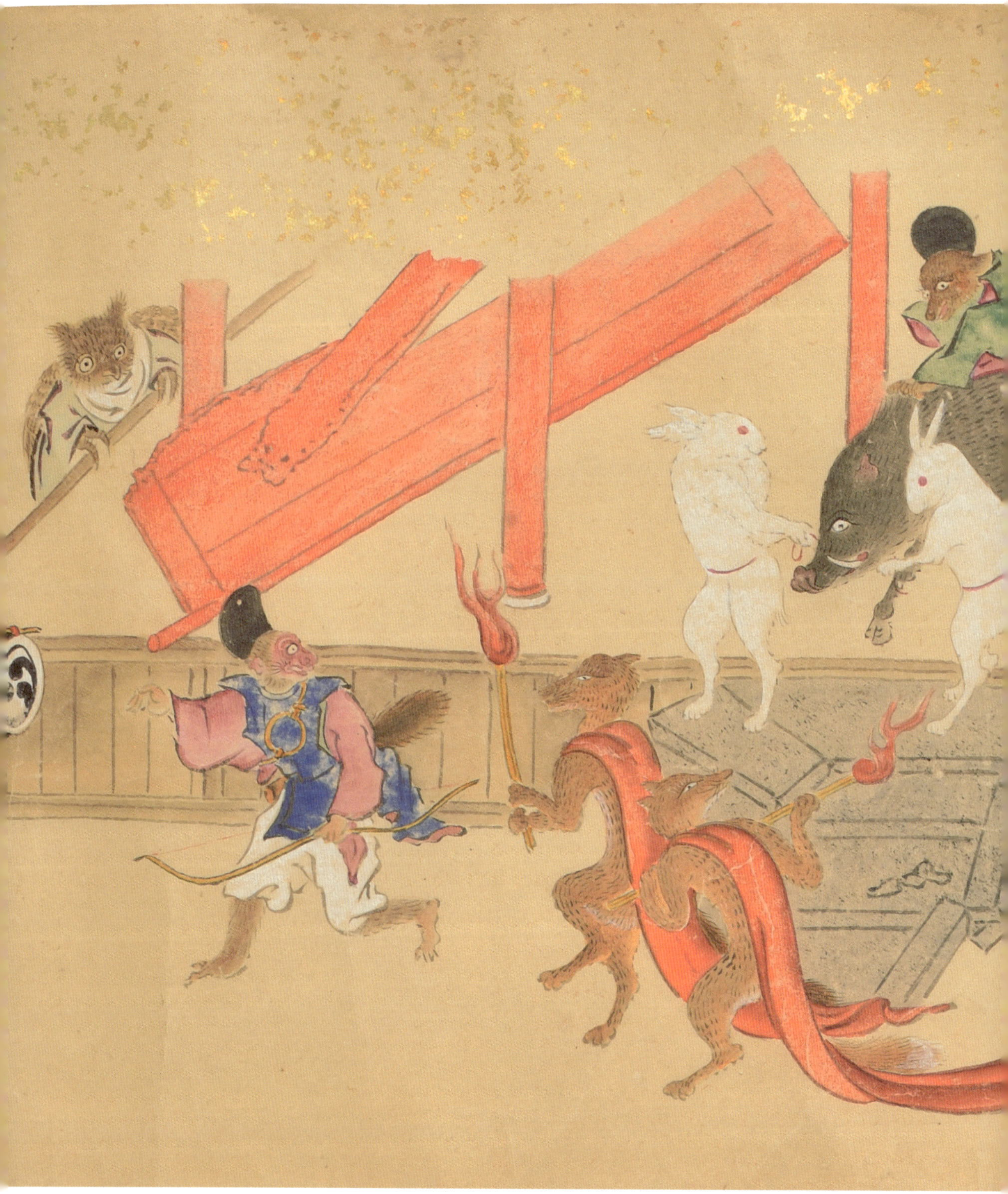

兎が引く猪に跨った猿、松明を持つ狐などの動物が朽ちた建物から外に向かっている。
A monkey drawn by a boar led by rabbits, foxes holding torches and other animals head out from a rundown building.

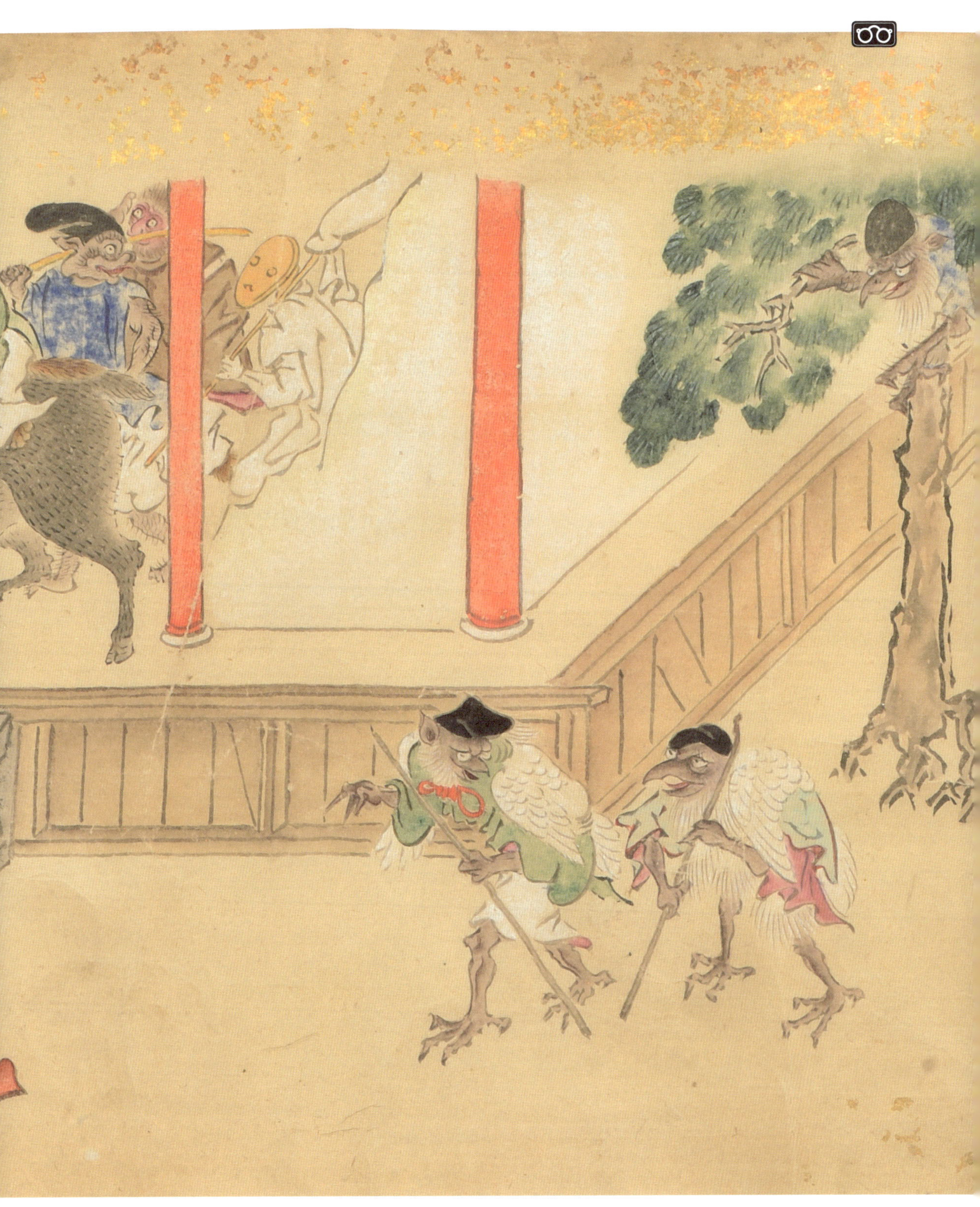

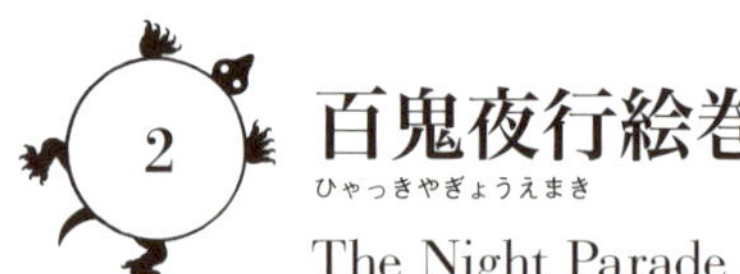

百鬼夜行絵巻
ひゃっきやぎょうえまき

The Night Parade of One Hundred Demons Picture Scroll

江戸時代　縦 31.5　長 493.0　Edo period, Height 31.5, Length 493.0

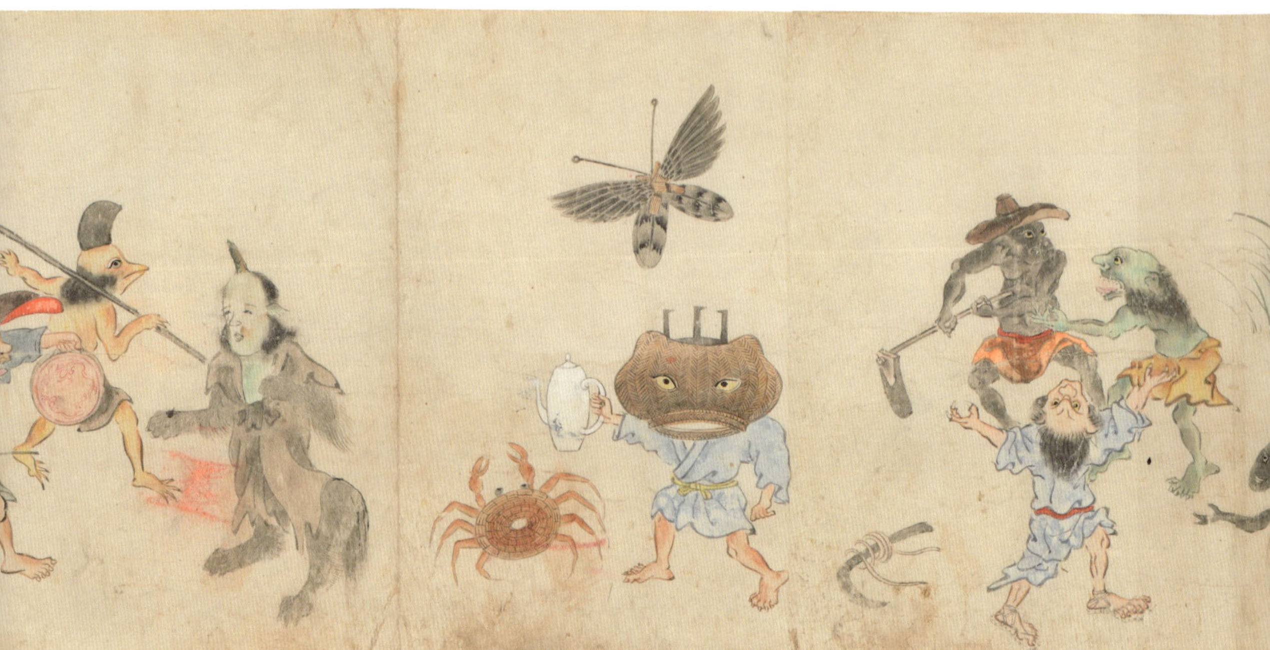

妖怪たちが騒いでいる横では籐で編んだ器物の妖怪たちが何処かに向かおうとしている。
Yokai of basket-weaving tools look over to see what the commotion is, caused by some rowdy characters next to them.

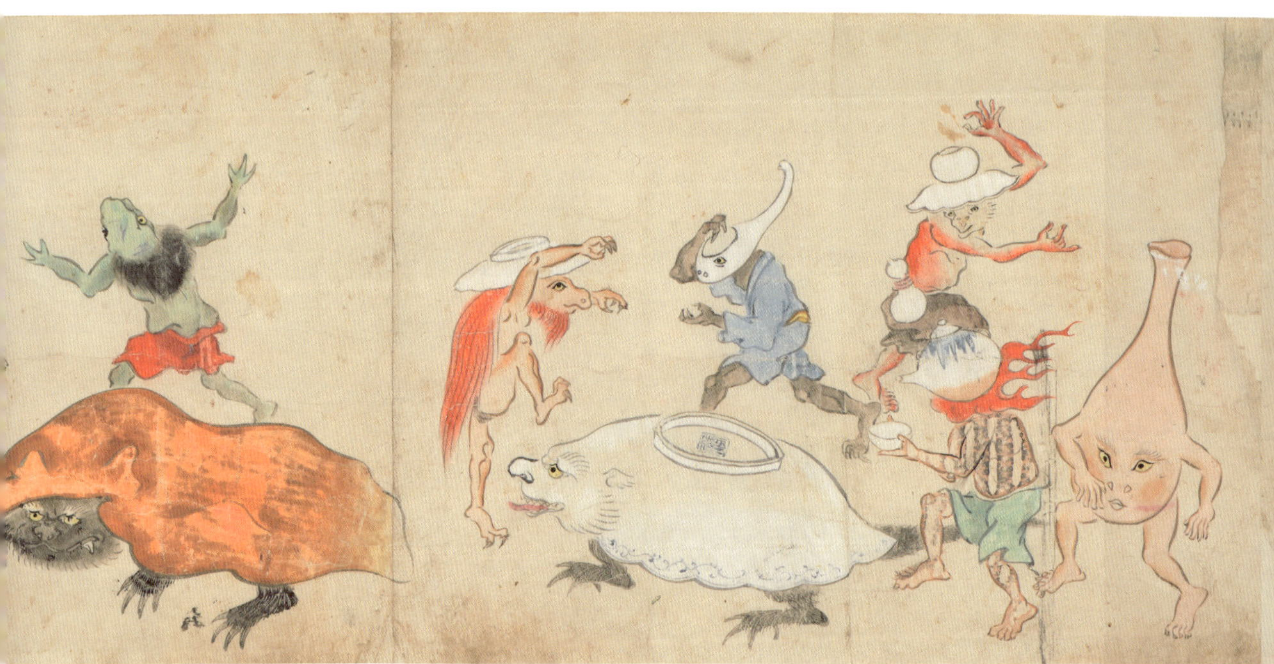

異形なものたちの田楽。
The harvest celebrations (*dengaku*) of strange beings.

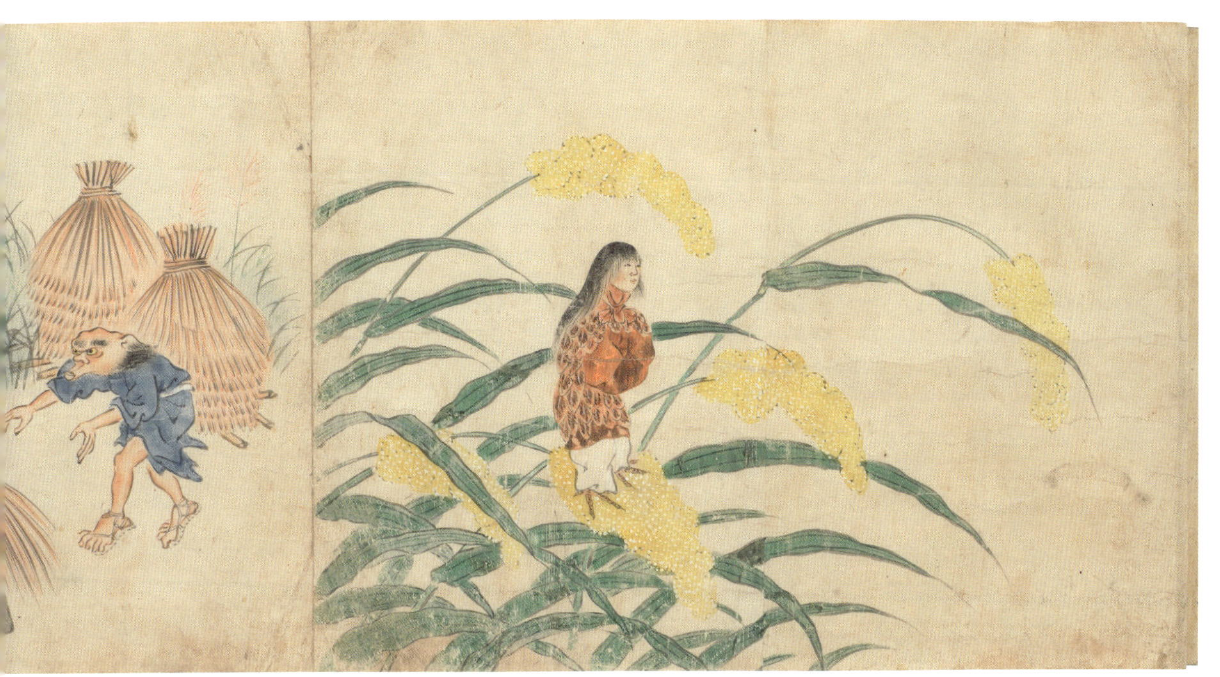

逃げ出した蓑を纏った鍬を追いかける妖怪。背後には藁塚がある。

A yokai chasing the run-away plow which is dressed in a straw raincoat. On its back are bundles of rice straw.

粟の実のうえに立つ雀の精。

Sparrow spirit standing on the ripe millet.

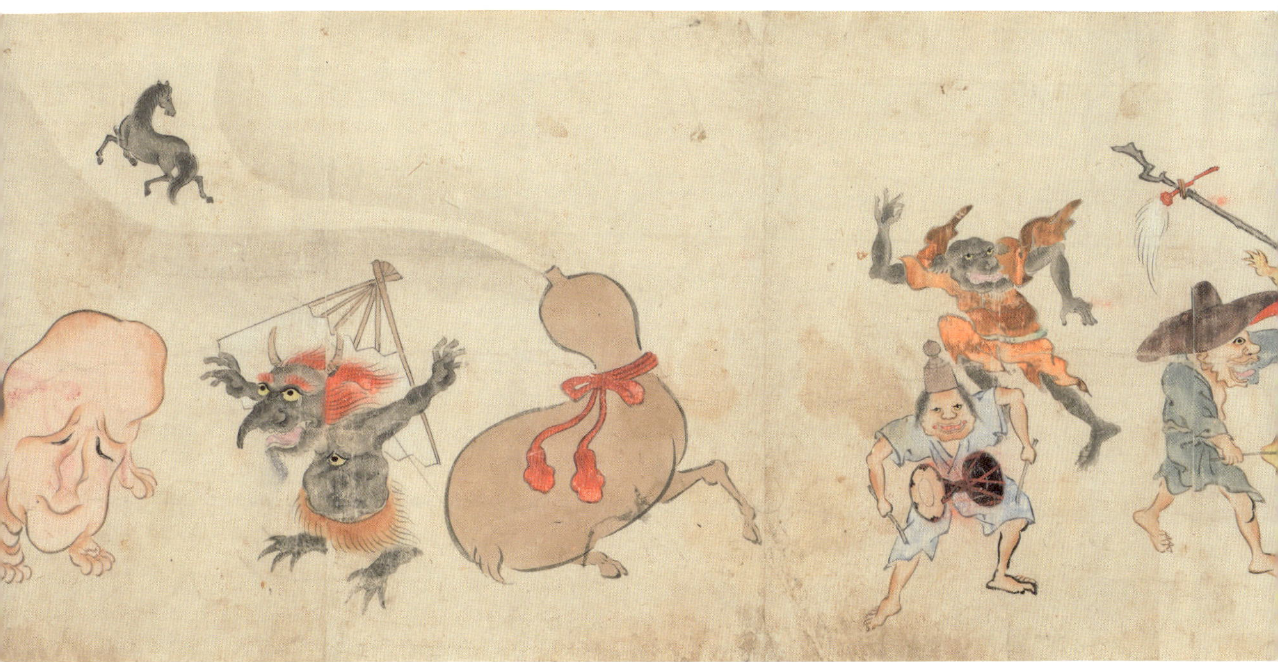

扇子の妖怪は真珠庵系百鬼夜行絵巻に登場するものを参考にしたものだろう。「ぬっぺっぽう」はよく知られたポピュラーな姿だ。

The folding fan yokai probably originates from the Shinjuan-style Night Parade of One Hundred Demons picture scroll. Nuppeppō, who looks like a saggy potato, is a well-known popular figure.

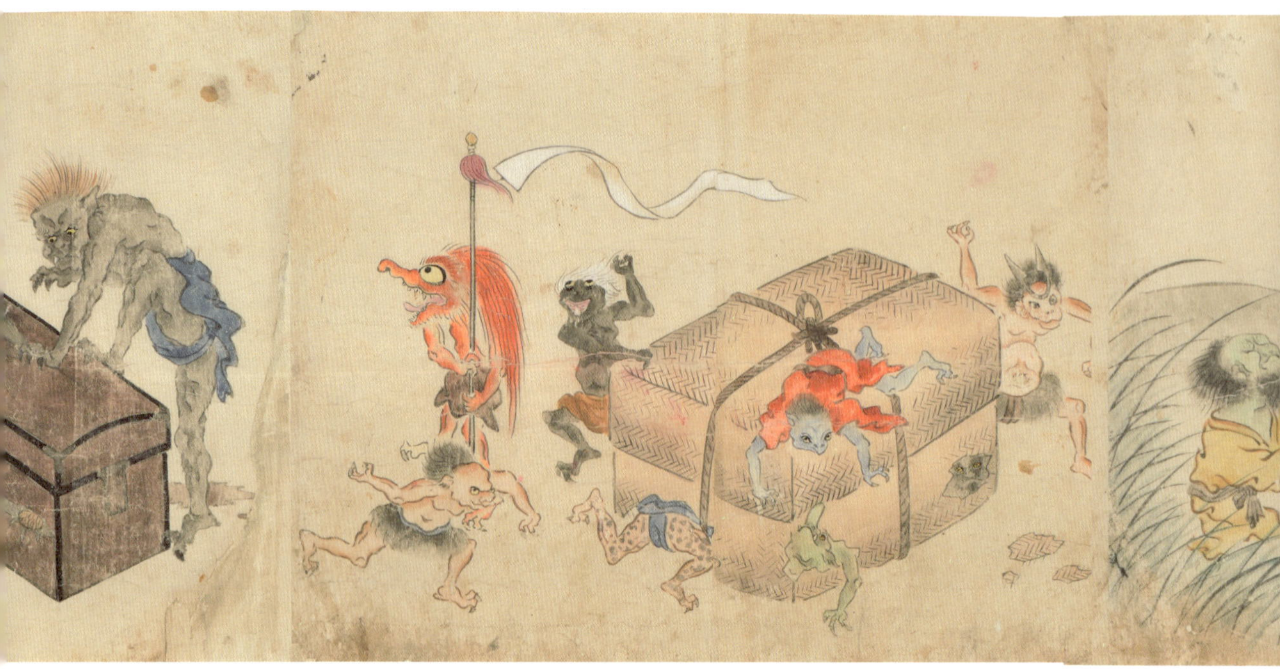

葛籠から出没する妖怪たちと幡をかざした妖怪。
Yokai infest a wicker box; one holds a Buddhist banner.

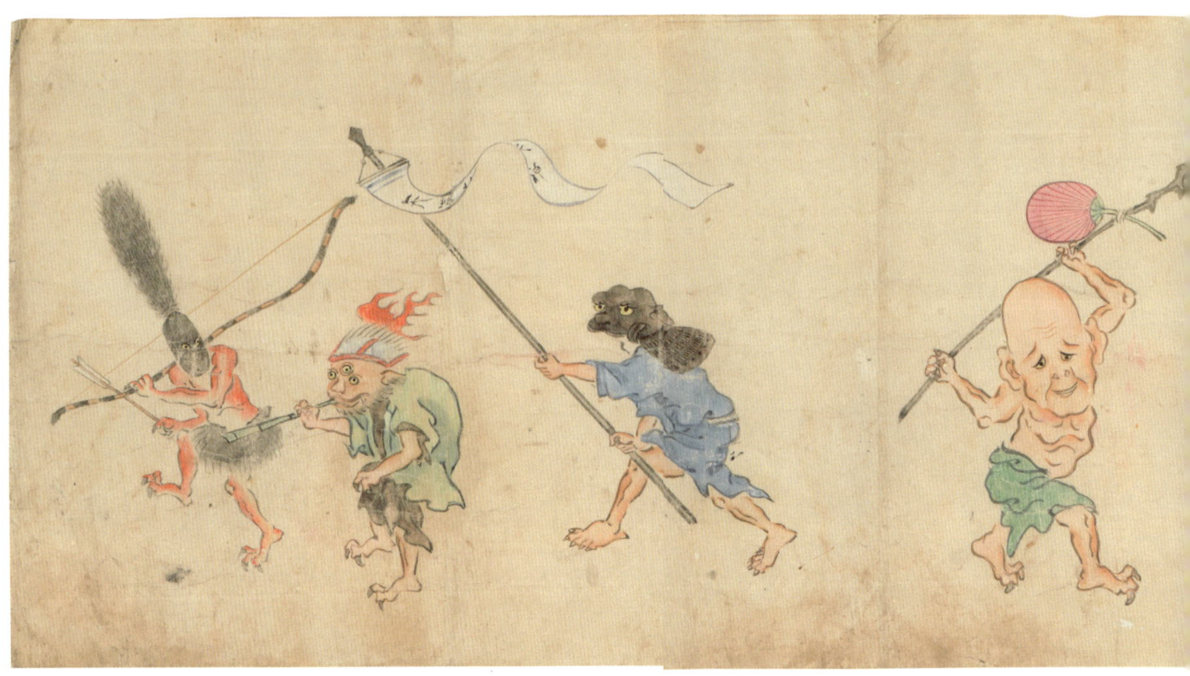

幡を掲げた妖怪、五徳の妖怪、弓を担いだ靫の妖怪。
A yokai raising a Buddhist banner, a *gotoku* (kettle tripod), and a quiver shouldering a bow.

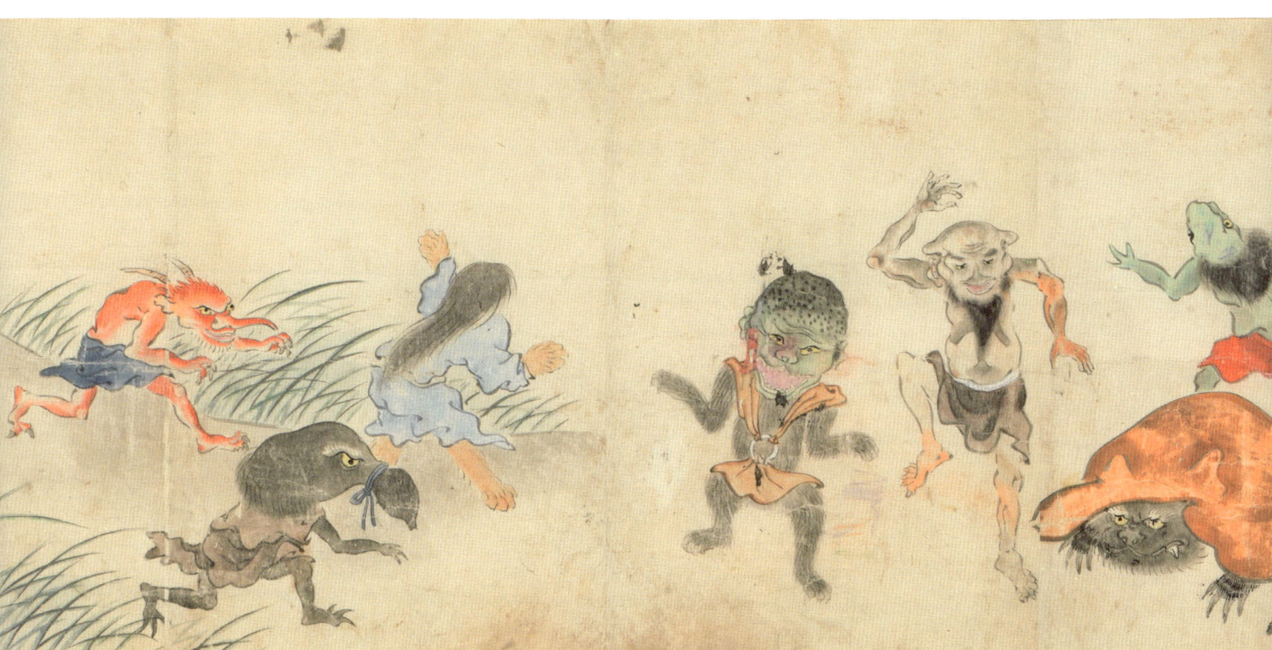

「手の目」が現れて逃げ惑う妖怪たち。
Yokai flee from a *tenome* (lit. ″eye hands″).

妖怪たちが踊っている。左の妖怪は「ひょうすべ」か。
Yokai dancing. The one on the left may be a *hyōsube* (a hairy river monster).

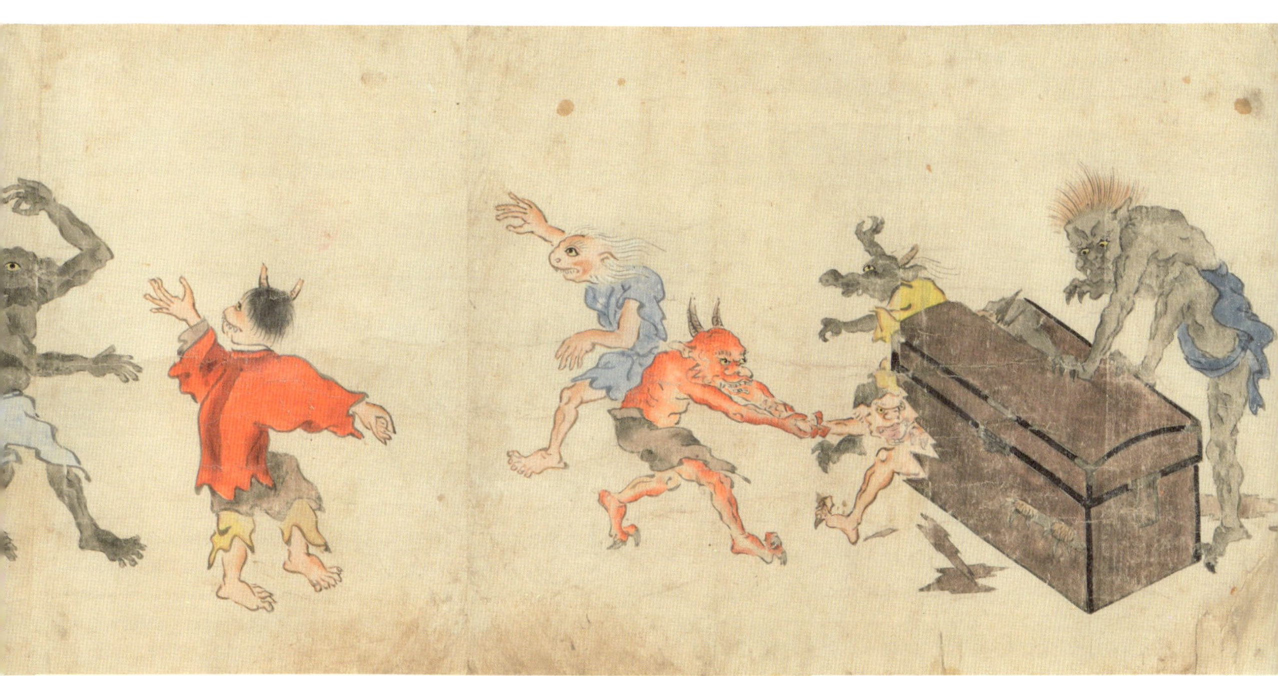

踊りに興ずる妖怪たち。団扇を縛り付けた枝を振り回す妖怪もみえる。
Dancing yokai. One is flapping a branch with a round uchiwa fan tied to it.

唐櫃をこじ開ける鬼。
唐櫃から逃げ出す妖怪の手を引っぱって助けている赤鬼もみえる。
An ogre is breaking open a Chinese-style chest (*karabitsu*). A red ogre is also giving the yokai a helping hand out of the chest.

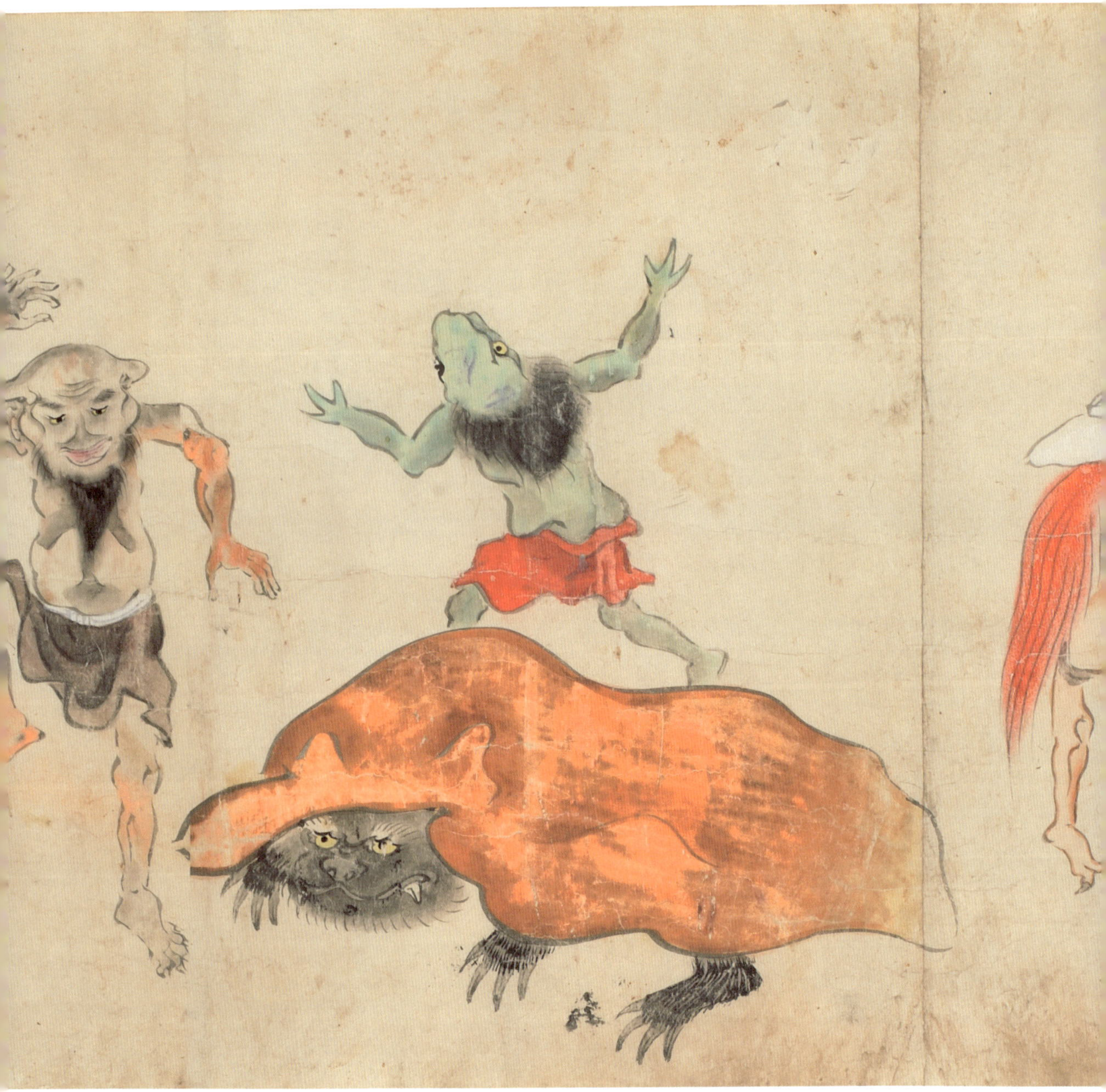

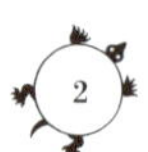

冒頭には実った粟のうえに立つ小さな童子が描かれているが、この童子は鳥の足で体は羽ということから雀の精だろう。続いて鍬の妖怪や異形な農夫らが登場し、妖怪の世界が展開されている。この絵巻は一般的な百鬼夜行絵巻とは大きく異なった内容で、現在のところ類例は確認できていない。描かれた妖怪は独自のものとポピュラーな百鬼夜行に登場するものとが入り混じっている。折本を絵巻にした可能性もある。江戸中期ころの作と思われる。

At the beginning of the scroll a small child-acolyte (*dōji*) stands on top of the ripe foxtail millet, but judging by its bird's feet and the feathers on its body it is probably a sparrow spirit. Next are some grotesque farmers and a plowshare yokai, which show the evolving world of yokai. The content of this scroll is very different to the usual Night Parade of One Hundred Demons picture scrolls; currently there are no known similar instances. Unique creatures are mixed in with popular characters from the Night Parade of One Hundred Demons. It is possible that this picture scroll was made from an *orihon* (folding book). Thought to be a work of the mid-Edo.

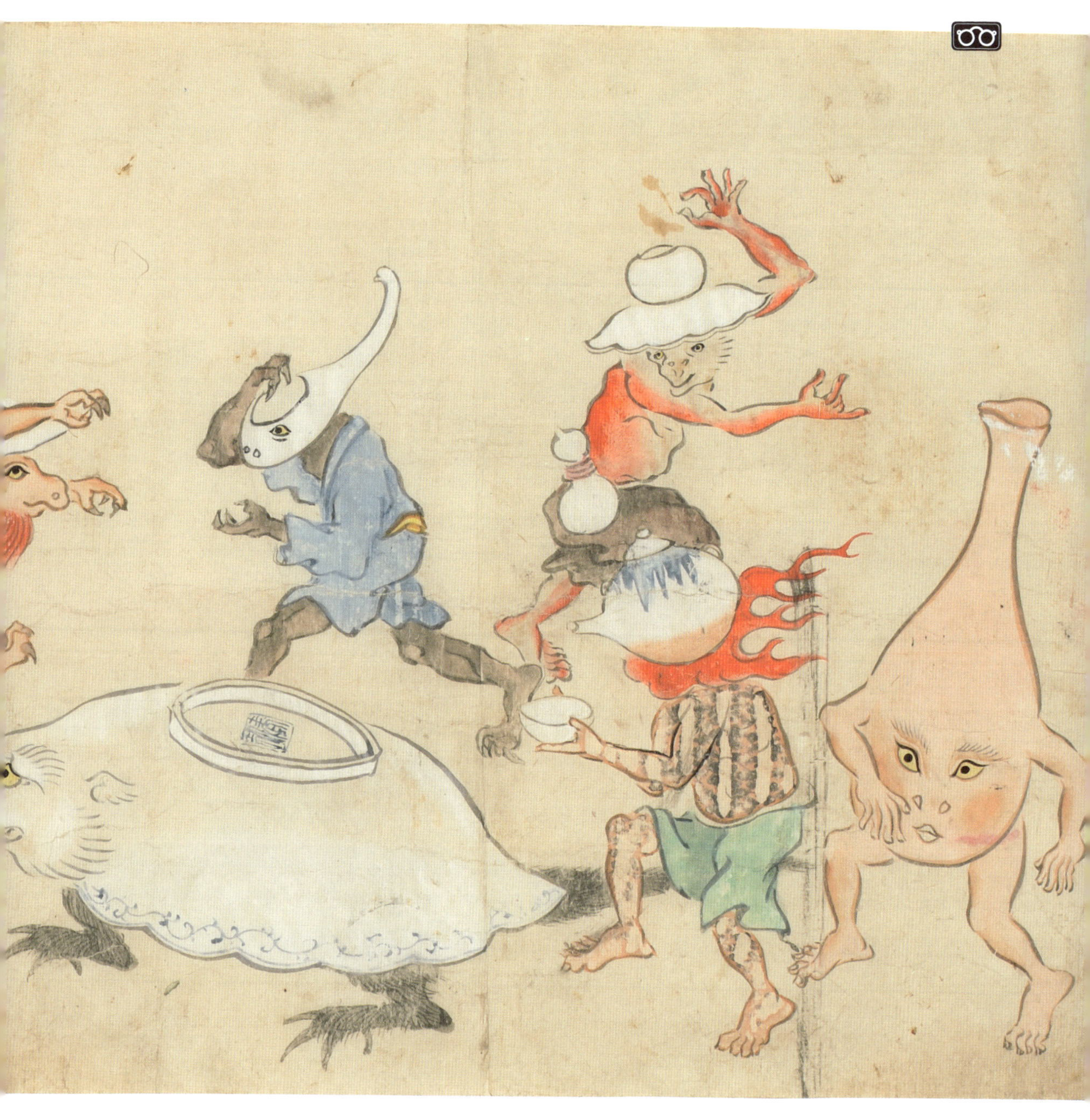

徳利、急須、大皿、蓮華など焼物たちがたむろし、妖怪たちが踊っている。布を被った妖怪は百鬼夜行絵巻を参考にしたのだろう。
A sake bottle, a tea pot, a platter, a Chinese spoon and other pottery items are hanging out. They are dancing. The yokai under a cloth in the foreground is likely to have been adapted from the Night Parade of One Hundred Demons scroll.

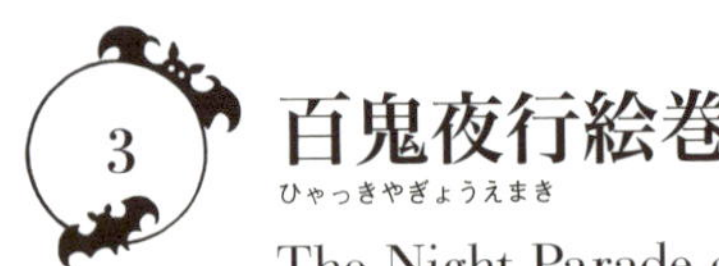

百鬼夜行絵巻
ひゃっきやぎょうえまき

The Night Parade of One Hundred Demons Picture Scroll

雲渓　江戸時代　縦 31.5　長 599.5　Unkei, Edo period, Height31.5, Length 599.5

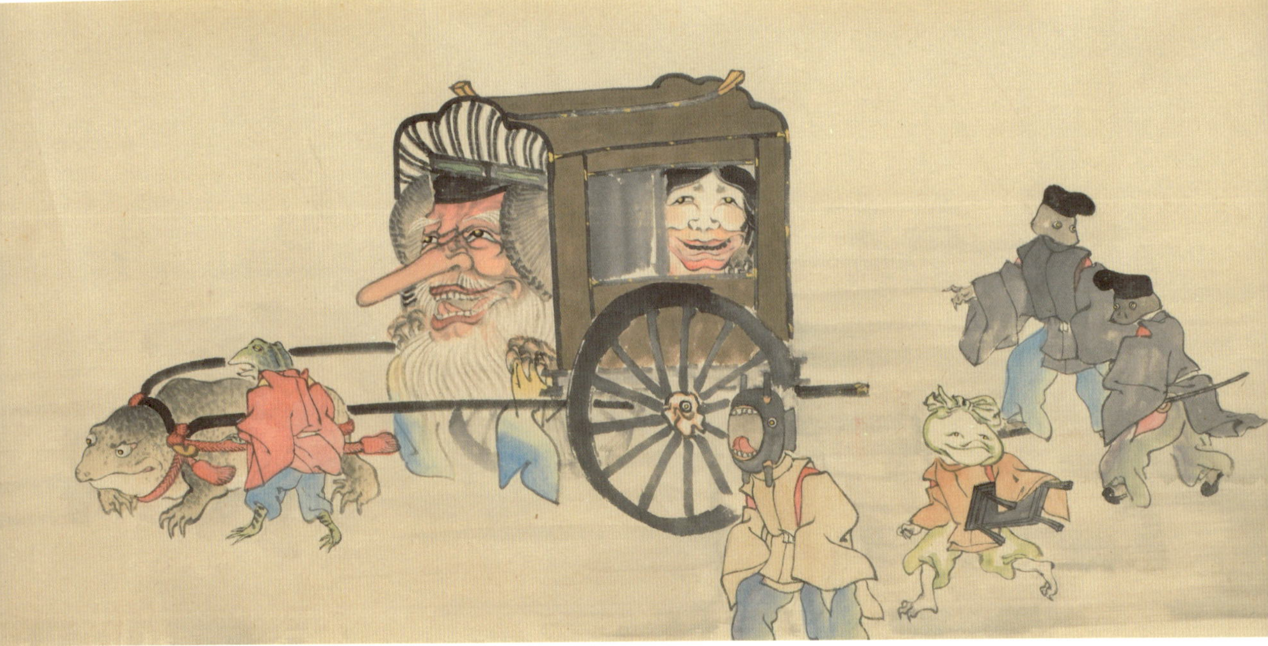

蝦蟇が引く牛車という構図は別の百鬼夜行絵巻を参考にしたものだろう。
The composition of the oxcart pulled by a toad is probably borrowed from another Night Parade of One Hundred Demons picture scroll.

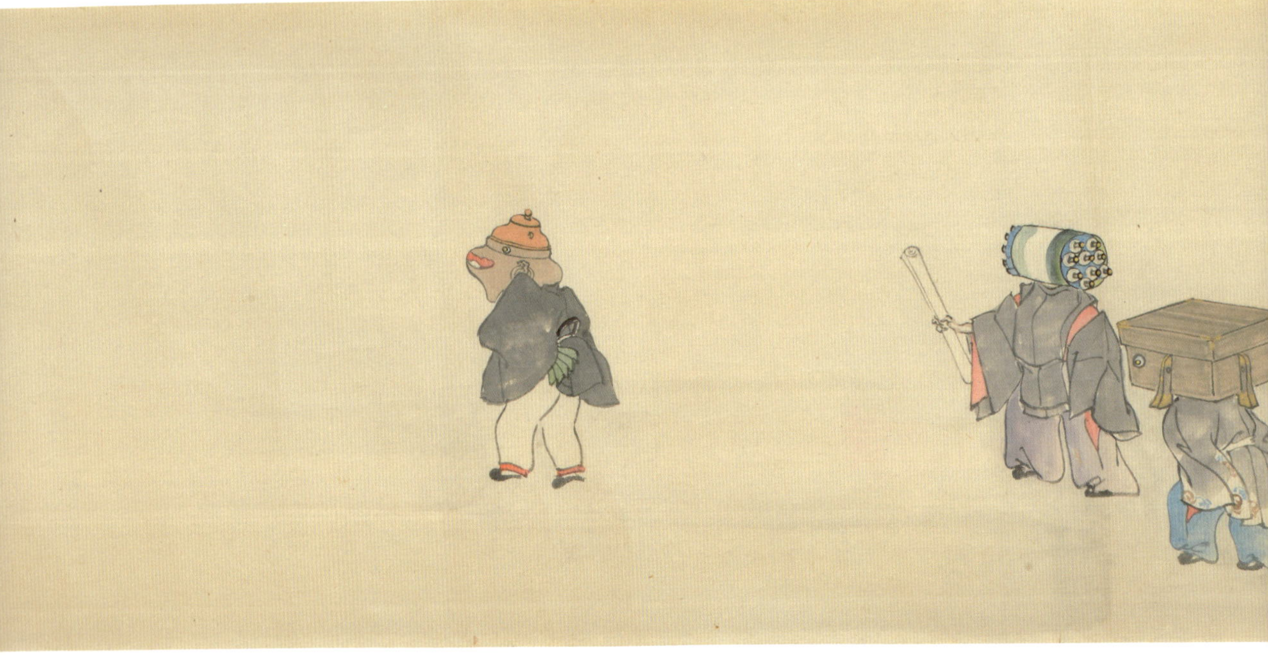

櫃、巻子、風炉らも何処かに行こうとしている様子だ。
A chest, a scroll yokai and a tea kettle are also on the move.

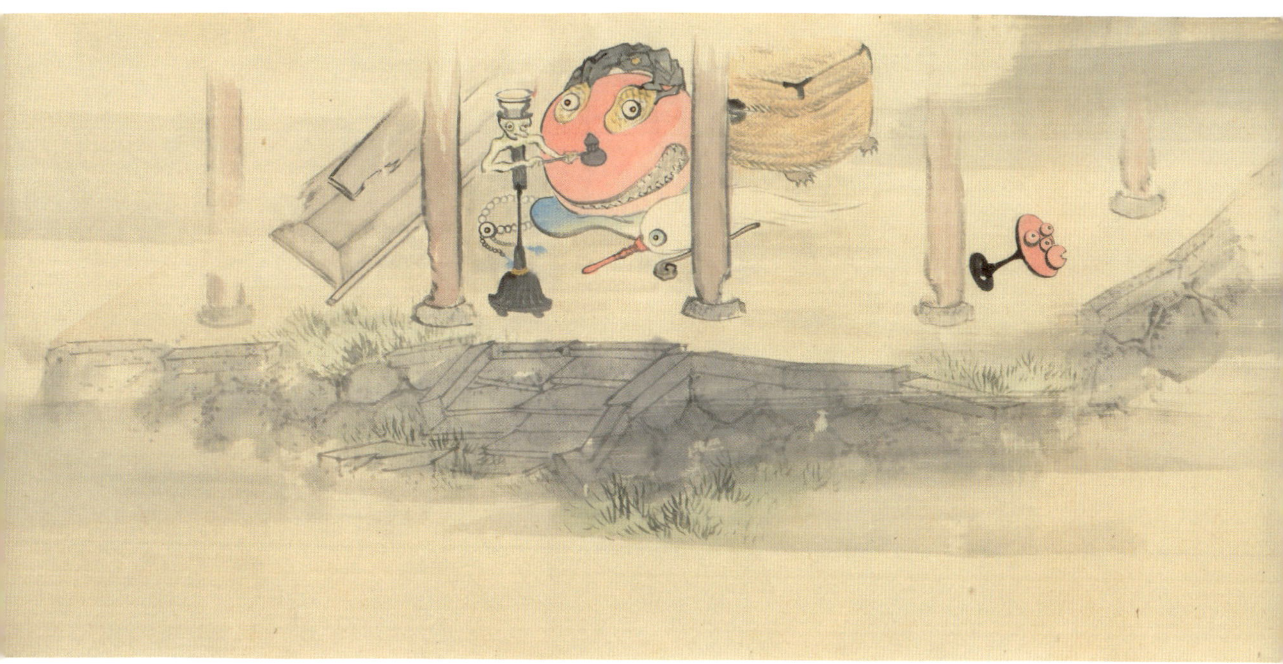

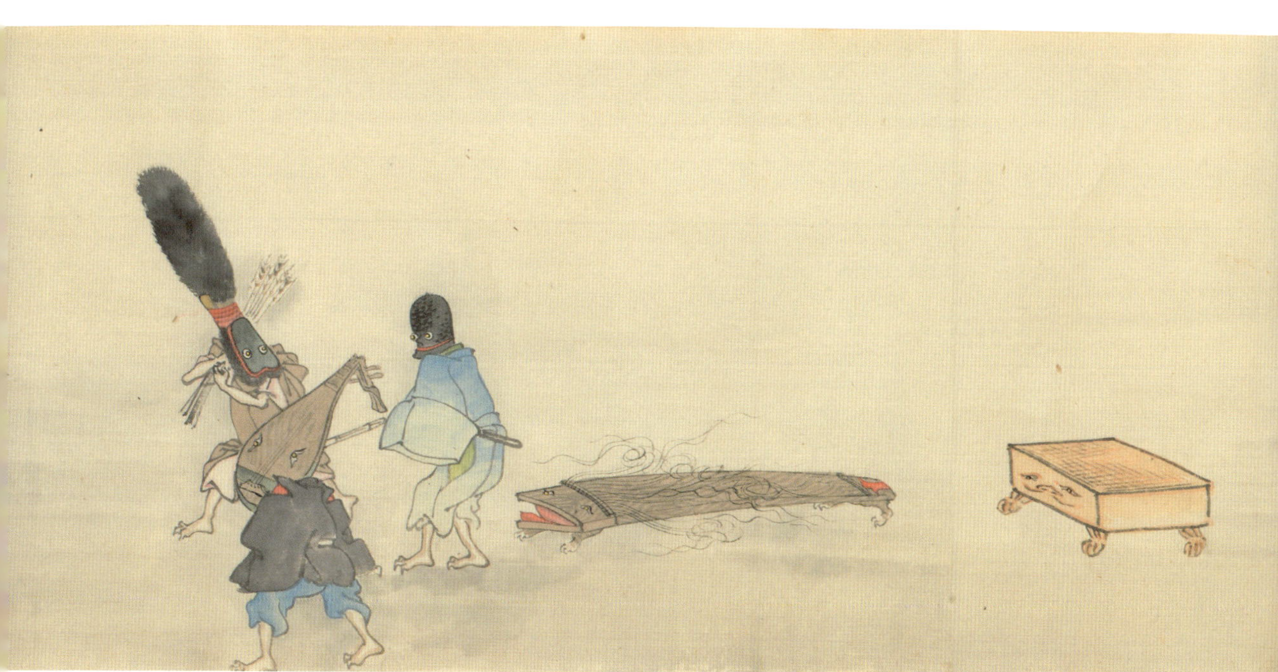

碁盤、琴、琵琶、靫などの妖怪が行列して何処かに向かっている。
Checkerboard, *koto*, *biwa* (Japanese lute) and quiver yokai are on their way somewhere.

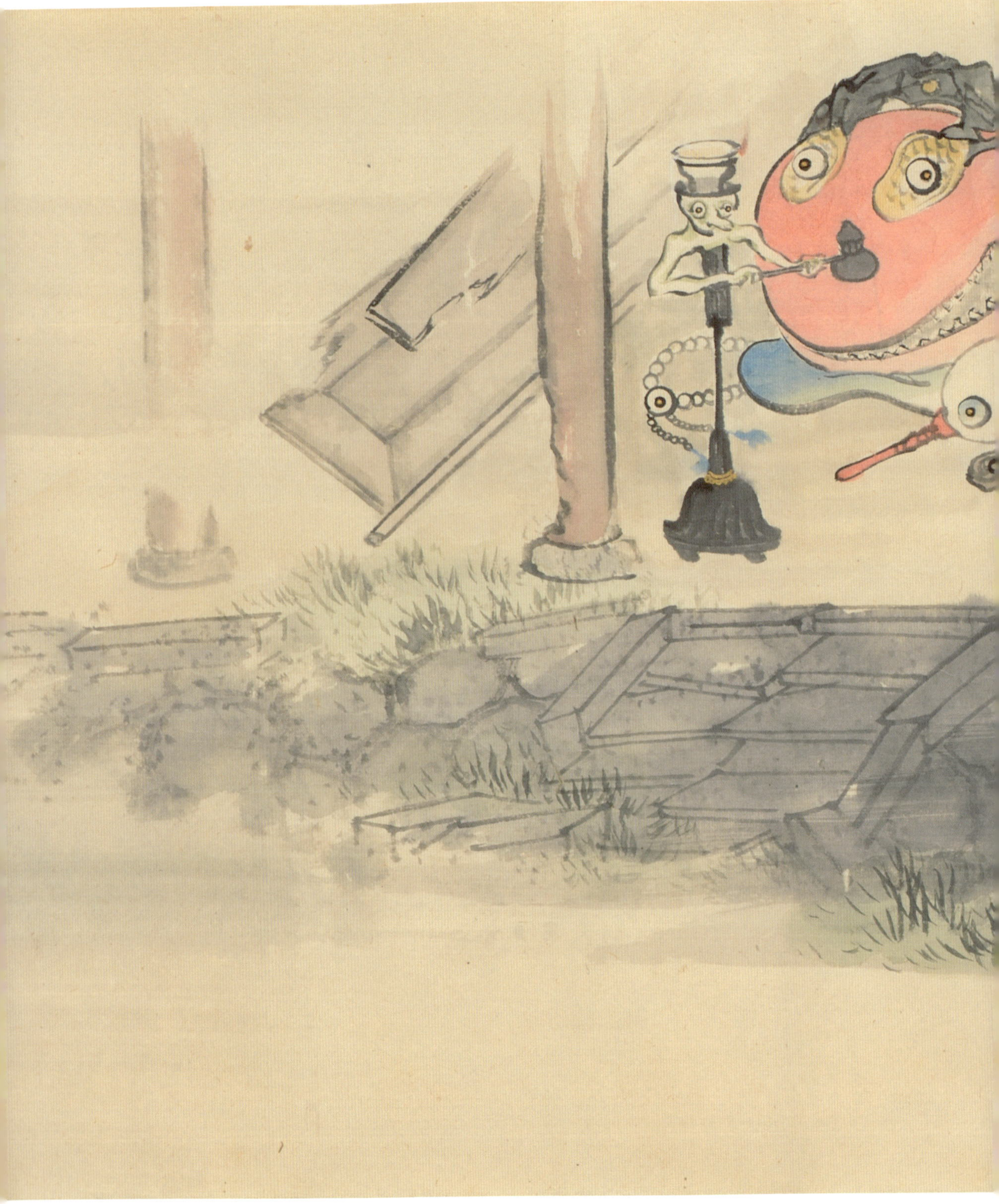

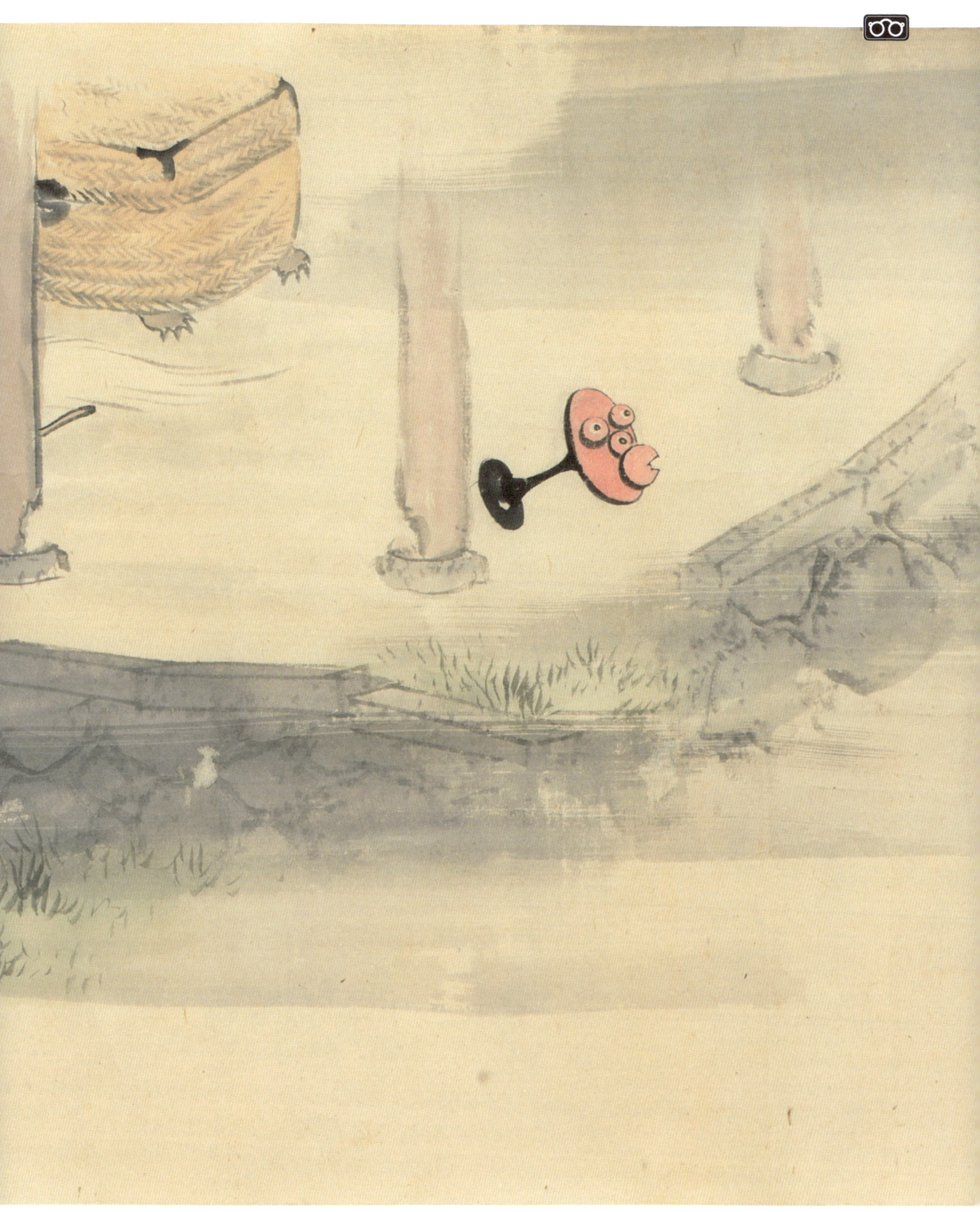

木魚、払子などが柱さえも崩れそうな廃寺で妖怪と化している。
Mokugyo (a wooden fish-shaped drum), *hossu* (a brush to drive away insects during meditation) and other altar items are changing into demonic creatures in a ruined temple which looks as if even the pillars are on the verge of collapse.

4 百鬼夜行絵巻
ひゃっきやぎょうえまき

The Night Parade of One Hundred Demons Picture Scroll

江戸時代　縦 38.0　長 1253.0　Edo period, Height 38.0, Length 1253.0

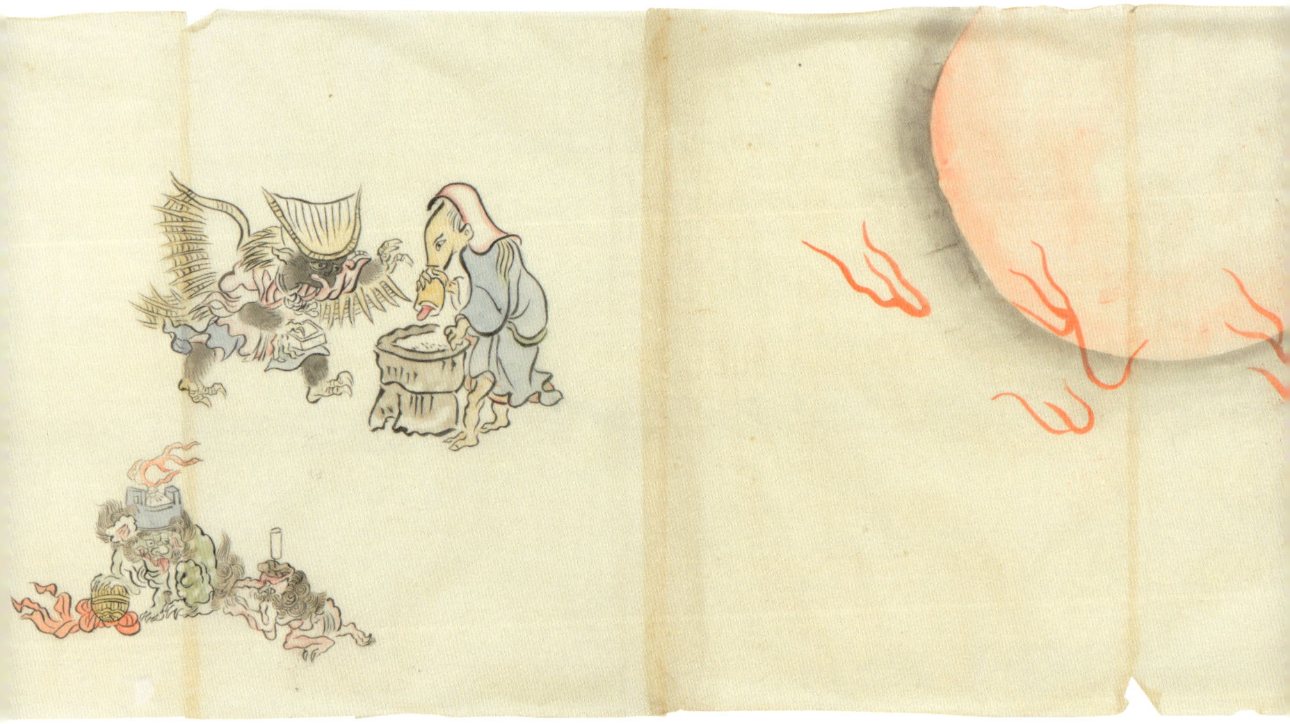

左右に百器夜行絵巻を配して真ん中に火の玉があるといった珍しい場面。
The rare scene of the *Night Parade of One Hundred Artifacts* continuing on to the left and right, with a fireball right in the middle.

真珠庵系の百鬼夜行絵巻と器物の妖怪を描いた百器夜行絵巻の場面が登場するスタイルだ。こうした事例は散見されることから妖怪絵巻の広がりがみてとれるが、この絵巻の最大の特徴は、通常は最後に描かれる巨大な火の玉が絵巻の中間で登場することだ。こうした事例の検証も百鬼夜行絵巻の研究には必要といえよう。

Scenes from the *Night Parade of One Hundred Artifacts* and the Shinjuan-style *Night Parade of One Hundred Demons* picture scrolls appear in this scroll. This shows the spread of yokai through scrolls, but the most distinctive characteristic of this scroll is that the huge fireball usually drawn at the very end appears midway through. More research into the *Night Parade of One Hundred Demons* scrolls is needed for the provenance of examples like this.

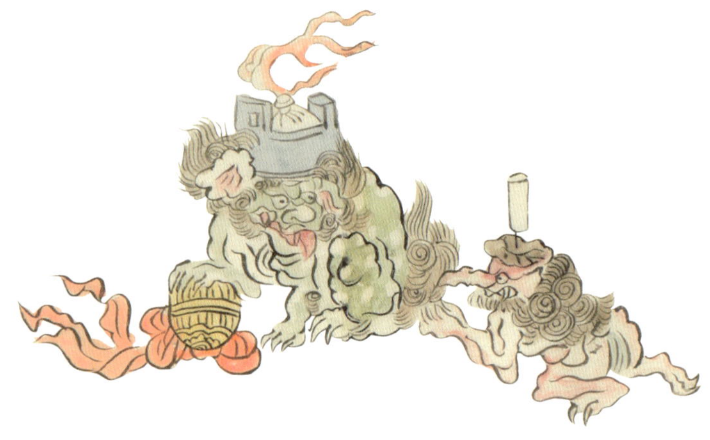

杵、箕、桶、砧などの妖怪が描かれているが、これらは百器夜行絵巻に登場するものだ。
Yokai from the *Night Parade of One Hundred Artifacts*: a pestle, winnowing basket, tub, and washing mallet (*kinuta*).

百器夜行絵巻に描かれている場面と同じもので、妖怪たちの後方には鹿の皮が掛かった衣桁も
みえる。その左端に火の玉があるのがわかる。
A scene from the *Night Parade of One Hundred Artifacts*: at the rear of the yokai, a rack with a
deerskin on it can be seen. On the left edge is a fireball.

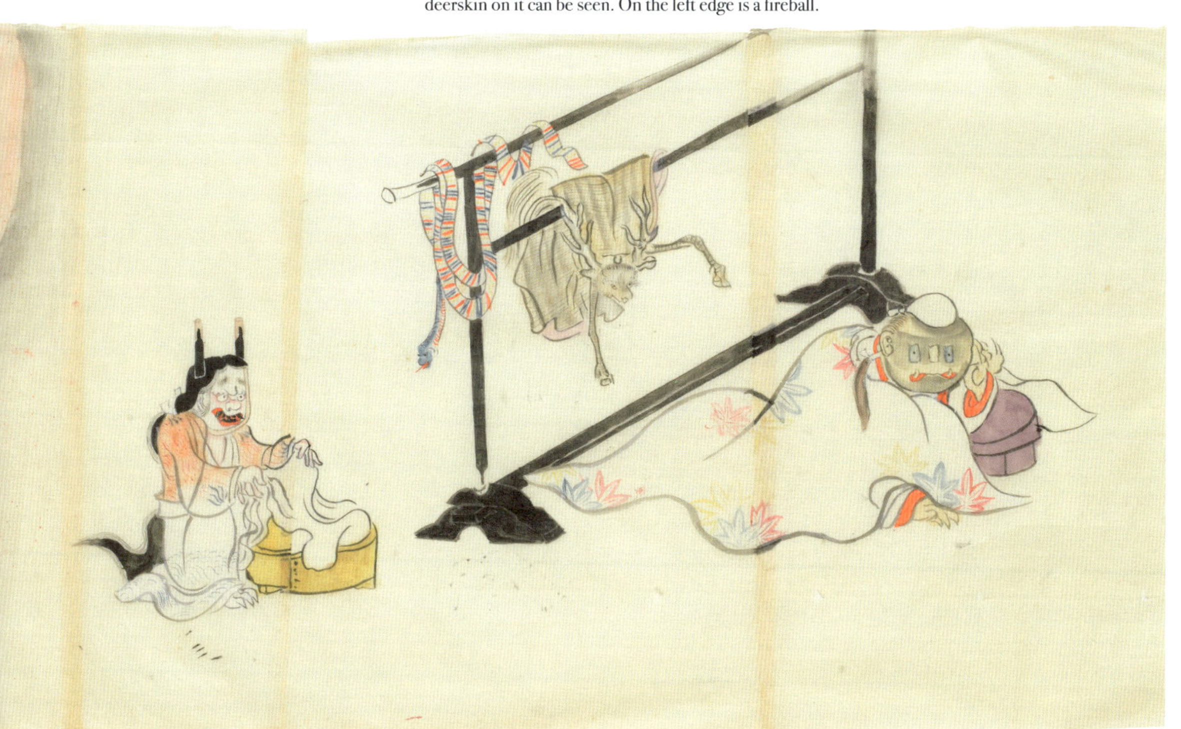

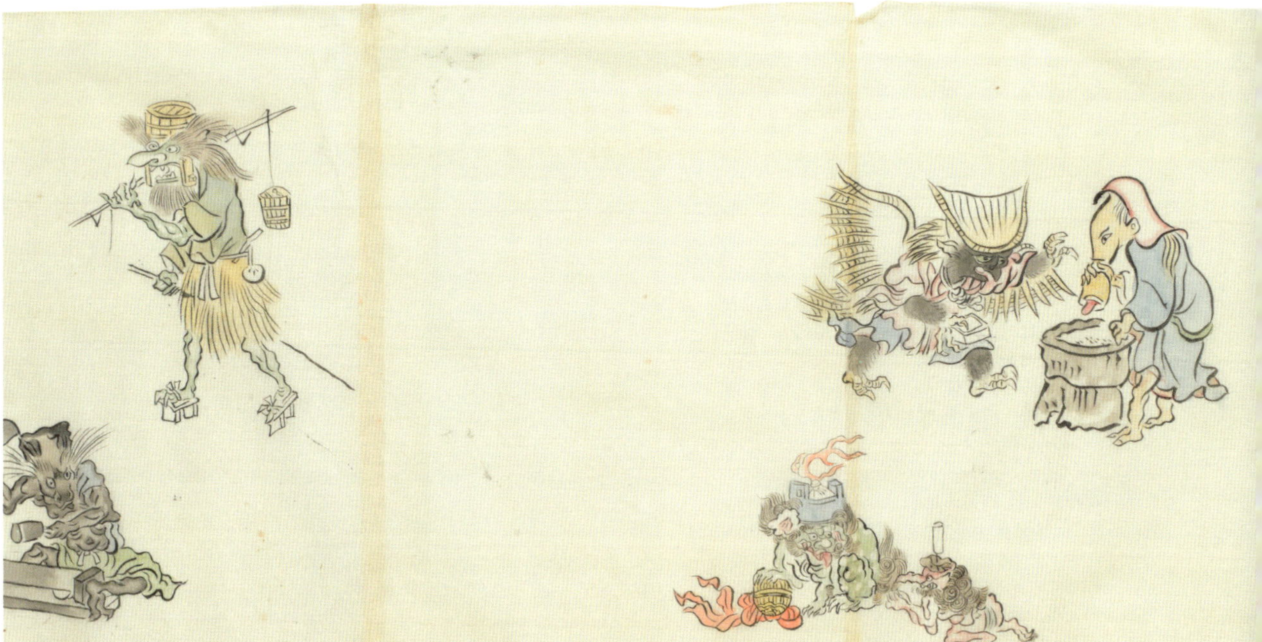

5 百鬼夜行絵巻
ひゃっきやぎょうえまき

The Night Parade of One Hundred Demons Picture Scroll

嘉永7（1854）年9月　縦26.5　長679.5　Ninth month of 1854 (Kaei 7), Height 26.5, Length 679.5

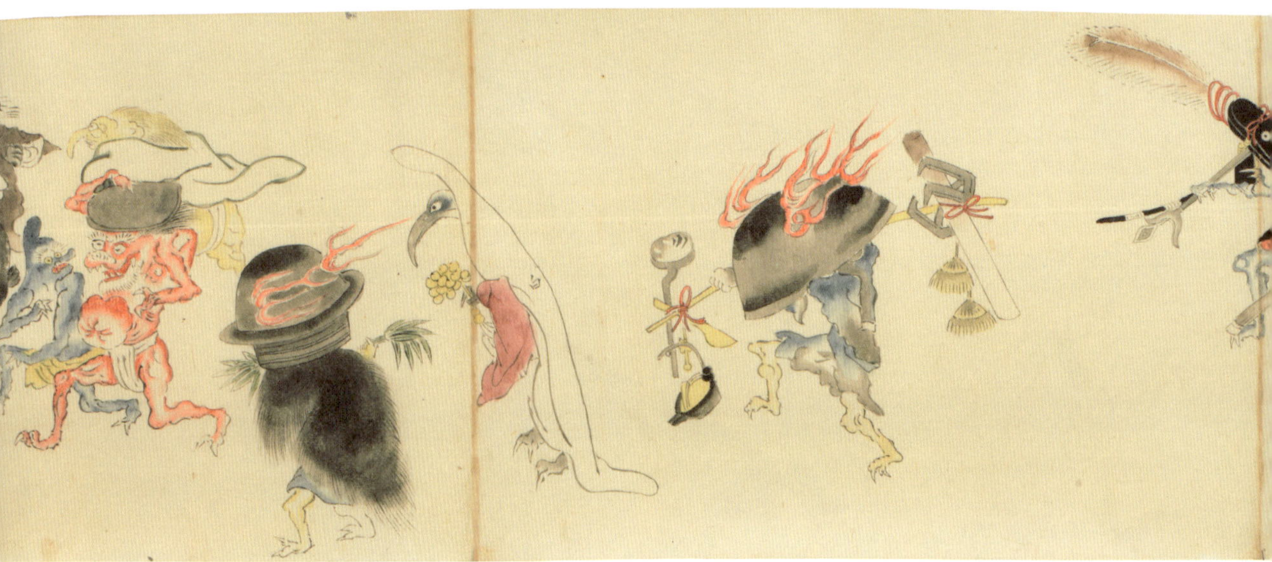

これは一般的な場面で、靫、鍋、釜などの行列が描かれている。

A common scene of a quiver, pot, bowl and other yokai in procession.

この絵巻の最大の特徴である巻末の場面だ。巨大な火の
玉を見て驚愕、逃げ去る妖怪ではなく、相手は縁側に座
した武者だ。彼は弓を握りしめ臨戦態勢のようだ。妖怪
退治譚に登場する武者は源頼光、源頼政、俵藤太、渡辺
綱など、少なからずいるが、ここに描かれた人物は必ず
しも特定できない。弓を持っていることがヒントかもし
れないが、研究課題だ。

This is the scene at the end, which is the most distinctive
feature of this scroll. Rather than yokai fleeing in dismay at
the sight of a huge fireball, the yokai encounter a warrior
sitting on the veranda. Bow in hand, he looks ready for battle.
Many warriors appear in tales of yokai defeats, among them
Minamoto no Yorimitsu, Minamoto no Yorimasa, Tawara no
Tōta, and Watanabe no Tsuna, but this warrior cannot be
definitively identified. The bow may provide a hint, but this
remains a question for future research.

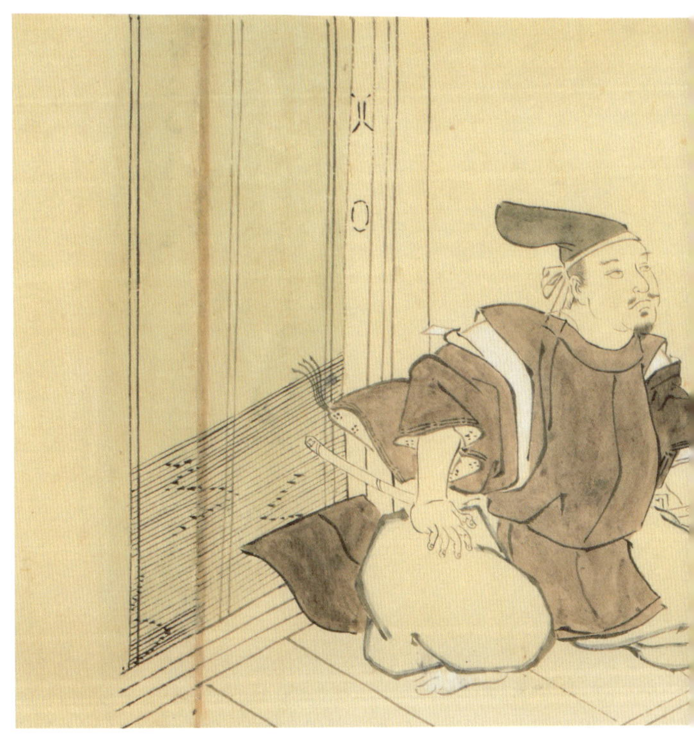

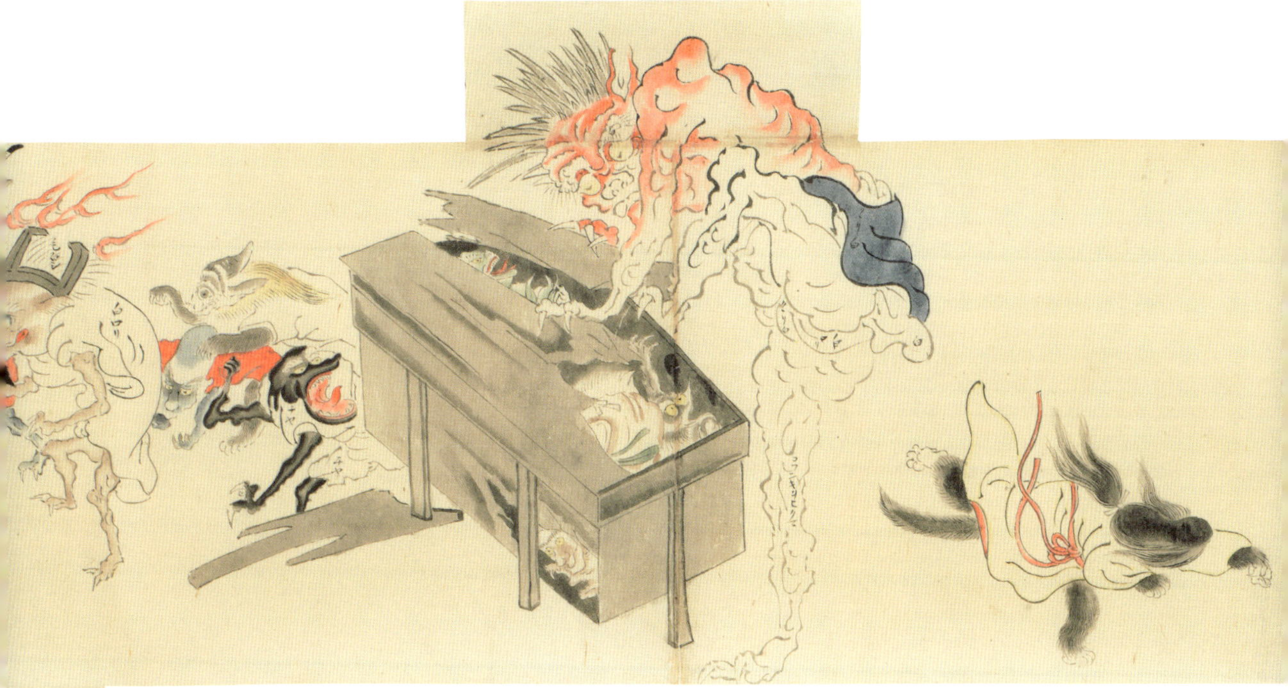

鬼が唐櫃をこじ開ける一般的な場面だが、鬼の体を描くために上部に紙を足している。こうしたタイプは他にも確認できる。
The standard scene of an ogre prying open a Chinese-style chest, except that extra paper has been added to fit in the ogre's upper body.
There are other examples of this technique.

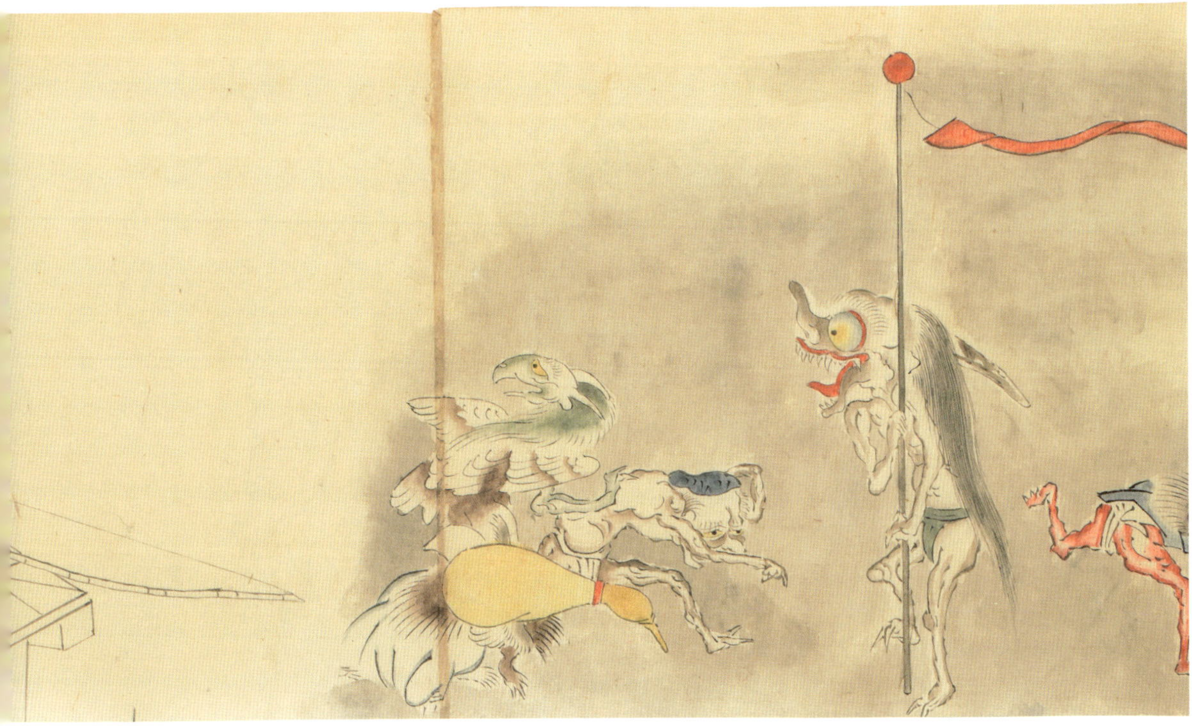

百鬼夜行図下絵　３点

ひゃっきやぎょうずしたえ

Three Sketches for the Night Parade
of One Hundred Demons

江戸時代以降　各縦 35.0　横 136
Post-Edo period, Height 35.0, Width 136 each

百鬼夜行絵巻は他の妖怪絵巻よりも多く下絵が残っているが、多くの場合は絵巻と同じ構図で色指定が書き込まれていたりする（『今昔妖怪大鑑』収録）。いっぽう、この作品は必ずしも全身像ではなく、一つ一つの妖怪を大きく描いているのが特徴だ。いずれも真珠庵系の百鬼夜行絵巻に登場する妖怪である。百鬼夜行絵巻の全容を明らかにするにはこうした下絵資料は重要である。

There are sketches for other yokai scrolls still in existence, but in most cases the compositions are the same as the final products, with color-coding directions written in (please refer to *Yokai Museum*). In contrast, the special characteristic of this work is that the yokai are drawn so large, their bodies extend beyond the borders of the page. All of these yokai appear in the Shinjuan-style Night Parade of One Hundred Demons picture scroll. Sketches such as these are of great interest in the quest to reveal the full picture of the scrolls of the Night Parade of One Hundred Demons.

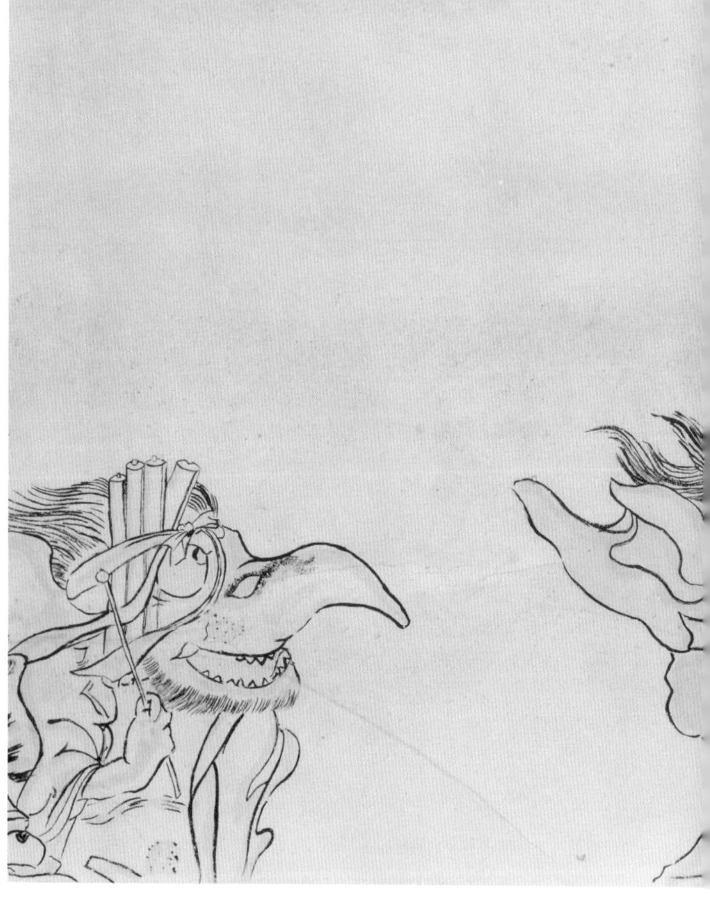

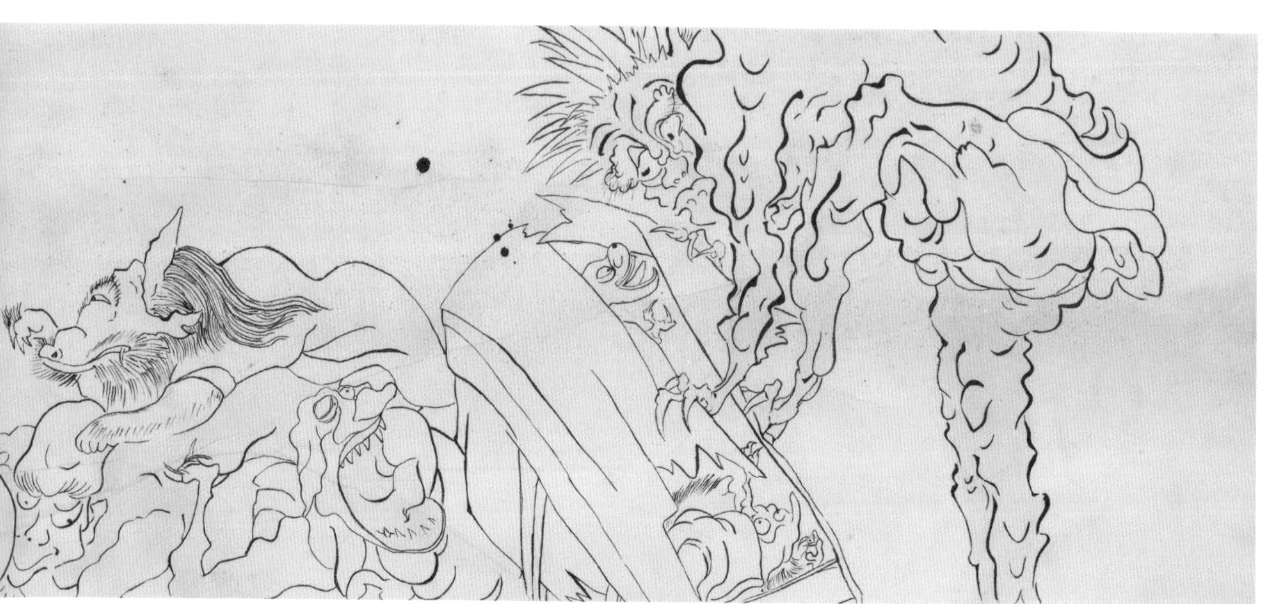

からびつ
唐櫃をこじ開ける赤鬼と逃げ出す妖怪たち。
As a red ogre forces open a Chinese-style chest (*karabitsu*), yokai make a break for freedom.

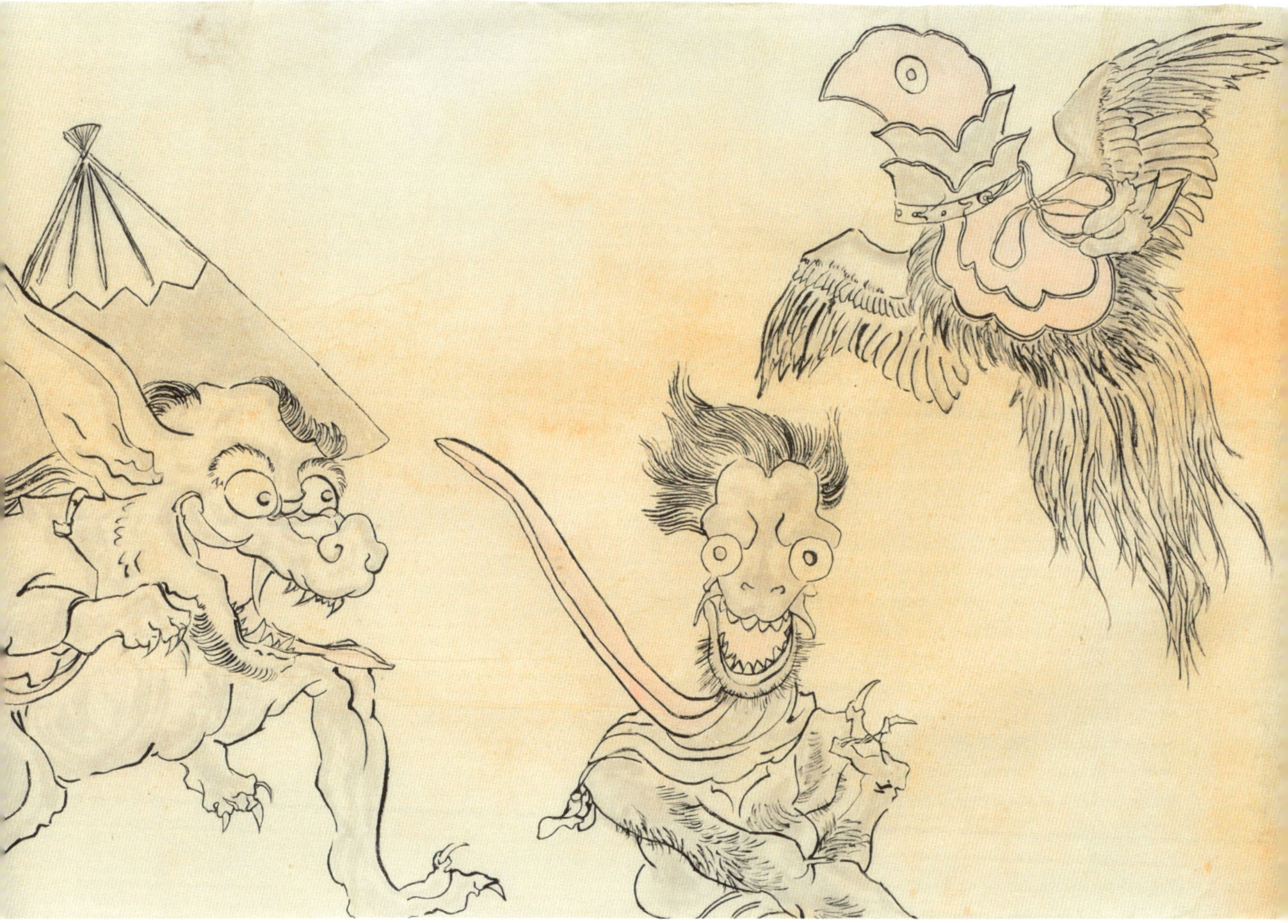

右から迦陵頻伽の姿をした鳥兜の妖怪。匙の妖怪。扇の妖怪。経巻を頭に載せた天狗のような妖怪。

From the right, a traditional bird helmet (*torikabuto*) cuts a figure like the fantastic immortal creature Kalavinka. A spoon. A folding fan. A yokai that looks like a long-nosed goblin (*tengu*) with sacred scrolls tied to its head.

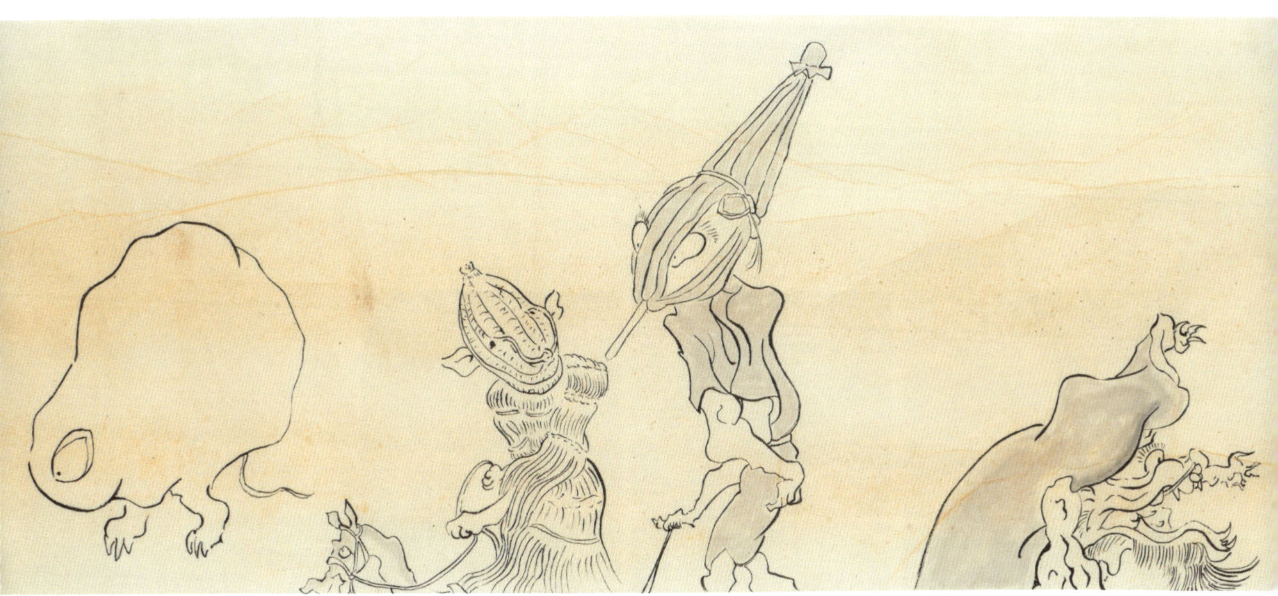

右から布を全身に纏った妖怪。杖をついた破れ傘の妖怪。藁の甲冑を身に着けた草履の妖怪。前足だけの異様な妖怪。

From the right, a yokai with its whole body covered in cloth. A ragged umbrella with a cane. A *zori* sandal wearing straw armor. A bizarre yokai missing its back legs.

百鬼夜行図
ひゃっきやぎょうず

The Night Parade of One Hundred Demons
(*Hyakki Yagyō Zu*)

礫川散人　明治時代以降　各縦 89.0　横 49.5
Rekisen-sanjin, Post-Meiji period, Height 89.0, Width 49.5 each

百鬼夜行図は大きな火の玉の出現や朝日が昇って妖怪たちが逃げ去るというスタイルが、この作品では太陽を背景に仏が現れて光が降り注いで妖怪が四散している。これは大錦 6 枚続の迫力ある作品として知られる「後鳥羽法皇の夢中に現れたる妖怪図」（『今昔妖怪大鑑』に収録・参考図参照）と同様だが、描かれた妖怪たちもこの錦絵のものと同じである。参考図では仏が左端上部に描かれているが、ここでは仏の左側にも妖怪を配した構図となっている。「辛未春日 礫川散人写」とあるが、「辛未」は明治 4 年か昭和 6 年と思われる。

This picture of the Night Parade of One Hundred Demons follows the pattern in which yokai flee at the appearance of the rising sun or a large fireball, but in this work, Buddha appears with the sun as background, the light beams down and yokai scatter in all directions. This work bears a strong similarity to Yokai Appearing in a Dream to the Retired Emperor Go-Toba (please refer to the image below from *Yokai Museum*), an impressive work which consists of six large-format *nishiki-e*, down to the yokai depicted. In that work, Buddha is placed leftmost in the upper corner, but in this composition, there are yokai positioned to the left of Buddha. The text reads "Eighth Year of the Sexagenary Cycle, Spring Day: Copy of Rekisen-sanjin"; the Eighth Year in question is thought to be either Meiji 4 (1871) or Shōwa 6 (1931).

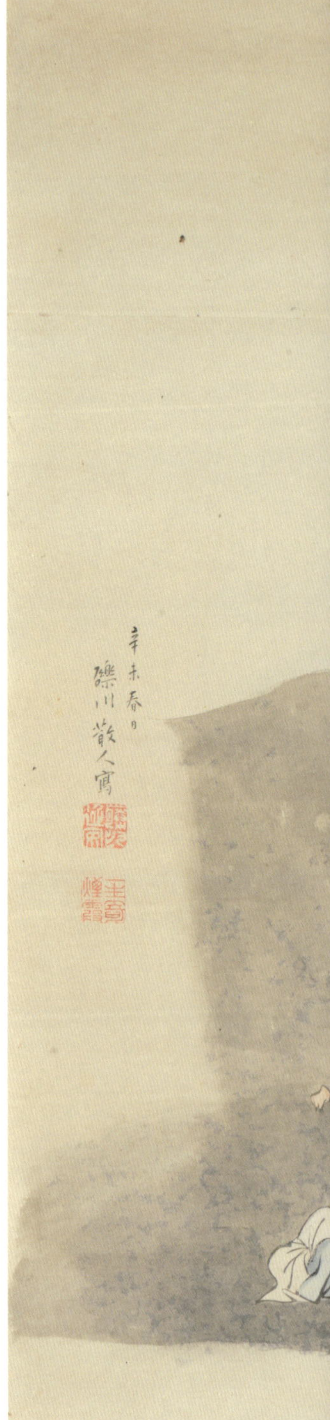

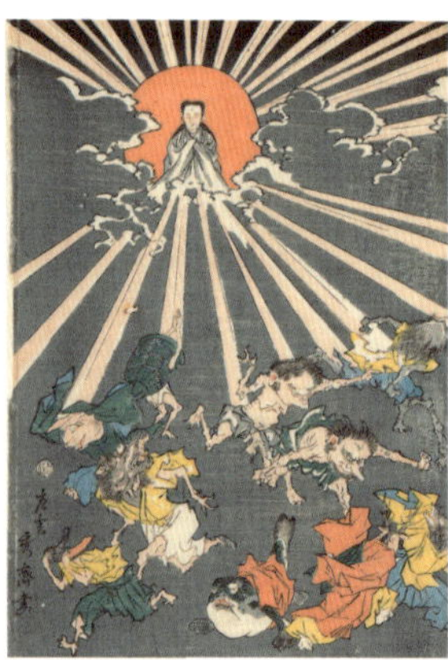
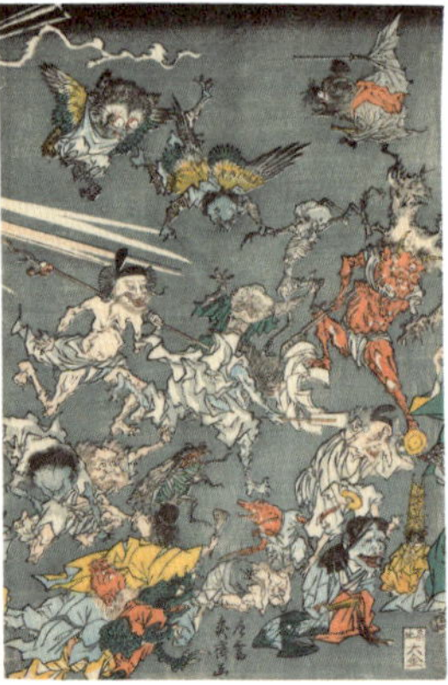
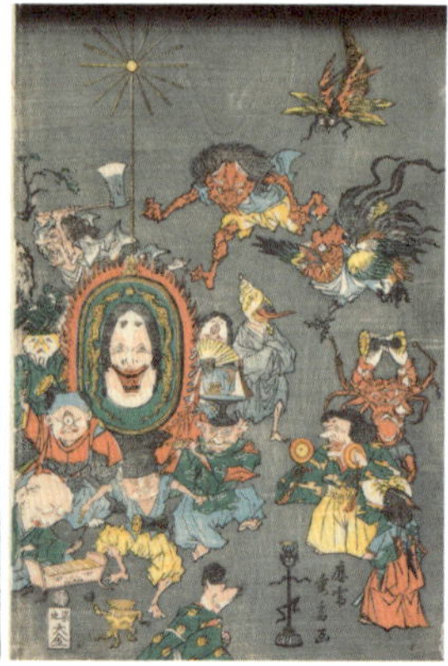

参考図版

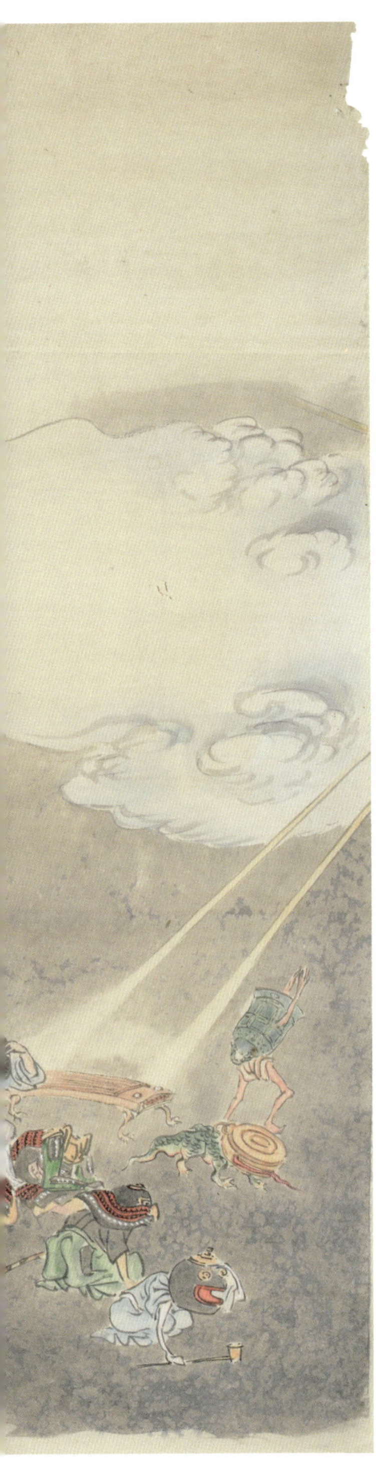

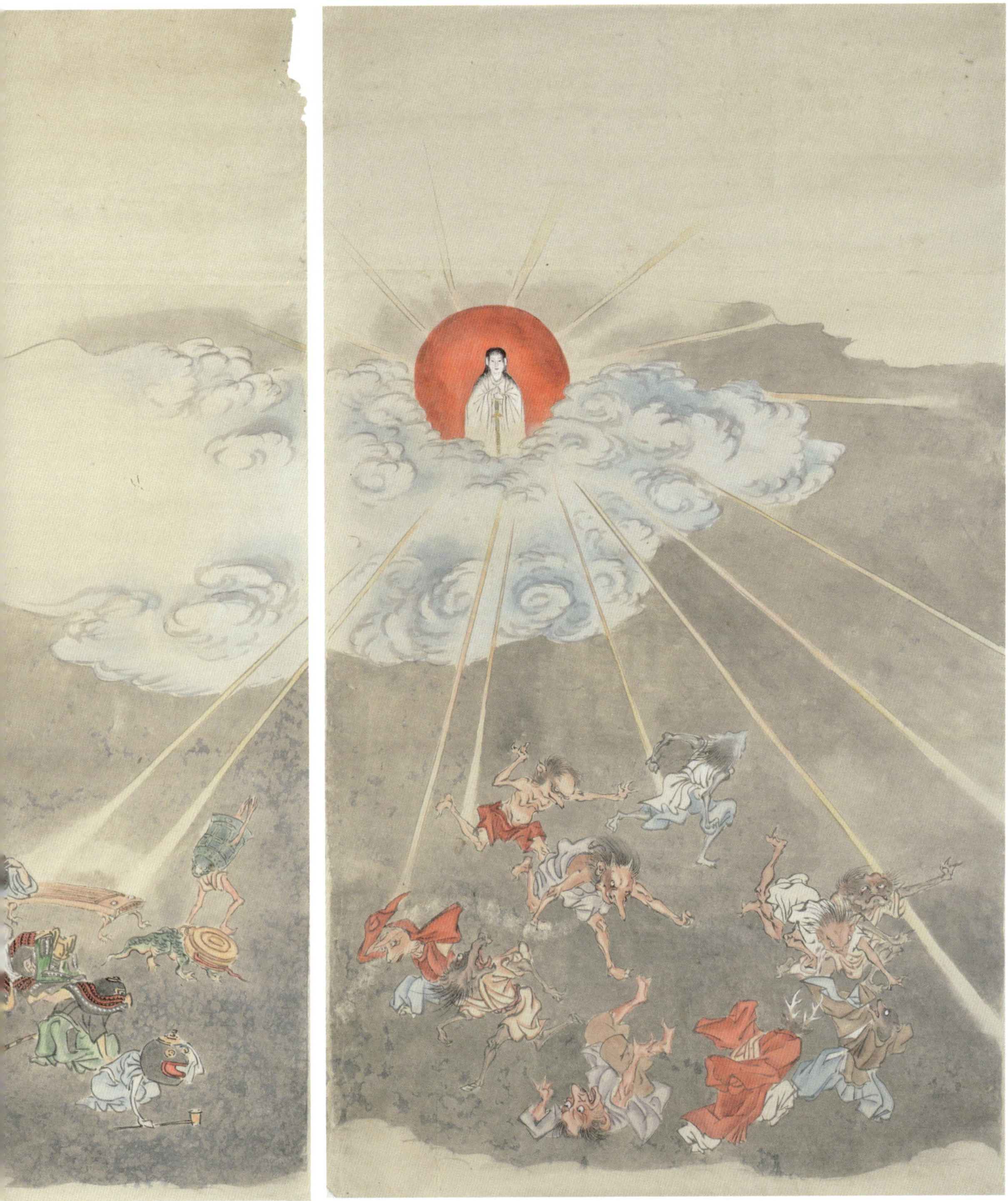

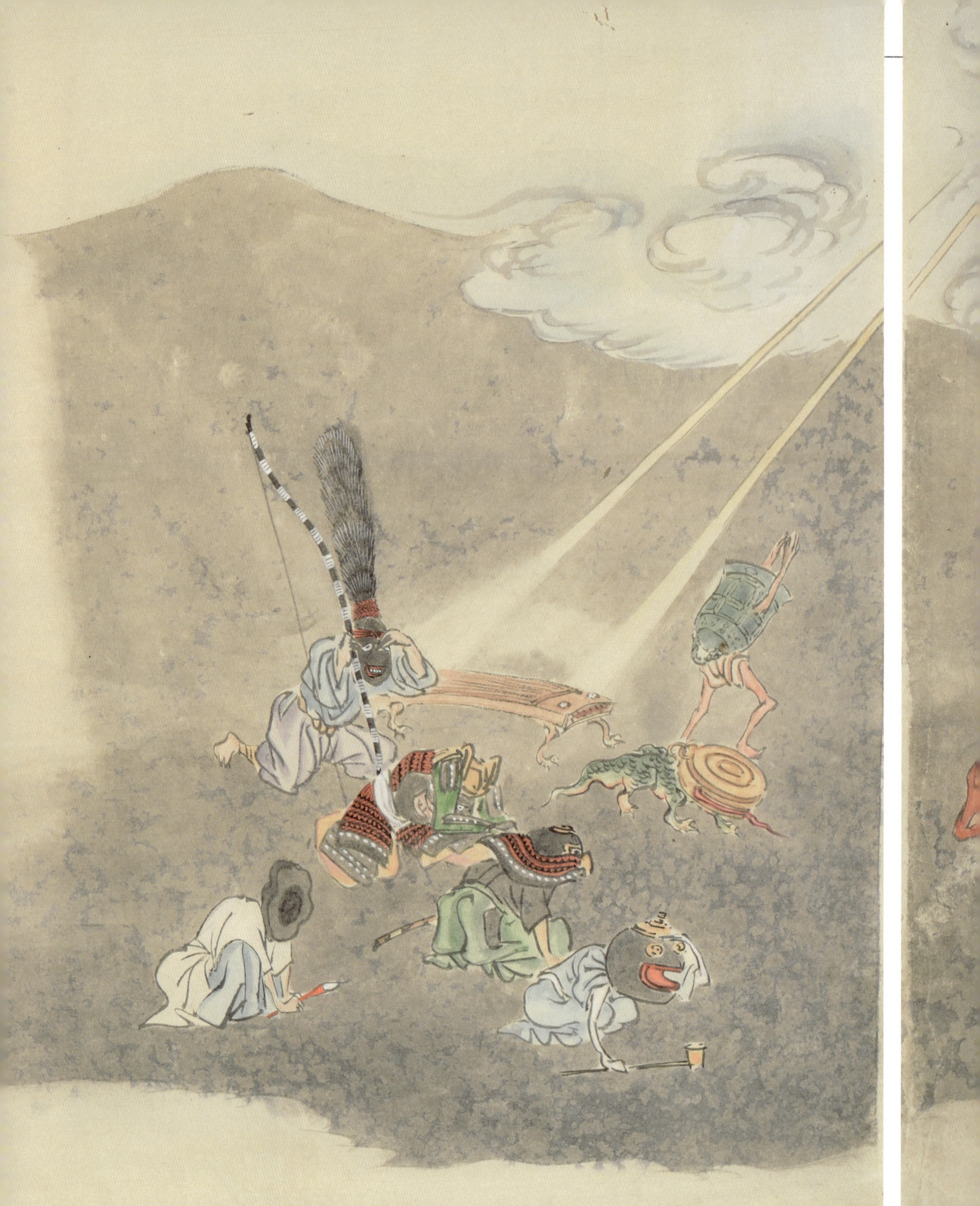

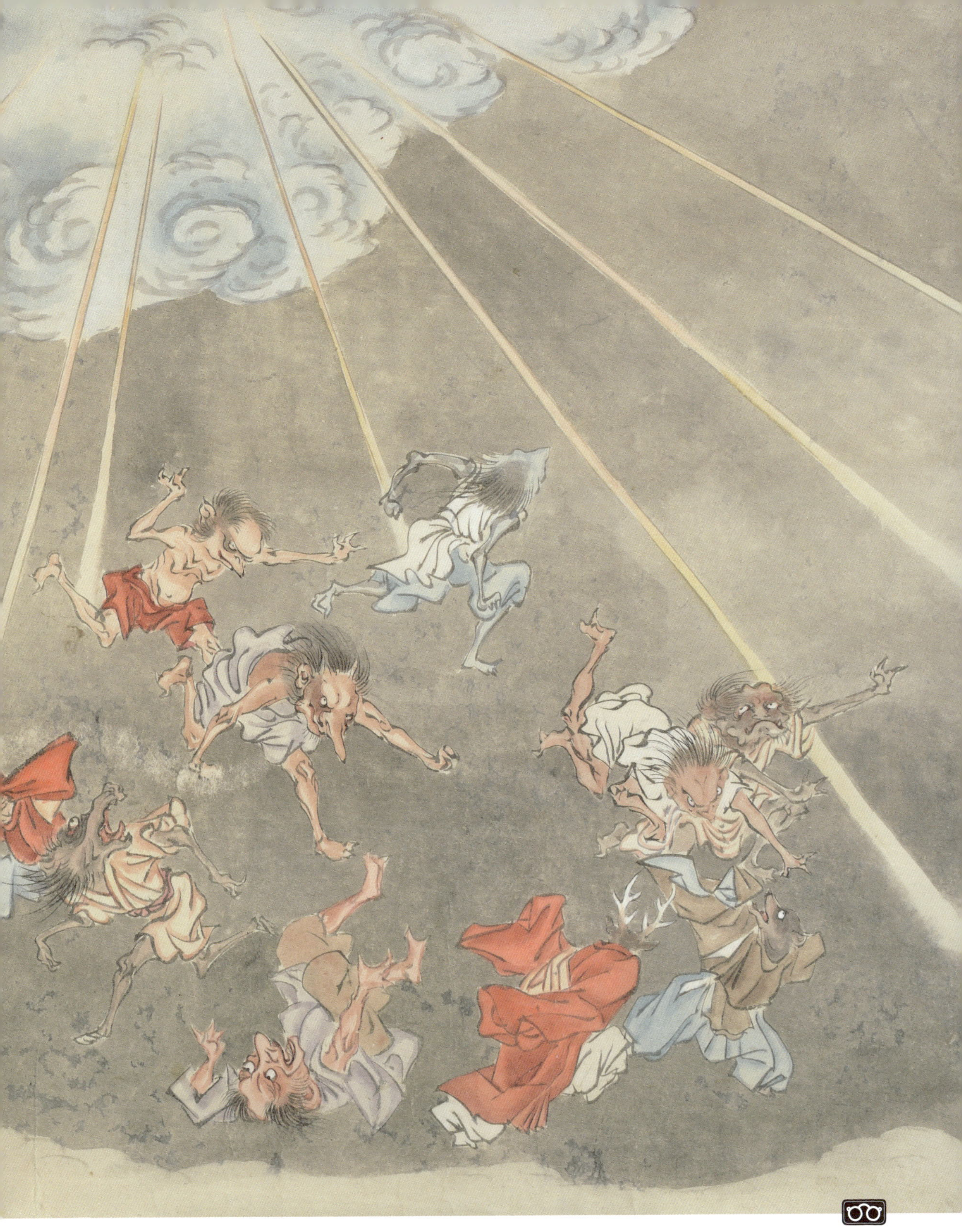

百鬼夜行図
ひゃっきやぎょうず

The Night Parade of
One Hundred Demons

淡島椿岳　明治時代　縦 141.3　横 40.5
Awashima Chingaku, Meiji period,
Height 141.3, Width 40.5

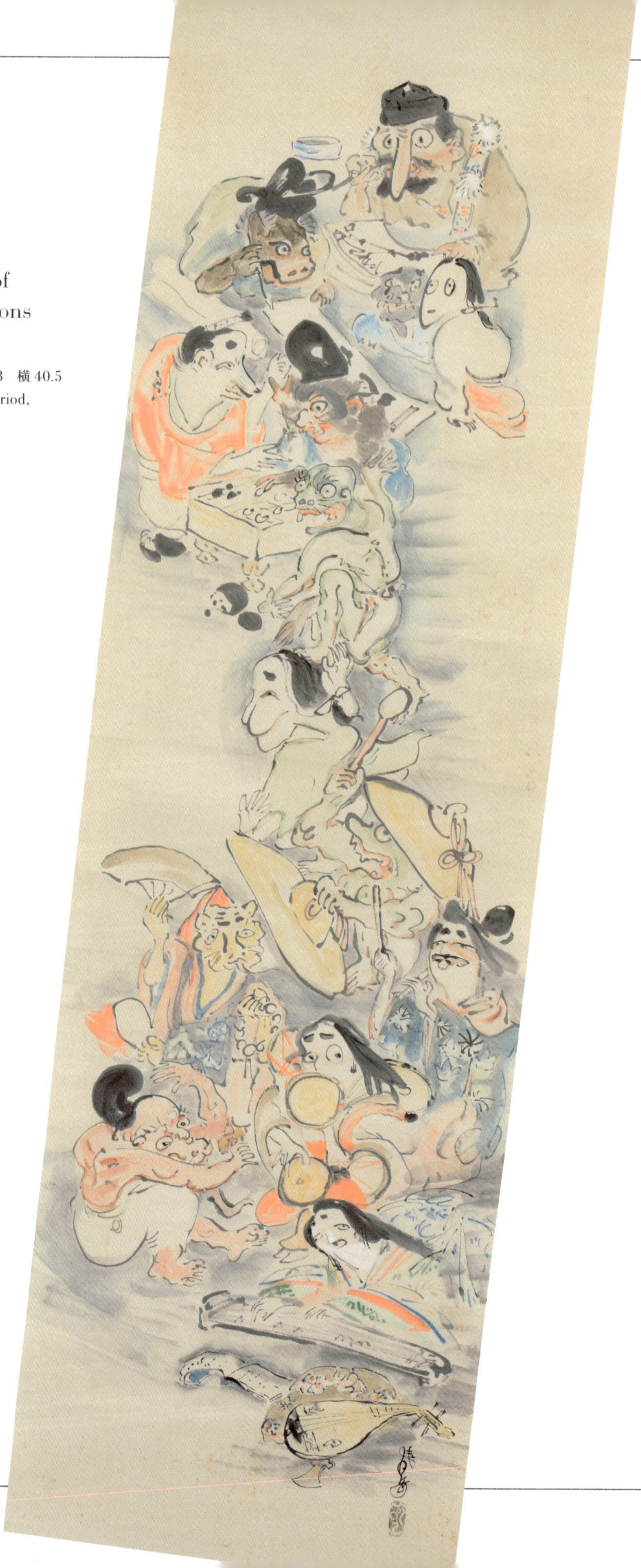

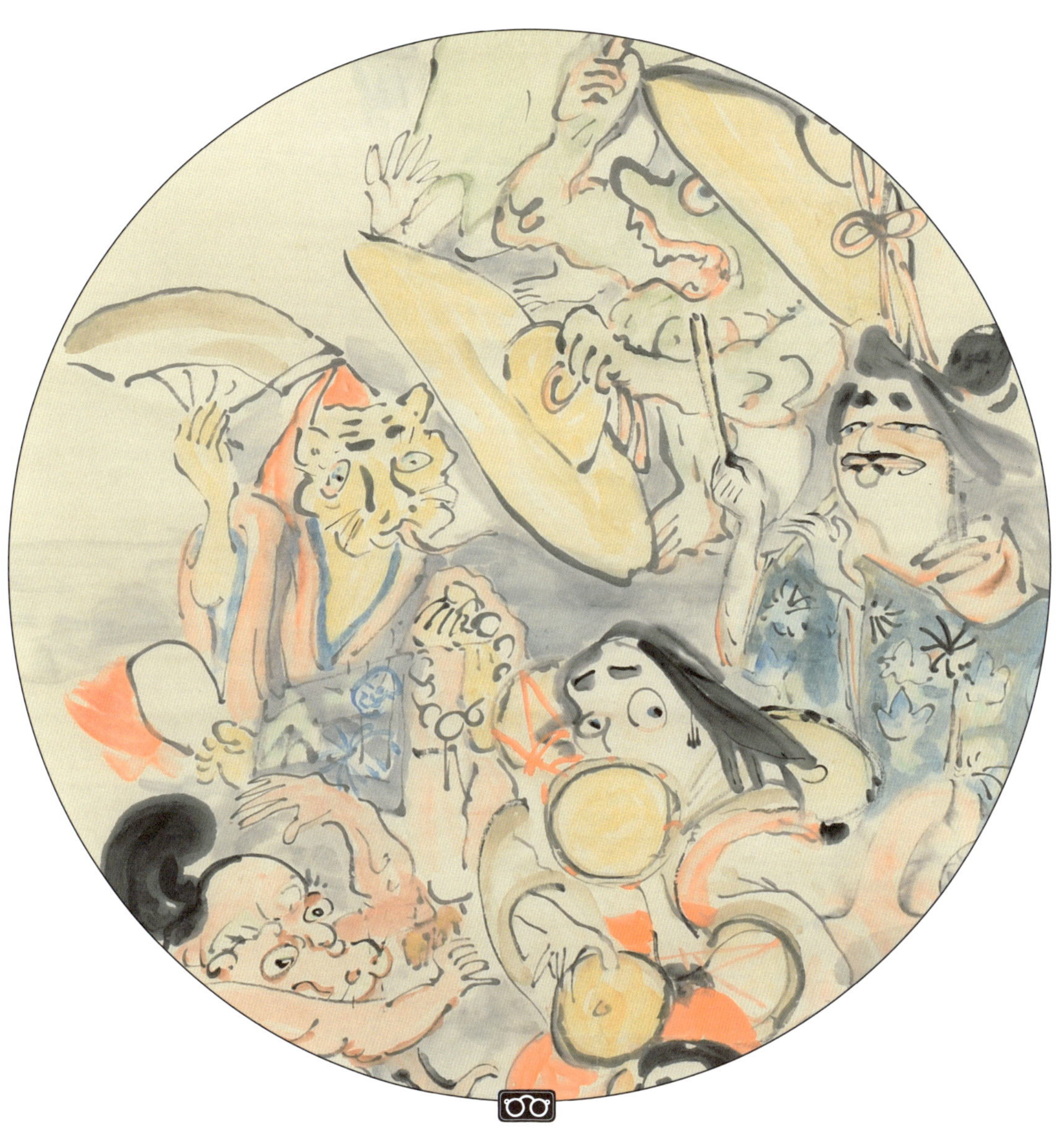

楽器を奏でる妖怪、舞に興ずる妖怪、碁を打つ妖怪、書を揮毫する
妖怪などが跋扈する様が縦長の構図のなかで描かれている。登場す
る妖怪は愛嬌のある姿で、古くからの百鬼夜行のイメージとは異な
る椿岳の妖怪世界が展開されている。

Yokai run riot in this long vertical composition: playing musical instruments, dancing, playing *go*, and doing brush calligraphy. The creatures appearing here are lovable figures of fun which draw us in to the world of Chingaku yokai, a very different world to the age-old Night Parade of One Hundred Demons.

百鬼夜行絵巻、こんなものも！！

The Night Parade of One Hundred Demons, as you've never seen it before!

真珠庵系の百鬼夜行絵巻は数多く残されているが、それだけに卓越した技量の持ち主によって描かれたものから技量の劣る作品まで千差万別の観がある。この作品も上質なものとはいえず、彩色も数色のみで施されている。しかし、こうした作品もあることが百鬼夜行絵巻がいかに広く描かれていったかを示す資料でもあるのだ。

Many scrolls of the Shinjuan style of Night Parade of One Hundred Demons remain; an endless variety is found in these, ranging from those by artists of sublime skill to works of inferior technique. This work cannot be described as high quality, and uses only a few different colors. However, the fact that a work such as this exists shows just how often the Night Parade of One Hundred Demons scroll was recreated.

百鬼夜行絵巻　江戸時代以降　縦39.5　長912.0
The Night Parade of One Hundred Demons Picture Scroll　Post-Edo period, Height 39.5, Length 912.0

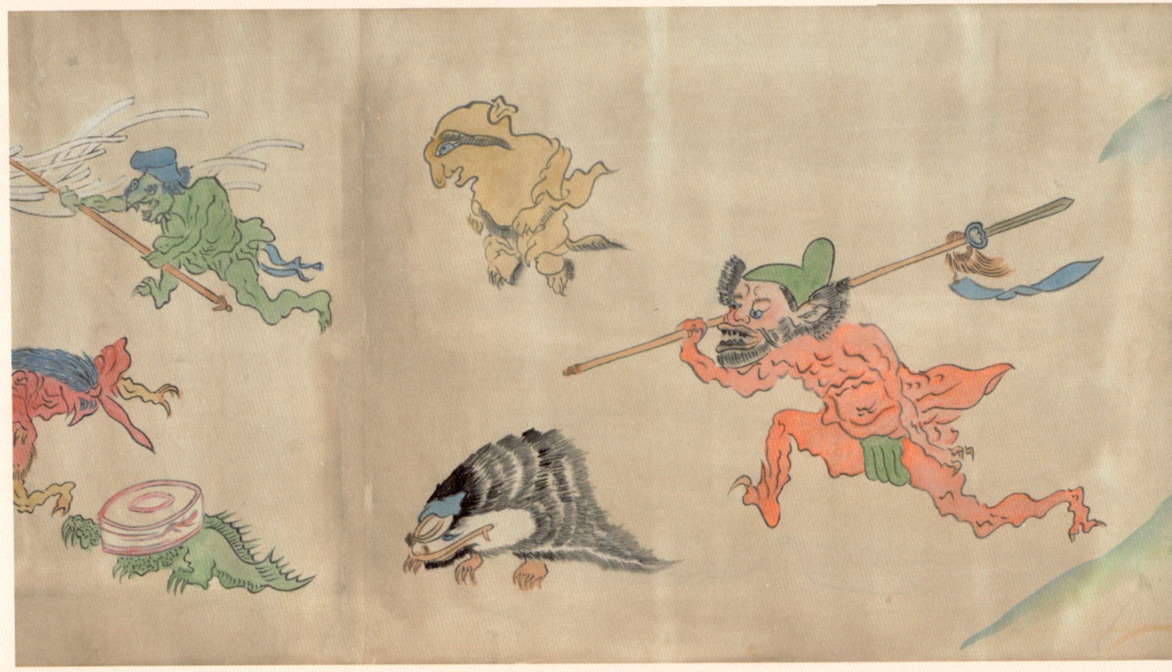

前図の妖怪を色だけ変えて再び登場させている。体の色を青から赤に変えたのは青鬼と赤鬼の意か。

The previous yokai changes its color to appear again. The change in body color may signify the story of the blue ogre and the red ogre.

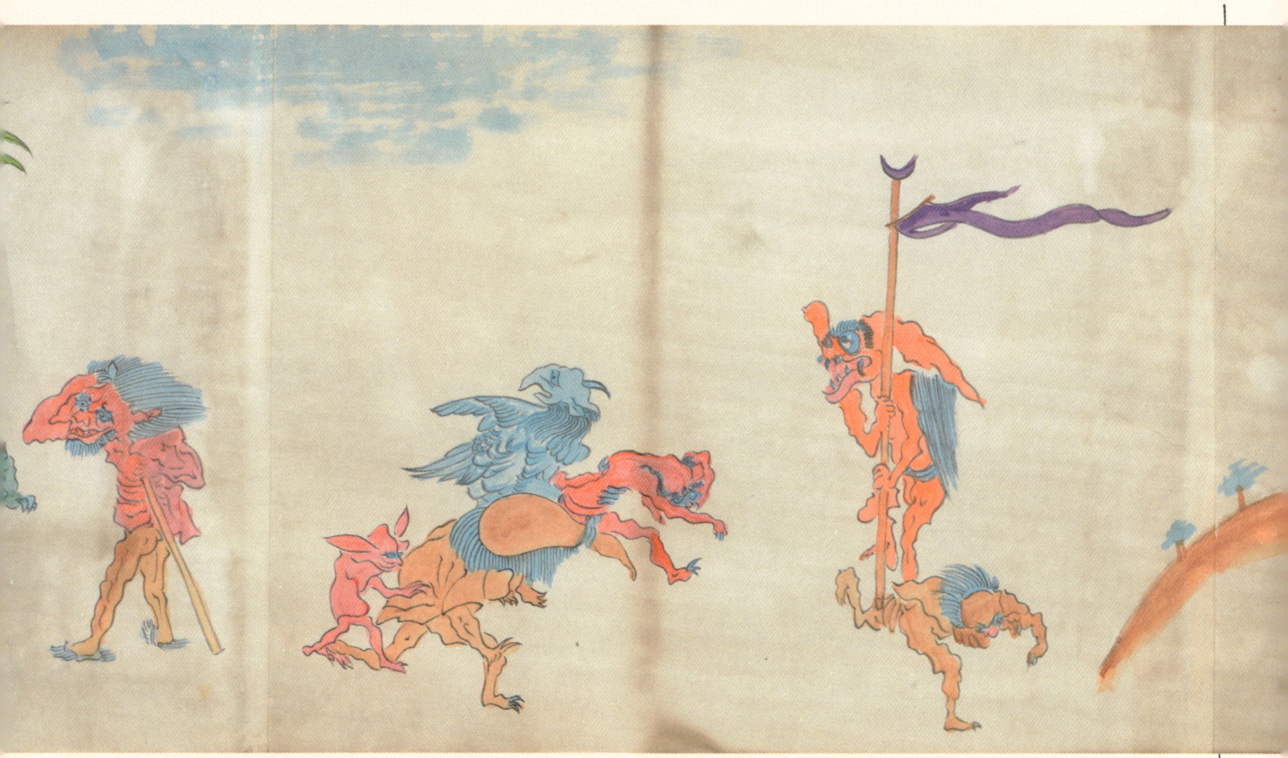

幡を持った妖怪はお馴染みの妖怪だが、ここでは体が毛と目以外は
一色で塗り潰されている。ほかの妖怪も同様で簡易に作られた作品
であることが一目瞭然だ。

The yokai holding a Buddhist banner is familiar, but here its body is painted all the same color except for its fur and eyes. It is obvious at a glance that the other yokai are done in a similar manner in this simply-made work.

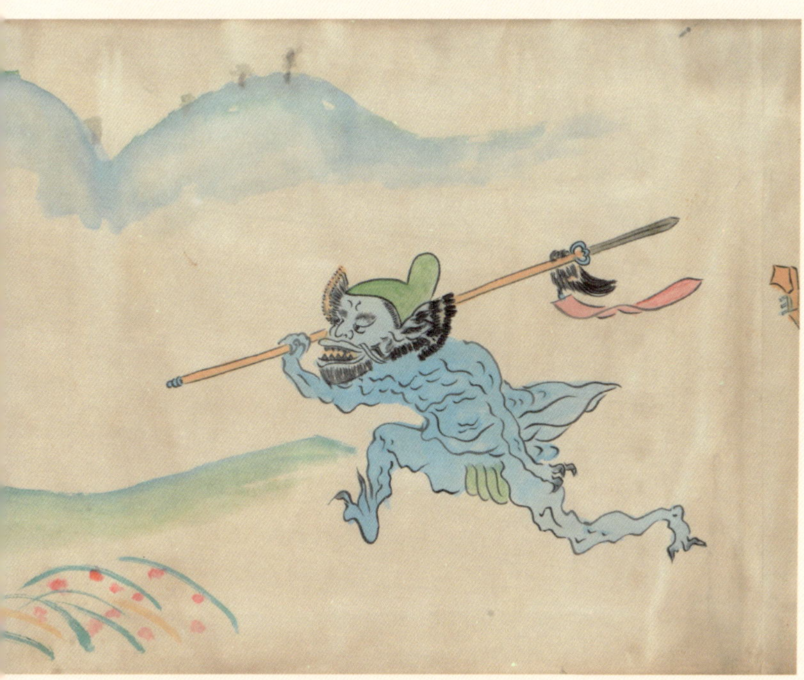

剣を担いだ妖怪が駆けて行く場面だが、地面やそこに生えた草や背
景に山並みを描いている。これは大きな意味もなく付け加えられた
ものだろう。簡易な作品だけにそうしたことを自由にやっているのだ。

A running yokai holds a blade; the ground, the grass growing on it and a row of mountains in the background have been sketched in. These were probably just added on for no particular reason. In a basic work, things like that can be done without putting too much thought in.

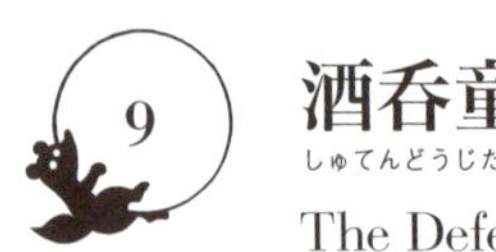

酒呑童子退治図

しゅてんどうじたいじず

The Defeat of Shuten-dōji

江戸時代以降　縦 77.3　横 68　Post-Edo period, Height 77.3, Width 68

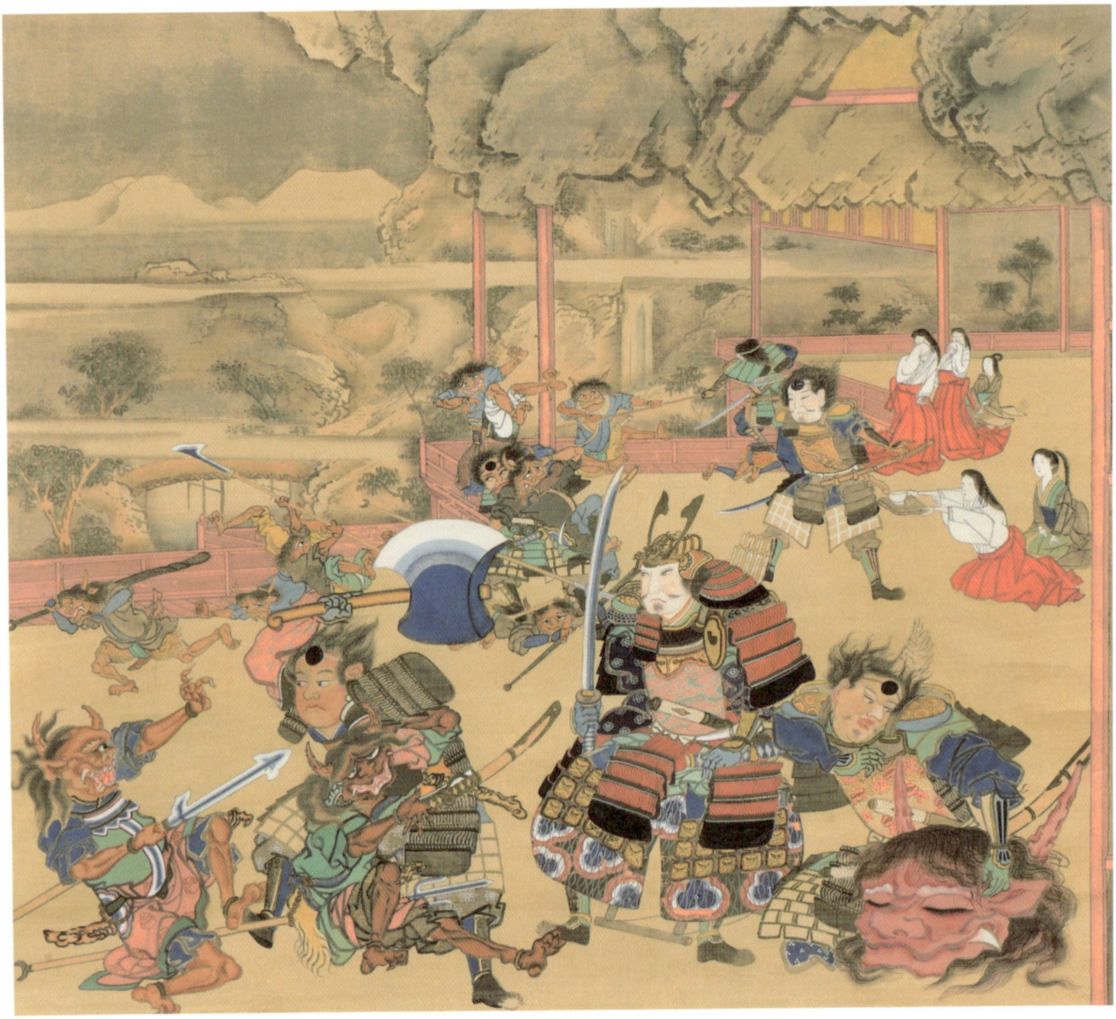

源頼光たちが酒呑童子を退治する話をテーマとしている。右には斬り落とされた酒呑童子の大
きな首が転がり、郎党の鬼たちも逃げ回っている。酒呑童子退治のクライマックス場面を描い
ている。

Minamoto no Yorimitsu and his company defeating Shuten-dōji is the theme of this work. Shuten-
dōji's huge decapitated head rolls on the right, and his ogre minions are on the run. This is the climactic
scene of Shuten-dōji's defeat.

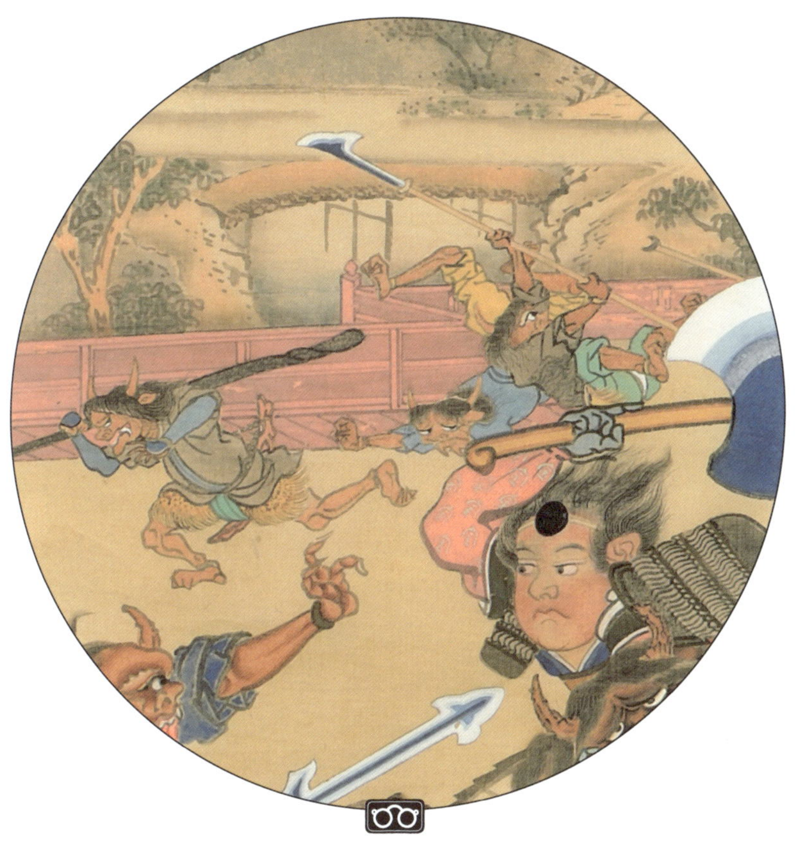

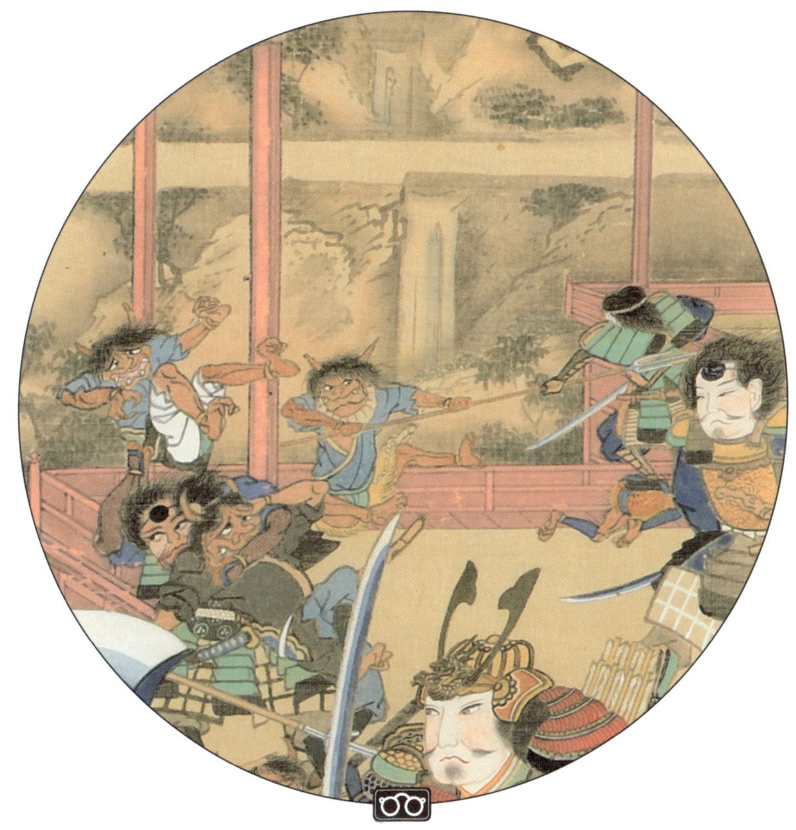

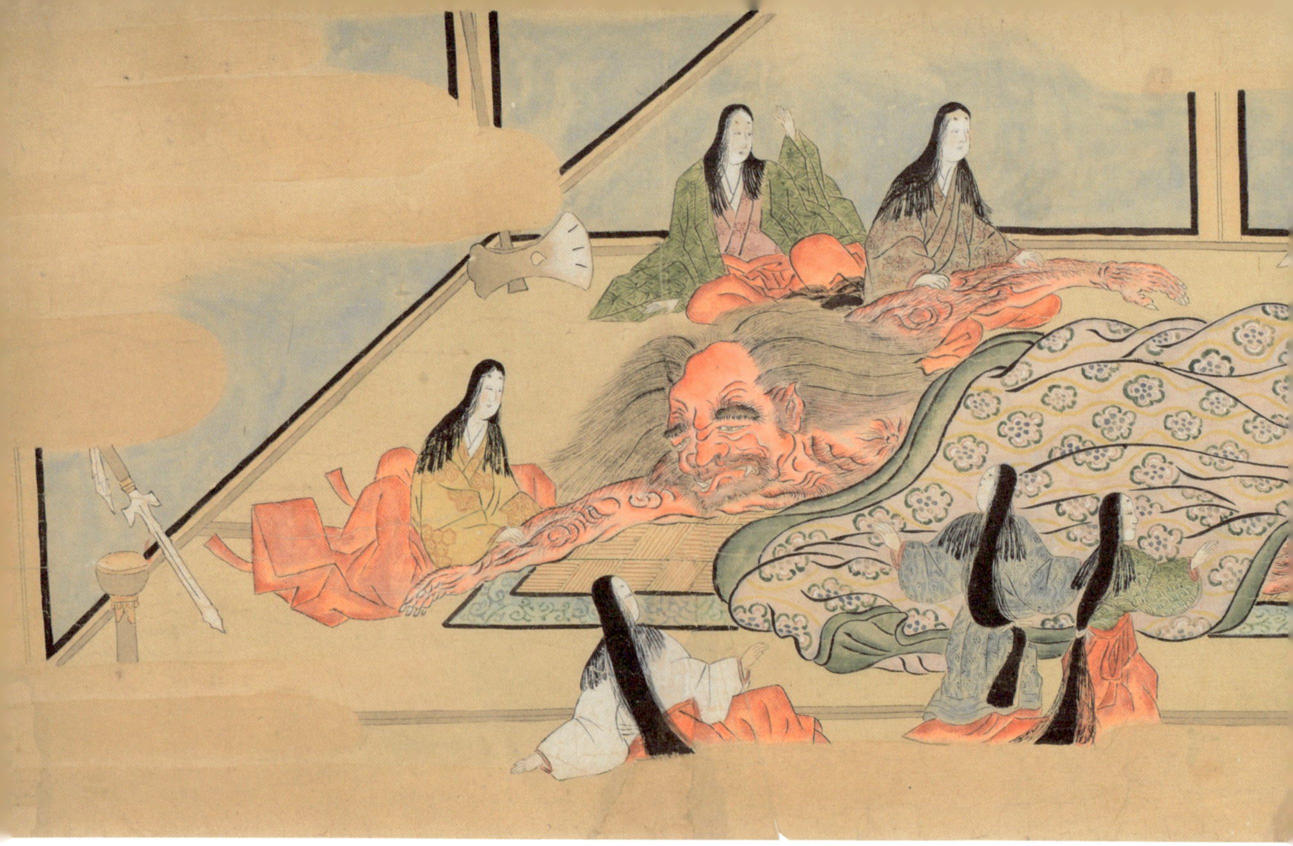

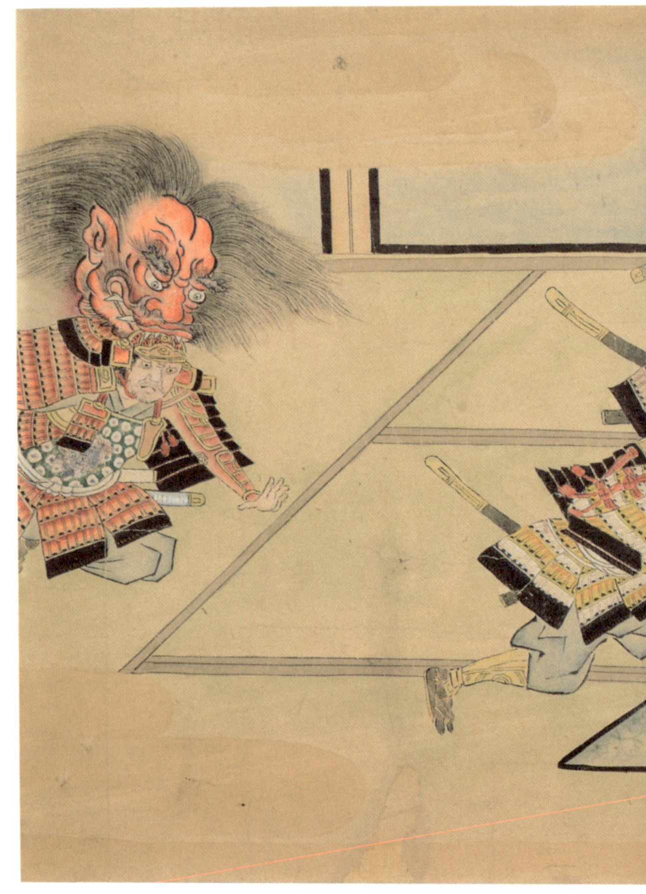

大江山絵巻 上巻（3巻のうち）
おおえやままえまき

Mount Ōe Picture Scroll:
First of Three Scrolls

宅間悠山　寛延元（1748）年　縦 32.0　長 1155.5
Takuma Yūzan: Kan'en 1 (1748),
Height 32.0, Length 1155.5

源頼光が酒呑童子を退治するストーリーの絵巻は「酒呑童子
絵巻」などと題されて中世から連綿と描かれ継がれているが、
この作品もその一つで、丁寧な筆致で仕上げられている。
詞書はなく、絵だけで展開されるスタイルで、下巻の巻末に
「寛延元戊辰年中秋日 宅間悠山七十一才画」とある。

The picture scroll of the story of how Minamoto no Yorimitsu
defeated Shuten-dōji was re-created over and over again from the
middle ages onward under titles such as Shuten-dōji Picture Scroll;
this work is one of these, executed with meticulous brushwork.
There is no accompanying text section (*kotobagaki*); this style
only uses images, but the end of the final scroll has this inscription:
"1748, 5th Year of the Sexagenary Cycle, 15th Day of the 8th
Lunar Month: By Takuma Yūzan, 71 years of age".

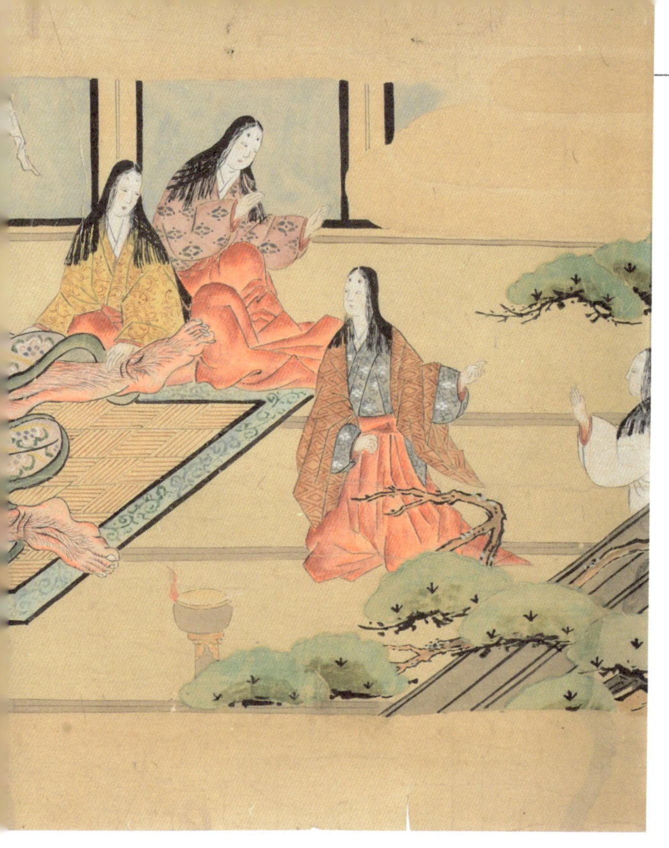

酒宴後に寝入った酒呑童子。巨大な鬼の姿を露わにして
いる。
Shuten-dōji fallen fast asleep after a bout of drinking. The
huge ogre is revealed.

寝入った酒呑童子を急襲した頼光たち。首を斬り落とさ
れた酒呑童子だが、首だけになっても頼光を襲うほどの
凄さだ。
The sleeping Shuten-dōji is set upon by Yorimitsu and his
companions. Even though Shuten-dōji's head has been cut
off, his power is so strong that his severed head strikes back at
Yorimitsu.

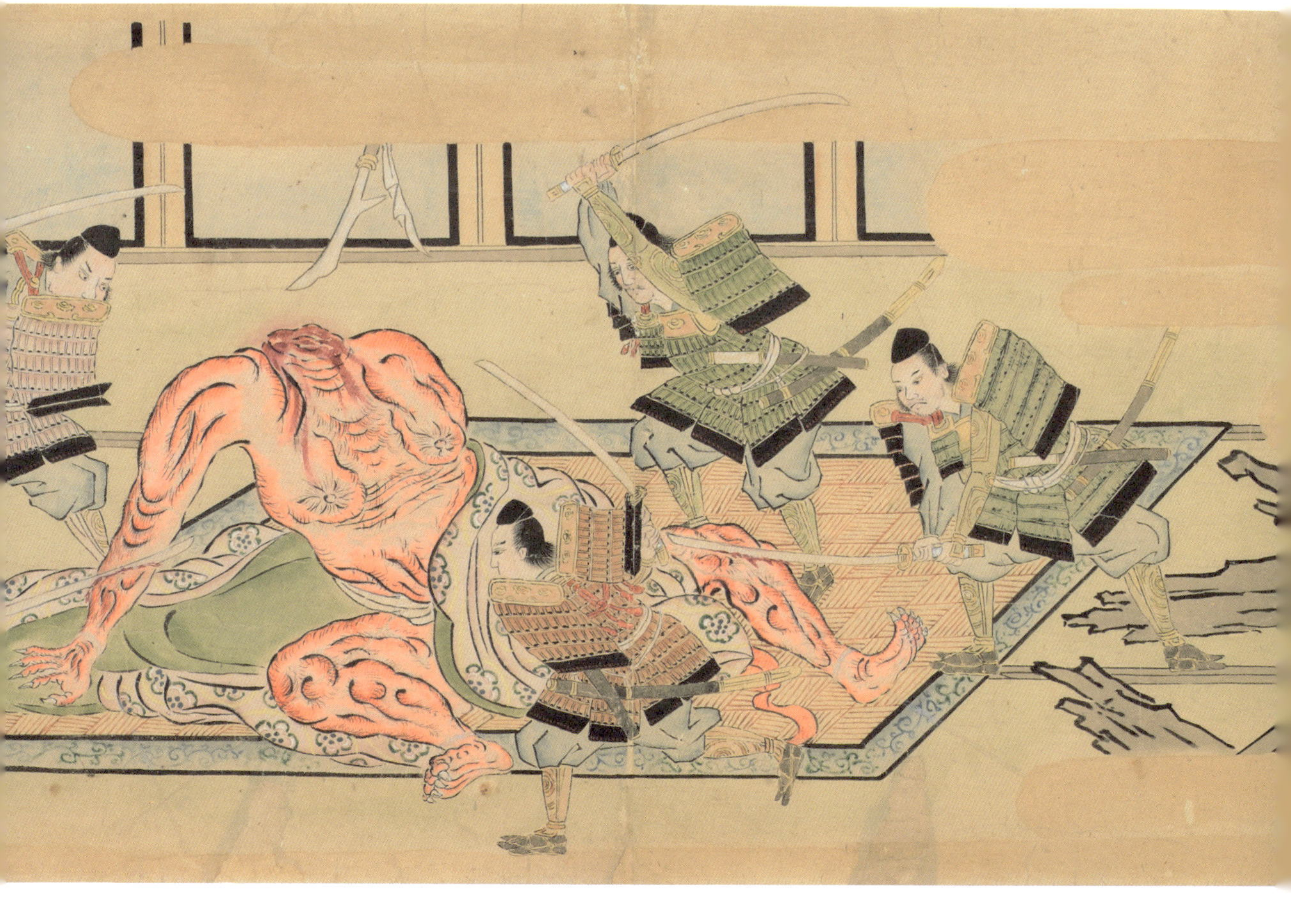

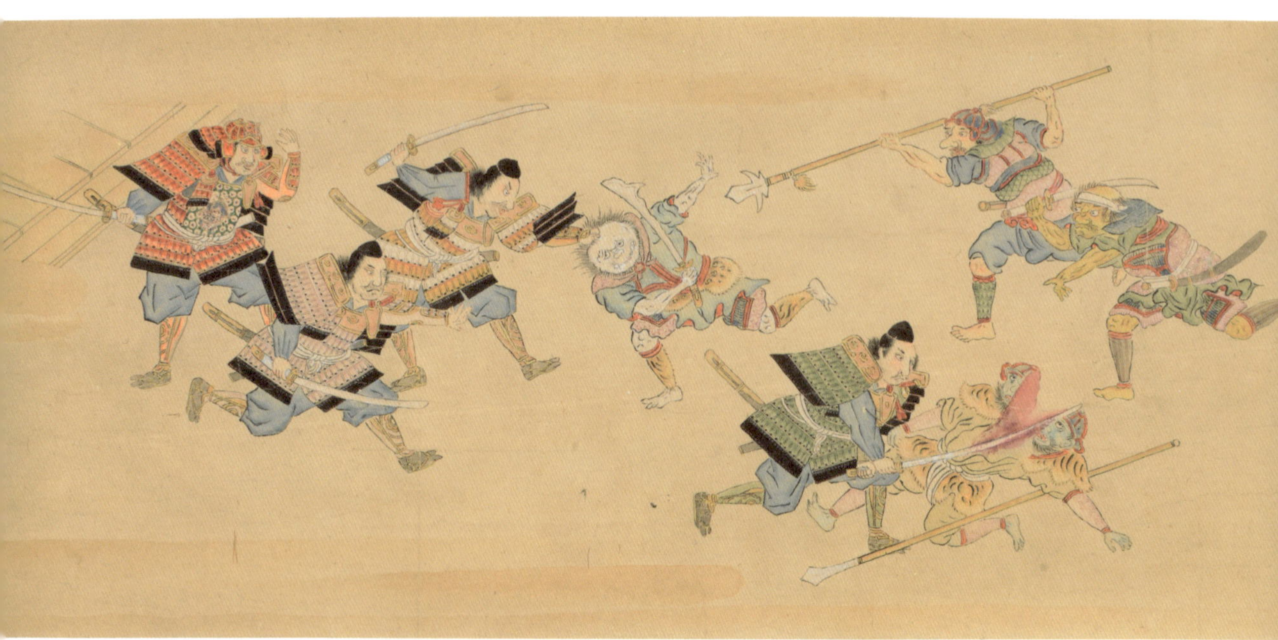

大挙して頼光らを襲う酒呑童子の手下の鬼たちと戦う頼光たち。鬼を胴体から真っ二つにしている場面も描かれている。
Yorimitsu and his companions fight with Shuten-dōji's swarming ogre minions. An ogre entirely cut in half through its torso is depicted.

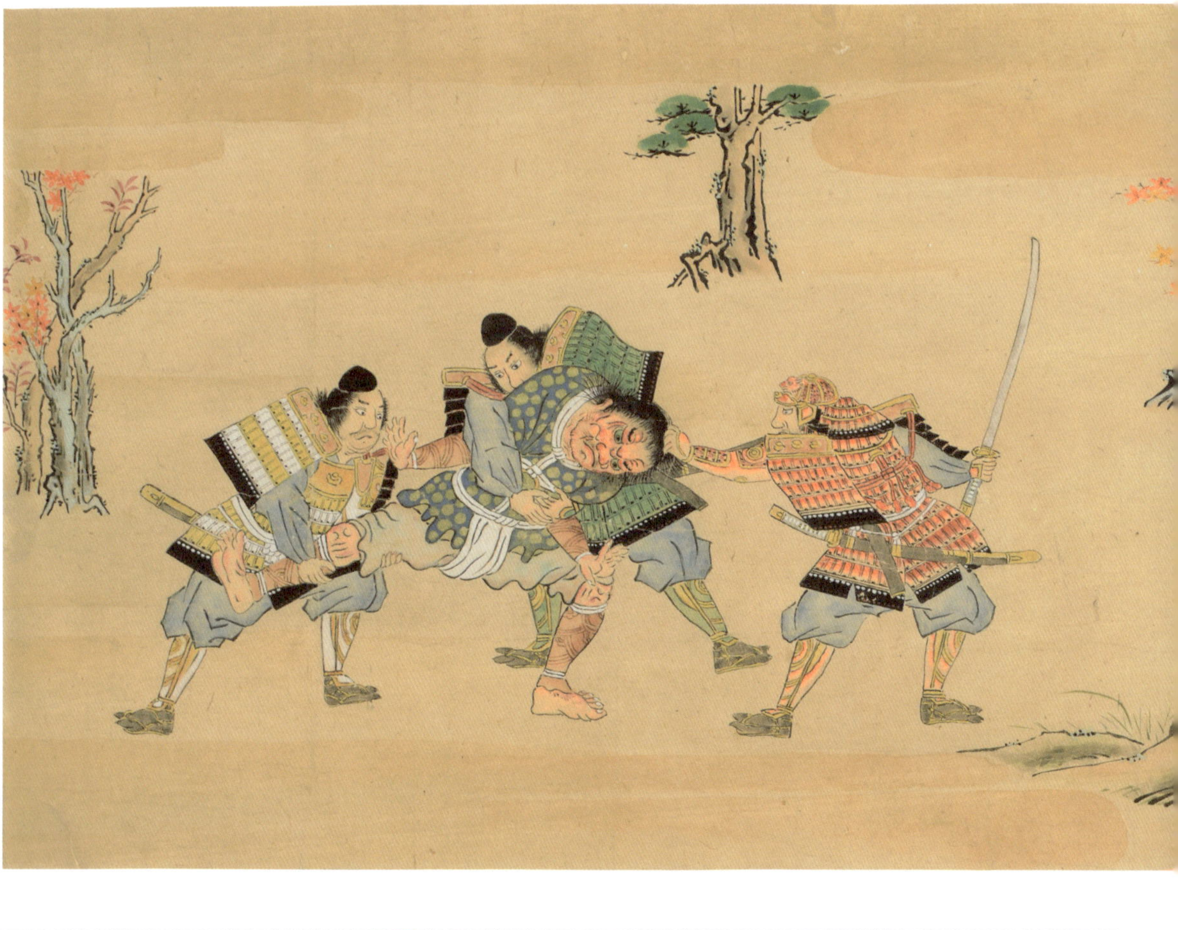

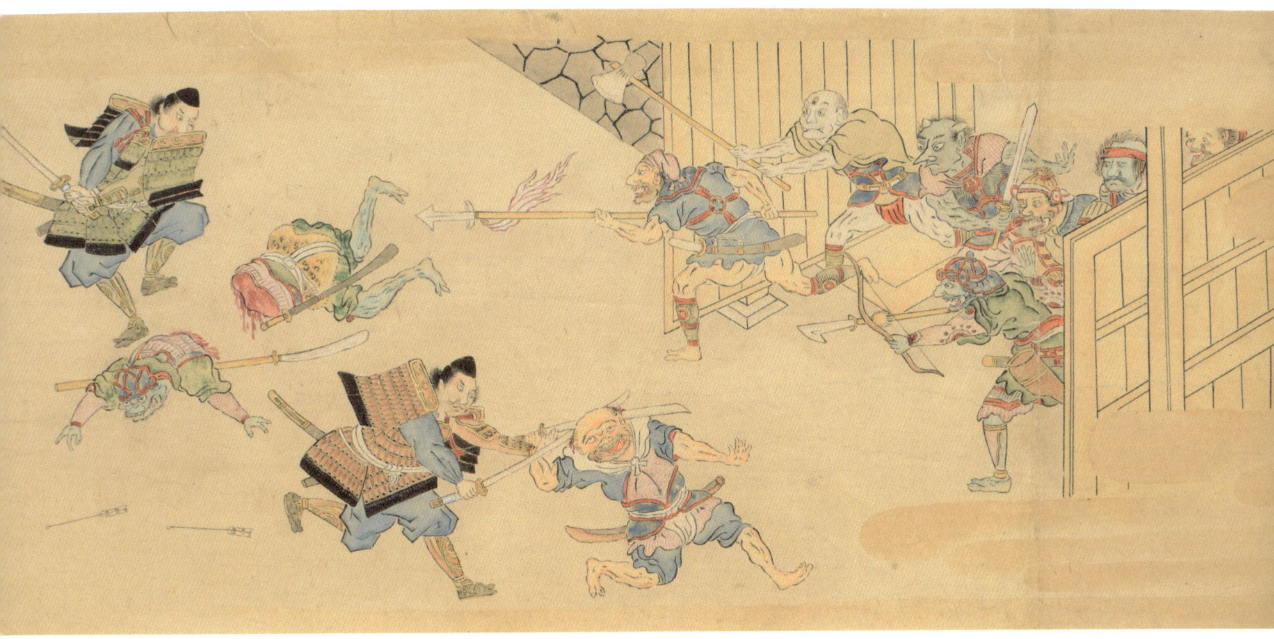

鬼との戦いの場面。
Scenes of the fight with the ogres.

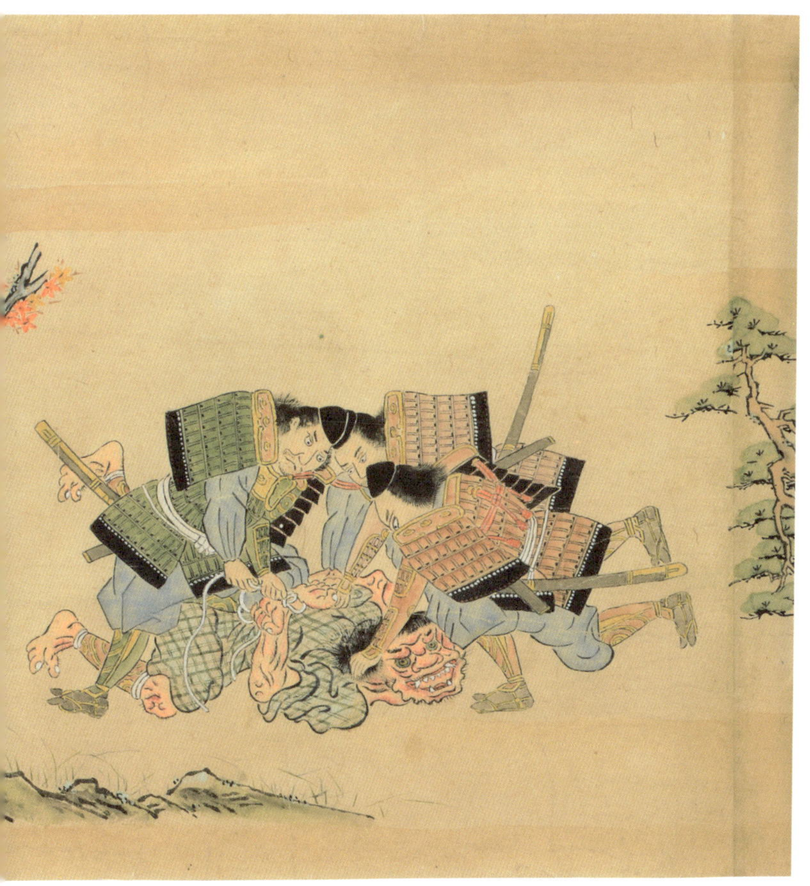

やがて、鬼たちは頼光らに敗れ、酒呑童子の残
党も一掃されて頼光らは都に凱旋を果たす。
At long last, the ogres have been defeated;
Yorimitsu and his men deal with the remainder of
Shuten-dōji's followers before returning to the
town for a heroes' welcome.

酒呑童子絵巻下絵
しゅてんどうじえまきしたえ

Shuten-dōji Picture Scroll Design

江戸時代　縦 31.0　長 1075.5　Edo period, Height 31.0, Length 1075.5

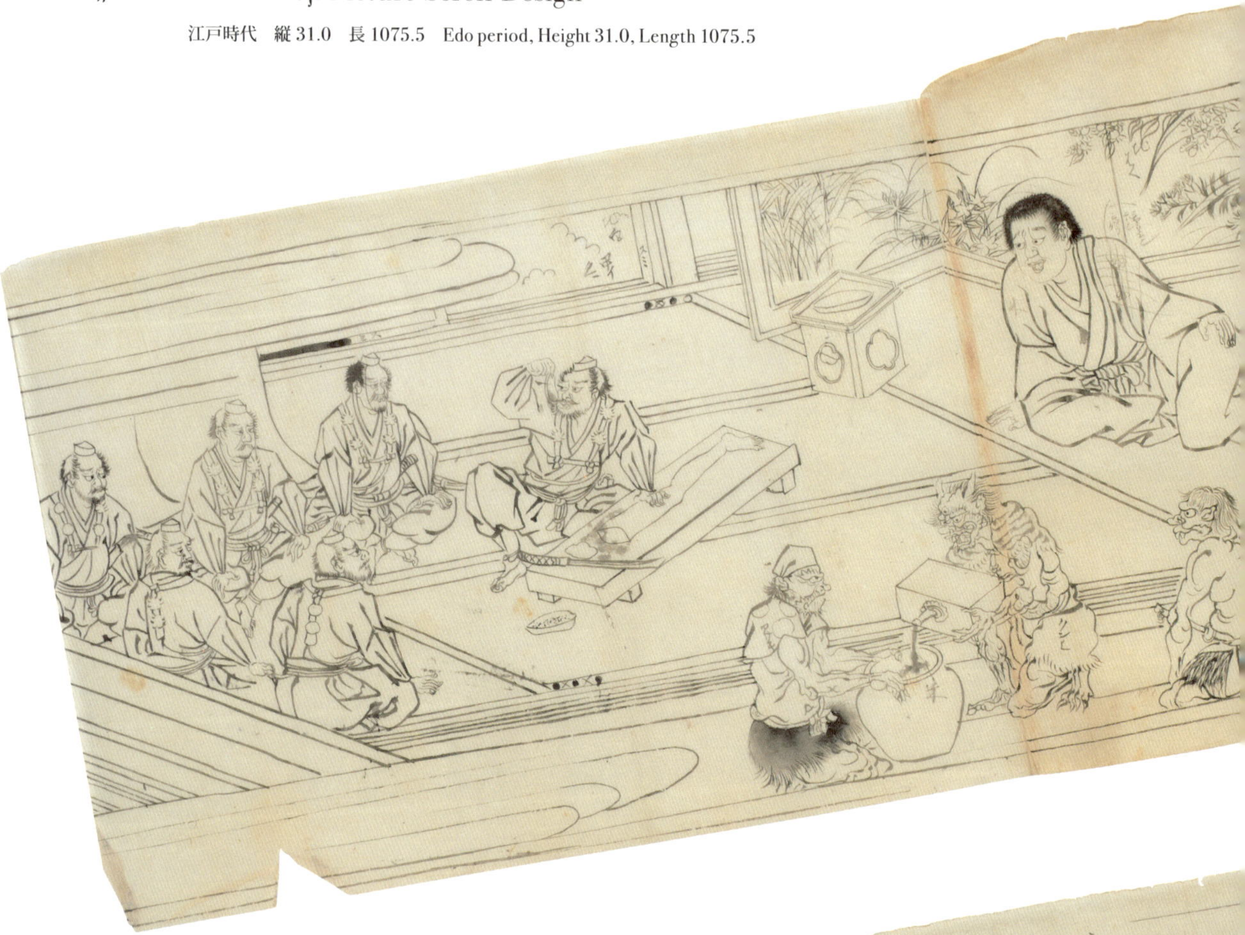

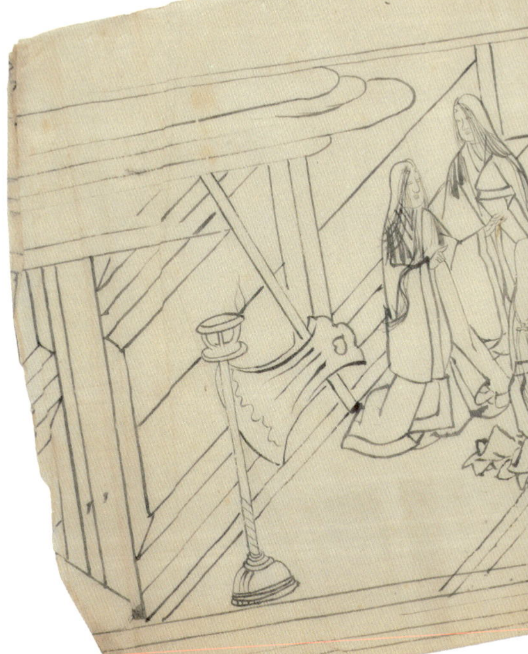

酒呑童子の館で鬼たちと酒宴を繰り広げる源頼光たち。
酒肴に人の足が料理されている。

Minamoto no Yorimitsu and his party are involved in a
drinking party with ogres at Shuten-dōji's mansion. A human
leg is being prepared as hors d'oeuvres.

妖怪絵巻のなかには白描の下絵が散見できるが、そのほとんどは百鬼夜行
絵巻や酒呑童子絵巻のものだ。それだけこれらの絵巻が描き継がれていっ
たということであろう。

There are some sketches for yokai picture scrolls drawn in ink lines; these are
almost always of the Night Parade of One Hundred Demons or Shuten-dōji. Those
themes alone may have continued to be drawn as picture scrolls.

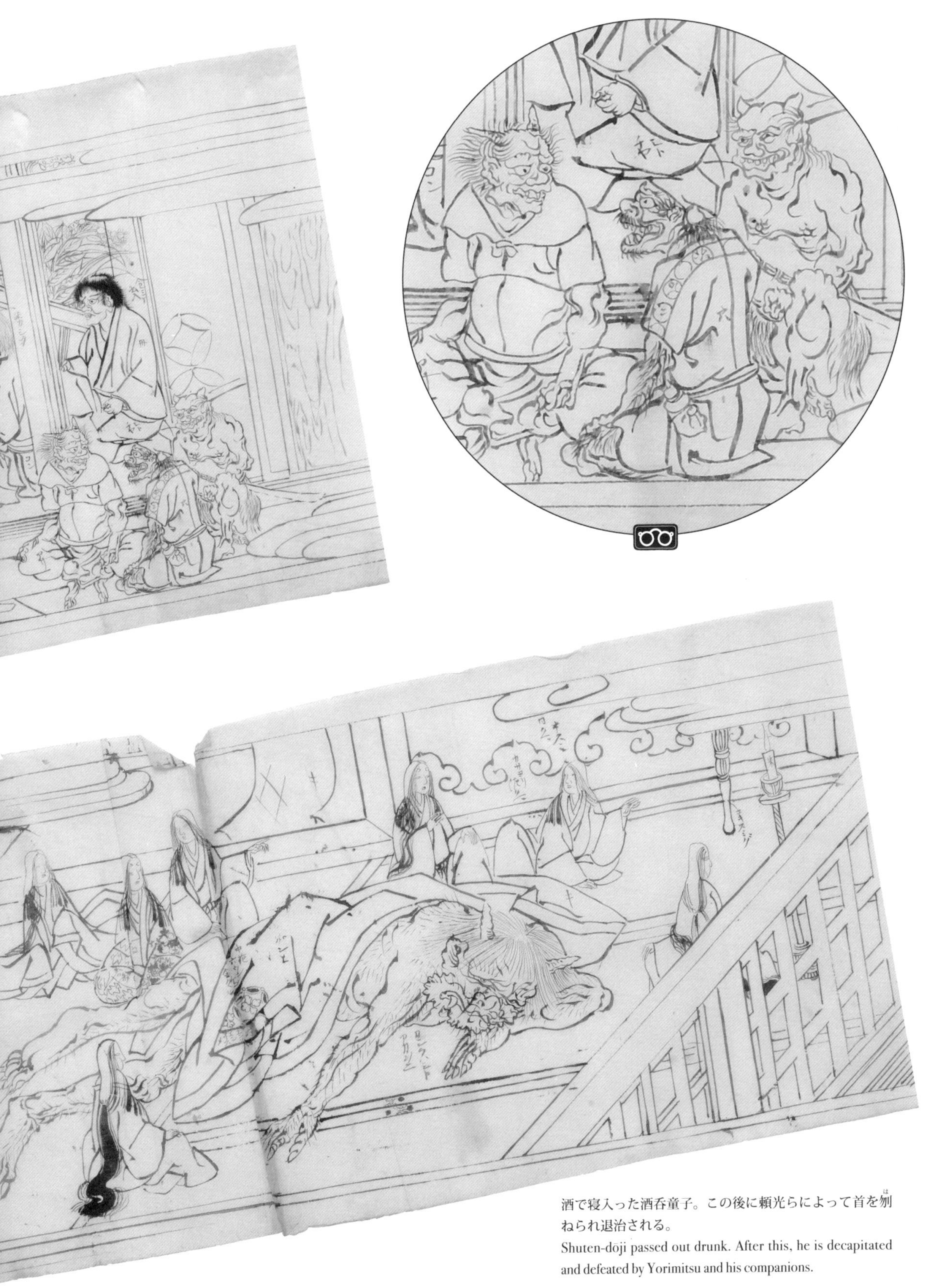

酒で寝入った酒呑童子。この後に頼光らによって首を刎ねられ退治される。
Shuten-dōji passed out drunk. After this, he is decapitated and defeated by Yorimitsu and his companions.

蜘蛛退治巻物

くもたいじまきもの

Scroll of the Spider's Defeat (*Kumo Taiji Makimono*)

江戸時代　縦 30.5　長 1061.5　Edo period, Height 30.5, Length 1061.5

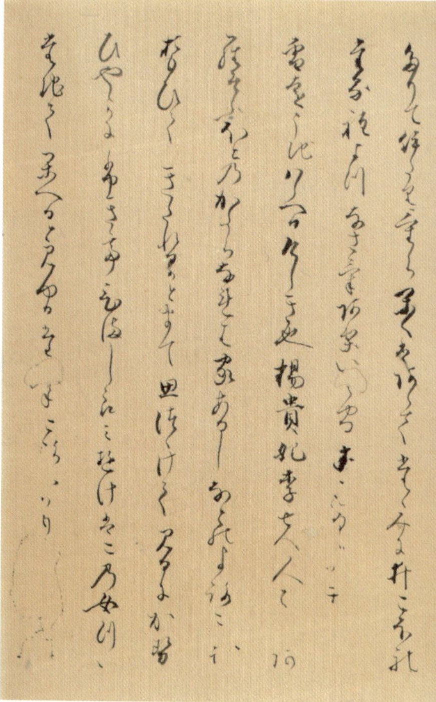

源頼光が北山蓮台野の屋敷で美女に変じた土蜘蛛の怪に悩まされ、やがて土蜘蛛の棲む洞窟を発見して退治するというストーリーを描いたもので、東京国立博物館蔵の「土蜘蛛草紙」の模写と思われ、詞書の欠字部分も忠実に写している。題簽には「蜘蛛退治巻物 古土佐 壱巻」とあるが、箱蓋の表には「土蜘蛛草紙 摸本」、裏には「下條桂谷翁旧蔵」との箱書がある。下條桂谷は幕末明治期の画家で軍人。巻末にはこの絵巻の原本は左近将監長隆の筆だったことなどが記されているが、朱色の落款も墨で模写されているので、模写を模写して伝えられた作品と思われる。

This scroll depicts the story of how Minamoto no Yorimitsu was enspelled by a *tsuchigumo* (lit. "earth spider") who took the form of a beautiful woman at the mansion of Kitayama Uradaino, and how at last he found the *tsuchigumo*'s lair and defeated her, and is thought to be a copy of *Tsuchigumo Zōshi* of the Tokyo National Museum: missing parts of that text (*kotobagaki*) have been transcribed faithfully. The label reads "Scroll of Tsuchigumo's Defeat: Kotosa Ikkan", but on the box lid is written "A copy of *Tsuchigumo Zōshi*", and on the back is "Previous Owner: Gejō Kei koku ō". Gejō Kei koku was a soldier and artist of the late Edo and Meiji periods. Lieutenant Nagataka of the Left Division of Inner Palace Guards is recorded as the artist of the original at the end of this scroll, but as the vermilion seal is copied in ink, this work is thought to be a copy of a copy.

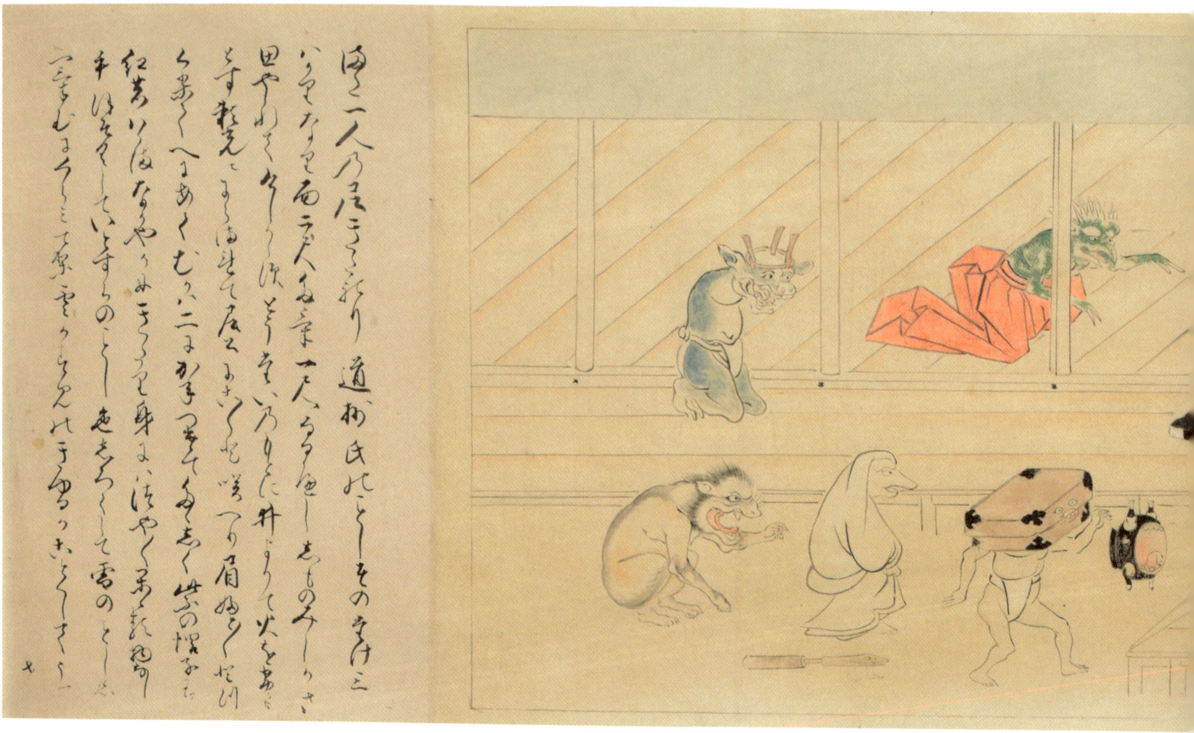

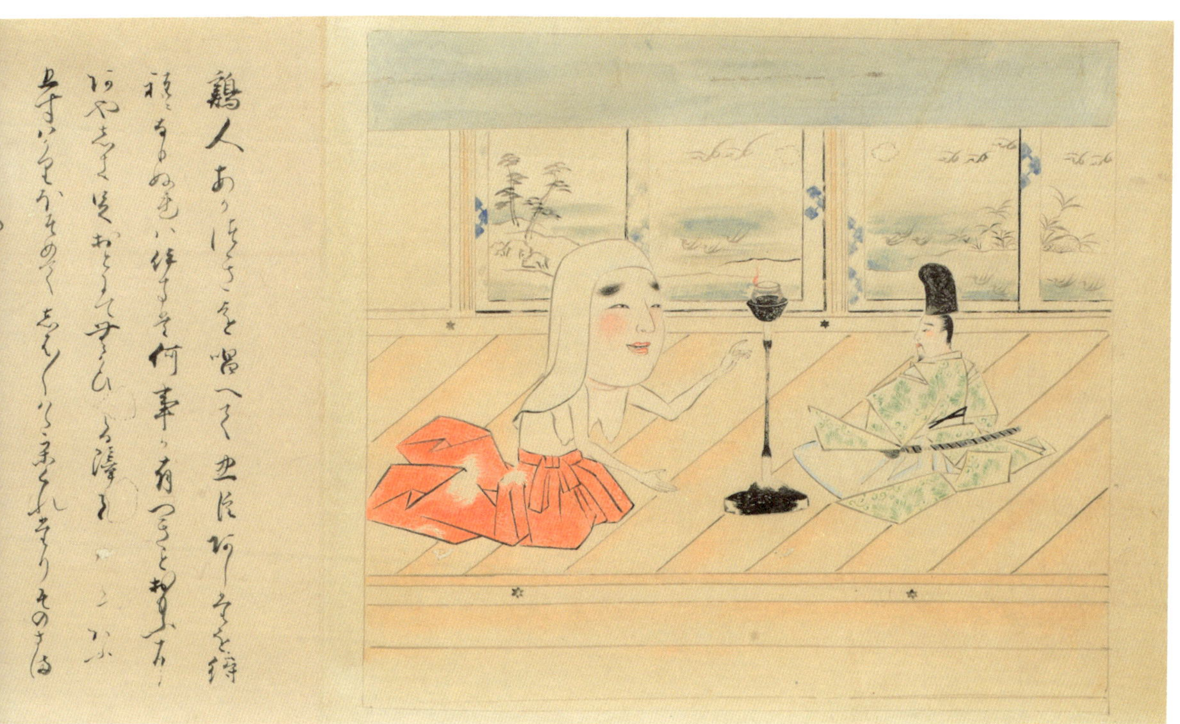

巨大な顔の尼が出現して頼光に笑いかけて消え去った。
燭台を挟んで頼光が睨みつけている。

A nun with a huge head appears, laughs at Yorimitsu, and vanishes. Yorimitsu is glaring at her from behind the lamp.

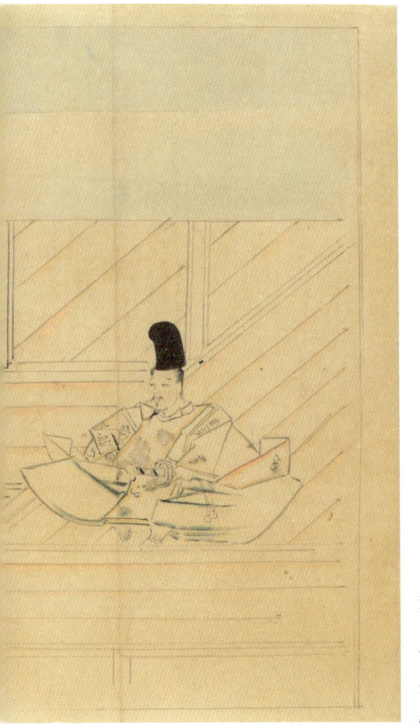

頼光の前に現れた妖怪。五徳や行李といった付喪神もみえる。

Yokai have appeared in front of Yorimitsu. Spirits of inanimate objects (*tsukumogami*), a *gotoku* (kettle tripod) and *kouri* (wicker trunk) can be seen.

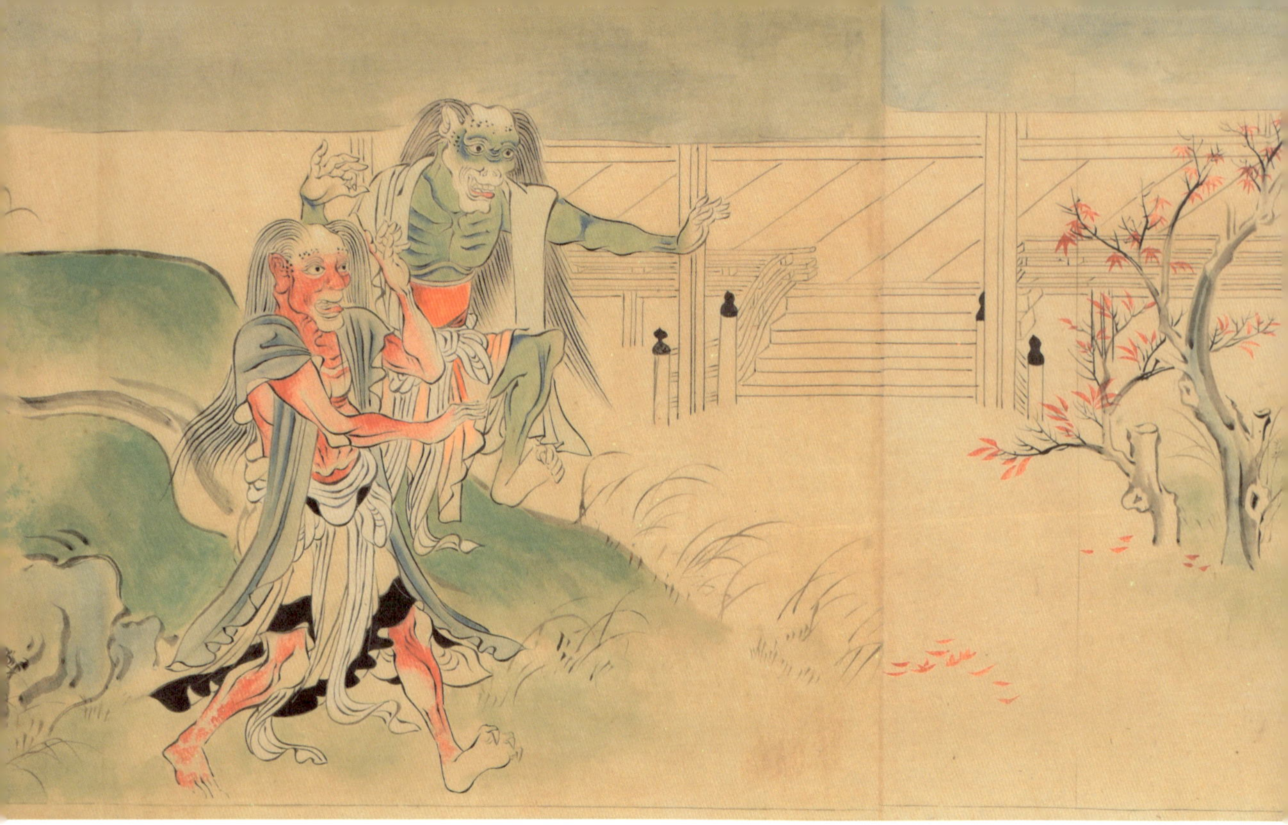

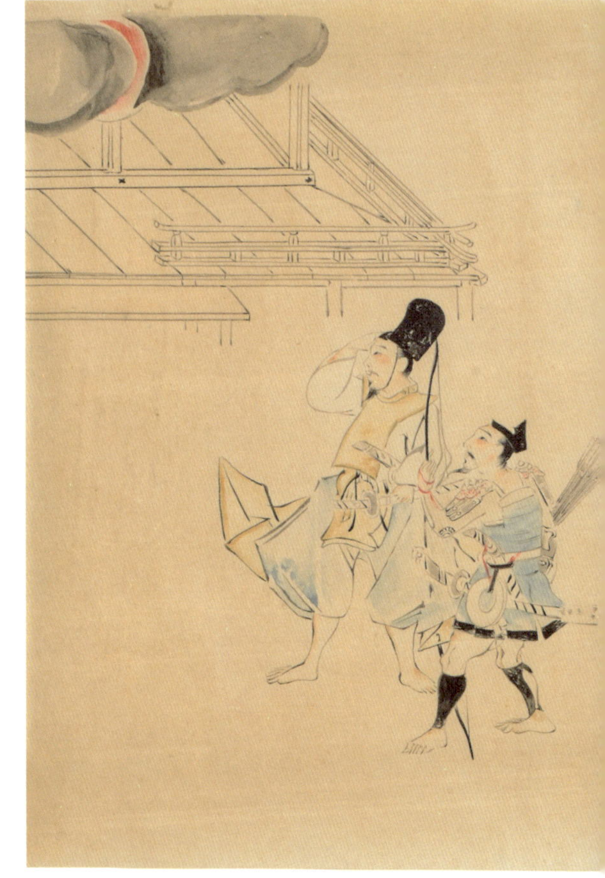

土蜘蛛を退治すると胎内から多数の髑髏が出てきた。
When the *tsuchigumo* is defeated, a number of skulls spill
out from inside her body.

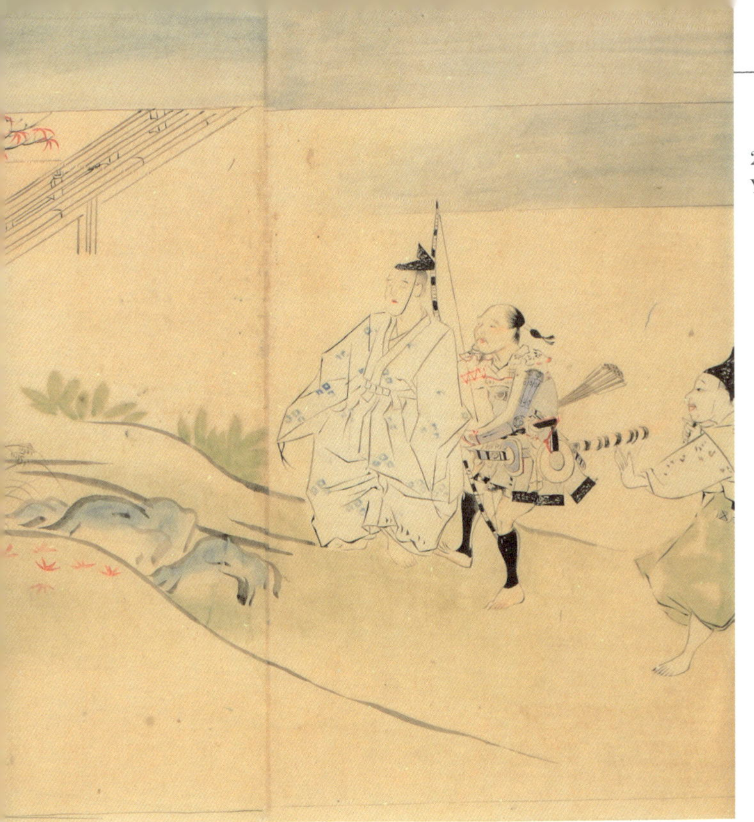

20 丈もある巨大な妖怪が頼光の前に現れた。
Yorimitsu is confronted by two hundred foot tall yokai.

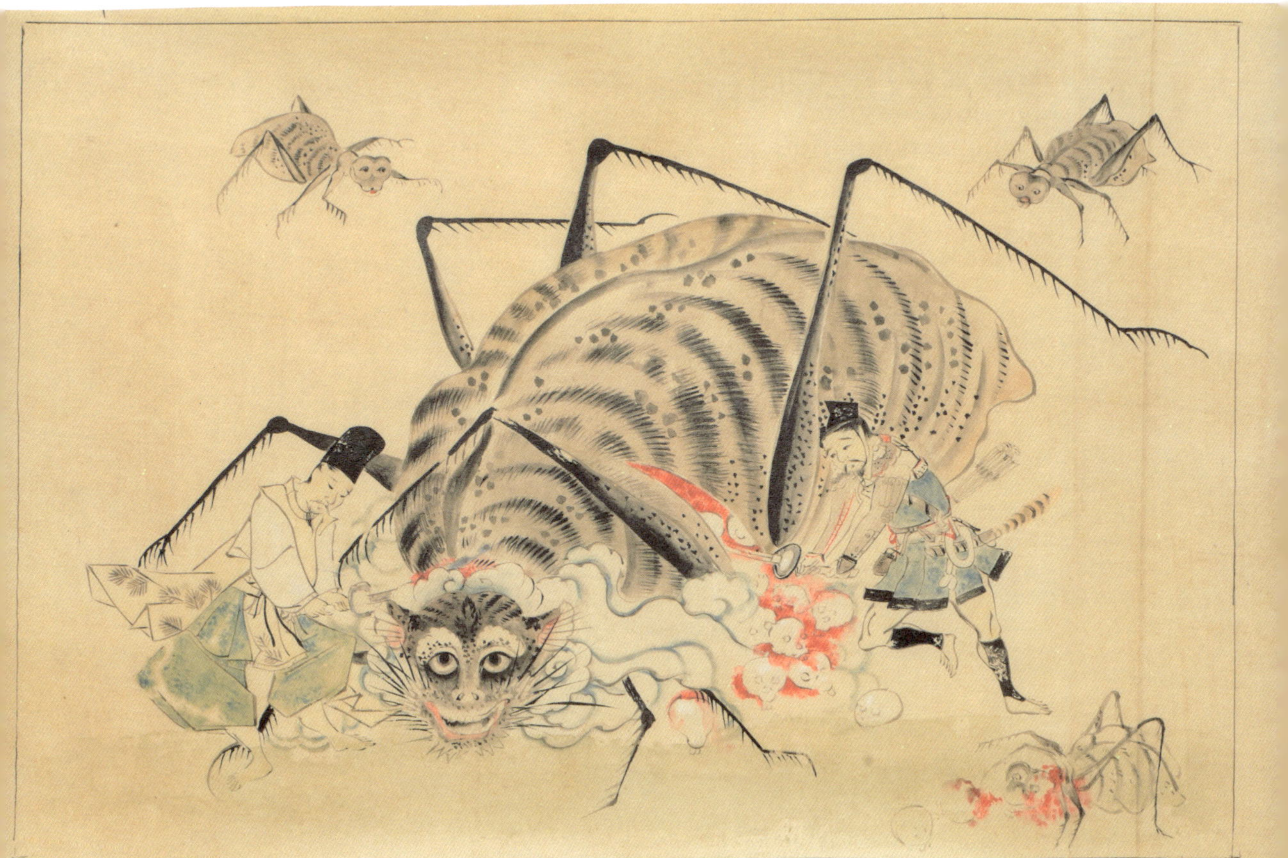

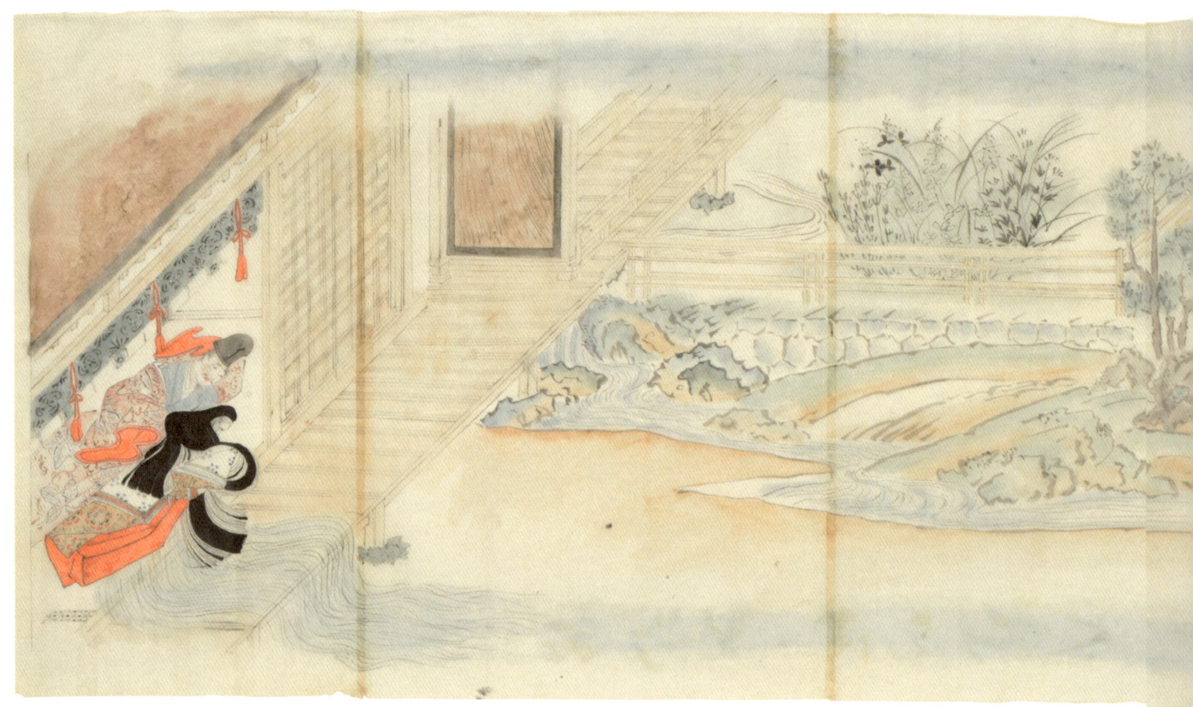

13　中納言長谷雄卿図巻
ちゅうなごんはせおきょうずかん

A Scroll of Pictures of Counselor of the Second Rank Lord Haseo
(*Chūnagon Haseo Kyō Zukan*)

淇川伴有造　弘化 5（1848）年 2 月　縦 38.0　長 1116.5
Kisen Bannoyuzo, Second month of 1848 (Kōka 5), Height 38.0, Length 1116.5

双六の名手・長谷雄が朱雀門で双六勝負を申し込まれる。負ければ全財産を差し出し、勝てば絶世の美女を得るという約束で勝負するが勝ったことで相手が美女を差し出す。100 日間は美女に触れるなと言う相手との約束をした長谷雄だったが守れず触れると美女は水と化して消えてしまう。双六の勝負をしたのは朱雀門に棲む鬼だったのだ。その後、長谷雄の乗る牛車の前に鬼が現れて約束を守らなかったことを責めたが、長谷雄が北野天神に祈ることによって鬼を退散させるといったストーリーで、絵巻としても少なからず描かれている。この絵巻は詞書と絵で構成されている。巻末に淇川伴有造なる人物が描き写したことが記されている。

Master of sugoroku Haseo is challenged to a game. He enters into the match at Suzakumon Gate on a bet that if he loses, he will forfeit all his worldly possessions, but if he wins, he will gain the most beautiful woman in the world; and as he wins, his opponent grants him the beautiful woman. Haseo vows not to touch her for 100 days, but breaks his vow and touches her, only to see her turn into water and drain away. His opponent was the ogre living in the Suzakumon Gate. The story continues with the ogre appearing in front of Haseo's oxcart to accuse him of breaking his vow, but Haseo prays to Kitano-tenjin to save him; this scene has been depicted in scrolls many times. This scroll features both text (*kotobagaki*) and pictures. At the end of the scroll the name of copyist Kisen Bannoyuzo is recorded.

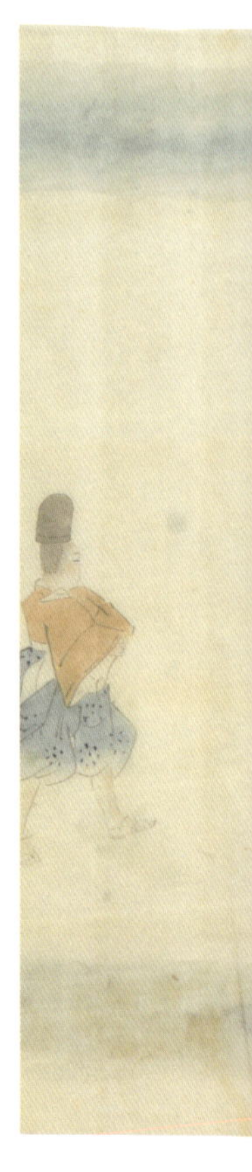

長谷雄の牛車の前に現れて長谷雄を責める朱雀門の鬼。
The ogre of the Suzakumon Gate appears in front of Haseo's oxcart to accost him.

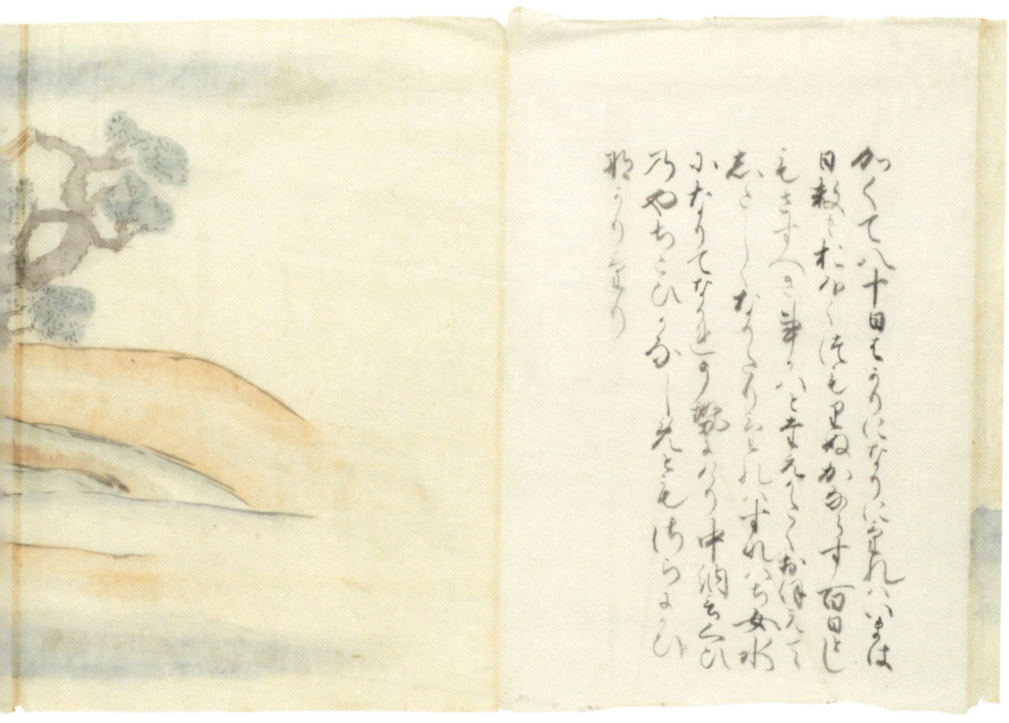

双六勝負に勝って得た美女に触れたために水に変じる美女。縁から水が流れ出し、美女が消えようとしている。
The beautiful woman who Haseo won in the *sugoroku* match transforms into water at his touch.
She melts away as the water flows out from the veranda.

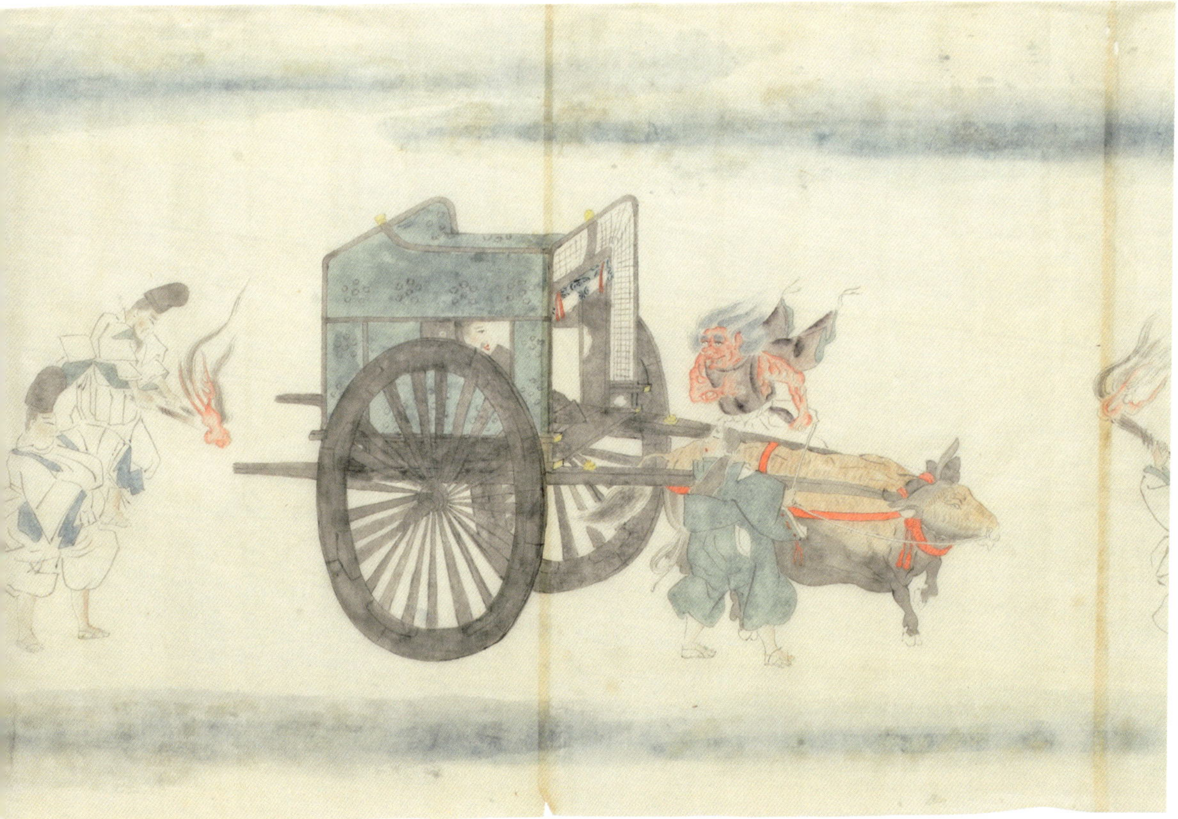

⑭ 道成寺絵巻
どうじょうじえまき

Dōjōji Temple Picture Scroll

天保 4（1833）年　縦 25.5　長 566.5　1833 (Tenpō 4), Height 25.5, Length 566.5

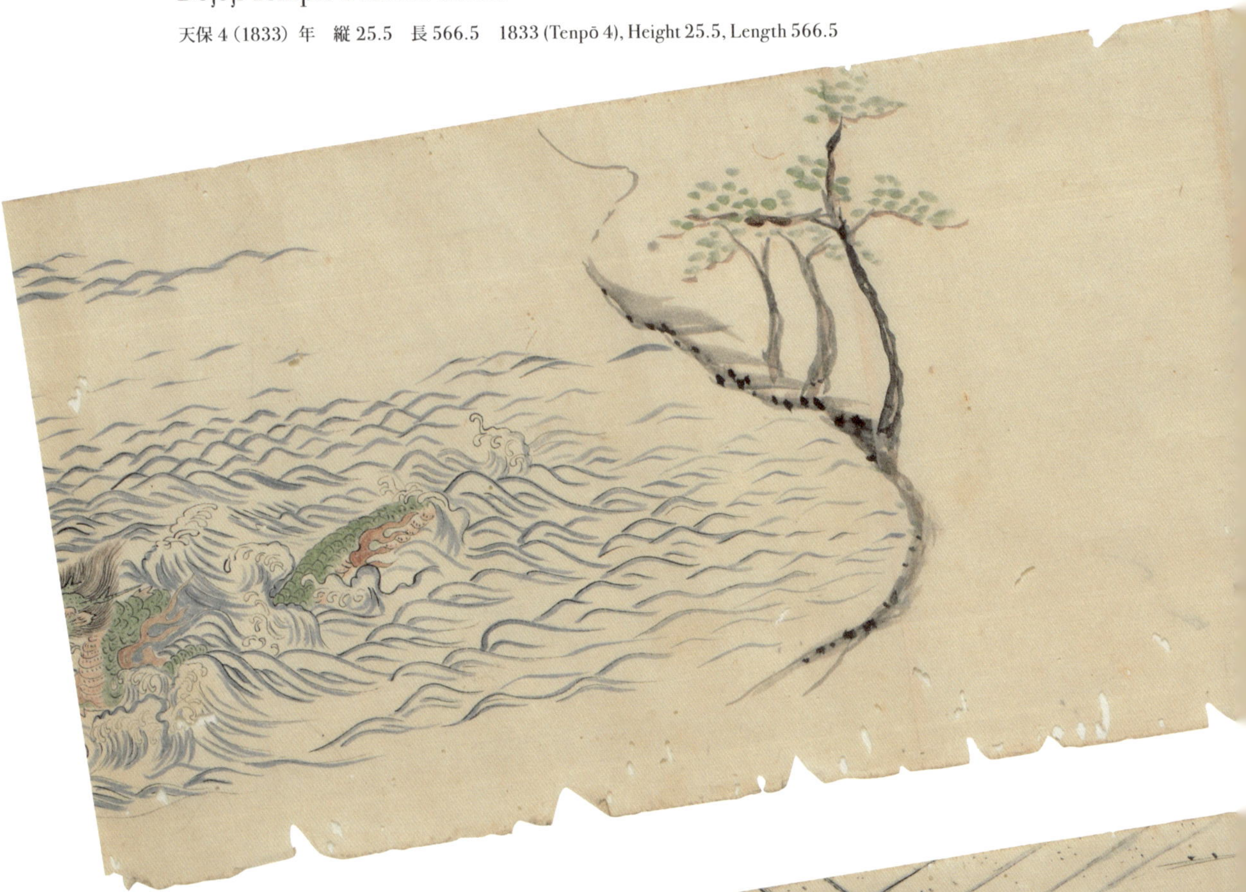

蛇となって日高川を渡る清姫。
Princess Kiyohime changes into a snake to
cross the Hidakagawa River.

安珍の隠れる鐘をぐるぐる巻きにして焼き殺そ
うとしている清姫。道成寺の坊主たちは逃げ出
している。
Princess Kiyohime coils around and around the bell
Anchin is hiding in to burn him to death. The
monks of Dōjōji Temple are running away.

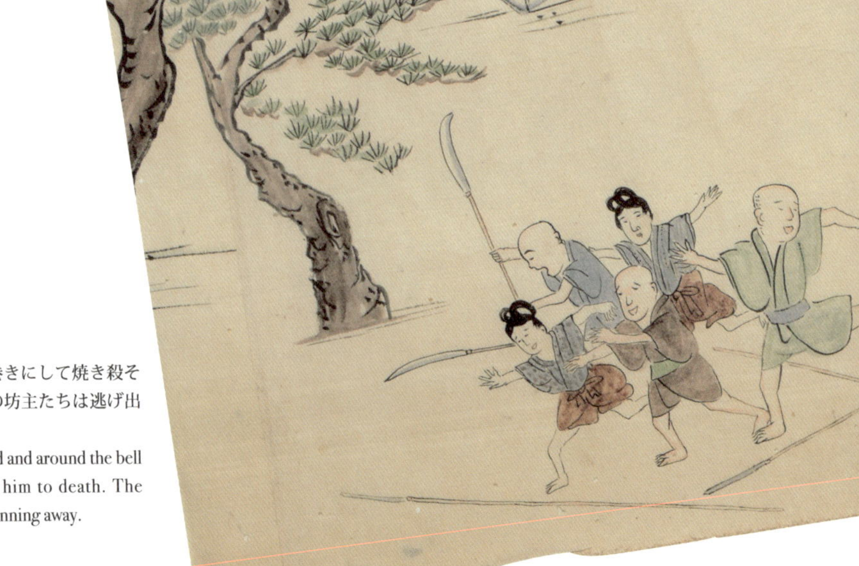

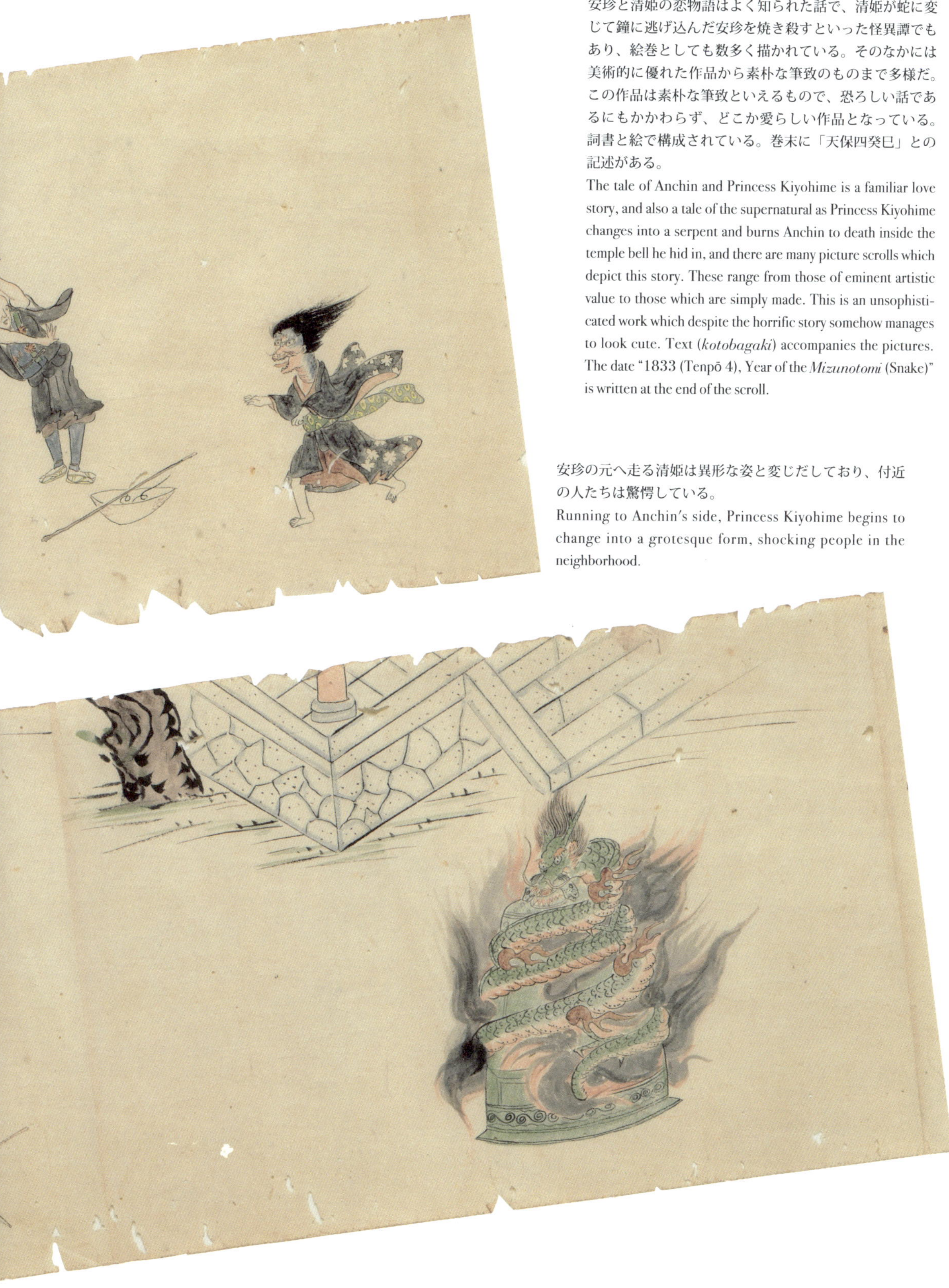

安珍と清姫の恋物語はよく知られた話で、清姫が蛇に変じて鐘に逃げ込んだ安珍を焼き殺すといった怪異譚でもあり、絵巻としても数多く描かれている。そのなかには美術的に優れた作品から素朴な筆致のものまで多様だ。この作品は素朴な筆致といえるもので、恐ろしい話であるにもかかわらず、どこか愛らしい作品となっている。詞書と絵で構成されている。巻末に「天保四癸巳」との記述がある。

The tale of Anchin and Princess Kiyohime is a familiar love story, and also a tale of the supernatural as Princess Kiyohime changes into a serpent and burns Anchin to death inside the temple bell he hid in, and there are many picture scrolls which depict this story. These range from those of eminent artistic value to those which are simply made. This is an unsophisticated work which despite the horrific story somehow manages to look cute. Text (*kotobagaki*) accompanies the pictures. The date "1833 (Tenpō 4), Year of the *Mizunotomi* (Snake)" is written at the end of the scroll.

安珍の元へ走る清姫は異形な姿と変じだしており、付近の人たちは驚愕している。

Running to Anchin's side, Princess Kiyohime begins to change into a grotesque form, shocking people in the neighborhood.

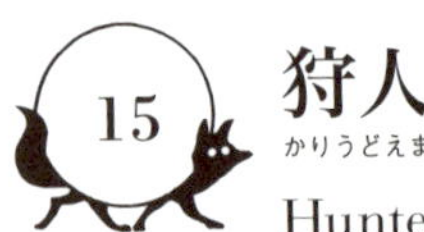

狩人絵巻
かりうどえまき

Hunter Picture Scroll

狩野休甫　江戸時代　縦 27.0　長 1583.5　Kanō Kyūho, Edo period, Height 27.0, Length 1583.5

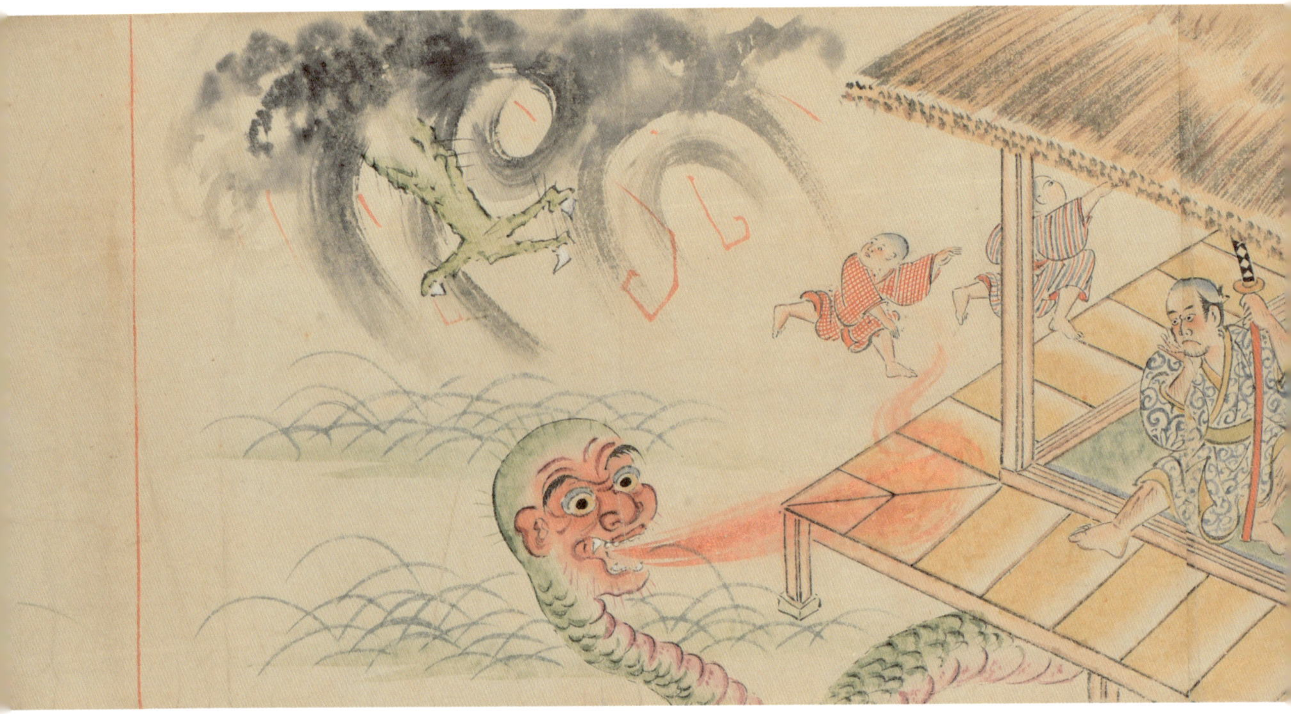

縁の下から出現した妖怪。蛇のような形状をした長くのびた体で、人の顔を持つ。口から火を吹き出して襲いかかろうとしている。暗雲からは龍を思わせる腕が出て、子どもたちが逃げ回っている。

A yokai has emerged from under the edge of the house. Its body is elongated into a snake-like form with a human face. On the attack, it spews fire from its mouth. The claw of what may be a dragon looms out of dark clouds, sending the children running.

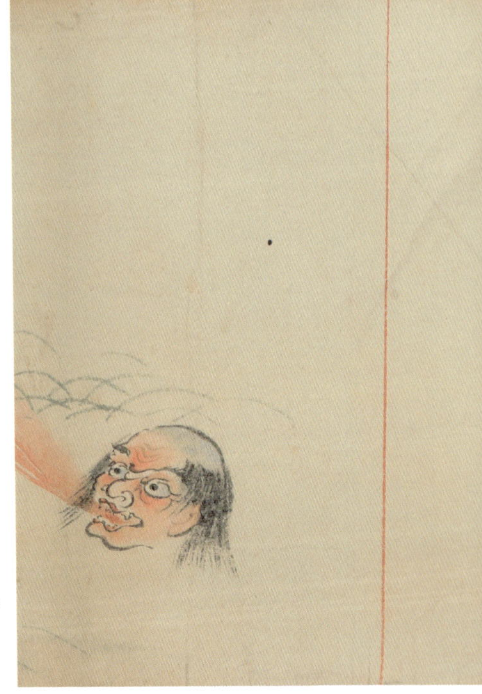

突風のなかに暗雲が漂い、巨大な女の顔が出現して睨みつけている。風で笠や下駄は吹き飛んでいる。

The huge face of a woman appears, staring down from a dark cloud borne on a gust of wind. A hat and *geta* sandals are sent flying in the wind.

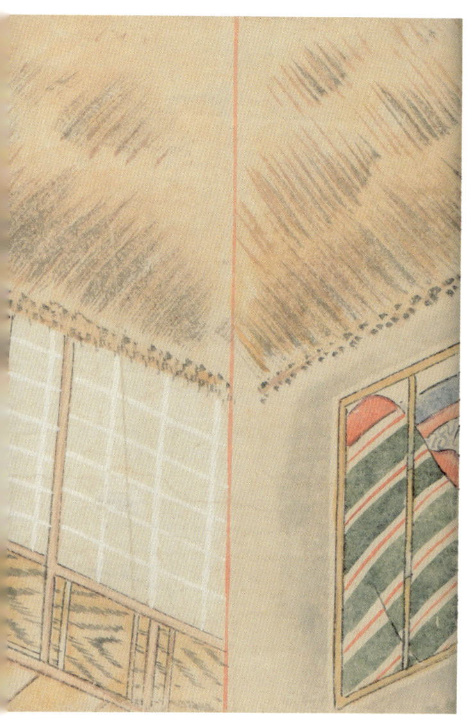

狩人が鉄砲で狐を狙ったことをきっかけに怪異が続発するというストーリー。詞書はなく、巻末には「宝暦四年正月二十二日ヨリ同二十五日マデニ出来ス」と記されている。これは怪異が起こった時期を書いたものであろうが、何処で起こった怪異かは不明。絵巻の箱は新しいが、以前の箱の蓋が絵巻と一緒に新しい箱に保存されている。その箱書きには「狩人御巻物　一軸　狩野休甫」とある。大石兵六絵巻や変化絵巻（ともに『今昔妖怪大鑑』に収録）など、狐にまつわる怪異を記録した絵巻は散見されるが、この作品は類例がないと思われる。狩野休甫については狩野派の絵師なのだろうが詳細は不明。

The story of a string of supernatural occurrences sparked off by a hunter taking aim at a fox with his gun. There is no accompanying text portion (*kotobagaki*), but "Done on the first month (New Year) 22 to 25, 1754 (Horeki 4)" is inscribed at the end of the scroll. This work was probably drawn around the time the supernatural phenomena occurred, but where they occurred is not known. The scroll box is new, but the previous box's cover has been preserved along with the scroll in the new box. On the original box was written "Hunter Picture Scroll (one scroll): Kano Kyūho". There are other scrolls which record supernatural phenomena involving foxes, such as the Ōishi Hyōroku and Henge picture scrolls (both are collected in *Yokai Museum*), but there are no known examples similar to this work. It is possible that Kano Kyūho was an artist of the Kano school.

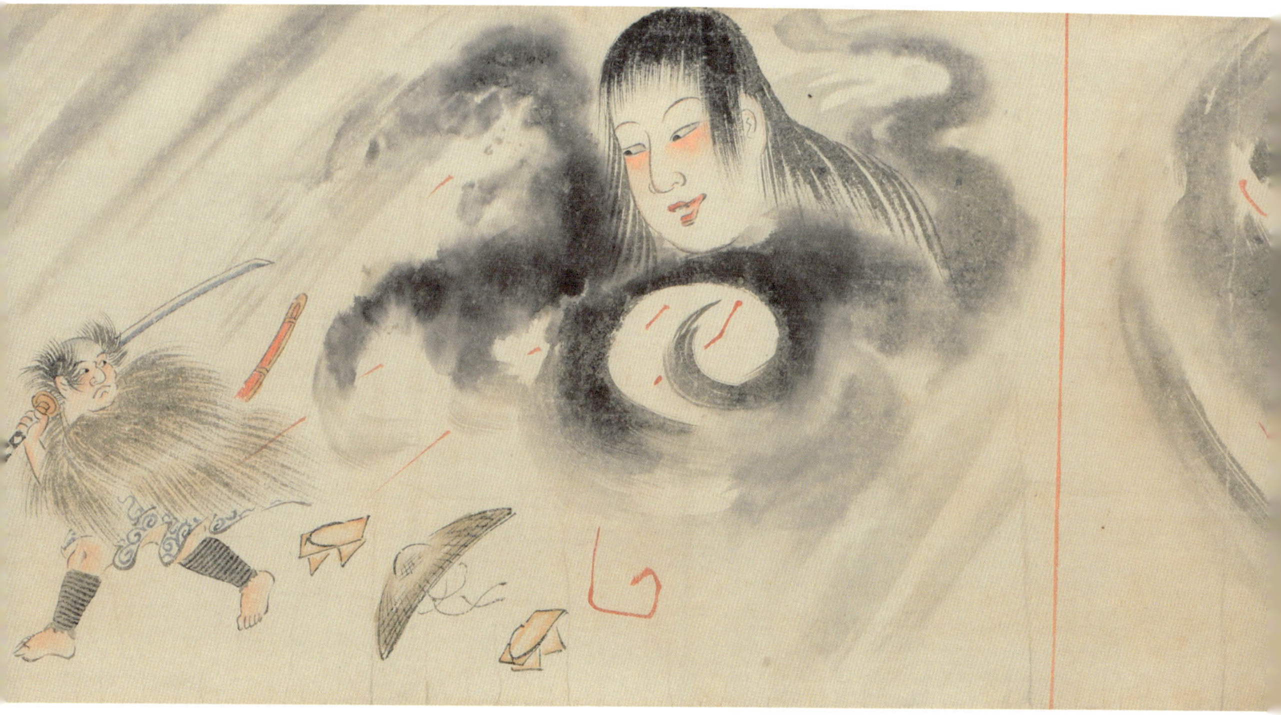

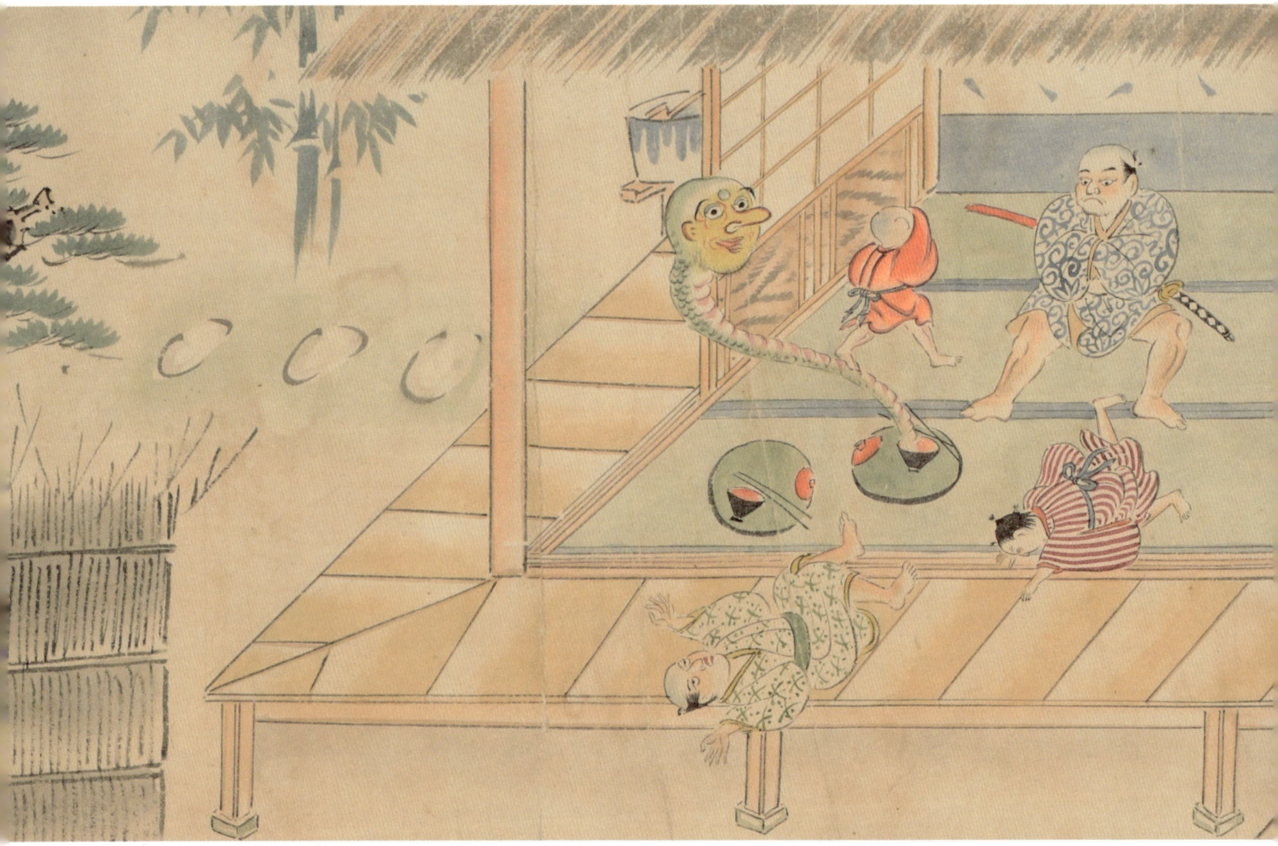

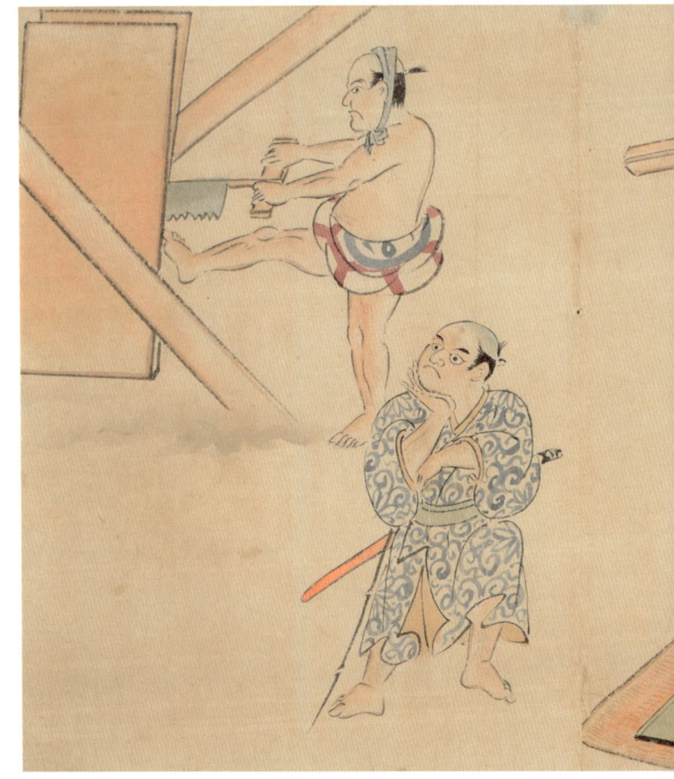

柱が蛇に変じ、道具箱からは顔が出現。大工たちの作業
場にも怪異が起こっている。
A beam changes into a snake, and a head pops out of a tool
box. Even the carpenters' workshop is not free of
supernatural phenomena.

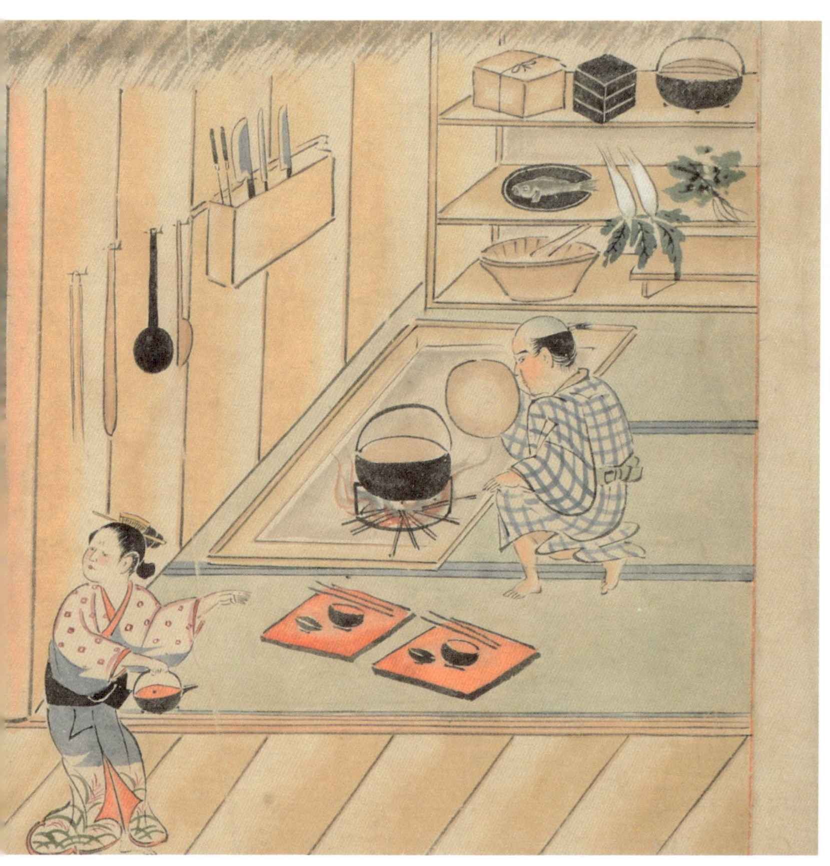

食事中の椀からろくろ首のような妖怪が出
現してパニック状態だ。椀から出た妖怪は
縁の下から出た妖怪と同じく蛇の体のよう
な形状だ。
Panic reigns as a creature like a *rokurokubi*
slithers out of a bowl during the meal. The
snaky body of this yokai is similar to the one
which came out from under the house.

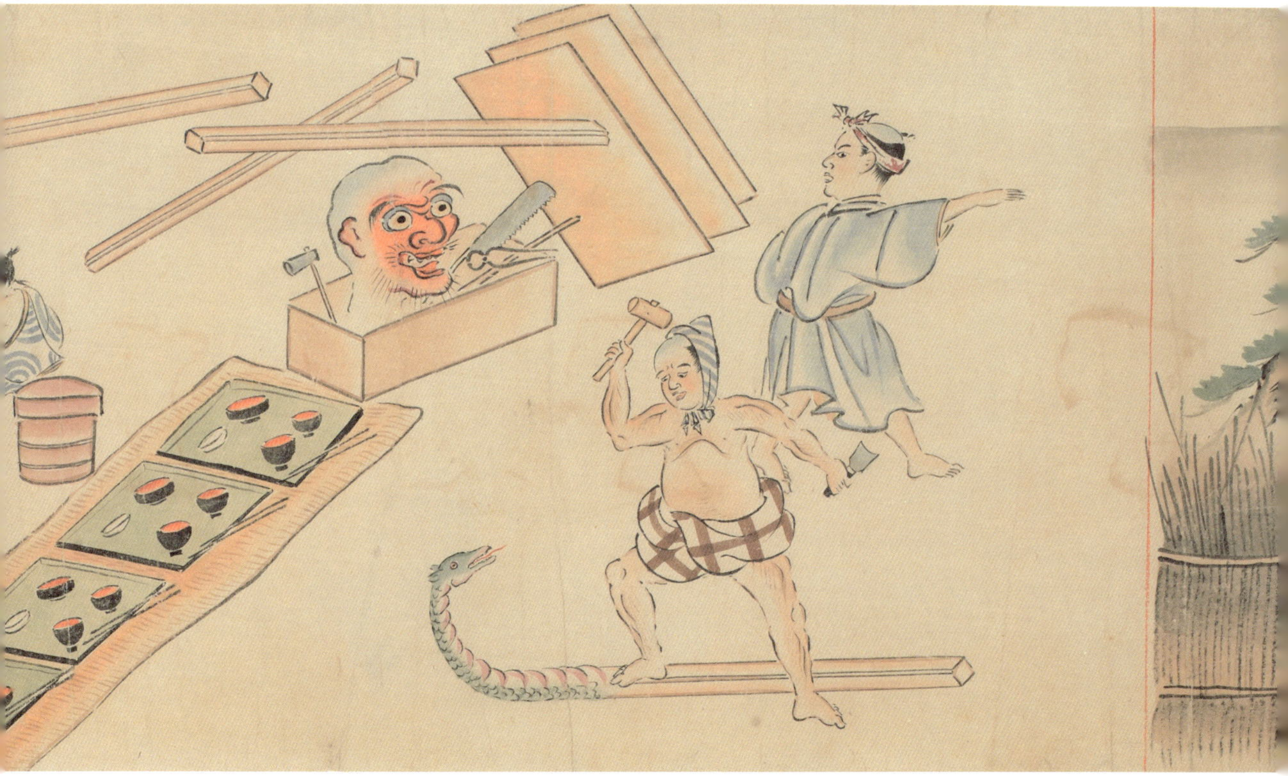

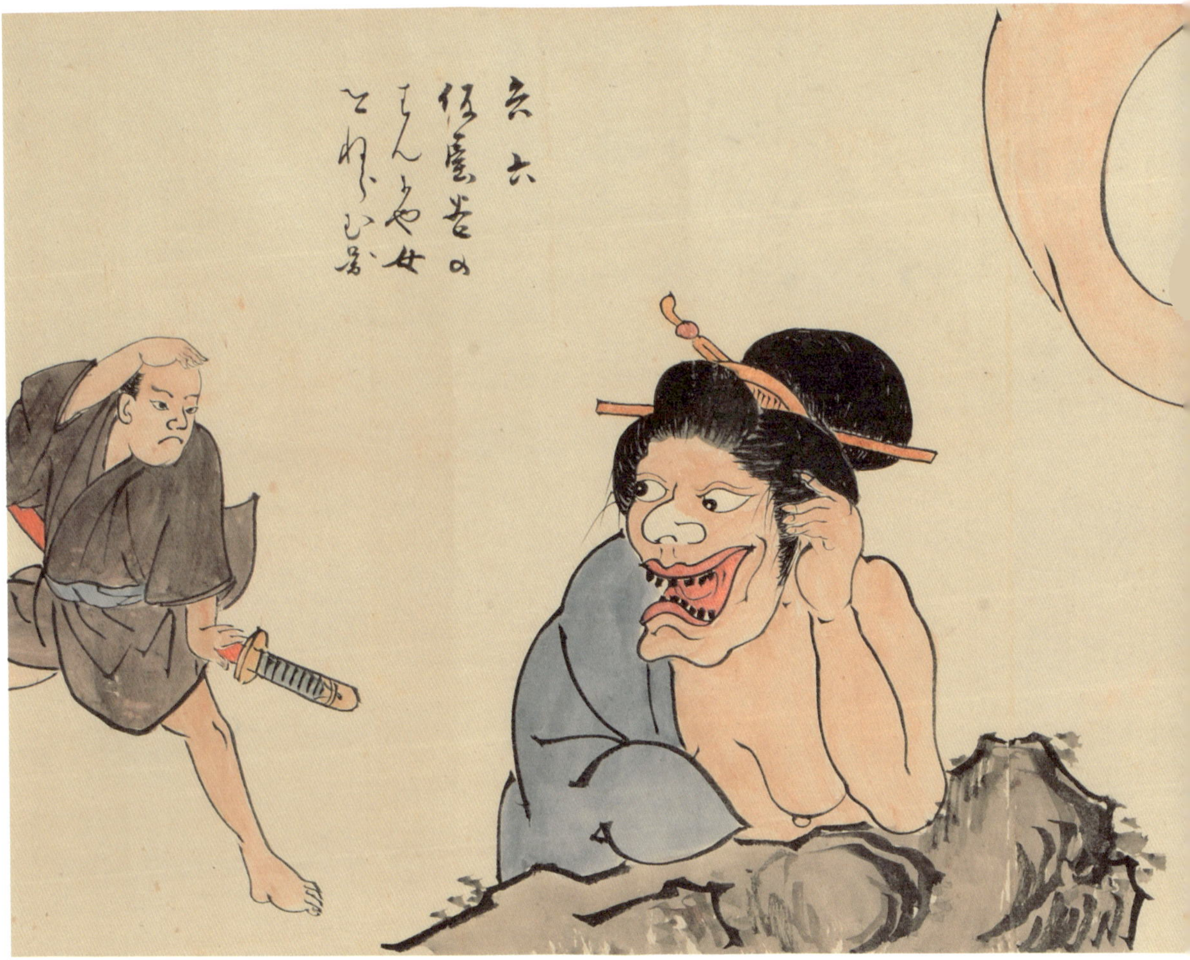

巨大な般若女と対峙する兵六。キャプションには「兵六 仮屋谷のはんにゃ女をねらむ図」とある。
Hyōroku faces off against a giant *han'nya* (demon woman). The caption is "Hyōroku glaring at a Kariyadani *han'nya*."

16 吉野兵六戯画絵巻
よしのひょうろくぎがえまき

Yoshino Hyōroku Caricature Scroll
明治時代以降　縦 27.0　長 1167.0　Post-Meiji period, Height 27.0, Length 1167.0

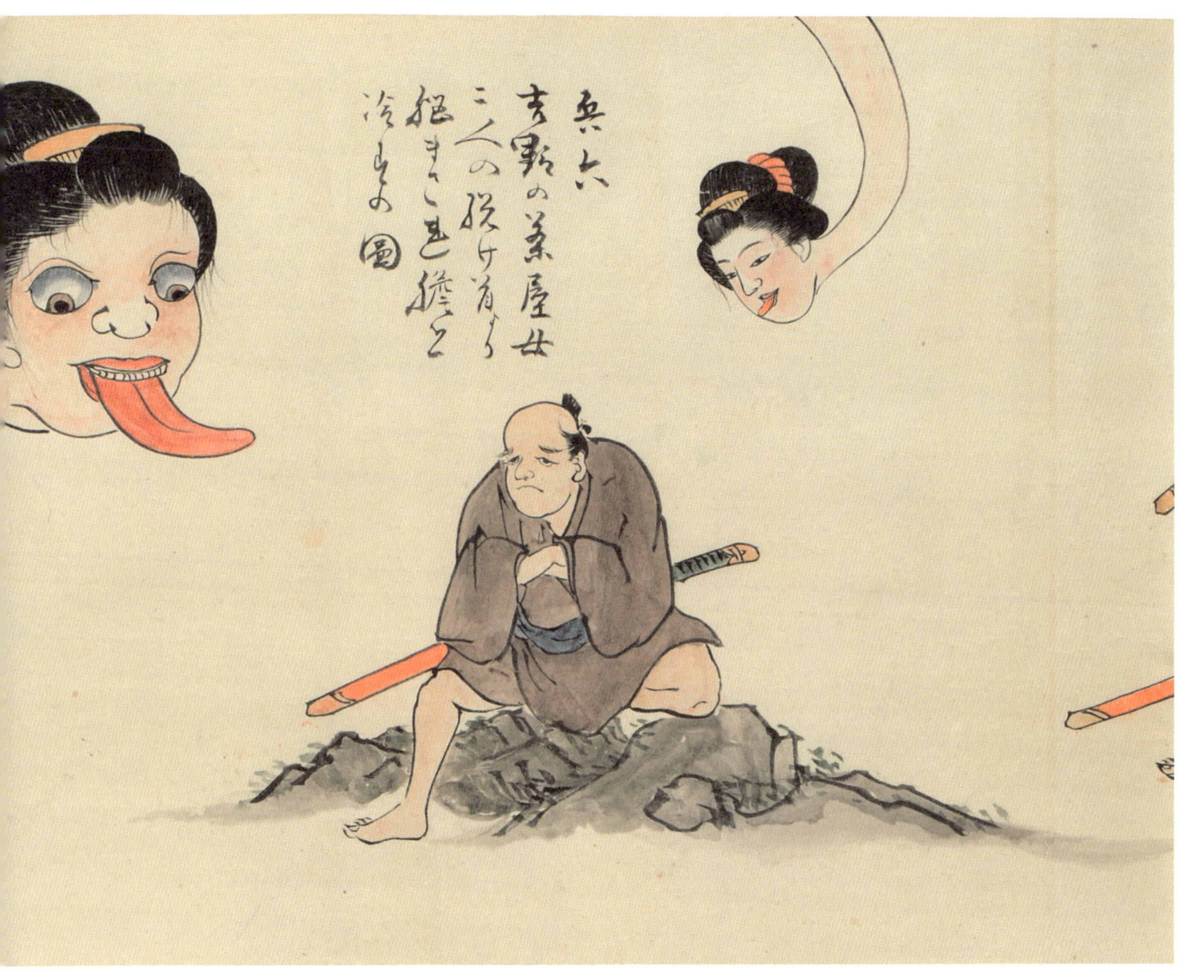

２人の女の首が出現して兵六を襲っている。左の首は巨大で赤い舌を出して兵六を威嚇している。
「兵六 吉野の茶屋女二人の抜け首より悩まされ膽を冷すの図」とのキャプションが添えられている。
Two female heads appear, attacking Hyōroku. The head on the left is huge and menaces Hyōroku, sticking out her red tongue.
A caption accompanies the image: "Hyōroku plagued by the disembodied heads of two Yoshino theahouse women".

薩摩国の武士・大石兵六が狐によるさまざまな怪異や妖怪の出現にめげず狐退治を行って仲間のところに凱旋するといったストーリーで、絵巻や写本としても伝えられている。この絵巻は一般的な絵巻とは異なりタイトルに「戯画」とあるように兵六の活躍と出現する妖怪を面白可笑しいスタイルで描いている。「吉野」は狐による怪異が起こったところ。詞書はない。

The story of how Ōishi Hyōroku, a warrior of Satsuma Province, overcame the supernatural visitations and yokai inflicted on him by a fox, vanquished the fox and returned to his friends victorious has been conveyed through scrolls and copies. This scroll differs from the usual; a caricature as the title states, it depicts Hyōroku's heroics and the yokai in a comical manner. Yoshino is the name of the place where the phenomena occurred. There is no text section (*kotobagaki*).

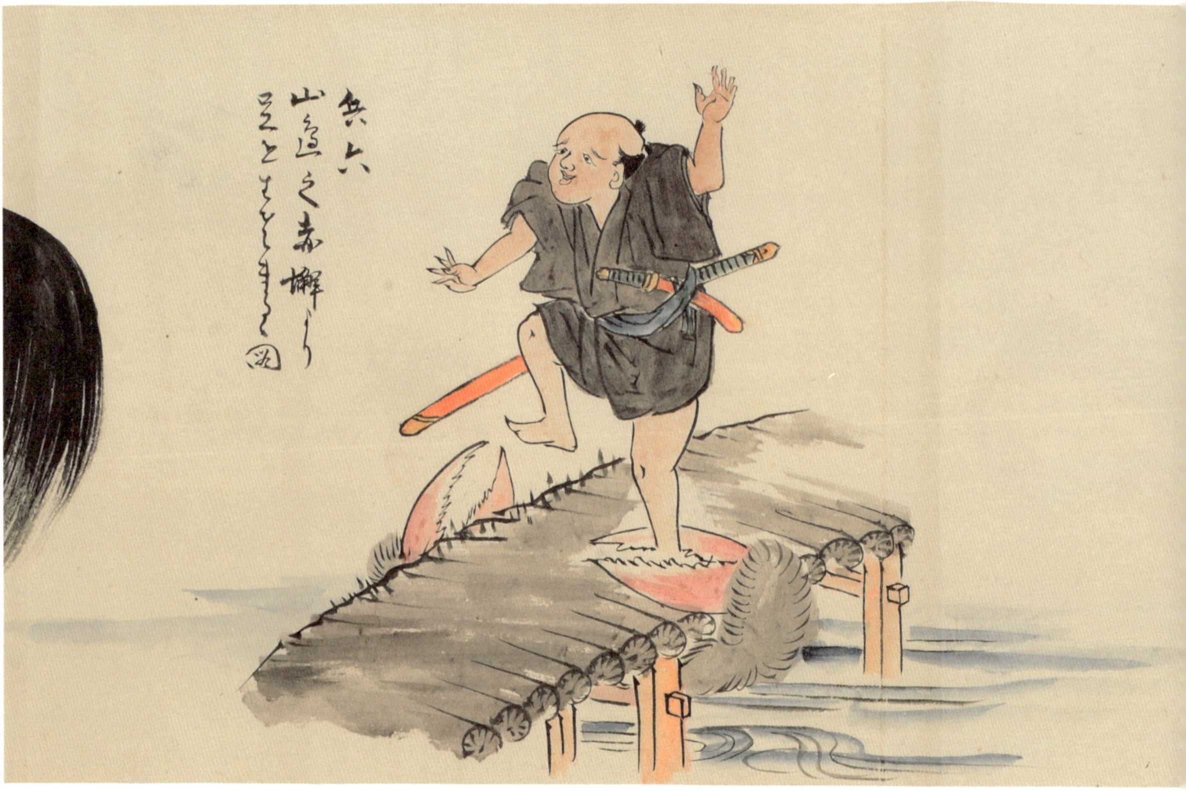

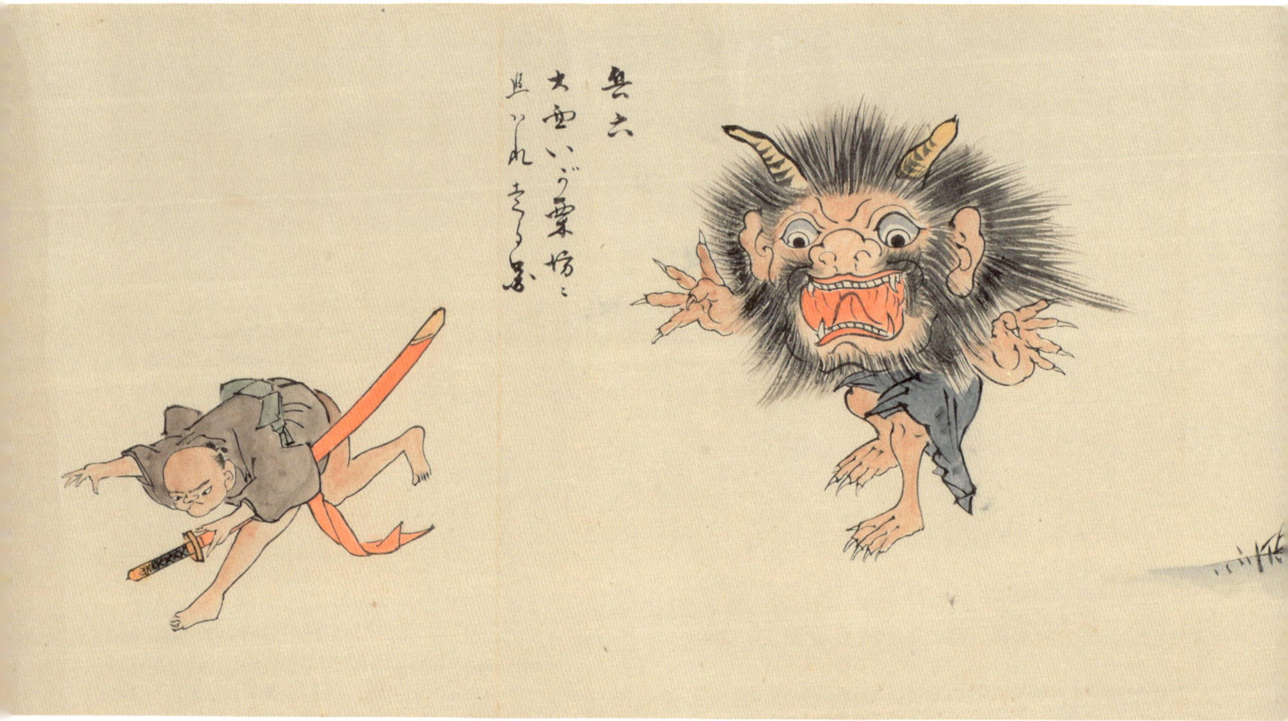

右端には兵六を化かした３匹の狐。毬栗の妖怪が兵六を襲う。キャプションには「兵六 大西いが栗坊に追はれ走る図」とある。
On the right edge are three foxes who have bewitched Hyōroku. A chestnut yokai attacks Hyōroku.
The caption is "Hyōroku running, pursued by an Ōnishi chestnut monk."

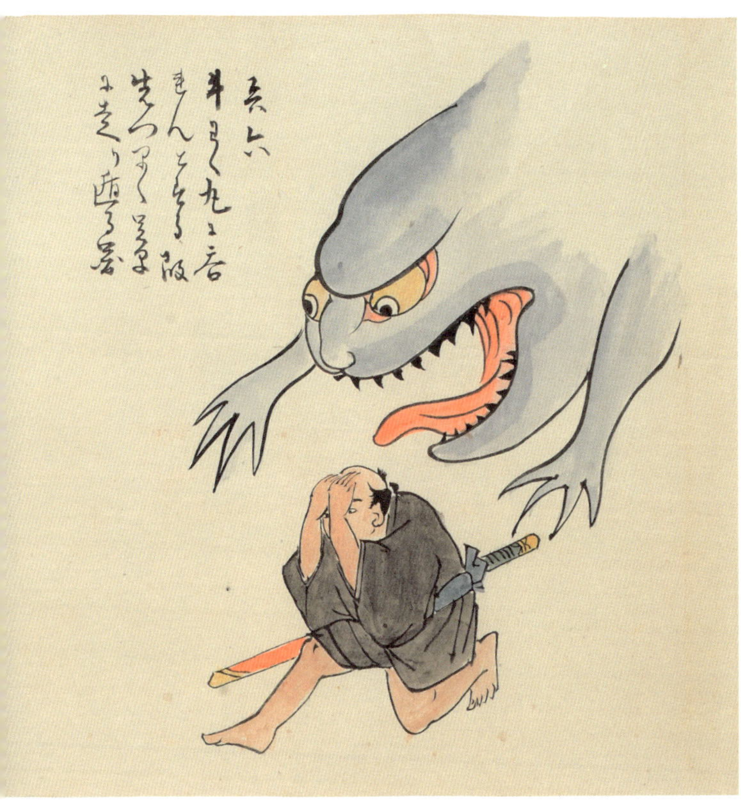

巨大な蝦蟇に襲われて呑み込まれそうになっている
兵六。腰を屈めて恐れている。キャプションには「兵
六 牛わく丸に呑れんとする故先つ早々足早に走り遁
る図」とある。
橋の下から出た大蟹の鋏に足をはさまれた兵六。キャ
プションには「兵六 山辺之赤蟹より足をはさまるる
図」とある。

Hyōroku is attacked by a gigantic toad, and he seems
about to be swallowed up. His legs give way in fear. The
caption is "Hyōroku rushing as fast as he can to avoid
being swallowed whole by bullfrog Ushiwakumaru."
Hyōroku with his leg in a huge crab's claw sticking out
from under the bridge. The caption is "Hyōroku with his
leg trapped by a Yamabe red crab."

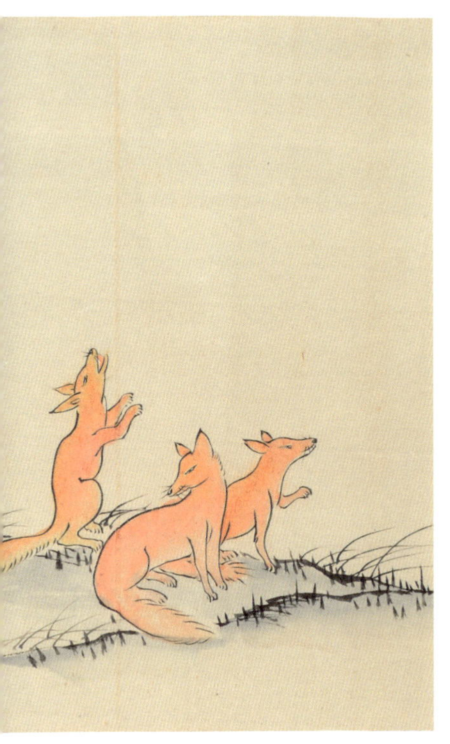

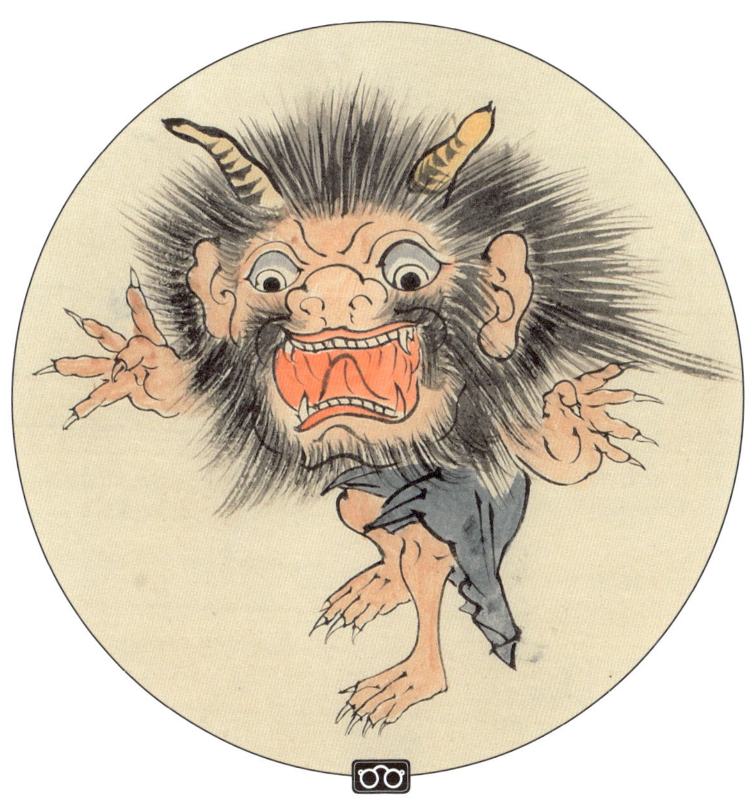

17　狐怪草紙絵巻
こかいぞうしえまき

Supernatural Foxes Picture Scroll (*Kokai Zōshi Emaki*)
明治28（1895）年　縦38.0　長561.5　1895 (Meiji 28), Height 38.0, Length 561.5

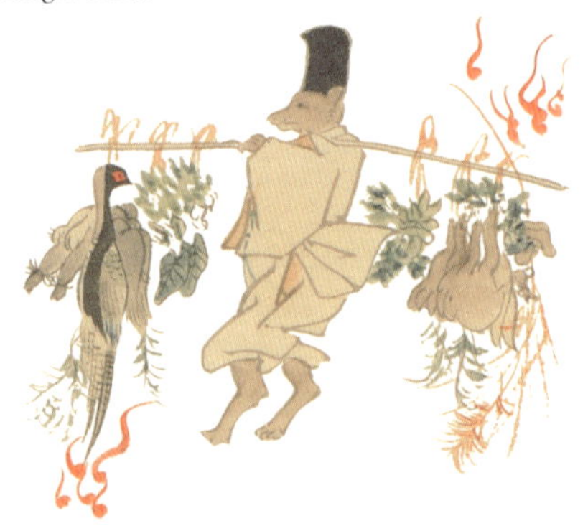

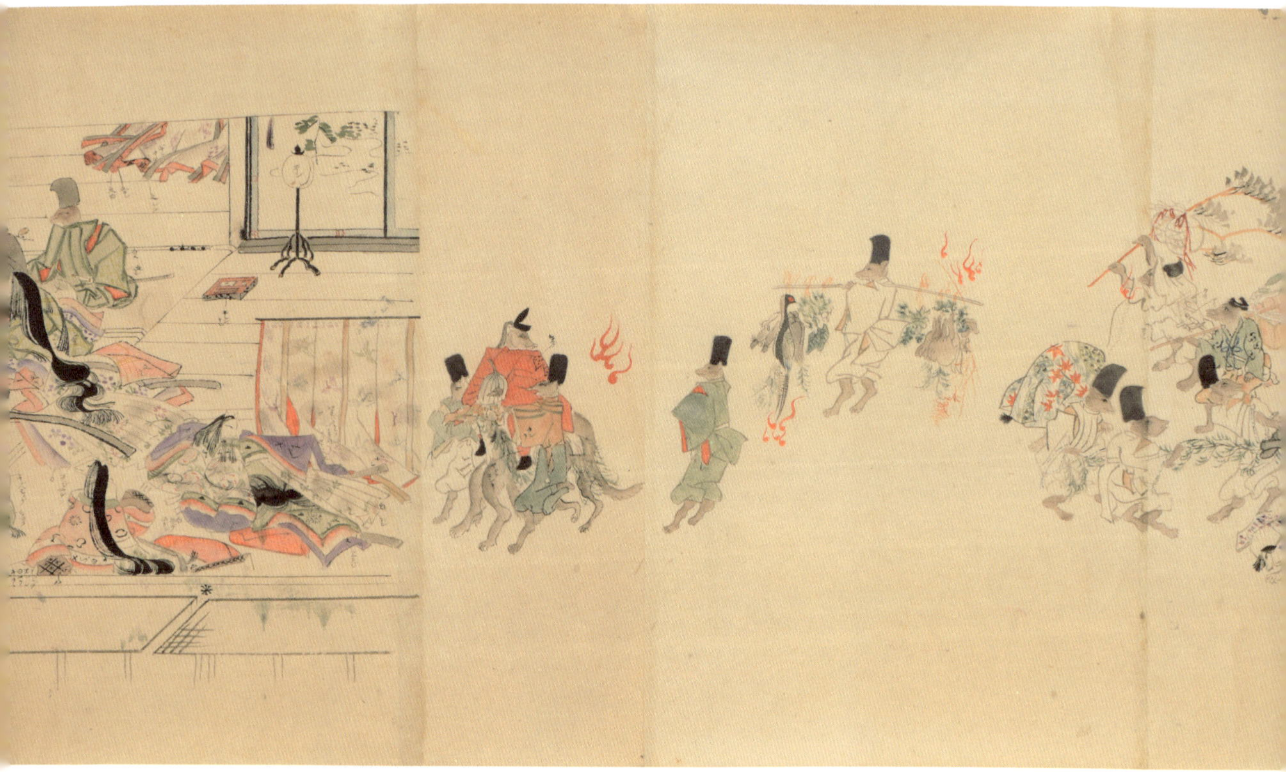

行列が御殿の場面に移り、高貴な狐たちの宴が始まる。その後、朝日が昇り宴は終焉を迎える。
The procession moves to the palace, where the aristocratic foxes start the revelry. Following this, the morning sun brings the feast to a close.

題簽には「狐怪草紙」とあるが、絵巻の冒頭では「狐怪双紙」と記されている。巻末に「明治弐十八年秋写す」とあるが作者名は記されていない。高貴な姿をした狐たちの御殿での生活を中心に描いている。最後は朝日が昇り出して終わっている。朝日から出た火焔も多く描かれているので、百鬼夜行絵巻からのイメージだろう。白描で色指定などが記された場面も混在するので完成品ではないのだろう。

Different kanji characters are used for the title and the heading at the beginning of the scroll. At the end of the scroll are the words ″Copied in autumn of 1895 (Meiji 28)″ but the name of the author is not recorded. The scroll focuses on noble-born foxes living in a palace. In the end it concludes with the morning sun rising. The flames licking from the sun imply that it hails from the *Night Parade of One Hundred Demons* picture scroll. This does not seem to be a finished work, as some scenes sketched out in ink lines with color-coding are mixed in.

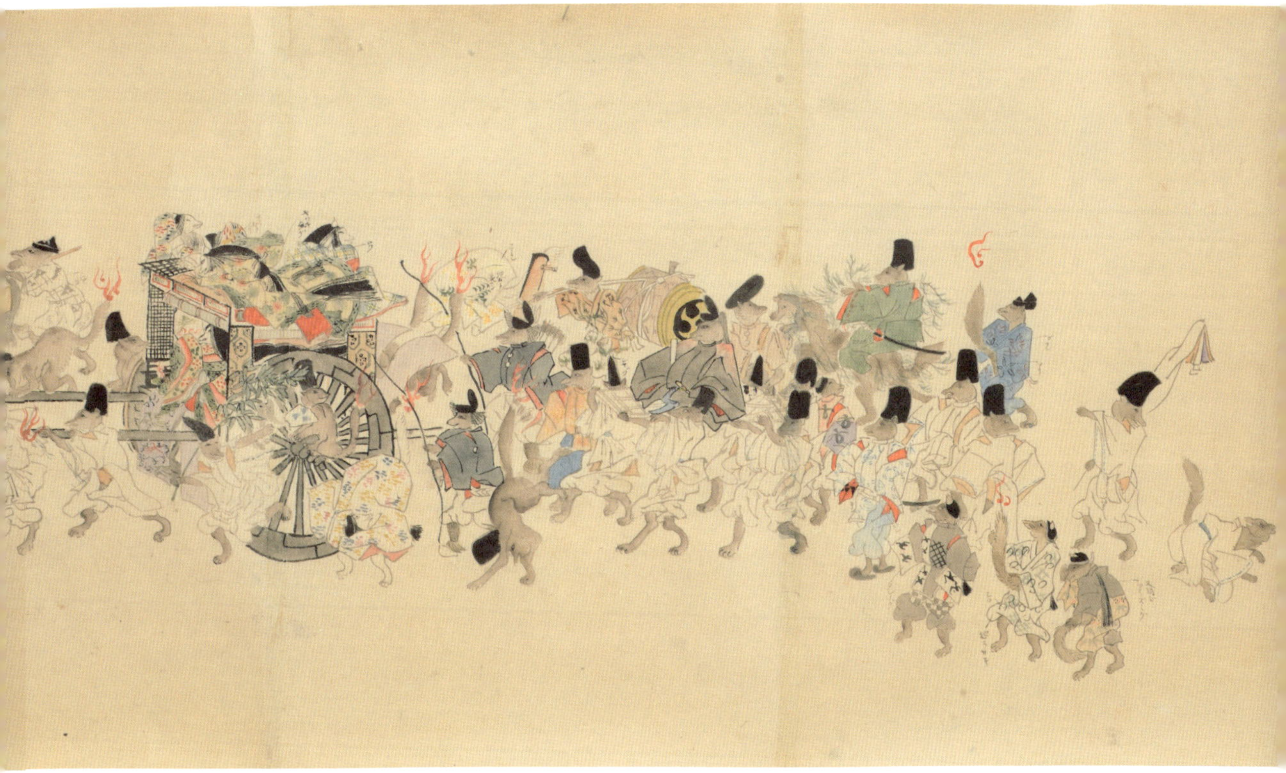

姫の乗る牛車の豪壮な行列。高位の狐も牛車に従って御殿へと向かっている。
尻尾を立てて狐火を掲げているものもいる。牛車の上には姫の御付きたちの姿もみえる。
Grand procession of the princess′s oxcart. High-ranking foxes follow the oxcart, heading for the palace.
Some raise their tails with fox fire on them. The princess′s attendants can be seen on top of the oxcart.

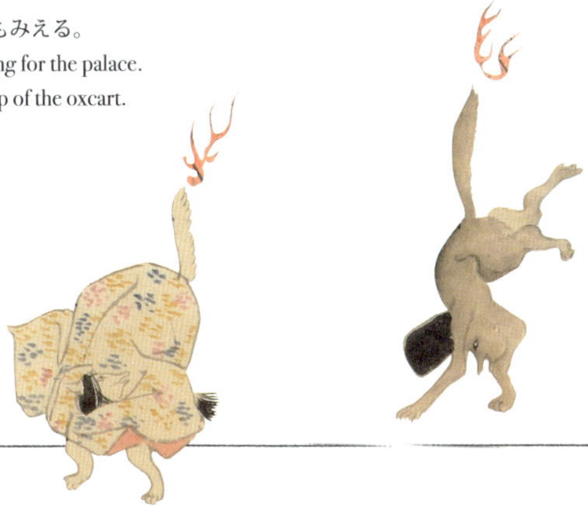

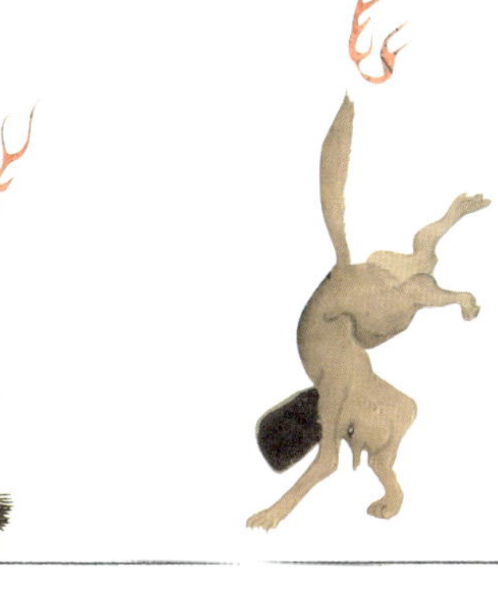

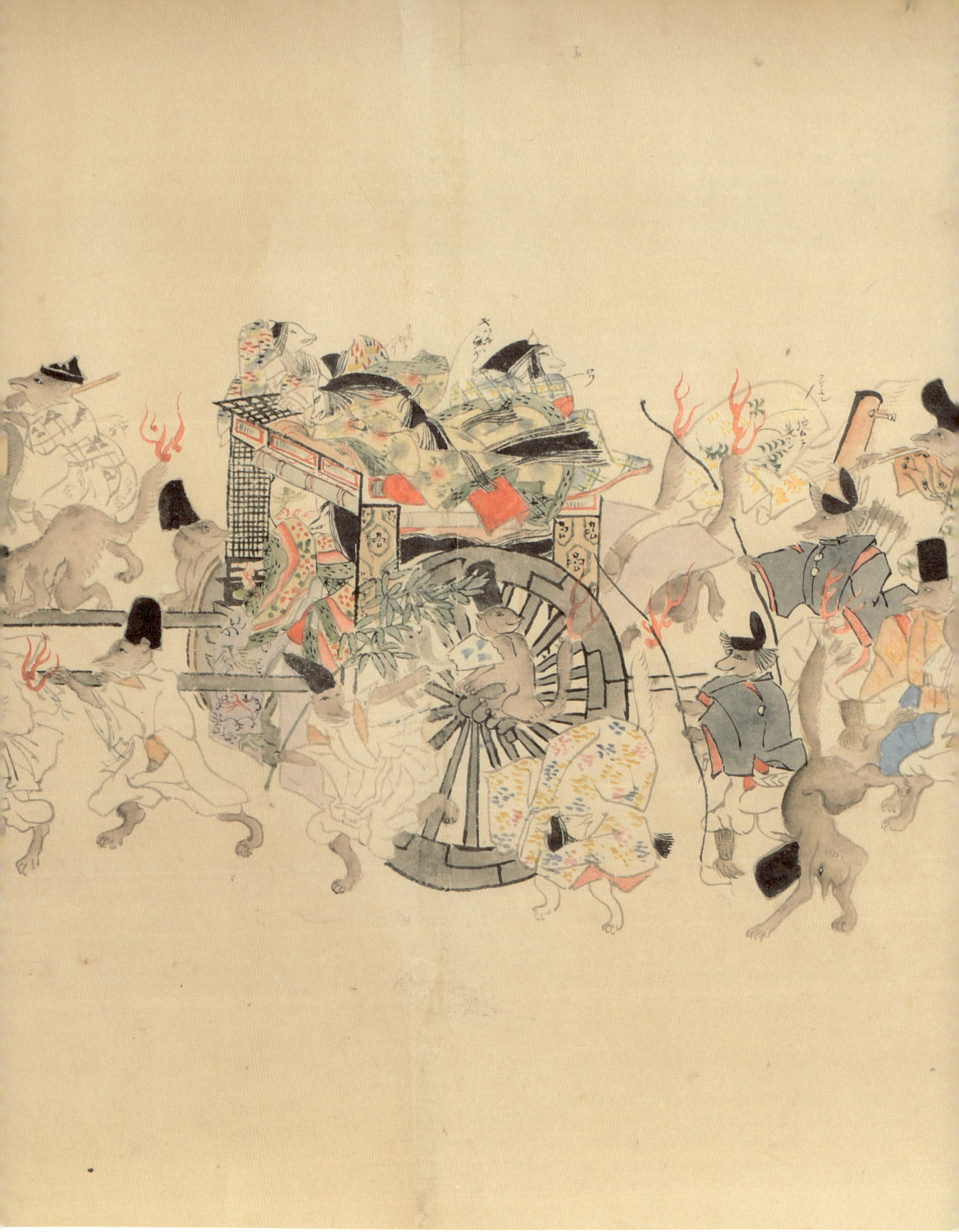

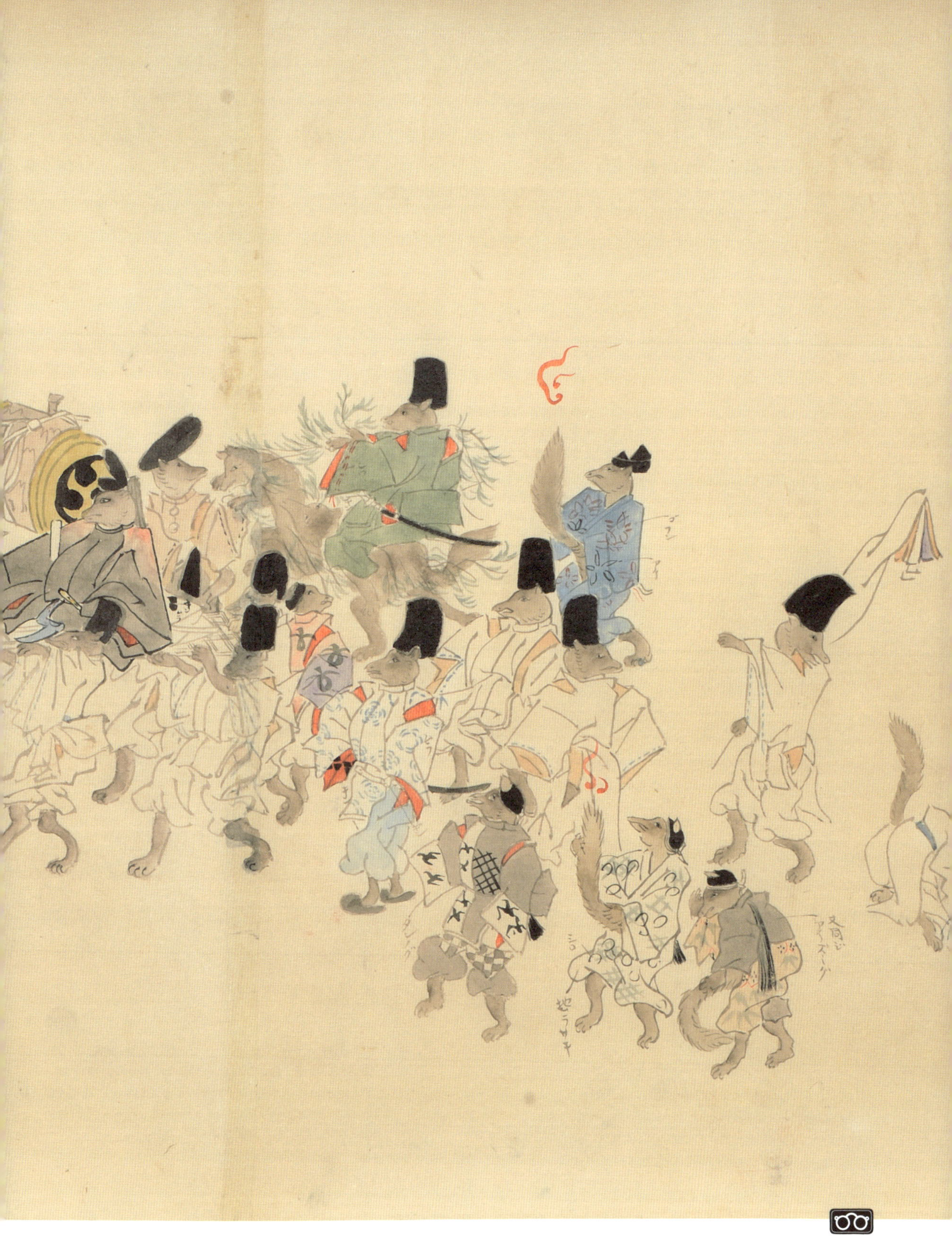

妖怪絵巻
ようかいえまき

Yokai Picture Scroll

江戸時代　縦 29.0　長 346.0　Edo period, Height 29.0, Length 346.0

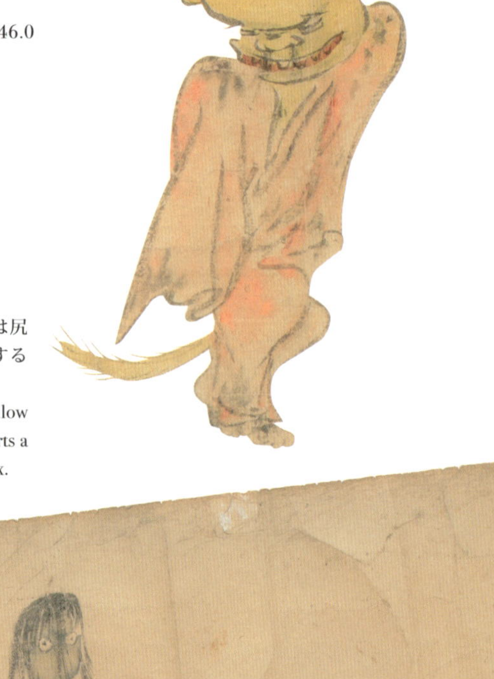

右の黄色い顔で大きな耳の妖怪は尻尾を出しているが、顔付きからすると狐ではないようだ。
The yokai on the right with the yellow complexion and prominent ears sports a tail, but judging by its face is not a fox.

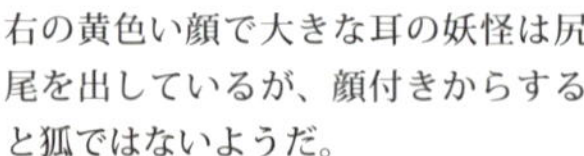

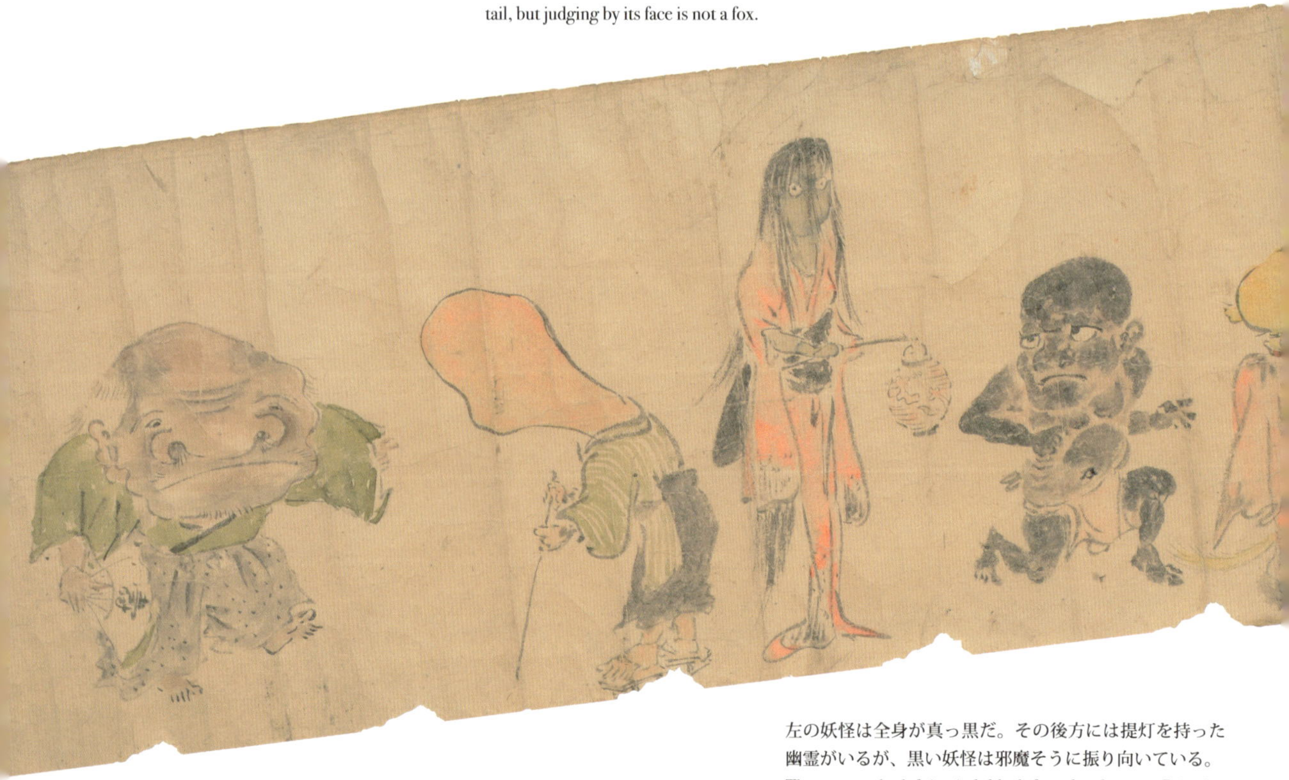

右は座頭の妖怪、左は扇子を持った老人のような妖怪。
To the right is a low-ranking blind yokai (*zatō*), and to the left is what looks like an old person holding a folding fan.

左の妖怪は全身が真っ黒だ。その後方には提灯を持った幽霊がいるが、黒い妖怪は邪魔そうに振り向いている。
The one on the left is pitch black from head to toe. Bringing up the rear is a ghost holding a lantern; the black yokai is turning back to glare at it, as if it is bugging him.

大きな顔で胴体がほとんどなくて足となる妖怪が異様に
大きな手を掲げて向かい合った妖怪を威嚇しているよう
だ。いっぽうで左の妖怪は極端に長い頭で手を幽霊のよ
うに垂らして相対している。

With a massive head and legs that dominate its torso, a yokai
raises its oversized hands as if to threaten the creature facing
off against it. Meanwhile, the yokai opposite it on the left with
the extremely long head hangs its hands like a ghost.

右側に蛸のような妖怪、左には不気味な動物のような妖
怪が描かれている。

On the right side is a creature like an octopus, and on the left
a freakish animal.

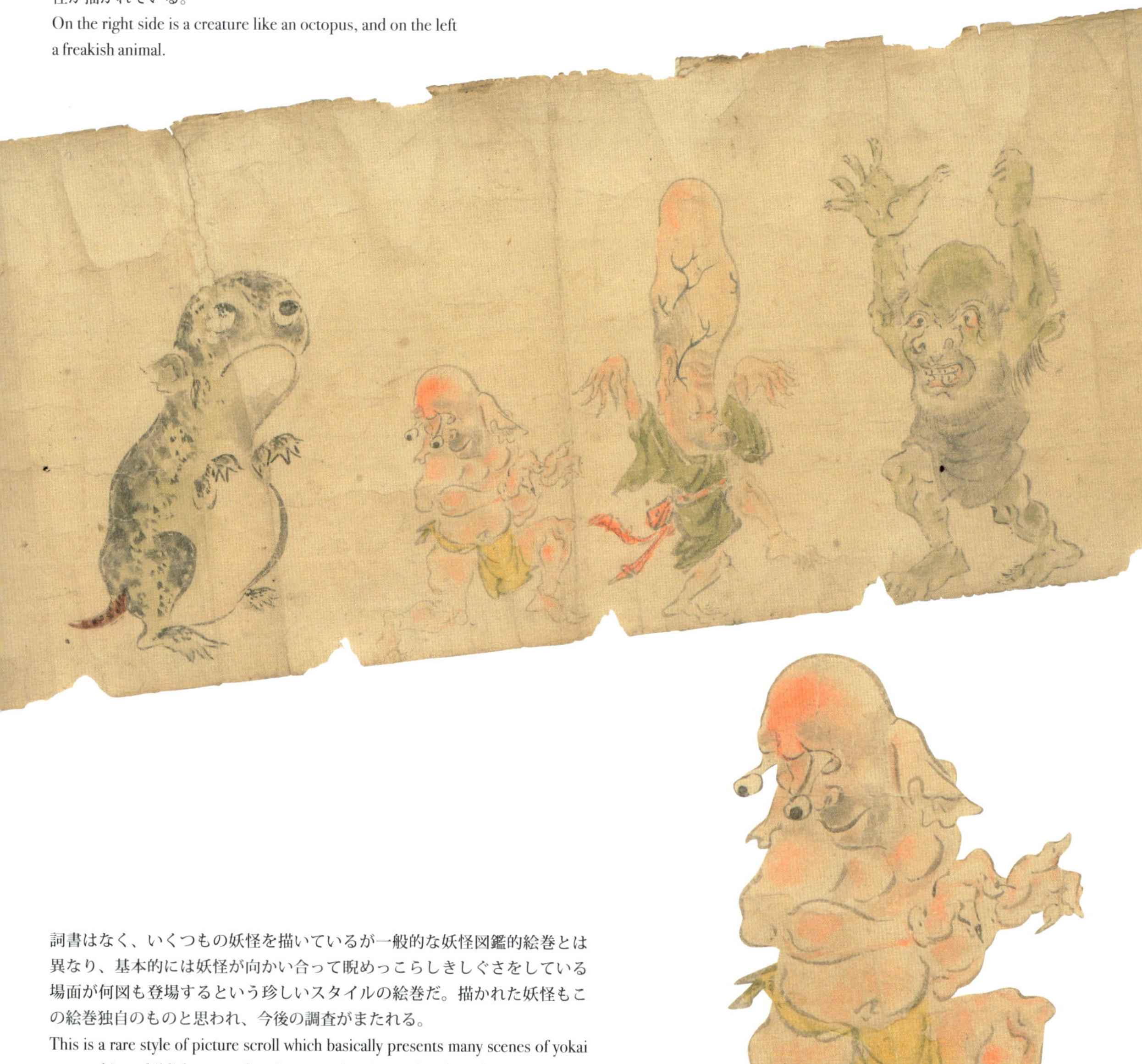

詞書はなく、いくつもの妖怪を描いているが一般的な妖怪図鑑的絵巻とは
異なり、基本的には妖怪が向かい合って睨めっこらしきしぐさをしている
場面が何図も登場するという珍しいスタイルの絵巻だ。描かれた妖怪もこ
の絵巻独自のものと思われ、今後の調査がまたれる。

This is a rare style of picture scroll which basically presents many scenes of yokai
engaged in a childish game of staring at each other and making faces; numerous
yokai are depicted, but in contrast to most illustrated yokai scrolls, there is no text
section (*kotobagaki*) written to accompany the images. The yokai depicted are
thought to be unique to this scroll, pending further investigation.

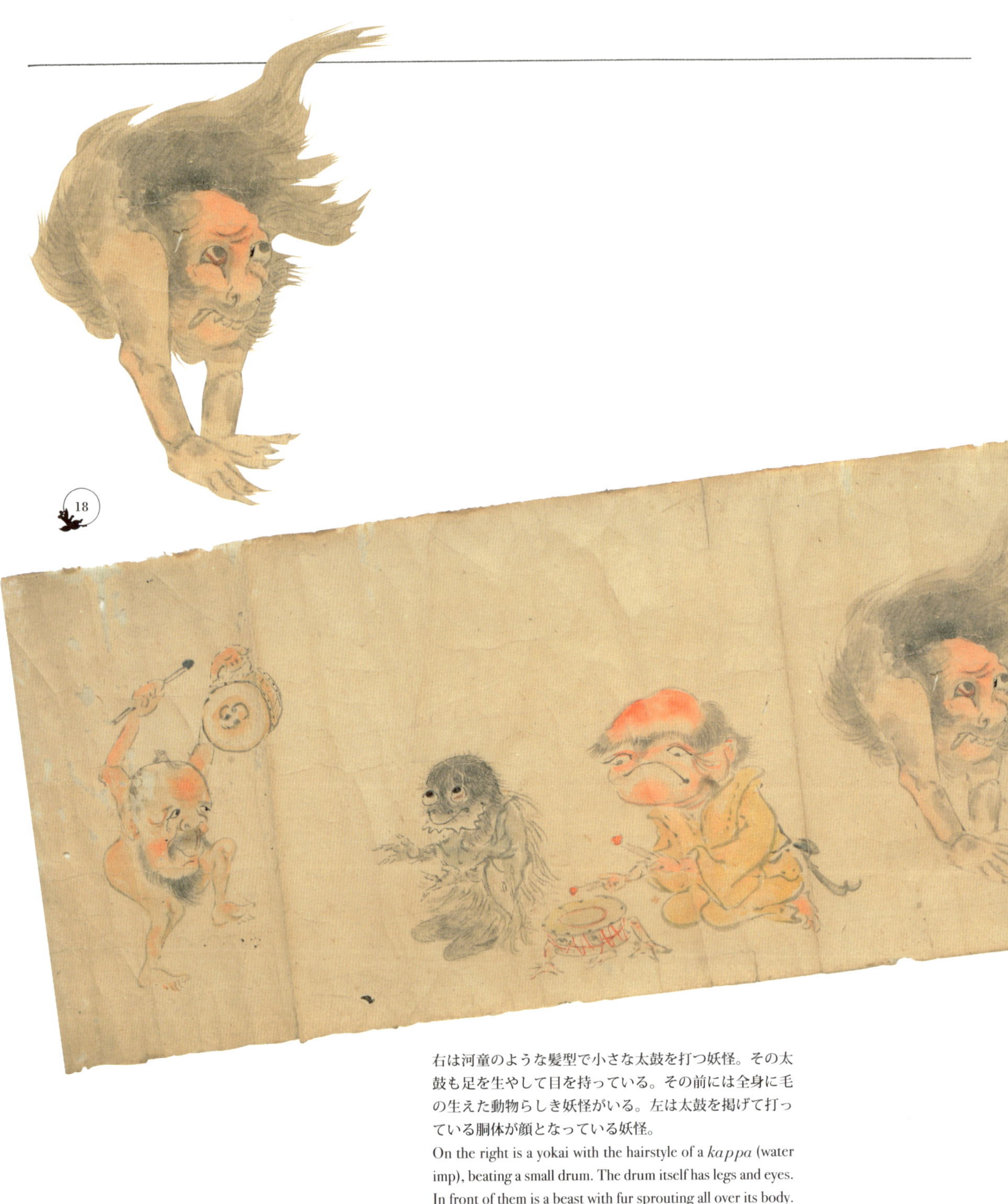

右は河童のような髪型で小さな太鼓を打つ妖怪。その太
鼓も足を生やして目を持っている。その前には全身に毛
の生えた動物らしき妖怪がいる。左は太鼓を掲げて打っ
ている胴体が顔となっている妖怪。

On the right is a yokai with the hairstyle of a *kappa* (water
imp), beating a small drum. The drum itself has legs and eyes.
In front of them is a beast with fur sprouting all over its body.
On the left is a yokai whose face has merged into its body,
banging on a drum held high.

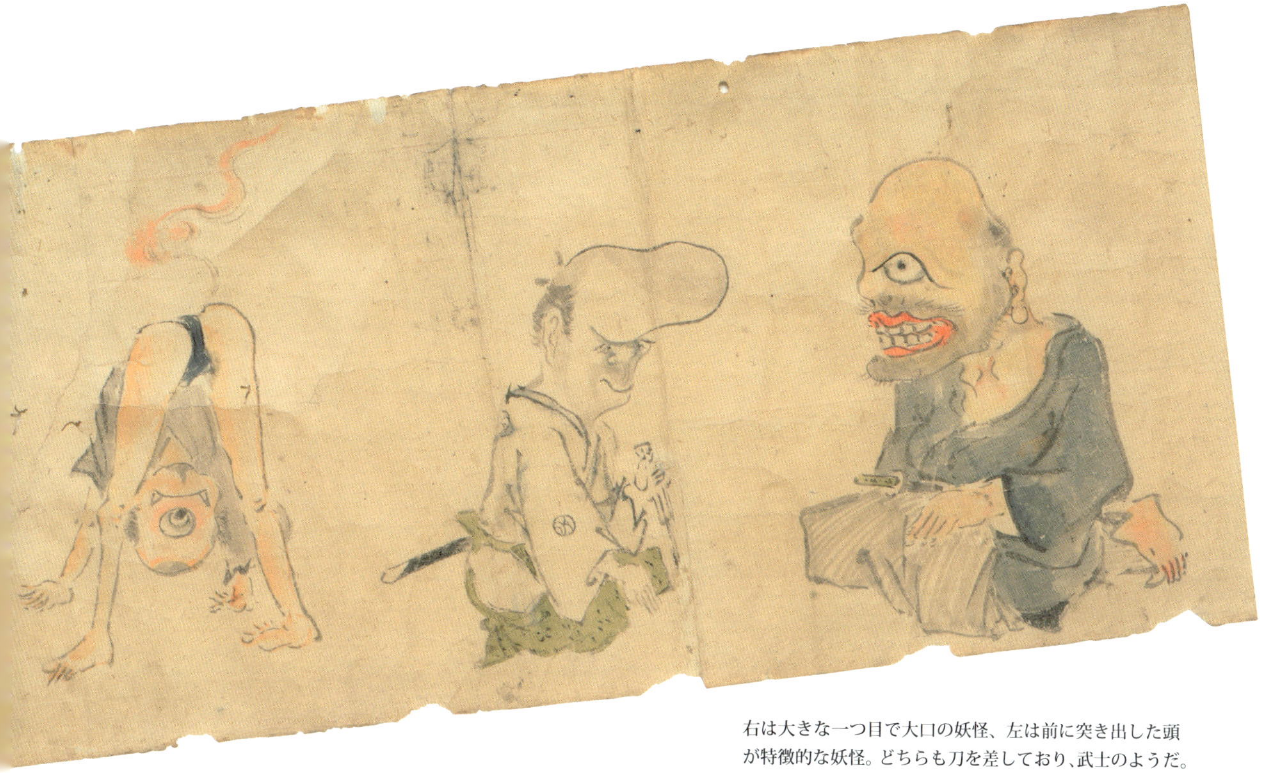

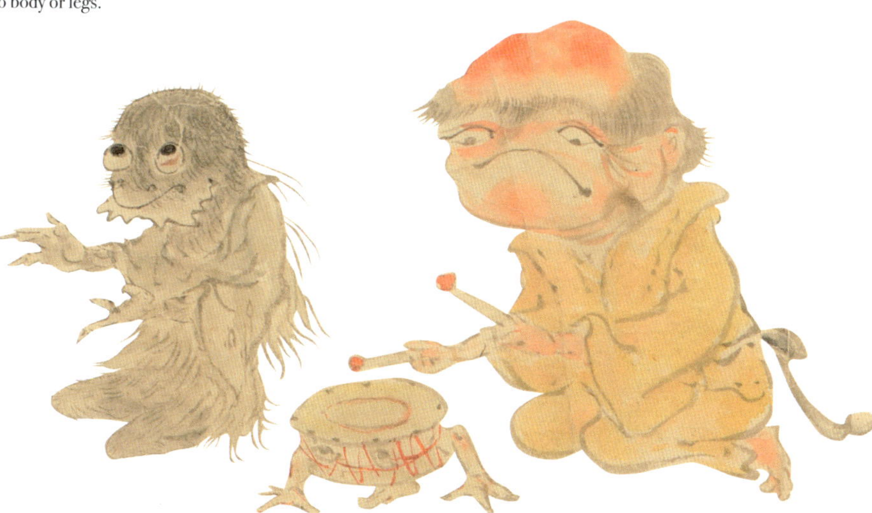

右は大きな一つ目で大口の妖怪、左は前に突き出した頭が特徴的な妖怪。どちらも刀を差しており、武士のようだ。
A yokai with one enormous eye and a huge mouth (right), and a yokai distinguished by its forward-jutting forehead (left). Both appear to be warriors as they are wearing swords.

右は股覗きをしている牙の生えた一つ目の妖怪、左は髪を振り乱して逆立ちしているが胴体や足のない妖怪。
On the right is a one-eyed, fanged creature peeking through its own legs, and on the left is a yokai with hair flying everywhere, standing on its hands as it has no body or legs.

化物絵巻

ばけものえまき

Bakemono Picture Scroll

江戸時代　縦 27.5　長 612.0　Edo period, Height 27.5, Length 612.0

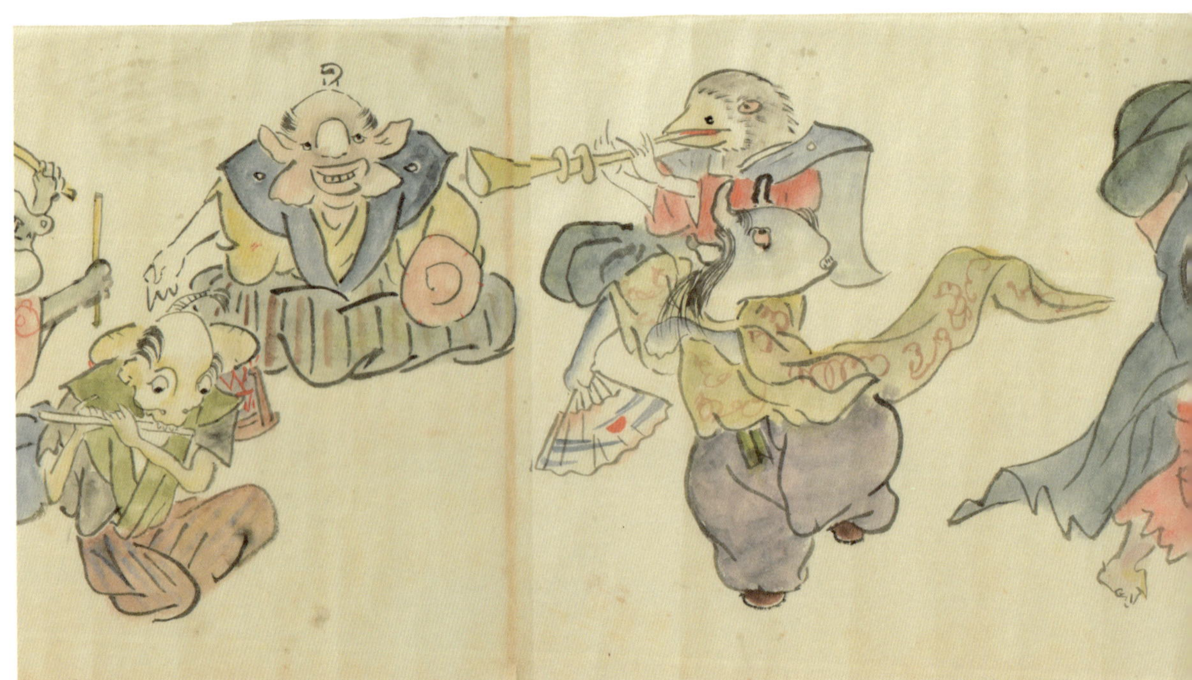

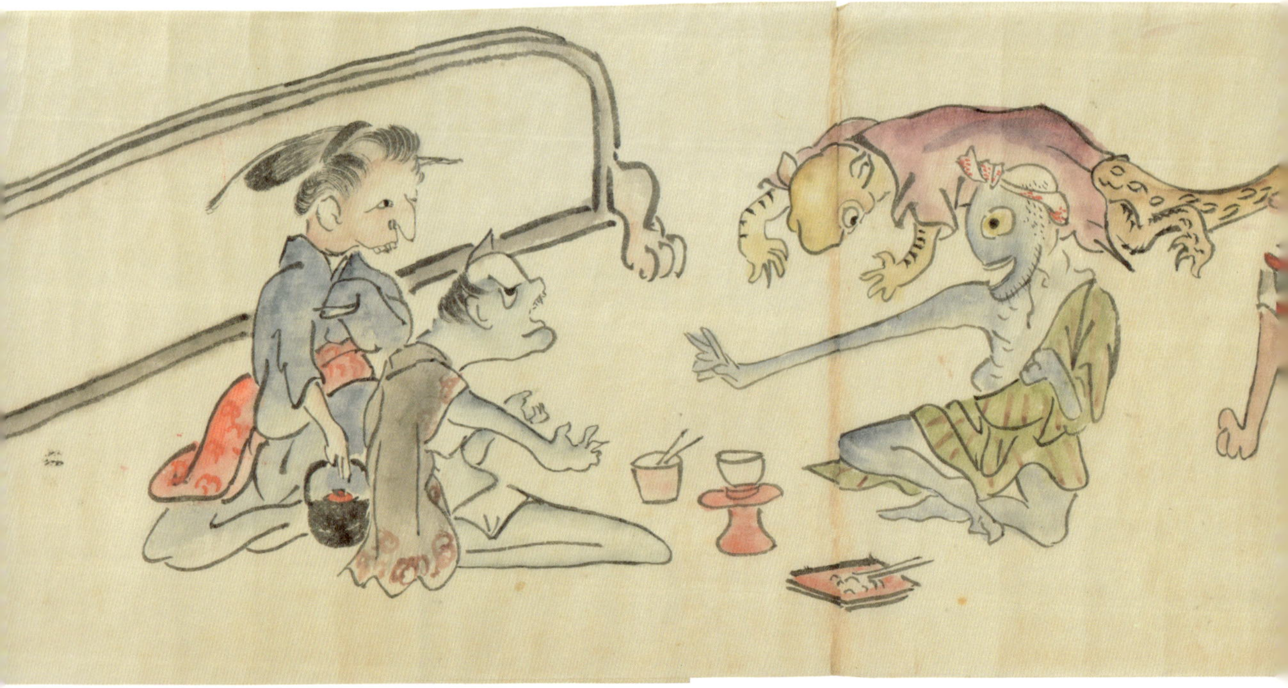

こちらでは酔った勢いで議論でもしているのだろうか。後ろには衣を纏った蜥蜴のようなものもみえる。
Here a heated drunken argument seems to be developing. In the background is what looks like a lizard wearing clothes.

宴もたけなわ。座を崩して座興の踊りに見入っている。
The party is in full swing. These yokai have fallen into more comfortable positions to watch the entertainment.

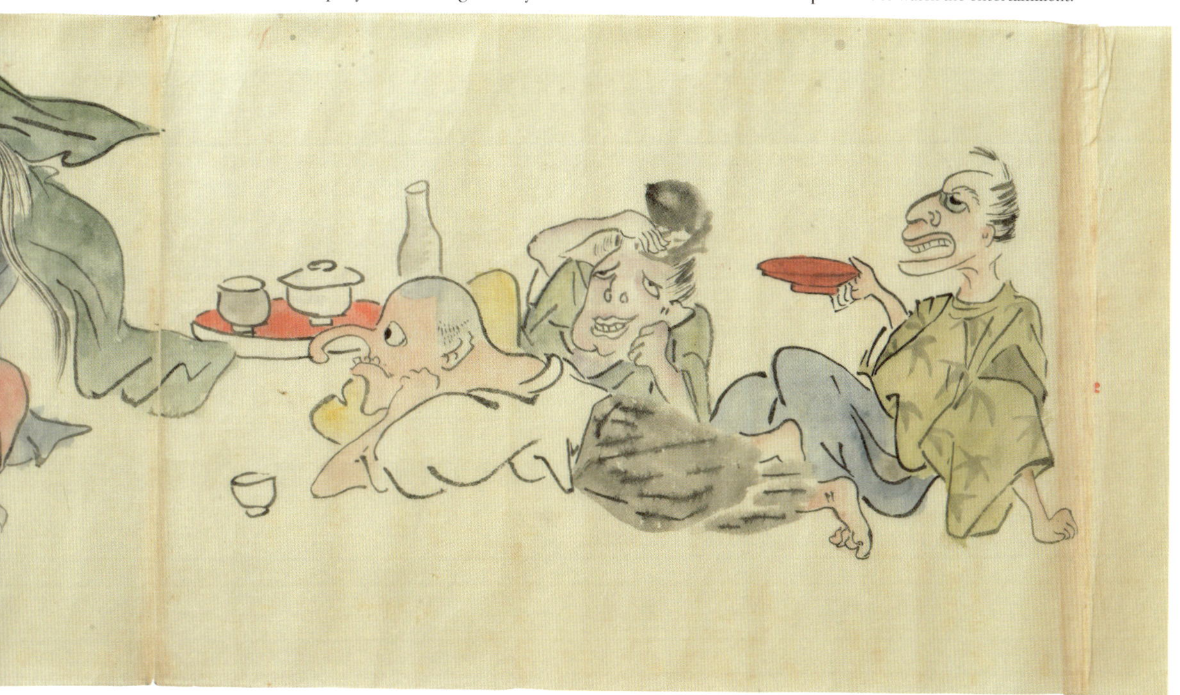

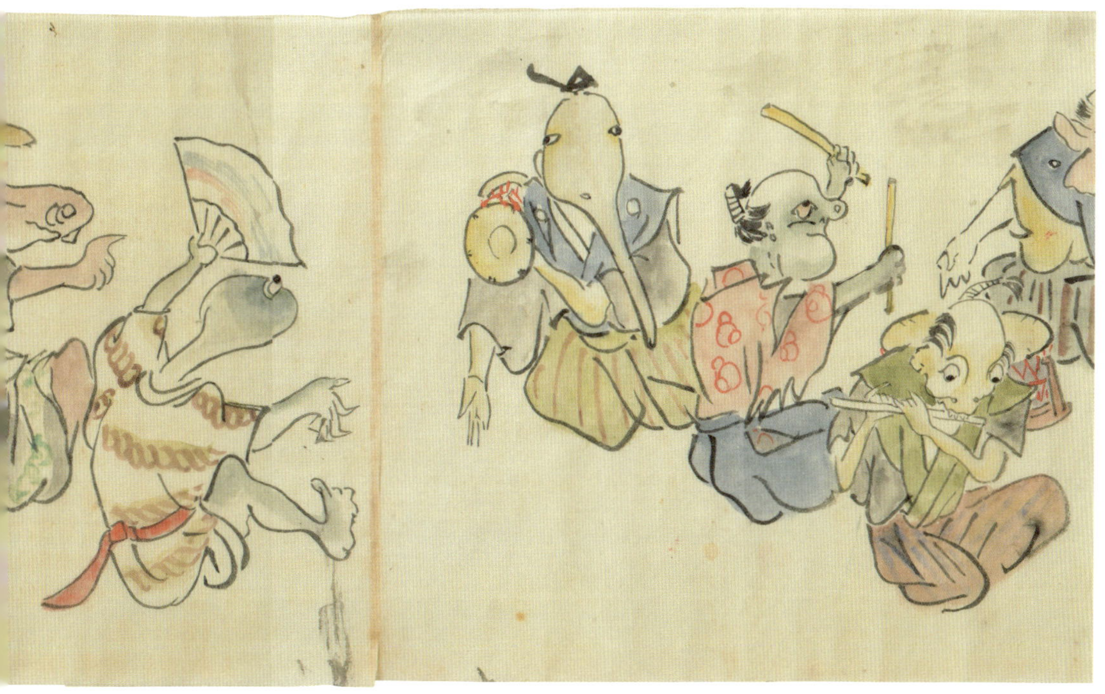

夢中に踊る人の横には笛、太鼓、鼓を奏でる者たち。
Musicians play a tune on flute, hand drum and stick drum to accompany the preoccupied dancers.

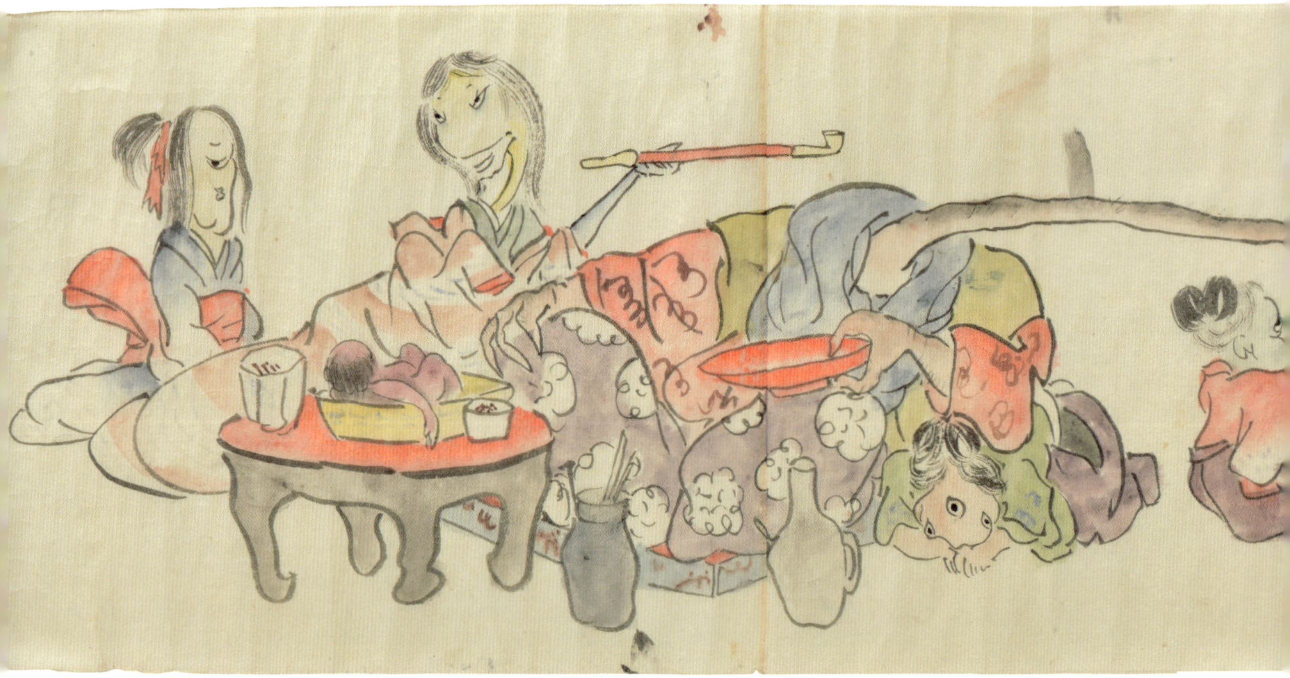

長い首の妖怪の膳には酒肴の赤子がみえる。不気味な宴会を象徴しているようだ。
A baby snack to accompany the alcohol can be seen in the dish of the long-necked yokai.
It is a symbol of the macabre drinking party.

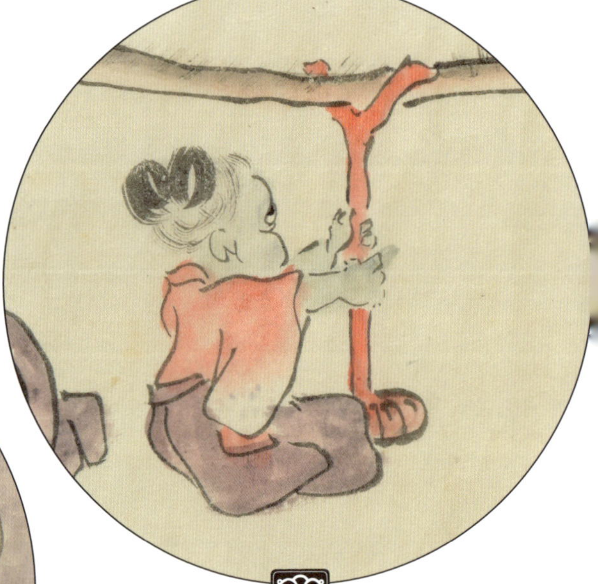

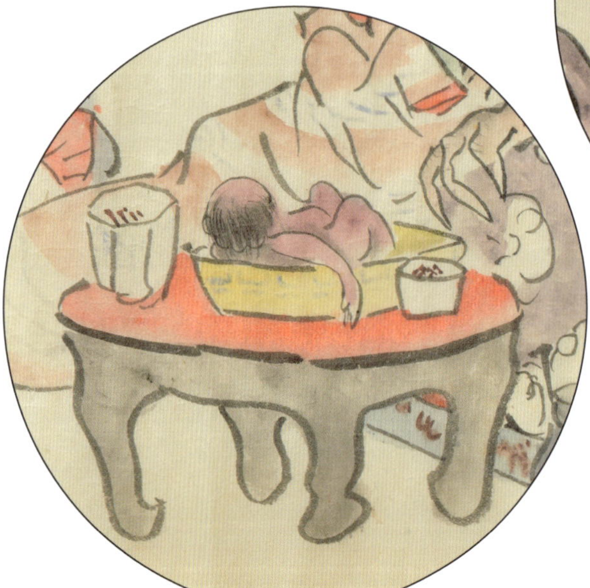

この絵巻は妖怪たちが酒宴を催し、どんちゃん騒ぎをしている様子を描いている。妖怪絵巻の形態としては主にストーリーが展開されているタイプ、妖怪図鑑的タイプ、いくつもの短いストーリーを収録した百物語的タイプの3種があるが、この絵巻は酒宴の一場面を描いていると思われる珍しいタイプだ。

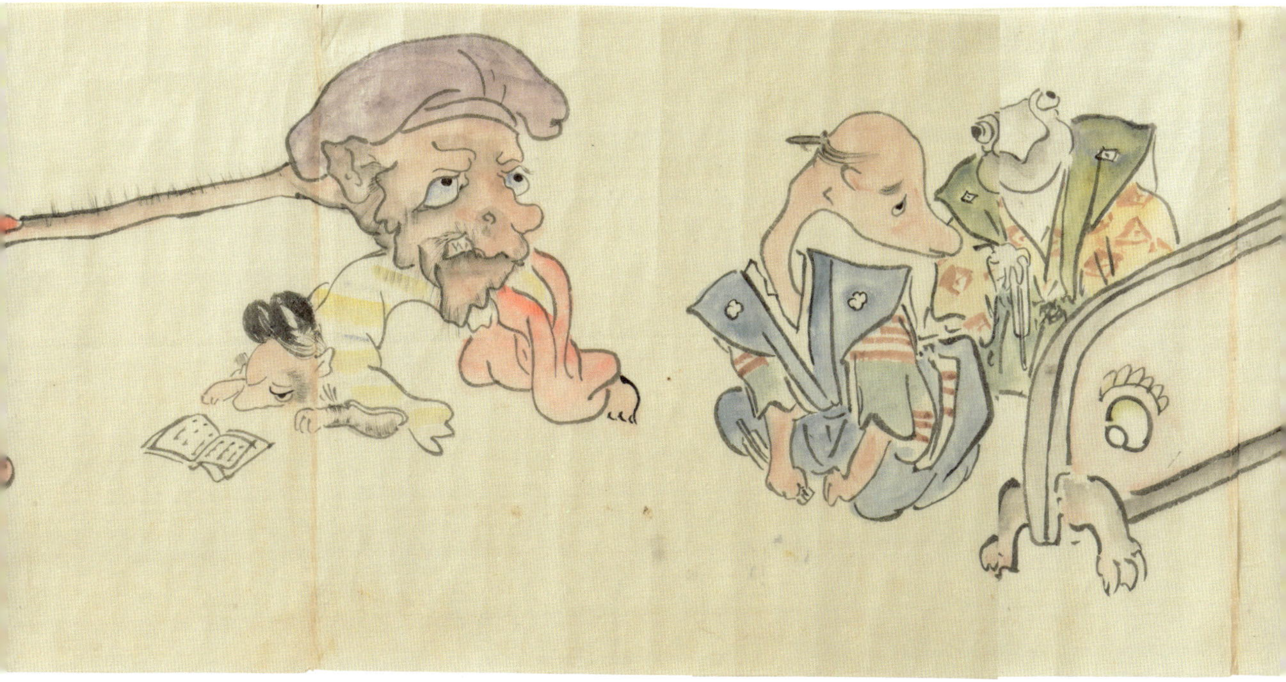

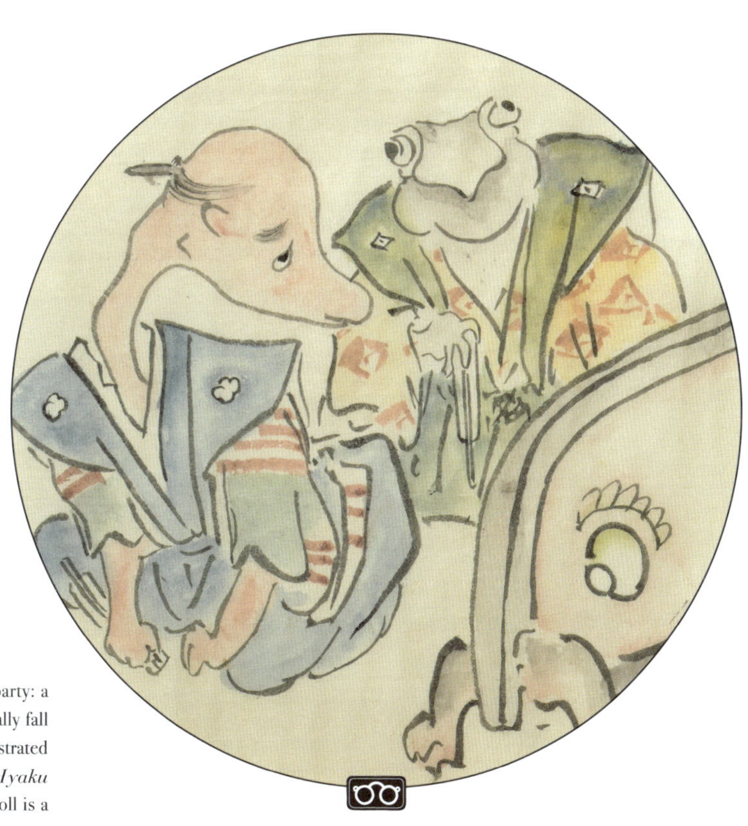

長い首が伸びて支えがないと不自由なようだ。
This head on a long neck is inconvenienced without support.

大きな衝立も付喪神のようだ。
A large screen appears to be an artifact spirit (*tsukumogami*).

This picture scroll shows yokai holding a drinking party: a scene of wild debauchery. Yokai picture scrolls usually fall under one of three types: those which tell a story, illustrated references, and anthologies of short stories like the *Hyaku Monogatari* (One Hundred Tales); this picture scroll is a rarity which features a single scene of a drinking party.

20 化物絵巻
ばけものえまき

Bakemono Picture Scroll

江戸時代　縦 28.0　長 678.0　Edo period, Height 28.0, Length 678.0

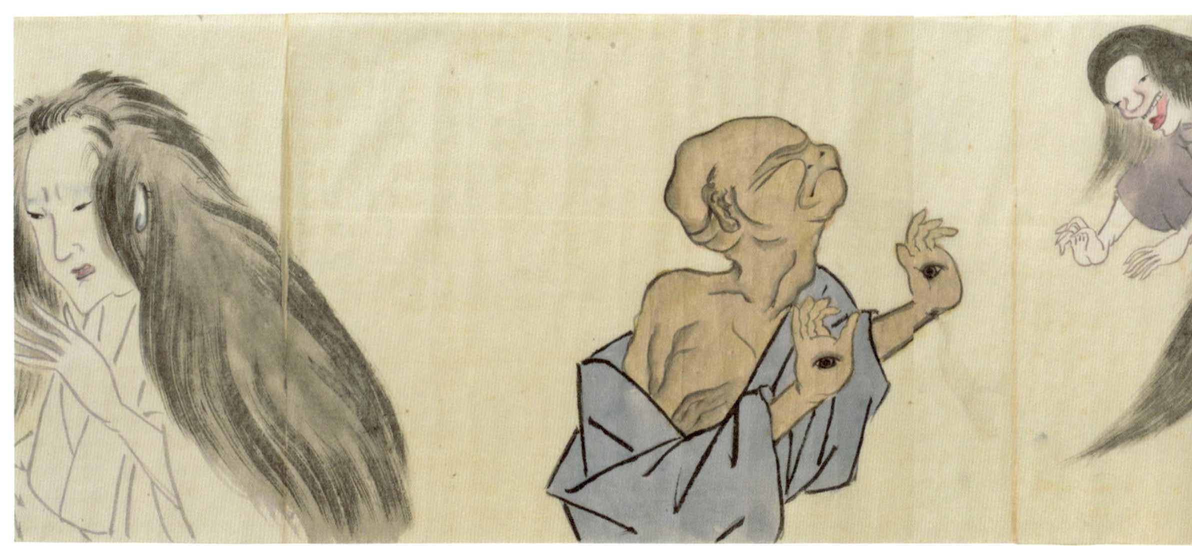

左は幽霊。『画図百鬼夜行』では多数の朽ち果てた塔婆の上に柳が茂る中から現れた幽霊が描かれているが、ここでは幽霊の上半身だけを描いている。雪女のようなイメージも入っているようだ。

On the left is a ghost. In the *Gazu Hyakki Yagyō*, the ghost is depicted on top of a dilapidated pagoda in the midst of willow trees, but here only the upper body is shown. This evokes the image of the *yukionna* (lit. "snow woman").

手の目。『画図百鬼夜行』では草むらから出てきたところだが、ここでは手の目だけが描かれている。

Tenome (lit. "eye hands"). In the *Gazu Hyakki Yagyō*, the *tenome* emerges from tufts of grass, but here it is drawn separately.

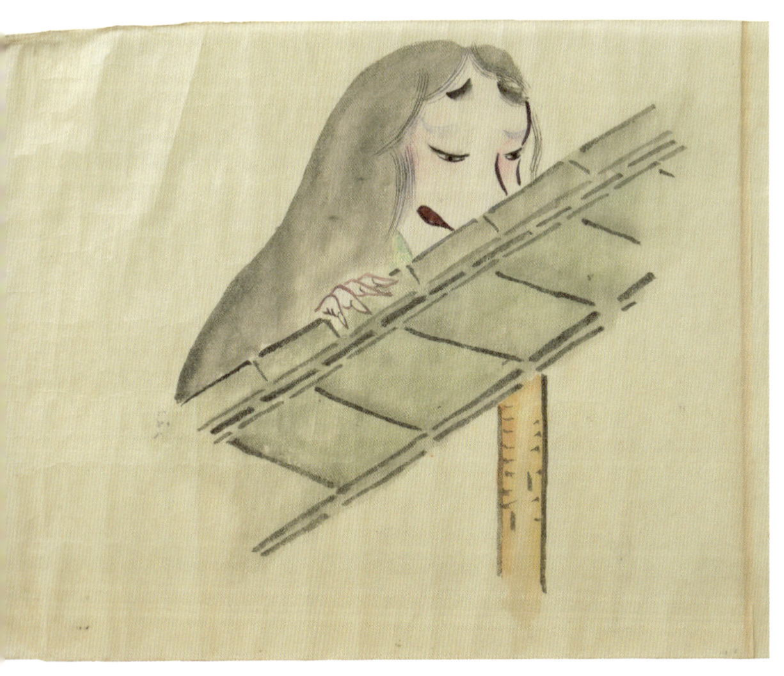

倩兮女。垣から覗く倩兮女を描いているが、この妖怪は『今昔百鬼拾遺』に収録されている。

Kerakera-onna ("cackling woman"). *Kerakera-onna* is drawn peeping over a fence; this yokai is from the *Konjaku Hyakki Shūi* (Supplement to The Hundred Demons from the Present and the Past).

巻頭に「化物之図」とある。いくつもの妖怪を紹介した妖怪図鑑的絵巻で、主に『画図百鬼夜行』に収録された妖怪だが、異なった構図となっているものが多く、彩色ということもあってこの絵巻の世界が展開されている。

At the beginning of the scroll is written "*Bakemono no zu*" ("Monster pictures"). The numerous yokai of this picture scroll are mainly from the Night Parade of One Hundred Demons, but their world expands with many different compositions and colors.

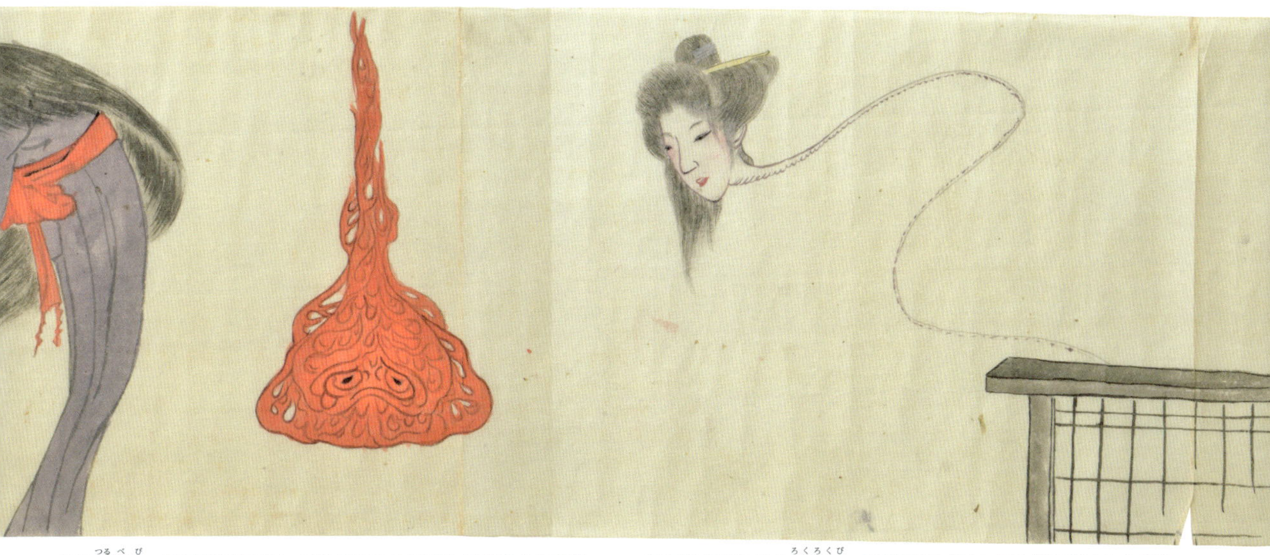

右は釣瓶火。『画図百鬼夜行』では岩場から伸びた松の近くに出現しているが、ここでは釣瓶火だけが真っ赤な姿で描かれている。
On the right is a *tsurubebi* (fireball spirit). In the *Gazu Hyakki Yagyō*, the *tsurubebi* appears on a tree growing from a rocky outcrop, but here it is depicted as a separate figure in bright red.

首だけが描かれた飛頭蛮。『画図百鬼夜行』では首の抜けた全身も描かれている。
The disembodied head of a *rokurokubi*. In the *Gazu Hyakki Yagyō* (Illustrated Night Parade of One Hundred Demons), the body that the *hitōban's* head leaves behind is also depicted.

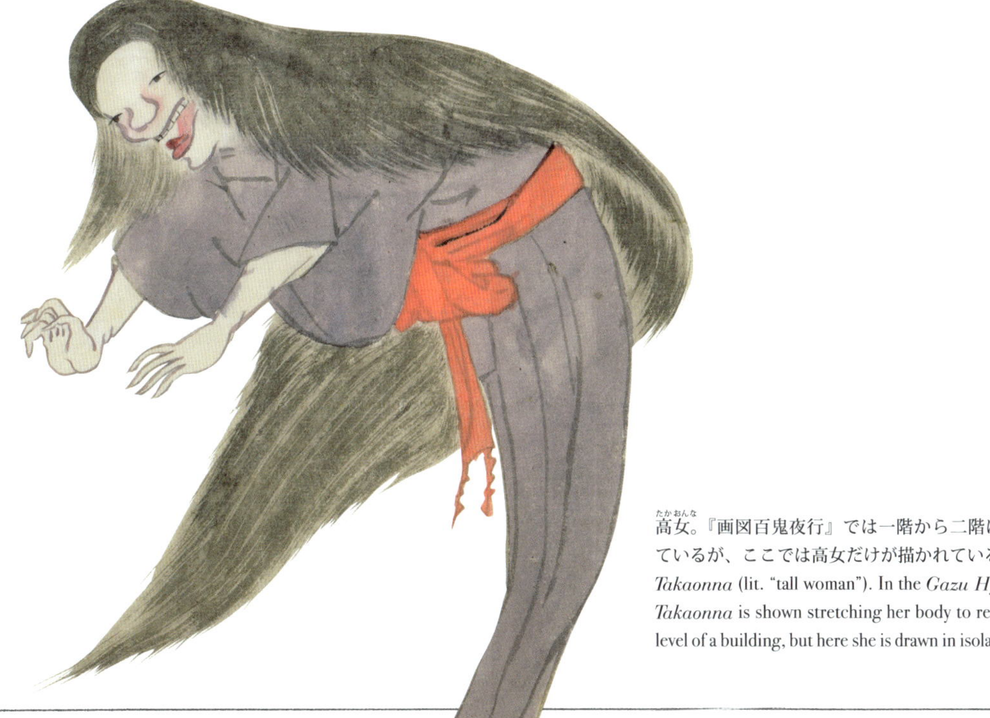

高女。『画図百鬼夜行』では一階から二階に身を伸ばしているが、ここでは高女だけが描かれている。
Takaonna (lit. "tall woman"). In the *Gazu Hyakki Yagyō*, *Takaonna* is shown stretching her body to reach the upper level of a building, but here she is drawn in isolation.

百鬼異形絵巻
ひゃっきいぎょうえまき

One Hundred Demon Forms Picture Scroll (*Hyakki Igyō Emaki*)

江戸時代　縦 37.0　長 1188.0　Edo period, Height 37.0, Length 1188.0

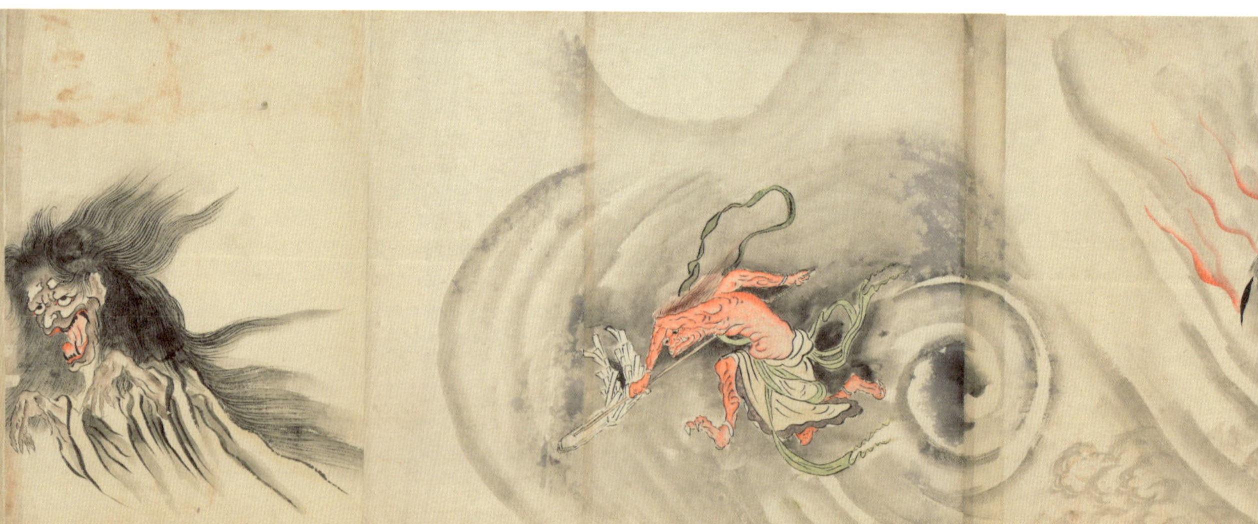

4番目に描かれた図なので「魔性」であろう。幽霊のような格好で口を大きく開いて襲いかかるような姿だ。

This is the fourth picture; an enchantress (*mashō*). A ghostly figure with mouth gaping wide as if about to attack.

3番目に描かれた図なので「鬼神」であろう。幣を突き出して突進するような姿だ。

This third picture is the *kishin* (ogre god). The ogre god charges, brandishing a Shinto wooden wand.

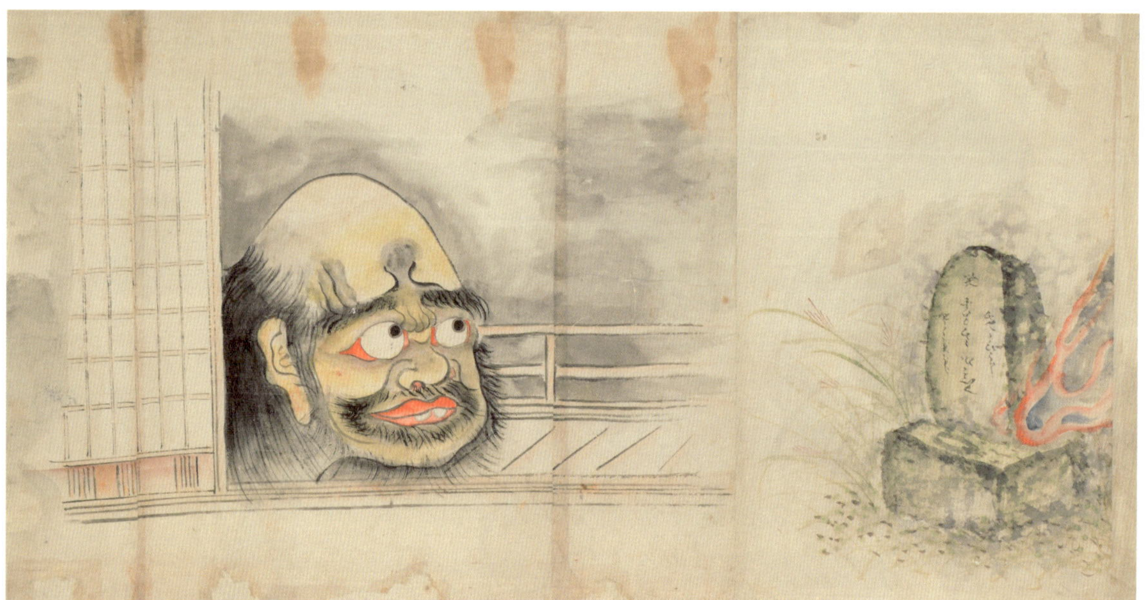

この図に至るまでに欠損があるために目次のどの妖怪かは不明。墓から怪火が出ている。この図の右側が欠損しているのでそこに妖怪が描かれているのかもしれない。
左には障子の外から巨大な顔が出現している。

We cannot be sure which yokai these are from the table of contents. A strange fire burns on a tombstone. The right side of this picture is missing; a yokai may have been drawn there.
On the left, a huge head appears outside the paper screen.

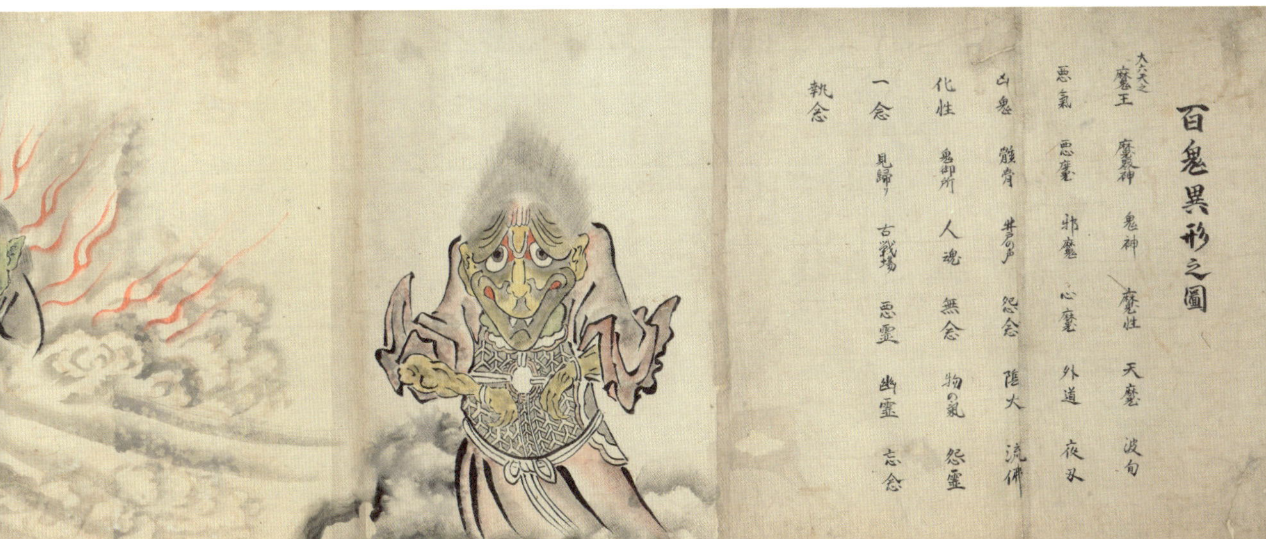

左上は 2 番目に描かれた図なので「魔界神」であろう。天狗のような長い鼻で牙もあり、体からは火焔を発している。

Following the order of the table of the contents, this second picture should be the *makaishin* (god of the devil world). Flames rise from its body; it has fangs and a nose as long as a *tengu* goblin's.

冒頭に描かれた妖怪なので「大六天之 魔王」であろう。暗雲から髪を逆立てて現れた魔王。

The first yokai at the beginning is probably the Demon King. He appears from a dark cloud with hair standing on end.

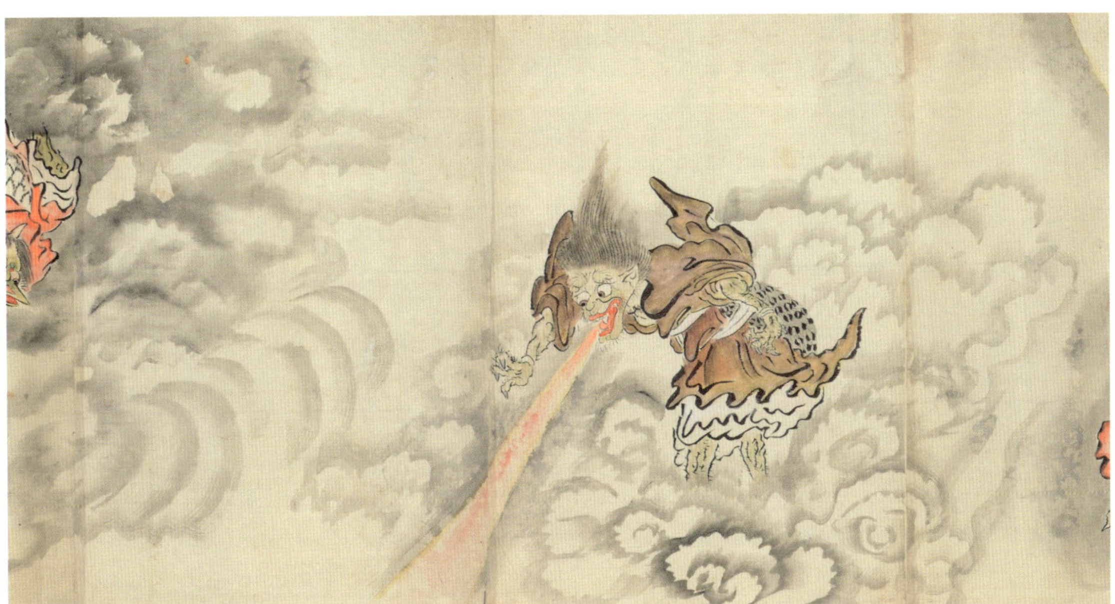

この図に至るまでに欠損があるために目次のどの妖怪かは不明。雲の上から下を見下ろして何かを狙うように火焔を吹きかけている。

It is not clear which yokai this is from the table of contents, as there are some omissions before this picture. From on top of a cloud, it looks down as if aiming at something and breathes fire.

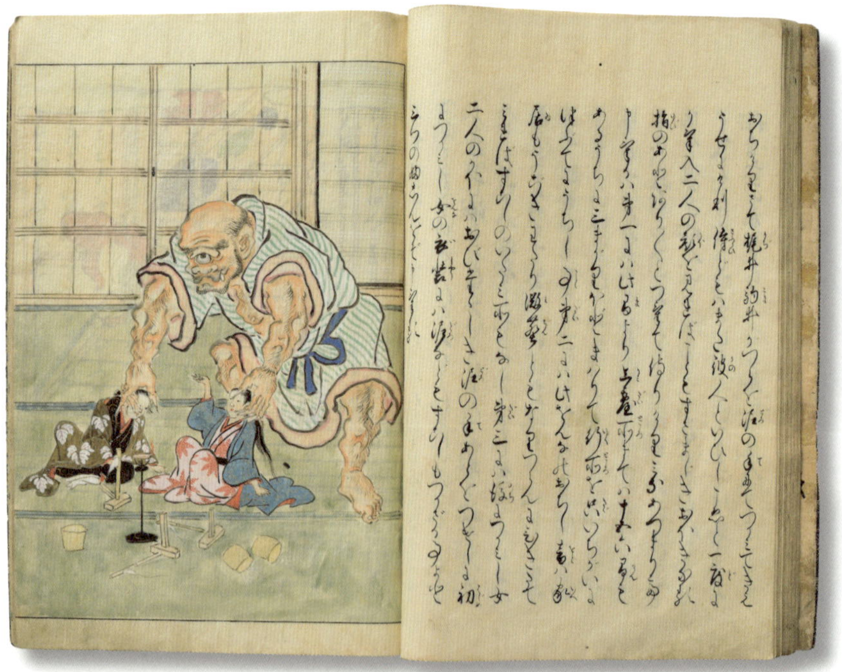

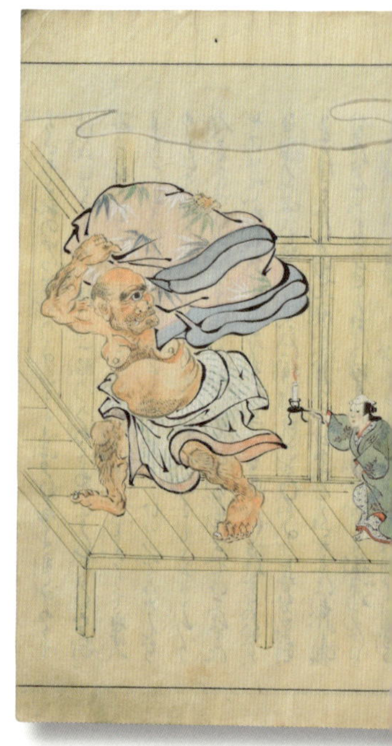

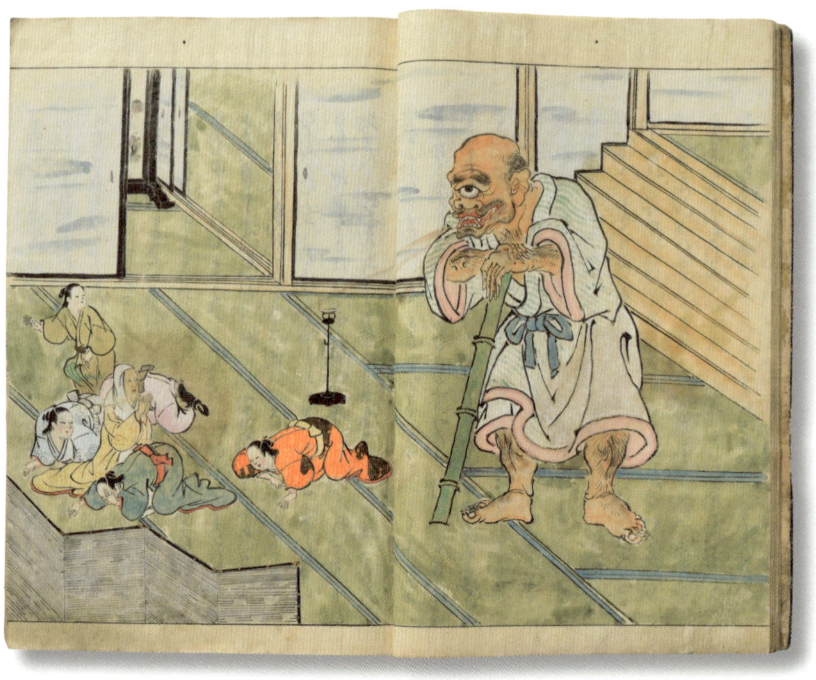

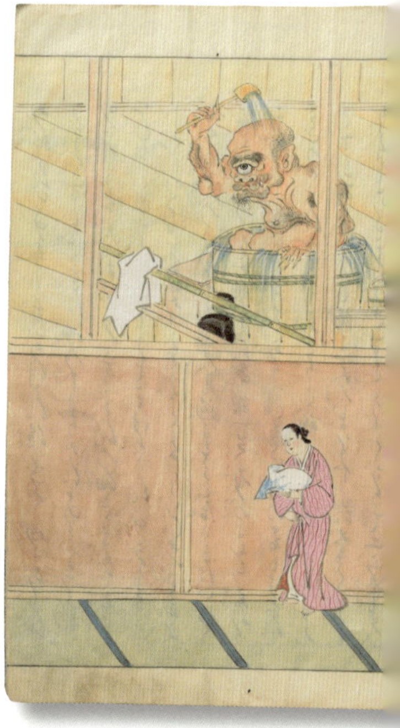

22 変化物語
へんげものがたり

Henge Monogatari

江戸時代　縦 31.2　横 21.5　Edo period, Height 31.2, Width 21.5

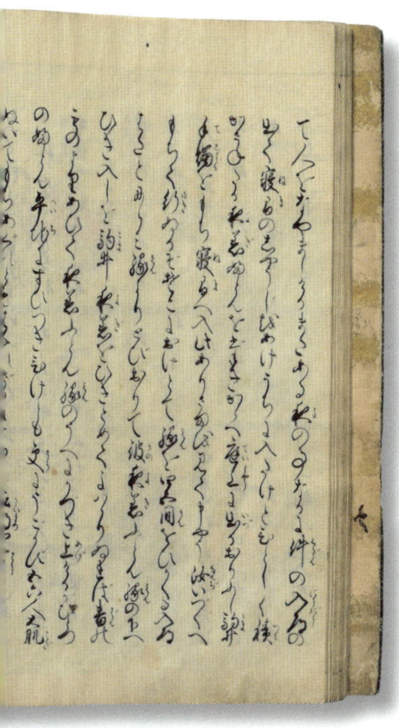

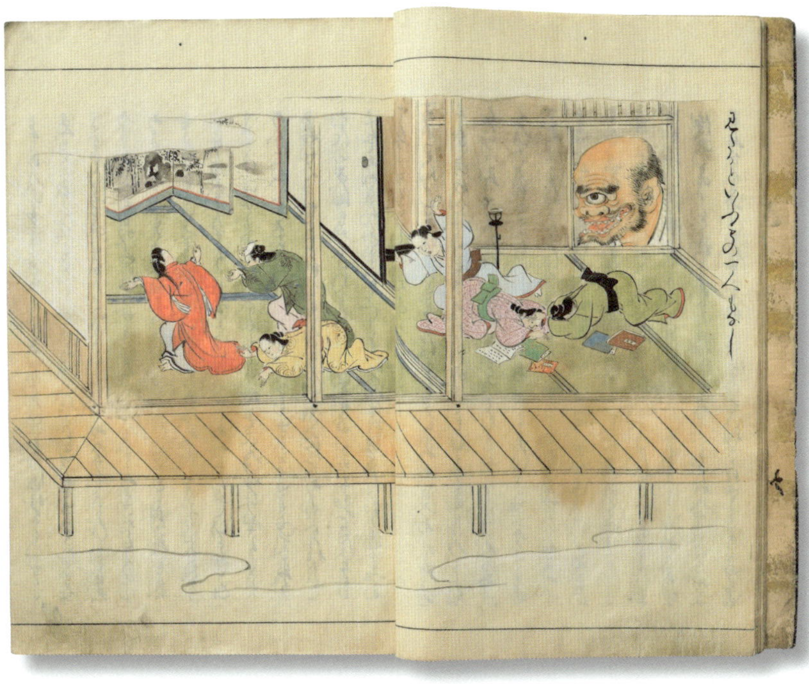

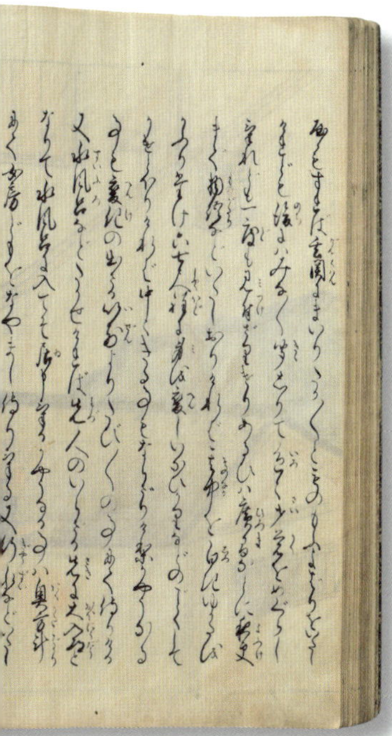

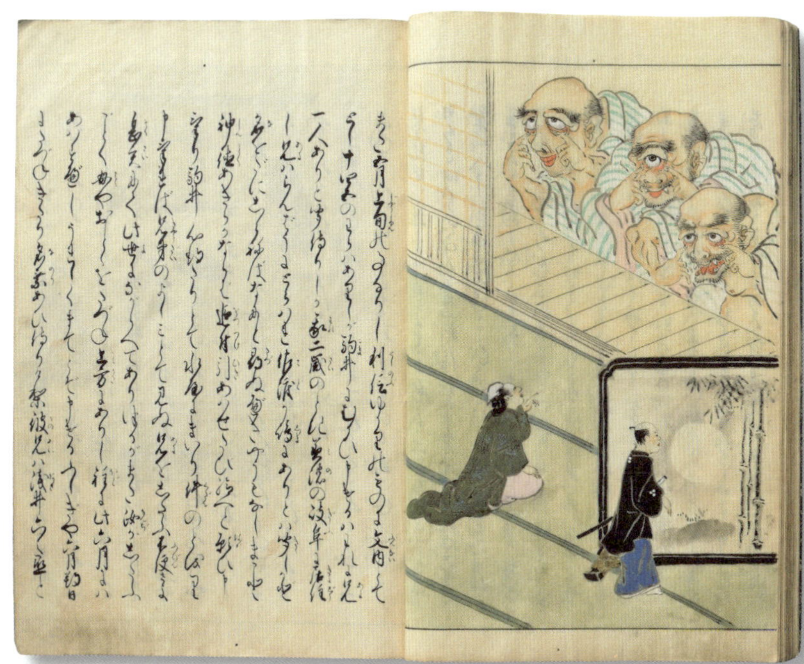

本書は上下2巻からなる丹後における妖怪譚を記し
たもので、丹後国の武士澤田将監利信の屋敷に起
こったさまざまな怪異を絵と文章で紹介している。
怪異が起こった原因は屋敷に棲みついた狐によるも
ので、巨大な一つ目入道の出現、ポルターガイスト
などが繰り返される。写本のほかに絵巻（『今昔妖
怪大鑑』収録）としても残されている。写本に「丹
後変化物語」との題名があるものも存在する。そも
そもは「変化物語」というタイトルであったが、広
く伝えられていくなかで、「丹後」という地名が加
えられて何処の地の話かを明示したともいわれ、「変
化物語」のほうが古いタイプとも考えられる。本書
は絵、文章とも丁寧にかかれており、江戸初期〜中
期の作品と思われる。海外からの里帰り品である。

This text is comprised of two scrolls of yokai tales from
Tango Province, which describe and illustrate various
supernatural occurrences at the mansion of samurai
Sawada no Shōgen Toshinobu of Tango. A huge one-
eyed priest, a poltergeist and other phenomena occurred
repeatedly, thought to be caused by a fox trapped in the
compound. Other copies and scrolls also remain (please
refer to *Yokai Museum*). There are also copies entitled
Tango Henge Monogatari. Originally the title was
Henge Monogatari, but as it spread to other regions
the placename Tango was added to make it clear where
the stories were from, therefore the *Henge Monogatari*
are thought to be older works. Dated sometime in the
early to mid-Edo, the text and illustrations are carefully
executed. This work has been repatriated from overseas.

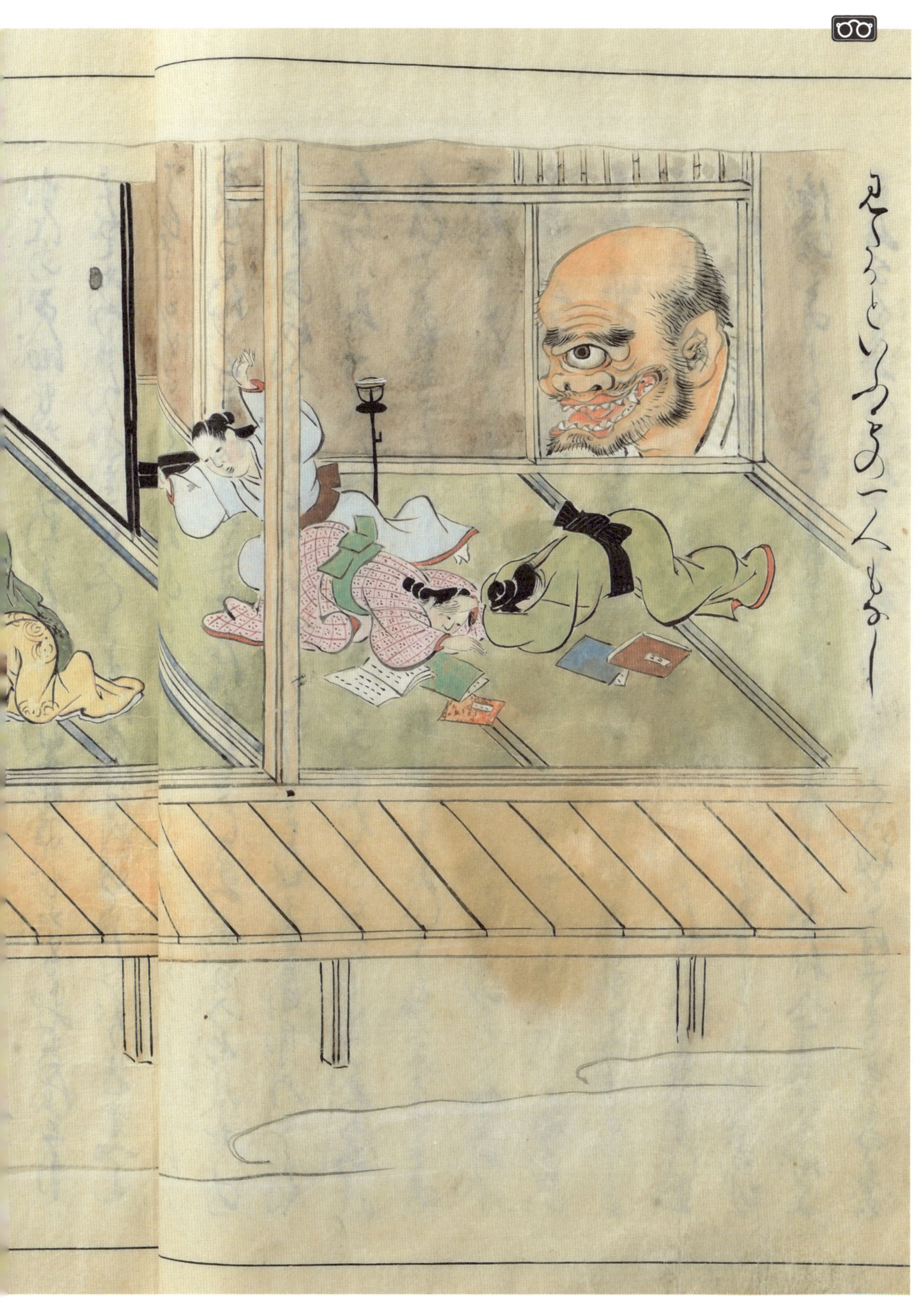

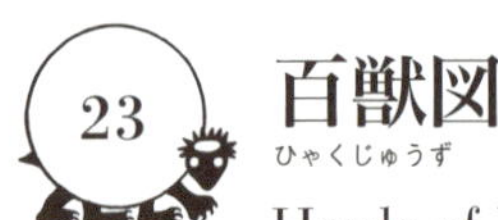

百獣図
ひゃくじゅうず

Horde of Beasts

洞堂美保　江戸時代　縦 86.8　横 49.4　Dōdō Yoshiyasu, Edo period, Height 86.8, Width 49.4

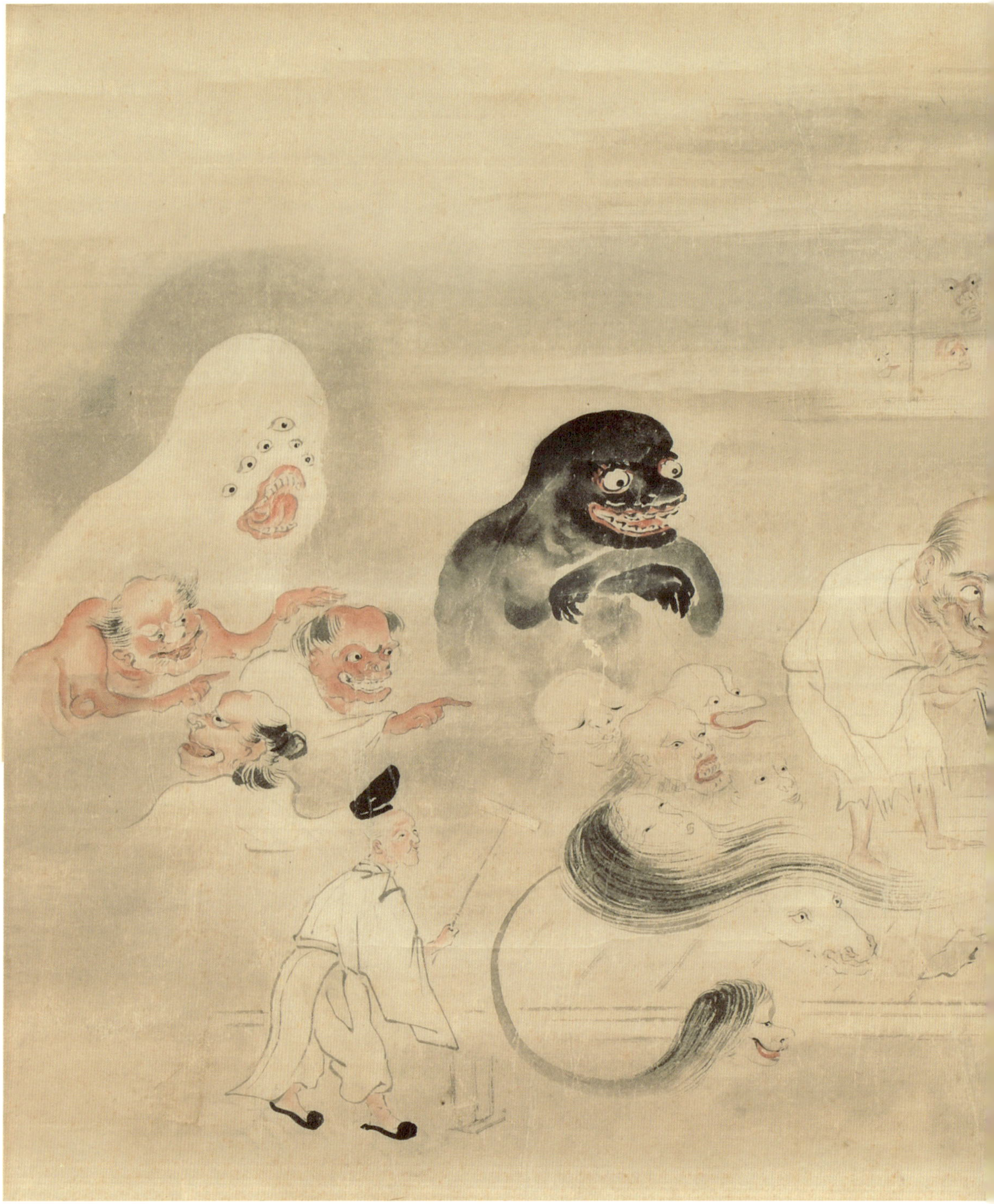

縁先で繰り広げられる怪異。庭や縁の下から不気味な妖怪たちが出
現しているが、獣のような姿もあり、箱書きの「百獣図」のイメー
ジだろう。部屋からも巨大な女の妖怪などが出現し、手前には小さ
な人の行列、襖にも顔が現れ怪異が満ち溢れている場面だ。この作
品には化物草紙絵巻の影響もみえる。

Grotesquerie revolving around a veranda. Ghastly yokai converge from
under the veranda and the garden, with beast-like shapes among them, as
this is probably an image from the box of artwork Horde of Beasts. The
scene is filled with strangeness; a giant female yokai emerges from the
room, a procession of small people are lining up in the foreground, and
faces appear on the sliding doors. This work shows the influence of the
Bakemono Zōshi picture scroll.

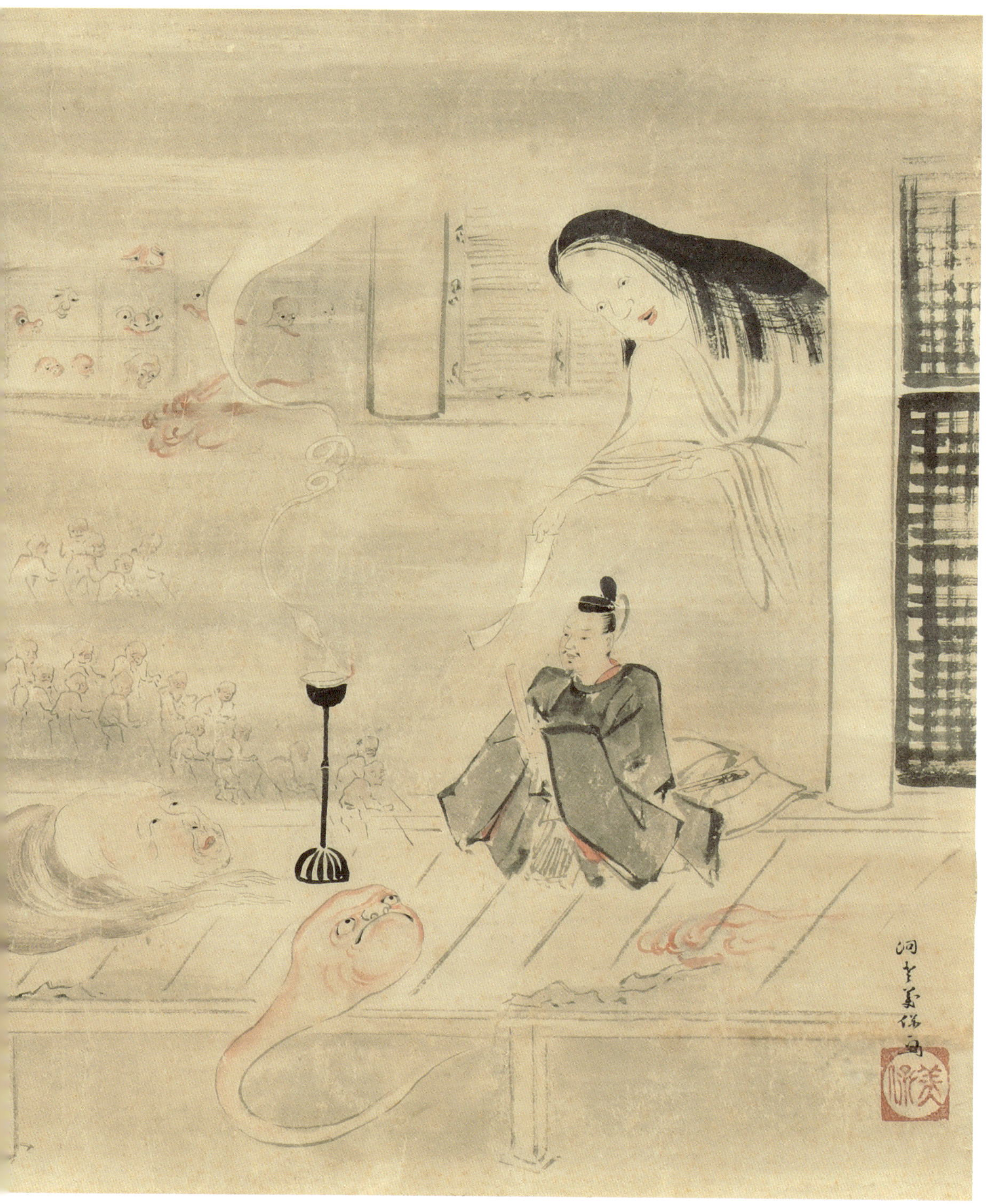

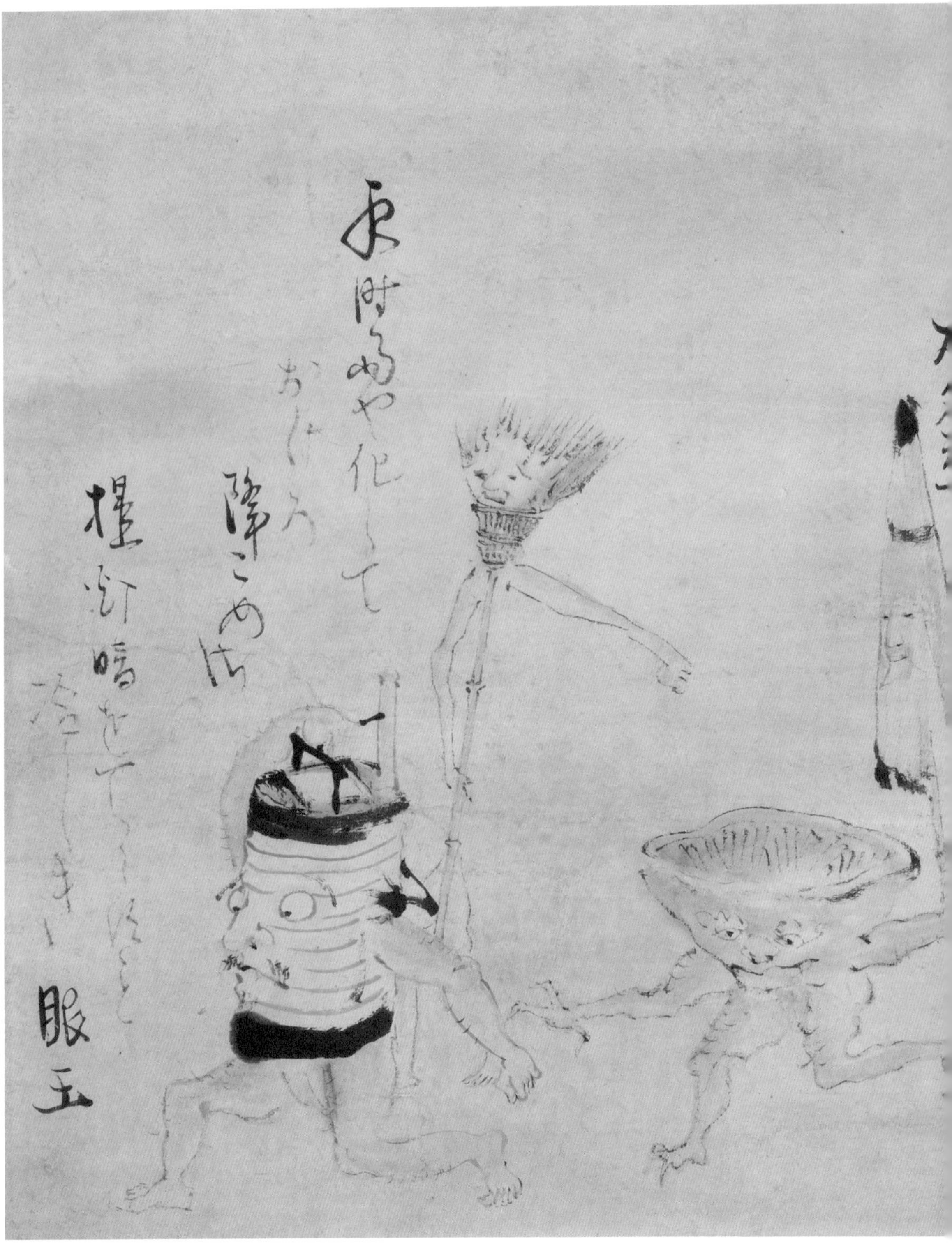

24 戯墨七怪図
ぎぼくななかいず

Seven Monsters in Ink with Nonsense Verses

十返舎一九　江戸時代　縦 32.5　横 54.3　Jippensha Ikku, Edo period, Height 32.5, Width 54.3

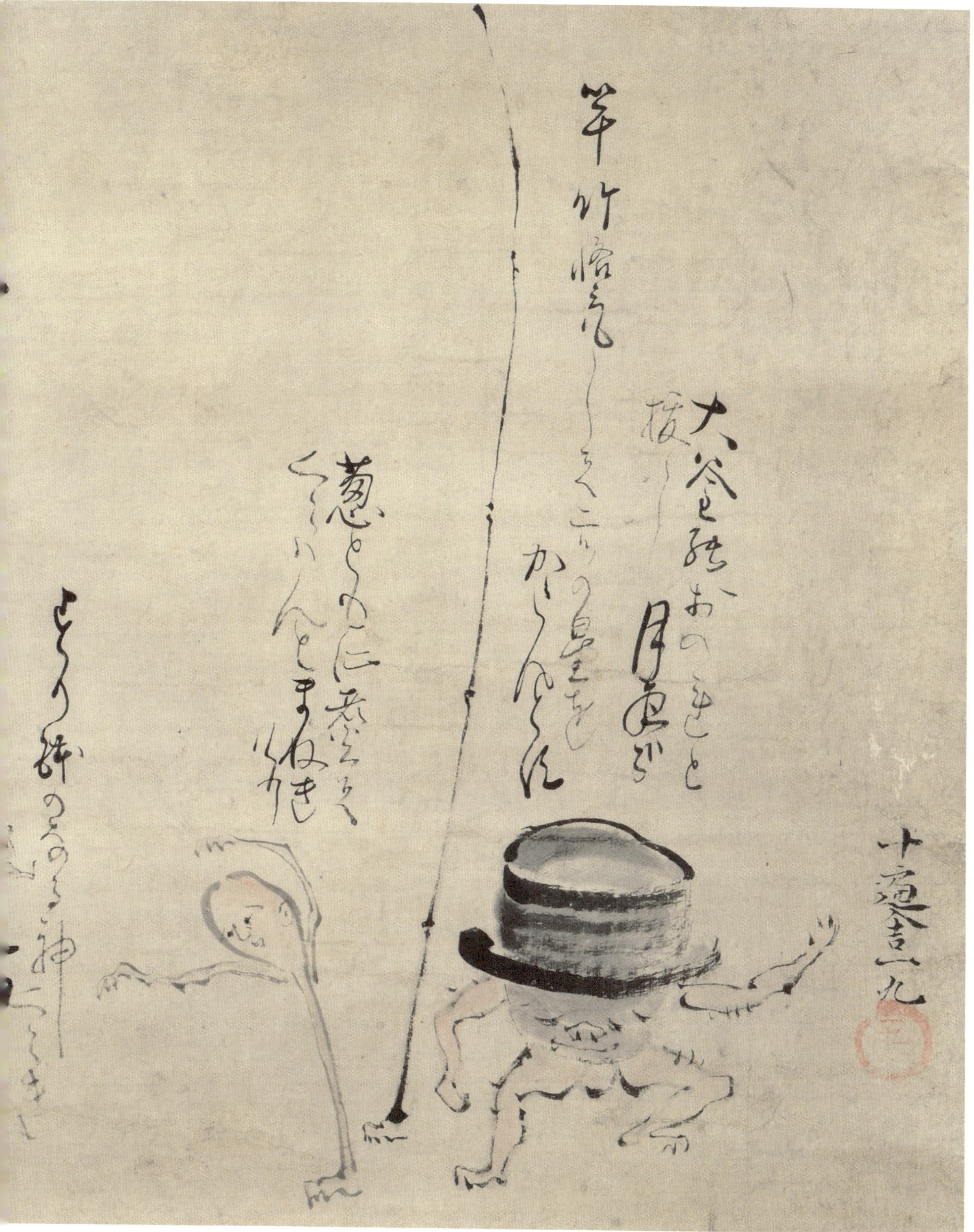

十返舎一九は江戸時代の戯作者で絵師としても活躍した。この作品は一九が7種の器物の妖怪を描いて狂歌を添えている一九らしさの出た作品となっている。

Jippensha Ikku was active as an artist and writer in the *gesaku* tradition in the Edo period. This work is characteristic of Ikku: seven types of household object yokai are drawn with *kyōgen* verse to accompany each one.

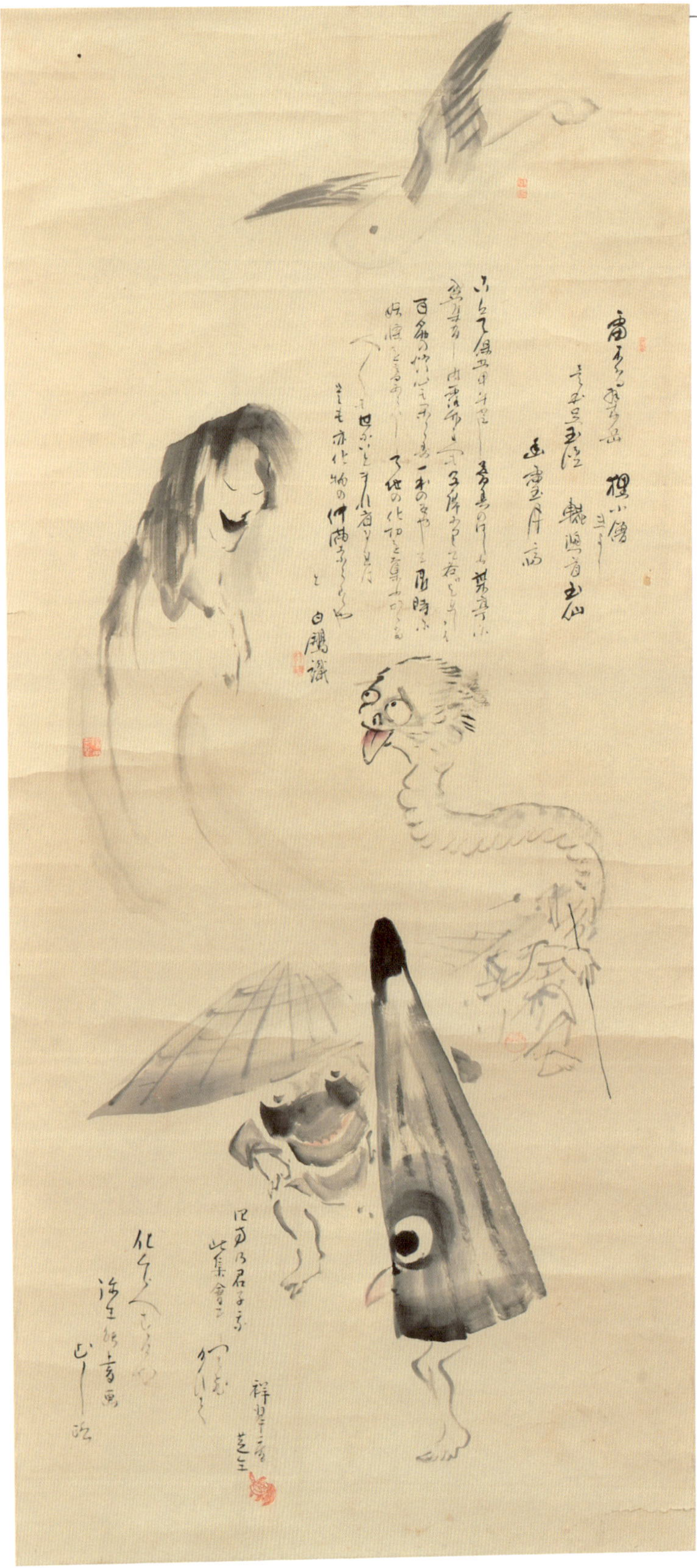

昔噺妖怪図
むかしばなしようかいず

Yokai of Ancient Tales

天保 5（1834）年　江戸時代
縦 133.3　横 60.6
Tenpō 5 (1834), Edo period,
Height 133.3, Width 60.6

江戸時代には百物語会や怪談会といった同好の士が
集まって怪談話や妖怪を詠む集まりが行われたが、
この作品も天保 5 年に開催されたそうした会の折に
制作されたもので、擂粉木鳥、狸小僧、一本足唐傘、
幽霊、轆轤首が描かれている。妖怪狂歌を収録した
版本、歌合せ妖怪絵なども残されていて、江戸時代
の妖怪遊びの広がりをみることができる。

In the Edo period clubs of like-minded enthusiasts
known as the *Hyaku Monogatari* (One Hundred Tales)
or *Kaidankai* gathered to invent yokai or ghost stories,
and this work was created on one such occasion in 1882,
featuring a *surikogi* bird, a raccoon dog monk, a one-
legged paper umbrella, a ghost, and a *rokurokubi*.
Books of collected *kyōka* (comic poems) and pictures
from *uta-awase* (poetry contests) on yokai also remain,
as a testament to the extent of the Edo period enthusiasm
for yokai amusements.

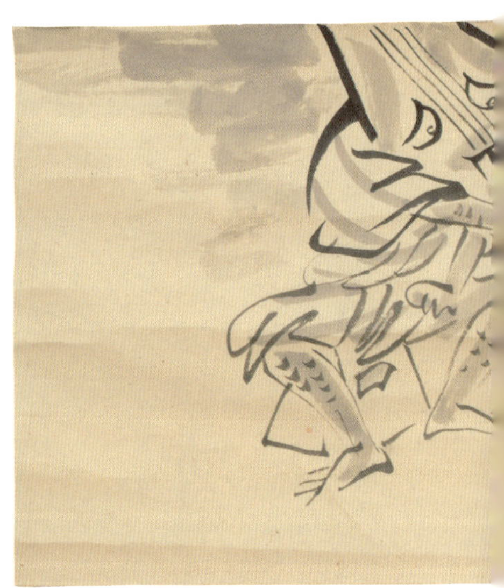

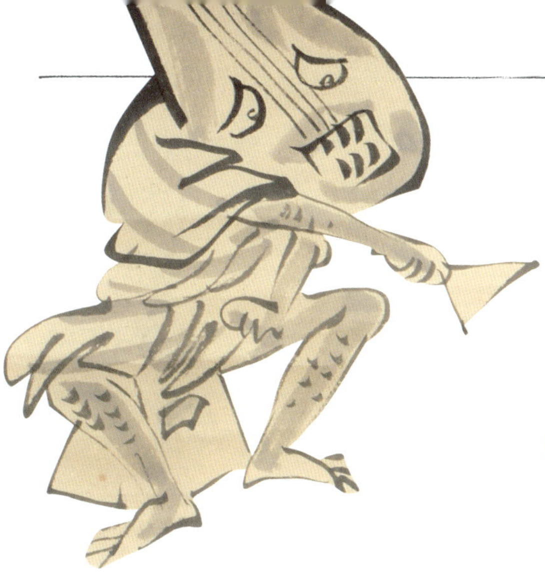

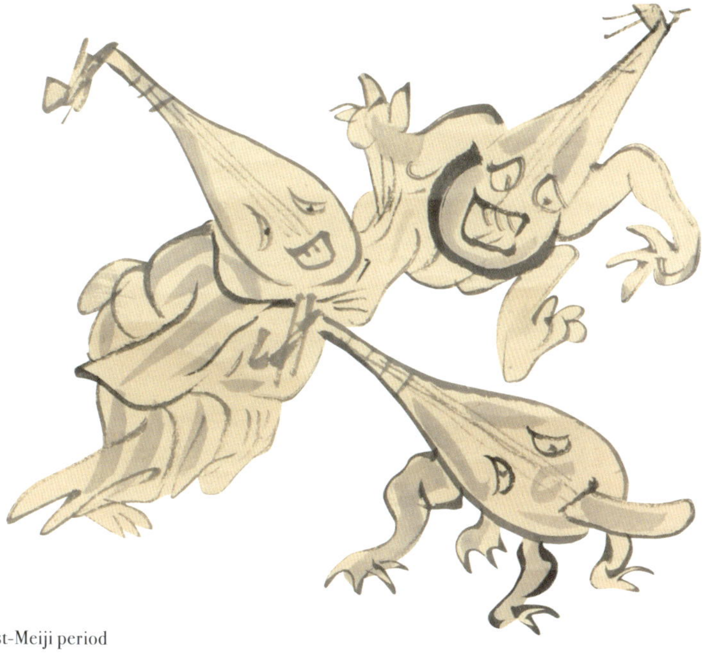

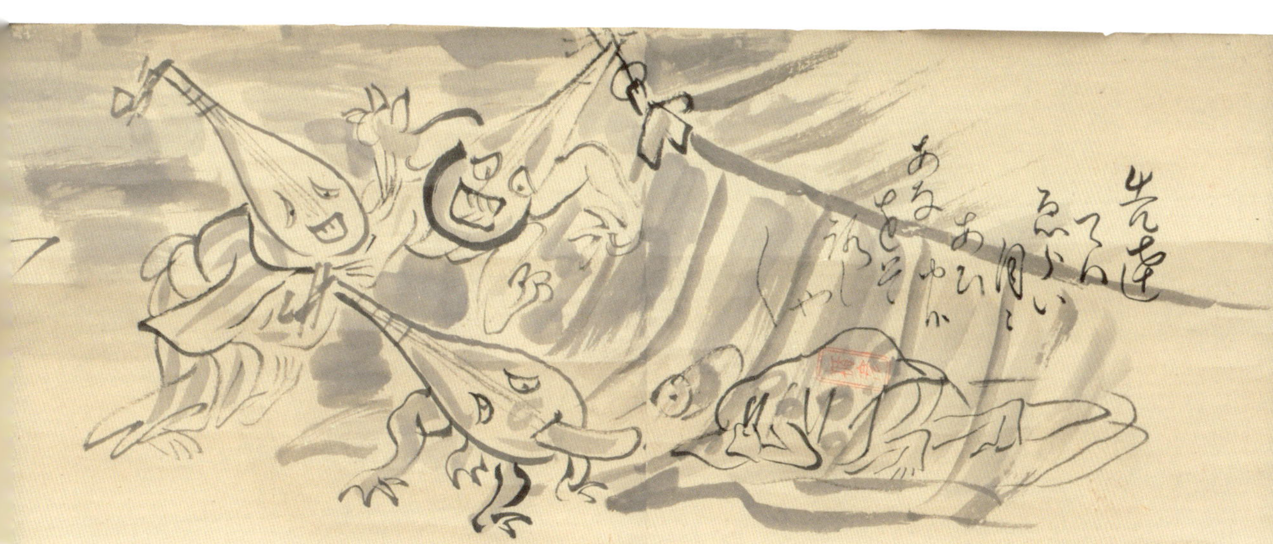

26 琵琶妖怪図
びわようかいず

Biwa Yokai

菅楯彦　明治時代以降　Suga Tatehiko, Post-Meiji period

蚊帳のなかで寝ているところを琵琶の妖怪たちが襲いに来ている。蚊帳の人物には「楯彦」と朱の落款がおされており、作者自身なのだろう。布団を頭から被って慄いているが、これは現実なのか夢なのか。楯彦は怯えながら、「先達てはえらい目にあひ申候 あなをそろしやをそろしや」とつぶやいている。琵琶たちはどこかユーモアがあるが、この軸の裏には「菅楯彦 琵琶のおどけ絵」とあるのも頷ける。

Biwa (Japanese lutes) are coming to assault the sleeper under the mosquito net. The red seal Tatehiko is imprinted on the person under the net, which may indicate that this is a self-portrait. His head is buried in the futon, trembling with fear; this could be reality or a dream. Tatehiko is muttering " The other day was awful, it's so scary, so scary..." in his terror. There is something amusing about the lutes; on the back of the sleeve is written "Suga Tatehiko: Funny Picture of Biwa".

妖怪尽くし絵巻
ようかいづくしえまき

Yokai Zukushi Picture Scroll

東海坊散人　昭和時代　縦 20.0　長 276.0　Tōkaibō Sanjin, Shōwa period, Height 20.0, Length 276.0

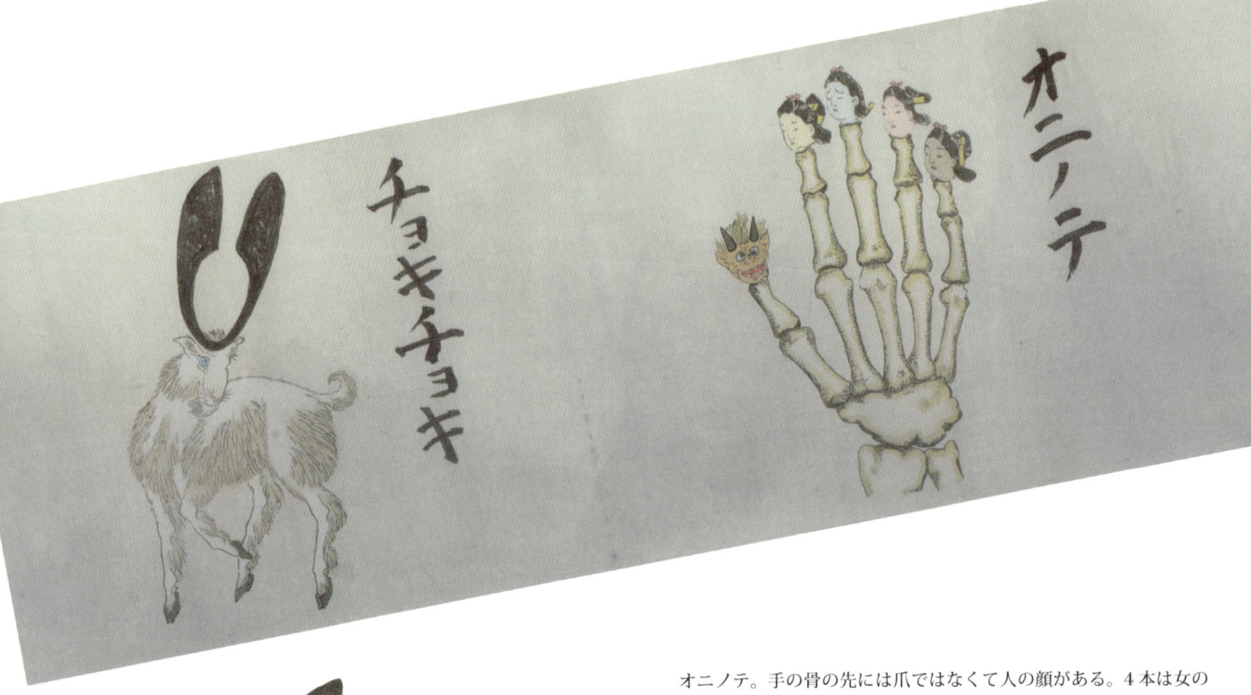

オニノテ。手の骨の先には爪ではなくて人の顔がある。4本は女の顔だが、親指だけは鬼の顔となっている。

Oni-no-te. Human heads take the place of nails on the ends of the skeletal fingers. Four are women; the thumb alone is an ogre.

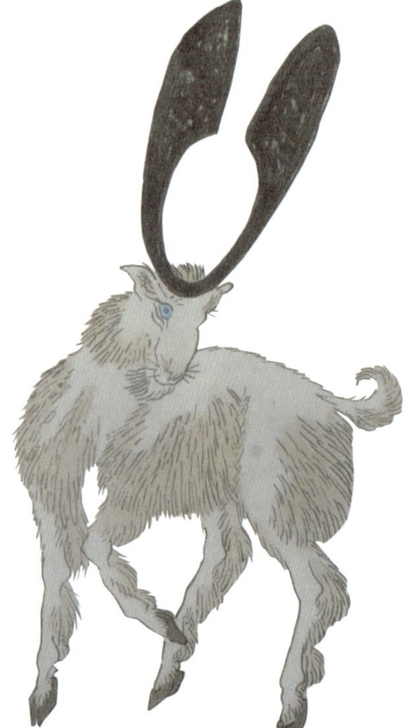

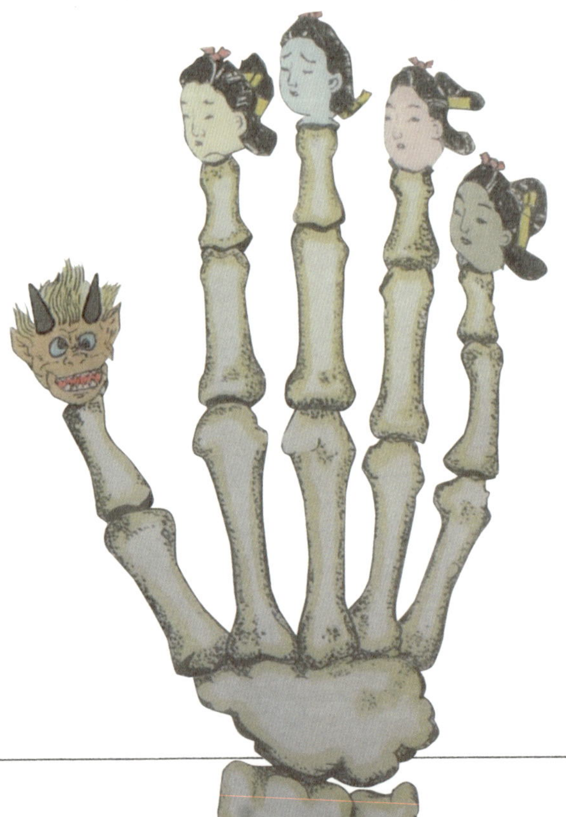

チョキチョキ。山羊の角が鋏となっている。
Choki-choki. The horns of this goat are scissors.

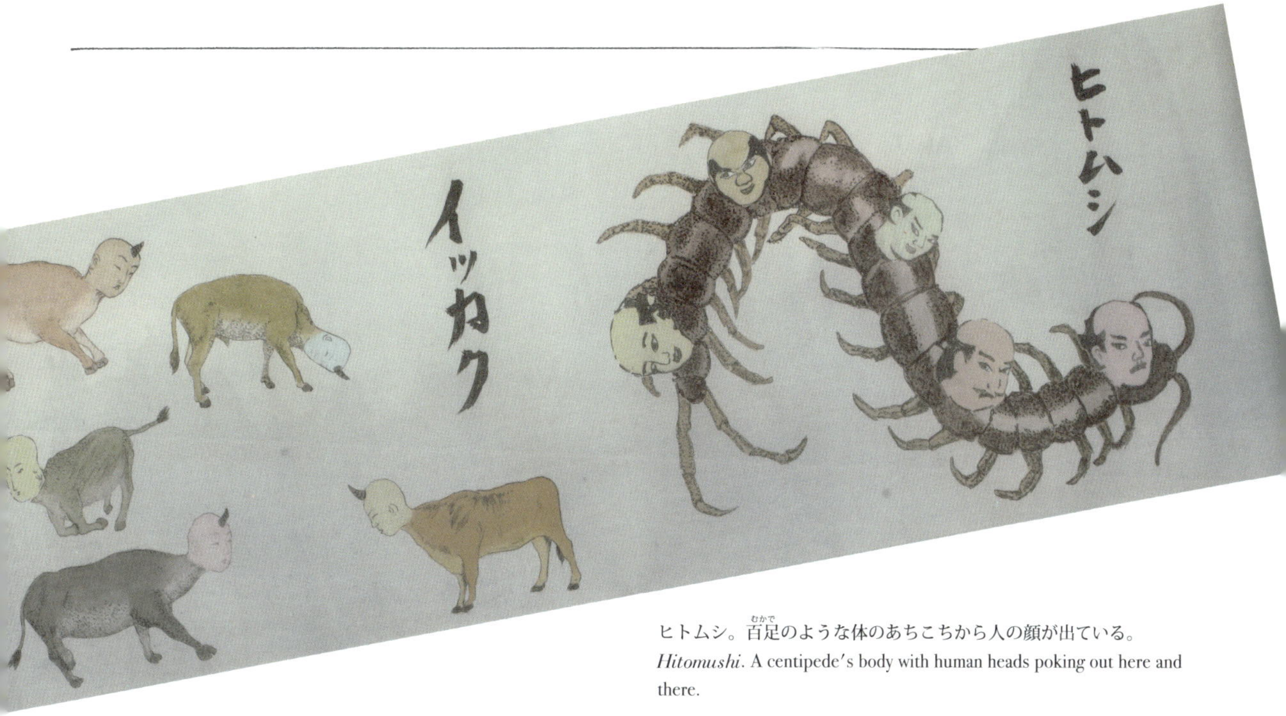

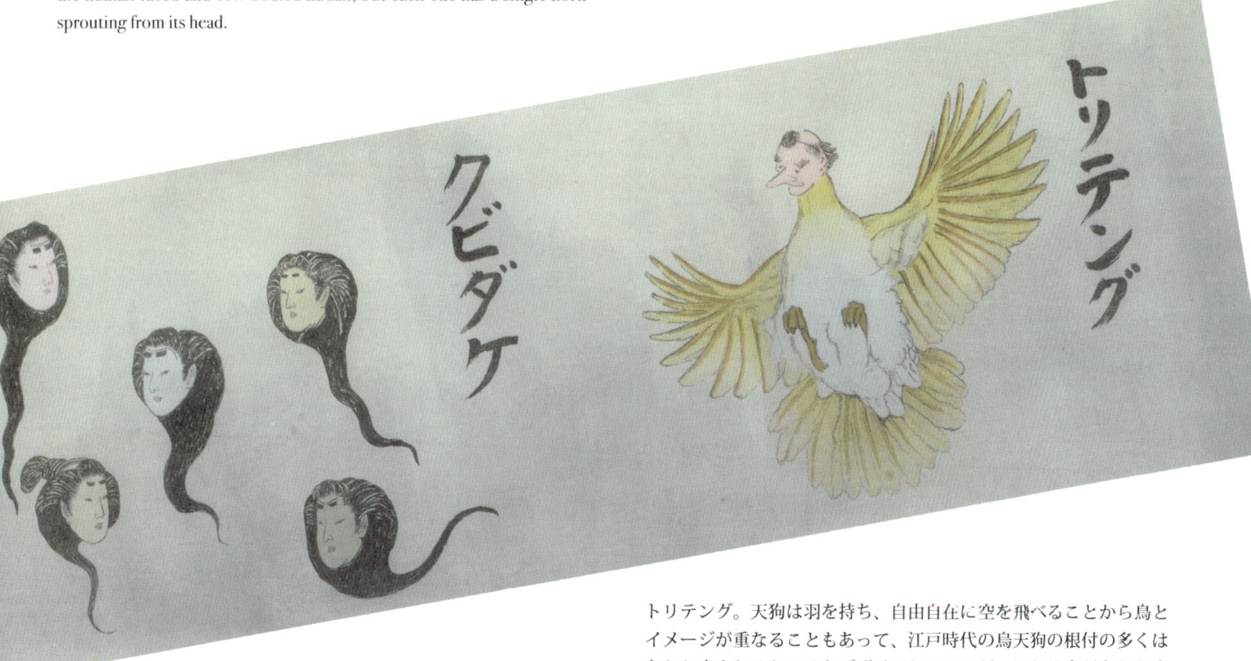

ヒトムシ。百足（むかで）のような体のあちこちから人の顔が出ている。

Hitomushi. A centipede's body with human heads poking out here and there.

イッカク。体は動物で顔は人ということでは人面牛体のクダンのようなものだが、どれにも頭から一本の角が生えている。

Ikkaku. With the body of an animal and a human face, these are similar to the human-faced and cow-bodied kudan, but each one has a single horn sprouting from its head.

クビダケ。その名の通り首だけが描かれている。火の玉のように尾を引いているが、実際は髪の毛が伸びた状態だ。

Kubidake. As the name *kubidake* suggests (lit. "head only"), these are disembodied heads. They drag tails behind them like comets, but these are just their long trailing hair.

トリテング。天狗は羽を持ち、自由自在に空を飛べることから鳥とイメージが重なることもあって、江戸時代の烏天狗の根付の多くは卵から産まれるところをデザインしているが、これは鳥が卵から産まれるので、烏天狗も同様だろうという考えからだ。しかし、ここに描かれたトリテングはまさしく鳥そのもので、顔だけが嘴（くちばし）のある人の姿だ。

Tori tengu. The images of *tengu* and birds overlap as the *tengu* has wings and flies freely in the sky; most *netsuke* of *karasu tengu* (crow goblins) of the Edo period showed them hatching out of eggs, and this is a bird hatched from an egg in the same way as *karasu tengu*. However, the *tori tengu* depicted here is completely a bird, except for its beaky-nosed human head.

28 妖怪尽くし絵巻
ようかいづくしえまき

Yokai Zukushi Picture Scroll

東海坊散人　昭和時代　縦 20.0　横 275.5　Tōkaibō Sanjin, Shōwa period, Height 20.0, Width 275.5

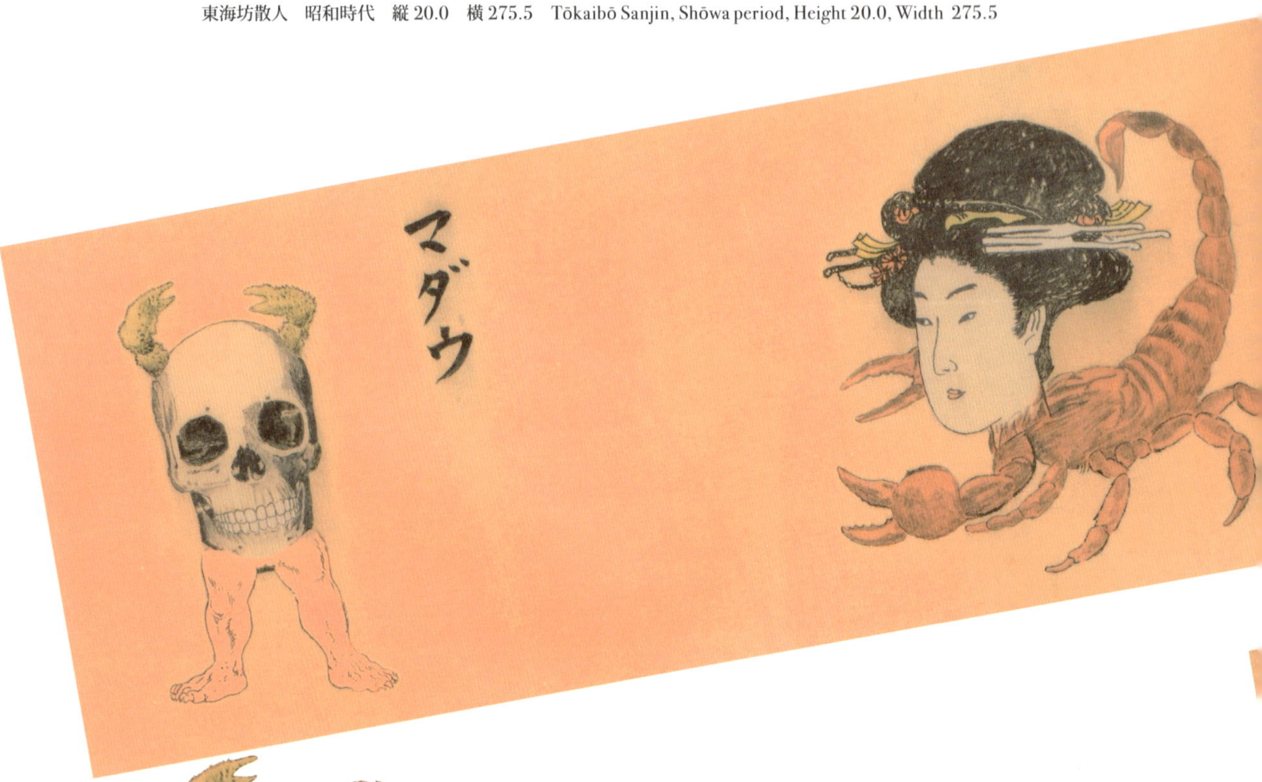

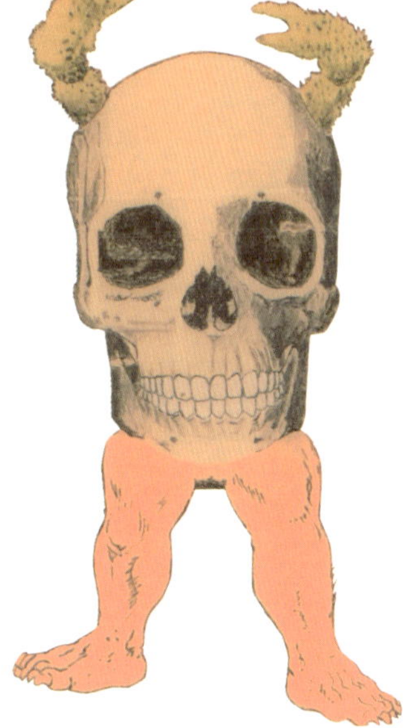

マダウ。巨大な髑髏が体と顔を形作り、足は人が踏ん張った
格好だ。頭蓋骨から伸びた 2 本の手は蟹のように鋏になって
いるが、手ではなくて角のようにも見える。

Madau. A huge skull forms the shape of a torso and face: the
human legs are braced apart. Two arms like crab claws extend from
the cranium, but these appear to be more in the nature of horns.

チクリ。サソリの体で芸者と思しき女の顔からチクリという
名なのだろう。

Chikuri. Named for *chikuri* (lit. "sting") with the head of a geisha
and the body of a scorpion.

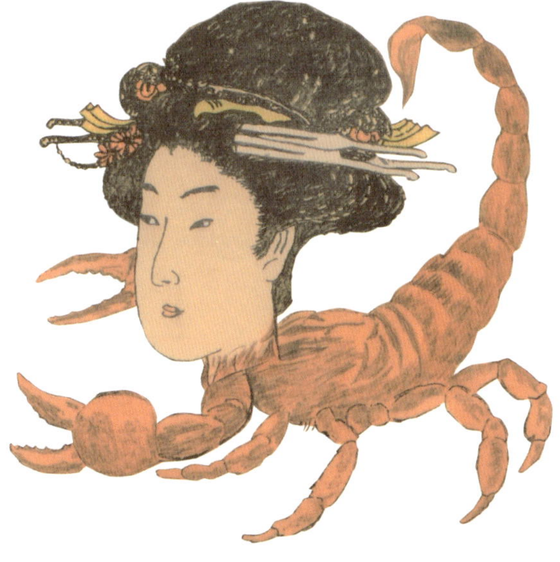

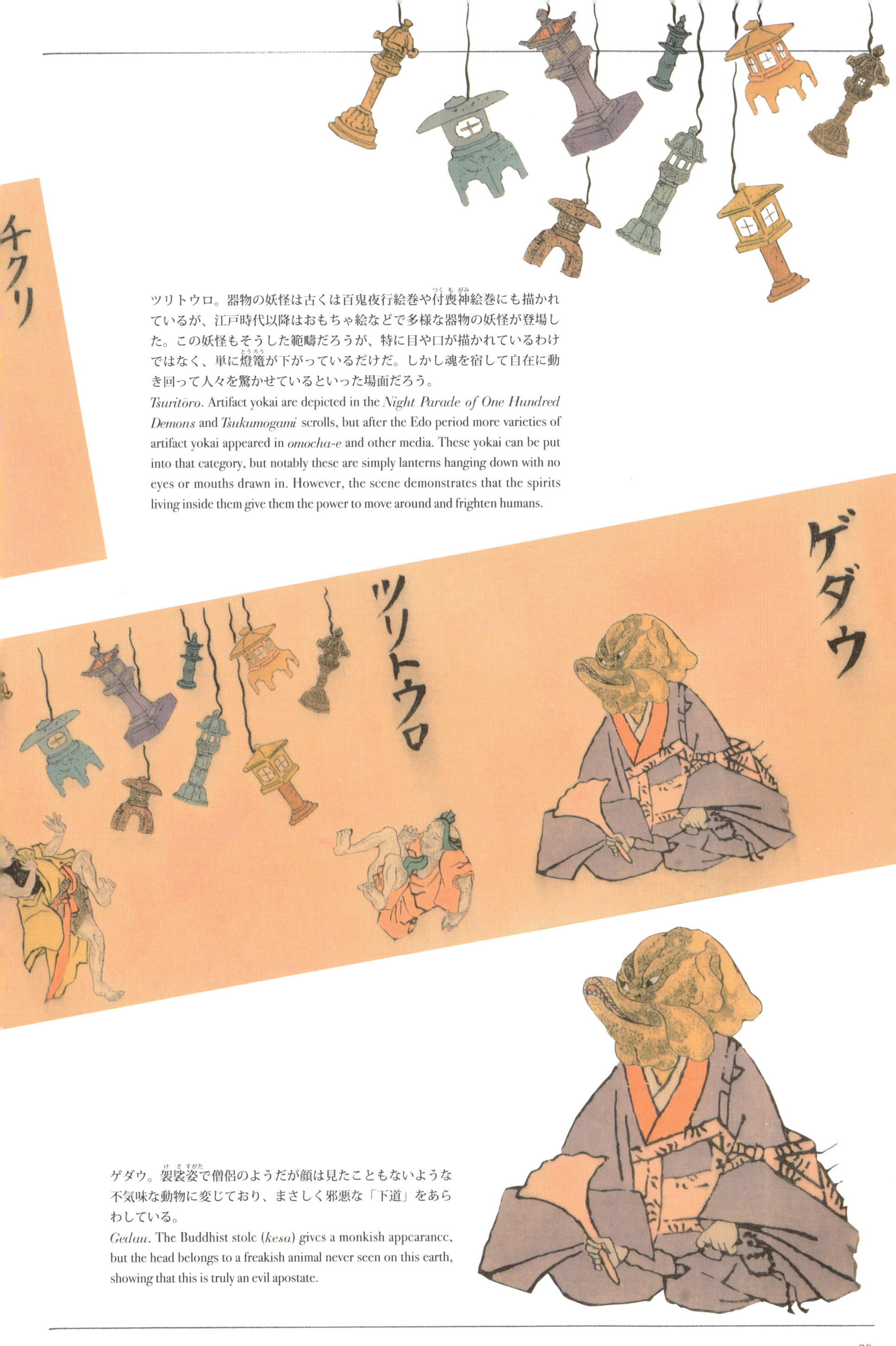

ツリトウロ。器物の妖怪は古くは百鬼夜行絵巻や付喪神絵巻にも描かれているが、江戸時代以降はおもちゃ絵などで多様な器物の妖怪が登場した。この妖怪もそうした範疇だろうが、特に目や口が描かれているわけではなく、単に燈篭が下がっているだけだ。しかし魂を宿して自在に動き回って人々を驚かせているといった場面だろう。

Tsuritōro. Artifact yokai are depicted in the *Night Parade of One Hundred Demons* and *Tsukumogami* scrolls, but after the Edo period more varieties of artifact yokai appeared in *omocha-e* and other media. These yokai can be put into that category, but notably these are simply lanterns hanging down with no eyes or mouths drawn in. However, the scene demonstrates that the spirits living inside them give them the power to move around and frighten humans.

ゲダウ。裂裟姿で僧侶のようだが顔は見たこともないような不気味な動物に変じており、まさしく邪悪な「下道」をあらわしている。

Gedau. The Buddhist stole (*kesa*) gives a monkish appearance, but the head belongs to a freakish animal never seen on this earth, showing that this is truly an evil apostate.

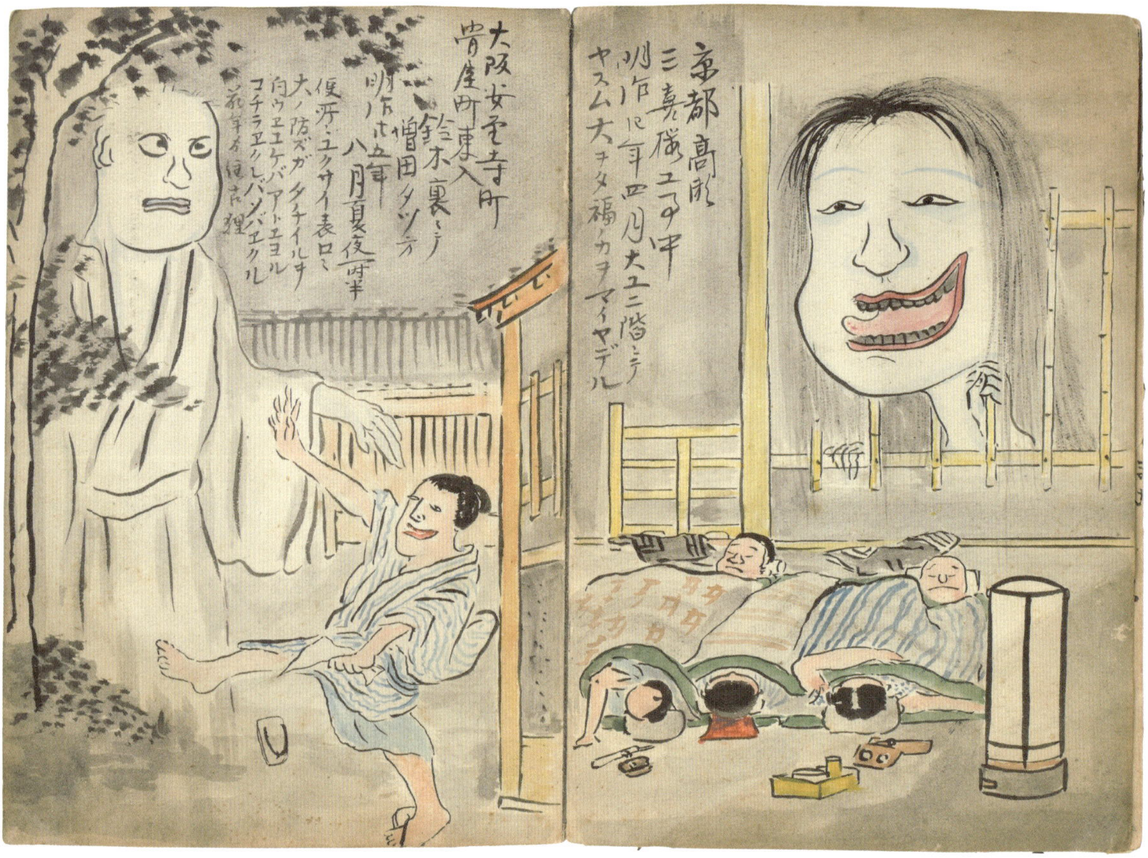

図1　Figure 1

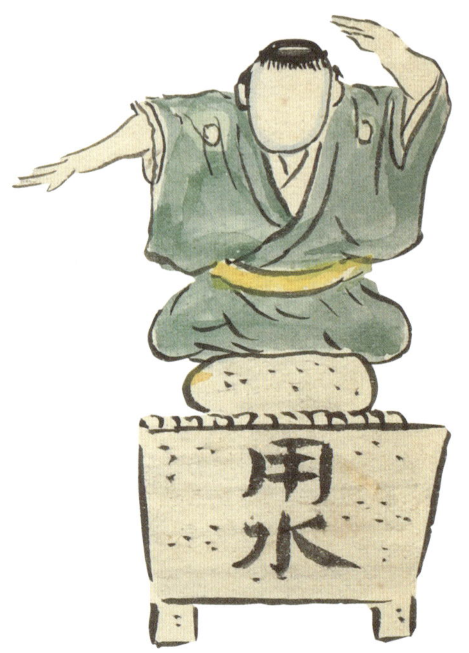

おばけおどけ

Supernatural Shenanigans (*Obake Odoke*)
鈴木嘉助　大正元（1912）年　縦 20.5　横 14.0
Suzuki Kasuke, 1912 (Taishō 1), Height 20.5, Width 14.0

折本スタイルで主に関西地方の怪異、妖怪を取り上げているが、その多くは明治時代の出来事で具体的な日付や場所なども記録されている。折本の裏面には「諸国名所」というタイトルで関西地方を中心に紹介されており、おそらくは鈴木嘉助という人物が関西方面を旅行した折に折本に描いて残したものと思われ、末尾に「大正元年八月 鈴木嘉助之書」と記されている。ここに収録された怪異や妖怪は庶民の描いた明治時代の記録として貴重な資料といえよう。

This *orihon* (folded book) mainly focuses on supernatural phenomena and yokai of the Kansai region, most of which have a concrete location and date in the Meiji period recorded. The title "Famous places all over the world" is written on the back cover, but it centers on the Kansai region; it seems that the individual known as Suzuki Kasuke travelled around the Kansai region, occasionally writing in this *orihon*, as at the end is written "August 1912 (Taishō 1), Suzuki Kasuke's book". As a Meiji-era record written by an ordinary person, this collection of supernatural phenomena and yokai is a precious resource.

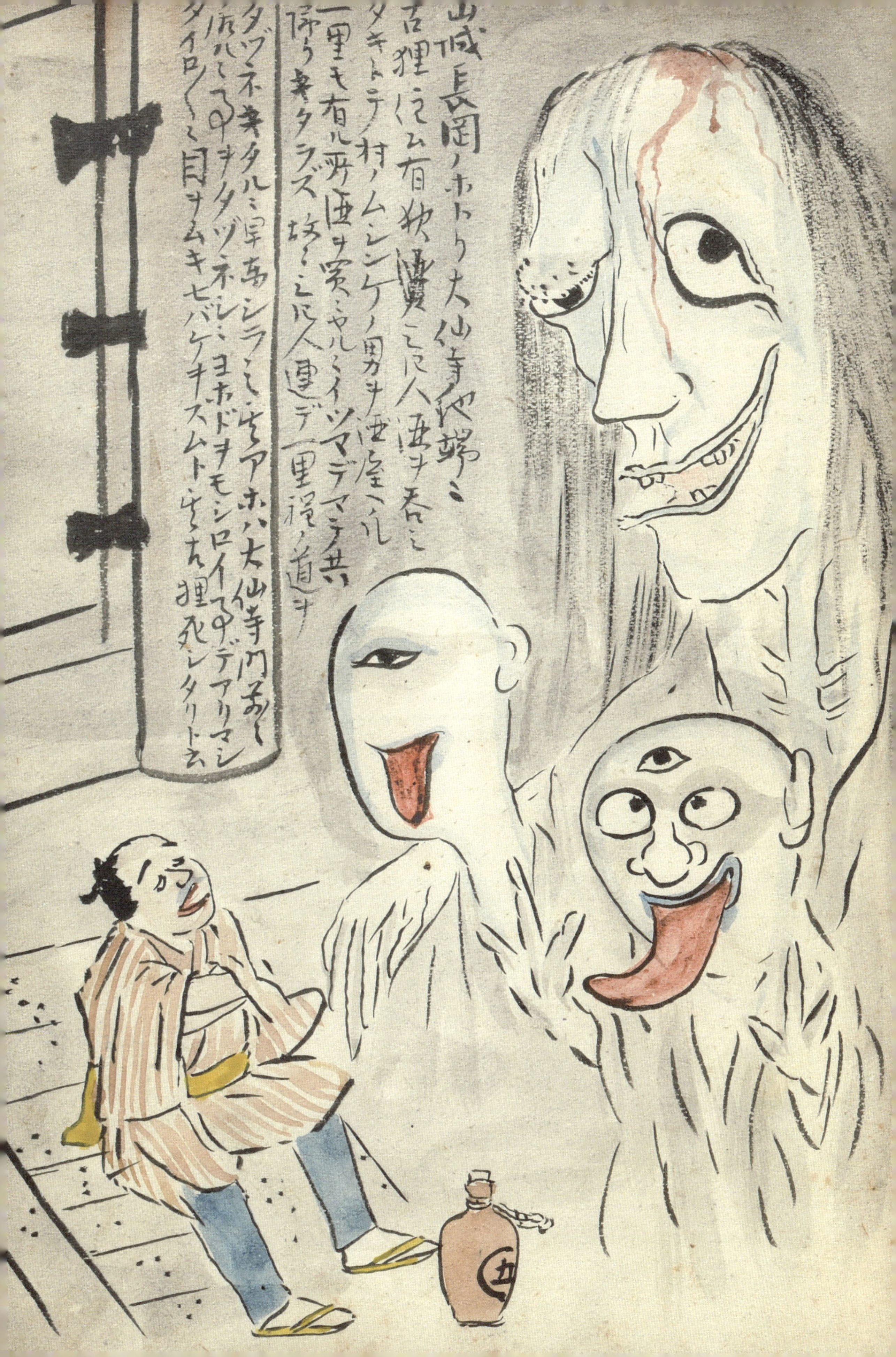

山城長岡ノホトリ大仙寺ノ地蠣ニ
古狸ニム有狼獲ニ二尺人誤ナ吞ニ
タキトテ村ノムシシケノ男ヲ世逢ヘル
一里モ有ル死涯サ寅シヤルイツマデマテ共
待り寺クラズ故ニ二人連デ一里程ノ道ナ
タブネ不幸タルニ宰寄シラニ土アホ六大仙寺ノ
流ヘテ中ニチタヅネレハヨホドヲモシロイテ中デアリマシ
タイロくく目サムキセバケチスムト生ス狸死レタリトエ

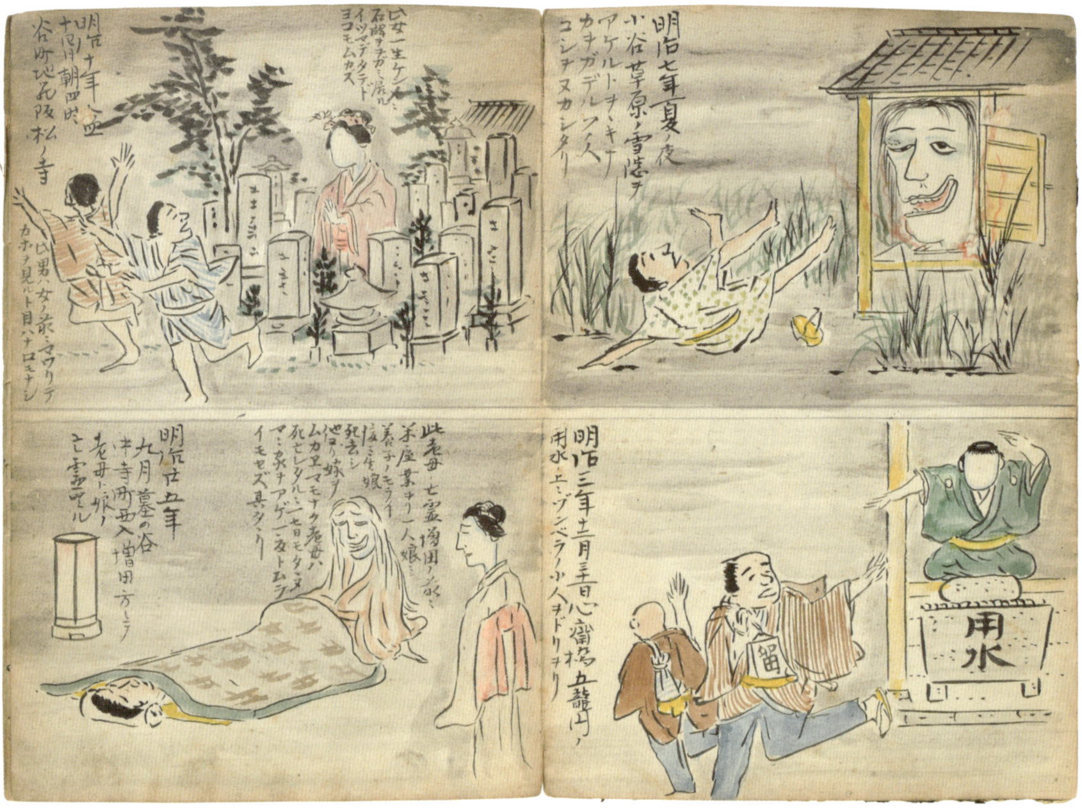

図2　Figure 2

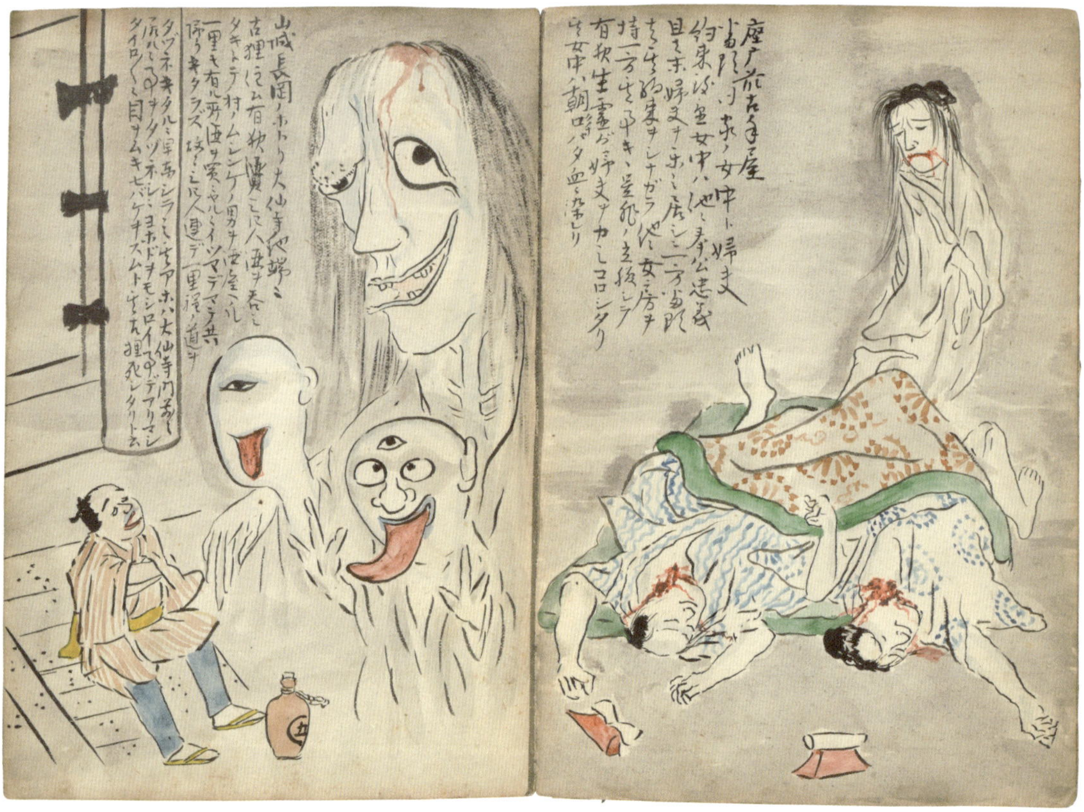

図3　Figure 3

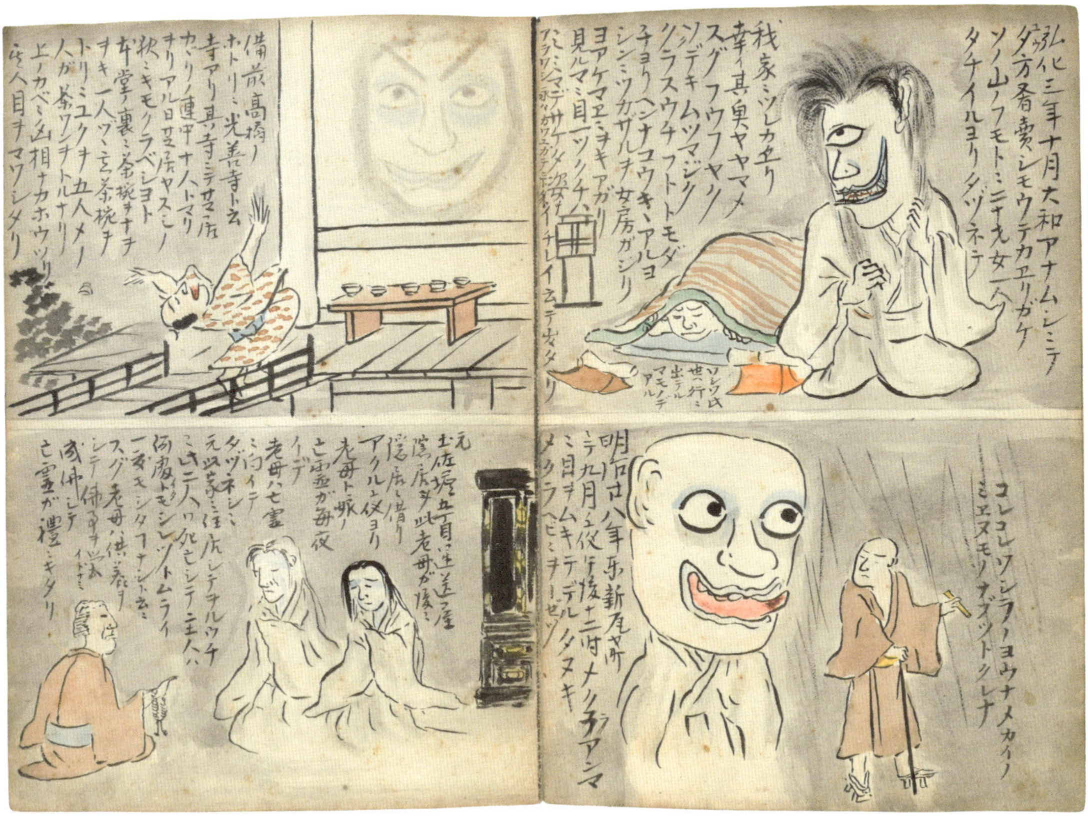

図4　Figure 4

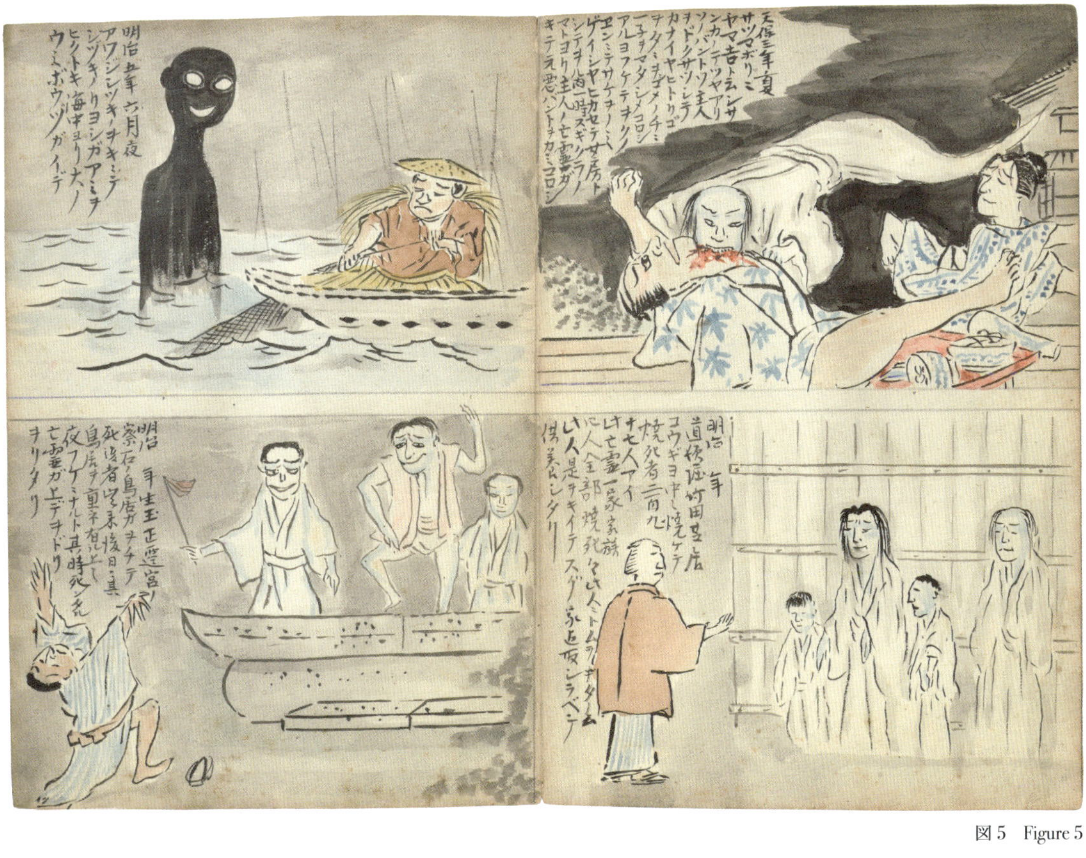

図5　Figure 5

30 「大阪妖怪画談」原画

「おおさかようかいがだん」げんが

"An Exploration of Osaka Yokai" (original illustration)

昭和8年（1933）縦18.5 横29.0　1933 (Shōwa 8), Height 18.5, Width 29.0（以下、原画の制作年と法量は同じ）

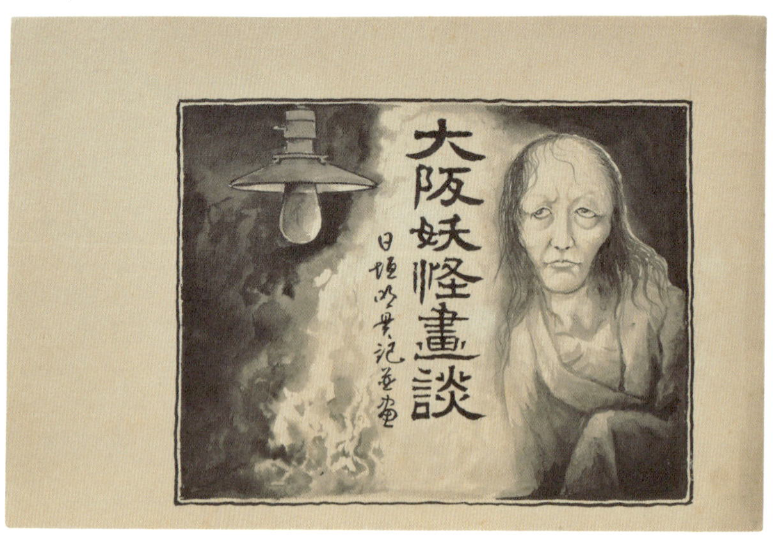

この原画は黒一色の濃淡だけで描かれており、作者の日垣は自ら解説した怪異譚以外のそれぞれの話にも目を通して1点1点描き上げたと思われる。

This original illustration is drawn in shades of gray; it is thought that the author Higaki drew this having looked through various stories above and beyond the supernatural tales he describes.

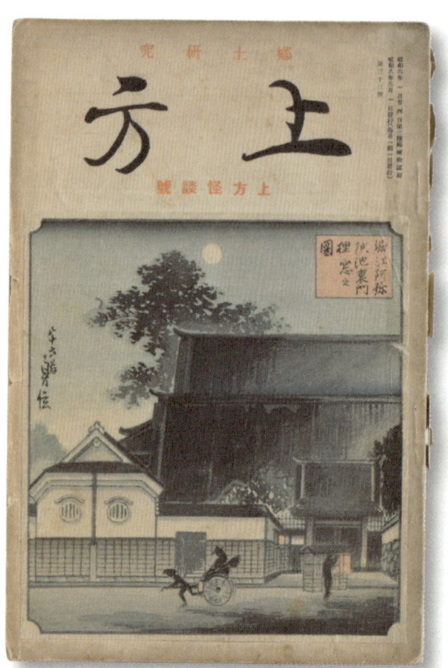

『上方』33号

Kamigata magazine, issue 33

昭和8年（1933）9月1日発行縦22.3 横15.2

September 1, 1933 (Shōwa 8),

Height 22.3, Width 15.2

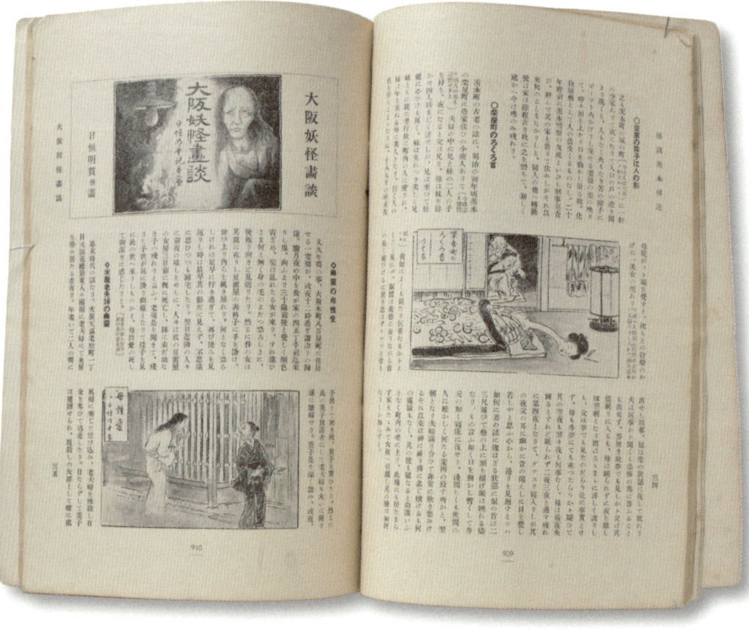

「上方怪談号」として出され、何人もの筆者が体験した上方の怪談を中心に紹介されている。収録された「怪談茨木附近」、「大阪妖怪画談」などの挿絵原画も残されている。いずれの絵も日垣明貫が描き、「大阪妖怪画談」は文も日垣が書いている。

This *kaidan* edition of *Kamigata* presents ghost stories of the Kyoto/Osaka region by numerous writers. *Ghost Stories of the Ibaraki Area*, *An Exploration of Osaka Yokai*, and other original illustrations drawn for this publication are collected here. The illustrations are by Higaki Akenuki, who also wrote the text for *An Exploration of Osaka Yokai*.

「道祖本の火の玉」原画
"The Fireball of Sainomoto" (original illustration)
「怪談茨木附近」の冒頭に収録された「道祖本の火の玉」の挿絵。蔵の屋根に 1 丈もある大男が座っていて、2 尺ほどの火の玉が出て回転したが、これは古狸によるものという内容。
Illustration for "The Fireball of Sainomoto" from the introduction to *Ghost Stories of the Ibaraki Area*. A ten-foot-tall giant sat on the storehouse roof, and a two-foot-wide fireball appeared and whirled about: these phenomena were the work of an old raccoon dog.

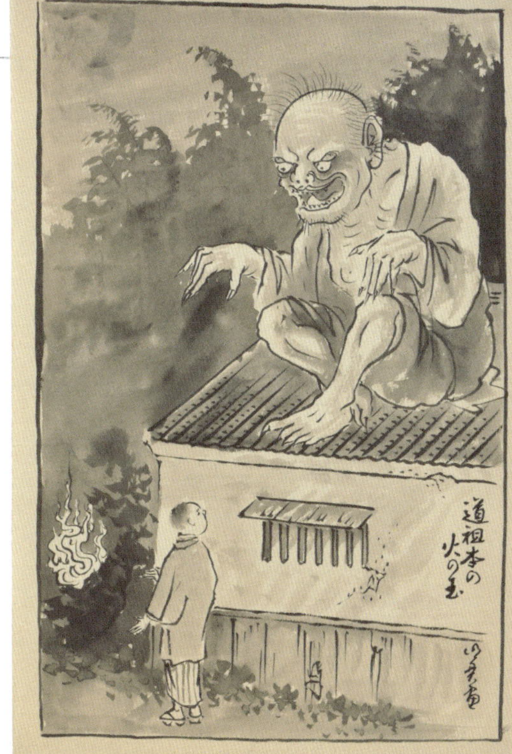

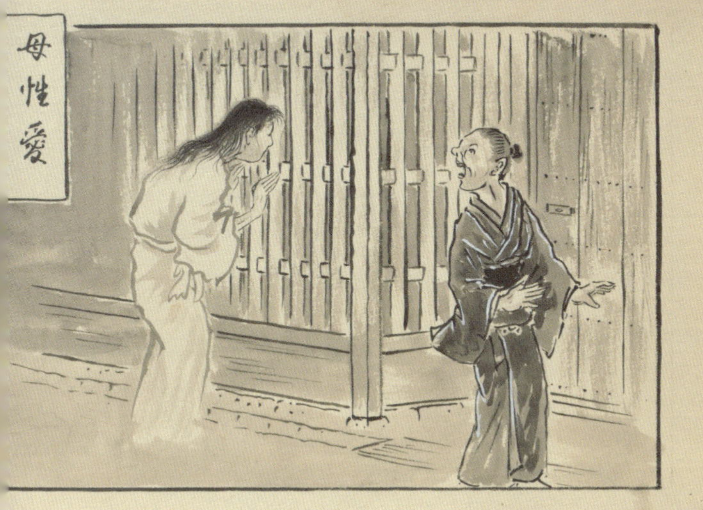

「母性愛」原画
"Mother's Love" (original illustration)
「幽霊の母性愛」という話の挿絵。文久年間の大坂本町八百屋町で目撃された幽霊。幼子をのこして死んだ豆腐屋の女房が店先から子どもを心配して中を覗いていたという実話。
Illustration for the story "A ghost mother's love". In the late nineteenth century (Bunkyū period), a ghost was seen in Yaoya-machi, Honmachi, Osaka. Based on the true story of a tofu maker's wife who left behind a young child when she died; worried about her child, her ghost would peep into the tofu shop.

「柴屋町のろくろ首」原画
"The *Rokurokubi* of Shibaya-machi" (original illustration)
「怪談茨木附近」に収録された「柴屋町のろくろ首」の挿絵。明治初年ころに茨木の柴屋町の商人の美人の娘が夜になると首が伸び、両親は神仏に祈るも甲斐なく、やがて町内で噂となって居たたまれずに大阪へ転居したという話。
Illustration for "The *Rokurokubi* of Shibaya-machi" from the introduction to *Ghost Stories of the Ibaraki Area*. In the early Meiji years, there was a beautiful maiden who was the daughter of a merchant of Shibaya-machi in Ibaraki, whose neck would lengthen when night fell despite her parents' prayers to Buddha, and eventually word got around and the family was forced to move to Osaka.

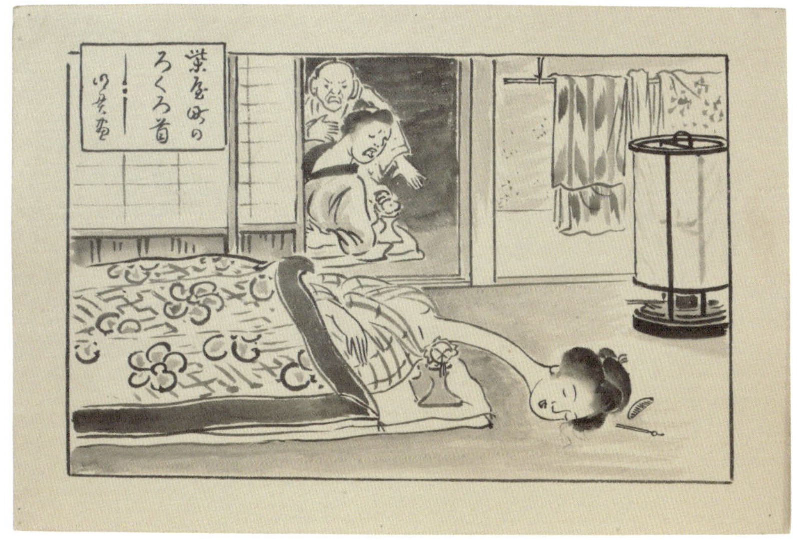

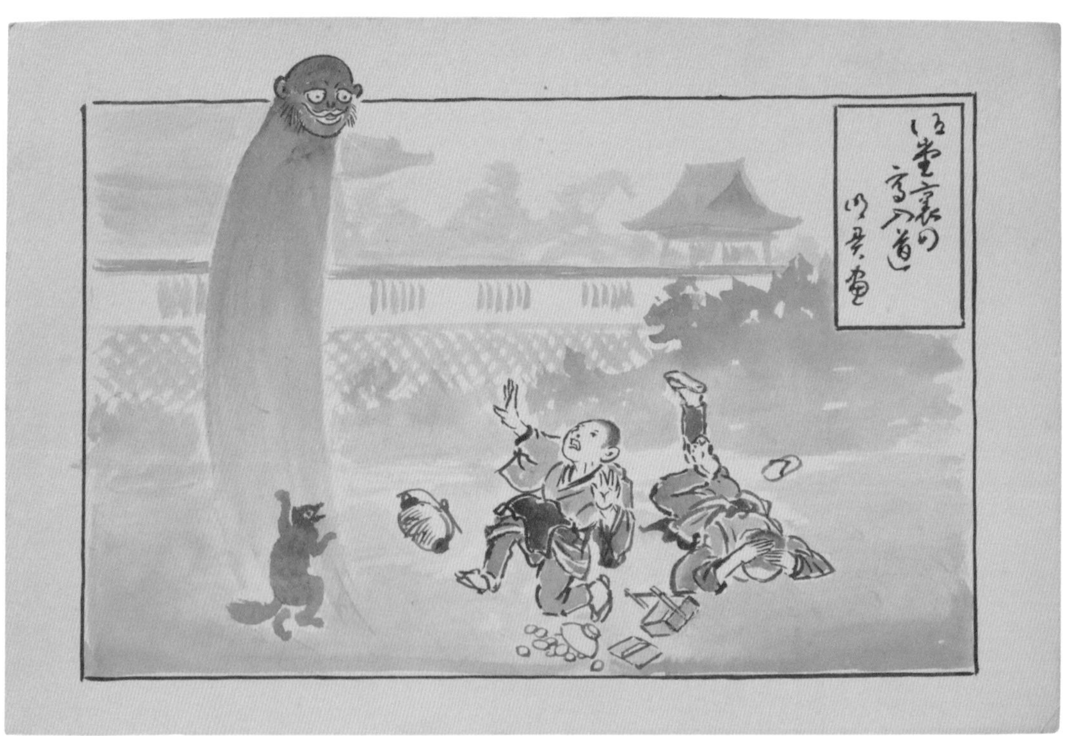

「御堂裏の高入道」原画　　"The Tall Priest Behind the Midō" (original illustration)

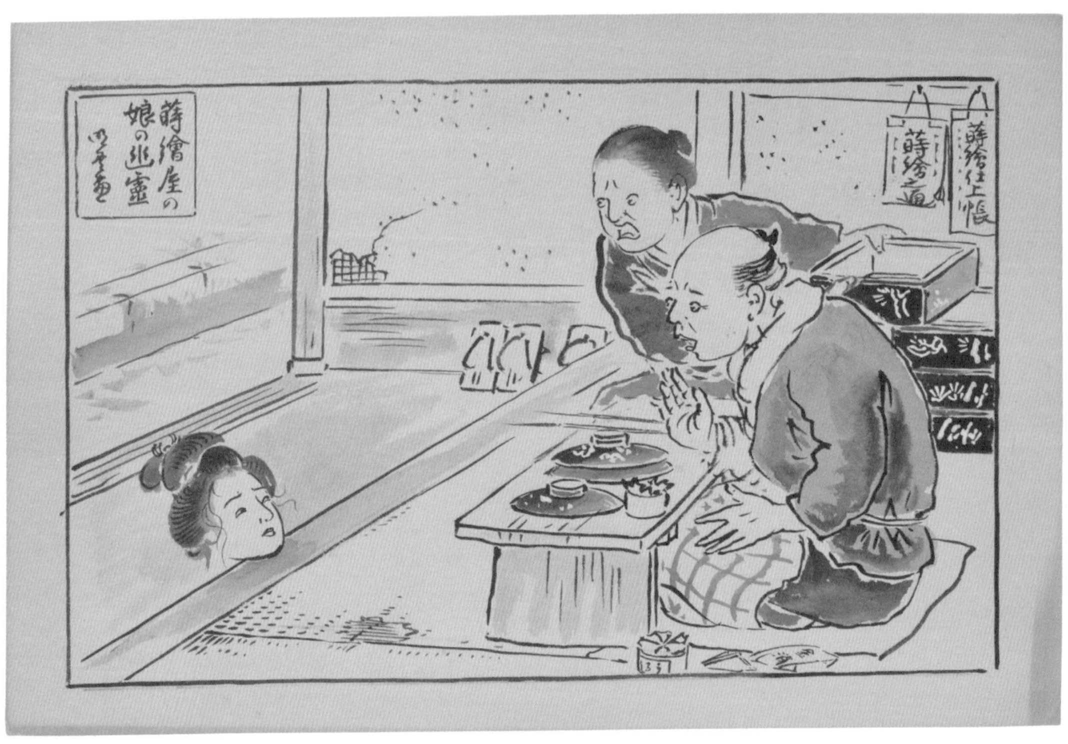

「蒔絵屋の娘の幽霊」原画　　"Ghost of the *Maki-e* Lacquerer's Daughter" (original illustration)

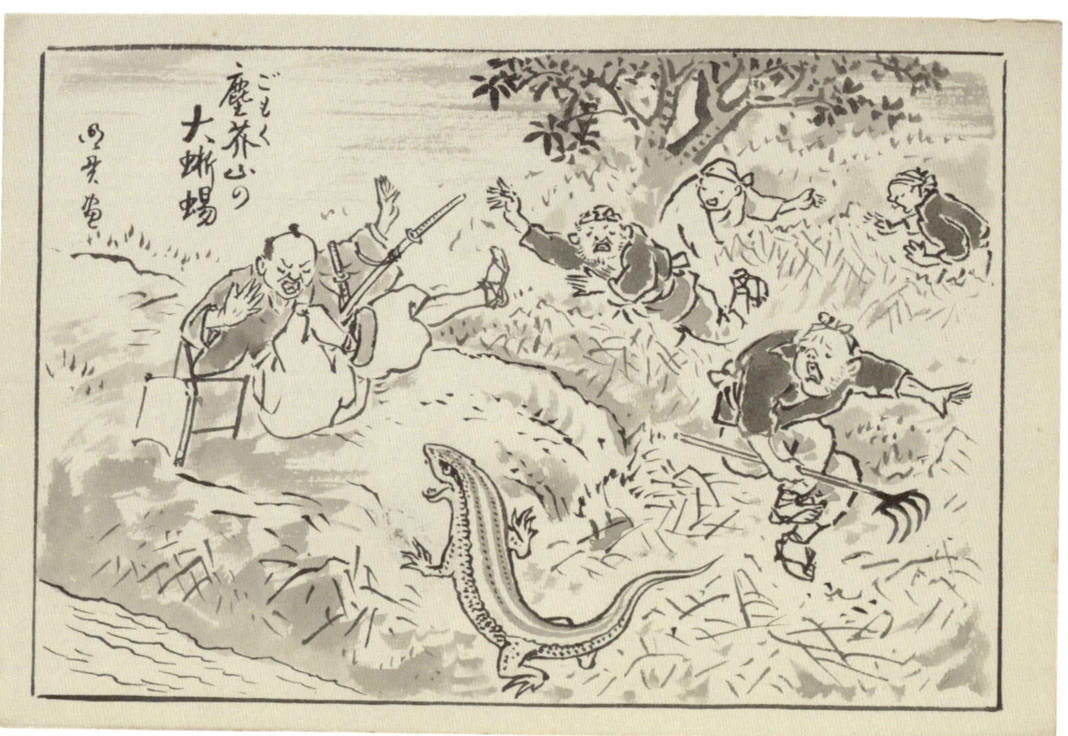

「塵芥山の大蜥蜴」原画　"The Giant Lizard of Trash Mountain" (original illustration)

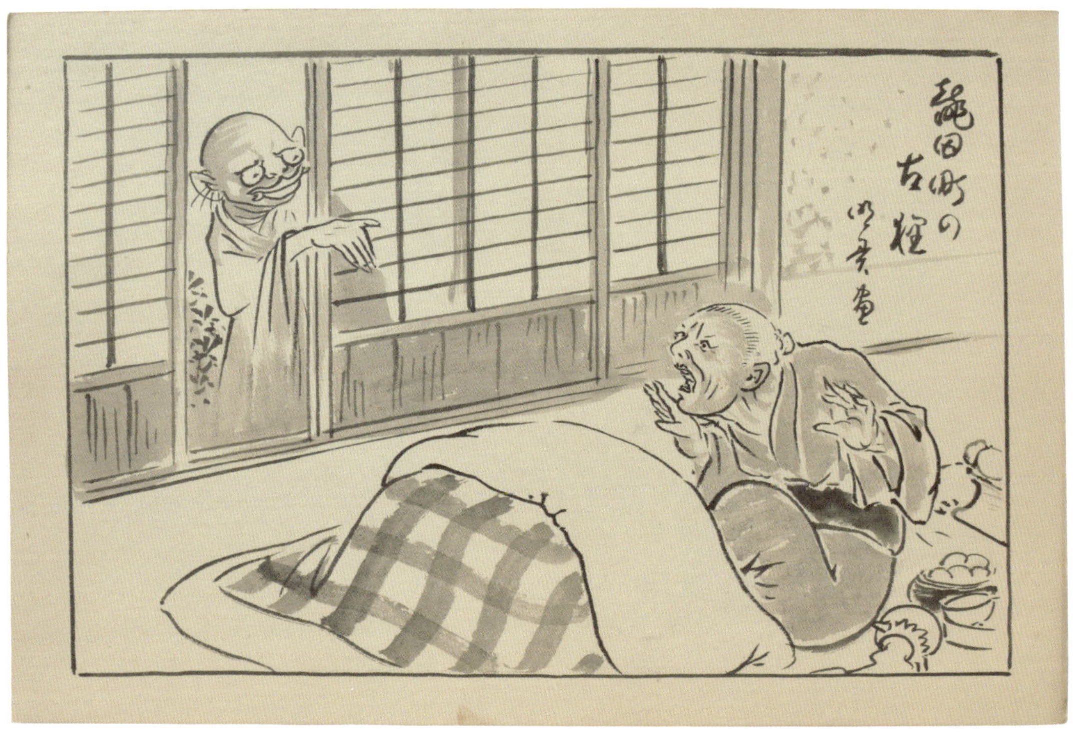

「龍田町の古狸」"The Old Raccoon Dog of Tatsuta-cho" (original illustration)

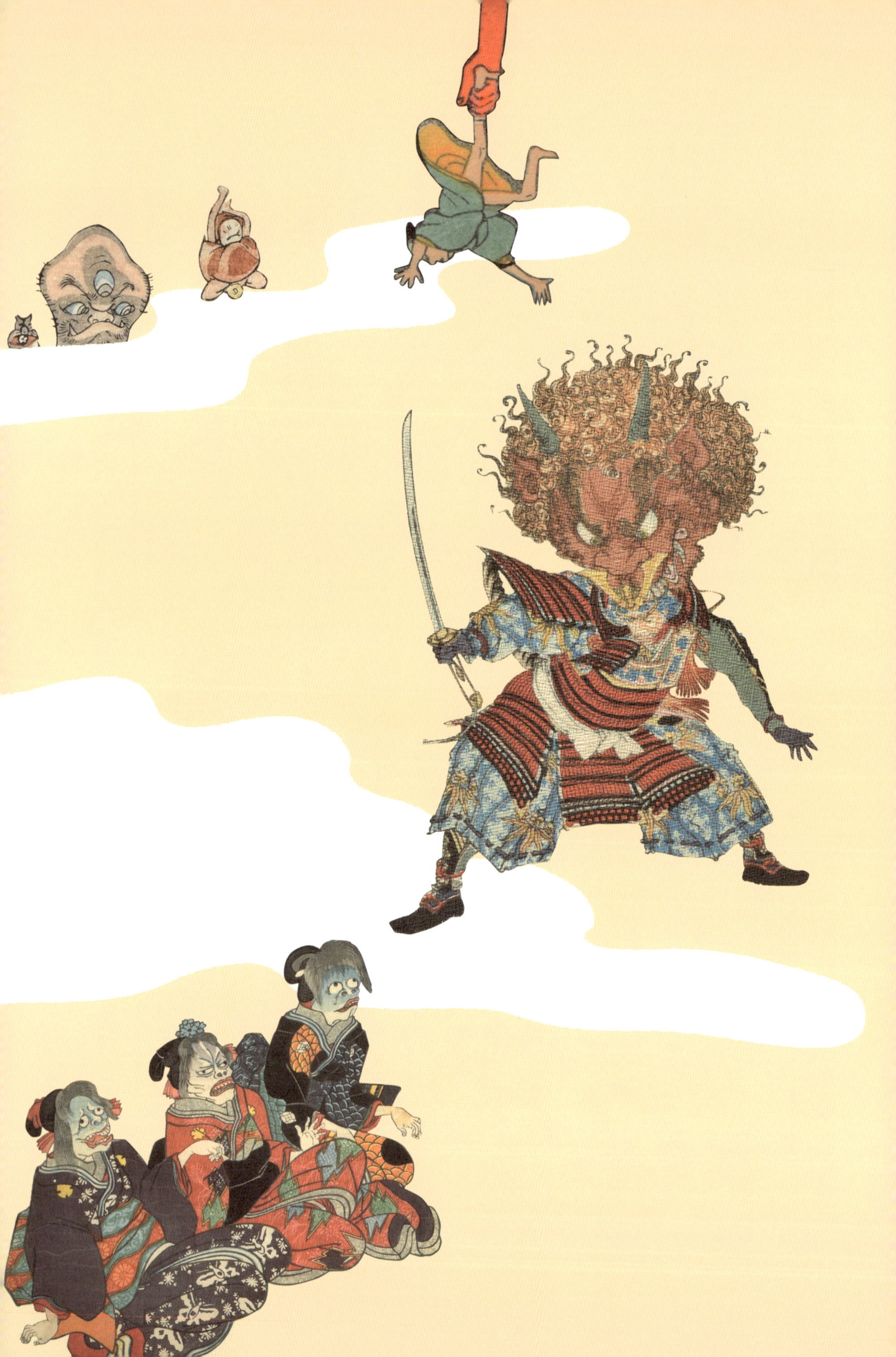

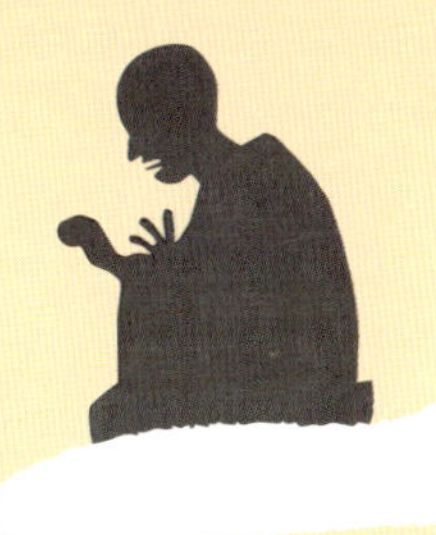

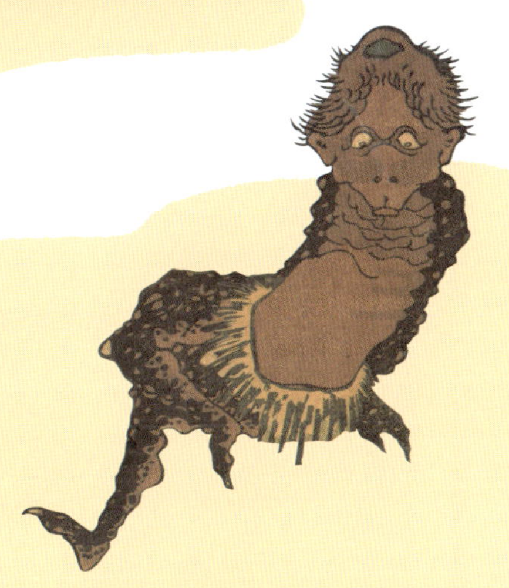

2

印刷の妖怪たち

Yokai of Prints

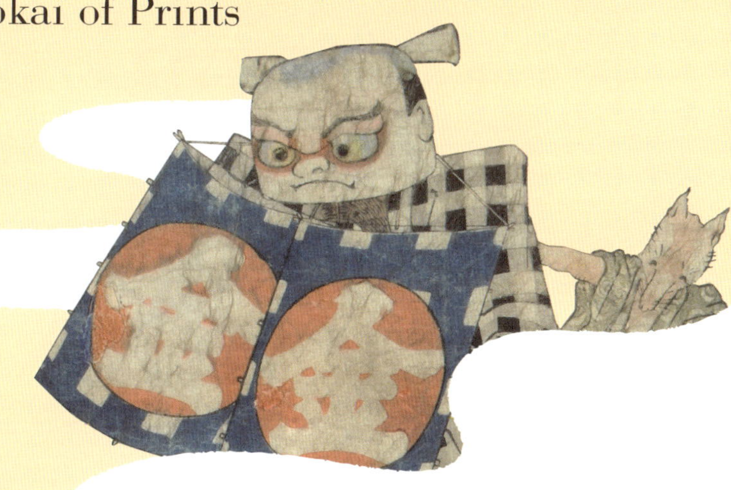

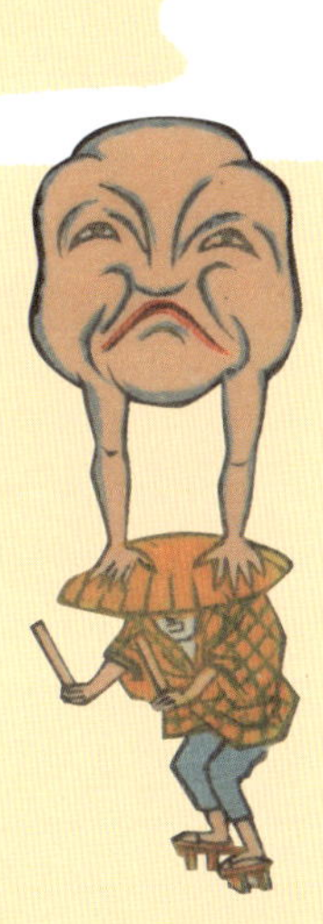

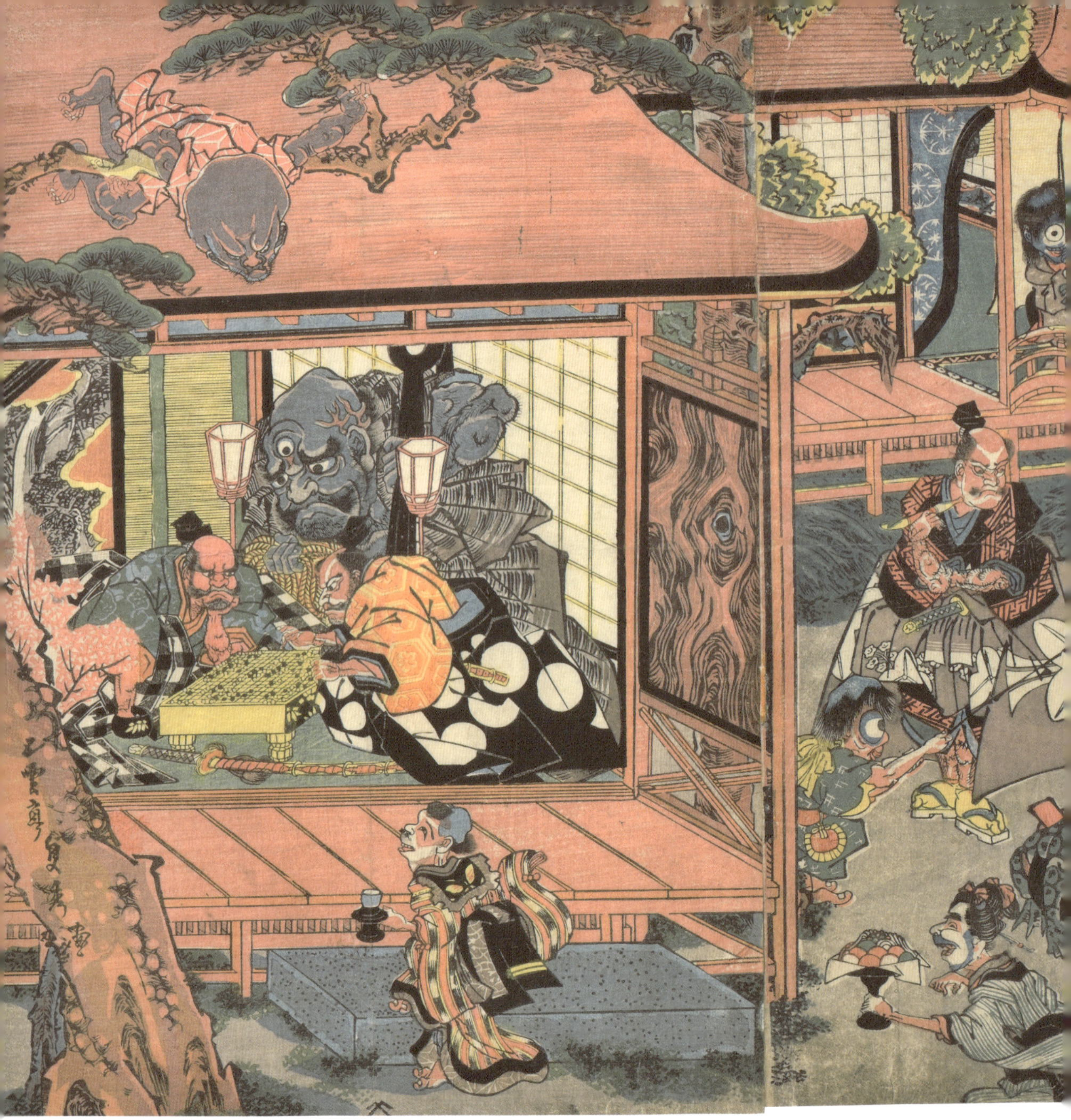

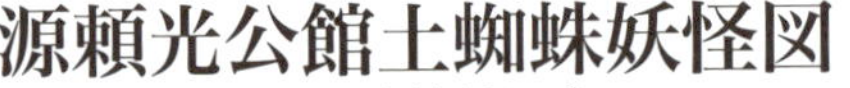

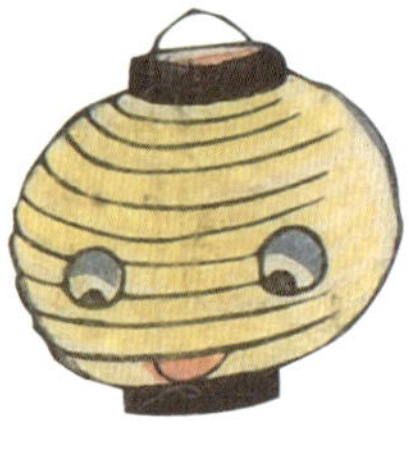

31 源頼光公館土蜘蛛妖怪図

みなもとのよりみつこうやかたつちぐもようかいず

The Yokai of Tsuchigumo at the Mansion of Minamoto no Yorimitsu

(Minamoto no Yorimitsu Kō Yakata Tsuchigumo Yōkai Zu)

歌川貞秀　江戸時代　大判錦絵 3 枚続　Utagawa Sadahide, Edo period, Large triptych

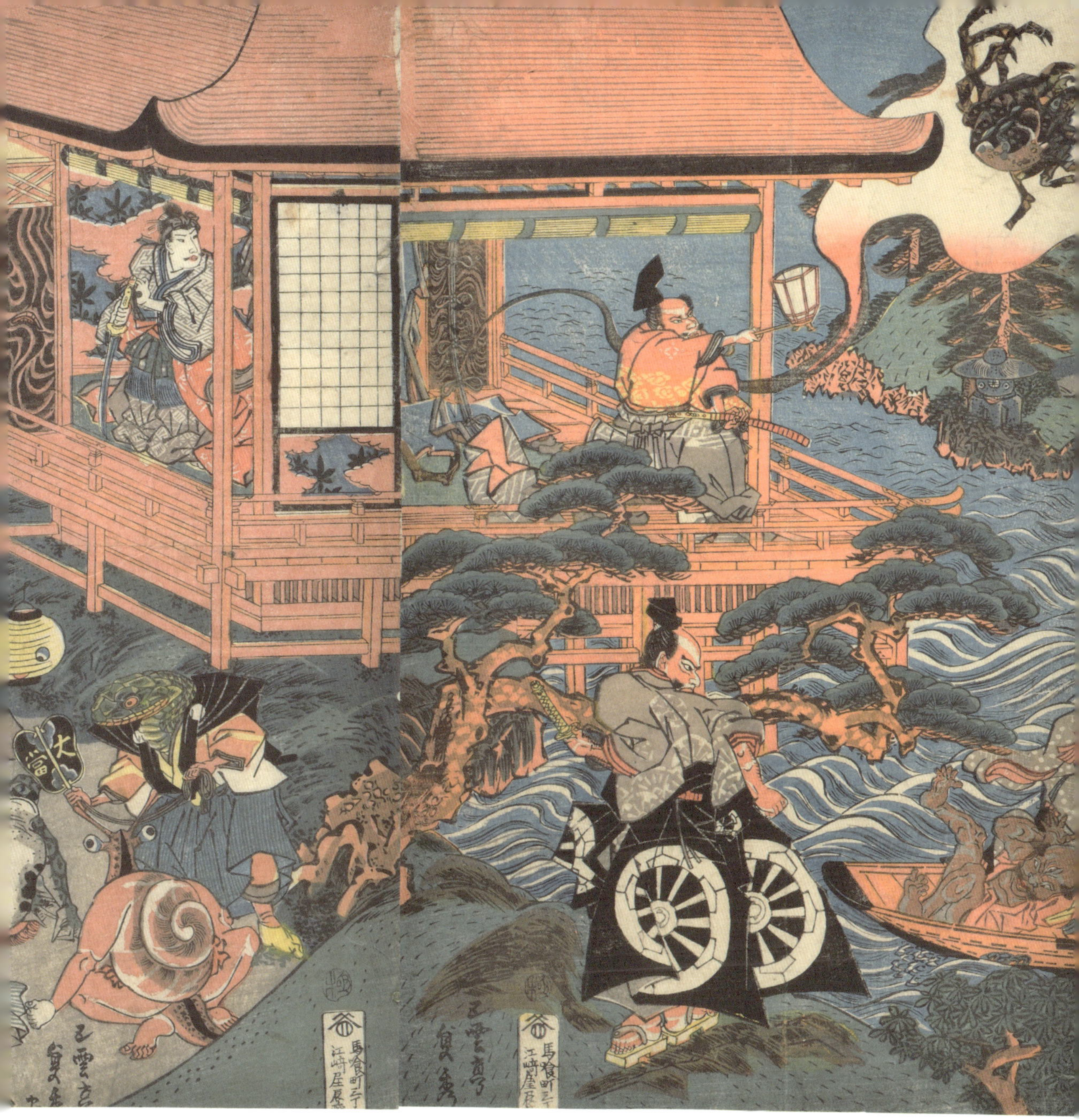

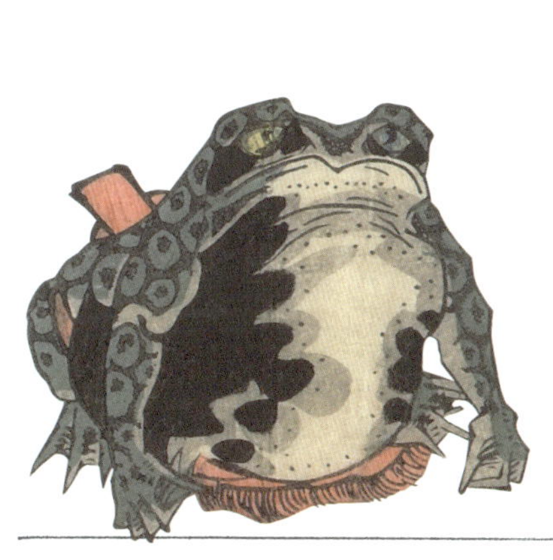

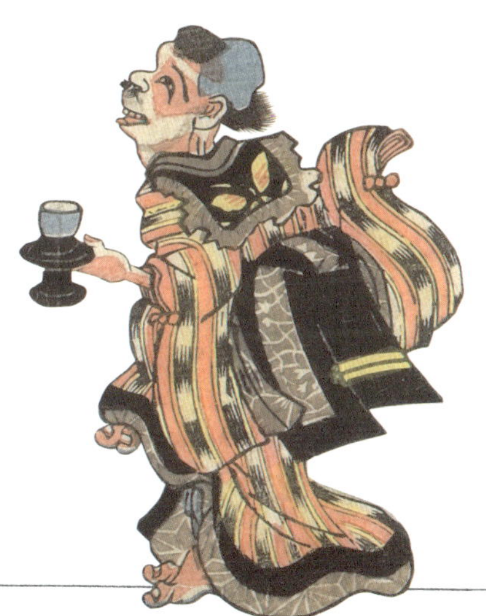

白縫譚
しらぬいものがたり

Shiranui Tales (*Shiranui Monogatari*)

歌川豊国（3代）　嘉永 5 年（1852）4 月　大判錦絵 2 枚続
Utagawa Toyokuni (III), April 1852(Kaei 5), Large diptych

芳年漫画　妖怪土蜘蛛図
よしとしまんが　ようかいつちぐもず

Yoshitoshi Manga: The Earth Spider (*Tsuchigumo*)

月岡芳年　明治 19 年（1886）　大判錦絵 2 枚続　Tsukioka Yoshitoshi, 1886 (Meiji 19), Large diptych

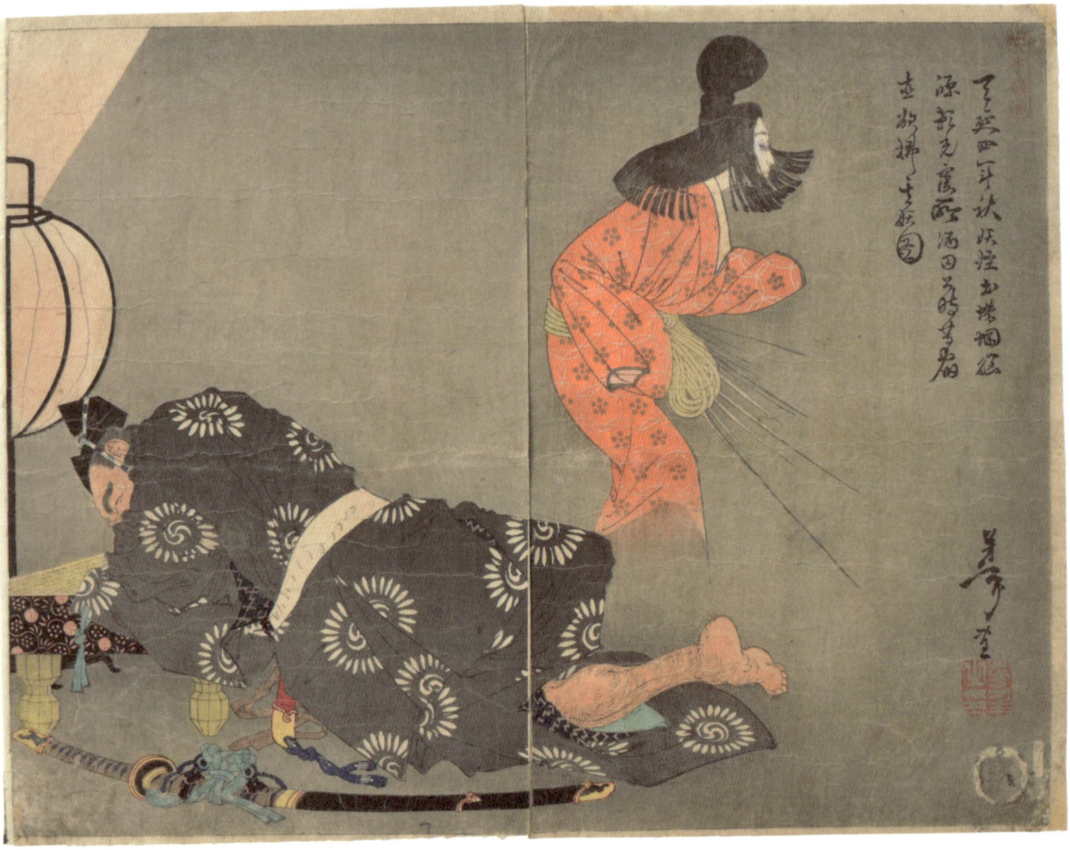

源頼光の館に出現する土蜘蛛から頼光を護るために泊まり込んだ坂田金時ら四天王。睡魔に襲われた坂田金時の横に現れた土蜘蛛の精は可憐な姿だが蜘蛛の糸が見え隠れしており、その正体がみてとれる。

Sakata no Kintoki and the other three loyal retainers keep the night watch, guarding Minamoto no Yorimitsu from Tsuchigumo's visitations to his mansion. By the side of Sakata no Kintoki who has been overcome by sleep, the spirit of Tsuchigumo manifests in a lovely guise betrayed by a telltale glimpse of spider's thread.

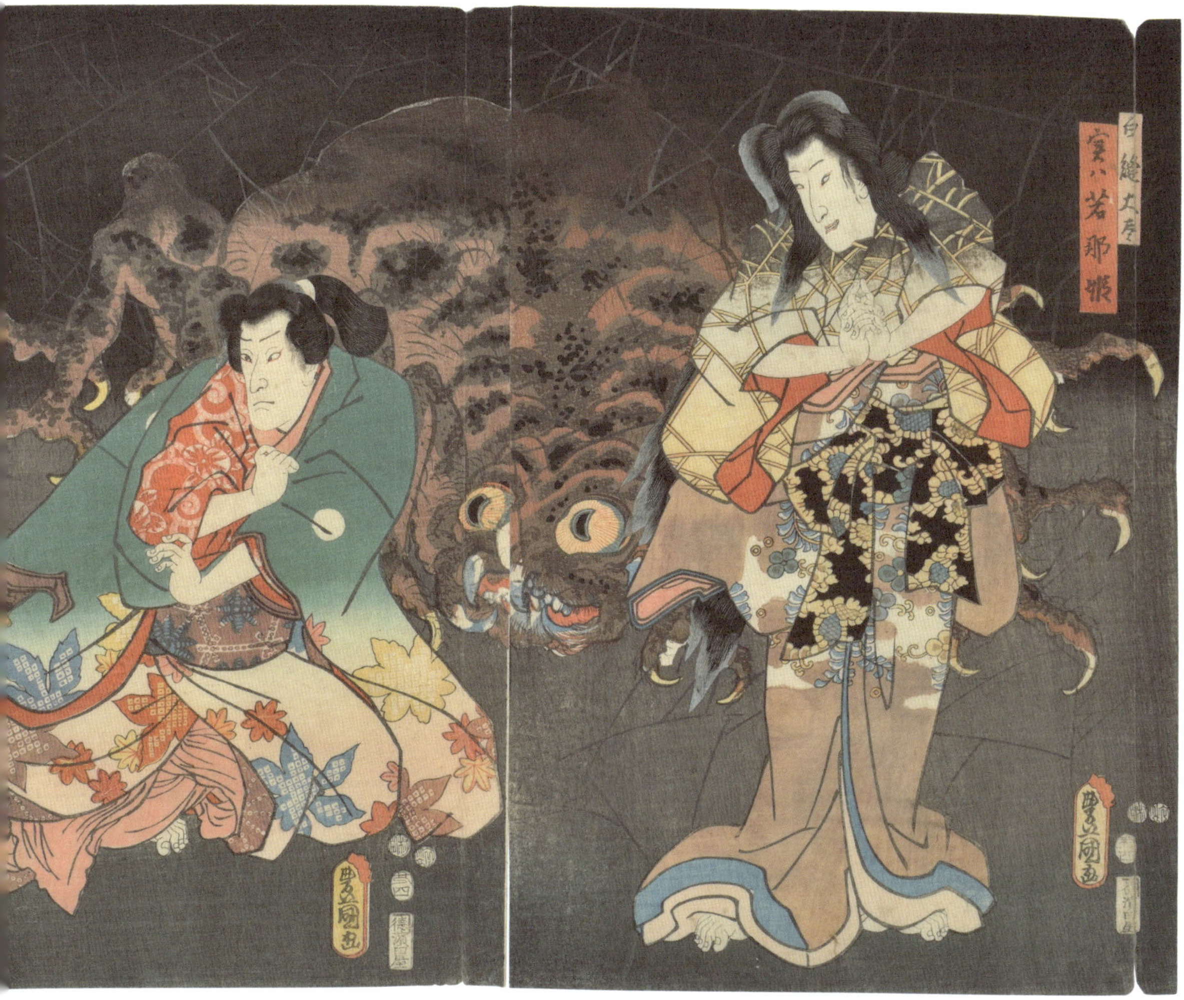

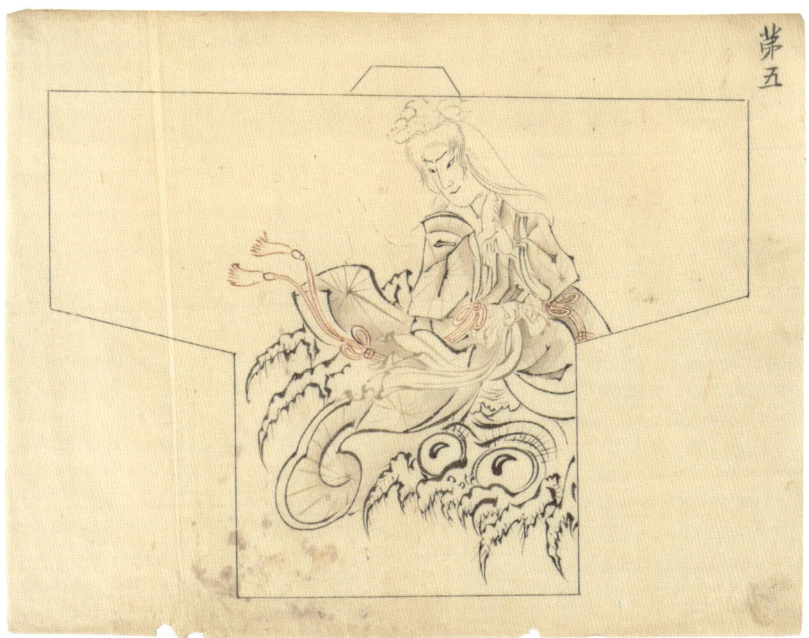

「白縫譚」着物下絵　江戸時代以降

Shiranui Tales Kimono Sketch
Post Edo period

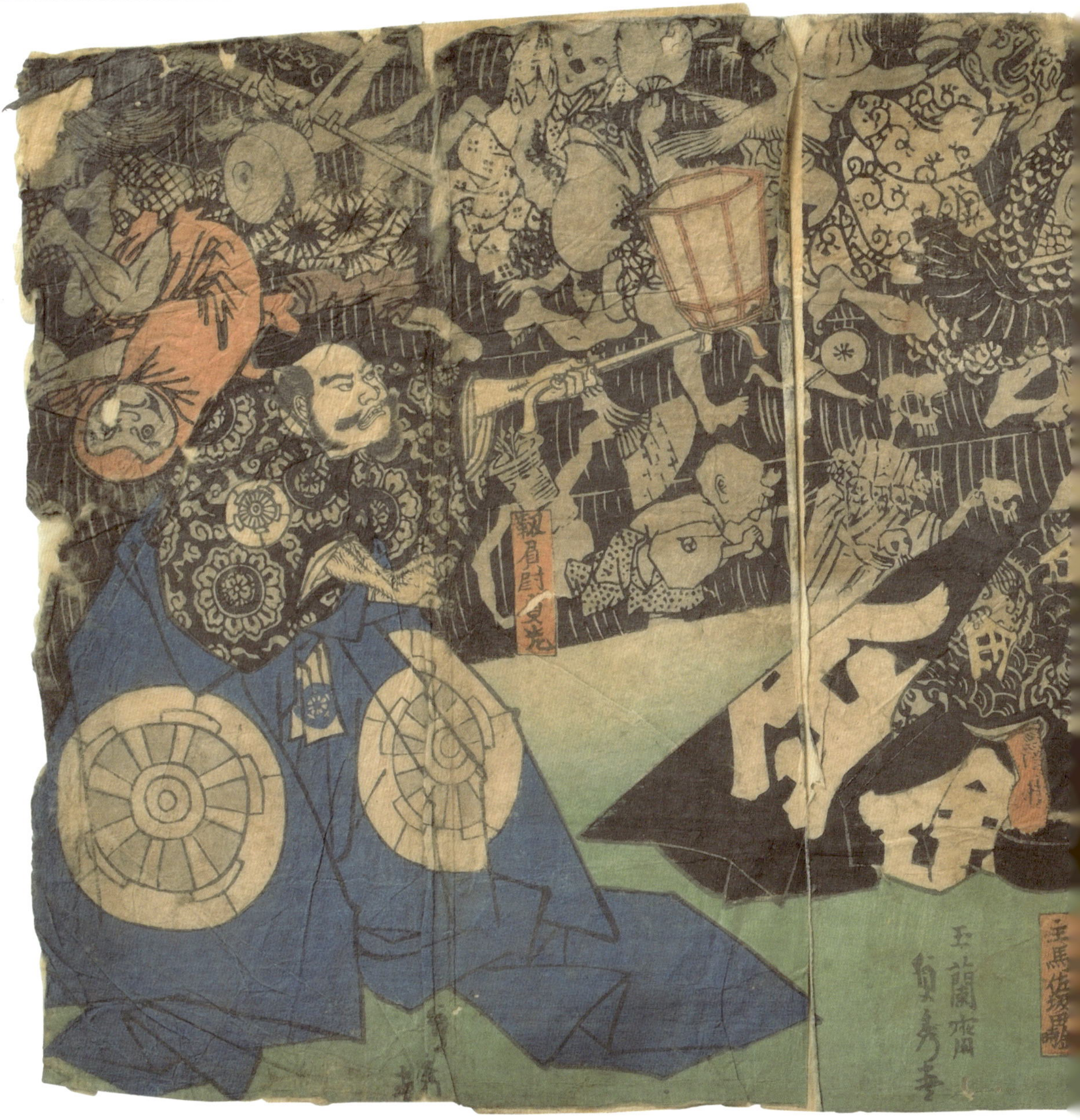

34 土蜘蛛妖怪図

つちぐもようかいず

Tsuchigumo and Yokai (*Tsuchigumo Yōkai Zu*)

歌川貞秀　江戸時代　大判錦絵 3 枚続　Utagawa Sadahide, Edo period, Large triptych

天保改革を風刺した歌川国芳の「源頼光公館土蜘作妖怪図」（『今昔
妖怪大鑑』収録。参考図版参照）は幕府に不満をもつ庶民の共感を
呼んで爆発的人気となり、海賊版も出されるほどだった。この作品
も「源頼光公館土蜘作妖怪図」の影響をうけて作られたものである
ことは構図からも一目瞭然だ。しかし、闇のなかに蠢いている妖怪
たちは独自の妖怪世界を展開している。幕府は為政者や政策に対す
る批判が広がることを恐れてこの作品を描いた貞秀と版元は逮捕さ
れて手鎖 20 日間、罰金 3 貫文に処せられ、作品は発禁処分となっ
ている。

Utagawa Kuniyoshi's satire of the Tenpō Reforms *Minamoto no
Yorimitsu in his Palace with Tsuchigumo and Yokai* resonated with
people dissatisfied with the Tokugawa shogunate and exploded in
popularity to the point where people made pirated versions. This work
shows the influence of *Minamoto no Yorimitsu in his Palace with
Tsuchigumo and Yokai* with a strikingly similar composition. However,
the yokai moving in the dark reveal a unique world of demonic creatures.
The Tokugawa shogunate feared that political dissent would spread; this
print was banned, and Sadahide and the printer were arrested and received
punishment of 20 days *tegusari* (home detention with handcuffs) and a
fine of 3 *kanmon*.

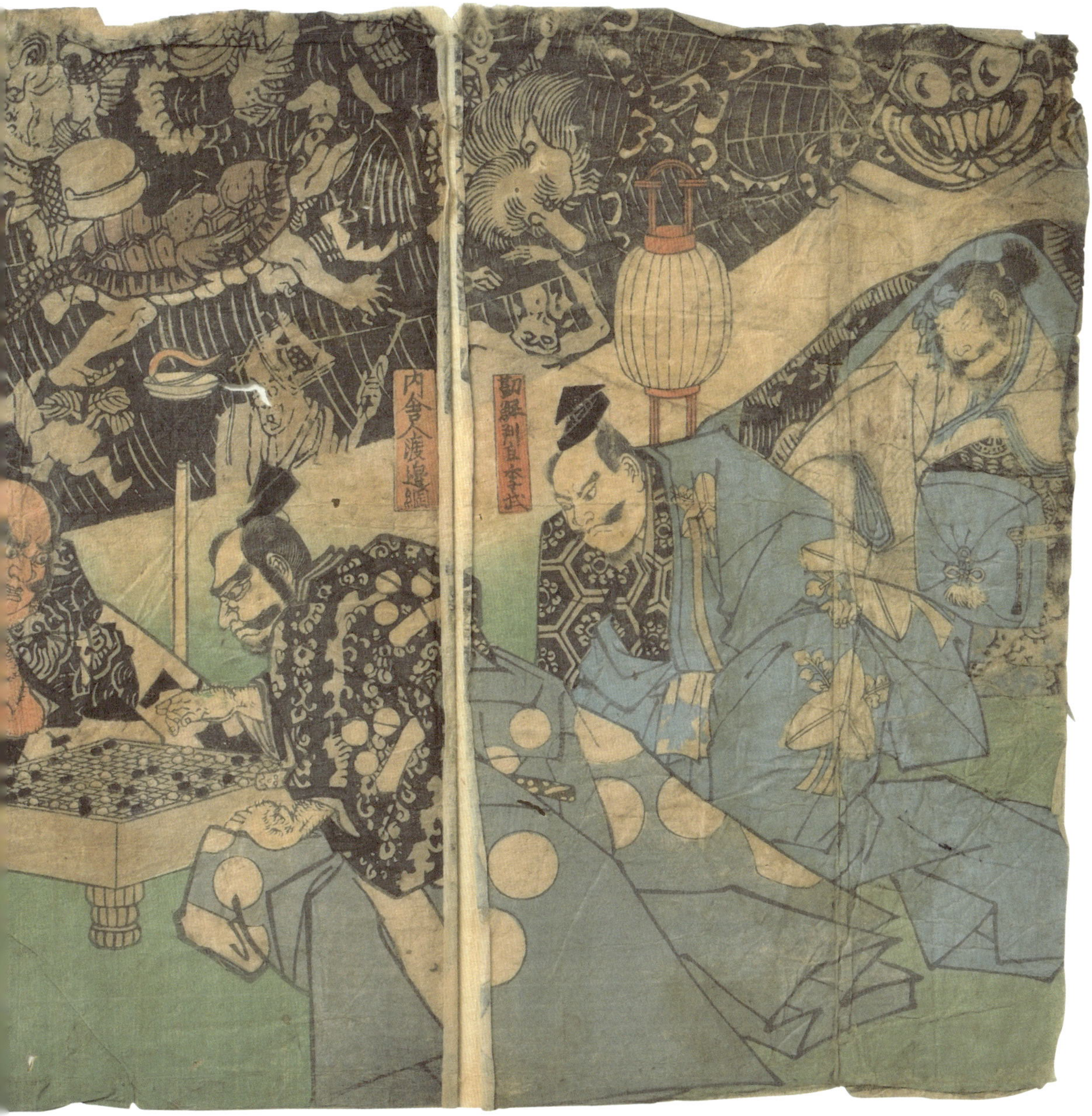

参考図版

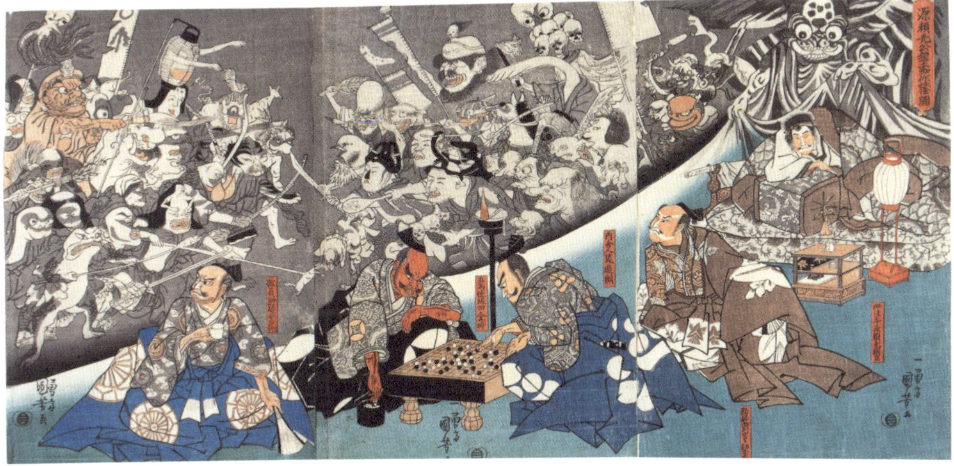

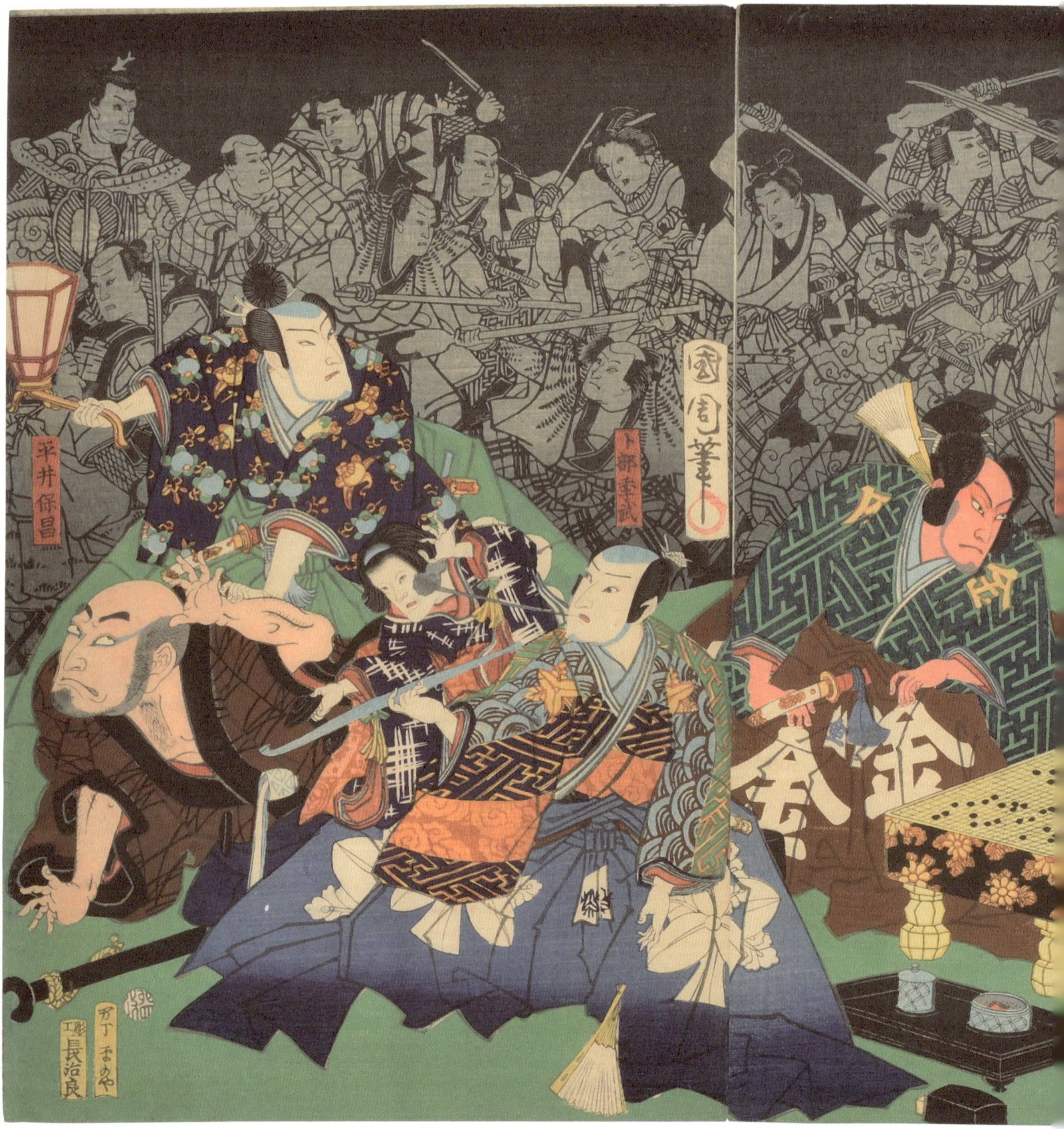

（35）頼光館土蜘怪異做図

よりみつのやかたつちぐもかいいをなすのず

Tsuchigumo Causes Mysterious Phenomena in the Mansion of Minamoto no Yorimitsu (*Yorimitsu no Yakata Tsuchigumo Kaii wo Nasu no Zu*)

豊原国周　慶応3年（1867）4月　大判錦絵3枚続　Toyohara Kunichika, The fourth month of 1867 (Keiō 3), Large triptych

この作品は歌舞伎の「土蜘蛛」を題材としたもので、源頼光の館における土蜘蛛による怪異の場面を描いている。右端に土蜘精を配し、その傍らに源頼光、頼光を警護する四天王は碁盤を中心に左右2人ずつ描かれた構図は歌川国芳の「源頼光公館土蜘作妖怪図」（P.105参考図版参照）を真似たことが一目瞭然だが、そこには描かれていない平井保昌と蜘蛛が化けた僧・智疇が登場しているのは歌舞伎の内容に沿ったものだ。「源頼光公館土蜘作妖怪図」はその後の錦絵に大きな影響を及ぼしたが、この作品もそうしたなかの一つといえる。誰もがこの作品に「源頼光公館土蜘作妖怪図」を重ねて見ていたことは想像に難くない。

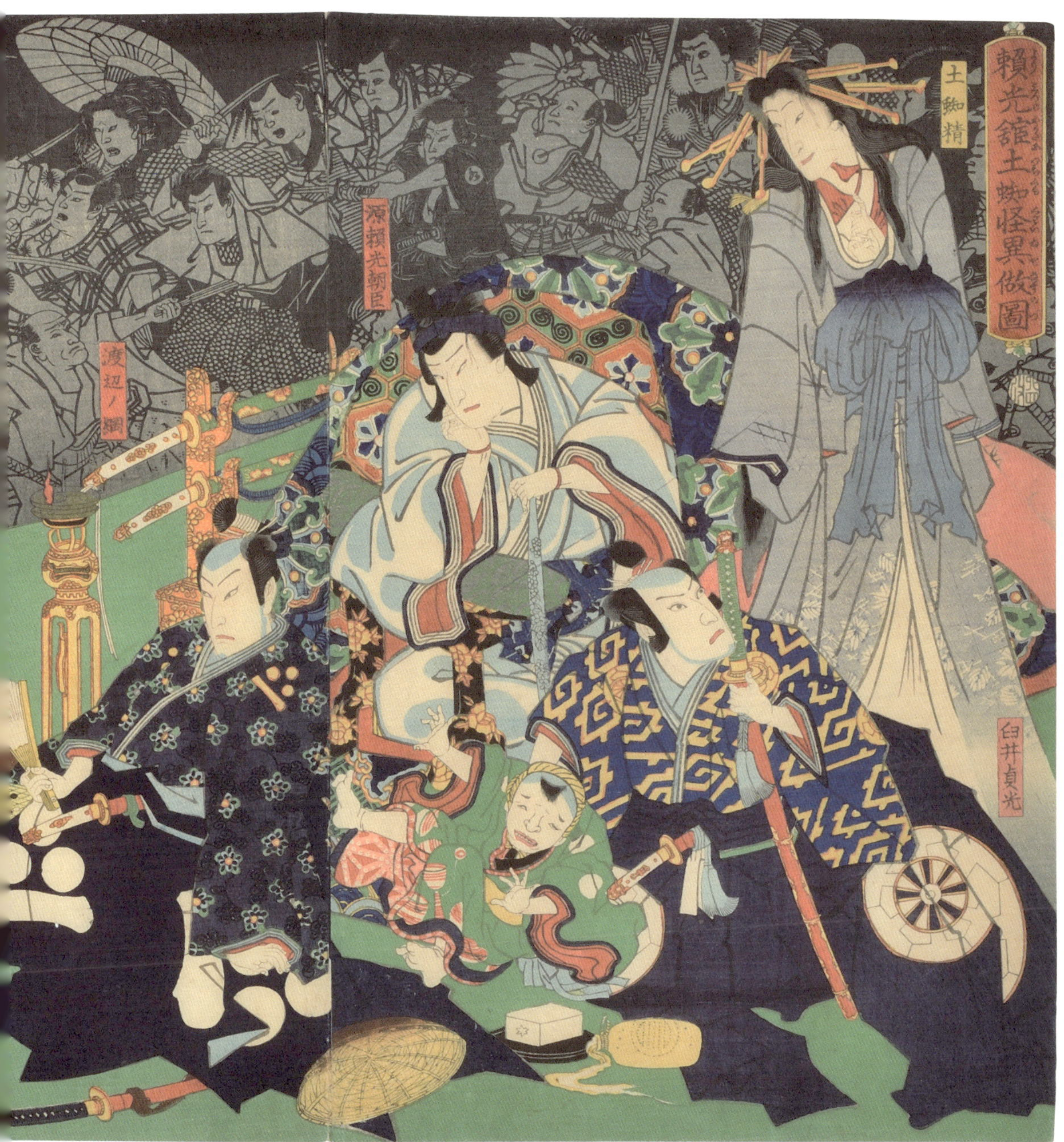

This work depicts a scene of the earth spider's supernatural powers unleashed in Minamoto no Yorimitsu's mansion from the kabuki play *Tsuchigumo*. There is an immediately striking resemblance to the composition of Utagawa Kuniyoshi's *Minamoto no Yorimitsu in his Palace with Tsuchigumo and Yokai* (please refer to p105); the spirit of Tsuchigumo is placed in the right-hand corner with Minamoto no Yorimitsu beside her, and his guard (the Raikō Shitennō) are set out two on each side of the *go* board, however, the additional presences of Hirai no Yasumasa and spider-turned-priest Chichū are in keeping with the kabuki play. *Minamoto no Yorimitsu in his Palace with Tsuchigumo and Yokai* had a strong influence on later works. It is easy to imagine that that work was referred to repeatedly in the creation of this one.

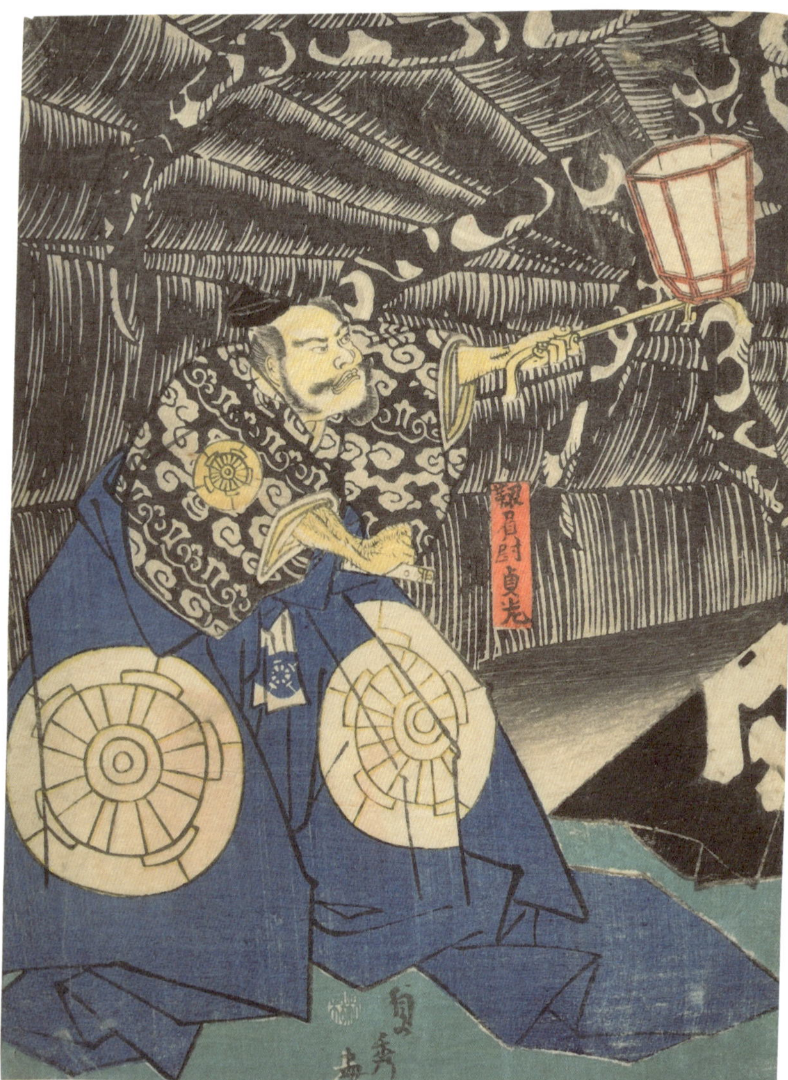
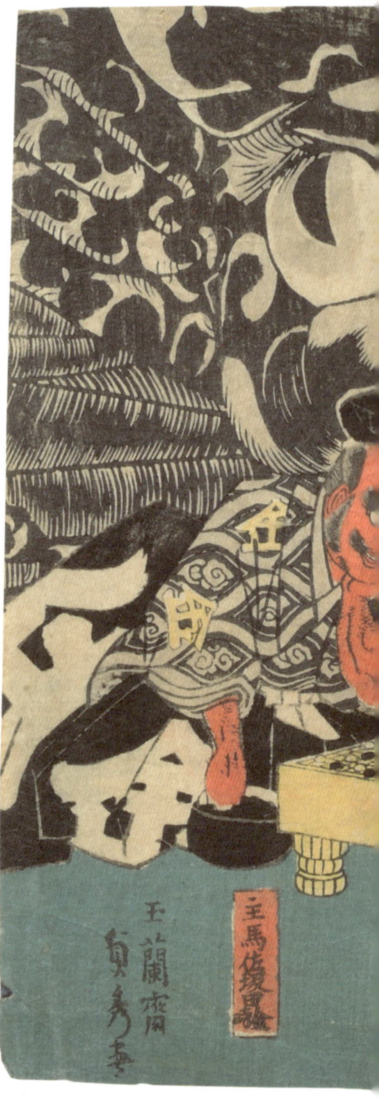

36 源頼光館土蜘蛛図

みなもとのよりみつやかたつちぐもず

Tsuchigumo at the Mansion of Minamoto no Yorimitsu
(*Minamoto no Yorimitsu Yakata Tsuchigumo Zu*)

歌川貞秀　江戸時代　大判錦絵 3 枚続　Utagawa Sadahide, Edo period, Large triptych

碁を打ちながら源頼光を護る四天王。その背後には巨大な土蜘蛛が画面いっぱいに描かれて不気味な迫力を醸し出している。土蜘蛛をテーマとした錦絵は多くあるが、この作品はそのなかでも土蜘蛛の怪を見る者に強く印象付ける一品だ。

The Raikō Shitennō are playing *go* while guarding Minamoto no Yorimitsu. Behind them a huge *tsuchigumo* is drawn to fill the scene, projecting an uncanny tension. There are many *nishiki-e* on the theme of *tsuchigumo*, but this one strongly impresses the horror of Tsuchigumo on the viewer.

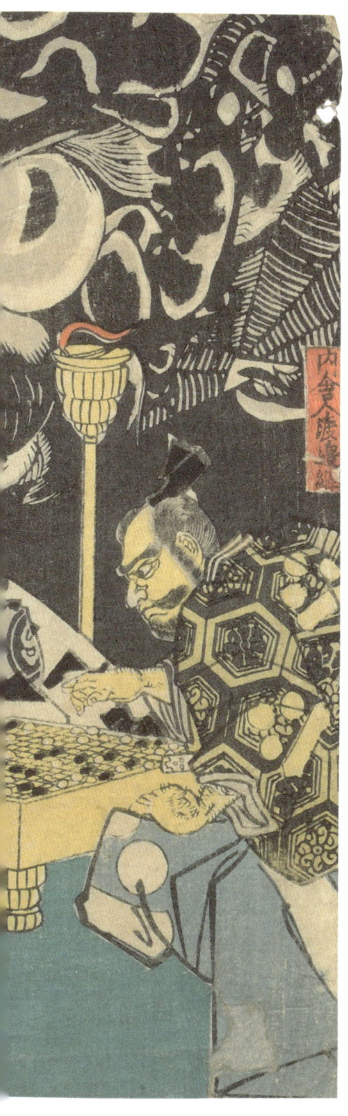
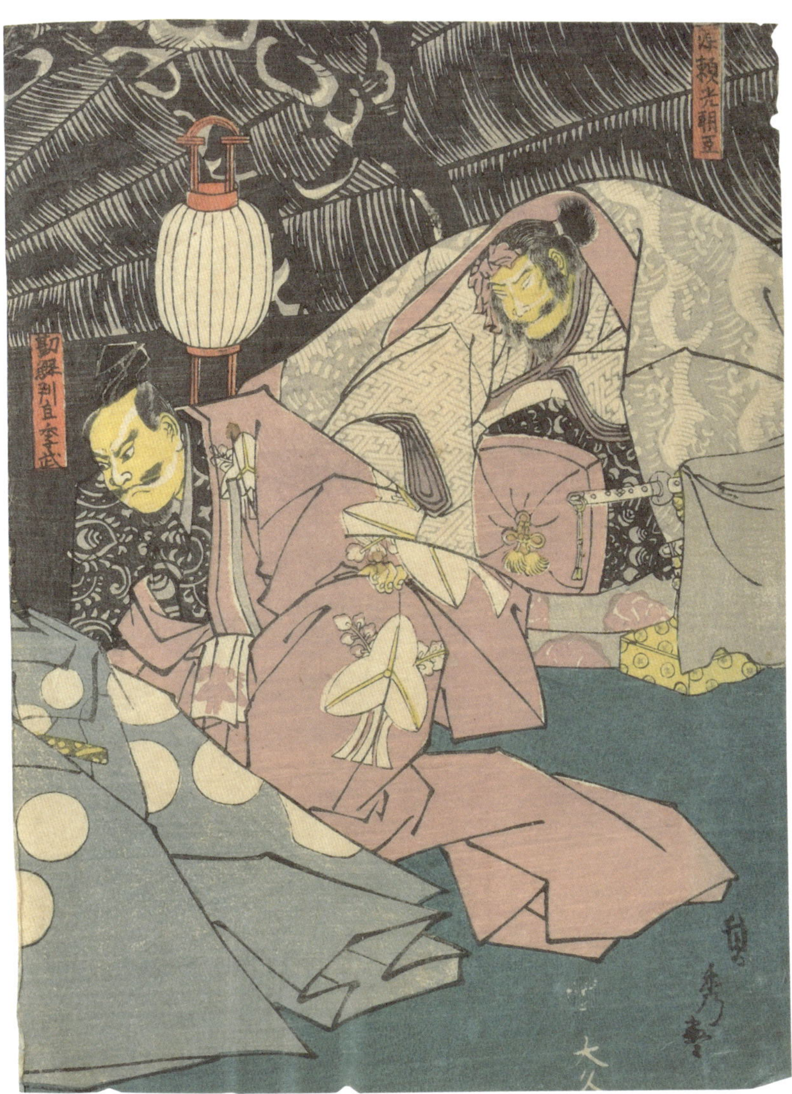
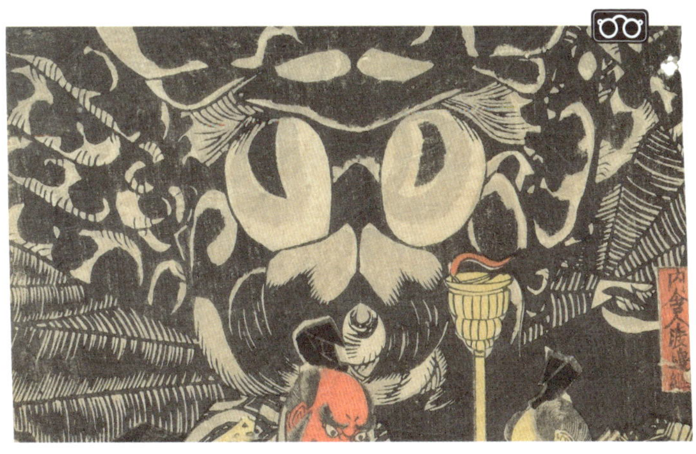

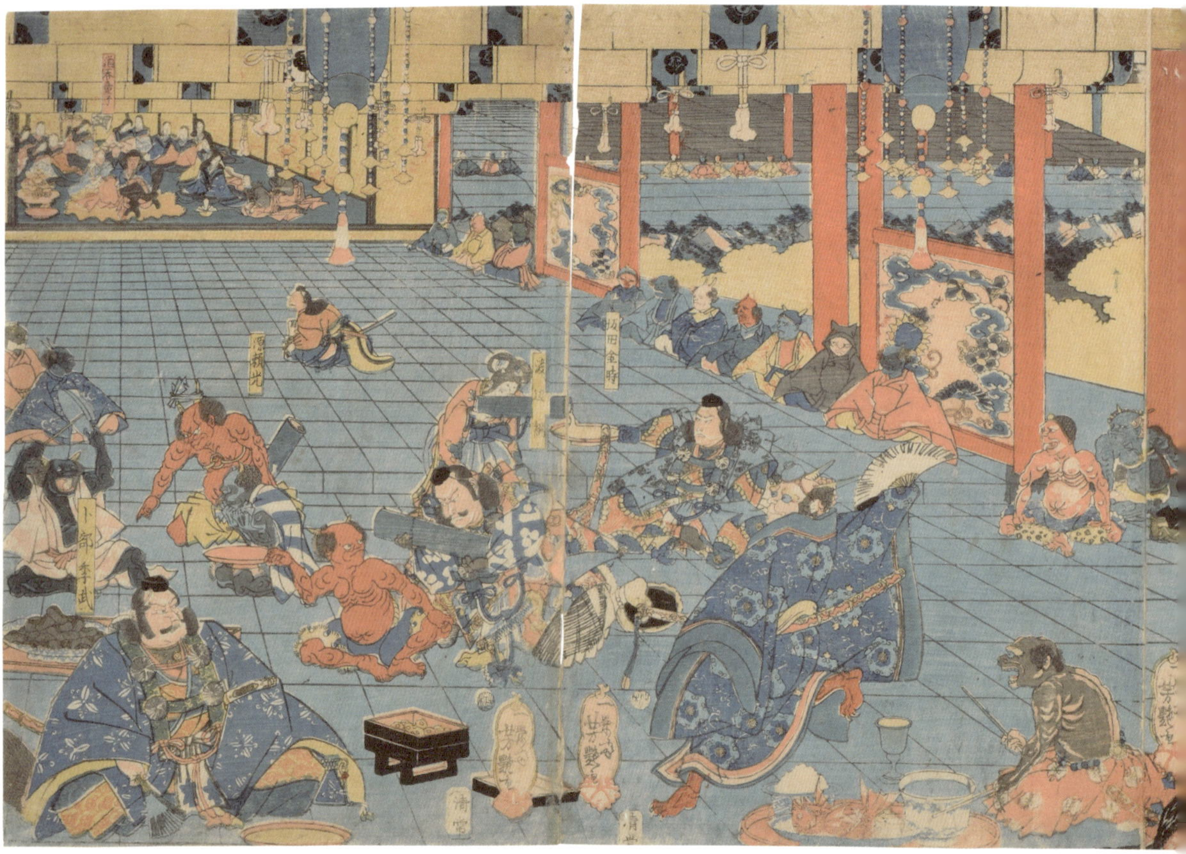

37 丹波国大江山之図
たんばのくにおおえやまのず

Mount Ōe of Tanba Province (*Tanba no Kuni Ōe Yama no Zu*)

歌川芳艶　江戸時代　大判錦絵 3 枚続　Utagawa Yoshitsuya, Edo period, Large triptych

38 川上演劇歌舞伎座中幕大江山
かわかみえんげきかぶきざなかまくおおえやま

Middle Act of Kawakami's Mount Ōe at the Kabuki-za

(*Kawakami Engeki Kabuki-za Nakamaku Ōe-yama*)

歌川豊斎　明治時代　大判錦絵 3 枚続　Utagawa Toyosai, Meiji period, Large triptych

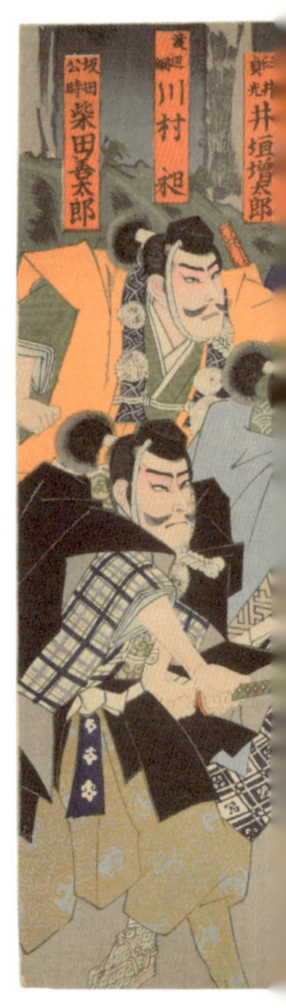

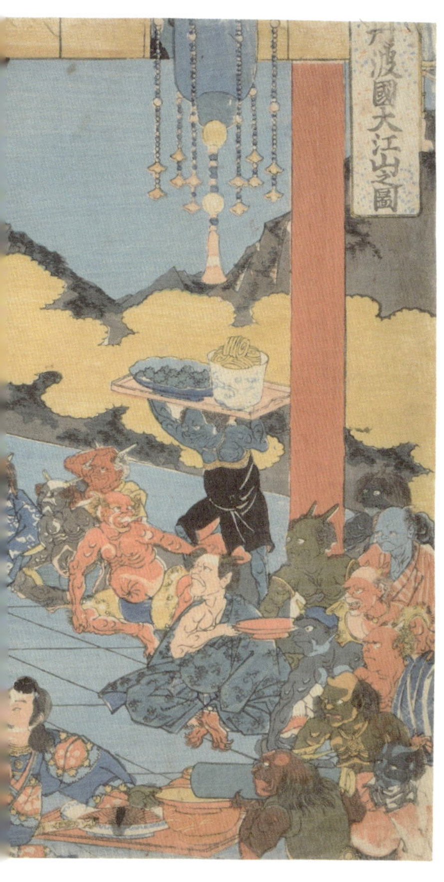

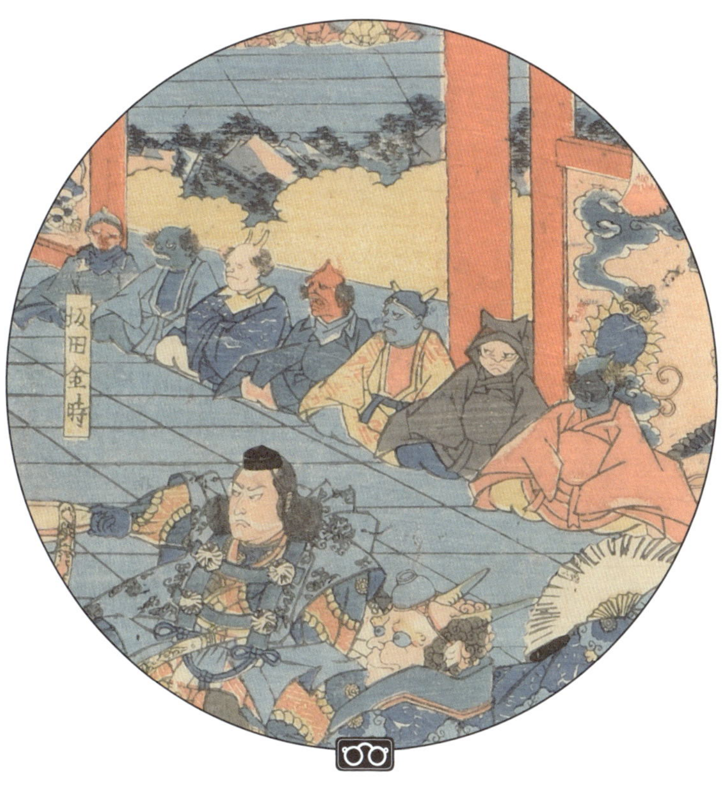
坂田金時

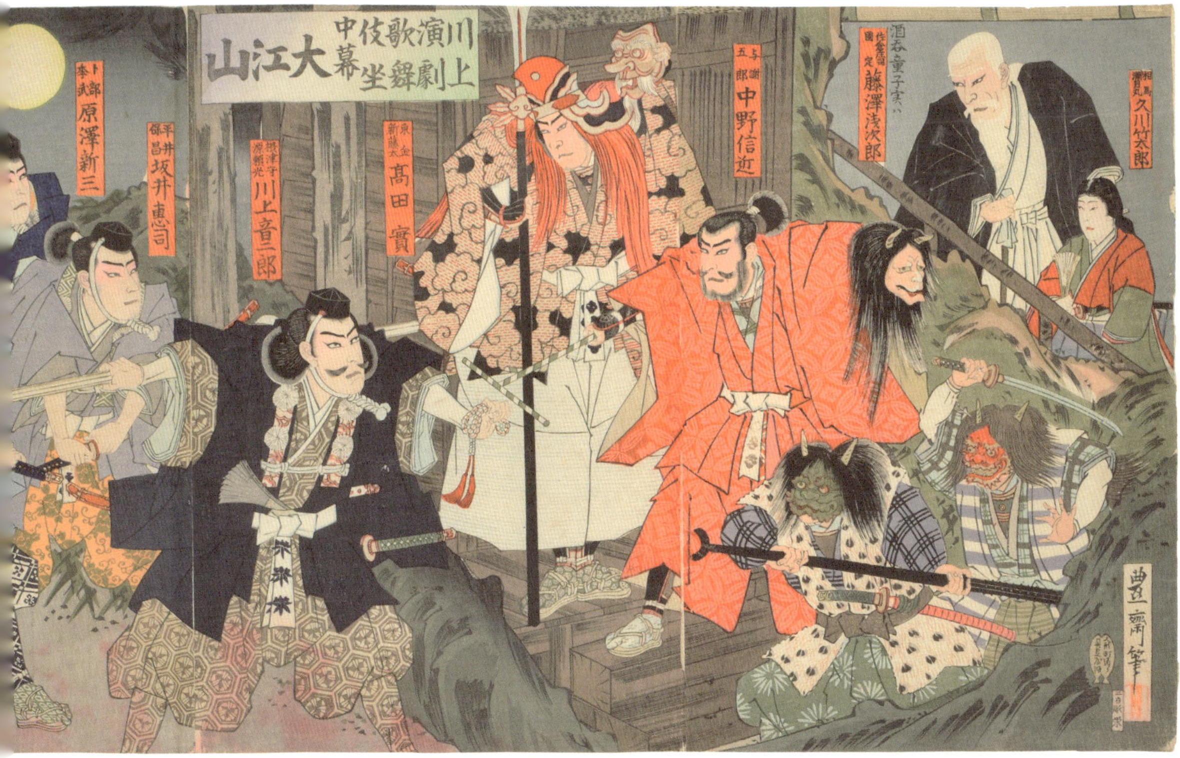

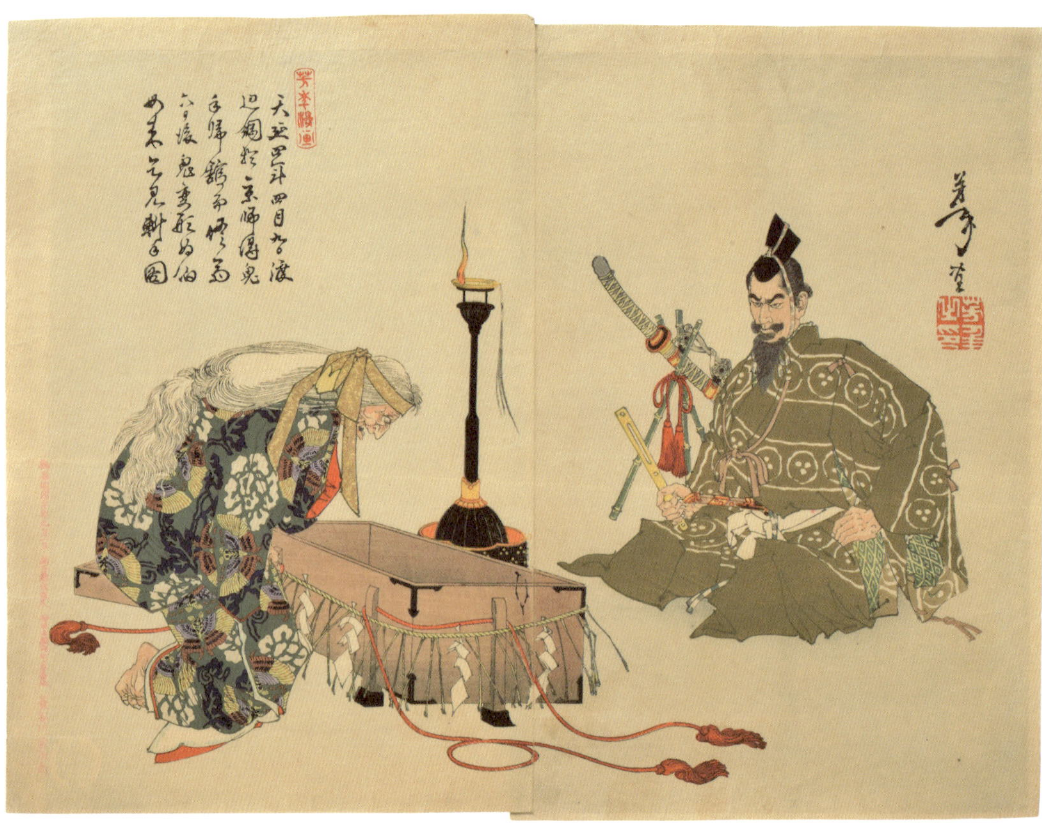

39

芳年漫画　渡辺綱と茨木童子
よしとしまんが　わたなべのつなといばらきどうじ

Yoshitoshi Manga: Watanabe no Tsuna and Ibaraki-dōji

月岡芳年　明治 18 年（1885）　大判錦絵 2 枚続
Tsukioka Yoshitoshi, 1885 (Meiji 18), Large diptych

渡辺綱によって腕を斬り落とされた茨木童子が綱の伯母に化けて綱
の館を訪ねて斬られた腕を取り戻して去るという有名な話をテーマ
としている。綱に見せられた自分の腕を見入る伯母に化けた茨木童
子の形相が恐ろしい。

The famous story of the ogre Ibaraki-dōji whose arm was cut off and stolen
by Watanabe no Tsuna, upon which the ogre disguised himself as Tsuna's
aunt and visited Tsuna's mansion to take his arm back. In the guise of the
aunt, Ibaraki-dōji's expression is frightening as he stares at his own arm
shown to him by Tsuna.

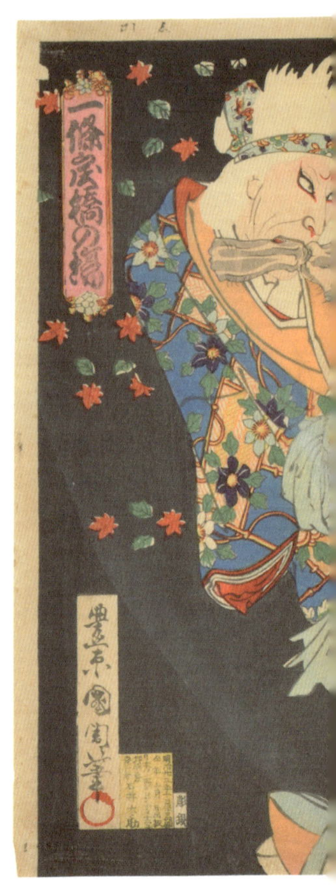

一條戻橋の場

いちじょうもどりばしのば

On Ichijō Modori Bridge
(*Ichijō Modori-bashi no Ba*)

豊原国周　明治 23 年（1890）10 月
大判錦絵 3 枚続
Toyohara Kunichika, October 1890
(Meiji 23), Large triptych

源頼光の四天王の一人である渡辺綱が茨木童子に襲われ
てその腕を斬り落としたという有名な伝説は錦絵の題材
としても多数描かれていったが、この作品は伝説をベー
スに明治 23 年に東京の歌舞伎座で初演された河竹黙阿弥
作「戻橋恋の角文字」の名シーンで、5 世尾上菊五郎（怪
童丸）と初世市川左団次（渡辺綱）だけをクローズアッ
プして描き緊迫感溢れる舞台を伝えている。

The famous legend of how one of Minamoto no Yorimitsu's
four loyal retainers Watanabe no Tsuna was attacked by
Ibaraki-dōji and cut off the ogre's arm has been depicted in
nishiki-e and other media; this work features the pivotal scene
from kabuki play *Modori-bashi Koi no Tsuno Moji* written
by Kawatake Mokuami based on this legend and premiered at
the Tokyo Kabuki-za in 1890, conveying the stage full of
tension with a close-up depiction of Onoe Kikugorō V (as
Kaidōmaru) and Ichikawa Sadanji I (as Watanabe no Tsuna).

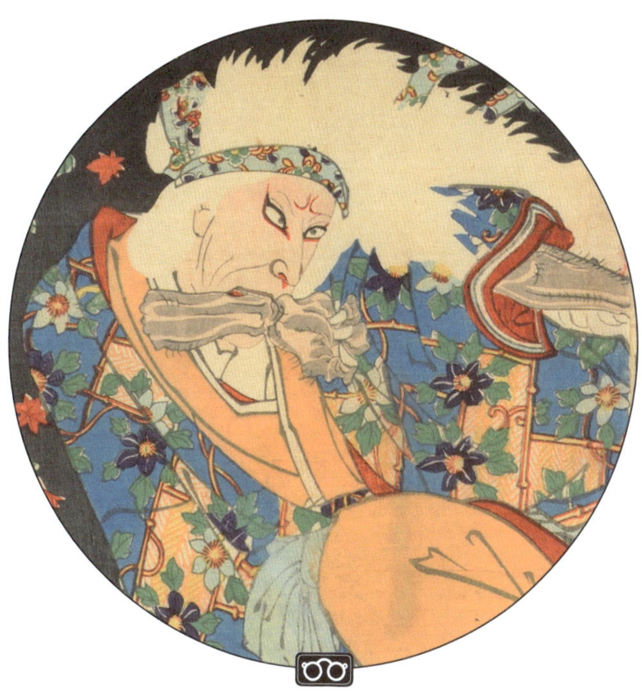

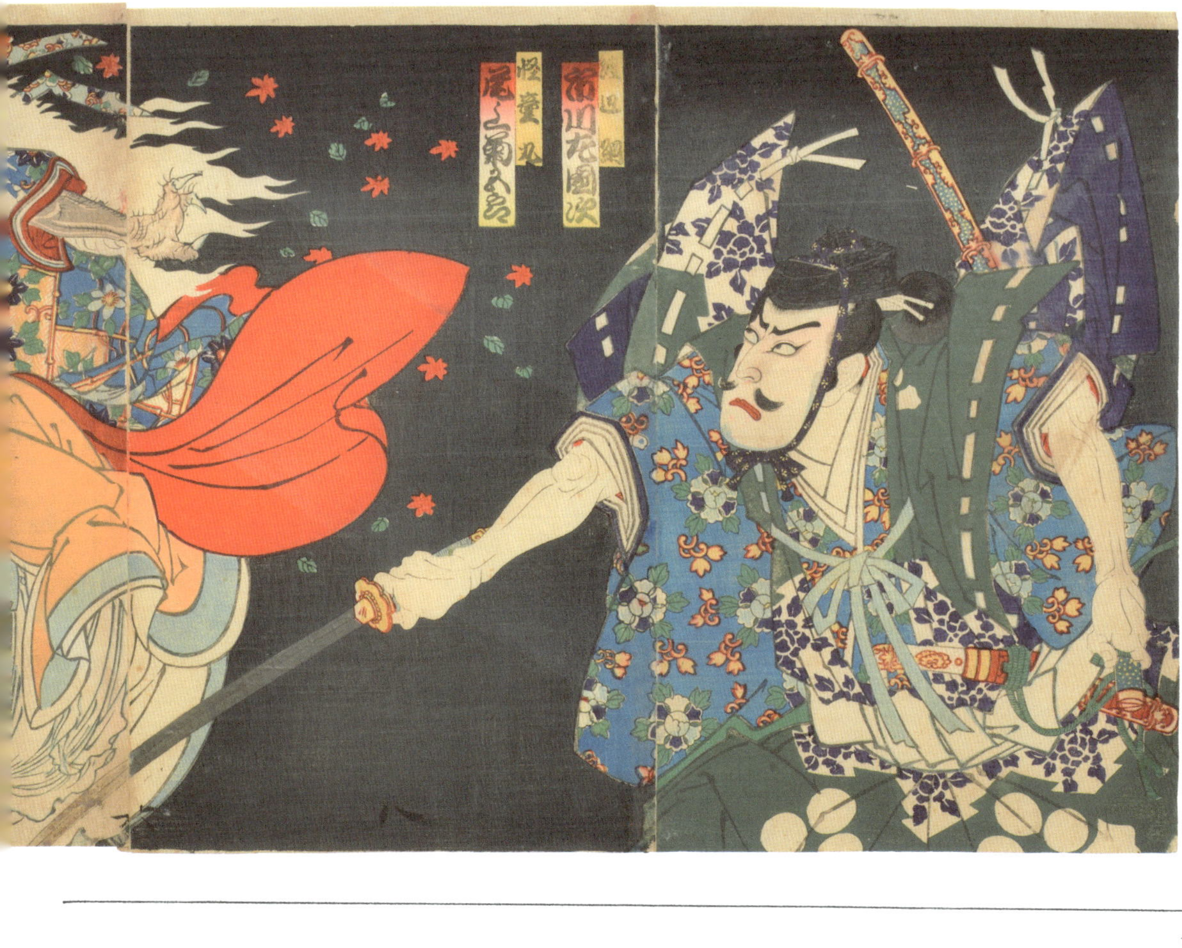

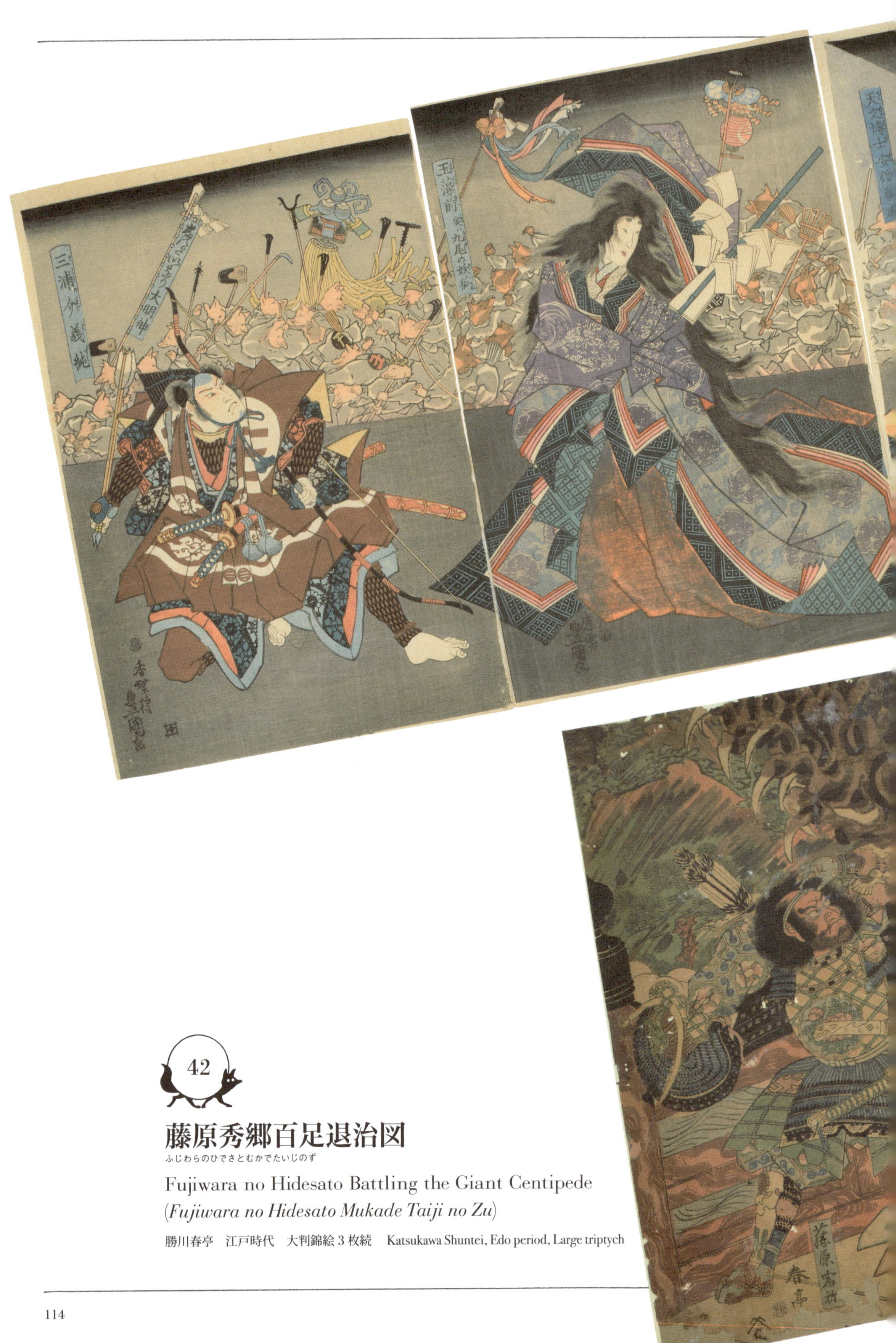

42

藤原秀郷百足退治図

ふじわらのひでさとむかでたいじのず

Fujiwara no Hidesato Battling the Giant Centipede
(*Fujiwara no Hidesato Mukade Taiji no Zu*)

勝川春亭　江戸時代　大判錦絵３枚続　Katsukawa Shuntei, Edo period, Large triptych

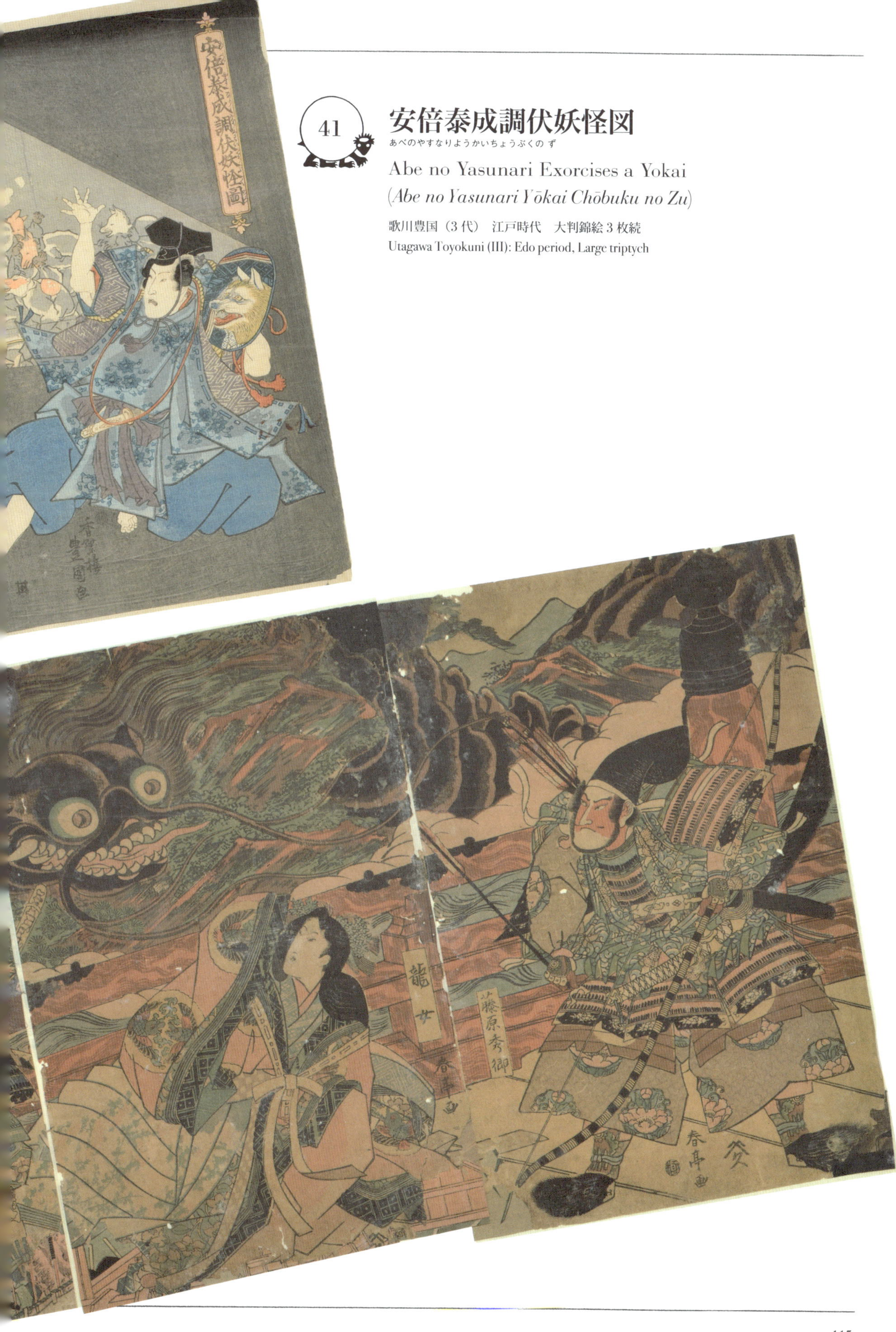

41 安倍泰成調伏妖怪図

あべのやすなりようかいちょうぶくのず

Abe no Yasunari Exorcises a Yokai

(*Abe no Yasunari Yōkai Chōbuku no Zu*)

歌川豊国（3代）　江戸時代　大判錦絵 3 枚続
Utagawa Toyokuni (III): Edo period, Large triptych

43

浅倉当吾亡霊図
あさくらとうごぼうれいず

The Ghost of Asakura Tōgo (*Asakura Tōgo Bōrei Zu*)

歌川国芳　江戸時代　大判錦絵 3 枚続　Utagawa Kuniyoshi, Edo period, Large triptych

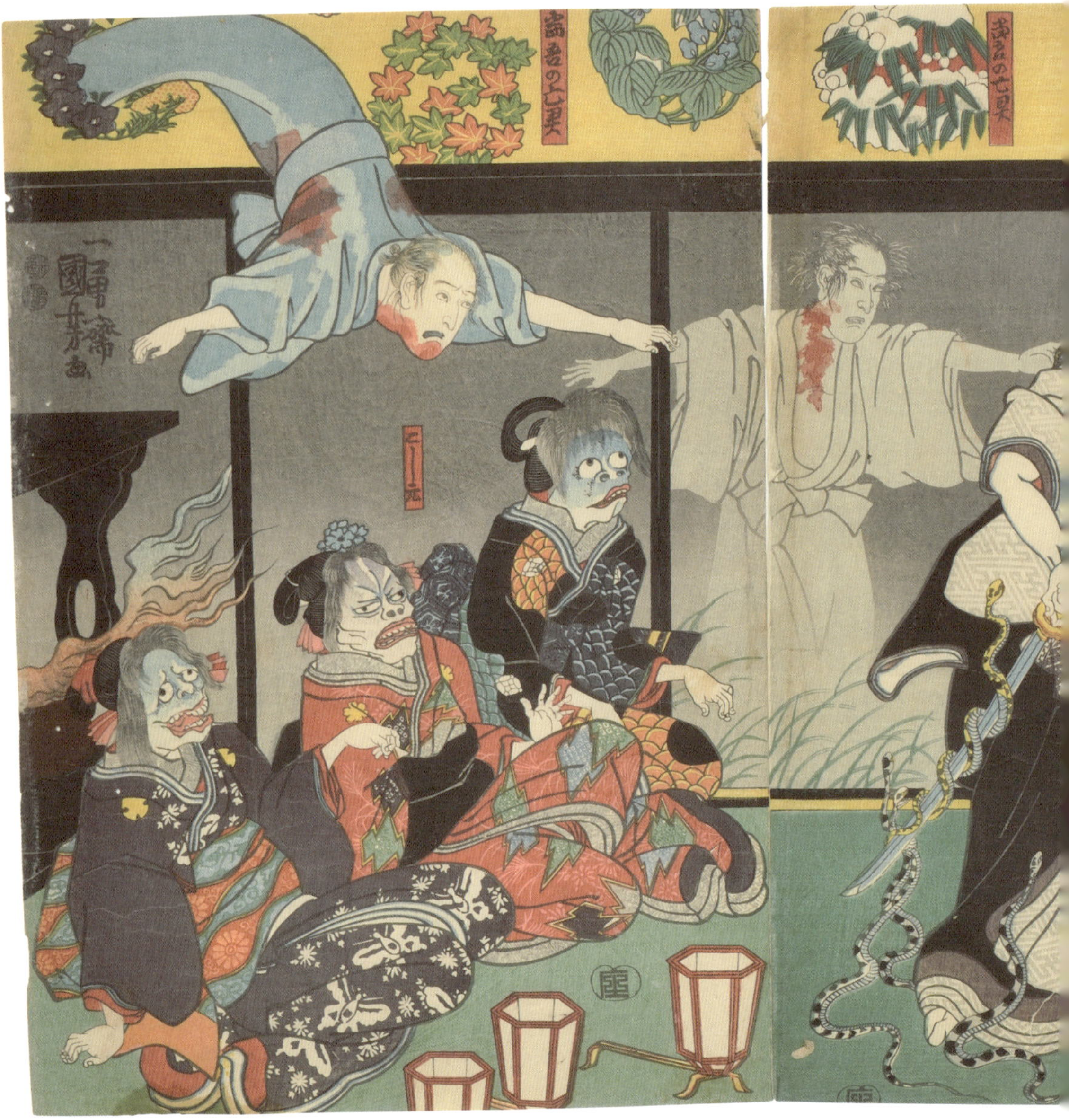

佐倉藩主の重税に苦しめられている農民を救うために名主の佐倉惣五郎は将軍に直訴したことによって死罪となったという義民伝説が庶民の心を掴み、歌舞伎としても上演されて大いに人気を博した。この作品は歌舞伎「東山桜荘子」を題材としたもので、浅倉当吾（佐倉惣五郎）の亡霊が出現して悩まされる織越大領政知（佐倉藩主・堀田正信）。政知は横の当吾の亡霊に気を取られているが、右からも左からも当吾の亡霊は姿を現しており深い恨みが表現されている。傍に侍る腰元たちも骸骨と化し、政知には何匹もの蛇がまとわりついて不気味さを醸し出している。

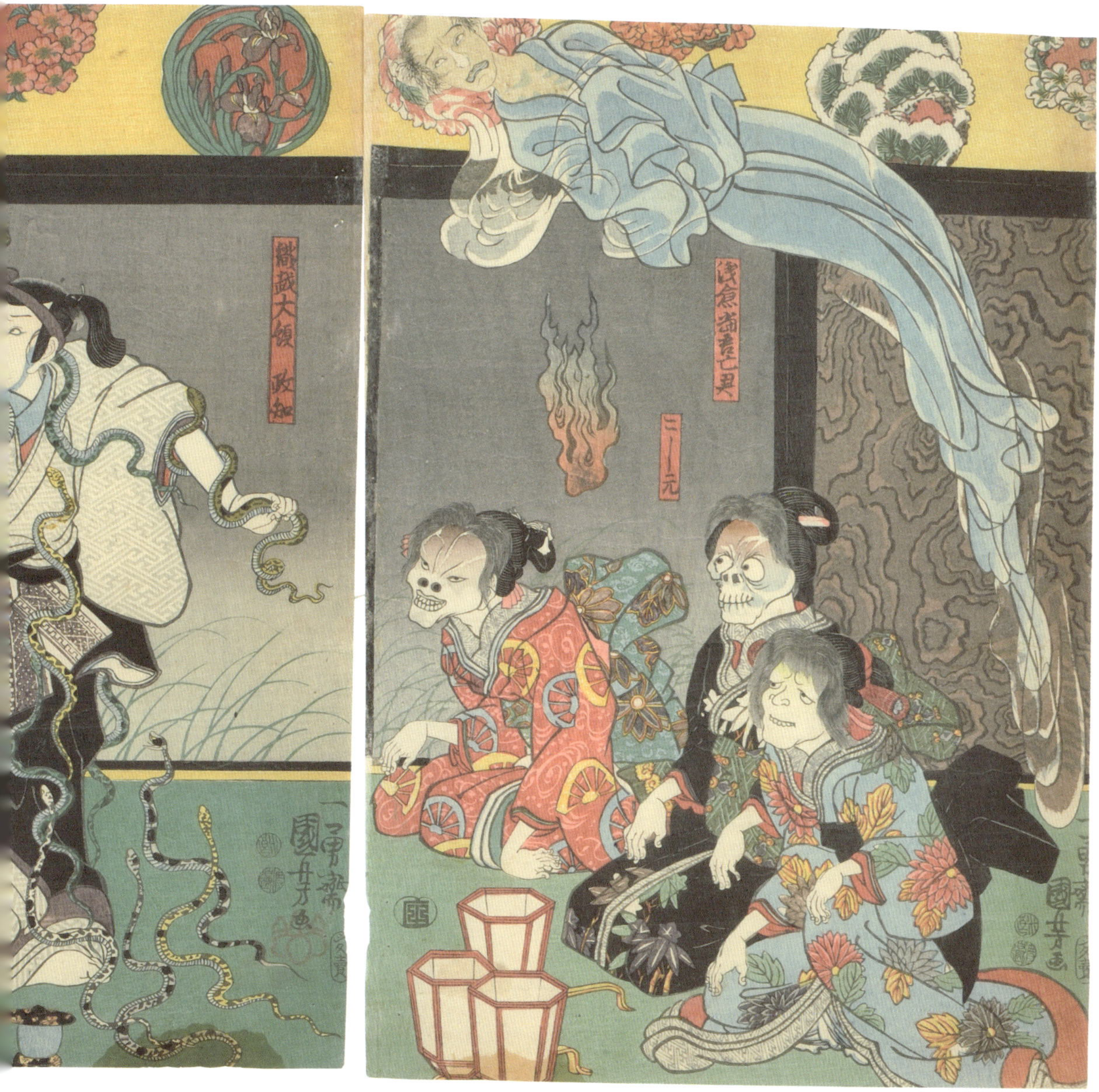

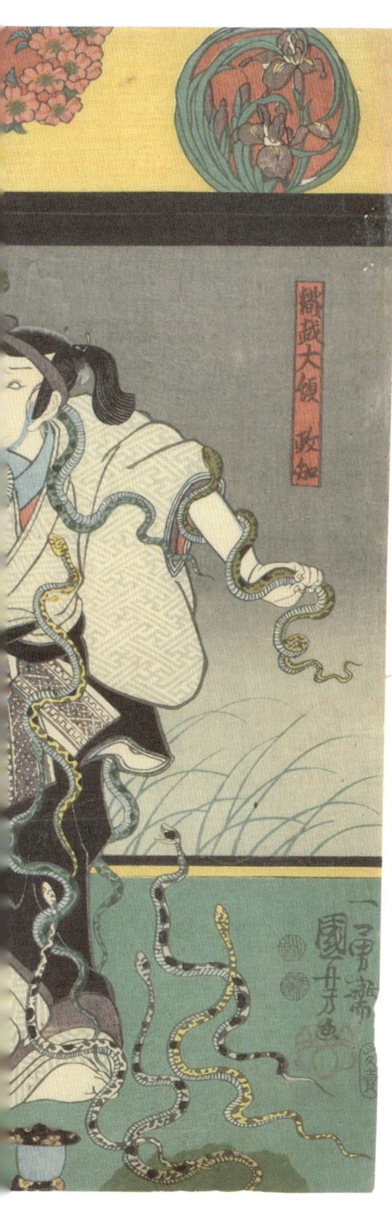

Self-sacrificing village headman Sakura Sōgorō made a direct appeal to the Shōgun to save the farmers suffering under the punitive taxes of the lord of the Sakura Domain and was sentenced to death; his stirring legend became very popular as a kabuki play. This work is based on the kabuki play *Higashiyama Sakura Soshi* (A Tale of Higashiyama Cherry Blossoms), in which Lord Orikoshi Masatomo (the lord of the Sakura Domain, Hotta Masanobu) is haunted by the ghost of Asakura Tōgo (Sakura Sōgorō). Masatomo's attention is held by the ghost of Tōgo on the side, but more ghosts of Tōgo appear from the left and right, illustrating how deeply the grudge runs. The female attendants nearby warp into skeletal forms, and a writhing mass of snakes clings to Masatomo's body, exuding eeriness.

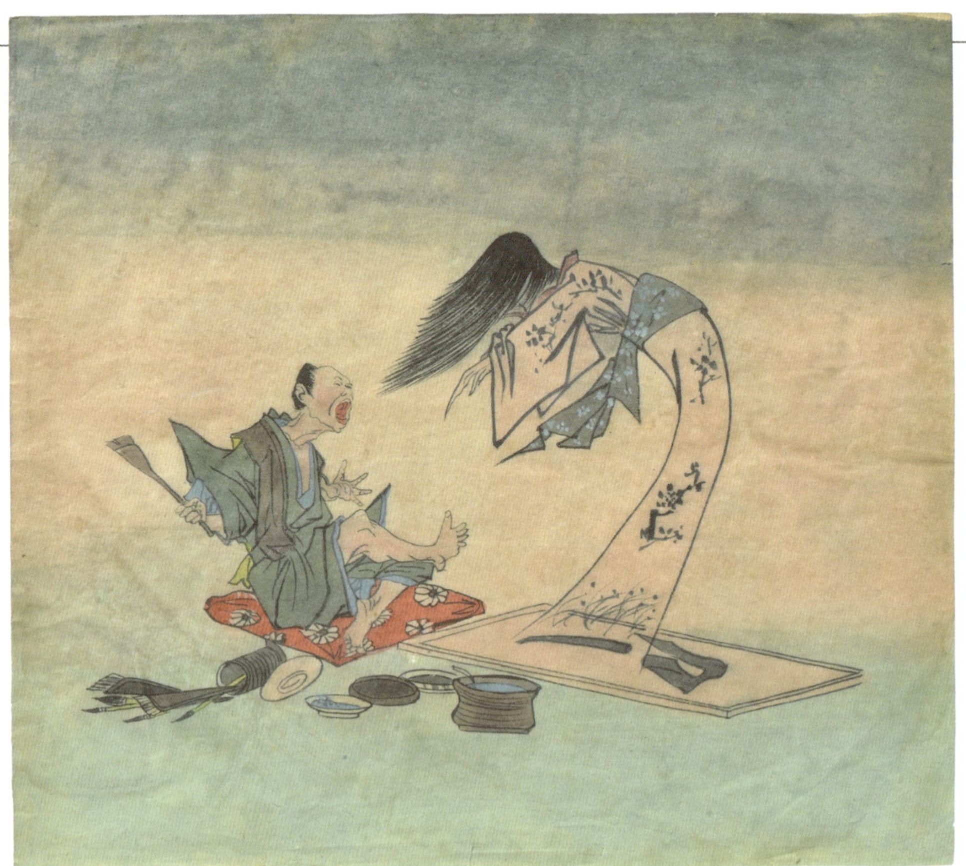

44 　応挙の幽霊
おうきょのゆうれい

Ōkyo's Ghost (*Ōkyo no Yūrei*)
明治時代 Meiji period

月岡芳年が描いた錦絵「応挙の幽霊」を大きなサイズの肉筆で描いた作品で、幽霊の着物に柄があるなどの細かな違いはあるものの、そっくりそのままの構図だ。作者は芳年本人か別人かは不明だが、このようなものも残されているという興味深い資料といえる。

A work based on the *nishiki-e* Ōkyo's Ghost by Tsukioka Yoshitoshi, which uses almost exactly the same composition drawn by hand to a larger size, although there are differences in details such as the pattern of the ghost's kimono. It is not known whether the artist was Yoshitoshi himself or someone else, but this is an interesting artefact.

45 　応挙之幽霊
おうきょのゆうれい

Ōkyo's Ghost (*Ōkyo no Yūrei*)

月岡芳年　明治 15 年（1882）　大判
Tsukioka Yoshitoshi, 1882 (Meiji 15), Ōban

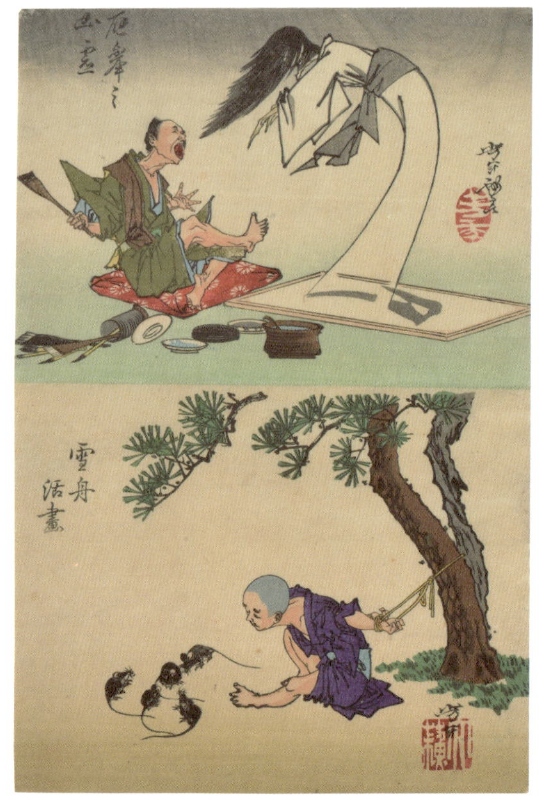

東京自慢十二ヶ月 七月 仲之街 廓の燈篭 小とみ

とうきょうじまんじゅうにかげつ　しちがつ　なかのまち　さとのとうろう　ことみ

"Kotomi of Nakanochō with a Lantern of the Pleasure District" (July)
from the calendar series *Pride of Tokyo's Twelve Months*
(*Tokyo Jiman Jūnikagetsu: Shichigatsu*)

月岡芳年　明治 13 年（1880）3 月　大判　Tsukioka Yoshitoshi, March 1880 (Meiji 13), Ōban

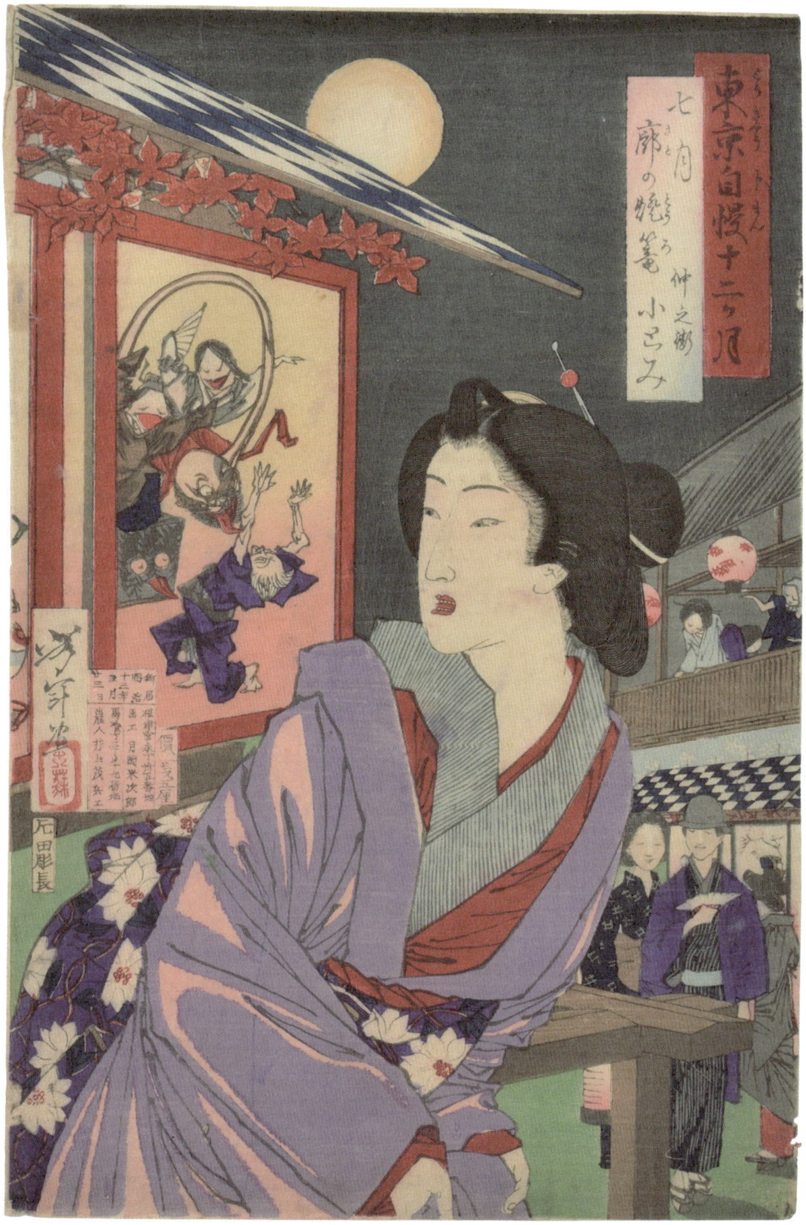

「東京自慢十二ヶ月」シリーズのうち吉原の芸者・小とみを描いた作品だが、小とみの横には大きな燈篭があり、その図柄は葛籠から飛び出したお化けたちだ。小とみの背後にも燈篭がみえるが、こうした吉原の燈篭のなかに図のような妖怪を扱ったものも存在したことが見てとれる資料だ。

Kotomi, a geisha of the Yoshiwara, is depicted beside a large lantern featuring monsters leaping out of a box. Other lanterns are visible behind her as well, but we can see that there were some Yoshiwara lanterns which had yokai on them.

外道化もの
百物かたり
げどうばけものひゃくものがたり

The One Hundred Tales held
by Heretic Monsters
(*Gedō Bakemono*
Hyaku Monogatari)

歌川国芳　江戸時代　大判
Utagawa Kuniyoshi, Edo period, Ōban

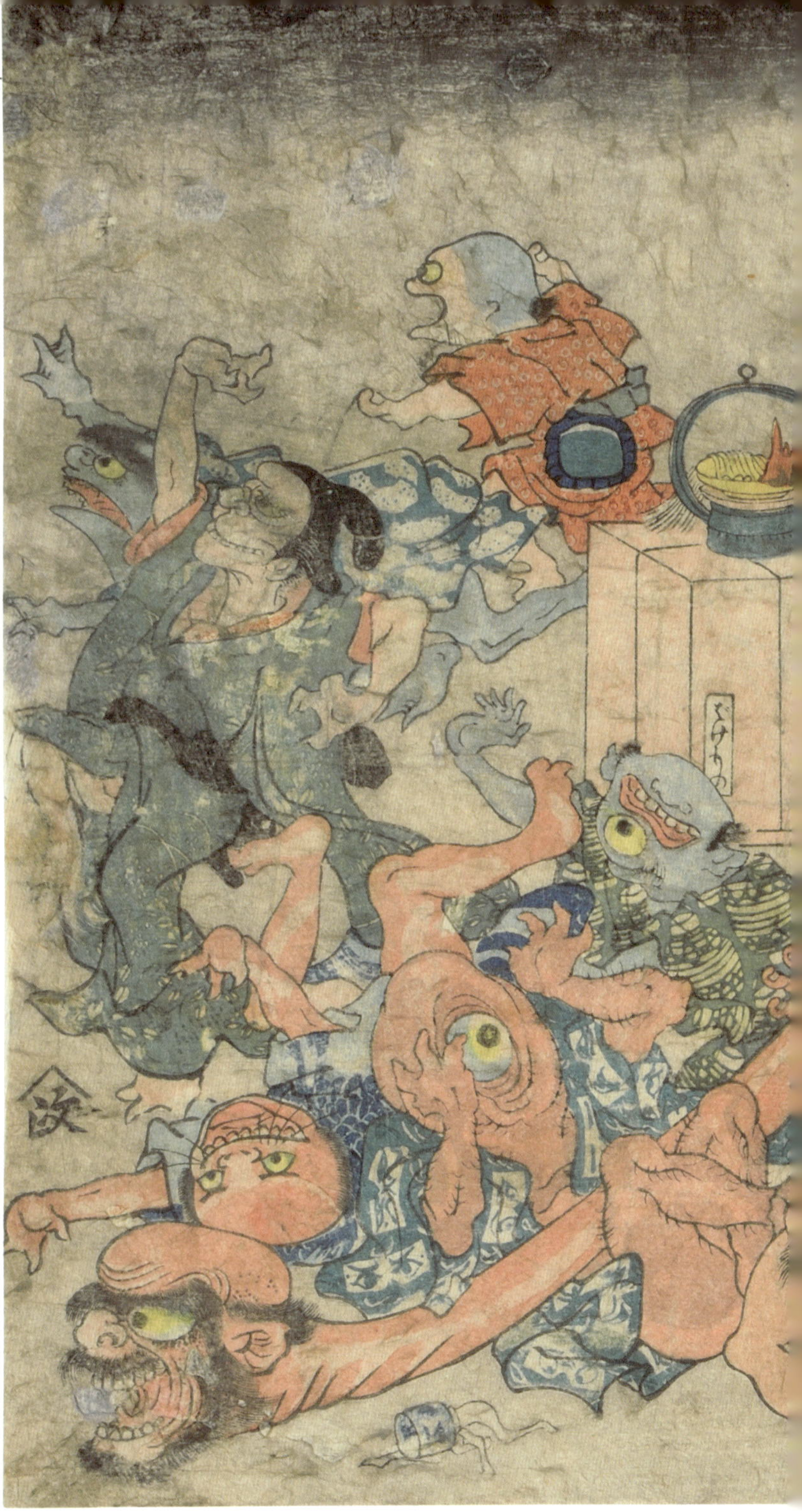

何人もが集まって順番に怪談を話し、一話終わるたびに一本ずつ灯りを消して行き、最後の一本が消えると怪異が起こるという言い伝えがあり、武士たちは肝試しとしてこの言い伝えを実践した。やがて誰もが怖さを楽しむ遊びとして百物語会、怪談会などと称して各地で行われていった。錦絵にも百物語会を描いたものは散見できるが、この作品は国芳の戯画として描かれたもので、化物たちが集まって百物語に夢中になっているところに化物など物ともしない勇猛な武士坂田金平（坂田金時の子）が突然現れて怪異が起こったかのよ

うに化物たちは逃げ惑っている。金平は屏風の裏から狸が突き出した作り物だ。国芳は狸の八畳敷をさまざまなものに擬える戯画を種々描いているが、この作り物も狸の八畳敷に違いない。慌てふためく化物たちはろくろ首、一つ目等々、勢ぞろいで、徳利もが逃げ出している。こんな戯画が描かれたのも百物語が広く流行していたからに他ならない。

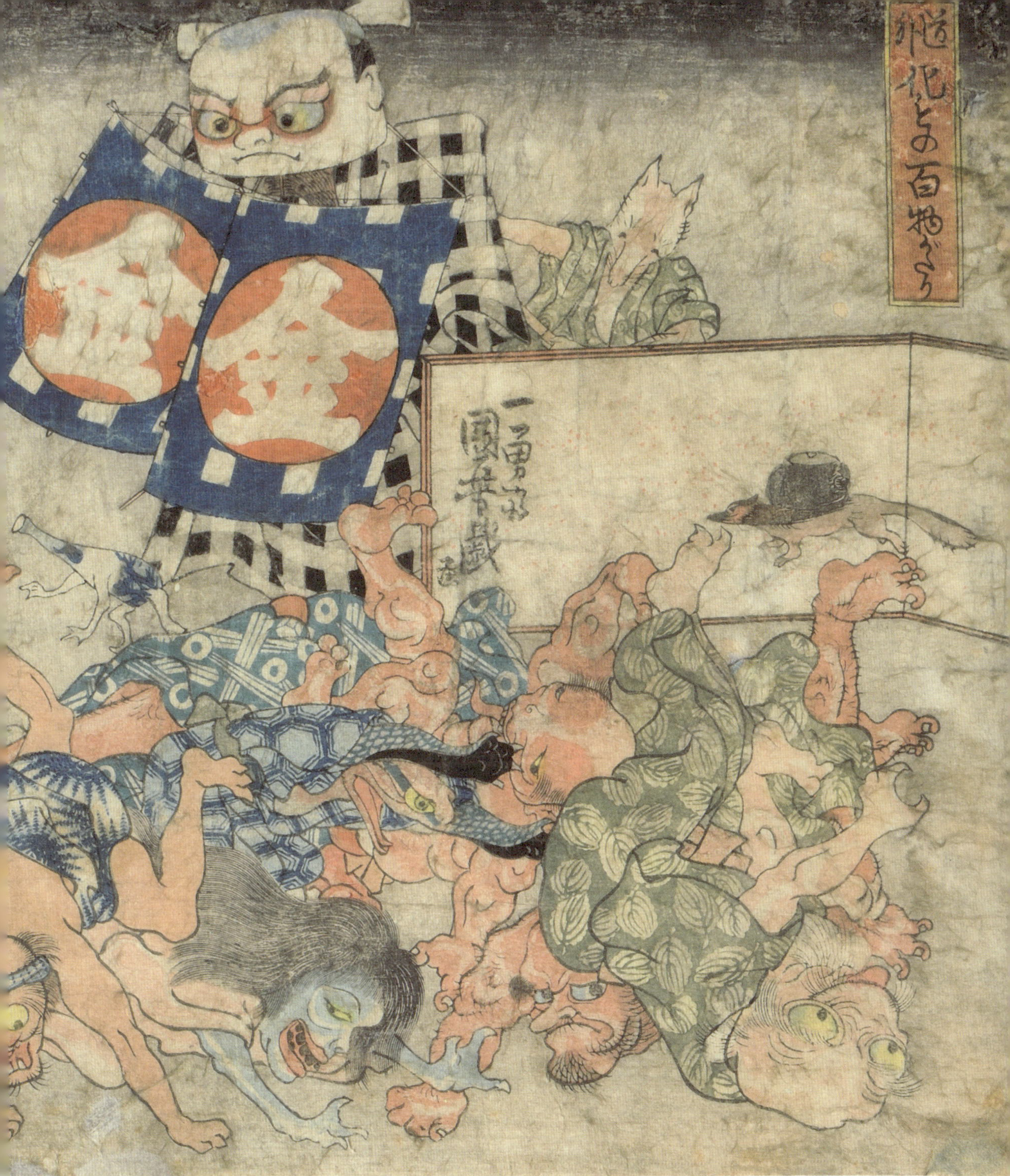

People gathered to tell ghost stories one after another, extinguishing one candle at the end of each tale, until as the last candle went dark supernatural phenomena were believed to occur; this was rumored to have been practiced by samurai as a test of courage. Eventually these gatherings came to be held all over Japan as a thrilling game of fear, known as the *Hyaku Monogatari* (One Hundred Tales) or *kaidankai* (ghost story gathering). There are many *nishiki-e* which depict ghost story gatherings, but this work by Kuniyoshi is a caricature with a gathering of monsters who are absorbed in the game when suddenly the brave warrior and monster-slayer Sakata no Kinpira appears (the son of Kintoki), and the monsters scramble to escape as if something horrible is after them. "Kinpira" is a fake, thrust out from behind a folding screen by a raccoon dog. Kuniyoshi drew a variety of caricatures with eight-tatami raccoon dogs imitating various things: this is unmistakably an eight-tatami raccoon dog. Among the monsters fleeing in panic is a *rokurokubi*, some one-eyed creatures, and even a sake bottle making a run for it. A caricature like this would only have fed the craze for *Hyaku Monogatari*.

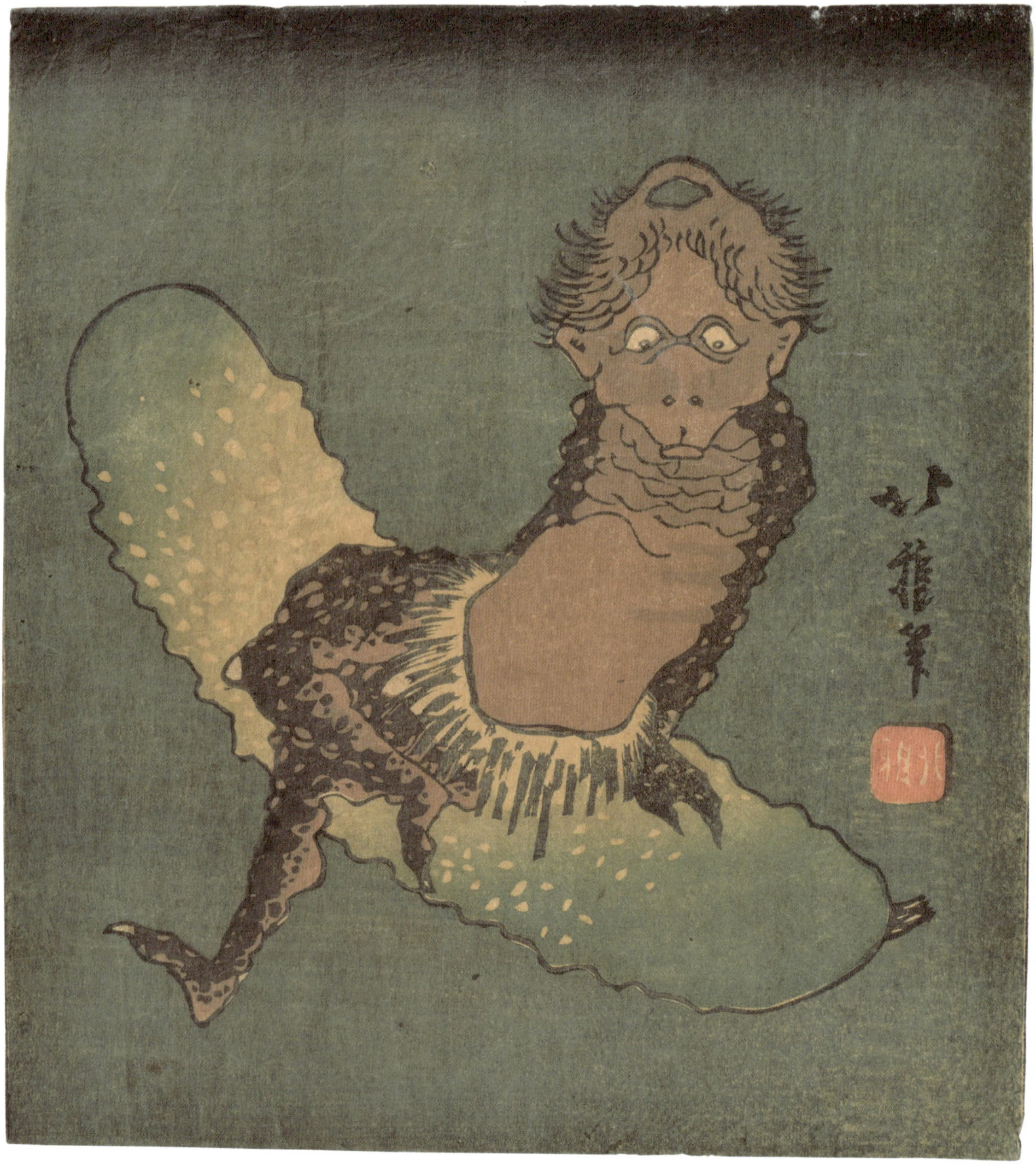

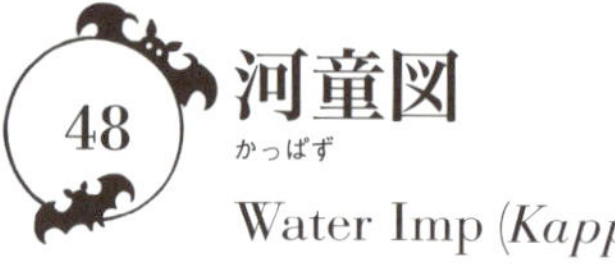

河童図
かっぱず

Water Imp (*Kappa*)

葛飾北雅　江戸時代　Katsushika Hokuga, Edo period

好物の胡瓜に座って足を組んでくつろぐ河童。腰には蓑を巻き、正面を見つめている。河童と胡瓜という構図は少なくないが、この作品もその一つで、ほぼ正方形の紙に描かれている。

A *kappa* lounges with legs folded on its favorite snack: a cucumber. It gazes directly out of the page, straw around its hips. Images of *kappa* with cucumbers are not uncommon, but this work is drawn on a piece of paper which is almost square.

49

妖怪ちりめん本
ようかいちりめんぽん

Creped Book of Yokai
(*Yōkai Chirimen Bon*)

明治時代　Meiji period

日本の昔話などを外国に紹介するために制作された和本スタイルの製本で和紙を縮緬状に加工している。ちりめん本のなかには源頼光の酒呑童子退治など、妖怪譚も何点かみられる。

This is a book produced to introduce local folktales to other countries, which is made of washi paper processed into creped sheets (*chirimen*) and bound in the Japanese style. Minamoto no Yorimitsu's defeat of Shuten-dōji and many other tales of yokai can be found inside.

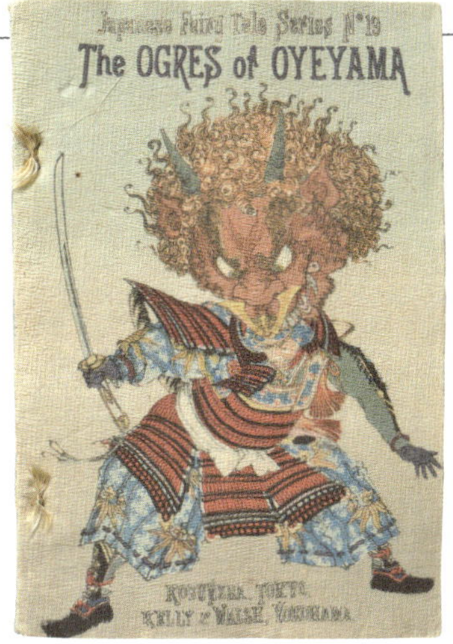

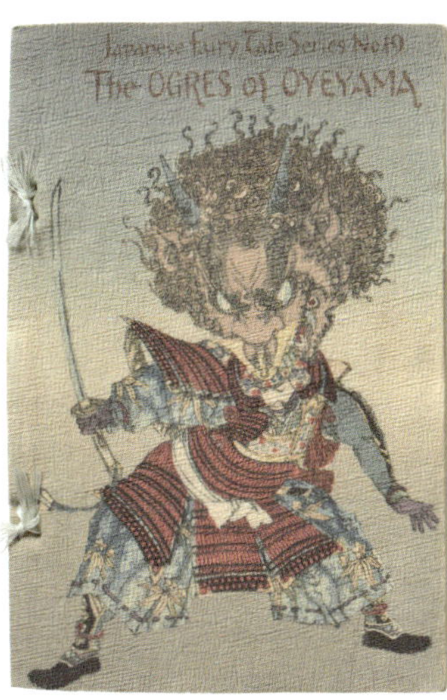

「大江山」縦 15.0　横 10.5　どちらも源頼光の酒呑童子退治をテーマとしている本の表紙。再版や増刷などで配色が異なっていることがわかる。

Ōe-yama Height 15.0, Width 10.5　Both of these covers depict Minamoto no Yorimitsu's defeat of Shuten-dōji. The differences in coloring show that the cover has been reprinted.

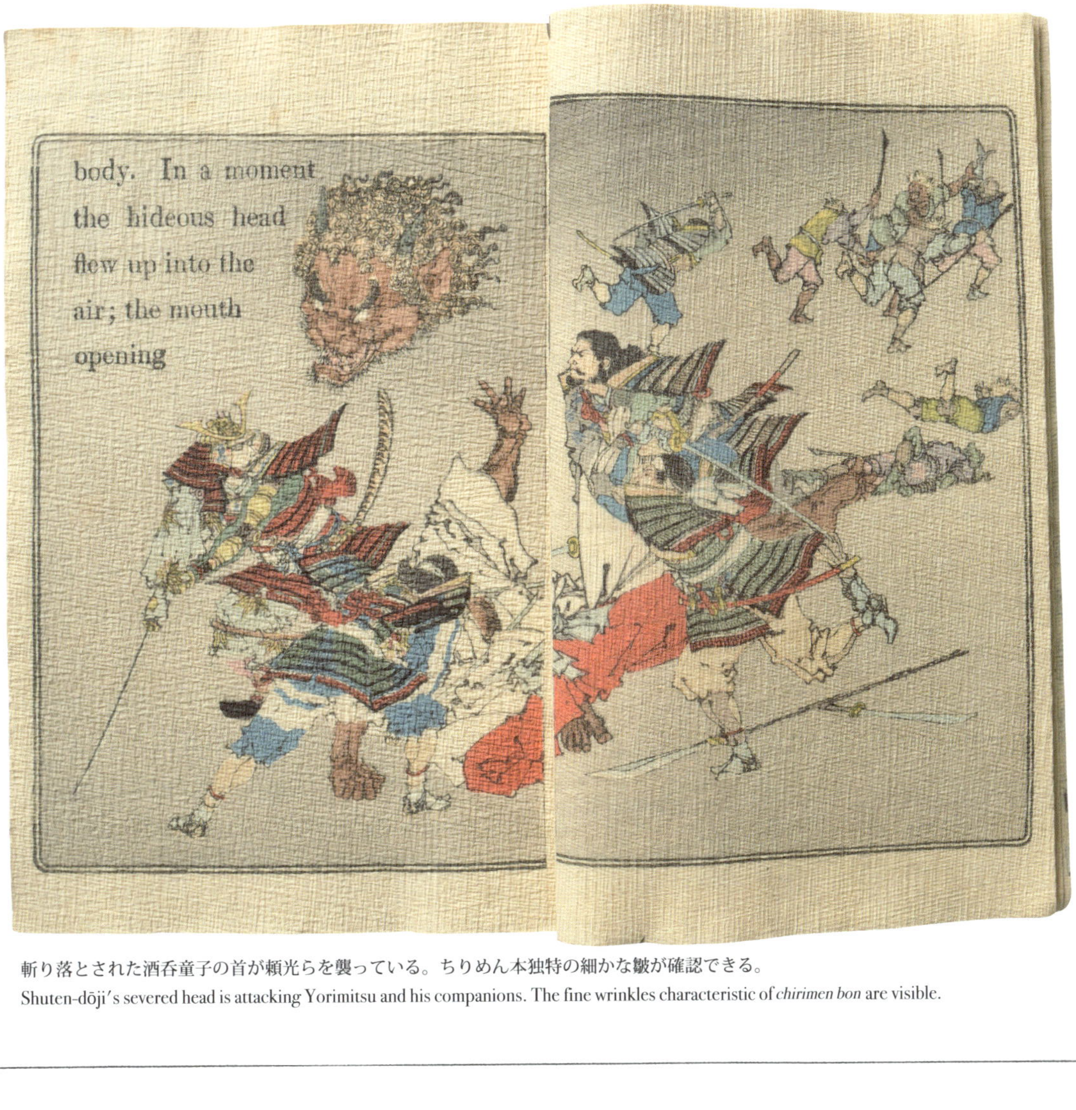

斬り落とされた酒呑童子の首が頼光らを襲っている。ちりめん本独特の細かな皺が確認できる。

Shuten-dōji's severed head is attacking Yorimitsu and his companions. The fine wrinkles characteristic of *chirimen bon* are visible.

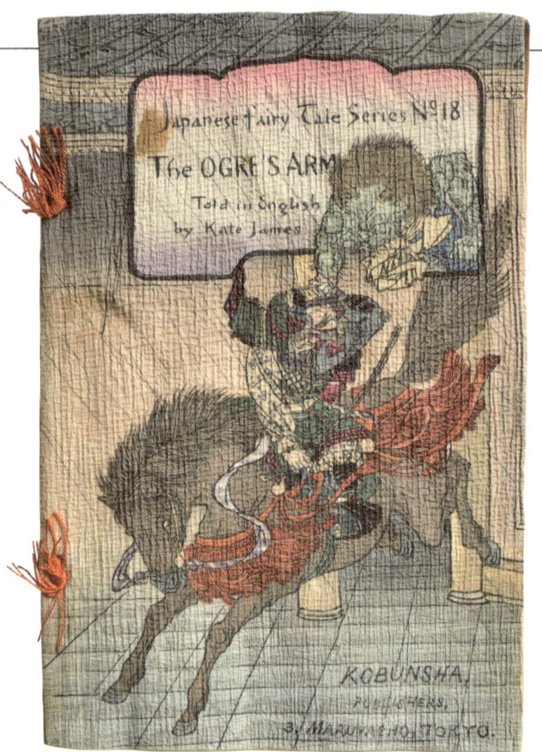

渡辺綱を襲う茨木童子をテーマとした本の表紙。羅生門の上から馬に乗った綱を狙う有名な場面を取り上げている。
This book cover pictures Ibaraki-dōji attacking Watanabe no Tsuna. This is the famous scene in which the ogre pounces on the mounted Tsuna from the top of the Rashōmon gate.

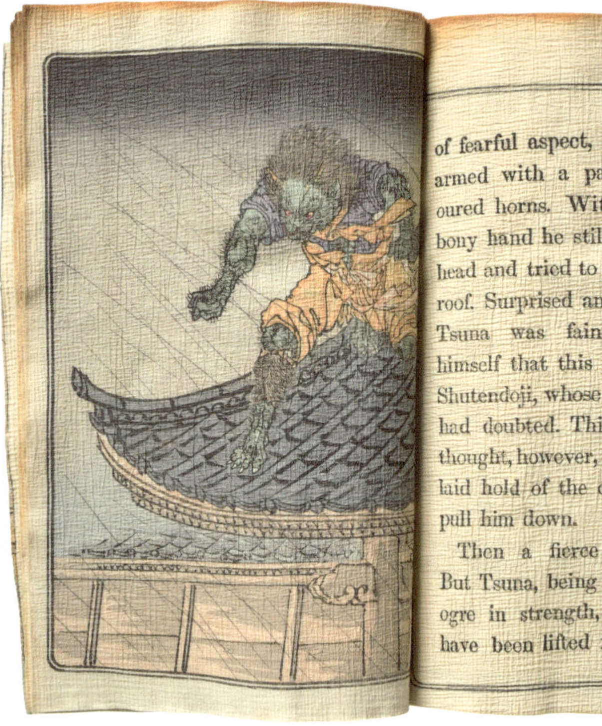

of fearful aspect, b
armed with a pai
oured horns. With
bony hand he still
head and tried to li
roof. Surprised and
Tsuna was fain
himself that this n
Shutendoji, whose v
had doubted. This
thought, however, a
laid hold of the og
pull him down.

Then a fierce
But Tsuna, being n
ogre in strength,
have been lifted fr

羅生門の屋根から綱を見下ろしている茨木童子。
Ibaraki-dōji looks down on Tsuna from the roof of Rashōmon.

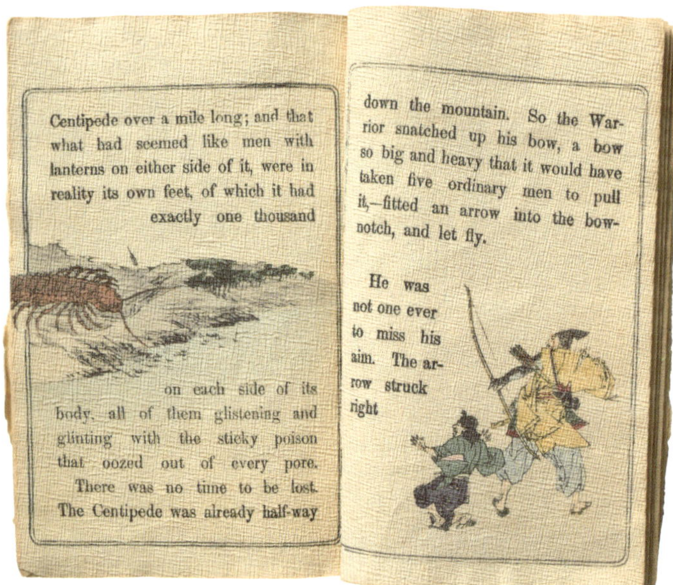

Centipede over a mile long; and that what had seemed like men with lanterns on either side of it, were in reality its own feet, of which it had exactly one thousand on each side of its body, all of them glistening and glinting with the sticky poison that oozed out of every pore. There was no time to be lost. The Centipede was already half-way down the mountain. So the Warrior snatched up his bow, a bow so big and heavy that it would have taken five ordinary men to pull it,—fitted an arrow into the bow-notch, and let fly.

He was not one ever to miss his aim. The arrow struck right

俵藤太の百足退治話で、左端には大百足、左には弓で百足を退治している藤太が描かれている。
The story of Tawara no Tōta's defeat of the centipede, showing the giant centipede on the left, and Tōta with his bow on the right.

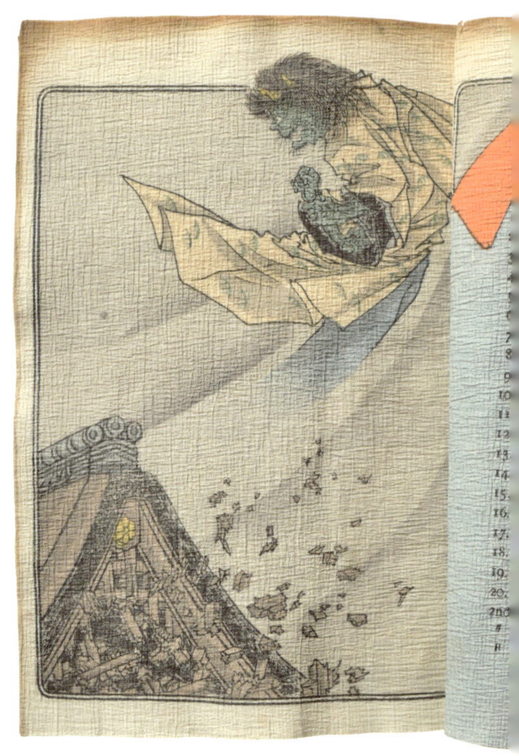

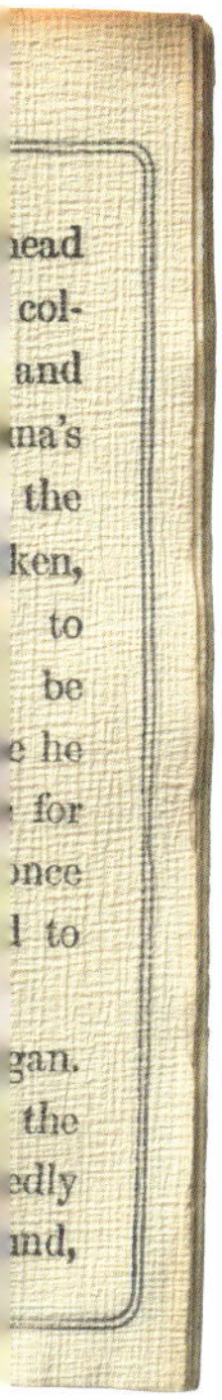

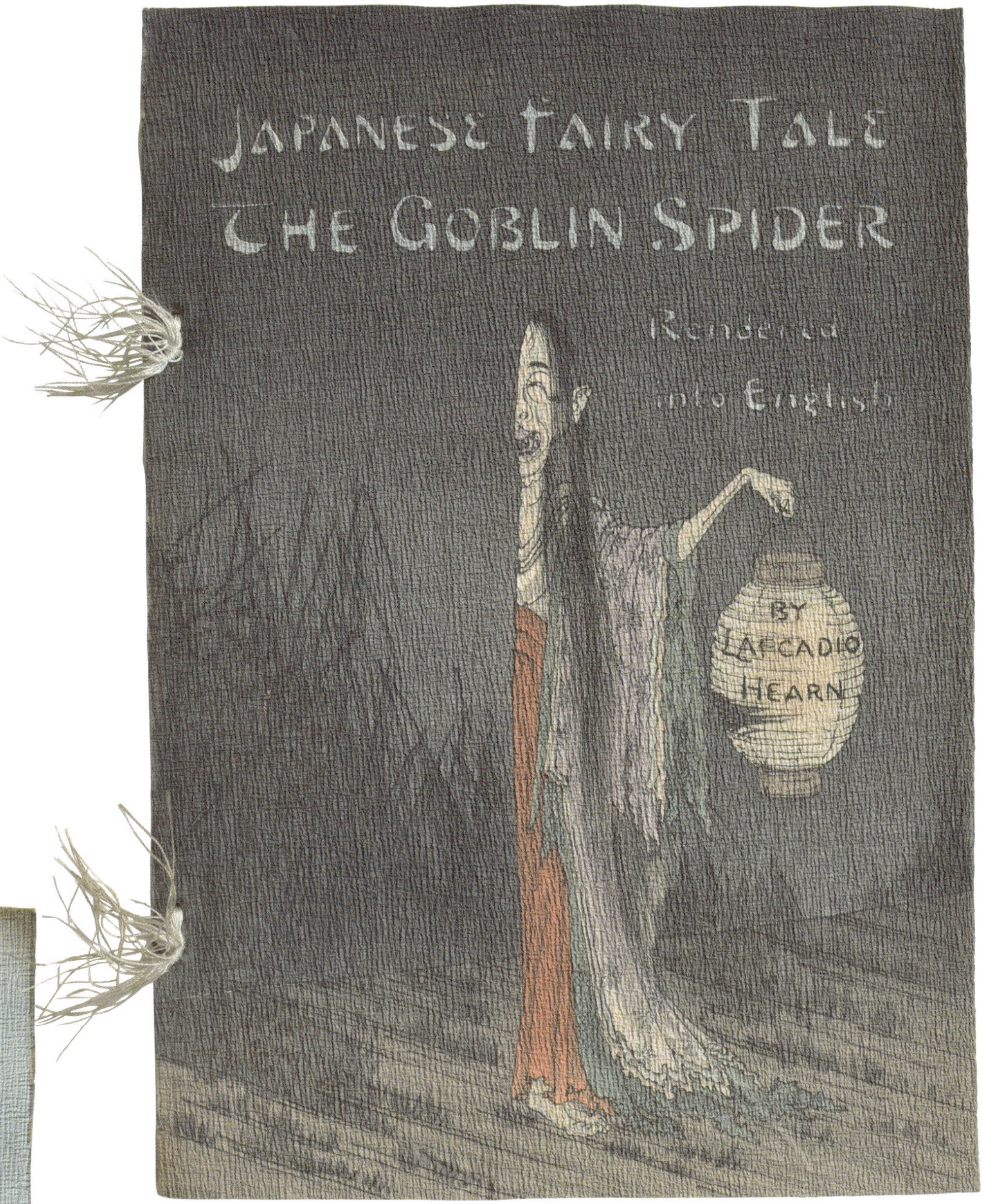

ラフカディオ・ハーンの書いた土蜘蛛の話をテーマとしたちりめん本。
一般的なちりめん本より一回り大きなサイズとなっている。
Chirimen bon (creped book) by Lafcadio Hearn: a tale of *Tsuchigumo*. This
book is slightly larger than most *chirimen bon*.

腕を斬り落とされた茨木童子が腕を取り返して空に消え去る有名な
場面。右ページにはちりめん本のシリーズも紹介されている。
The classic scene in which Ibaraki-dōji retrieves his stolen severed arm
and flees into the sky. On the page on the right, the whole series of books
is advertised.

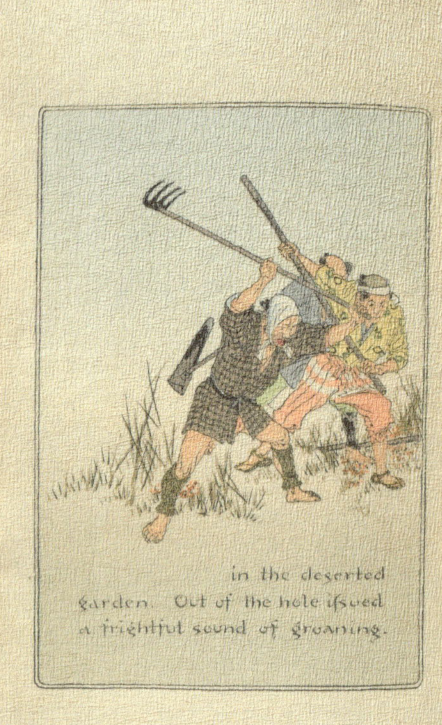

in the deserted garden. Out of the hole issued a frightful sound of groaning.

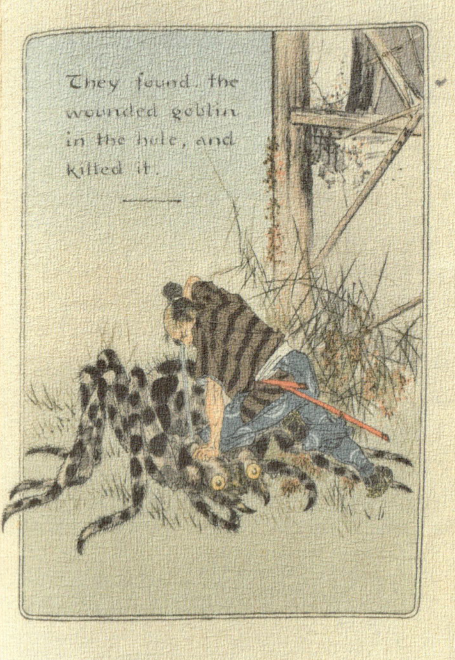

The priest, seeing him, burst out laughing, and said:—"So you thought I was a goblin? Oh no! I am only the priest of this temple; but I have to play to keep off the goblins.—Does not this *samisen* sound well? Please play a little."

And he offered the instrument to the samurai who grasped it very cautiously with his left hand. But instantly the samisen changed into a monstrous spider-web, and the priest into a goblin-spider; and the warrior found himself caught fast in the web by the left hand. He struggled bravely,

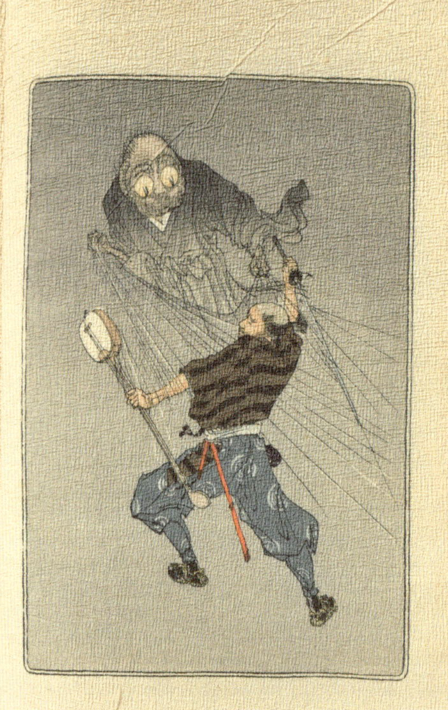

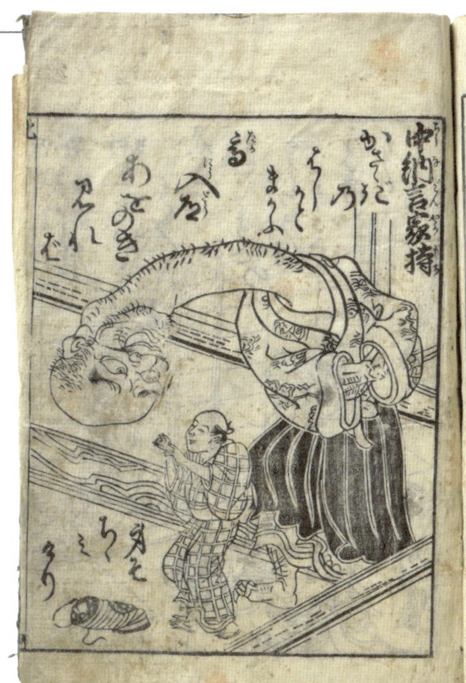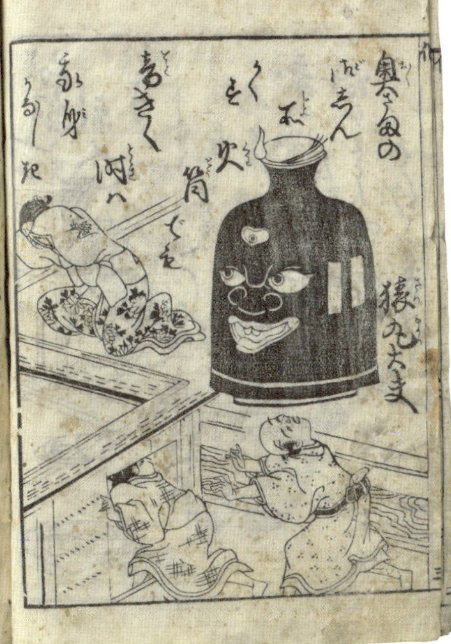

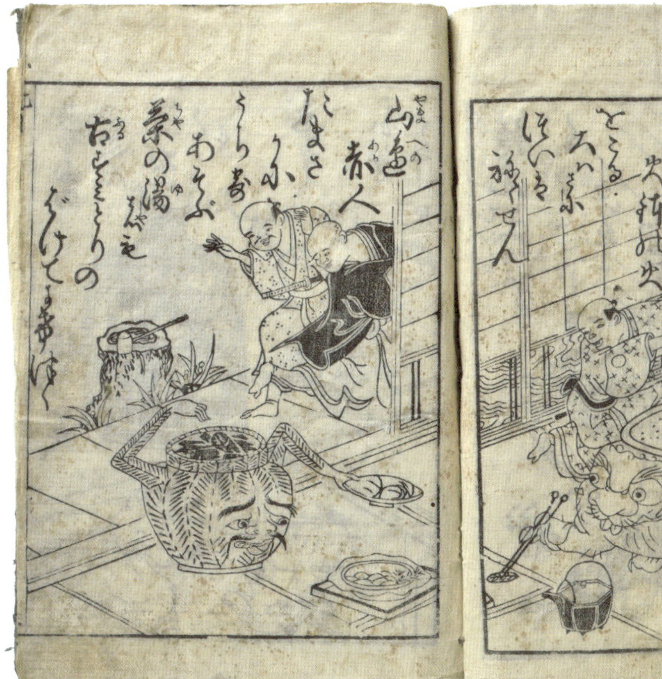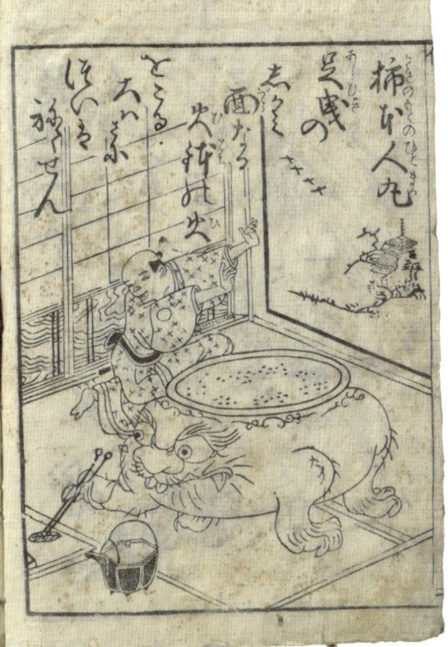

50 化物百人一首
ばけものひゃくにんいっしゅ

One Hundred Monster Poems by One Hundred Poets (*Bakemono Hyakunin Isshu*)

江戸時代　縦 21.5　横 15.3　Edo period, Height 21.5, Width 15.3

題簽はなく、柱に「化」とある。小倉百人一首の歌人たちの和歌の妖怪版パロディとなっている。江戸時代には妖怪をテーマとした狂歌遊びも行われたが、そうした流行のなかでこのような本もだされていったのだろう。

There is no title provided, but "*Bake*" is written on the center fold. This is a yokai parody of the anthology of *waka* poems by one hundred different poets *Ogura Hyakunin Isshu*. In the Edo period yokai were used as a theme for games of *kyōgen* verse, and books like this one were produced during the craze.

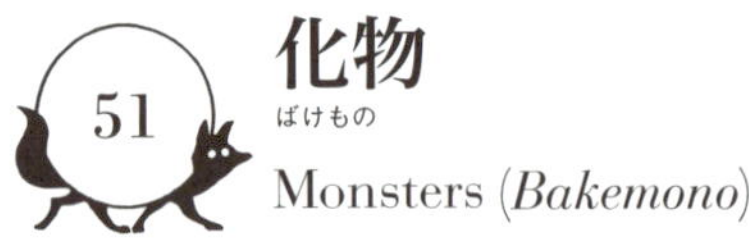

51 化物
ばけもの

Monsters (*Bakemono*)

江戸時代　縦 21.5　横 15.3　Edo period, Height 21.5, Width 15.3

題簽はないが柱に「化物」とある。器物の妖怪たちが暴れまわって人々を驚かせている内容。図 1 は煙草盆に押しつぶされている武士、常夜灯と戦う武士、用水樽が水を流して襲ってきたので逃げ出す武士。図 2 は室内で跋扈する鏡台、三味線、琵琶などで、侍女たちは怯えきっている。

No title is given, but on the center fold is written *"Bakemono"*. Inside, yokai of household objects are running riot and frightening people. Figure1 shows samurai being squashed under old-fashioned tobacco equipment (*tabako bon*), fighting with a night-light, and running away from a water-spitting cask. Figure 2 depicts a dresser, a *shamisen*, and a *biwa* (Japanese lute) intimidating a room of ladies-in-waiting.

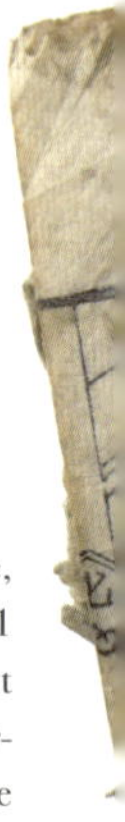

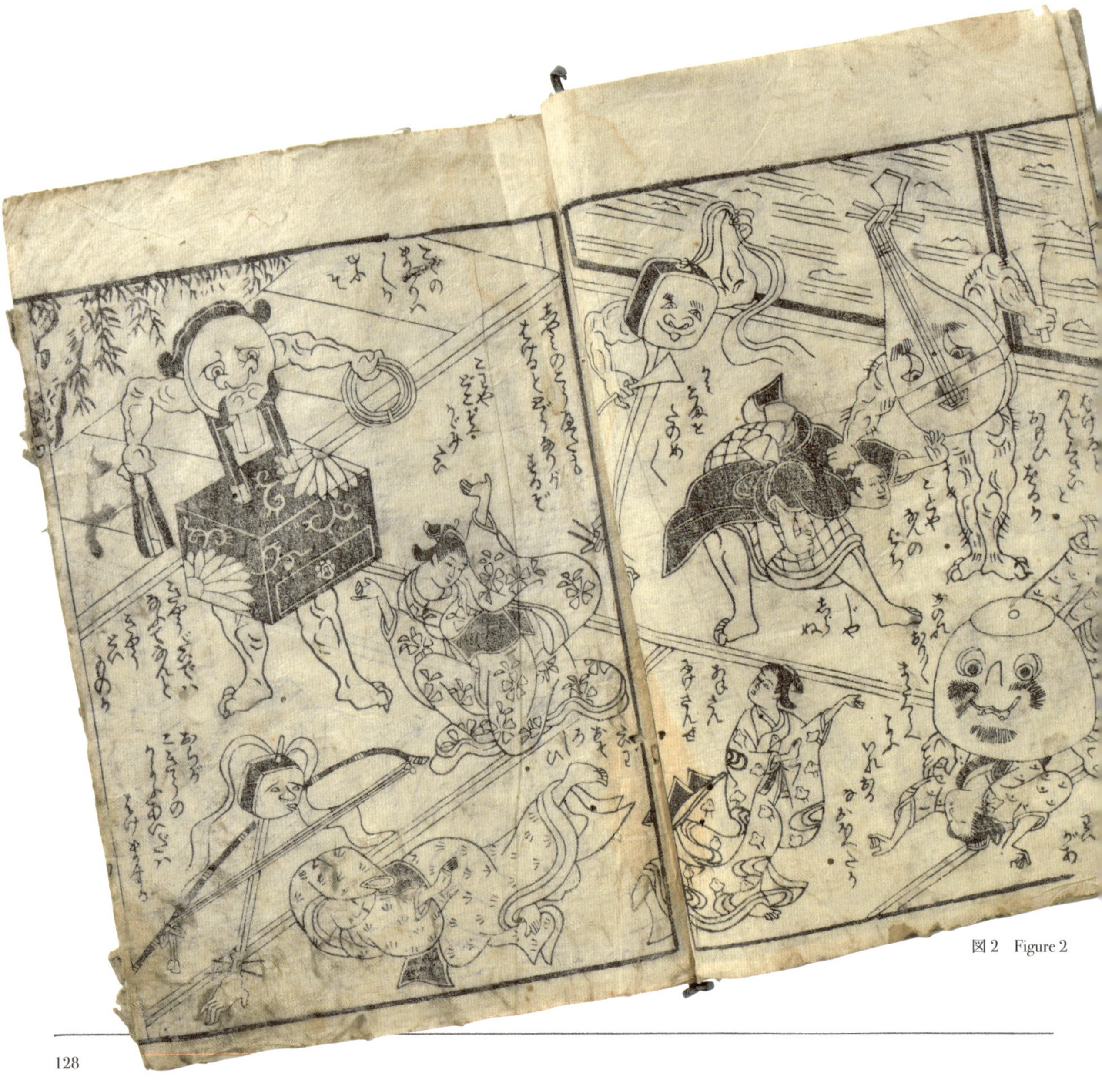

図 2　Figure 2

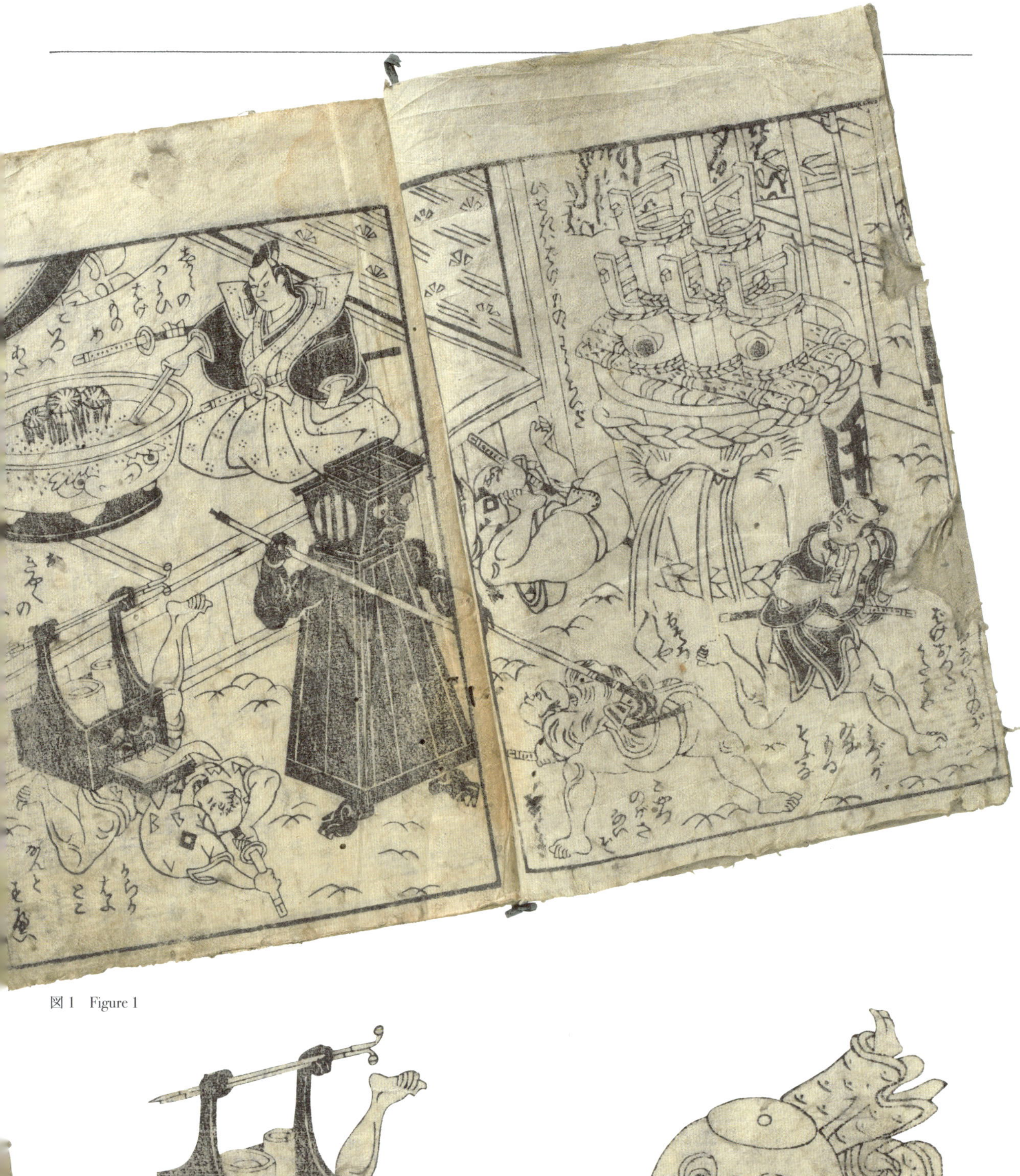

図1　Figure 1

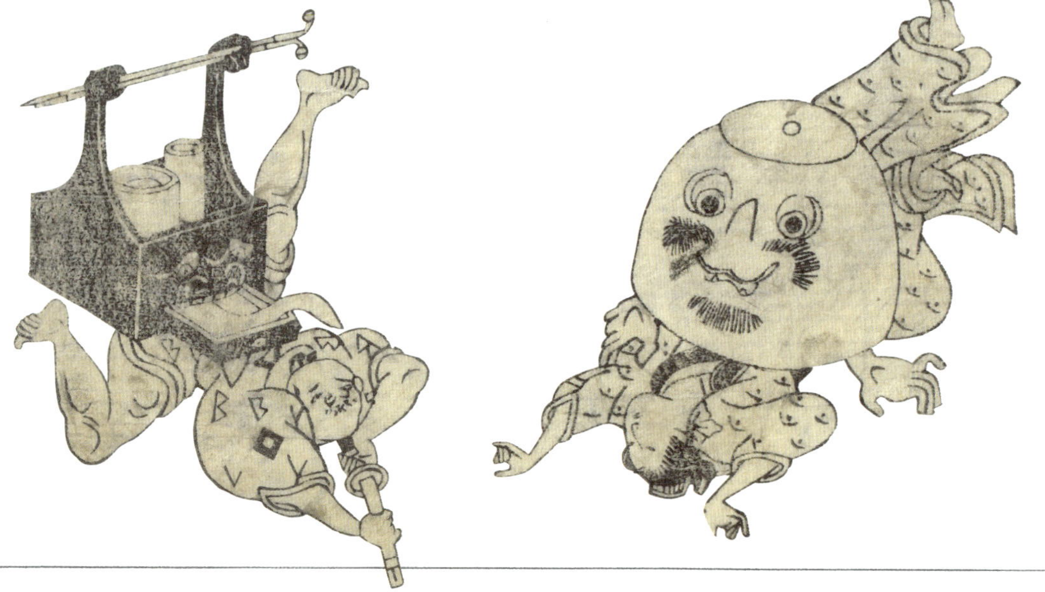

52 絵本怪談揃
えほんかいだんそろえ

Illustrated Book of Collected Ghost Stories
(*Ehon Kaidan Soroe*)

江戸時代　縦 21.5　横 15.6
Edo period, Height 21.5, Width 15.6

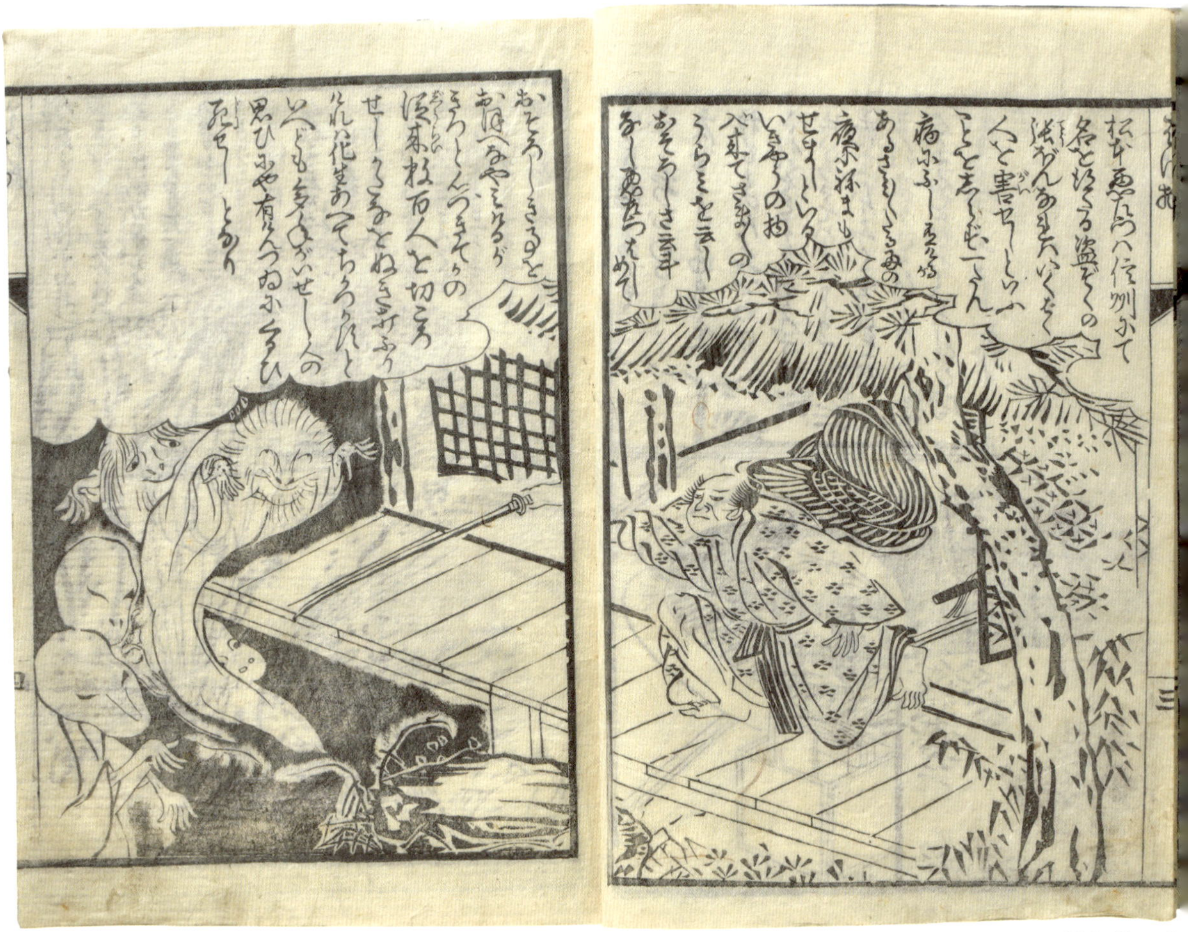

図1　Figure 1

表紙の題簽に「絵本怪談揃 全」とあるが、柱には「ばけ物」と書かれている。見開きで一話一話を紹介するスタイルとなっている。図1は信州の松本惣左衛門という盗賊の頭が数百人を殺め、その亡霊に悩まされて狂い死にするという内容。庭先に現れたいくつもの亡霊に刀を抜いて斬りかかる惣左衛門が描かれている。図2は伊賀国で病死した妻が毎夜のように生前の姿で現れるので夫が患ってしまったことを伝え聞いた友人の石川庄右衛門が泊まり込んで夜中に現れた死んだ妻に斬りつけると4〜5尺もある猫股だった。斬りつけられて顔や指は変じて正体を現す猫股。

On the cover is written *"The Illustrated Book of Collected Ghost Stories: Unabridged"* (*"Ehon Kaidan Soroe Zen"*). Each story is set out on a double-page spread. The first picture shows Matsumoto Sōzaemon, a bandit chief of the Shinshu region who killed hundreds of people and was driven to madness and death by their ghosts. Sōzaemon is pictured swinging his sword at the ghosts flocking in from the garden. The second one is the story of a wife who died of her illness in Iga Province but continued to appear in the form she had in life; when a concerned friend Ishikawa Shouemon heard of her husband's suffering he stayed over, slashed at the dead wife when she appeared in the middle of the night, and discovered that the visiting spirit was a forked cat (*nekomata*) about 4–5 feet tall. The face and hands of the nekomata have shifted shape under the onslaught, giving away her true form.

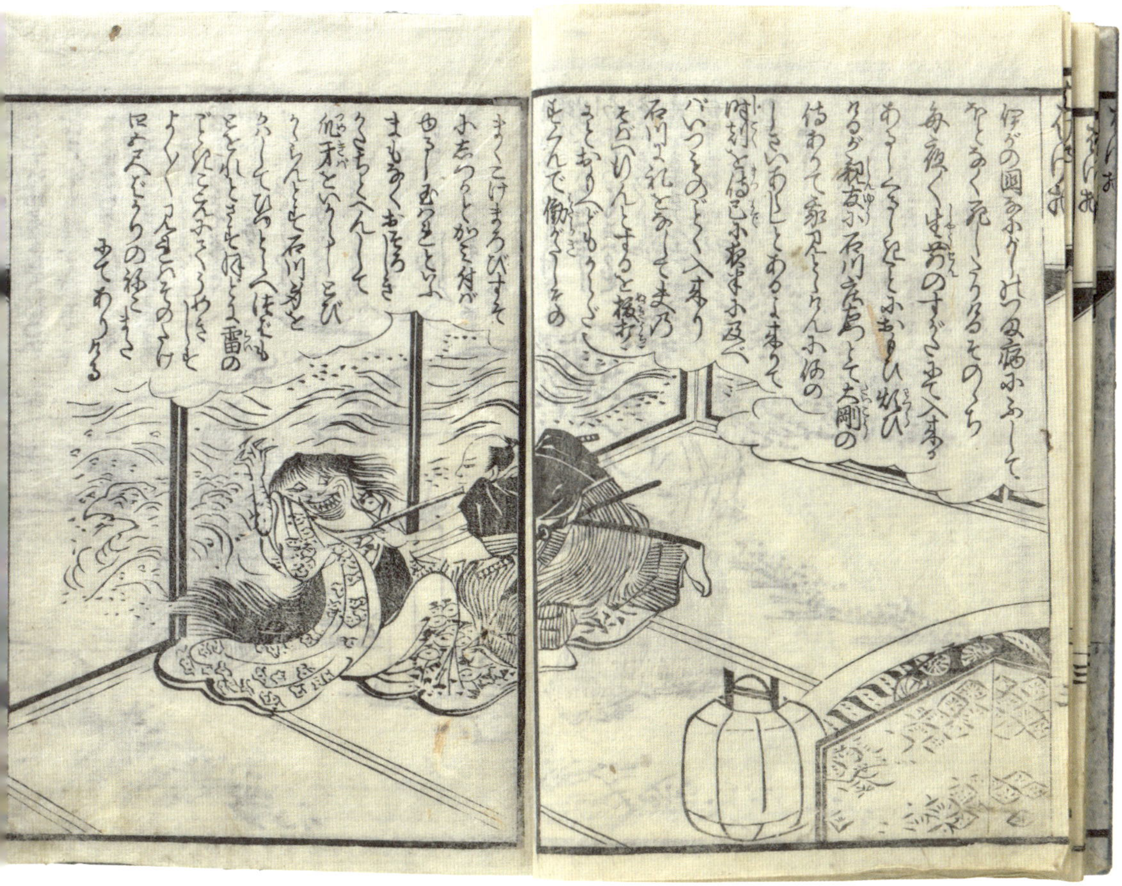

版木「花村座花川弥三郎」
はんぎ　はなむらざはなかわやさぶろう

Printing woodblock *Hanamura-za Hanakawa Yasaburō*

江戸時代　Edo period

印刷物の怪異、妖怪資料はさまざまなものが残されているが、それを刷った版木資料は極めて少ない。この版木は怪談の上演に関する刷り物のために作られたもので、幽霊が大きく彫られた上に「怪談」の文字がみえる。その版木による印刷物は確認できないが、版木だけしかないケースもあり、版木は貴重な資料といえる。

A multitude of prints of yokai and the supernatural remain to this day, but the woodblocks which created them are very rare. This woodblock was made for a print advertising a performance of spooky tales; above the large engravings of ghosts is the inscription *"Kaidan"* (ghost stories). As the woodblock alone remains, there are no prints made from this block to see, but this makes the relic all the more precious.

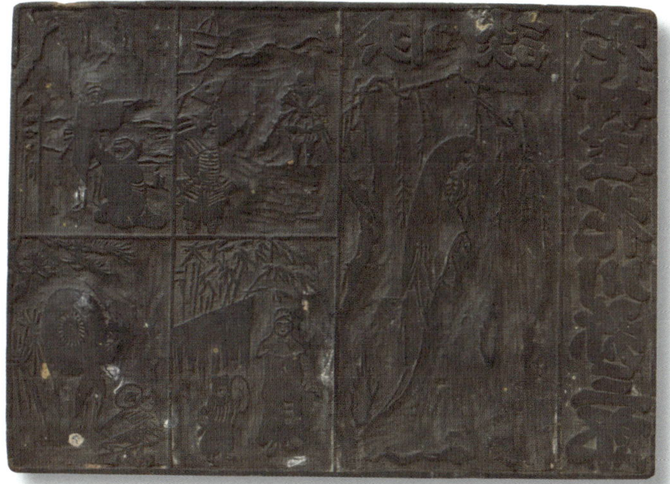

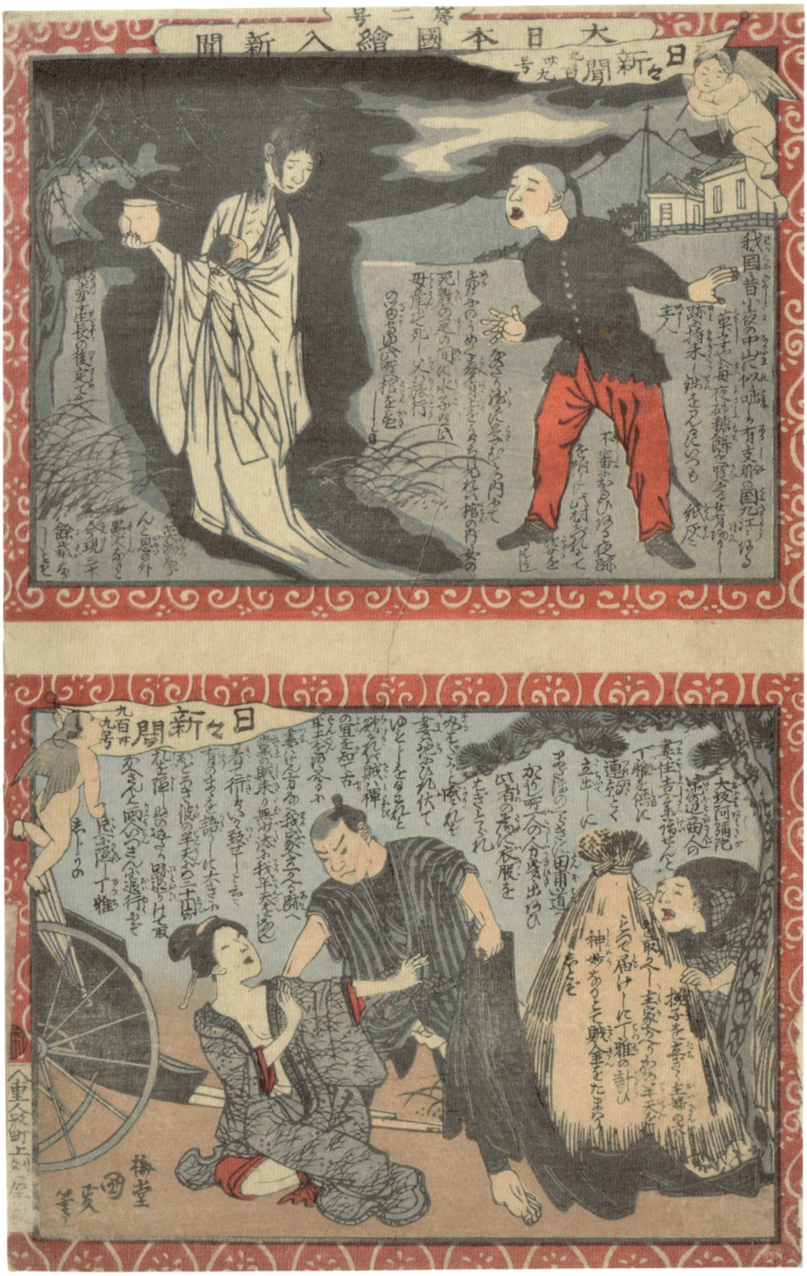

大日本国絵入新聞　第二号
だいにっぽんこくえいりしんぶん

Great Japan Illustrated News (*Dai-nippon-koku E-iri Shinbun*) Number 2

梅堂国政　明治時代　大判　Umedō Kunimasa, Meiji period, Ōban

「日々新聞」939 号（上段）と同じく 939 号（下段）の 2 つの記事を紹介した二丁掛の新聞錦絵。上段は中国での幽霊話で、九江というところの菓子屋に毎夜のように砂糖餅を買いに来る女性を不審に思った店主が女性の後をつけて行くと草むらに女性の死骸があり、女性はその傍らの赤子のために砂糖餅を買っていたのだった。その赤子は現在 30 余歳となって生きているということだ。

Two-panel news *nishiki-e* presenting two articles from *Nichinichi Shimbun* number 939. The upper panel is a ghost story from China: every night a woman comes to buy sugar rice-cakes at a sweet shop in Jiujiang, and when the shop owner grows suspicious and follows her, he finds the baby she had been buying the sugar rice-cakes for next to her corpse in the grass. It goes on to say that the baby is still alive and past the age of 30.

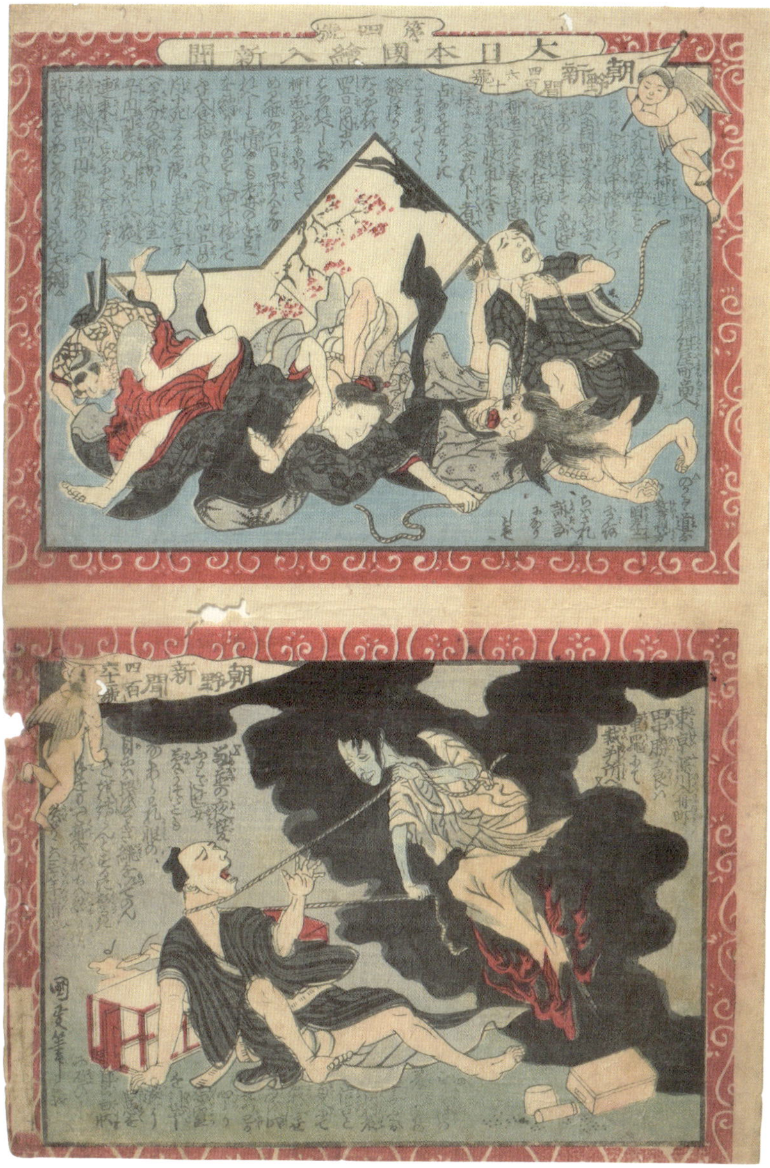

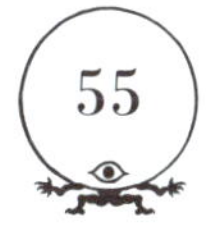

大日本国絵入新聞
第四号

だいにっぽんこくえいりしんぶん

Great Japan Illustrated News
(*Dai-nippon-koku E-iri Shinbun*)
Number 4

梅堂国政　明治時代　大判

Umedō Kunimasa, Meiji period, Ōban

「朝野新聞」460号（上段）と462号（下段）の2つの記事を紹介した二丁掛の新聞錦絵。下段には重罪で裁判所に留置かれた者に以前殺害した女性の幽霊が出現したためにその罪も白状したという記事を錦絵にしている。

Two-panel news *nishiki-e* presenting two articles from *Chōya Shimbun* numbers 460 (upper) and 462 (lower). The lower panel is a *nishiki-e* of an article in which a person detained at the courthouse on serious charges is visited by the ghost of a woman he murdered and driven to confess to her murder as well.

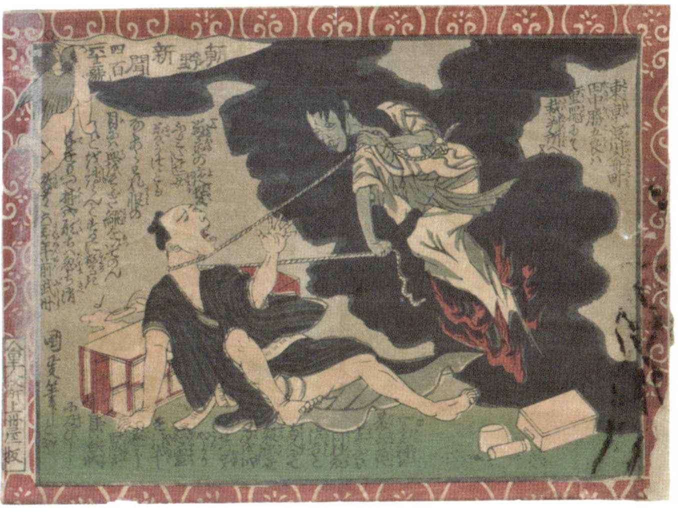

参考図版

56

大阪錦絵新聞 第四号
おおさかにしきえしんぶん

*Osaka Nishiki-e Shimbun
Number 4*

笹木芳光　明治時代　Sasaki Yoshimitsu, Meiji period

大阪天満で人力車に乗せた客が到着地まで来ると消えていたという話。狐に化かされたものだろうが、お稲荷さまから幸運がもたらされるだろうとの車夫の感想も記事にしている。人力車に乗せた客が消えたという話題は当時の新聞に散見できる。

A passenger riding in a rickshaw from Tenma in Osaka vanished when he reached his destination. Comments from the rickshaw man also made the news: he believed the passenger had turned into a fox, but he had been blessed by Oinari-sama (the fox god). Articles on the rickshaw passenger who vanished can be found in the newspapers of the day.

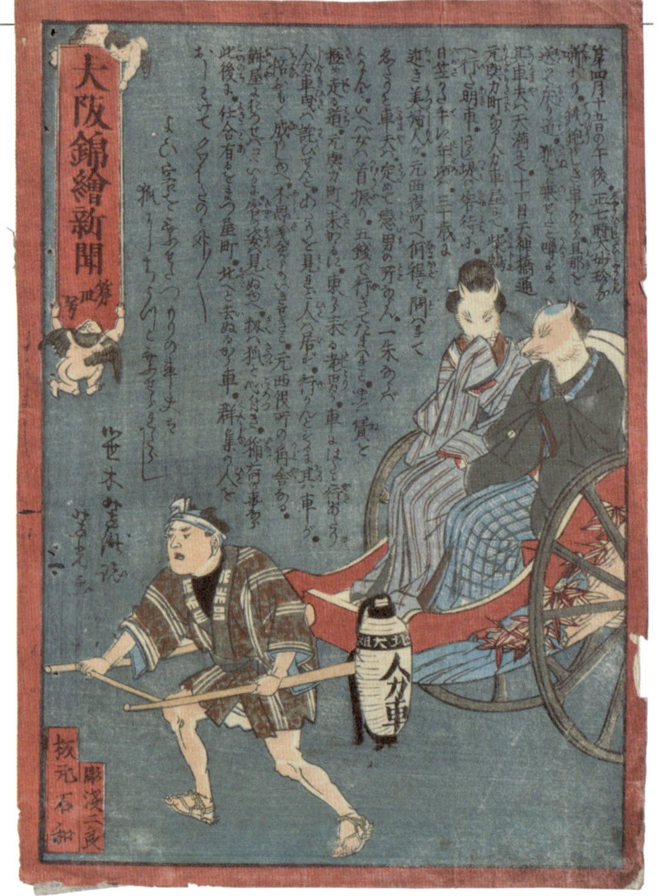

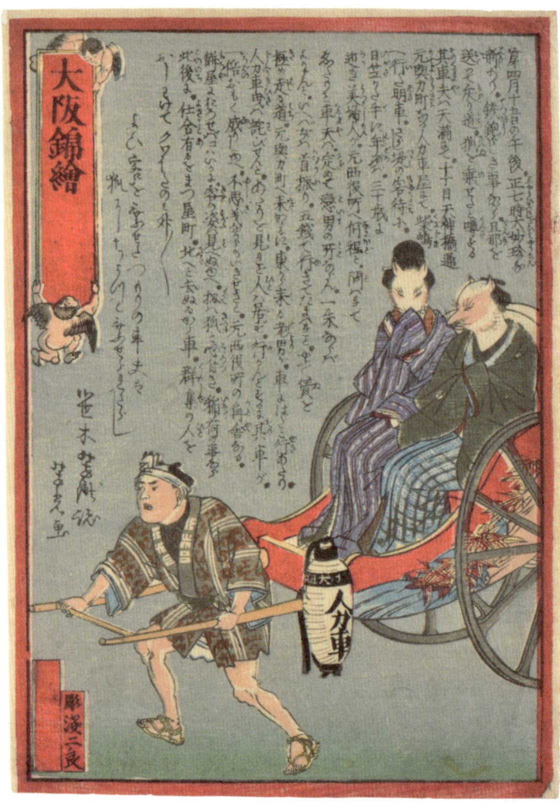

57

大阪錦絵
おおさかにしきえ

Osaka Nishiki-e

笹木芳光　明治時代　Sasaki Yoshimitsu, Meiji period

「大阪錦絵新聞 第四号」と記事の絵も同じものだが、タイトルは「大阪錦絵」となっており、「版元 石和」という文字も消されている。こうした改変したスタイルの錦絵新聞はいくつか出されているのは人気があったからなのだろう。

The same illustration from *Osaka Nishiki-e Shimbun* Number 4, but the title is *Osaka Nishiki-e*, and the text "Printer Isawa" is missing. Due to the popularity of news *nishiki-e* many were reproduced with slight alterations.

大阪日々新聞紙 第十三号

おおさかにちにちしんぶんし

Osaka Nichinichi Shimbunshi
Number 13

長谷川貞信（2代）　明治時代
Hasegawa Sadanobu II, Meiji period

東京伝馬町の大工棟梁の家に毎夜 12 時ころに現れる黒
坊主の怪を取り上げた新聞錦絵。
News *nishiki-e* on the phenomenon of the black monk who
appeared at midnight every night in a master carpenter's
house in Tenma-chō, Tokyo.

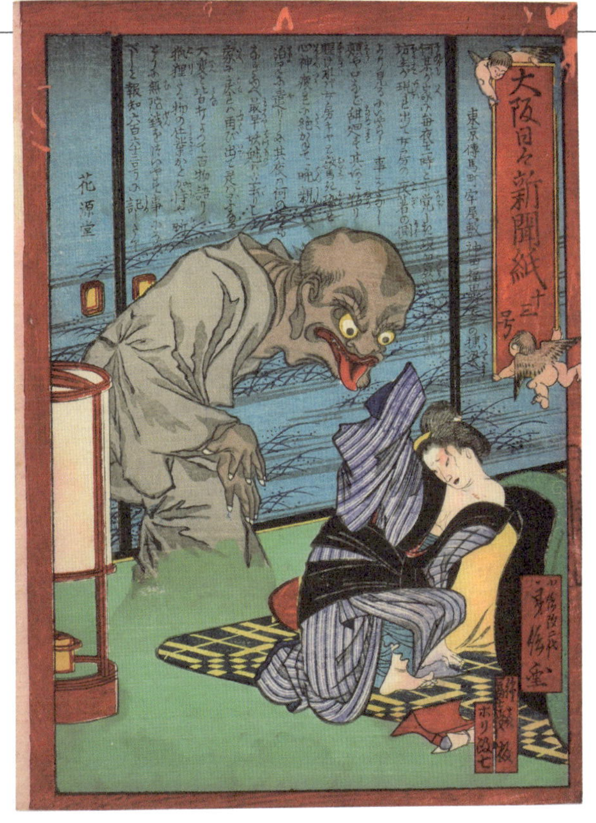

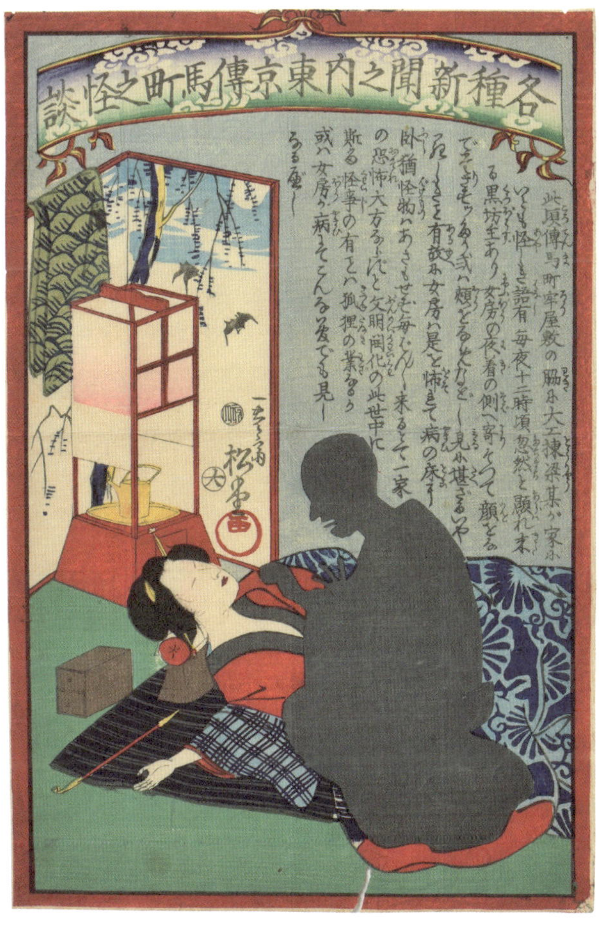

各種新聞之内
東京伝馬町之怪談

かくしゅしんぶんのうちとうきょうでんまちょうのかいだん

A Ghost Story of Tenma-chō, Tokyo, from
various news sources (*Kakushu Shinbun
no Uchi: Tokyo Tenma-chō no Kaidan*)

松堂　明治 8 年（1875）4 月　大判
Shodō, April 1875 (Meiji 8), Ōban

東京伝馬町の大工棟梁の家に毎夜 12 時ころに黒坊主が現れると
いう記事は新聞錦絵の「郵便報知新聞」（『今昔妖怪大鑑』掲載）、
「大阪日々新聞紙」などにも紹介されているほど話題になった。
同じ話題を取り上げながら絵がそれぞれに大きく異なっている
のが興味深い。
In the household of a master carpenter of Tenma-chō in Tokyo, every
night around midnight a black monk would appear; this phenomenon
became so topical that articles on it appeared in news *nishiki-e Yubin
Hōchi Shimbun* (please refer to *Yokai Museum*) and *Osaka Nichinichi Shimbunshi* among others. Even though the illustrations cover
the same topic, they arc remarkably different.

文明開化 "東京怪異" あれやこれや
Enlightenment and "Tokyo Mysteries": a bit of this and that

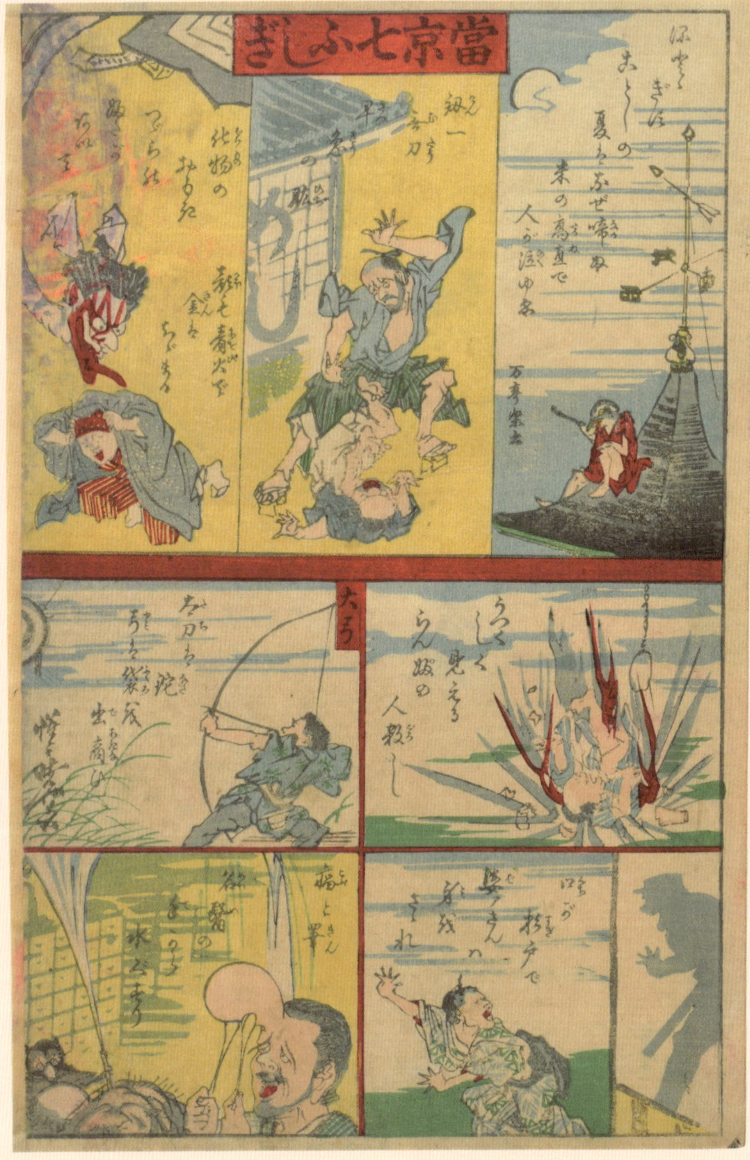

当京七ふしぎ
河鍋暁斎　明治時代　大判
Seven Mysteries of Tokyo
(*Tōkyō Nana Fushigi*)
Kawanabe Kyōsai,
Meiji period, Ōban

「当京」は「当世の東京」という意を込めたもので、文明開化の時代における風俗や社会の動きなどを7つ取り上げて「七ふしぎ」として錦絵化したもの。その内容は米価の高騰、新しい照明器具であるランプによる火事や火傷事故など、日々の生活に密着した事項を面白可笑しく紹介した内容で、直接的には怪異や妖怪とは関係ないが、わざわざ「七ふしぎ」と名付けたのは「本所七不思議」「麻布七不思議」「麹町七不思議」など、東京のあちこちに伝わる怪異譚が七不思議としてよく知られていたことからだ。それくらいに江戸には不思議があちこちにあったのだ。

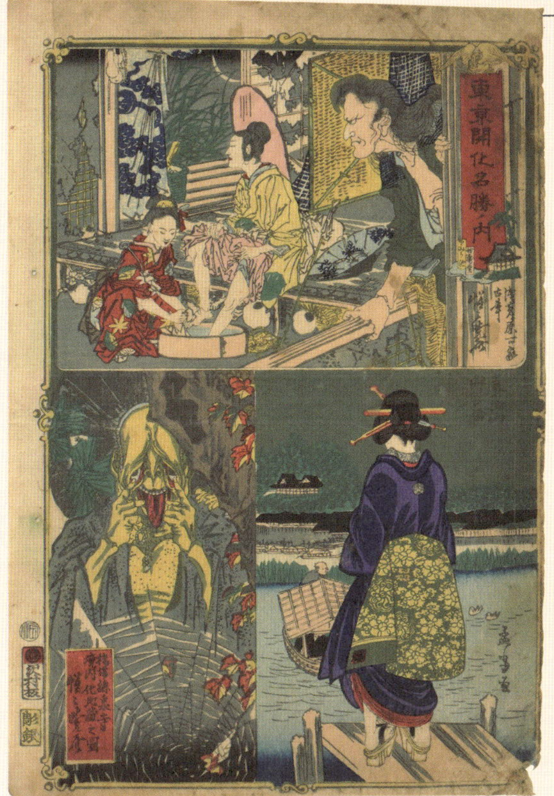

東京開化名勝之内 橋場総泉寺境内化地蔵之図
河鍋暁斎　明治 8 年（1875）　大判
'Ghostly Jizō of Sōsenji Temple in Hashiba' from the series *Beautiful Places of Advanced Tokyo* (*Tokyo Kaika Meishō no Uchi: Hashiba Sōsen-ji Keidai Bakejizō no Zu*)
Kawanabe Kyōsai, 1875 (Meiji 8), Ōban
明治時代に入って文明開化が声高に叫ばれた時世においても東京各所の不思議な言い伝えなどを描いた錦絵が各種出されていった。この作品は浅草橋場にあった総泉寺にあった化地蔵を紹介している。総泉寺の化地蔵は 3 メートルもあり、被っている大きな笠がいつのまにか動いているなどの噂があって化地蔵と呼ばれたという。総泉寺は板橋区に移ったが化地蔵は現在も当地に残っている。
Despite the much-talked-about "cultural enlightenment" as Japan entered the Meiji period, prints of local Tokyo superstitions abounded. This work shows a ghostly *jizō* (Buddhist deity of children) at Sōsenji Temple in Hashiba, Asakusa. The *jizō* of Sōsenji Temple stood three metres tall and wore a huge hat that was said to move on its own, and so became known as the *bakejizō*. Sōsenji Temple relocated to Itabashi Ward, but the *bakejizō* still remains on the original site today.

東京開化名勝之内 金丹院龍女之古事
河鍋暁斎　明治 8 年（1875）　大判
'Dragon Lady' from the series *Beautiful Places of Advanced Tokyo* (*Tokyo Kaika Meishō no Uchi: Kintan'in Ryujo no Koji*)
Kawanabe Kyōsai, 1875 (Meiji 8), Ōban

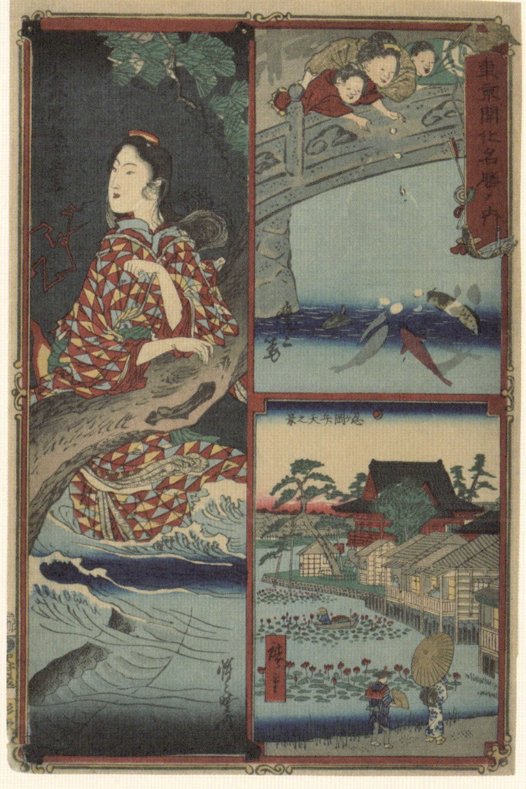

The non-standard spelling of "Tōkyō" stands for *Tōsei no Tōkyō* (Contemporary Tokyo), a *nishiki-e* which covered seven social trends or public morals in the era of cultural enlightenment under the name "Seven Mysteries". The subject matter is a comical look at the dramas of everyday life, such as the surging price of rice, or the fires and burns caused by a new type of lamp; these topics are not directly related to yokai or the supernatural, but the name "Seven Mysteries" is a nod in that direction, as such a title was well known to signify stories of the supernatural handed down from various locations in Tokyo, such as the Seven Mysteries of Honjo, Seven Mysteries of Azabu, and Seven Mysteries of Kojimachi. As you can see, strange things were all around in Tokyo.

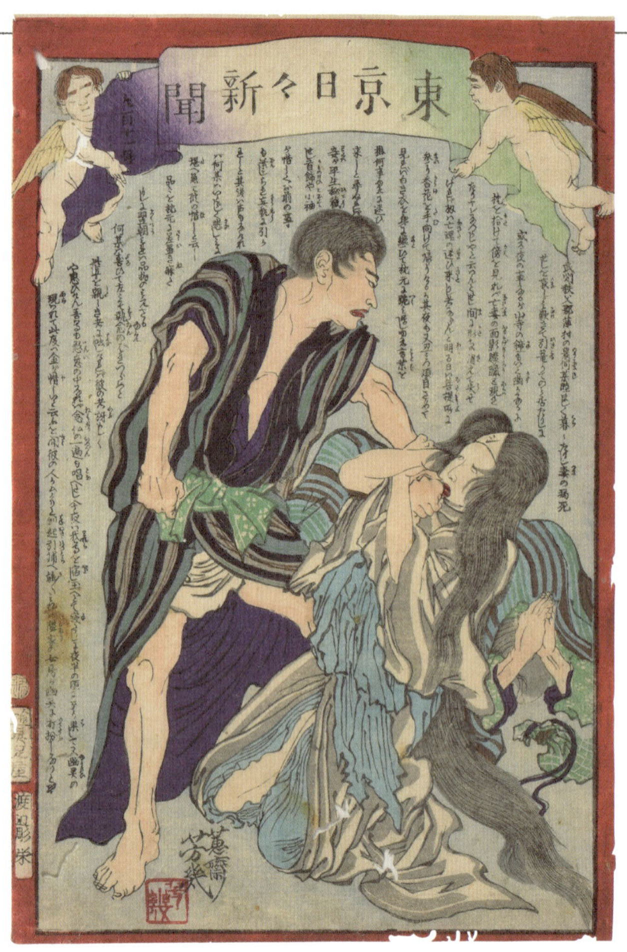

東京日々新聞 第九百十一号
とうきょうにちにちしんぶん

Tokyo Nichinichi Shimbun
Number 911

落合芳幾　明治時代　大判
Ochiai Yoshiiku, Meiji period, Ōban

武州秩父郡薄村の農夫の妻が病死したが、幽霊として枕元に立って生前愛用していた首飾りや小袖が惜しくて成仏できないと夫に伝えた。それに応じて枕元に要望した物を置いて寝ると翌朝にはなくなっていた。しかし、本当は幽霊ではなく隣家の女房が物欲しさに幽霊に化けて持ち去ったものであったという記事をもとに描かれた新聞錦絵。

In the village of Susuki in Chichibu-gun, Bushū (present-day Saitama), a farmer's wife died of illness, but her husband reported that she stood by the bed as a ghost, unable to enter paradise without her beloved necklaces and short-sleeved kimono. When he placed her favorite things by the bedside to appease her and went to sleep, the next morning they were gone. However, based on a news article this *nishiki-e* goes on to show that this was no ghost, but the wife from next door who wanted these things and disguised herself as a ghost to get them.

東京日々新聞 第九百九号
とうきょうにちにちしんぶん

Tokyo Nichinichi Shimbun
Number 909

落合芳幾　明治時代　大判
Ochiai Yoshiiku, Meiji period, Ōban

武州秩父郡横瀬村の農家の娘のもとに毎夜のように通う美少年は狸が化けたものか、という噂を掲載した新聞記事をもとに描かれた新聞錦絵。

Was the beautiful youth who came to visit the daughter of a farming family every night in the village of Yokoze in Chichibu-gun, Bushū (present-day Saitama) really a shape-shifting raccoon dog? News *nishiki-e* based on an article which covered this rumor.

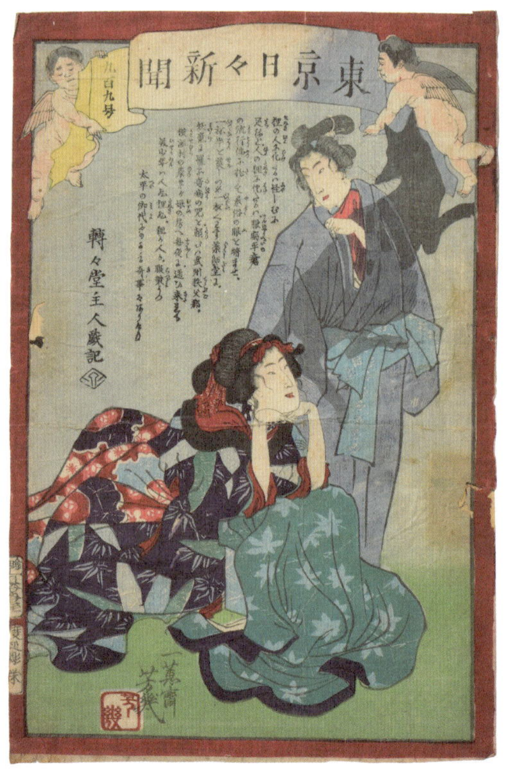

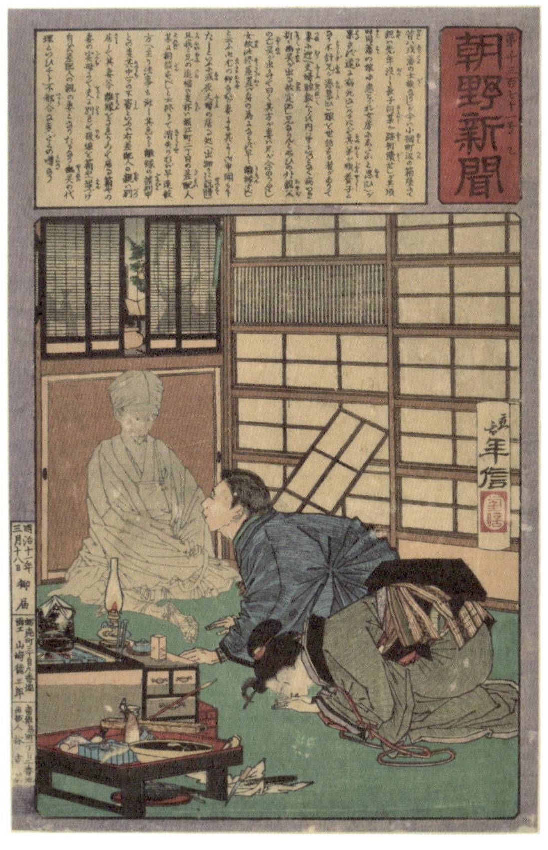

62

朝野新聞
第千三百七十一号 乙
ちょうやしんぶん

Chōya Shimbun Number 1371

山崎年信　明治 11 年（1878）3 月　大判
Yamazaki Toshinobu, March 1878 (Meiji 11), Ōban

病死した兄が恋した女性と結婚した弟のもとに父親の幽霊が
出て兄の念があるので離縁するようにと諭したという話をも
とに新聞錦絵化した作品。
Adapted from a news *nishiki-e* in which a woman whose lover had
died of his illness, and his younger brother who she had married
were visited by the ghost of his father, who urged them to divorce
out of fraternal duty.

63

郵便報知新聞
第五百二十七号
ゆうびんほうちしんぶん

Yūbin Hōchi Shimbun Number 527

月岡芳年　明治時代　大判
Tsukioka Yoshitoshi, Meiji period, Ōban

伊勢国の某は妻が病で乳飲み子を養うことも無理なのに遊里
通いばかりで、妻が病死すると乳母を雇って乳を飲ませてい
たが子が痩せ細ってしまうと死んだ妻が幽霊となって現れて
子に乳を含ませたという記事を錦絵化したもの。
Set somewhere in Ise Province, this news *nishiki-e* tells how a
woman was so sick she could not nourish her breastfed baby, but
kept going to the red-light district regardless; when she died of her
sickness a wet nurse for the baby was found, but when the child
began to starve she returned as a ghost to put the child to her
breast.

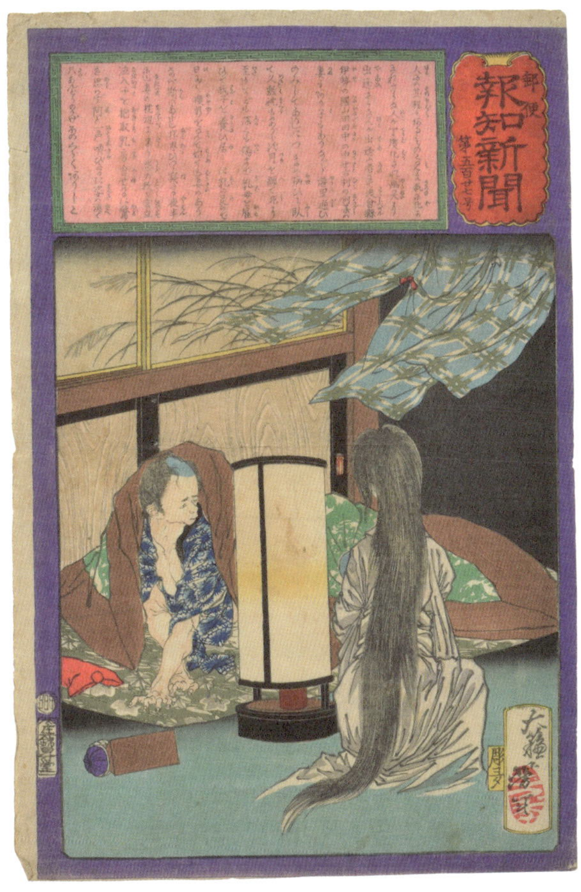

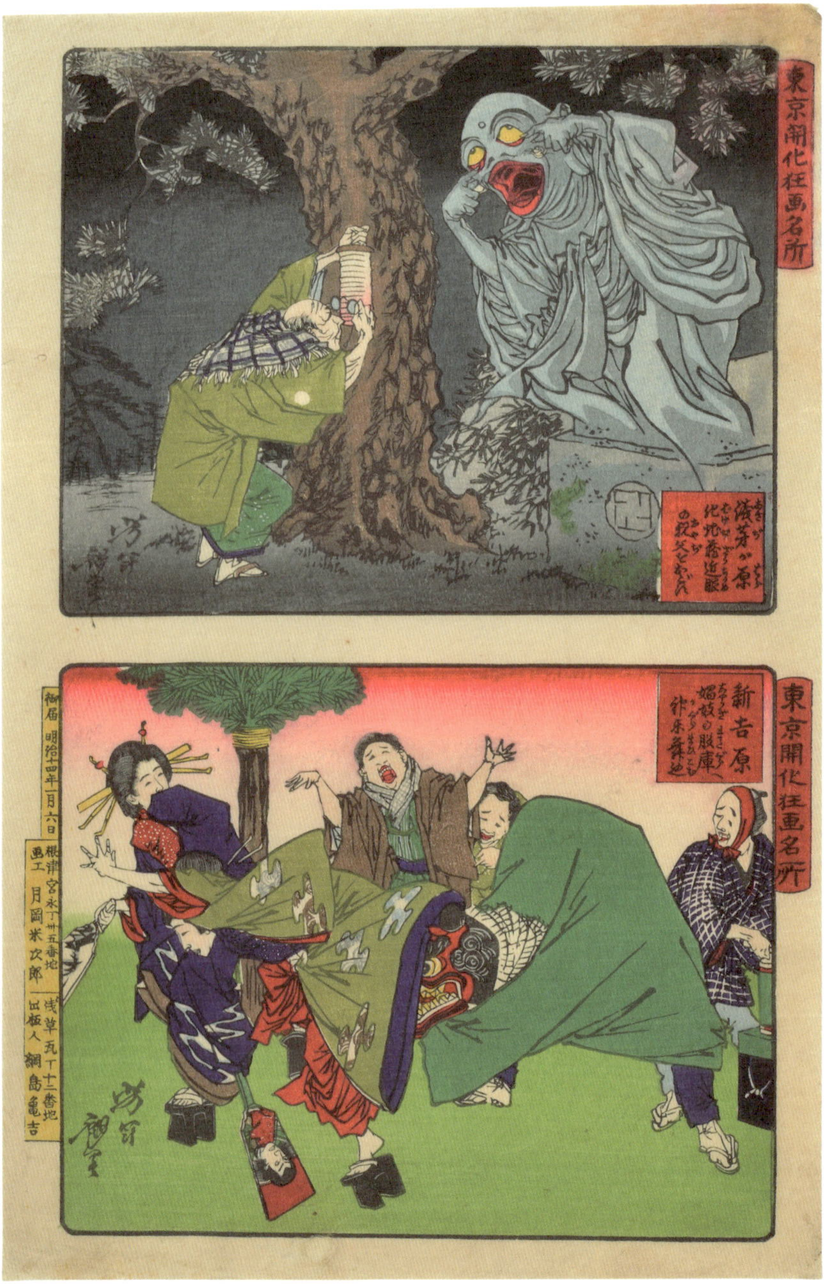

64 東京開化狂画名所
とうきょうかいかきょうがめいしょ

Thrilling Pictures of Famous Places in Tokyo (*Tokyō Kaika Kyōga Meisho*)

月岡芳年　明治 14 年（1881）1 月　大判　Tsukioka Yoshitoshi, January 1881 (Meiji 14), Ōban

二丁掛で上段が「浅茅が原の化地蔵 近眼の親父をおどす」という内容。この化地蔵は「東京開化名勝の内」にも取り上げられている。それくらいに有名だった。ここでは近くを通った親父を脅かそうとしている化地蔵だが、相手は近眼なので怖がらないといった具合だ。面白い名所を紹介しているので「狂画名所」というタイトルとなっている。

The upper panel of the two has the caption "The *bake jizo of* the bleak field scares a short-sighted old man." This notorious ghostly *jizo* also features in Beautiful Places of Advanced Tokyo (*Tōkyo Kaika Meisho no Uchi*). Try as he might to frighten an old man passing by, the man is too short-sighted to appreciate it. *Kyōga meisho* ("Thrilling Pictures of Famous Places") in the title of this work signals that places of interest are showcased.

65

『東京パック』「妖怪号」
（第七巻第二十六号）
とうきょうぱっく　ようかいごう

Tokyo Puck: Yokai Edition (volume 7, issue 26)

北沢楽天　明治 44 年（1911）9 月
Kitazawa Rakuten, September 1911 (Meiji 44)

漫画家・北沢楽天が主筆となって出された明治時代を代表する漫画雑誌『東京パック』の「妖怪号」。政治風刺、社会風刺などを妖怪に擬して描いている。
Manga artist Kitazawa Rakuten was chief editor of the yokai edition of Tokyo Puck, the archetypal manga magazine of the Meiji era. Yokai were used for socio-political satire.

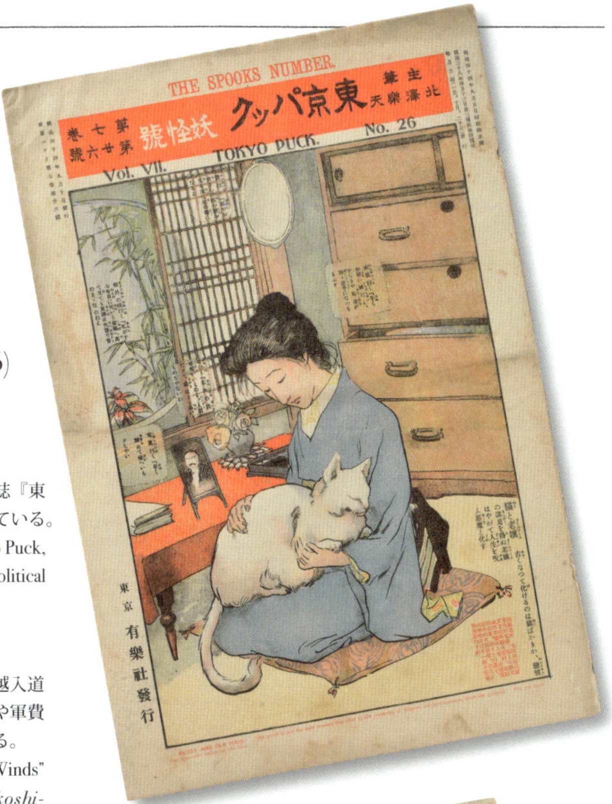

中央見開きページに大きく描かれた「腥さい風」と題された作品。見越入道や九尾の狐が跋扈して人々が翻弄されている。キャプションから悪税や軍費や不景気の風に悩む庶民の姿を描いて政策を風刺していることがわかる。
A work drawn large over a center-page spread, under the heading "Bloody Winds" (translated as "Ministerial Change"). The people are at the mercy of a *mikoshi-nyudō* goblin and a nine-tailed fox running rampant. The caption indicates that this is a satirical cartoon on public policy, showing ordinary people suffering in the winds of economic recession, war expenditure and exorbitant taxes.

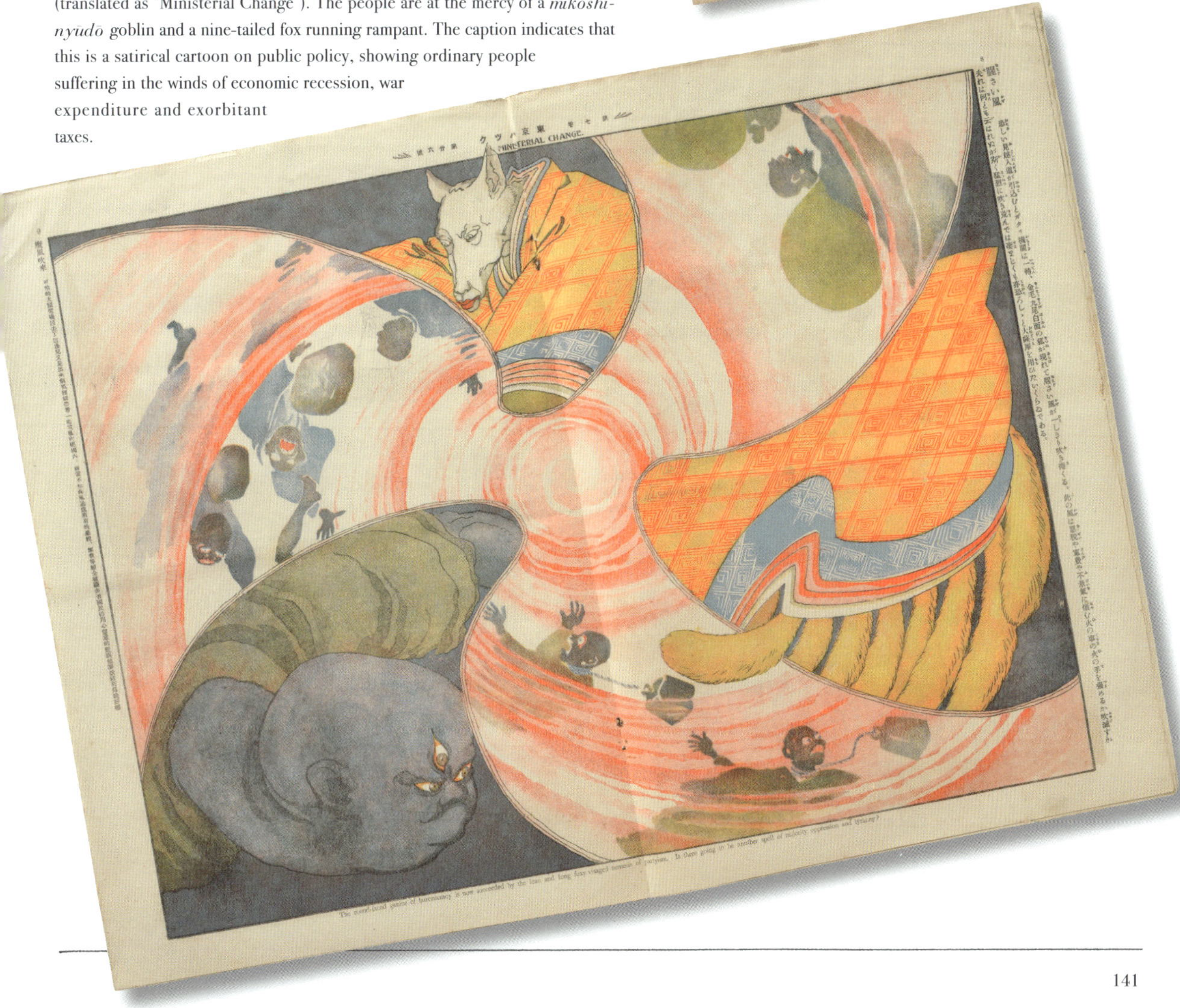

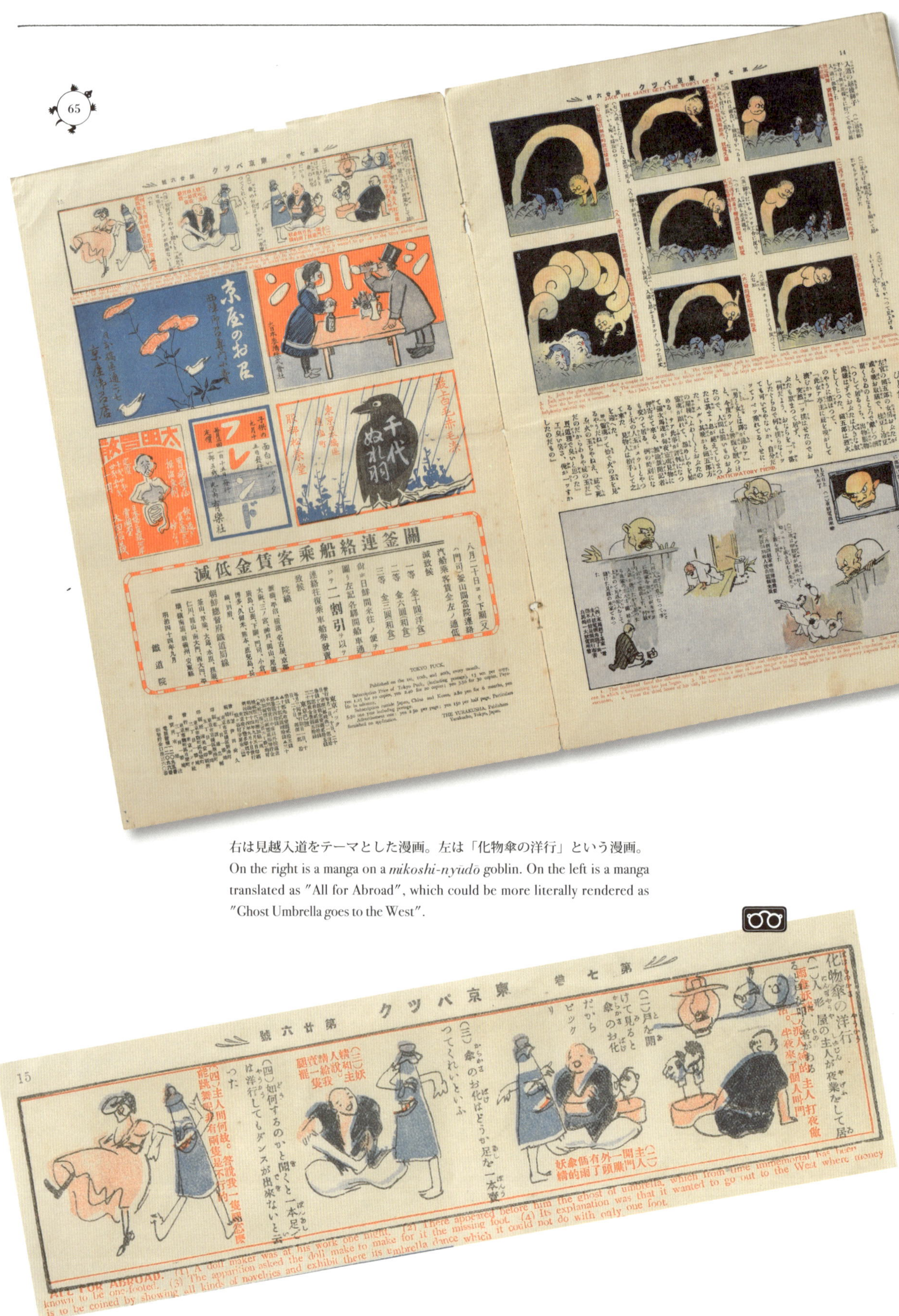

右は見越入道をテーマとした漫画。左は「化物傘の洋行」という漫画。
On the right is a manga on a *mikoshi-nyūdō* goblin. On the left is a manga
translated as "All for Abroad", which could be more literally rendered as
"Ghost Umbrella goes to the West".

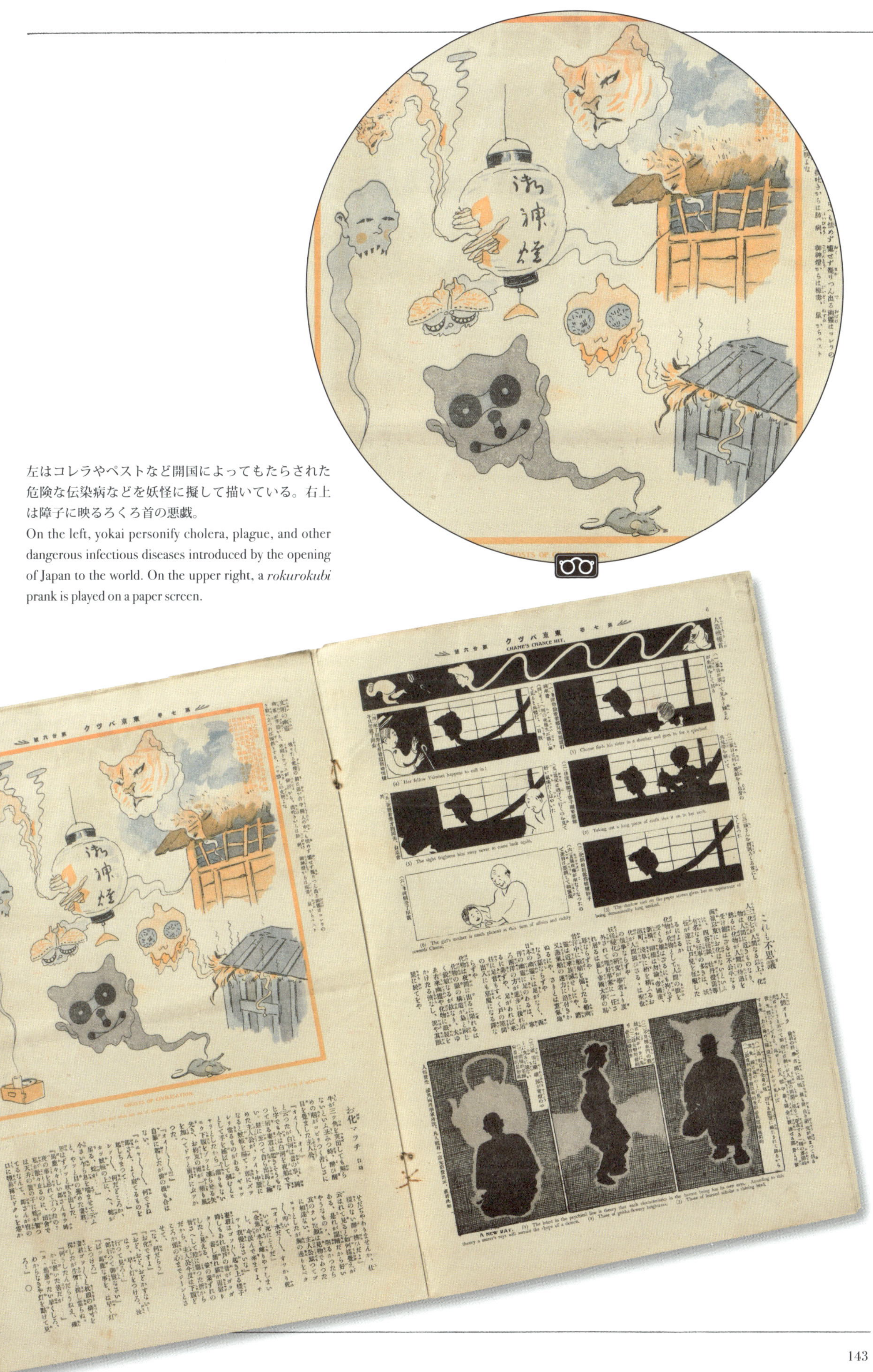

左はコレラやペストなど開国によってもたらされた
危険な伝染病などを妖怪に擬して描いている。右上
は障子に映るろくろ首の悪戯。
On the left, yokai personify cholera, plague, and other
dangerous infectious diseases introduced by the opening
of Japan to the world. On the upper right, a *rokurokubi*
prank is played on a paper screen.

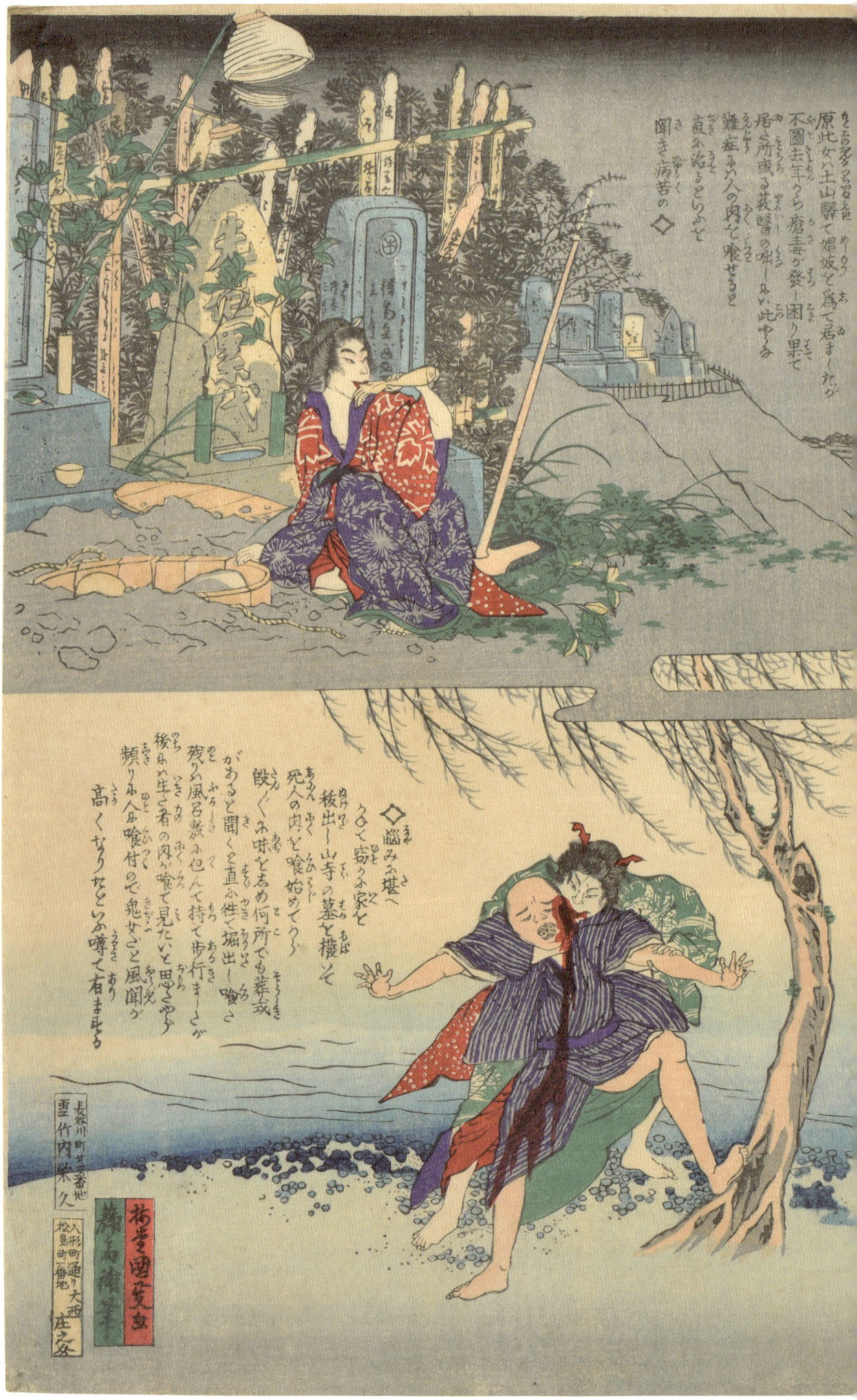

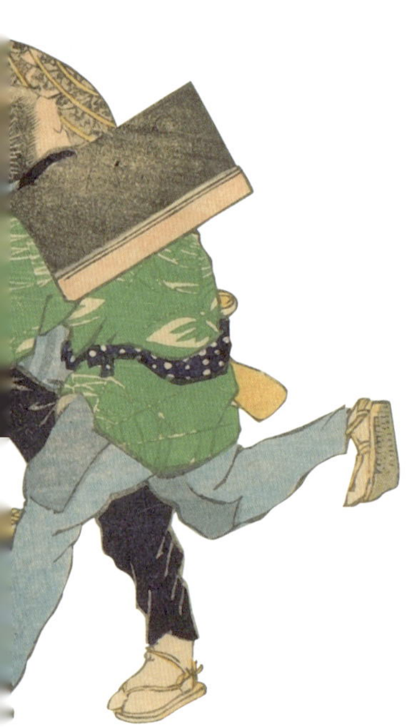

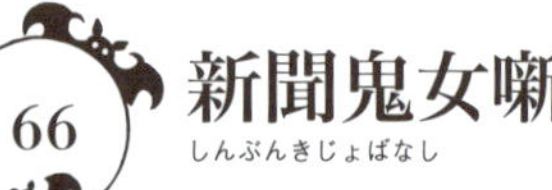

66 新聞鬼女噺

Newspaper: The Story of an Ogress (*Shinbun Kijo-banashi*)

明治時代　大判錦絵 2 枚続　Meiji period, Large diptych

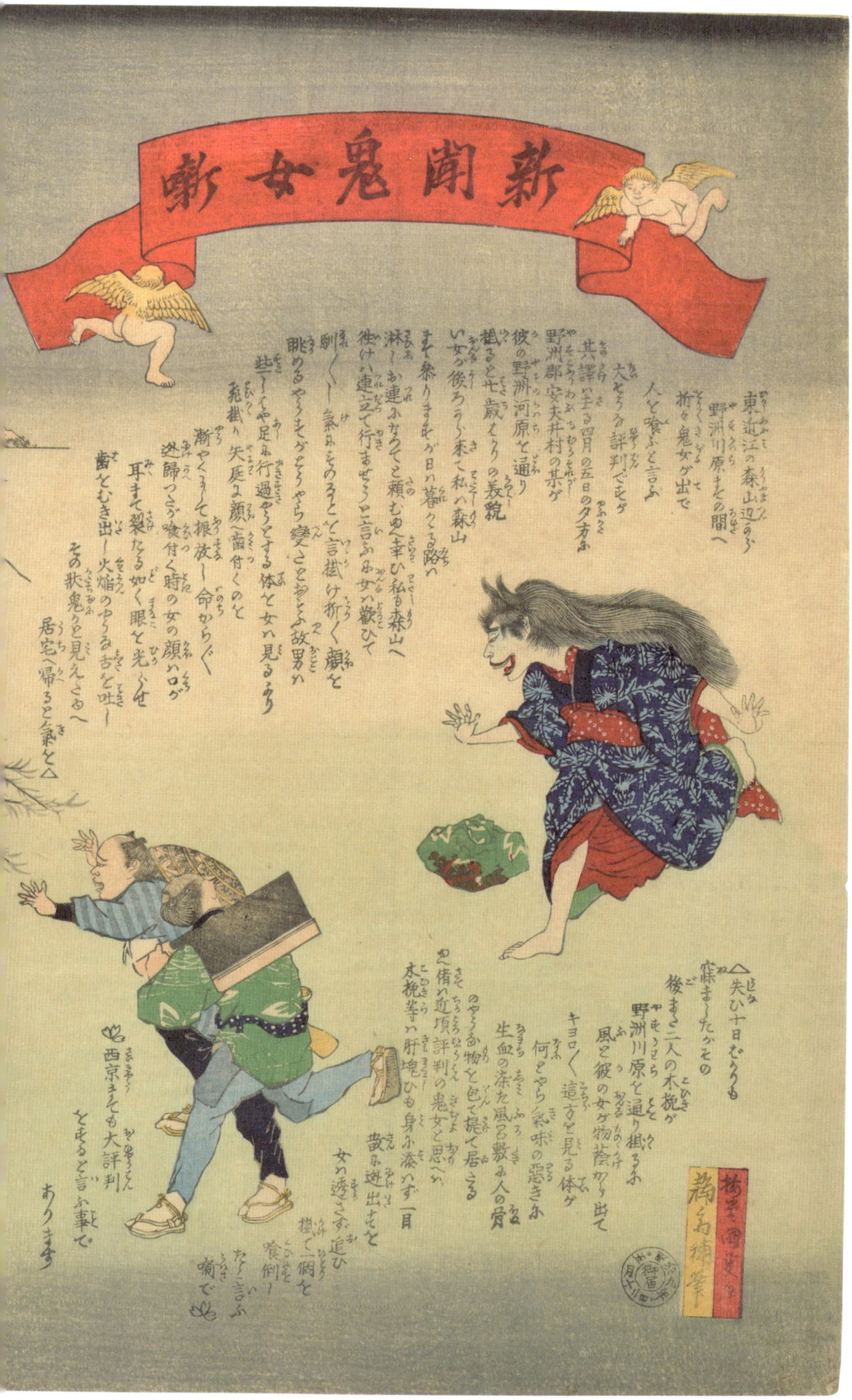

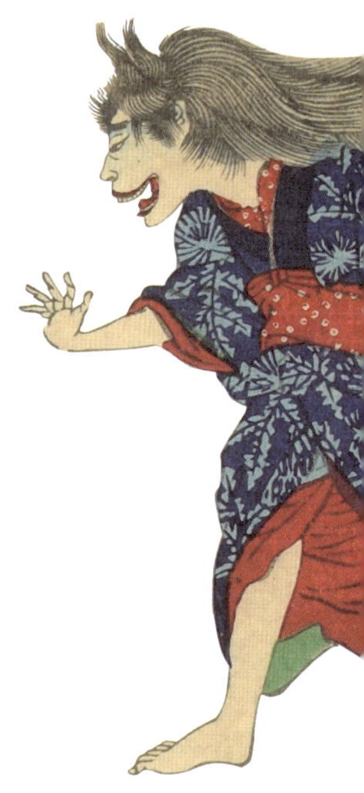

一般的な錦絵新聞とは違ったスタイルで、新聞報道をベースとしながら右に鬼女が出現して人を襲うという事件を掲載し、左ではその鬼女が疱瘡を発病した女で、人肉を食すると治癒するという言い伝えを信じて墓を掘り返して屍の肉を口にしたのをきっかけに生きた人の肉を食べたいというまでとなり人を襲ったと、事件の背景を報じている。

In a different style to most news *nishiki-e*, the right panel is based on a news report of the case of an ogress attacking people, and the left panel gives her backstory, reporting that the ogress started out as a woman infected with smallpox who believed the myth that eating human flesh would cure her, and so dug up a grave to eat dead flesh, subsequently acquiring a taste for fresher meat and preying on the living.

67

東海道中栗毛弥次馬
とうかいどうちゅうくりげやじうま

Shank's Mare on the East Sea Road (*Tōkaidochū Kurige no Yajiuma*)

歌川芳幾　万延元年（1860）10月　大判　Utagawa Yoshiiku, Tenth month of 1860 (Man'en 1), Ōban

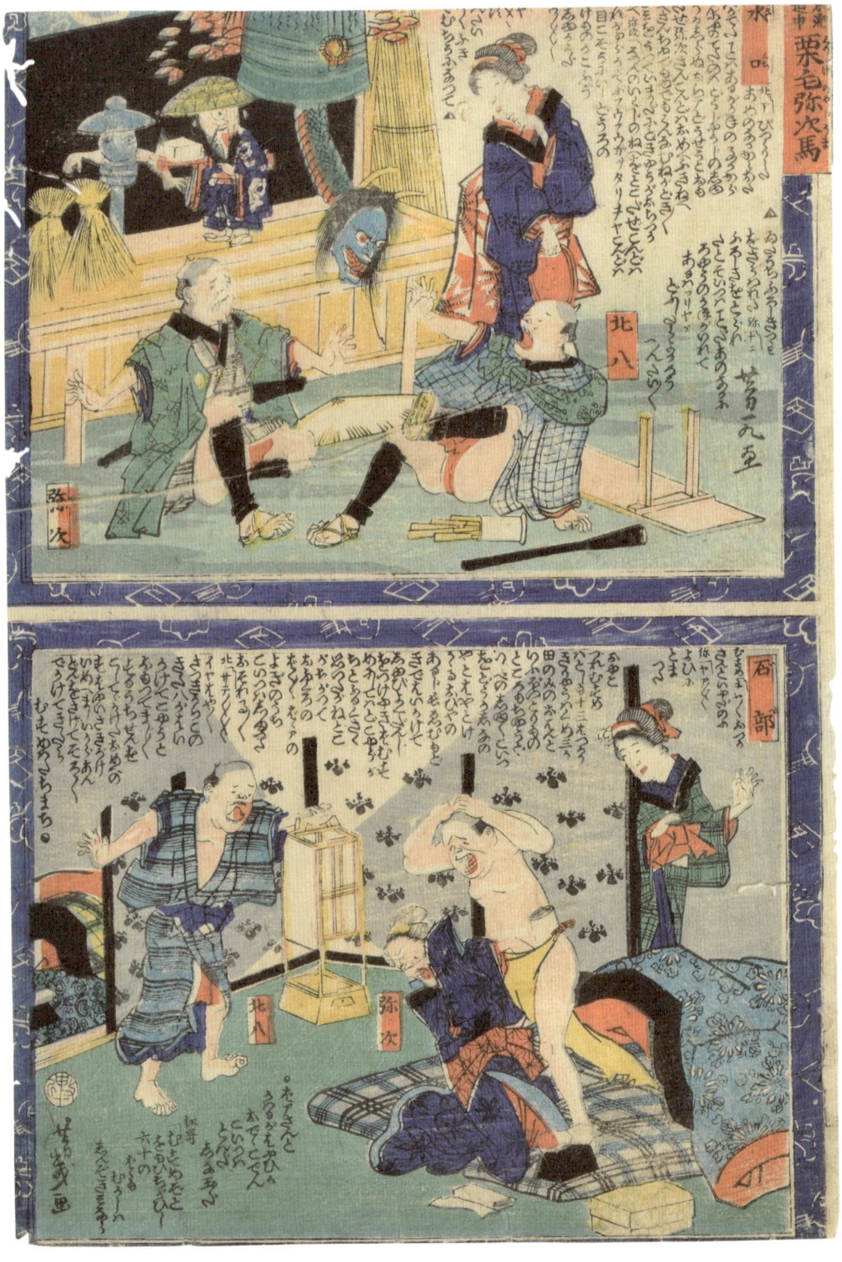

「東海道中栗毛弥次馬」シリーズで、二丁掛の上部「水口」には吹矢遊びに興じる弥次と北八が矢が的に当って鐘から蛇に変じた清姫が姿を現し、びっくりして腰を抜かしている様子が描かれている。清姫のほかにも豆腐小僧、お化け燈篭などもみえる。こうした遊びのなかにも妖怪は登場している。

In the upper panel "Minakuchi" from the series *Shank's Mare on the East Sea Road*, Yaji and Kitahachi hit a target in a blowgun game and Princess Kiyohime in snake-form pops out from a bell, startling them so much they fall over. As well as Princess Kiyohime, Tofu-Kozo (a spirit child carrying a block of tofu) and a ghostly stone lantern (*tōrō*) can be seen. Yokai feature in these kind of games too.

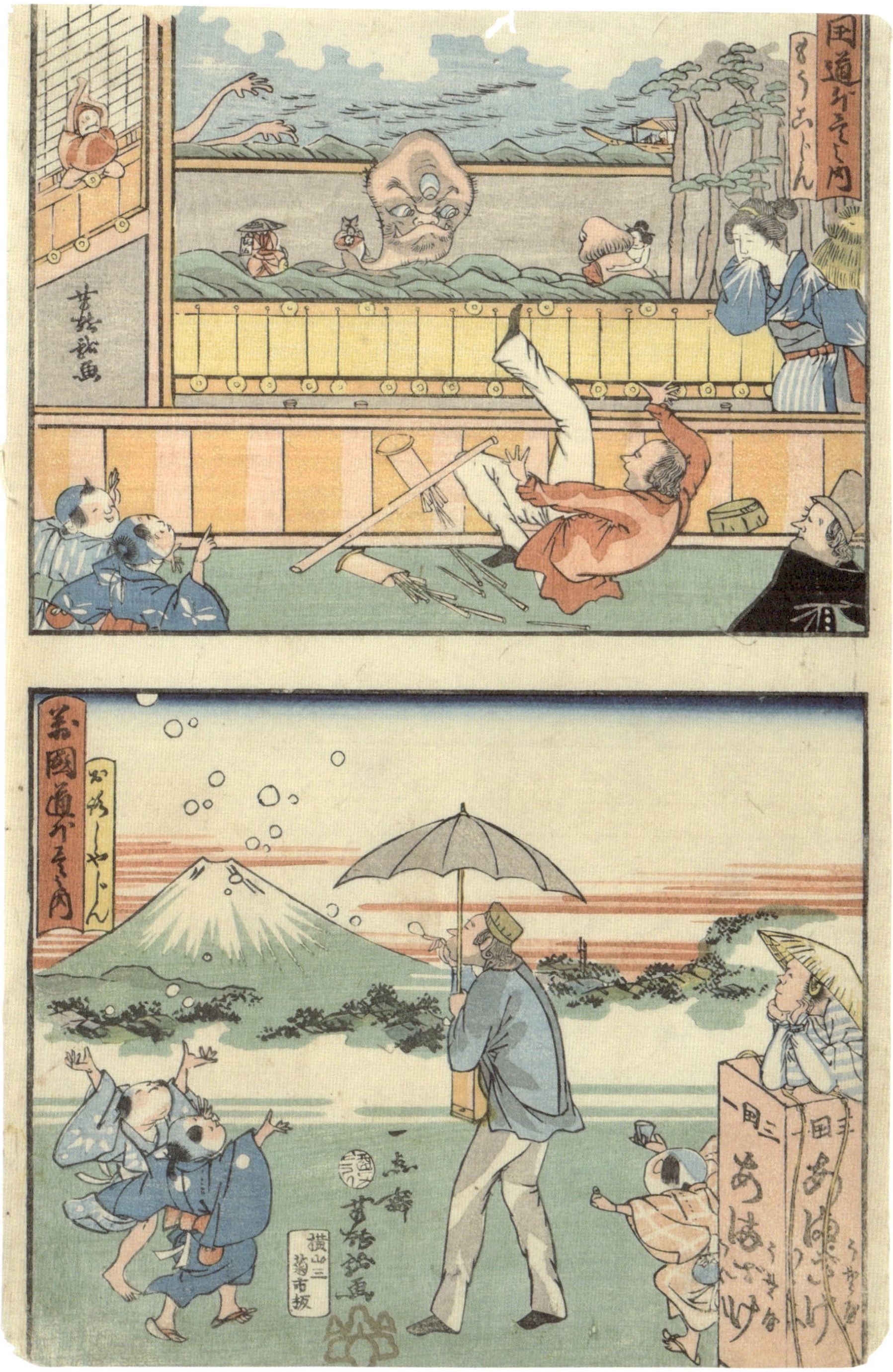

萬国道下尽之内 もうこじん
ばんこくどうけつくしのうち　もうこじん

'The Mongol' from A Series of Caricatures of Nationalities
(Bankoku Dōke Tsukushi no Uchi: Mōkojin)

中井芳瀧　文久元年（1861）3 月　大判　Nakai Yoshitaki (also known as Utagawa Yoshitaki), Third month of 1861 (Bunkyū 1), Ōban

69

おもちゃ絵「新聞錦絵（錦絵新聞）」

おもちゃえしんぶんにしきえ（にしきえしんぶん）

Omocha-e (news *nishiki-e*)

明治 7 年（1874）から十数年の短い間に出された錦絵のなかに新聞記事を扱った新聞錦絵（錦絵新聞）といわれるものがある。東京では「東京日々新聞」「郵便報知新聞」「朝野新聞」、大阪では「大阪錦絵新聞」「日々新聞」「錦画百事新聞」等々、何種類もが出されている。そのいくつかは本書や『今昔妖怪大鑑』でも紹介しているが、この新聞錦絵（錦絵新聞）をベースに小さなサイズにしたおもちゃ絵も各種刷られた。新聞錦絵（錦絵新聞）は多色刷の絵を交えてニュースを記したもので、報道としての役割を持っていたのに対して、おもちゃ絵「新聞錦絵（錦絵新聞）」はサイズが小さく、記事の文章も極端に省略されていることからニュース情報源として使われたものではなく、単に面白い刷物として出された錦絵といえるが、ここにも妖怪や怪異を扱ったものが散見できる。刷りは決して良質とはいえず、色や図柄がずれているものも散見できるほどだ。

Among the *nishiki-e* produced in the ten-odd years from 1874 on were news *nishiki-e* (*shinbun nishiki-e* or *nishiki-e shinbun*), colored woodblock prints which covered articles of news. Many publications were produced: in Tokyo, *Tokyo Nichinichi Shimbun*, *Yubin Hochi Shimbun*, and *Chōya Shimbun*, and in Osaka, *Osaka Nishiki-e Shimbun*, *Nichinichi Shimbun*, *Nishiki-ga Hyaku-ji Shimbun* and so on. Many of these are collected in this book and in *Yokai Museum*; based on news *nishiki-e* many varieties of smaller-sized *omocha-e* (lit. "toy pictures") were also printed. In terms of actual news coverage, news *nishiki-e* delivered news sprinkled with multi-colored pictures; *omocha-e* were not primarily used as a source of news due to their small size and extremely abbreviated article text, but rather as interesting prints, like the examples shown here featuring yokai and supernatural phenomena. The prints are not high quality; in many the colors and designs are out of alignment.

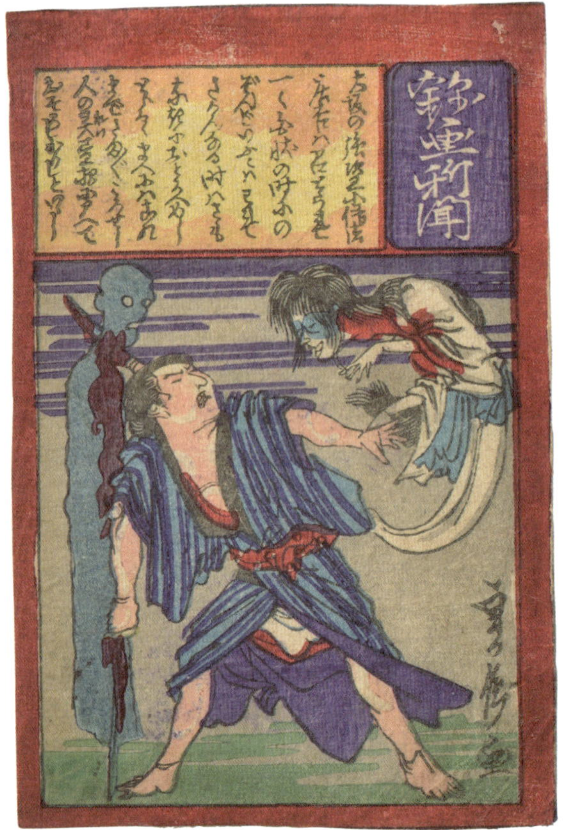

錦画新聞　殺した相手が幽霊となってあらわれて犯人を悩ましている。

Nishiki-e Shimbun　A murder victim returns as a ghost to torment their murderer.

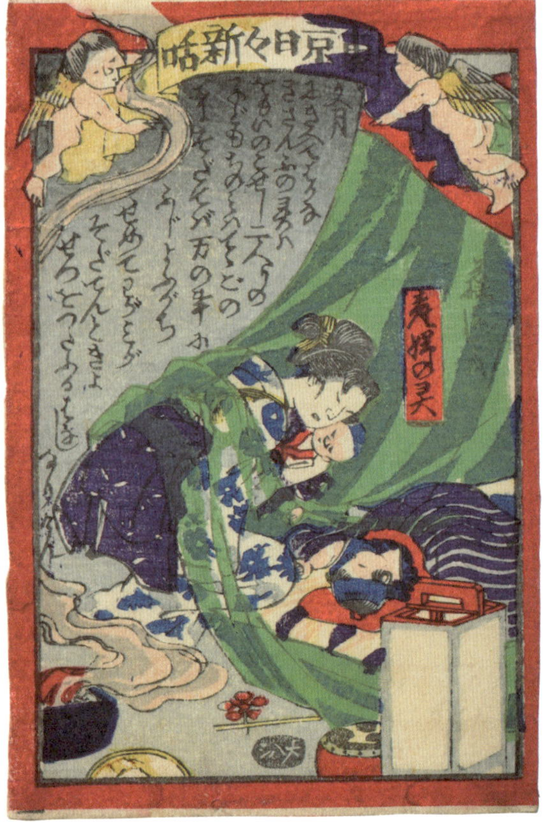

東京日々新咶　小さな子をのこして死んでいった母親が幽霊となって授乳にあらわれた。

Tokyo Nichinichi Shimbun　A mother who died leaving behind a small child returns from the dead to breastfeed.

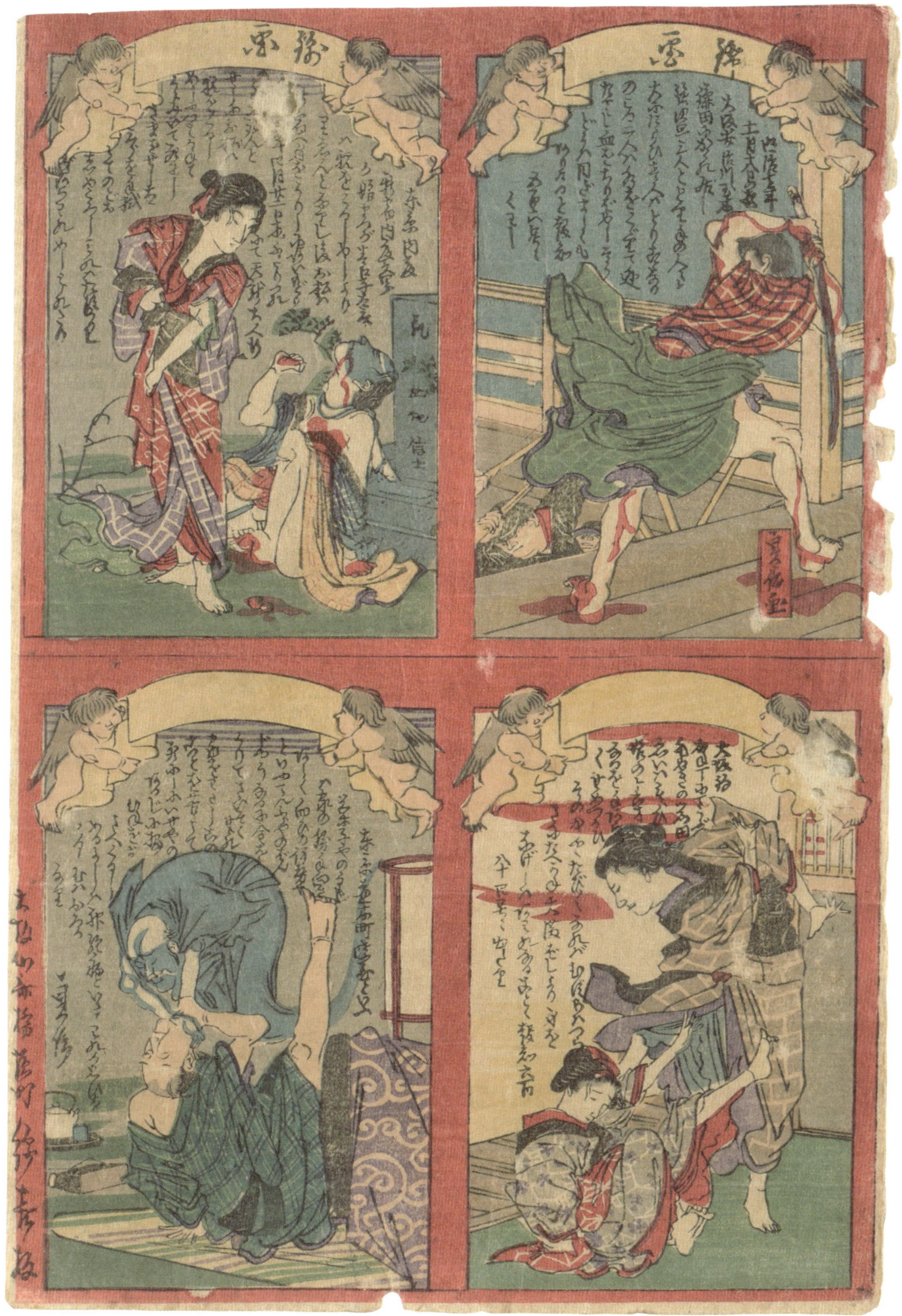

おもちゃ絵「新聞錦絵（錦絵新聞）」　明治時代　各縦 28.5　横 21.0
錦絵新聞をおもちゃ絵化したもの。この作品は一枚のなかに 4 つの錦絵新聞が刷られており、まだ 4 つに切り離されていないものだ。
左下に幽霊出現の話題があるが、これは錦絵新聞「大阪錦画日々新聞紙 26 号」（『今昔妖怪大鑑』参照）のおもちゃ絵化である。
Omocha-e (news *nishiki-e*)　Meiji period, Height 28.5, Width 21.0 each
News *nishiki-e* reworked as *omocha-e* (lit. "toy picture"). Four are printed on a single sheet, not yet cut and separated. On the lower left a ghost is featured; this is an *omocha-e of Nichinichi Shimbun Number* 17.

戦争と妖怪
Yokai and War

妖怪文化は長い時間のなかで広く浸透していったことは本書収録の幾多の資料からもみることができるが、そんななかでもここに掲げる絵馬と伝単は意外なものとして紹介したい。絵馬は戦時中の日本で敵の降伏を祈ってつくられたものだ。いっぽうで伝単はアメリカが日本国民を対象に為政者や軍部の欺瞞を直接訴えるために制作されたもので、飛行機から大量に撒いて多くの人たちの目に触れるような戦略的ビラだ。アメリカの伝単のなかには表は日本の流通紙幣そっくりで誰でも手にとってしまうが、裏には訴えたい内容が書かれているといったものさえある。

　戦争ではどんな手法もあり得るのだ。だからこそ日本でよく知られた怪猫譚を伝単に取りあげており、妖怪文化の広がりを印象づける興味深い資料といえよう。

Among the host of materials collected in this book which show the spread of yokai culture throughout the ages, these remarkable votive pictures (*ema*) and propaganda leaflets (*dentan*) deserve a special introduction. Ema (lit. "picture-horse") are small wooden Shinto plaques left hanging up as offerings at shrines, which in wartime in Japan people made to pray for the enemy's surrender. On the other hand, dentan were propaganda leaflets produced by the U.S. to convince the people of Japan that their own military and government were deceiving them, which were scattered from USAAF aircraft in large quantities to be seen by as many people as possible. Among the American leaflets were some which looked just like Japanese paper money on the front side so that anyone would pick them up, but a propaganda message was written on the back. All kinds of stratagems are possible in war. The well-known tale of a supernatural cat ended up being used on American propaganda leaflets in Japan; these are intriguing materials which convey the scope of yokai culture.

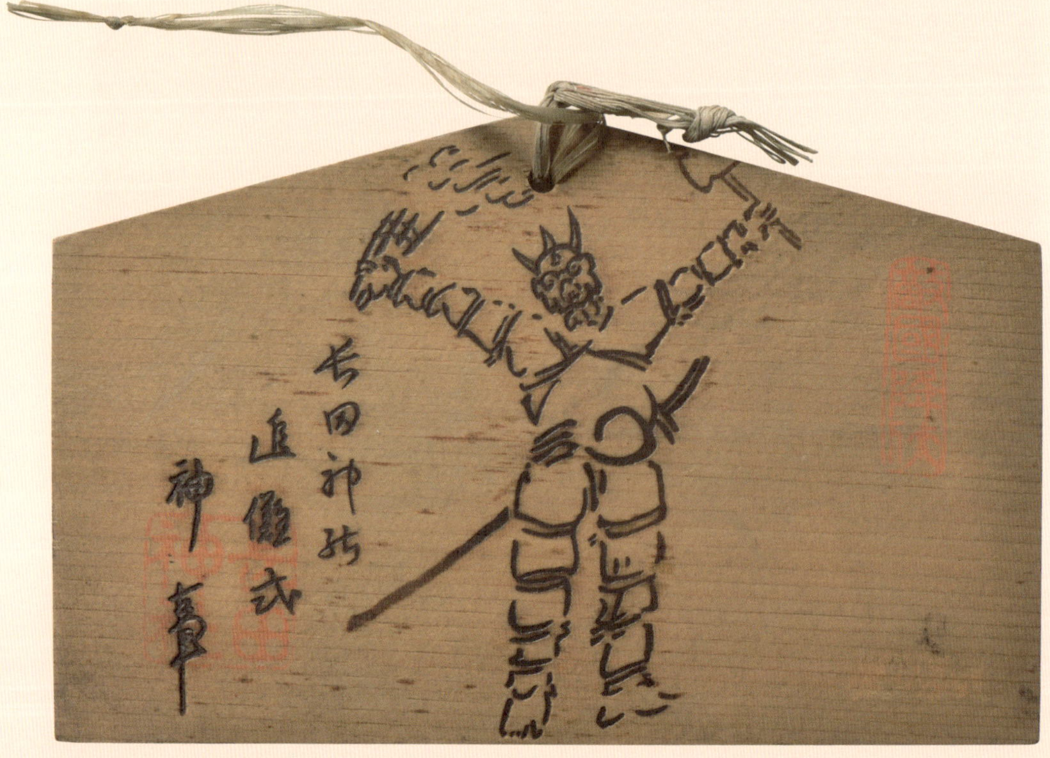

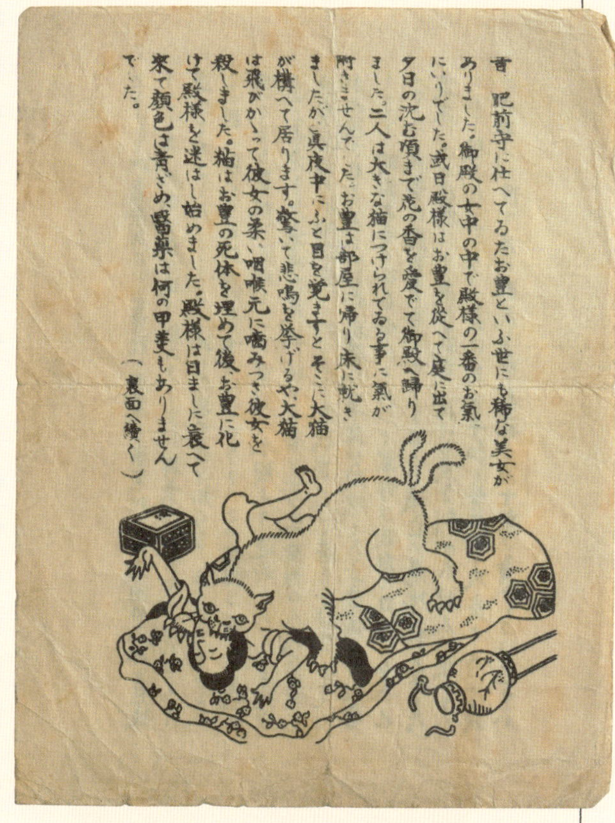

鍋島化け猫騒動（伝単）　昭和時代　縦 11.0　横 14.0
Leaflet on the Nabeshima Bakeneko Rebellion (*Nabeshima Bakeneko Sōdō Dentan*)
Shōwa period, Height 11.0, Width 14.0

伝単は戦時に敵の戦意喪失や混乱を狙って撒く戦略的ビラで、戦地における兵士ばかりでなく一般人も対象にして飛行機から大量に落下させることも多々あった。この伝単はアメリカが第二次世界大戦末期に日本本土に撒いたもので、日本人なら誰でも知っている鍋島化け猫騒動の話をもとに専横する軍部や為政者たちが悪行を働く化け猫であることを一般人に伝えようとしている。アメリカの伝単という意外なところにも日本の怪異譚が使われていたのだ。

Dentan were propaganda leaflets scattered in wartime to undermine the enemy's will to fight and cause confusion, targeting civilians as well as the military; they were often dropped in large volumes from planes. This leaflet was dropped on the Japanese mainland by the U.S. in the last days of WWII to communicate to the general public that their tyrannical government and military were causing harm like the monstrous Nabeshima cat, a tale that any Japanese person would have known. Japan's tales of the supernatural turn up in unexpected places such as American propaganda leaflets.

鬼図絵馬　昭和時代　縦 13.6　横 8.7　厚 0.2
Ogre Votive Tablet (*Ema*)　Shōwa period, Height 13.6, Width 8.7, Depth 0.2

戦争は妖怪の表現にも影響を与えている。この絵馬は第二次世界大戦中に作られたもので、鬼が災いを払うという長田神社の追儺式の神事を表現したもので、右上には「敵国降伏」の朱印が捺されている。敵国を鬼が退治するといった意で絵馬にも戦勝を祈る時代相がみられる。

Yokai left their mark as a means of expression in wartime. This votive tablet was made during WWII: it has a depiction of Nagata Shrine's Tsuinashiki ritual, a demon dance ceremony in which an ogre drives away evil spirits, and the red seal "Surrender of the enemy country" is stamped on the upper right. People praying for victory with a votive tablet of an ogre to defeat the enemy country reflects the social climate of the time.

妖怪ポチ袋
ようかいぽちぶくろ

Yokai Envelopes
(*Yokai Pochi Bukuro*)

明治時代以降　縦 9.5　横 6.0
Post-Meiji period, Height 9.5, Width 6.0

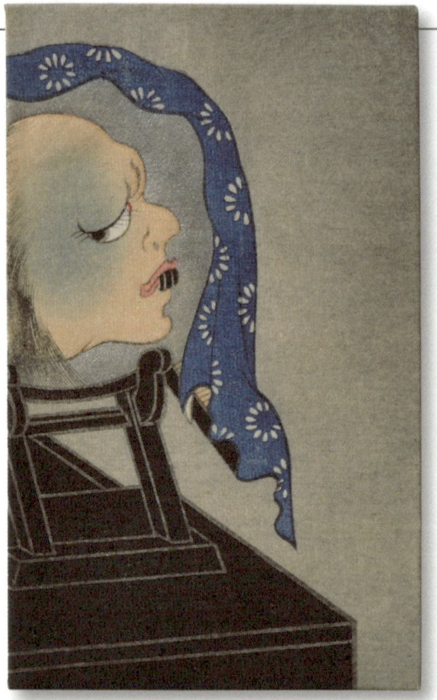

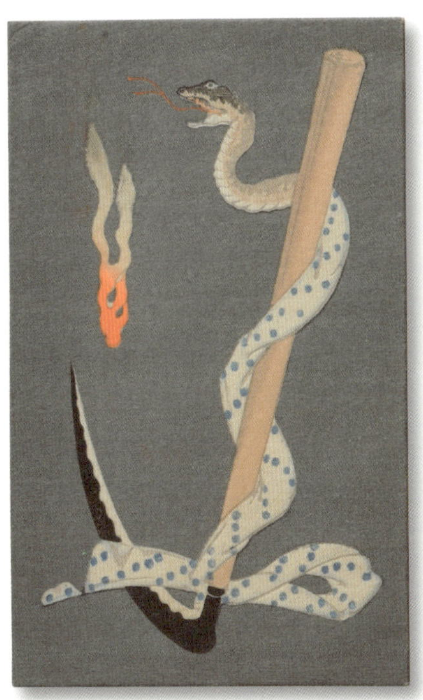

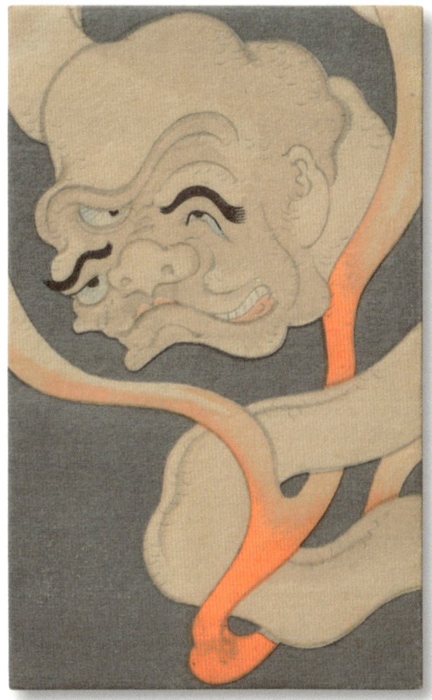

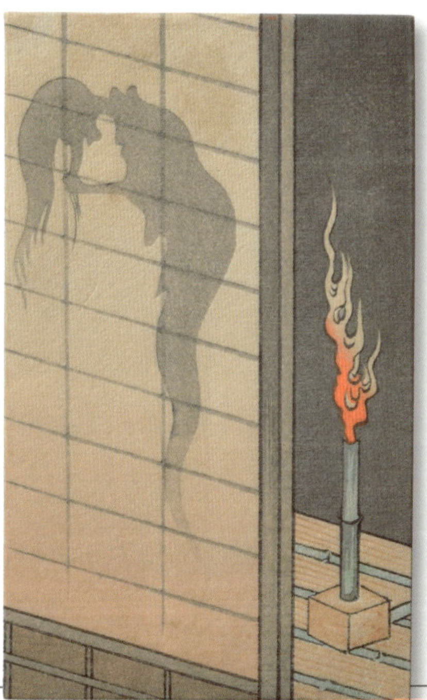

ポチ袋には多種多様なデザインがあるが、そのなかに妖怪柄のものも存在する。このポチ袋は鏡に映ったお岩の顔、障子に幽霊を蝋燭で映し出す遊び、ろくろ首、布が蛇と化して切り殺された恨みを晴らすように鎌にまとわりついた怪異などが刷られている。

These small envelopes come in a huge variety of designs, some featuring yokai. These are supernatural prints: Oiwa's face reflected in a mirror, the silhouette of a ghost candle behind a sliding screen, a long-necked *rokurokubi*, and cloth turning into a snake twining around a murder weapon to settle the score of the sickle's victim.

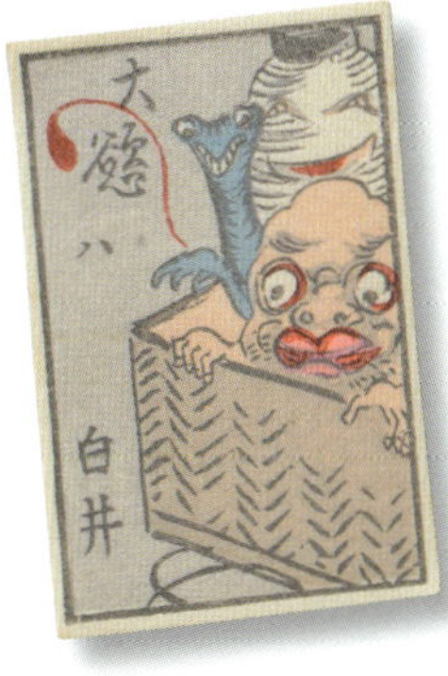 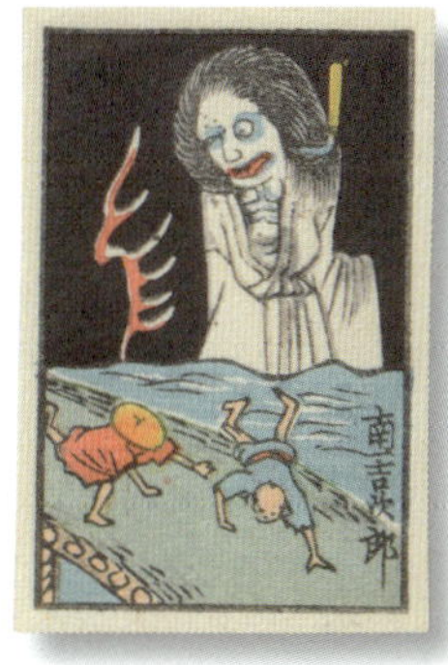 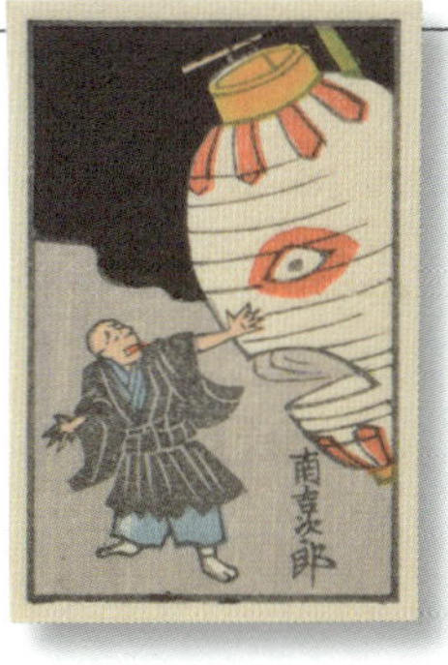 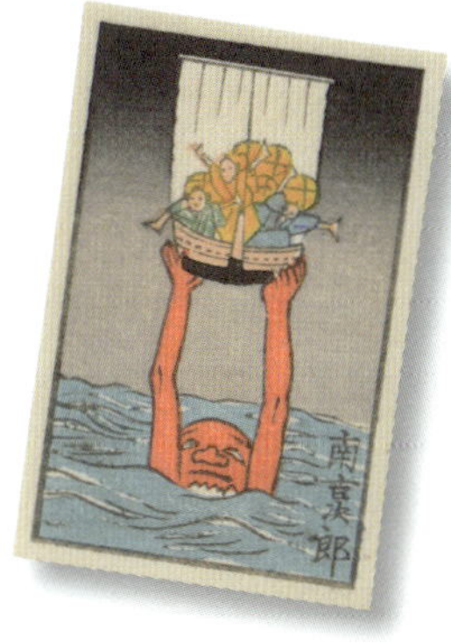

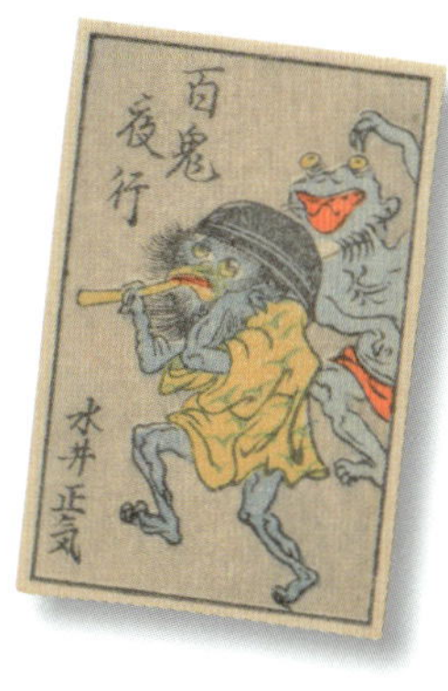 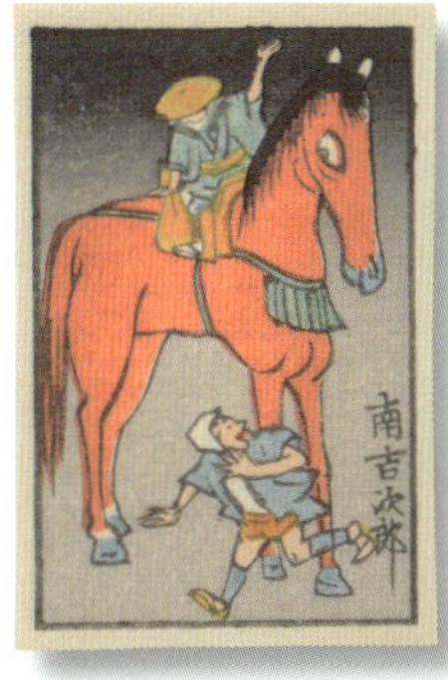 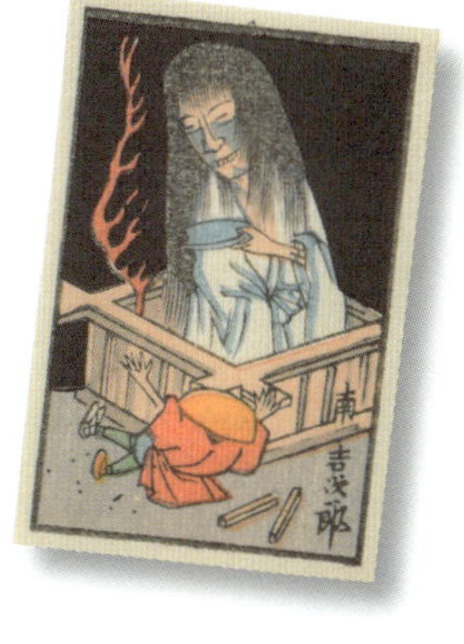 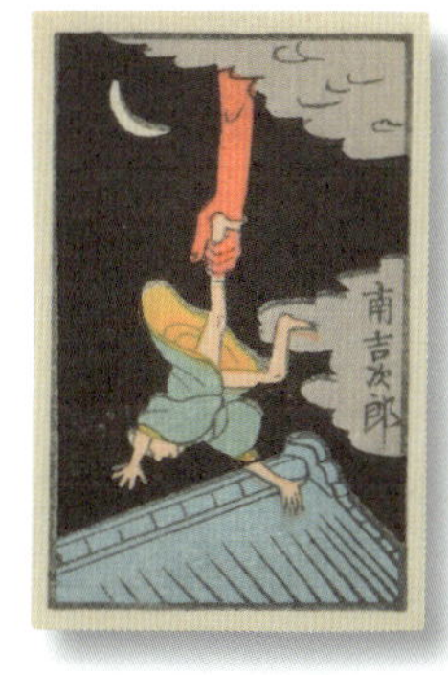

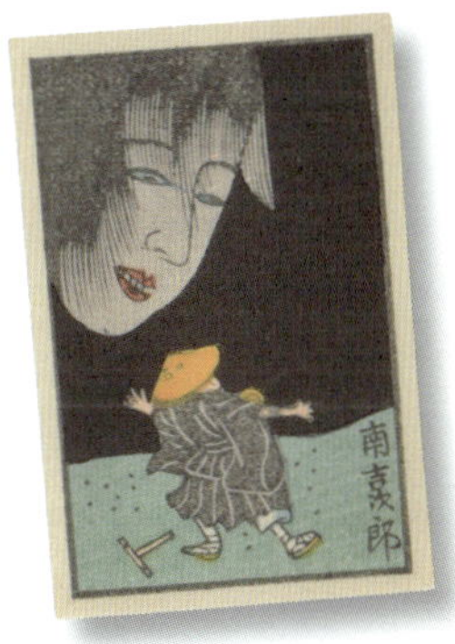 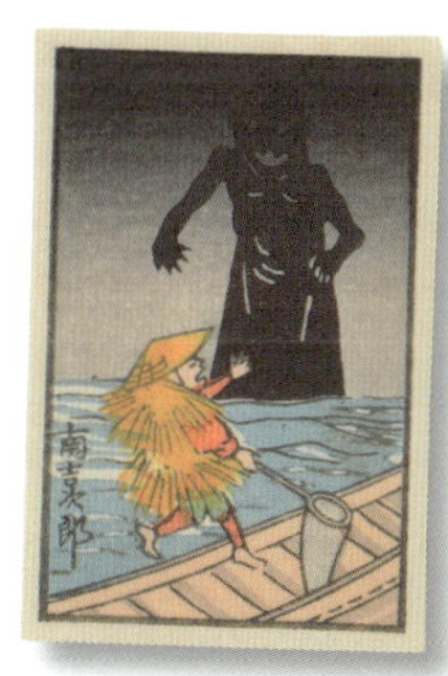 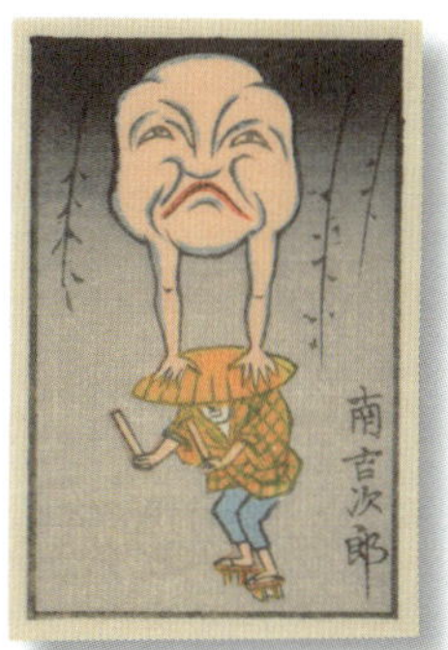 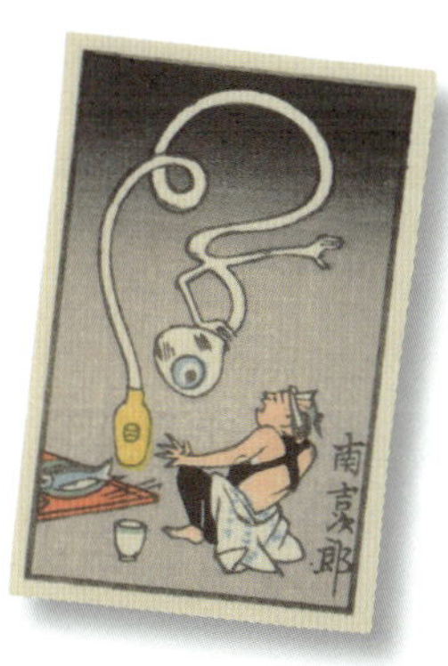

71 マッチラベル

まっちらべる

Matchbox Labels (*Macchi Raberu*)

昭和時代　縦 5.5　横 3.5　Shōwa period, Height5.5, Width 3.5

マッチ箱に貼られたラベルは広告として大きな役割を果たし、無数のデザインのラベルが作られたが、やがて趣味でのマッチラベル収集も行われるようになり、そのための多種多様なマッチラベルも制作された。この妖怪マッチラベルもそうした類のものだ。テーマは古くからの言い伝えが多いが、オリジナリティある描かれ方となっている。南吉次郎、三田村薫、水井正気、白井などの名前はラベルの制作者であろう。

The labels stuck on match boxes played a major role in advertising, and countless label designs were created, but eventually people began to collect matchbox labels as a hobby, and an abundant variety of labels were designed specifically for that purpose. These are collector's edition yokai matchbox labels. Their subjects are mainly myths, drawn with an original twist. The names Nankichi Jirō, Mita Murashi, Mizui Shōki, and Shirai on the labels are likely to be the names of their creators.

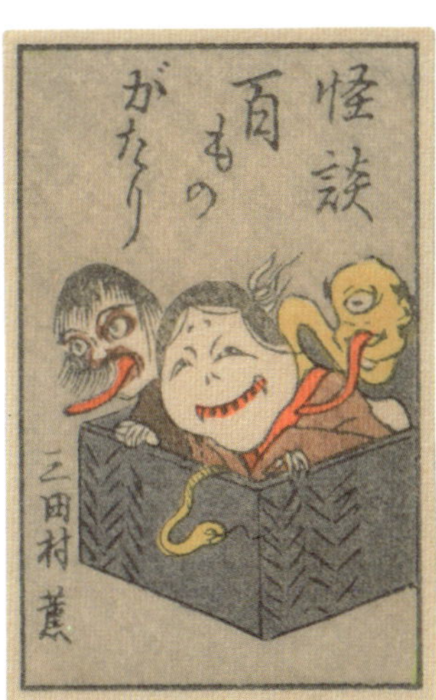

72 おばけろうそく説明書

おばけろうそくせつめいしょ

Ghost Candle Instructions
(*Obake Rōsoku Setsumei-sho*)

明治時代以降　Post-Meiji period

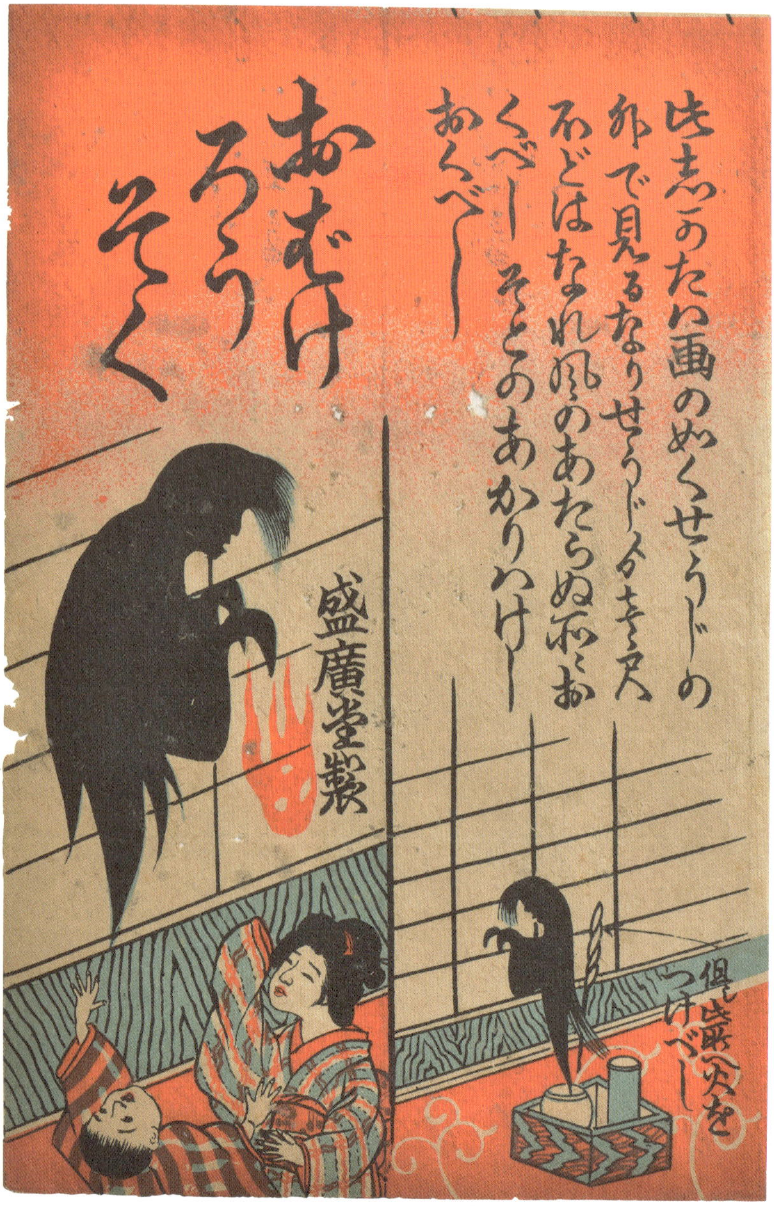

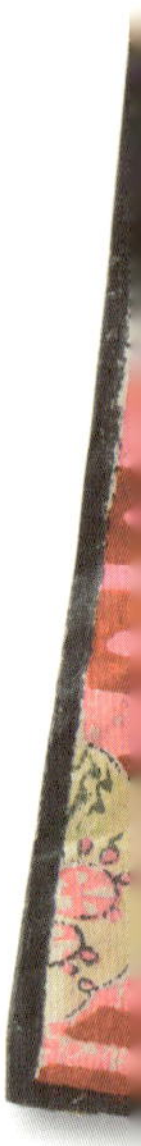

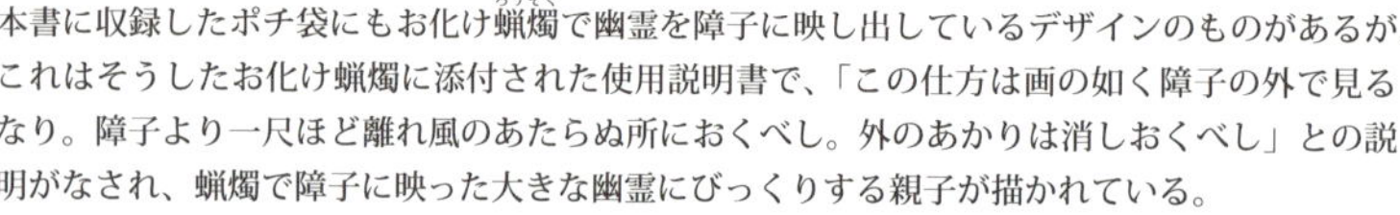

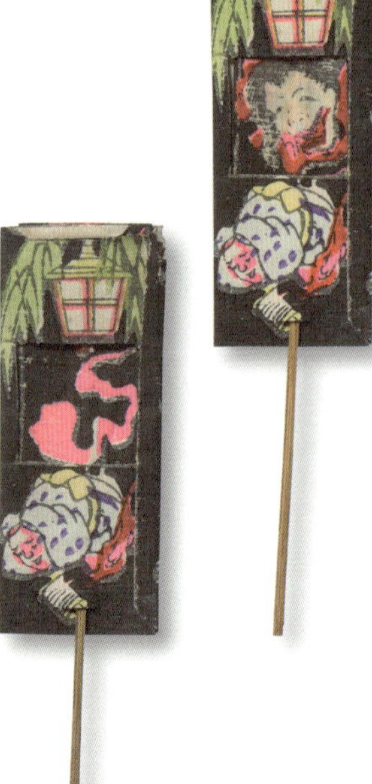

本書に収録したポチ袋にもお化け蝋燭で幽霊を障子に映し出しているデザインのものがあるが、これはそうしたお化け蝋燭に添付された使用説明書で、「この仕方は画の如く障子の外で見るなり。障子より一尺ほど離れ風のあたらぬ所におくべし。外のあかりは消しおくべし」との説明がなされ、蝋燭で障子に映った大きな幽霊にびっくりする親子が描かれている。

An envelope with the silhouette produced by a ghost candle on it is also collected in this book, but these are instructions for a ghost candle's use: "View from outside paper screen. Place approximately 30 cm from paper screen, away from drafts. Extinguish all other lights." The illustration shows a parent and child terrified by the large ghost silhouetted on the screen by the candle.

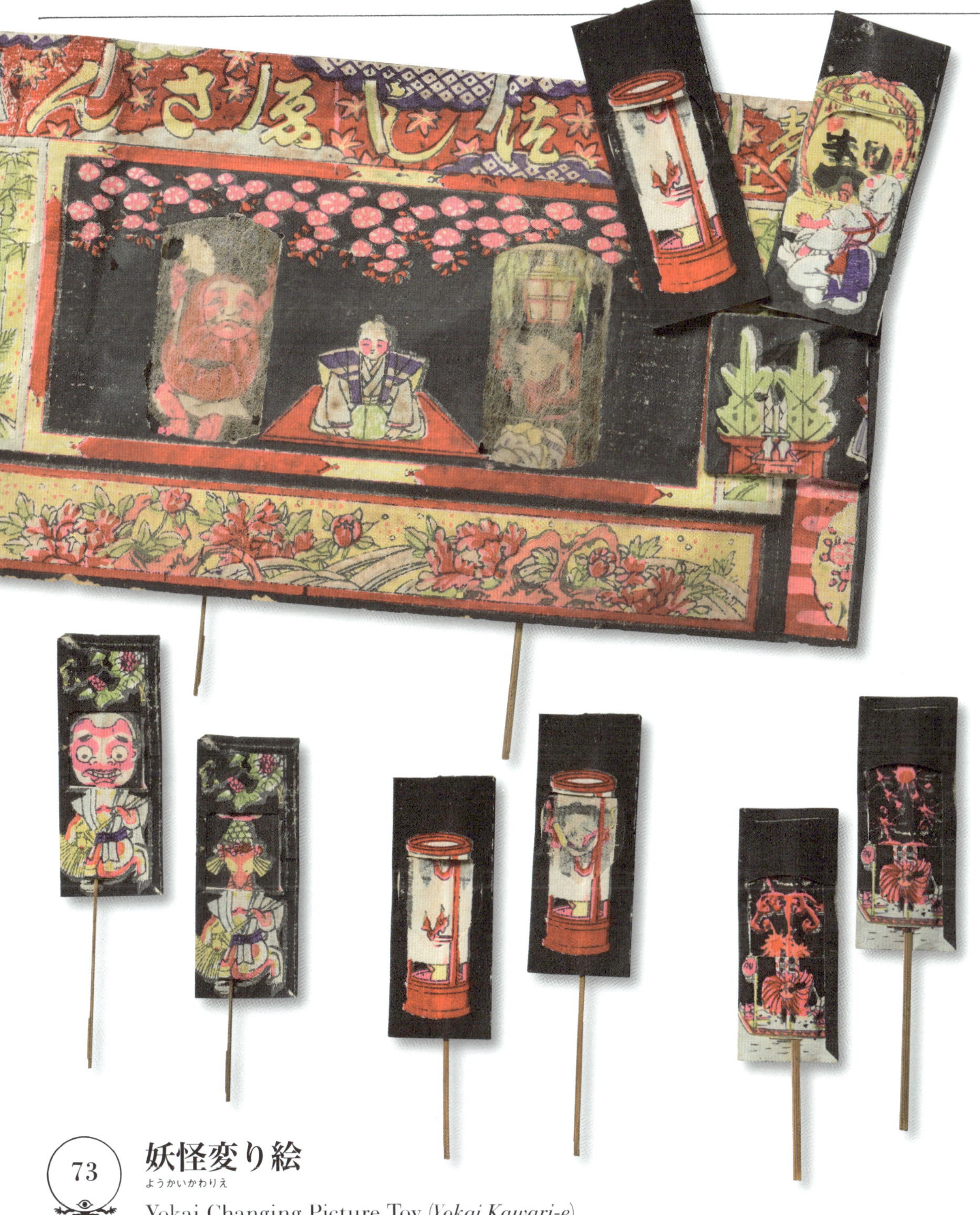

(73)

妖怪変り絵
ようかいかわりえ

Yokai Changing Picture Toy (*Yokai Kawari-e*)

明治時代以降　縦 12.5　横 23.5　Post-Meiji period, Height 12.5, Width 23.5

本書収録の「しん板かはりうつしえ」(p.156) と同様に画面を動か
して妖怪が出る趣向だが、この作品は舞台を設定して舞台上で行灯
に化け物が出たり、柳の下に幽霊が出て来るなどする遊びだ。舞台
の中央には挨拶する興行主を描き、左右に変り絵を入れるスペース
がある。変り絵のなかでも凝った作りといえよう。

This is a toy with a stage set up, where ghosts may appear in a lantern or
under a willow; the New Edition Magic Lantern Show (p.156) has a similar
mechanism by which the picture moves and yokai appear. In the middle of
the stage is the impresario greeting the audience, and on the left and right
are spaces for changing pictures. Even for a *kawari-e* the workmanship is
sophisticated.

しん板かはりうつしえ
しんばんかわりうつしえ

New Edition Magic Lantern Show (*Shinpan Kawari Utsushi-e*)

明治時代　縦 7.0　横 3.0　Meiji period, Height 7.0, Width 3.0

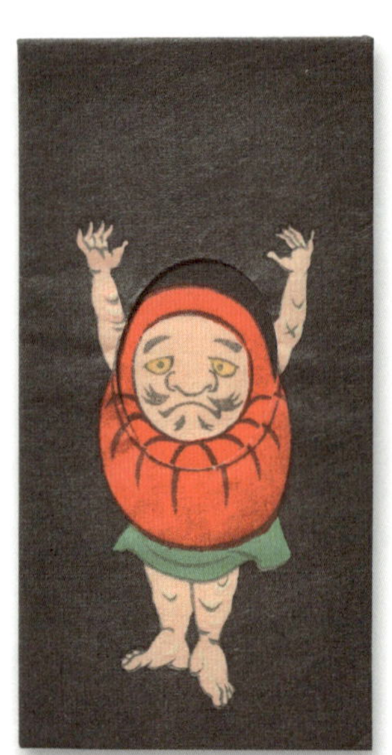

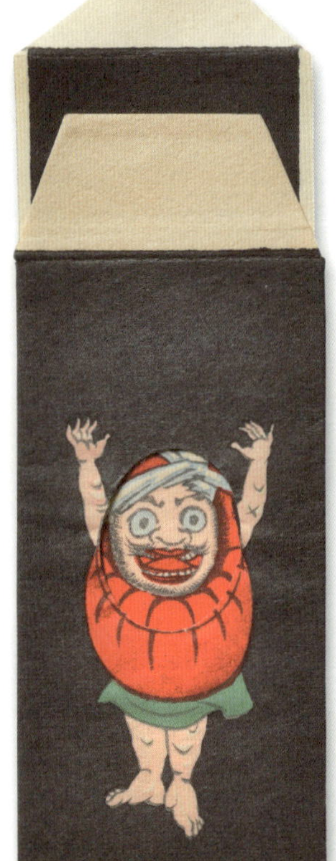

ポチ袋の中身の紙を引くと行灯に化け猫が出現
したり、狸が三つ目入道になったり、娘が骸骨
になったりする趣向の変り絵。変り絵には妖怪
を扱ったものも江戸時代からいくつか存在する。
遊びのなかでの妖怪の広がりを見ることのでき
る資料だ。

When the paper inside these envelopes is pulled,
the pictures transform: a monster cat appears in the
lantern, a raccoon dog changes into a three-eyed
priest, and a maiden turns into a skeleton. There
are a number of yokai *kawari-e* (lit., "changing
pictures") which date from the Edo period onwards.
This medium shows the spread of yokai into games.

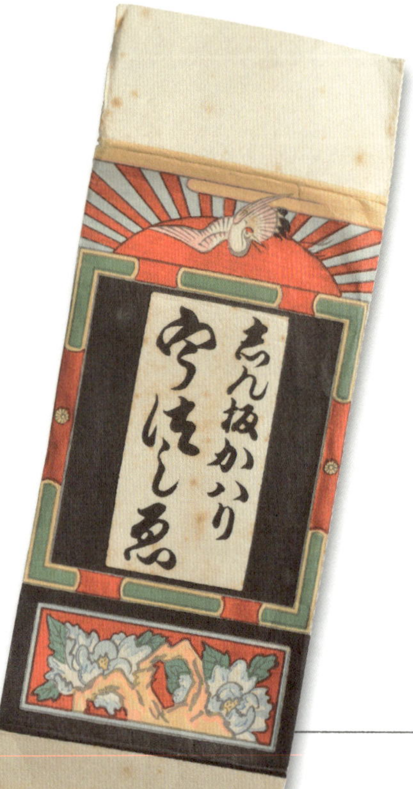

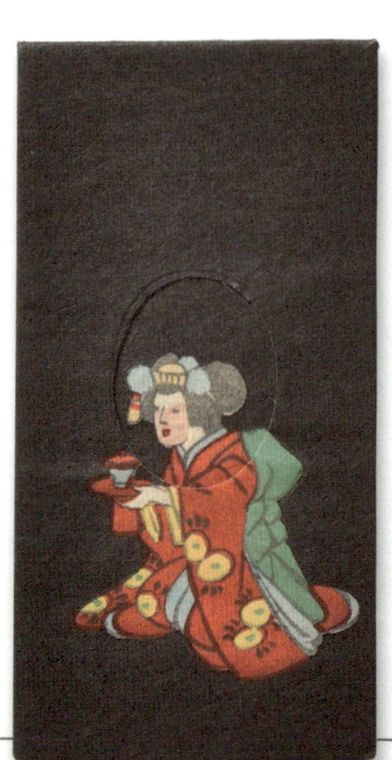

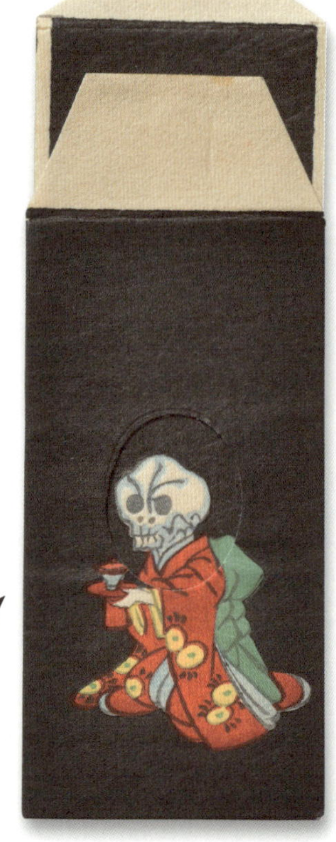

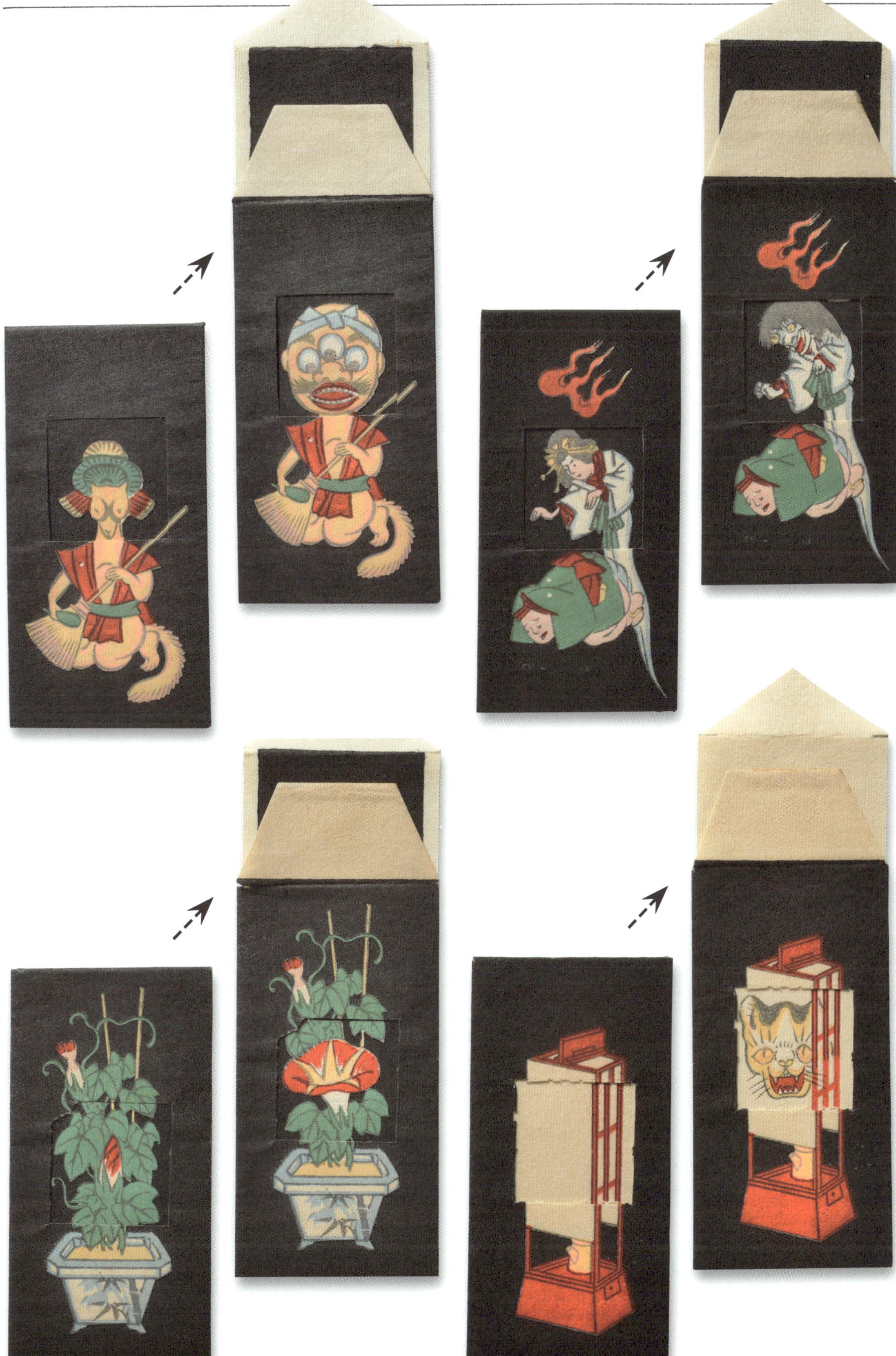

おばけかるた
Ghost Playing Cards (*Obake Karuta*)

江戸時代以降　箱：縦・横各 6.0 厚 5.0、札：縦 6.5　横 4.5
Post-Edo period, Case: Length and Width 6.0, Height 5.0,
Card: Height 6.5, Width 4.5

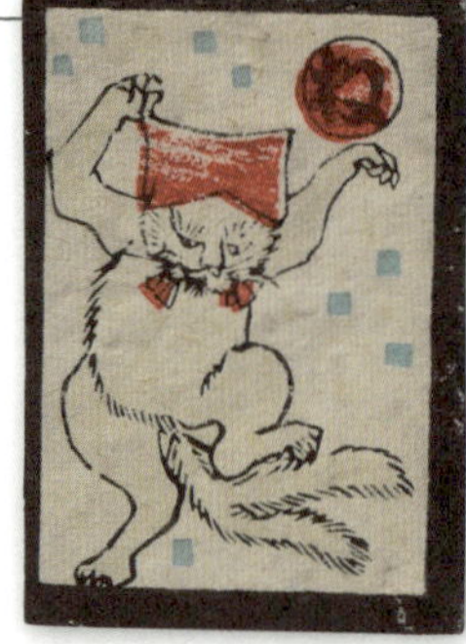
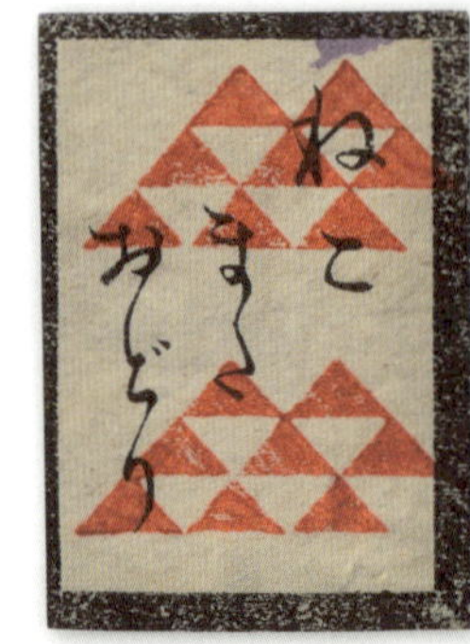
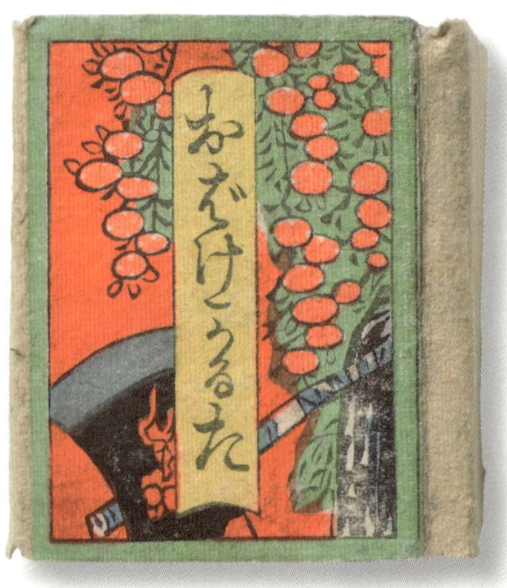
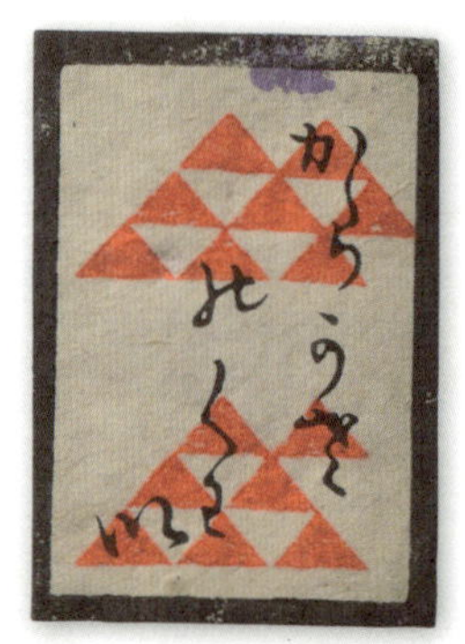
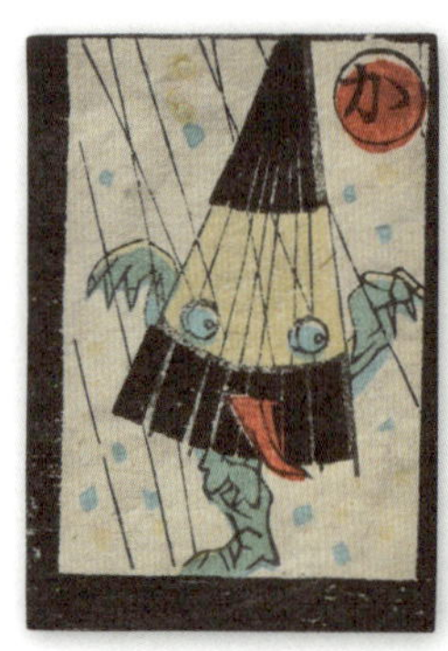
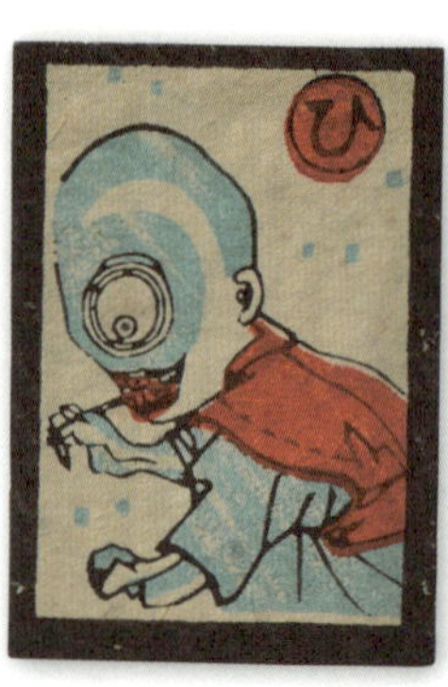
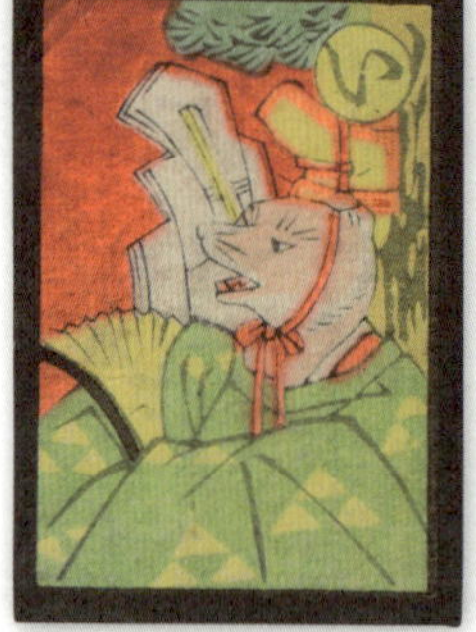
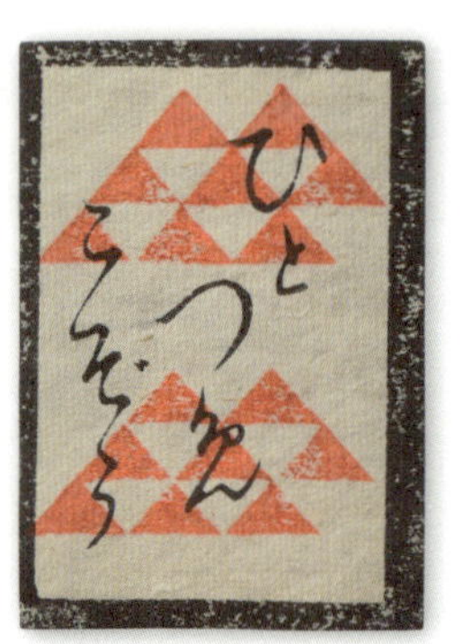
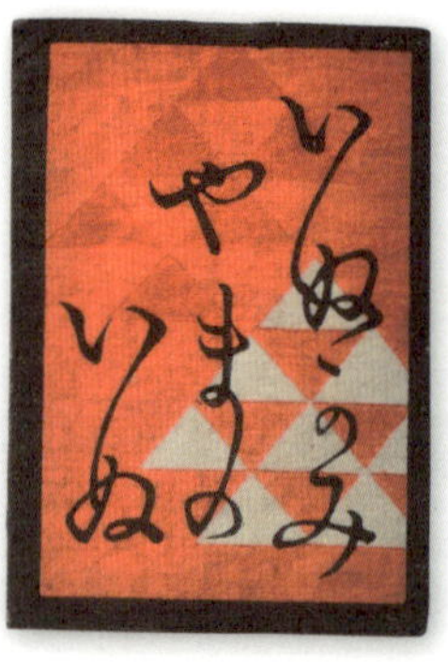
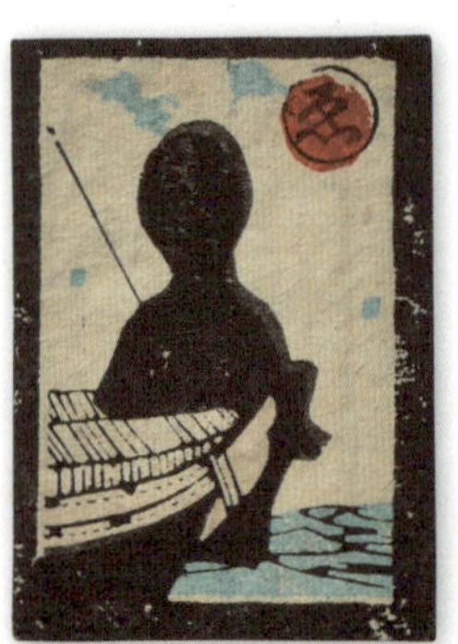
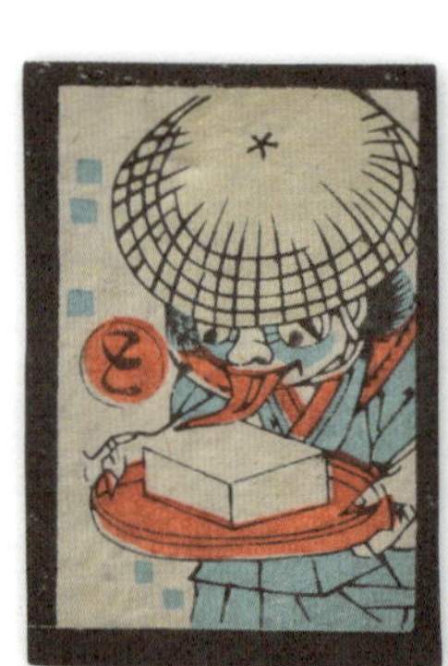
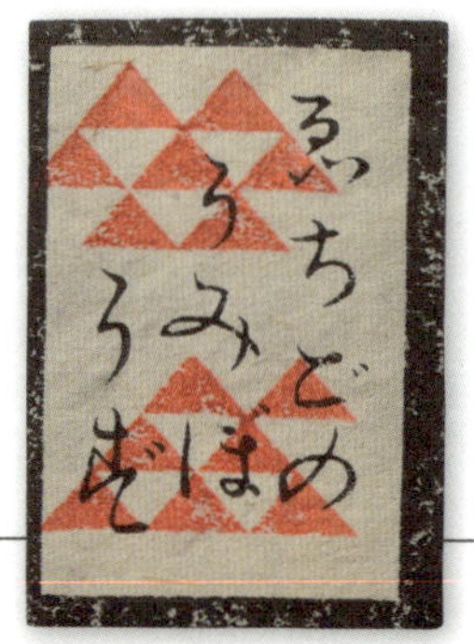

妖怪カルタは江戸時代から何種類もだされており、大きさも区々だが、
このカルタは平均的な大きさといえる。イロハの最初の「い」は絵札
も読札も他の札より丁寧な作りとなっている。
Yokai *karuta* have been produced in various types and sizes since the Edo
period; these cards are of average size. The picture and text on the first card
'i' of the 'i-ro-ha' (Japanese ABC) are more carefully drawn than the others.

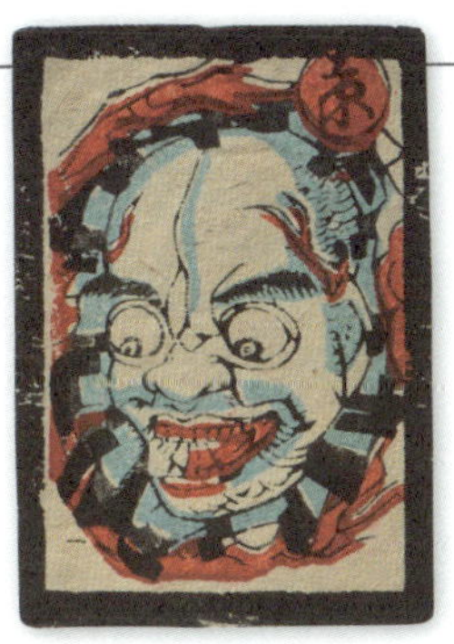

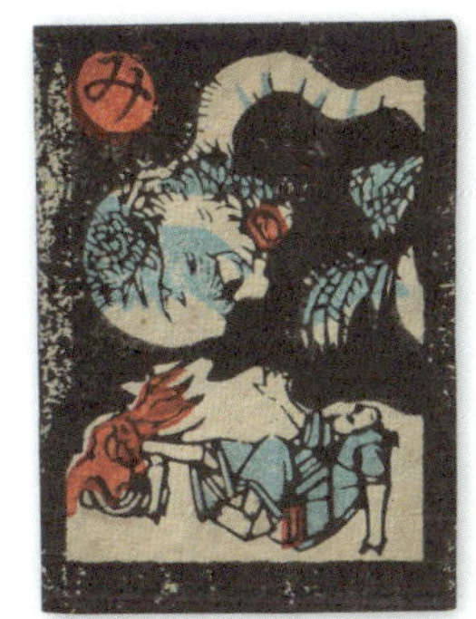

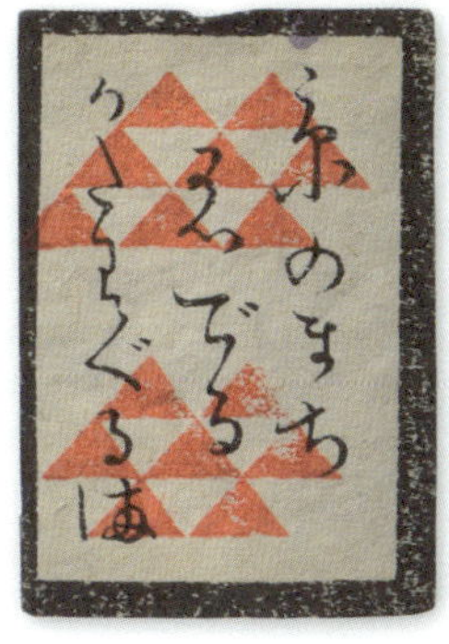

76 妖怪イロハカルタ

ようかいいろはかるた

A to Z Yokai Cards

(*Yokai Iroha Karuta*)

明治時代以降　箱：縦6.5　横5.5厚2.0、
札：縦4.0　横2.5
Post-Meiji period, Case: Length 6.5, Width 5.5, Height 2.0,
Card: Height 4.0, Width 2.5

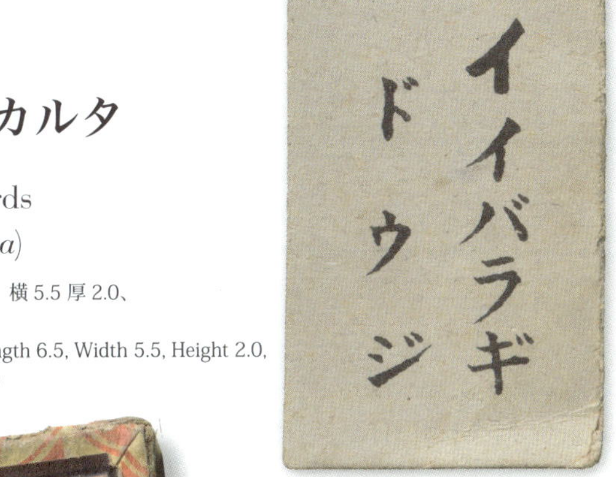

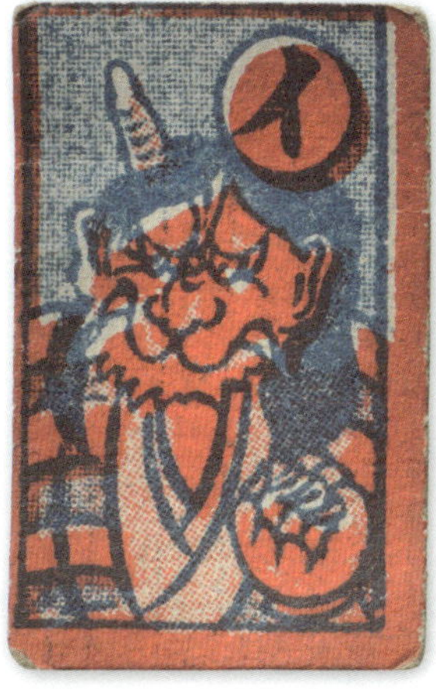

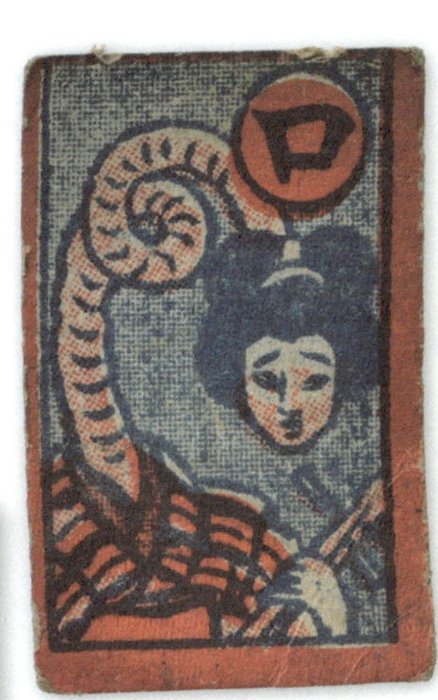

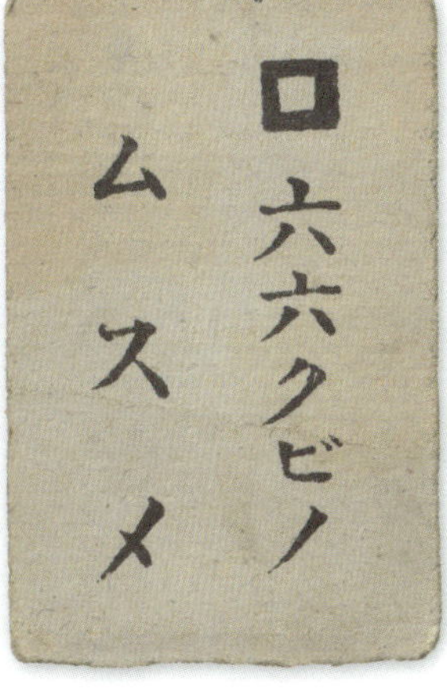

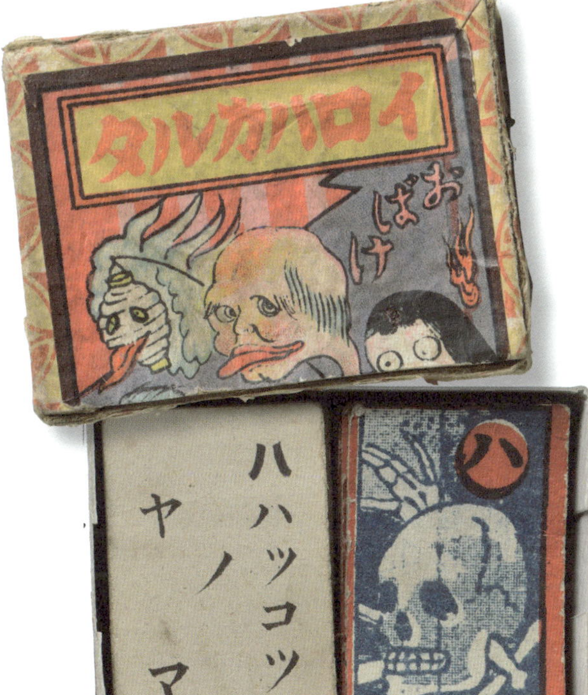

この妖怪カルタは読札は字だけ、絵札も赤と青の2色刷
で、サイズも小さく図版もズレているなど簡易な作りと
なっており、子どもが遊びで使ったものなのだろう。
These yokai cards were probably made for children's games;
they are small and basic with text on one side and a crudely-
printed picture in red and blue ink on the other.

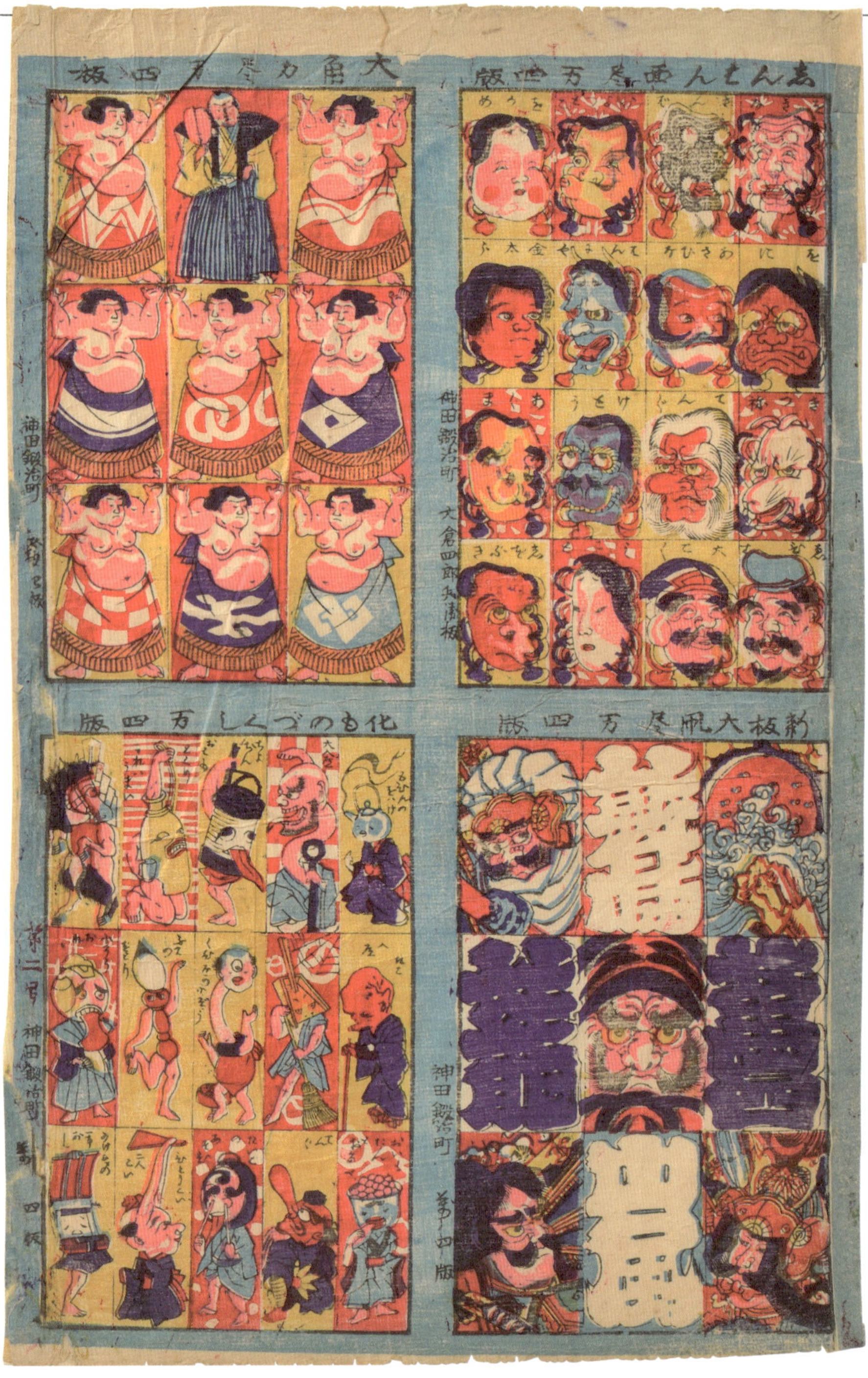

おもちゃ絵 化ものづくし

おもちゃえばけものづくし

Toy Pictures: Monsters Compendium (*Omocha-e: Bakemono Zukushi*)

江戸時代以降　大判　Post-Edo period, Ōban

「お化け尽くし」「化け物つくし」などのタイトルで、大判一枚のなかにさまざまな妖怪を描いたおもちゃ絵があるが、この作品は「面づくし」「角力づくし」「大凧づくし」とともに左下に配置されている。このように別なものと一緒に紹介されているケースも散見できる。

There are *omocha-e* of various yokai on a single large sheet with titles like Monster Tsukushi or *Bakemono Tsukushi*, but on this sheet masks, sumo wrestlers and giant kites join the monsters on the lower left. Occasionally, dissimilar things are presented together.

大新板ばけものず(づ)くし

だいしんばんばけものずくし

Daishinpan Bakemono Zukushi

明治時代　縦 36.5　横 16　Meiji period, Height 36.5, Width 16

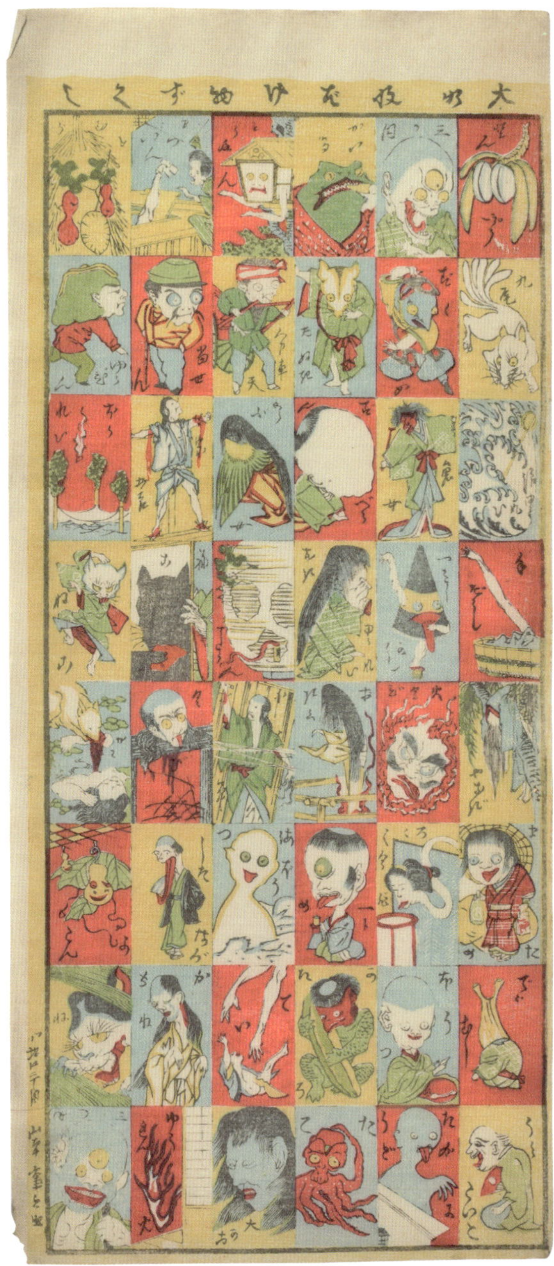

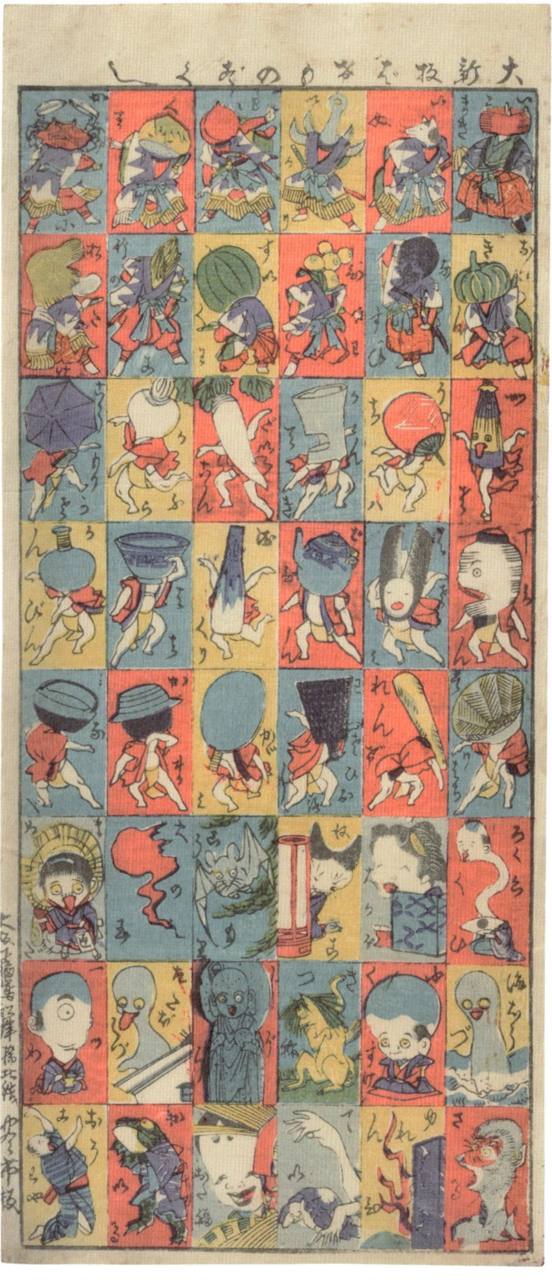

縦長のおもちゃ絵。さまざまな妖怪が描かれているが、そのなかに「こうもりがさ」や「人力車夫」の妖怪も登場していることから明治時代に入ってからの作品といえよう。

Vertically long *omocha-e* (lit. "toy picture"). Many different yokai are depicted, but this is identifiable as a work of the Meiji period by the yokai *Kōmorigasa* (Umbrella Bat) and Rickshaw Driver among them.

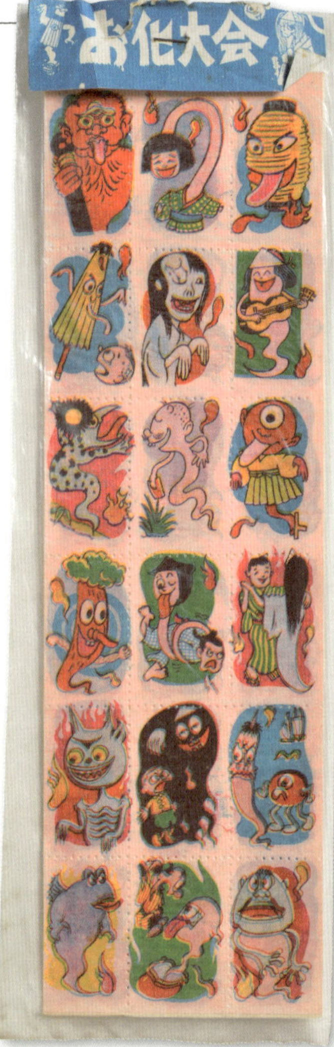

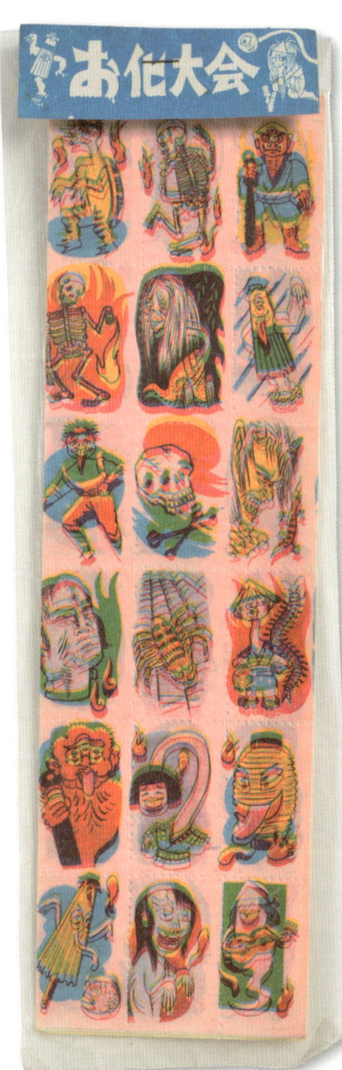

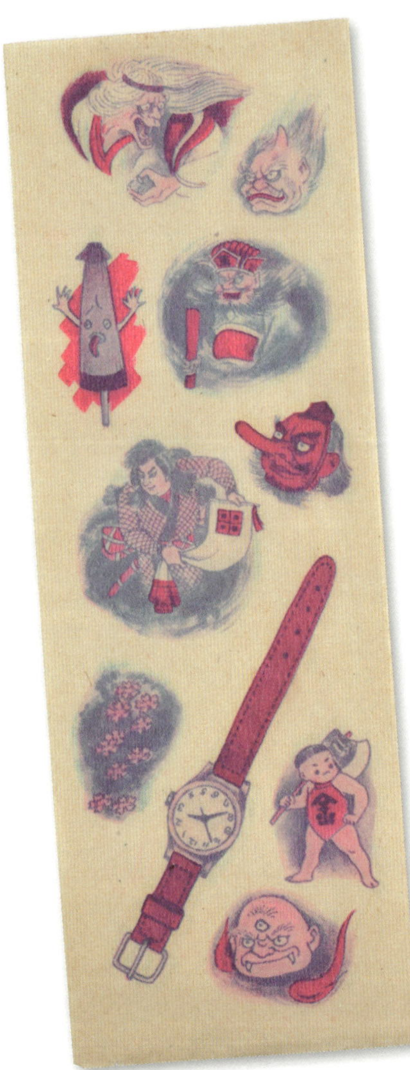

<table>
<tr><td>

80

妖怪シール
ようかいしーる

Yokai Stickers

昭和時代　縦 21.5　横 7.5
Shōwa period, Height 21.5, Width 7.5

</td></tr>
</table>

79

お化大会
おばけたいかい

Ghost Tourney (*Obake Taikai*)

昭和時代　縦 23.0　横 7.0　Shōwa period, Height 23.0, Width 7.0

子どもたちの遊びのためのシール。短冊形で江戸時代のおもちゃ絵のようにいくつ
もの妖怪を描いているが、一つ一つを切り離せるようにパンチ穴があけられている。
左右のシールを見比べると場所は違うものの提灯お化け、唐傘お化け、幽霊など同
じ図版が汎用されていることがわかる。印刷が大きくずれているなど簡易な制作で
あることがみてとれるが、これも子ども相手のグッズだったからであろう。
Stickers for a children's game. Many yokai are drawn on a strip like an Edo period
omocha-e, but holes are punched in the card so that each one can be separated. A
comparison of the stickers on the left and right reveals that some of the same plates have
been used in both cases but in different locations on the card. Made for children, it is
obvious from the degree of misalignment that these were crudely printed.

妖怪尽くし絵
ようかいづくしえ

Yokai Zukushi-e

明治時代以降　縦 54.2　横 19.1
Post-Meiji period, Height 54.2, Width 19.1

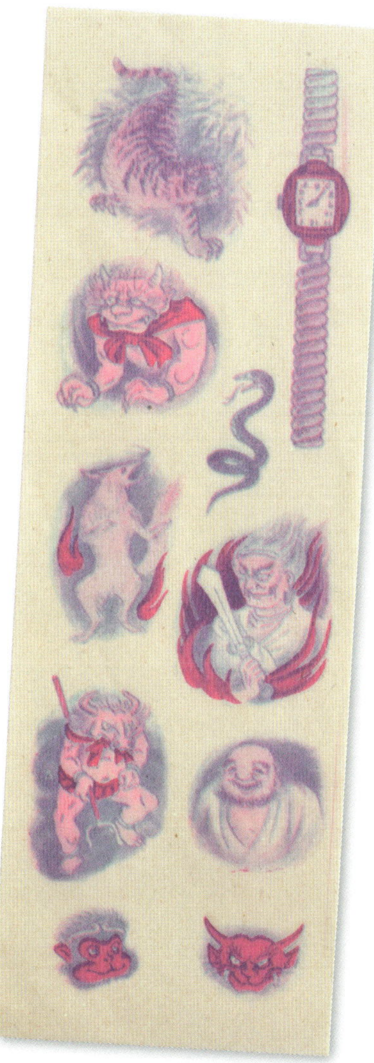

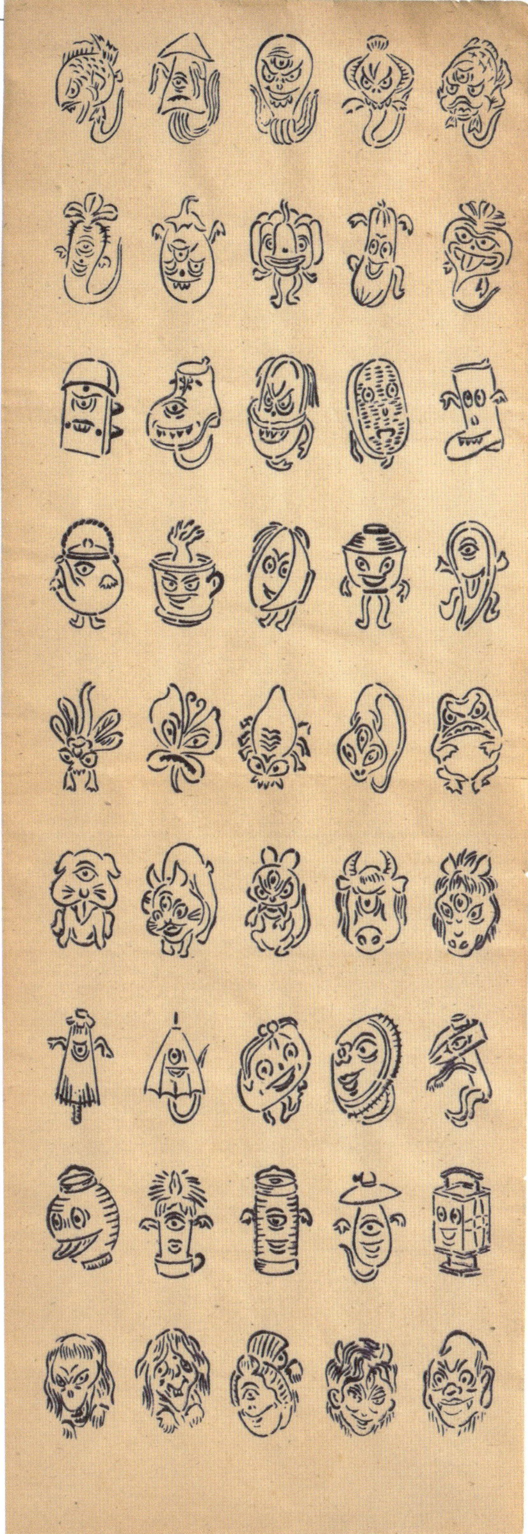

駄菓子屋で売っている子ども向けのシール。唐傘お
化け、三つ目入道、鬼、妖狐などが腕時計といっしょ
に描かれていて、ごちゃ混ぜの内容となっているが、
それも時代の反映といえるだろう。

Stickers for children which were sold at mom-and-pop
candy stores. A paper umbrella ghost, a three-eyed
priest, an ogre and a fox spirit are drawn all together in a
jumble which may be said to reflect the era.

さまざまな妖怪を描いているが上段は魚類、2 段目は野菜、3 段目
は履物、4 段目は器、5 段目は虫、6 段目は動物、7 段目は日常具、
8 段目は照明器具、9 段目は人間といった配置になっている。

This collection of yokai can be placed in nine categories from top to
bottom: sea creatures, vegetables, footwear, utensils, insects, animals,
everyday items, lights, and human-like creatures.

82

新板化物飛廻双六
しんぱんばけものとびまわりすごろく

New Edition Monster Board Game

(*Shinpan Bakemono Tobimawari Sugoroku*)

明治時代　Meiji period

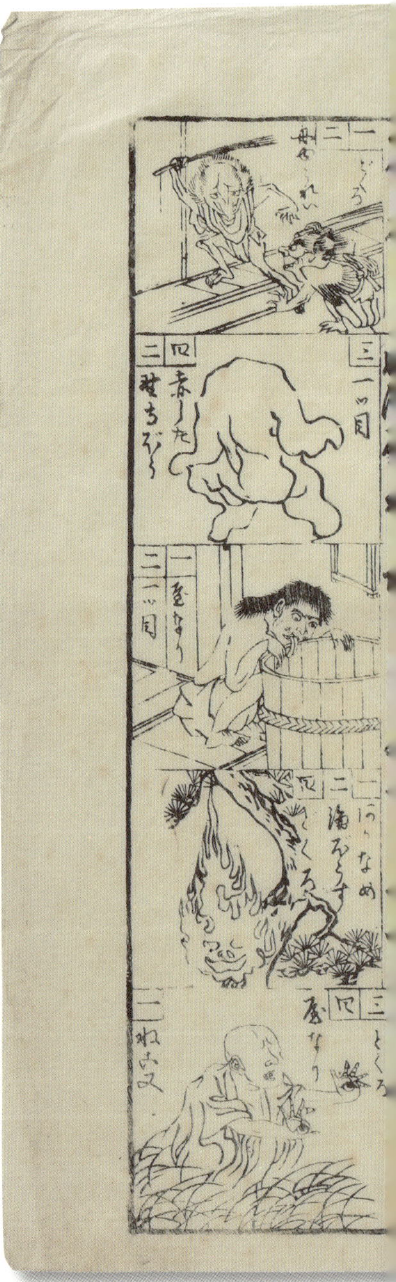

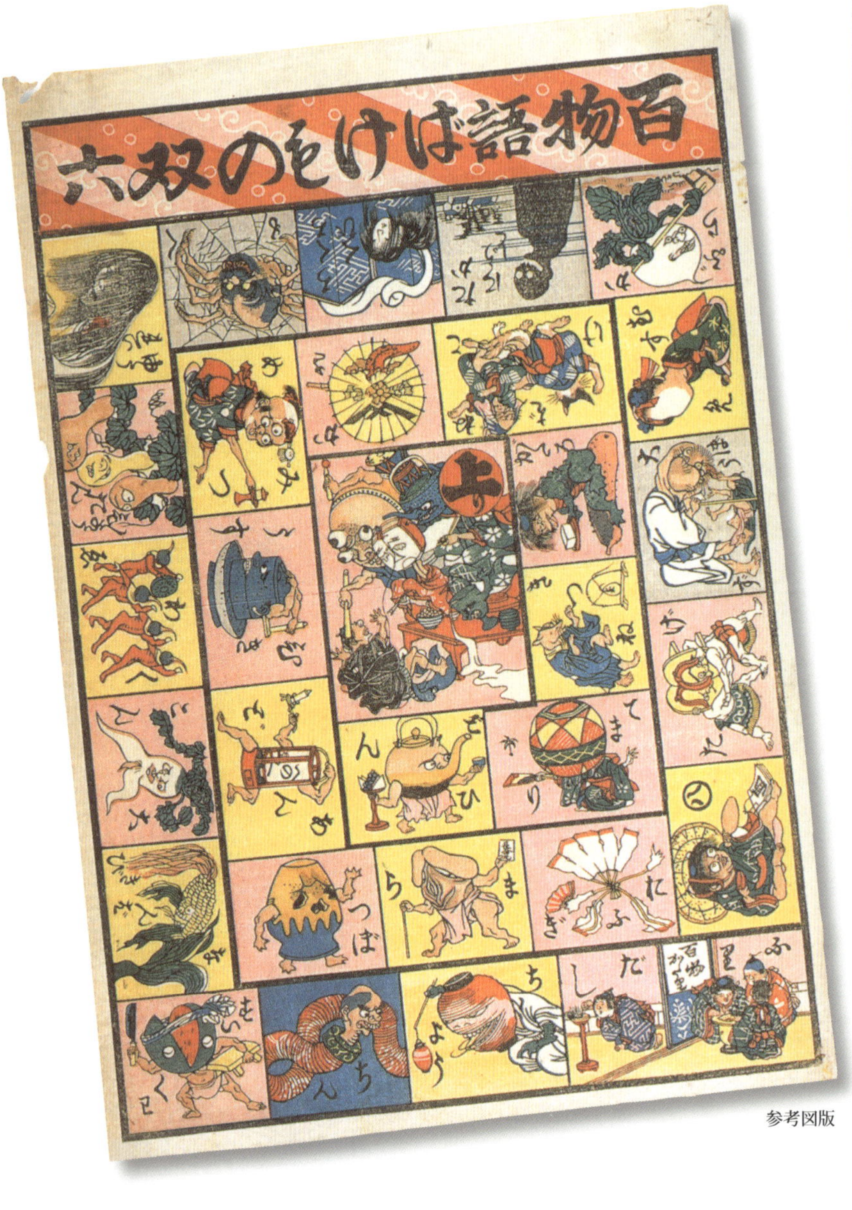

参考図版

百物語ばけもの双六　江戸時代以降　大判
タイトルに双六とあるが、サイコロの目数
は表示されていないので、実際に使うとい
うよりも双六スタイルのおもちゃ絵的なも
のといえよう。
One Hundred Tales Monster Board Game
(*Hyaku Monogatari Bakemono Sugoroku*)
Post-Edo period, *ōban* No dice numbers are
given: this is not an actual game to be played
but an *omocha-e* (lit. "toy picture") in the style
of a board game.

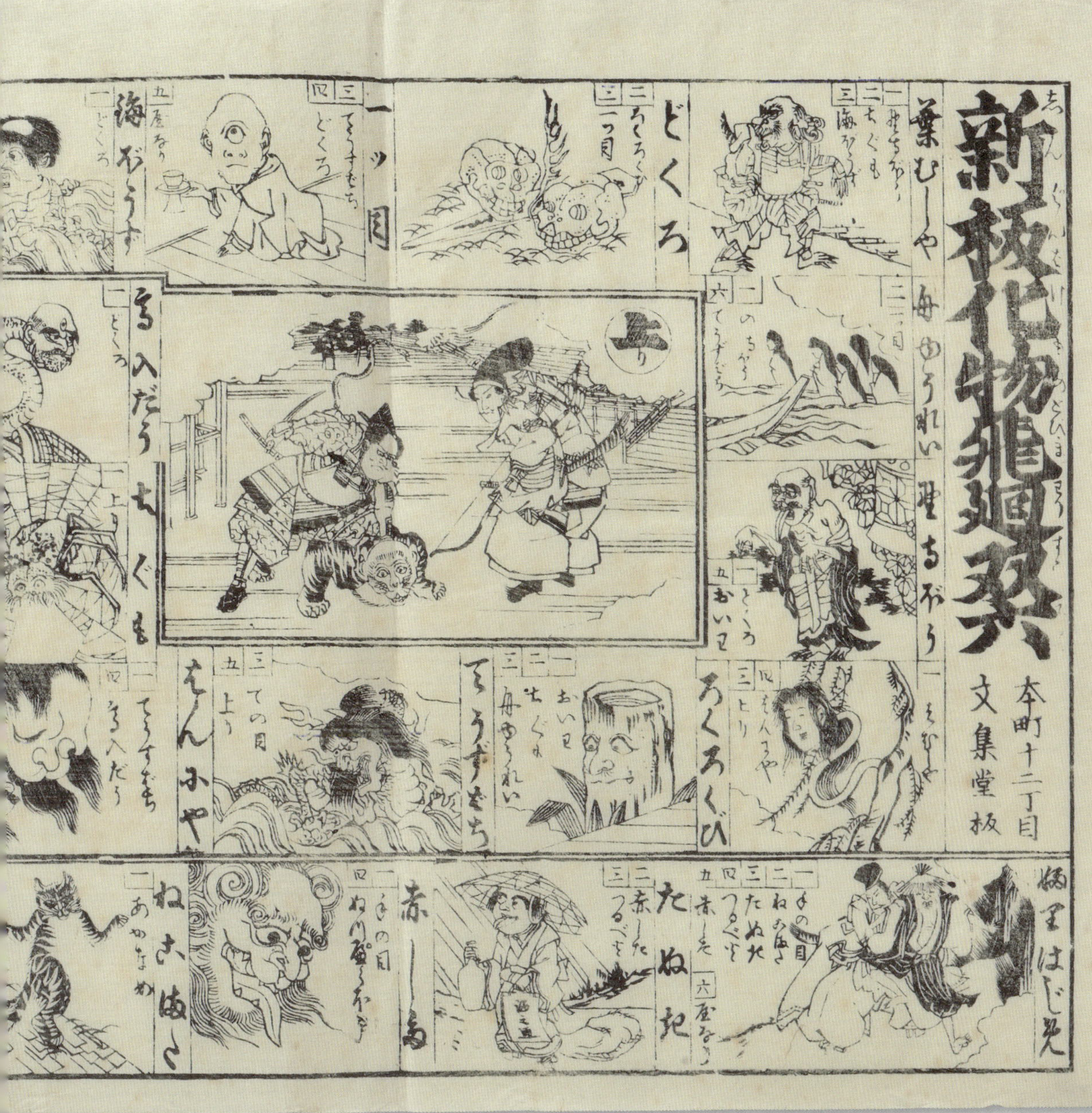

妖怪双六の一つで上りが鵺を退治した場面。描かれた妖怪はよく知られたものが多いが、「葉むしゃ」といったあまり聞きなれない妖怪も登場している。葉っぱを身に着けた武者姿なので、「葉武者」ということだろう。「海ぼうず」は何故か河童が描かれているようだ。

In this yokai board game, the winning square (*agari*) is the defeat of the Nue. The yokai are mostly familiar except for a relative unknown called Hamusha. As he is a warrior-like figure dressed in leaves, the name may mean "leaf warrior." For some reason "Umibōzu" is drawn as a *kappa*.

「新版妖怪飛巡双六」版木

しんぱんようかいとびまわりすごろくはんぎ

Printing woodblock for
New Edition Monster Board Game
(*Shinpan Yokai
Tobimawari Sugoroku: Hangi*)

明治時代　縦 57　横 32　厚 3.0
Meiji period, Height 57, Width 32, Thickness 3.0

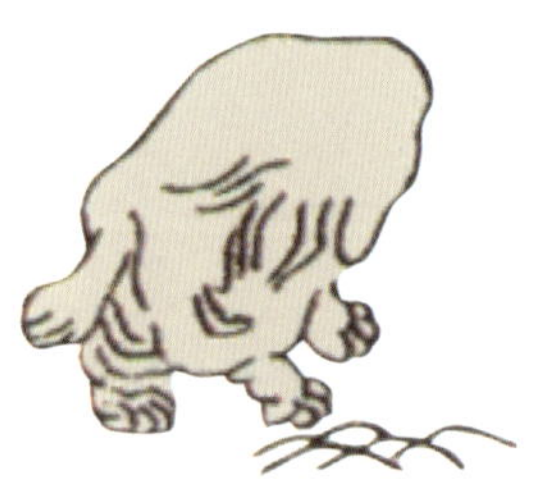

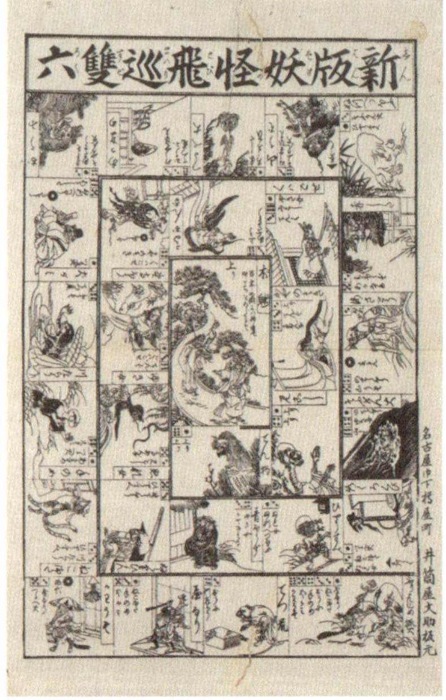

鳥山石燕の『画図百鬼夜行』に収録された妖怪を散りばめた双六の版木。（参考図版参照）
The yokai from Toriyama Sekien's *Illustrated Night Parade of One Hundred Demons* (*Gazu Hyakki Yagyō*) are strewn over this board game printing block (please refer to the print on the left).

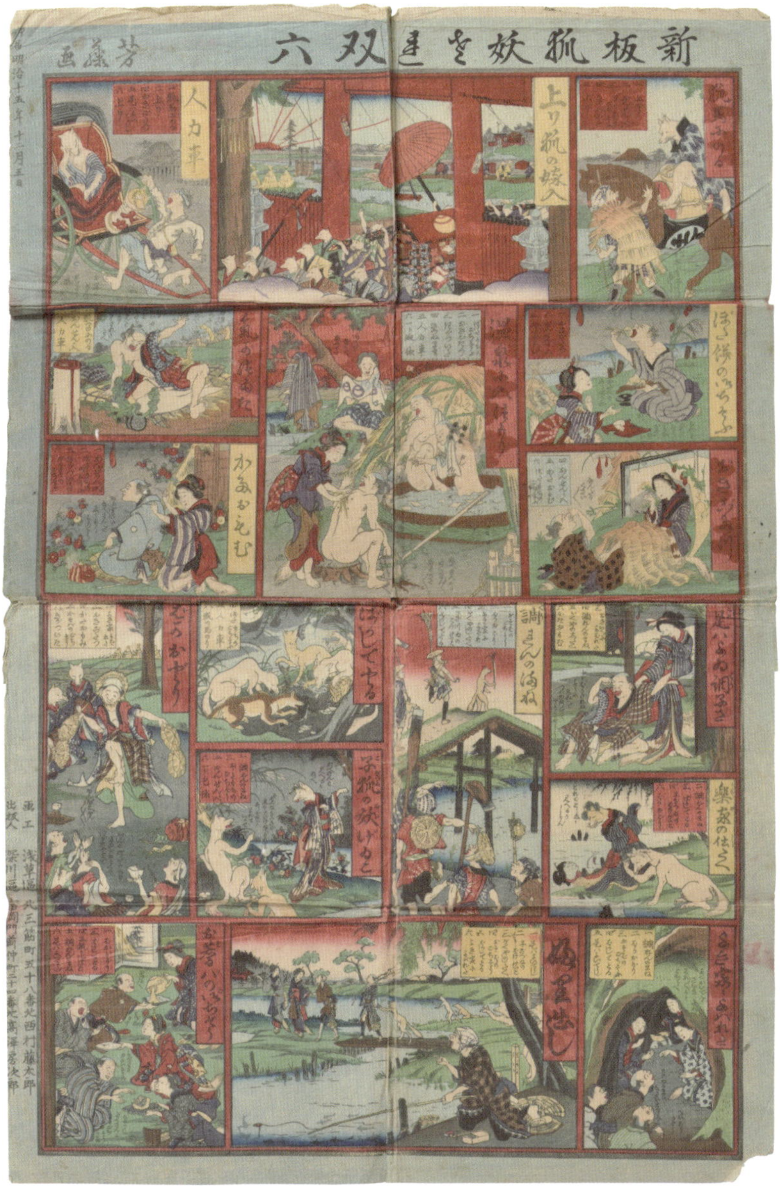

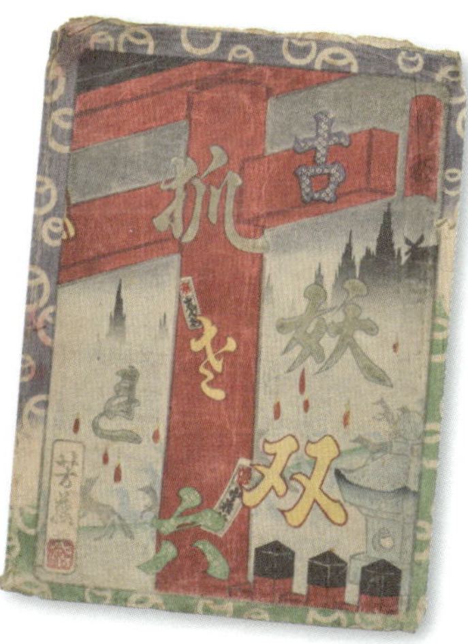

新板狐妖され双六
しんばんきつねばかされすごろく

New Edition Shapeshifting Fox Board Game (*Shinpan Kitsune Bakasare Sugoroku*)

歌川芳藤　明治 15 年（1882）12 月　縦 73.0　横 48.0　Utagawa Yoshifuji, December 1882 (Meiji 15) Height 73.0, Width 48.0

狐がさまざまに化かす姿を描き、上りは「狐の嫁入」となっており、豪壮な稲荷社へと向かう狐の嫁入りの行列となっている。時代を反映して人力車に乗った狐に驚く車夫の場面も登場する。この双六の袋では「新板古狐妖され双六」となっている。妖怪双六のなかには実際には使わずに見るだけのために制作されたものもあるが、この作品は実際に双六遊びに使われる目的でつくられた。

The myriad forms taken by the fox are illustrated; the winning square (*agari*) is "The Fox's Marriage", the wedding procession of foxes heading for the opulent Inari-sha Shrine. The scene of the rickshaw driver surprised that his passenger is a fox is a sign of the times. "New Edition Shapeshifting Fox Board Game" is written on the outer envelope. This was made to be used as a game, although some yokai *sugoroku* were made just to look at.

不二丸お化け双六
ふじまるおばけすごろく

Fujimaru and the Ghost Board Game
(*Fujimaru Obake Sugoroku*)

木下としお　昭和時代
袋：縦 29.5　横 21.5、
双六：縦 54.0　横 77.0
Kinoshita Toshio, Shōwa period,
Envelope: Height 29.5, Width 21.5,
Board Game: Height 54.0, Width 77.0

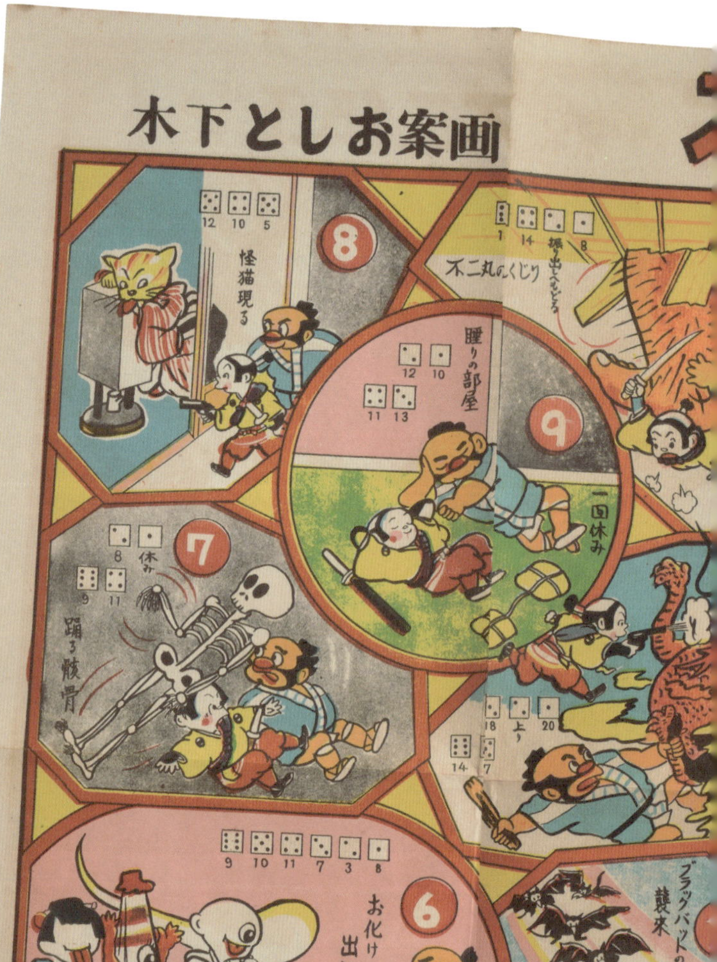

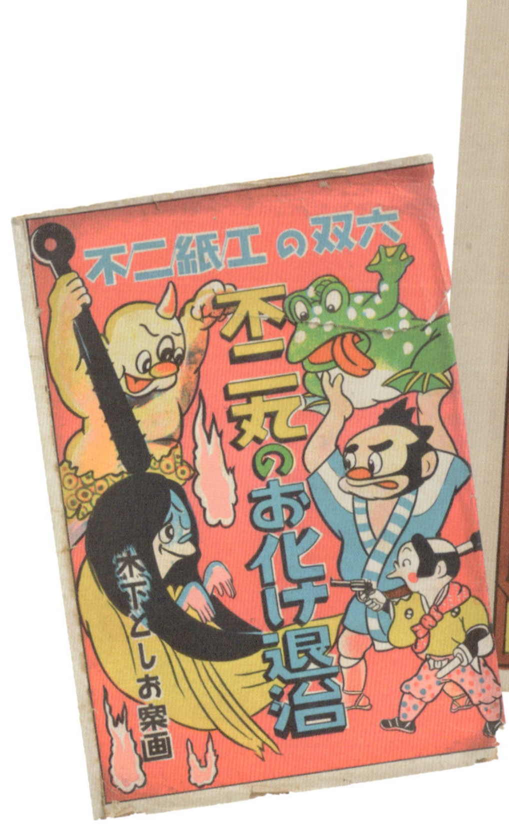

袋は「不二丸のお化け退治」となっている。子ども用の双六で振り出しで殿様にお姫様の救出を命じられた不二丸と赤鼻かん助がお化けと戦いながら救出を成功させるといったストーリーの双六。描かれたお化けたちはかわいい姿で幼少の子どもが遊ぶために制作されたものである。

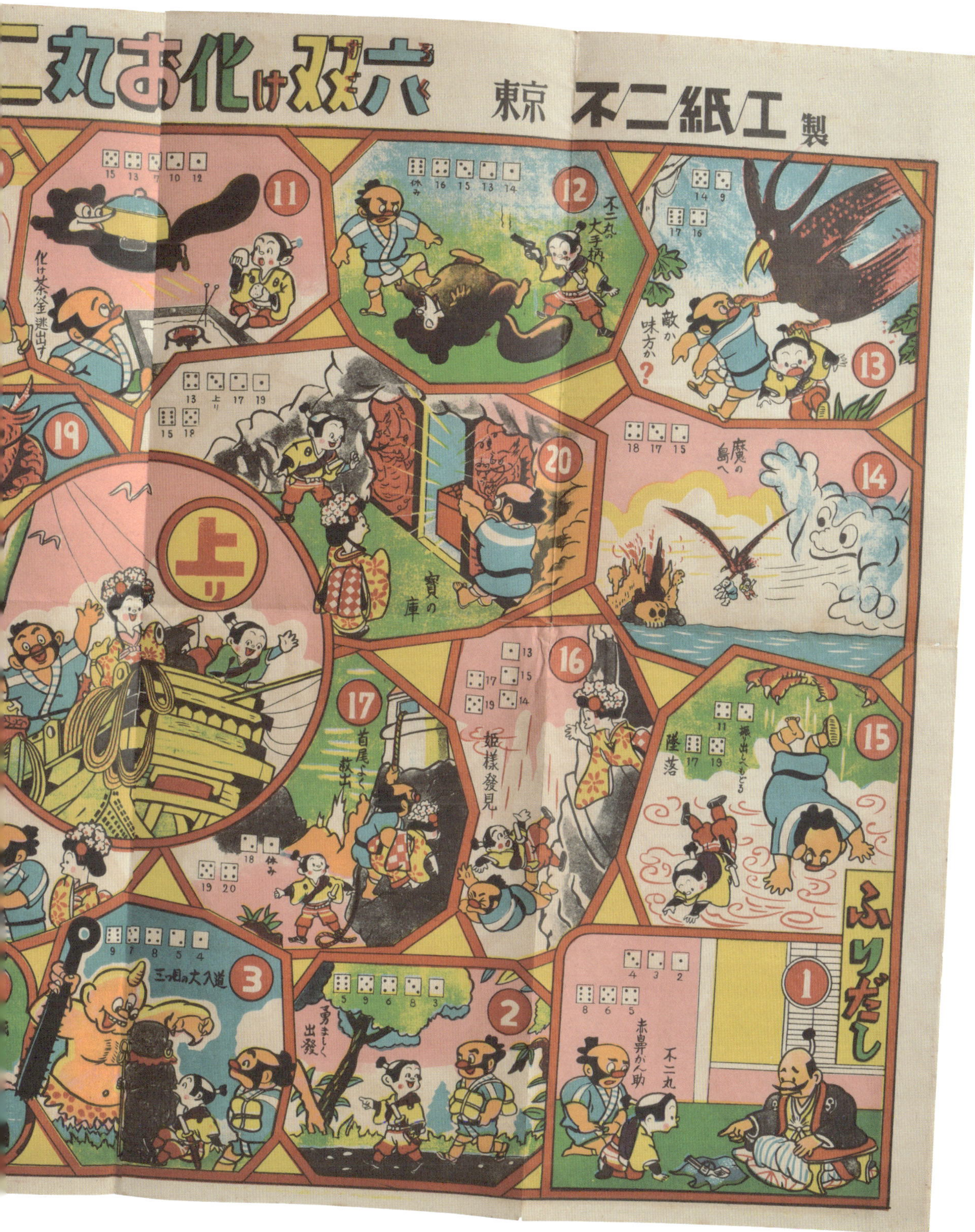

"Fujimaru Defeats a Ghost" is written on the bag. A board game for children to use: starting from square one, Fujimaru and Red Nose Kansuke are commanded by their lord to save a princess, and they fight a ghost to rescue her. Created for young children to play with, the ghosts depicted are cute.

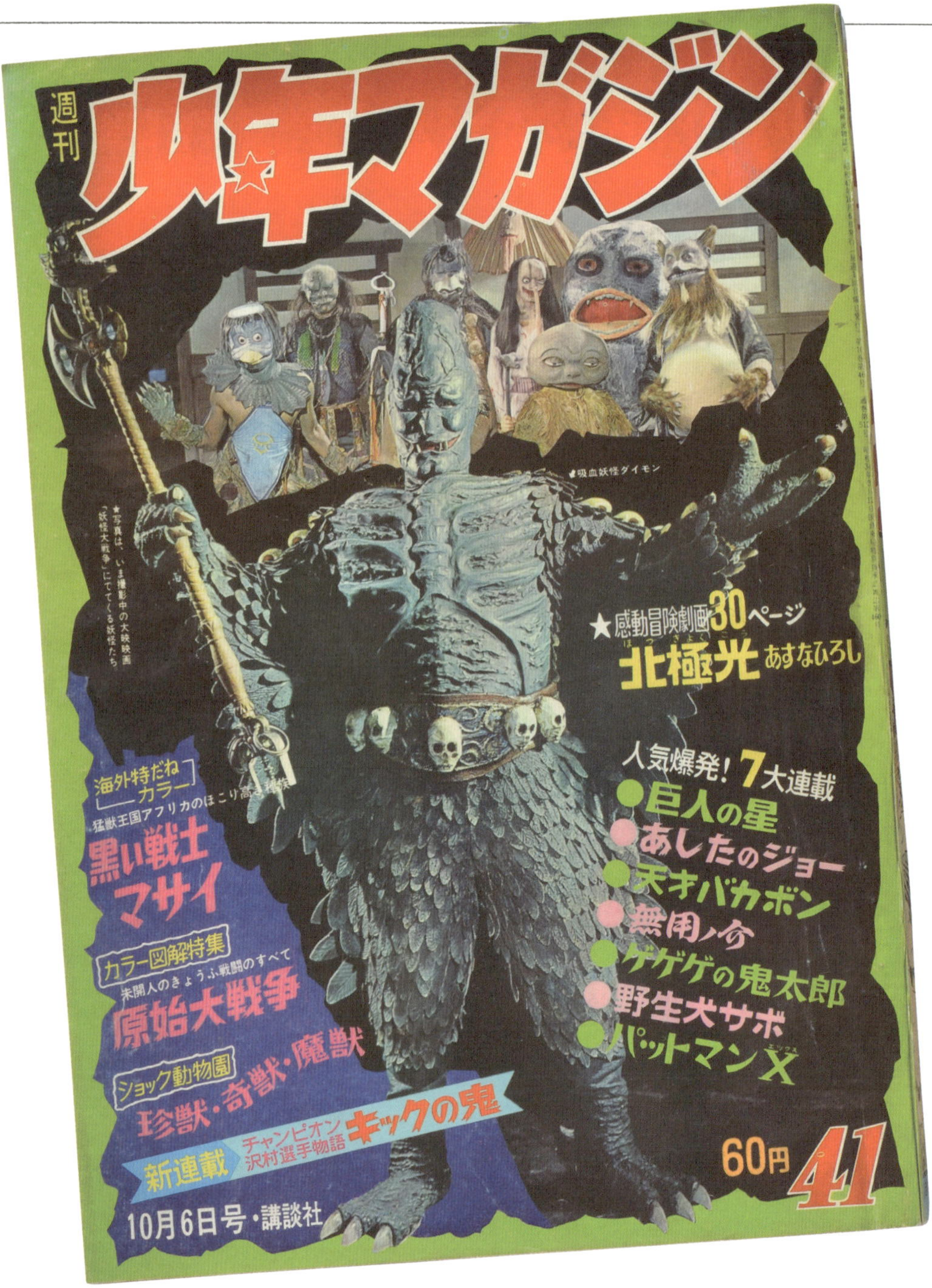

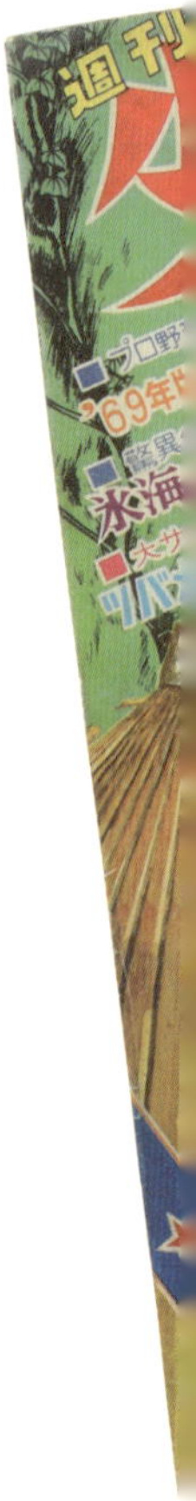

86 『週刊少年マガジン』10 巻 41 号

（昭和 43 年 10 月 6 日）

しゅうかんしょうねんまがじん

Weekly Shōnen Magazine volume 10 issue 41: October 6, 1968 (Shōwa 43)

少年漫画雑誌には人気となった妖怪映画を特集することもあり、映画の妖怪が表紙を飾るケースもみられる。この表紙は大映映画「妖怪大戦争」を扱ったもので、「写真は、いま撮影中の大映映画「妖怪大戦争」にでてくる妖怪たち」、中央の妖怪は「吸血妖怪ダイモン」と紹介されている。

Shōnen manga magazines (intended for young males) featured popular yokai movies, and occasionally yokai from movies made the cover. This cover promotes the Daiei motion picture The Great Yokai War (*Yōkai Daisensō*); the yokai in the center is introduced as Blood-sucking Yokai Daimon and the photo caption reads "*Yokai from currently filming Daiei motion picture Yōkai Daisensō*".

87

『週刊少年キング』6巻12号
（昭和43年3月17日）
しゅうかんしょうねんきんぐ

Weekly Shōnen King volume 6 issue 12:
March 17, 1968 (Shōwa 43)

妖怪を特集した号で、表紙には「写真は、すごい姿と超能力で人間をおどろかす妖怪たち。大映映画『妖怪百物語』より」として「うしおに」「一本足の傘」「青坊主」「油すまし」がキャプションを付されて紹介されている。
On the cover of this edition featuring yokai is written "Yokai frightening humans with their amazing physiques and supernatural powers. From Daiei Motion Pictures *Yōkai Hyaku Monogatari*", and the yokai *Ushioni*, One-legged Umbrella, Blue Monk, and *Abura-sumashi* are introduced.

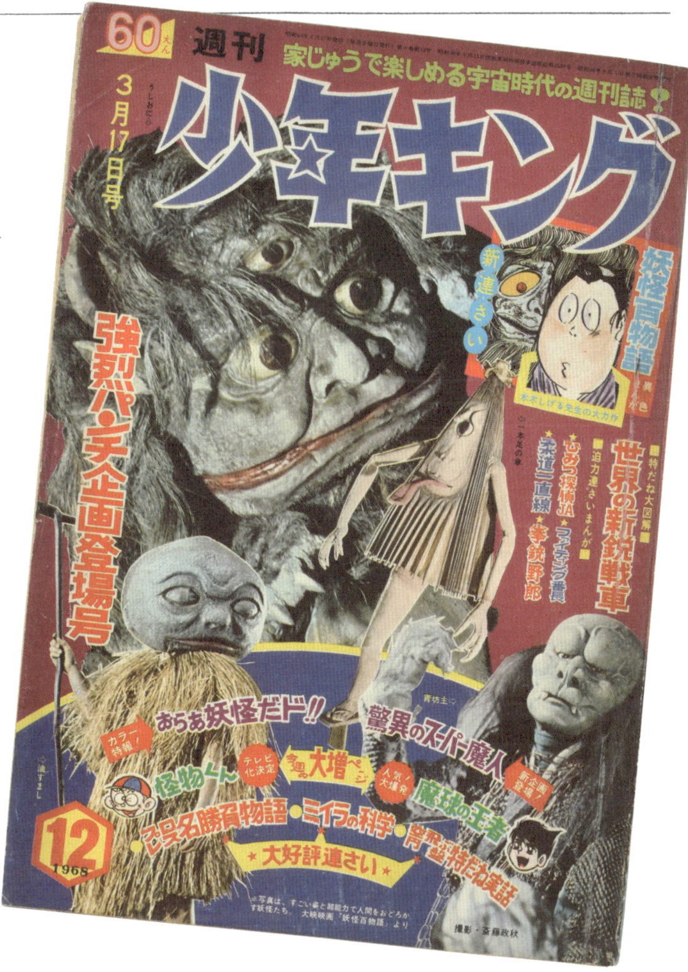

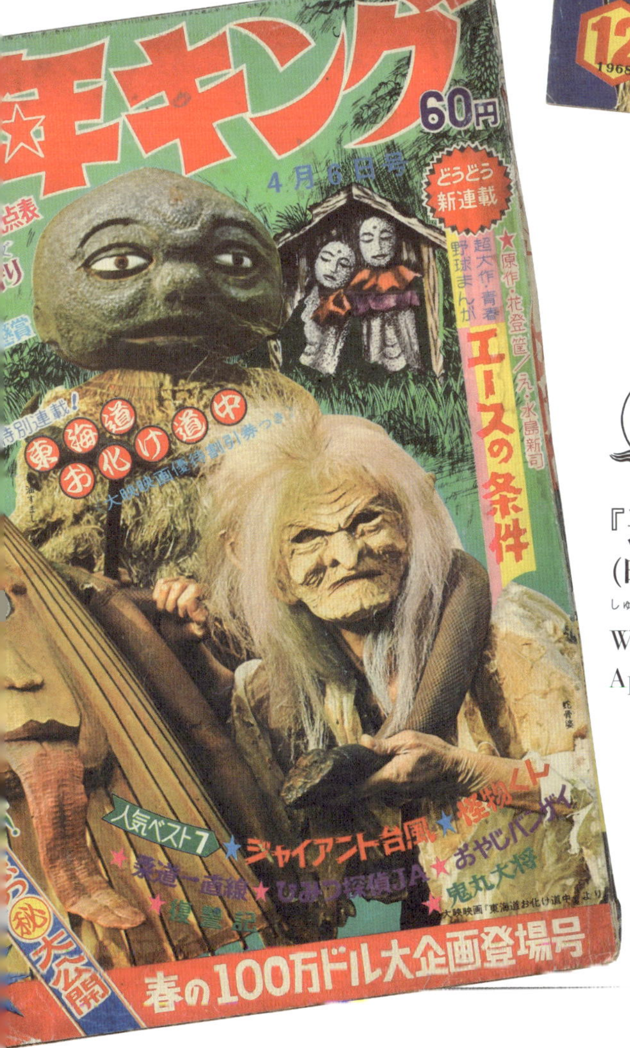

88

『週刊少年キング』7巻15号
（昭和44年4月6日）
しゅうかんしょうねんきんぐ

Weekly Shōnen King volume 7 issue 15:
April 6, 1969 (Shōwa 44)

「大映映画『東海道お化け道中』より」として映画に登場する「油すまし」「からかさ」「蛇骨婆」をキャプションを付して紹介している。
Abura-sumashi, *Karakasa* and *Jakotsu-Baba* (Snake Bone Hag) from Daiei Motion Pictures *Along with Ghosts on Tokaido Road (Tokaido Obake Dōchu)* are introduced in the captions.

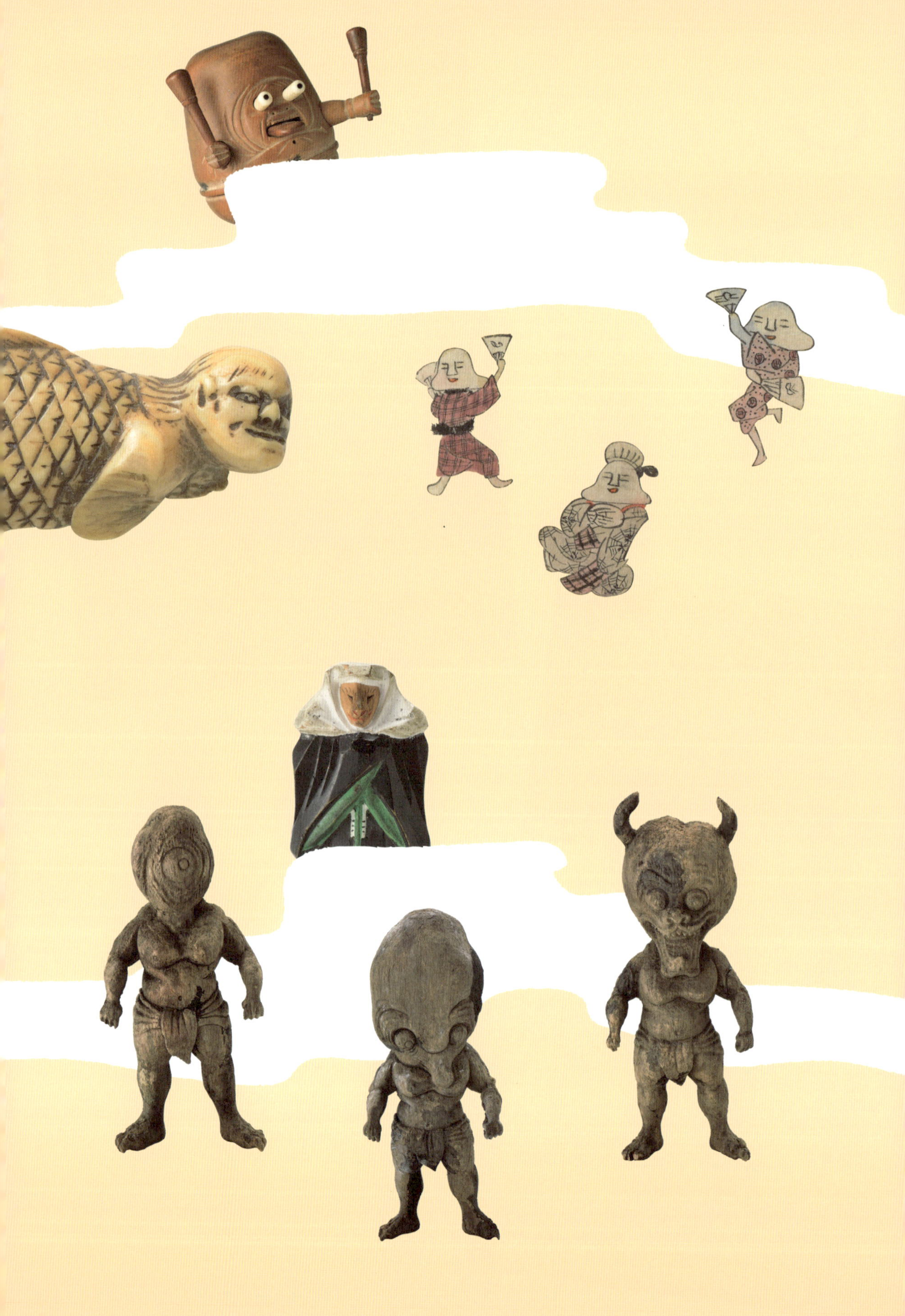

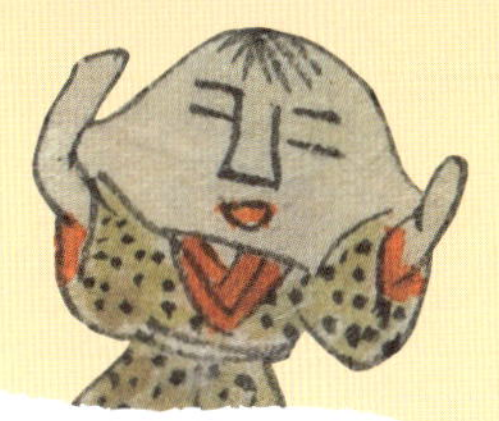

3

あらゆるモノになる妖怪

Yokai of Things

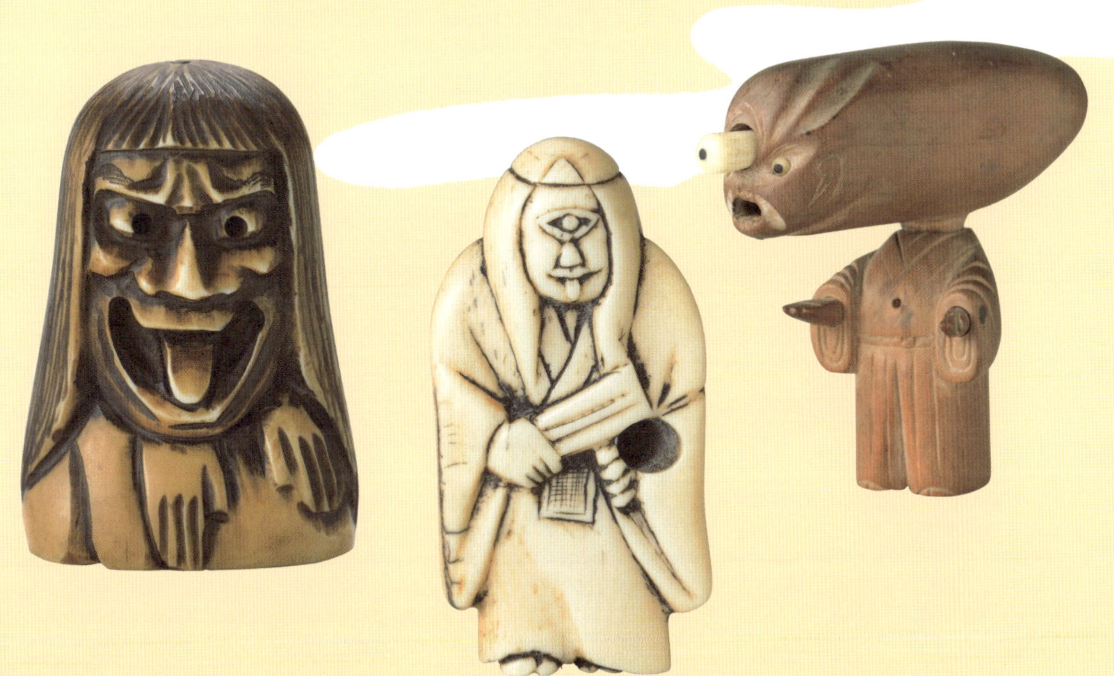

怪魚退治図刺子半纏

かいぎょたいじずさしこはんてん

Defeat of the Monster Fish *Hanten*

江戸時代以降　縦 91.0　横 117.0　Post-Edo period, Height 91.0, Width 117.0

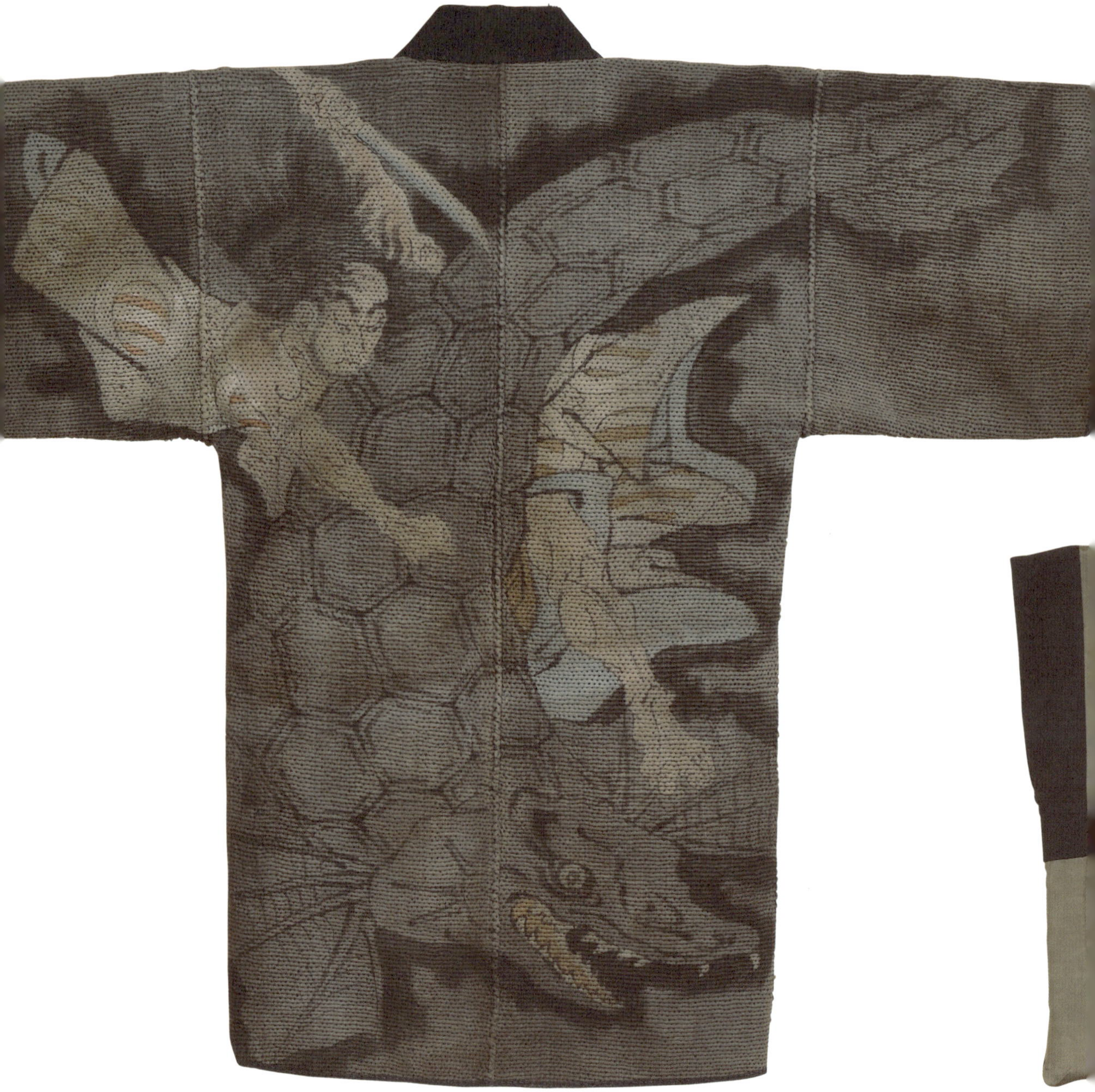

大きな口を開けた巨大な怪魚を退治する図柄。このデザインは裏地にあり、表は無地紺色となっている。刺子半纏は消火活動の折に着用するが、消火が終わるとリバースにして裏地の目を引く図柄を見せながら引き揚げていくために、びっくりさせるような妖怪柄などもデザインされたと思われる。

A design of the battle with the gigantic monster fish, its huge mouth wide open. The reverse side is solid dark blue. Quilted *hanten* were worn for fire fighting; when the fire fighting was over they were worn inside out so that the eye-catching designs would show when carrying out salvage work, and it is thought that the yokai designs were intended to startle people.

90 ぶんぶく茶釜図羽織

ぶんぶくちゃがまずはおり

Tea Kettle *Haori* (*Bunbuku Chagama Zu Haori*)

江戸時代以降　縦 110.0　横 133.0
Post-Edo period, Height 110.0, Width 133.0

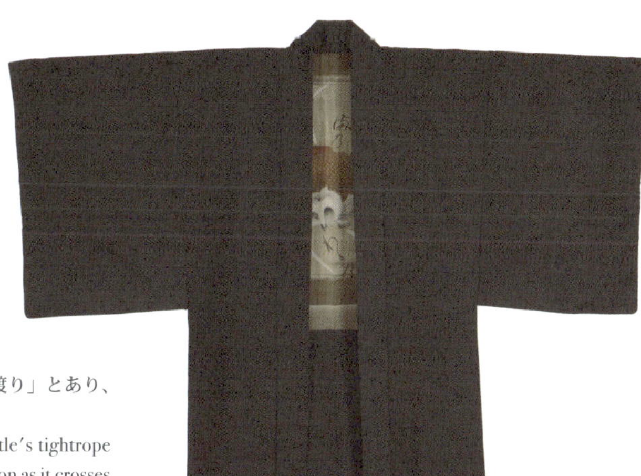

羽織の裏地がぶんぶく茶釜のデザイン。「ぶんぶく茶釜の綱渡り」とあり、茶釜の狸が綱を渡っている姿を正面から捉えている。
On the reverse side of this *haori* is a tea kettle design. "Tea kettle's tightrope walking" is written on it; a tea kettle raccoon dog is captured front-on as it crosses the ropes.

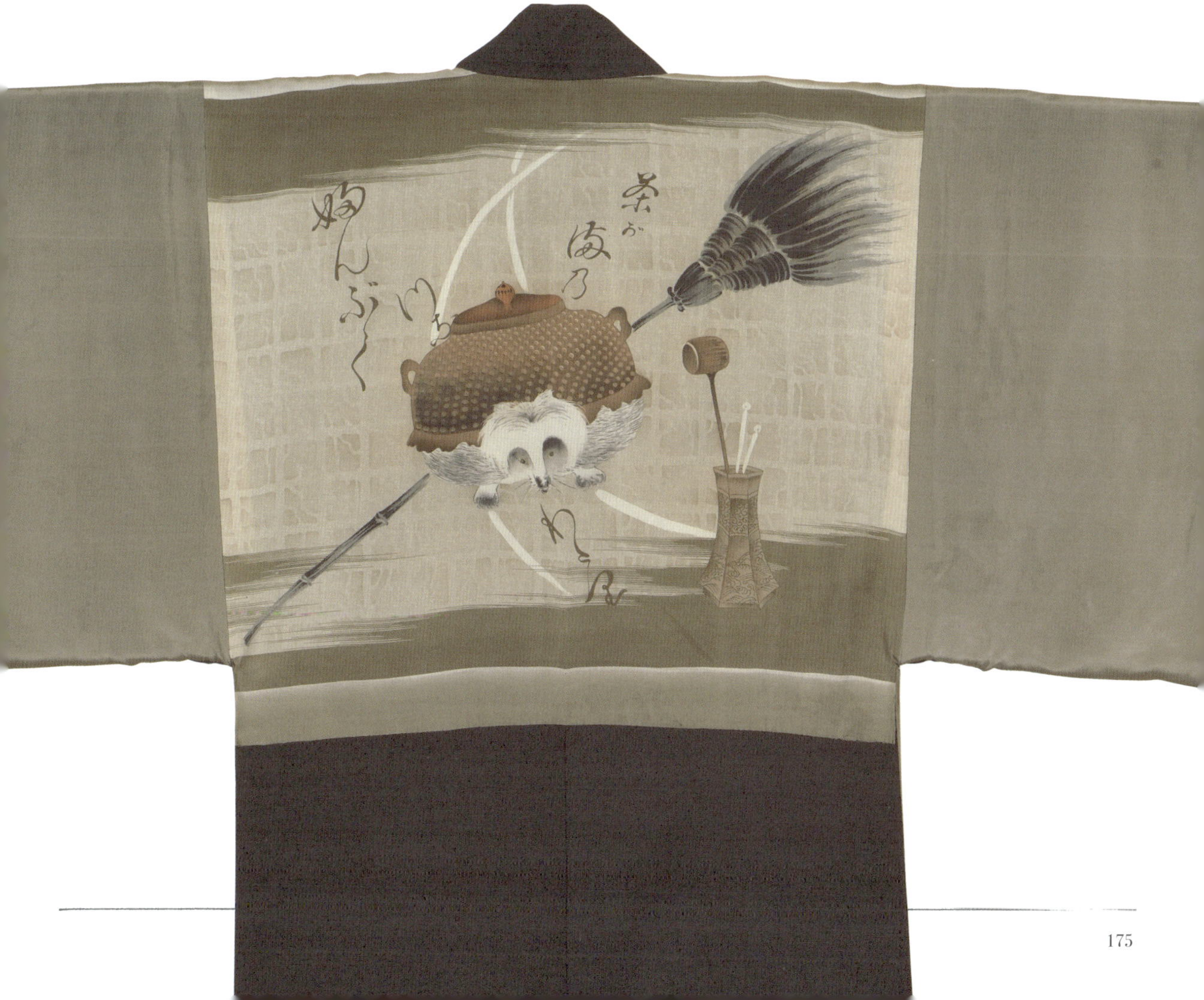

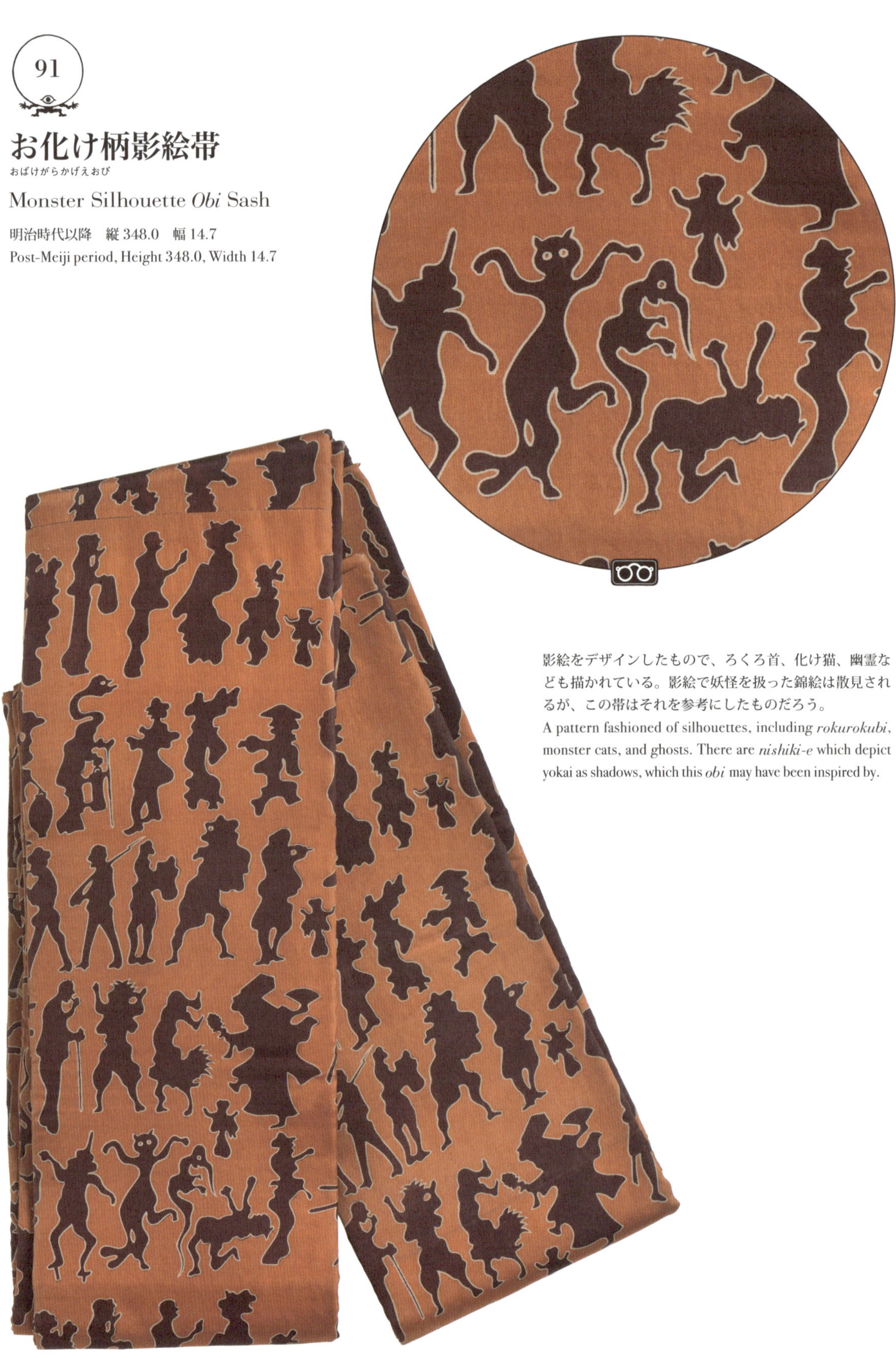

お化け柄影絵帯

おばけがらかげえおび

Monster Silhouette *Obi* Sash

明治時代以降　縦 348.0　幅 14.7
Post-Meiji period, Height 348.0, Width 14.7

影絵をデザインしたもので、ろくろ首、化け猫、幽霊な
ども描かれている。影絵で妖怪を扱った錦絵は散見され
るが、この帯はそれを参考にしたものだろう。
A pattern fashioned of silhouettes, including *rokurokubi*,
monster cats, and ghosts. There are *nishiki-e* which depict
yokai as shadows, which this *obi* may have been inspired by.

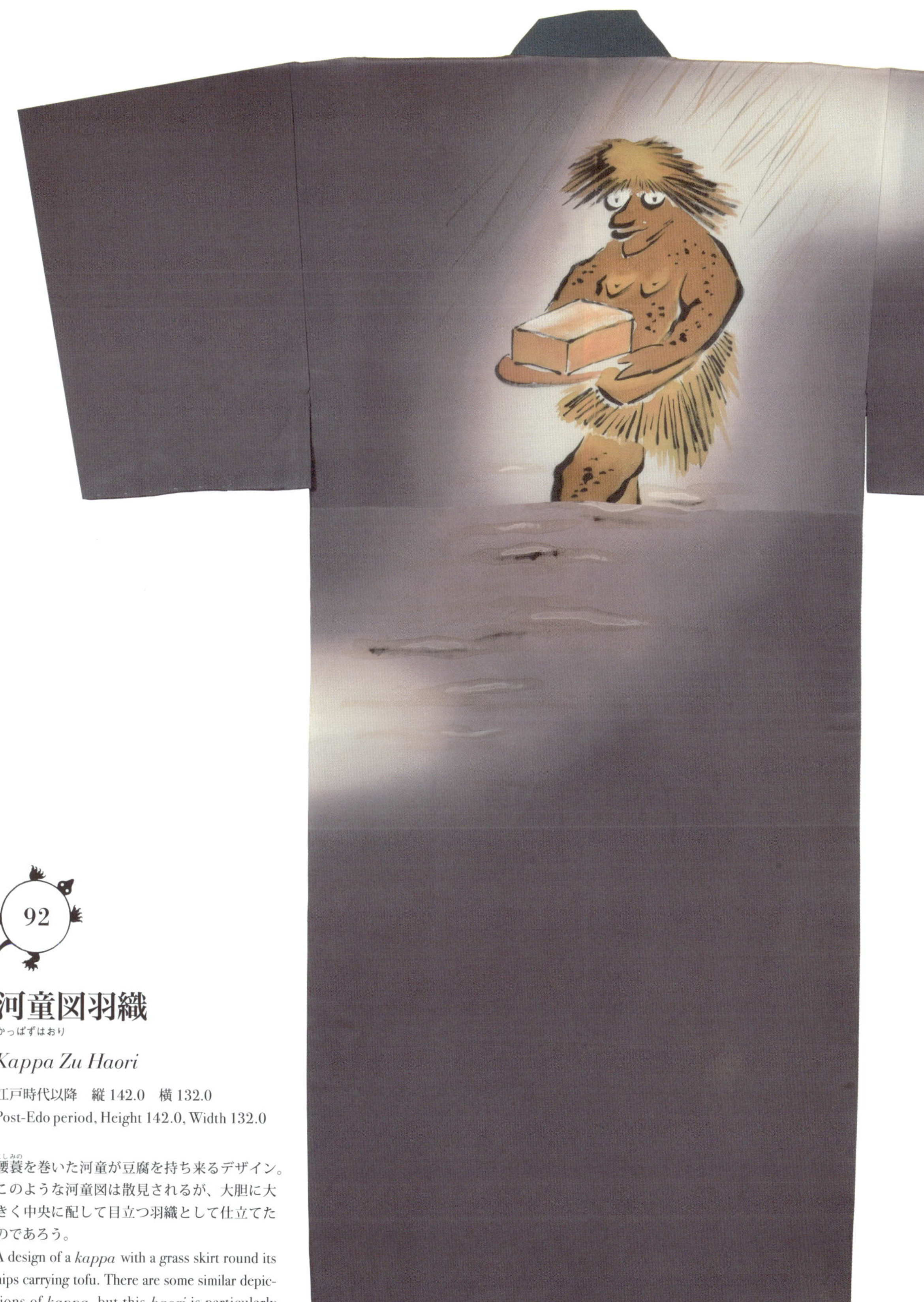

河童図羽織
かっぱずはおり

Kappa Zu Haori

江戸時代以降　縦 142.0　横 132.0
Post-Edo period, Height 142.0, Width 132.0

腰蓑を巻いた河童が豆腐を持ち来るデザイン。
このような河童図は散見されるが、大胆に大
きく中央に配して目立つ羽織として仕立てた
のであろう。

A design of a *kappa* with a grass skirt round its
hips carrying tofu. There are some similar depictions of *kappa*, but this *haori* is particularly
striking with its boldly-drawn large central image.

93

茨木童子図羽織
いばらきどうじずはおり

Ibaraki-dōji Zu *Haori*

江戸時代以降　縦 130.0　横 129.0
Post-Edo period, Height 130.0, Width 129.0

渡辺綱によって腕を斬り落とされた茨木童子という
鬼が、腕を取り戻しに綱の館に伯母に化けて入って
腕を持ち去るという伝説は錦絵などにも数多く描か
れた。この羽織の場面は、館から取り戻した腕を持っ
て空に逃げ去るというよく知られたシーンをデザイ
ンしている。図柄を中央に配して上下を薄黒にして
いることによって闇夜を強調しているのであろう。

The famous legend of how the ogre Ibaraki-dōji, whose
arm was stolen by Watanabe no Tsuna, visited Tsuna at
his mansion in the form of his aunt to get the arm back
has been represented in *nishiki-e* and other media; the
well-known scene on this *haori* is the ogre fleeing into
the sky from the mansion, holding the arm he has
reclaimed. The design is centered with dark gloom above
and below, which may be intended to emphasize that the
scene is set on a moonless night.

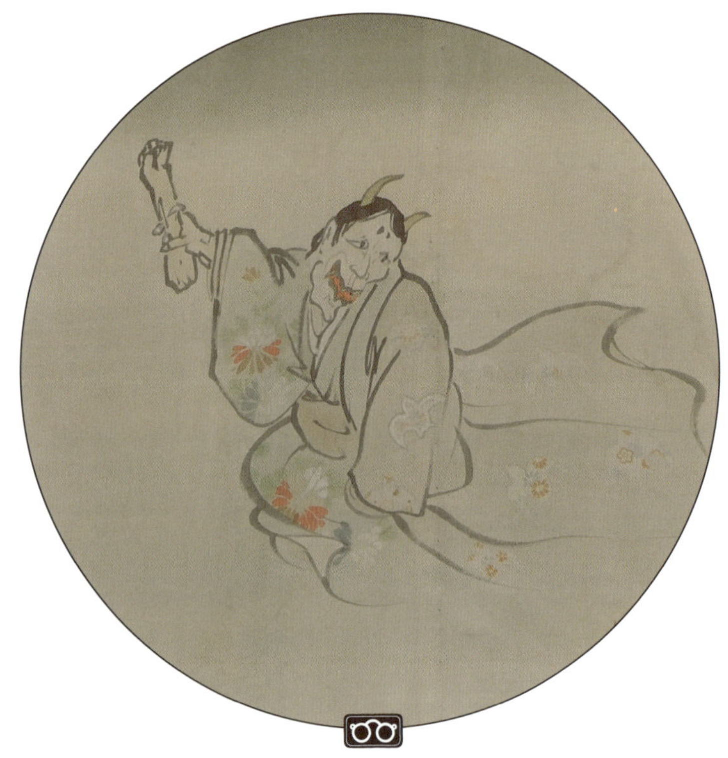

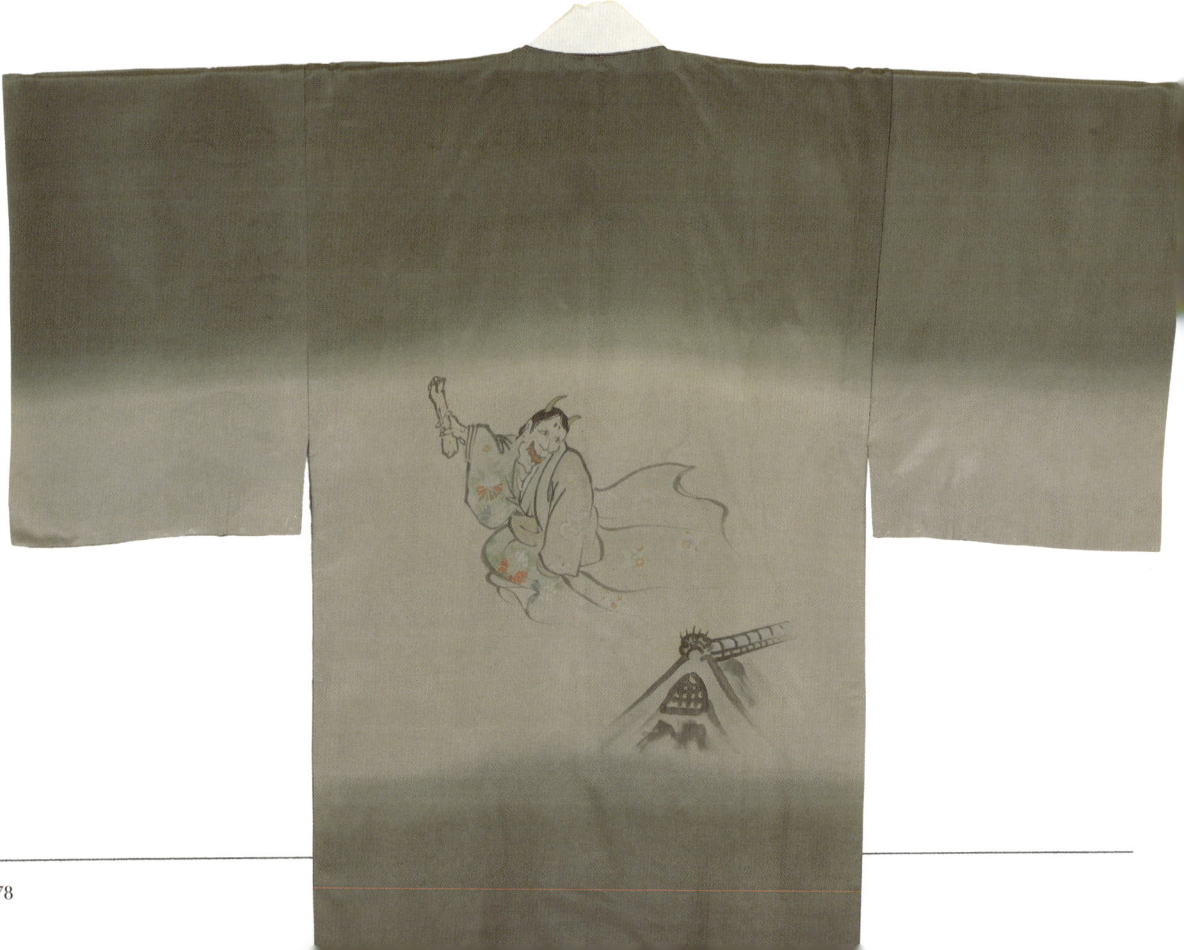

紅葉狩り図羽織
もみじがりずはおり

Hunting Momiji *Haori* (*Momijigari Zu Haori*)

江戸時代以降　縦 124.5　横 130.0
Post-Edo period, Height 124.5, Width 130.0

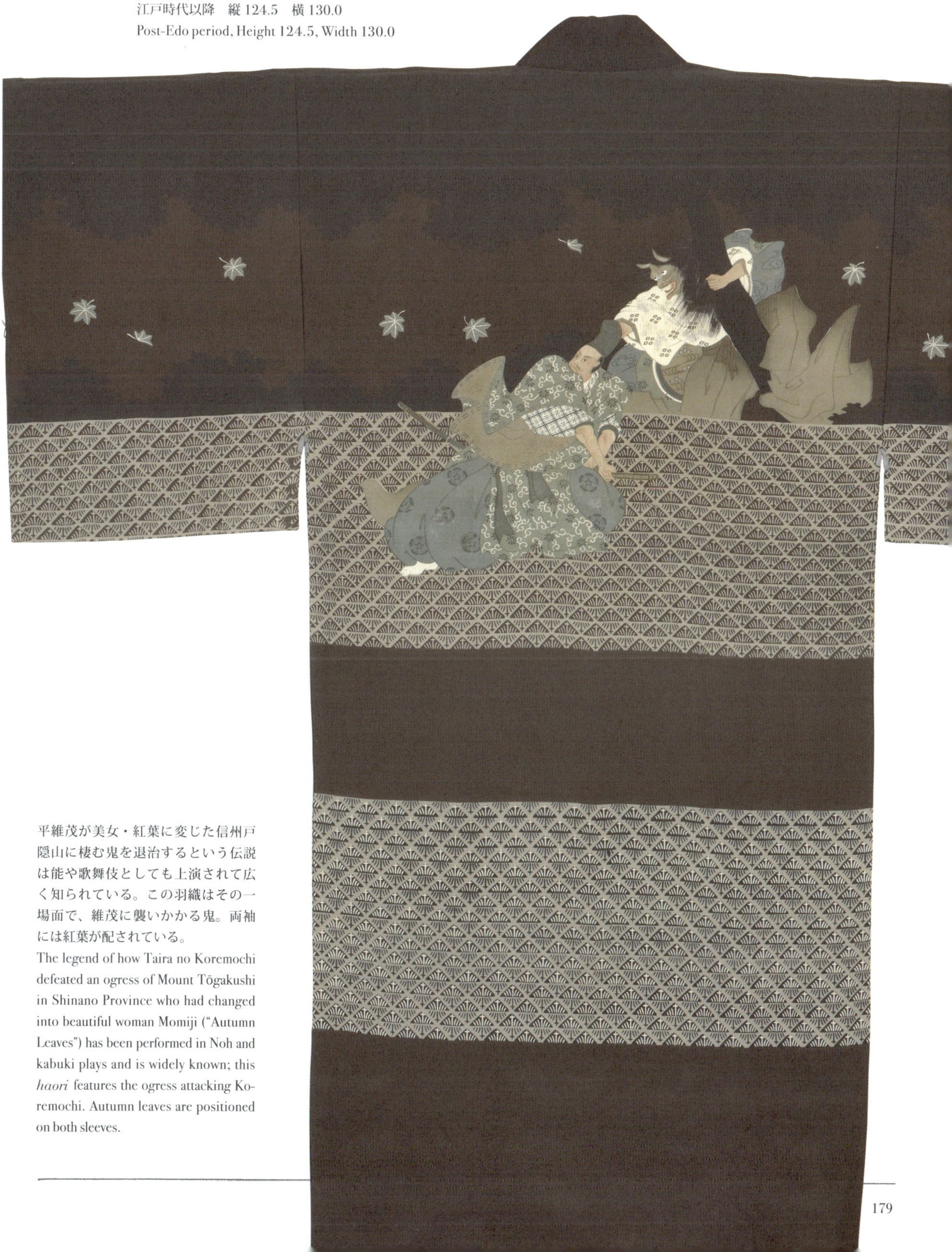

平維茂が美女・紅葉に変じた信州戸
隠山に棲む鬼を退治するという伝説
は能や歌舞伎としても上演されて広
く知られている。この羽織はその一
場面で、維茂に襲いかかる鬼。両袖
には紅葉が配されている。

The legend of how Taira no Koremochi
defeated an ogress of Mount Tōgakushi
in Shinano Province who had changed
into beautiful woman Momiji ("Autumn
Leaves") has been performed in Noh and
kabuki plays and is widely known; this
haori features the ogress attacking Koremochi. Autumn leaves are positioned
on both sleeves.

茨木童子図絵馬

いばらきどうじずえま

Ibaraki-dōji Votive Tablet (*Ema*)

宝暦元（1751）年　縦36.0　横48.0　厚2.2　Hōreki 1 (1751), Height 36.0, Width 48.0, Thickness 2.2

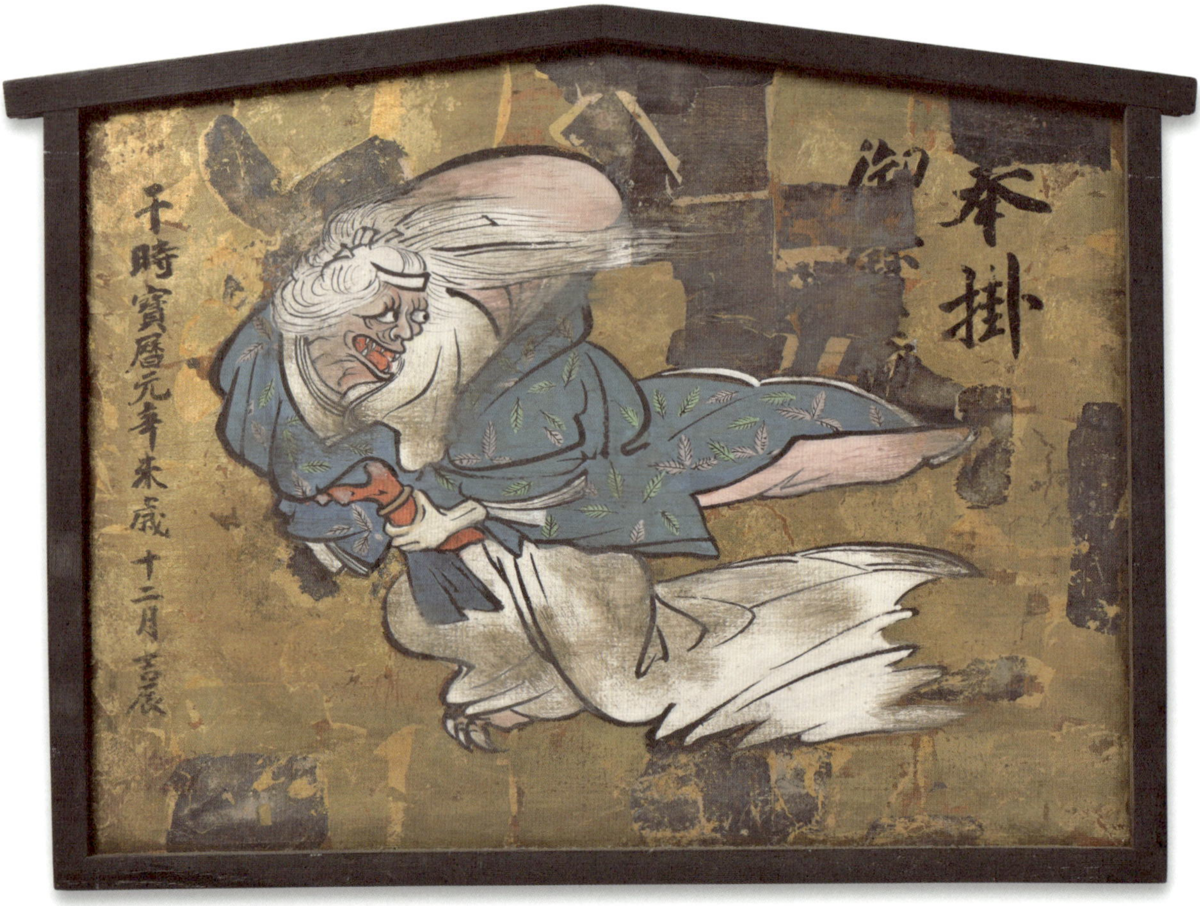

腕を斬り取られた茨木童子が渡辺綱の伯母に化けて腕を取り返して逃げ去る場面は多くの絵師によって
描かれているが、この絵馬もその有名な場面を取り上げている。丁寧に作られた作品といえる。

This votive tablet covers the famous scene illustrated by many artists in which the ogre Ibaraki-dōji disguised
himself as Watanabe no Tuna's aunt to steal back his severed arm and fled with it. It has been skillfully painted.

96 化け狐図絵馬
ばけぎつねずえま

Shapeshifting Fox Votive Tablet (*Ema*)

明治時代以降　縦 23.5　横 27.5　厚 1.8　Post-Meiji period, Height 23.5, Width 27.5, Thickness 1.8

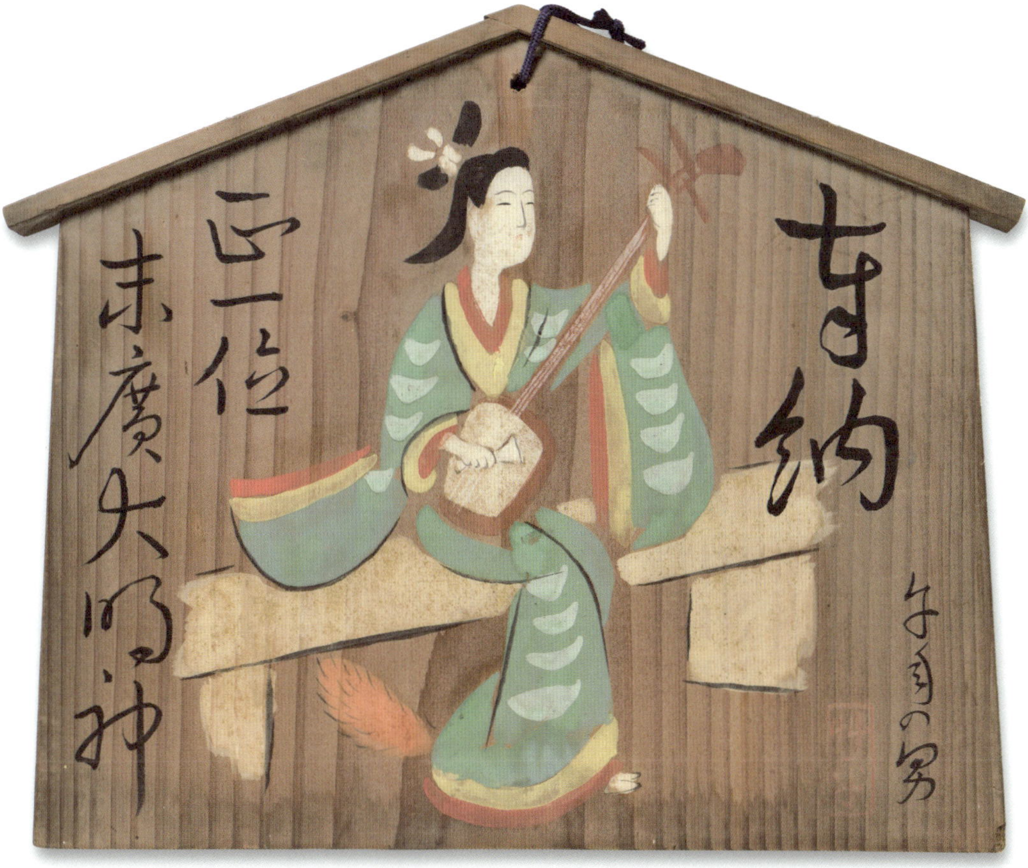

三味線を弾く芸妓のようだが、下から尻尾が出ているのがみえ狐が化けていたのだと分かる。こうした図は大津絵などにもみられる。末広大明神に奉納されたもので、裏面には多数の提灯も描かれており、初午の祭りを表現しているのだろう。裏面にも丁寧に絵がある絵馬は珍しい事例だ。

At first glance this appears to be a geisha playing a *shamisen*, but the tail poking out below betrays that she is actually a shapeshifting fox. This image can also be seen in *Otsu-e* folk art paintings. The tablet is dedicated to the guardian deity Suehiro Daimyojin; the many lanterns painted on the reverse side may be a representation of the Hatsu-uma Harvest Festival. It is rare for a votive tablet to have a carefully-executed picture on the back as well.

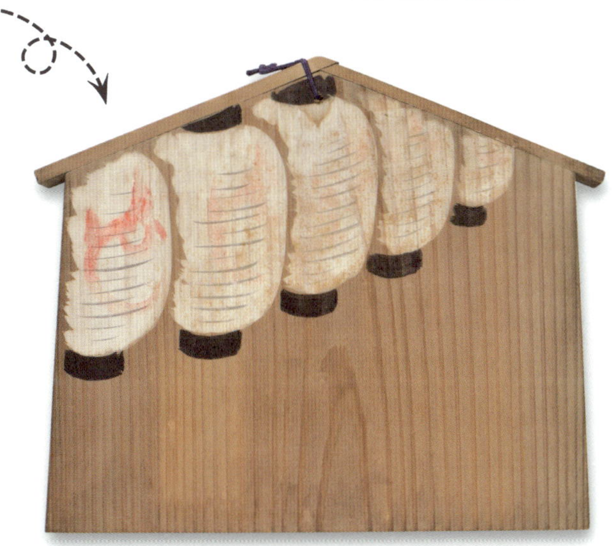

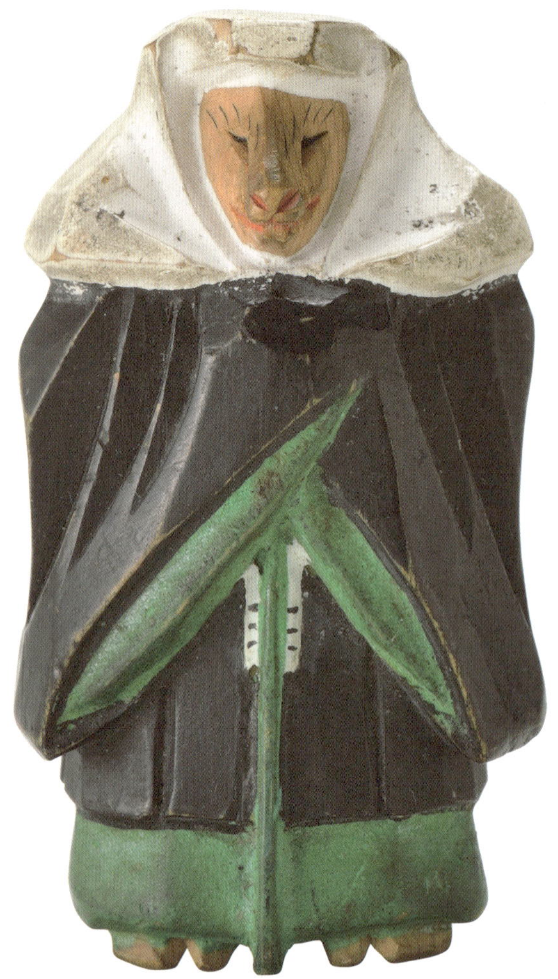

白蔵主根付
はくぞうすねつけ

Hakuzōsu Netsuke

明治時代以降　幅 5.3　奥行 2.4　高 10.5
Post-Meiji period, Width 5.3, Depth 2.4, Height 10.5

白蔵主は根付の題材として多数制作されている。一般的には木彫の場合でも彩色されないが、この作品は木彫彩色というスタイルとなっている。
The fox-spirit Hakuzōsu has been the subject of many *netsuke*. Generally colors are not used on wood carvings, but this work is the exception.

原寸大
Actual size

白蔵主香合
はくぞうすこうごう

Hakuzōsu Incense Case

江戸時代　幅 4.1　奥行 3.5　高 5.0
Edo period, Width 4.1, Depth 3.5, Height 5.0

白蔵主という僧に化けた狐を香合の蓋にデザインしている。
Hakuzōsu the fox who changed into a monk is incorporated into the design of the lid of this incense case.

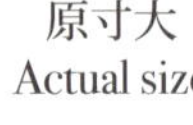

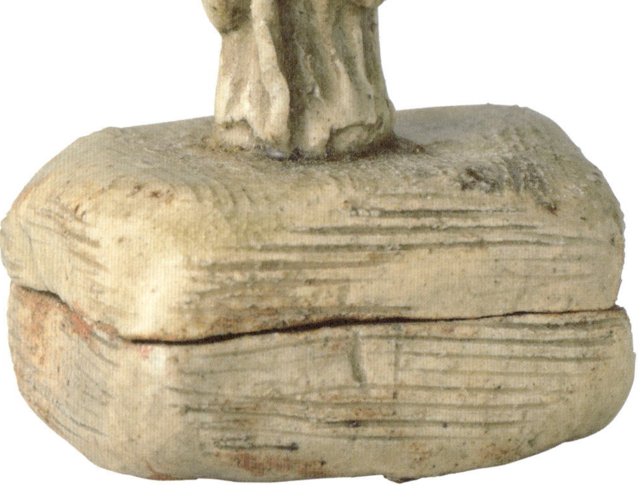

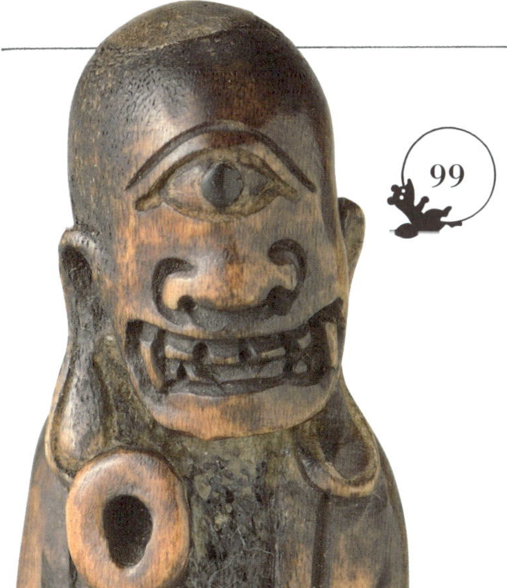

99 一つ目入道根付
ひとつめにゅうどうねつけ
One-eyed Priest Netsuke

江戸時代　幅 1.9　奥行 1.8　高 8.6
Edo period, Width 1.9, Depth 1.8, Height 8.6

100 一つ目妖怪根付
ひとつめようかいねつけ
One-eyed Yokai Netsuke

江戸時代以降　幅 2.7　奥行 1.5　高 5.3
Post-Edo period, Width 2.7, Depth 1.5, Height 5.3

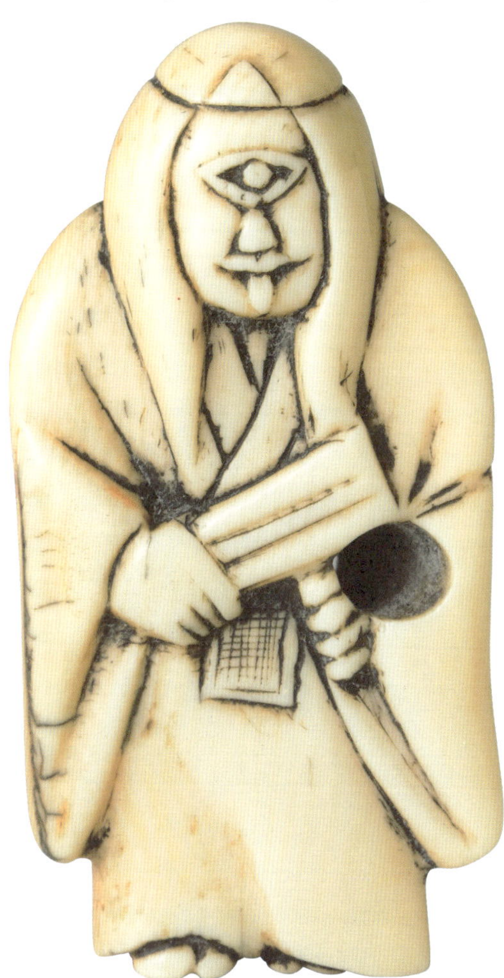

原寸大
Actual size

金棒を持った一つ目入道。このイメージは丹後国の妖怪譚を描いた変
化絵巻に登場する一つ目入道から来ていると思われる。

A one-eyed priest holding a studded war club (*kanabo*), thought to be the
one-eyed priest from the yokai of Tango Province in the Henge picture scroll.

長い髪で着物などから女の一つ目妖怪のようだ。右手に
扇のようなものを握っている。

Judging by the long hair and style of kimono, this is a female
cyclops. Her right hand grips what appears to be a folded fan.

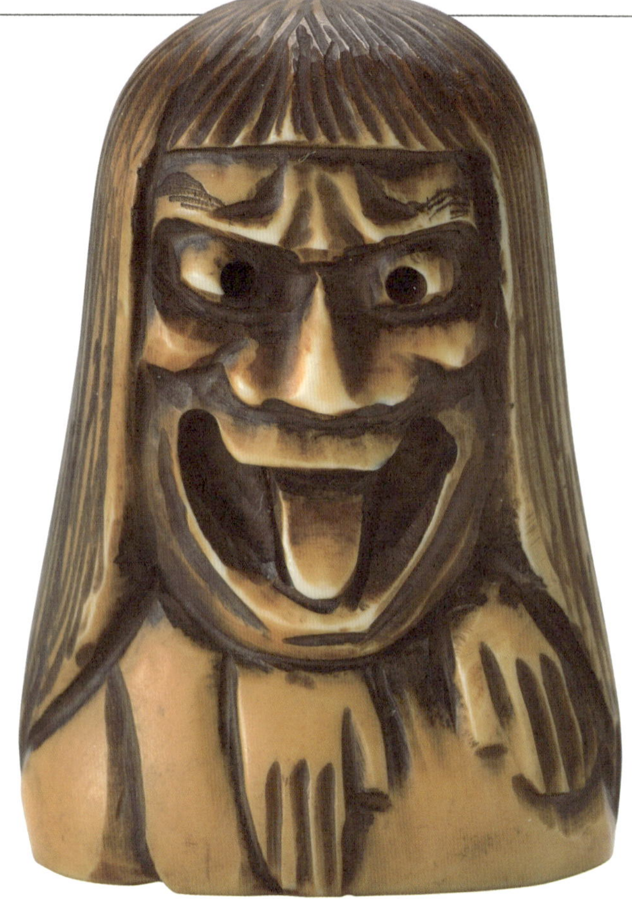

101

原寸大
Actual size

幽霊根付
ゆうれいねつけ

Ghost Netsuke

江戸時以降　幅 2.8　奥行 2.2　高 4.4
Post-Edo period, Width 2.8, Depth 2.2, Height 4.4

幽霊をデザインした根付は散見されるが、全身像が多い。
この作品は上半身だけとなっている。大きく口を開いて
いる不気味な顔つきだ。

Some *netsuke* use ghost designs, but most of these are full-body sculptures. This one is upper body only. The facial expression is eerie with mouth gaping wide.

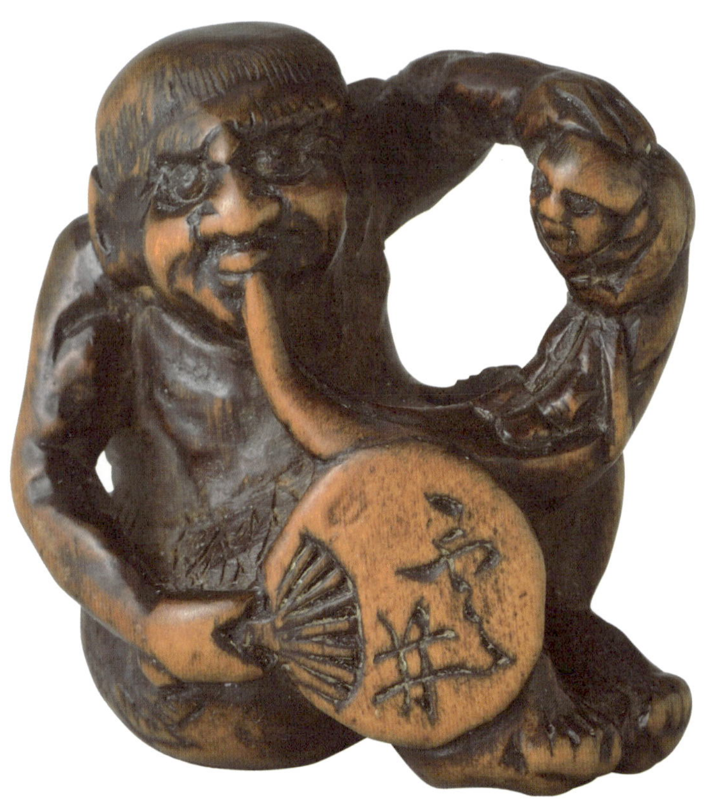

102

原寸大
Actual size

雲井根付
くもいねつけ

Kumoi Netsuke

江戸時代　幅 2.9　奥行 2.1　高 2.9
Edo period, Width 2.9, Depth 2.1, Height 2.9

雲を作り出す雲井が口から出しているのは生まれた
ばかりの雲だろうか？団扇で煽いで散らそうとして
いるのだろう。団扇には「雲井」と大きく書かれて
いる。

Is a new cloud being born from cloud-creator Kumoi's mouth? The round *uchiwa* fan may be for spreading out the clouds. "Kumoi" is written large on the fan.

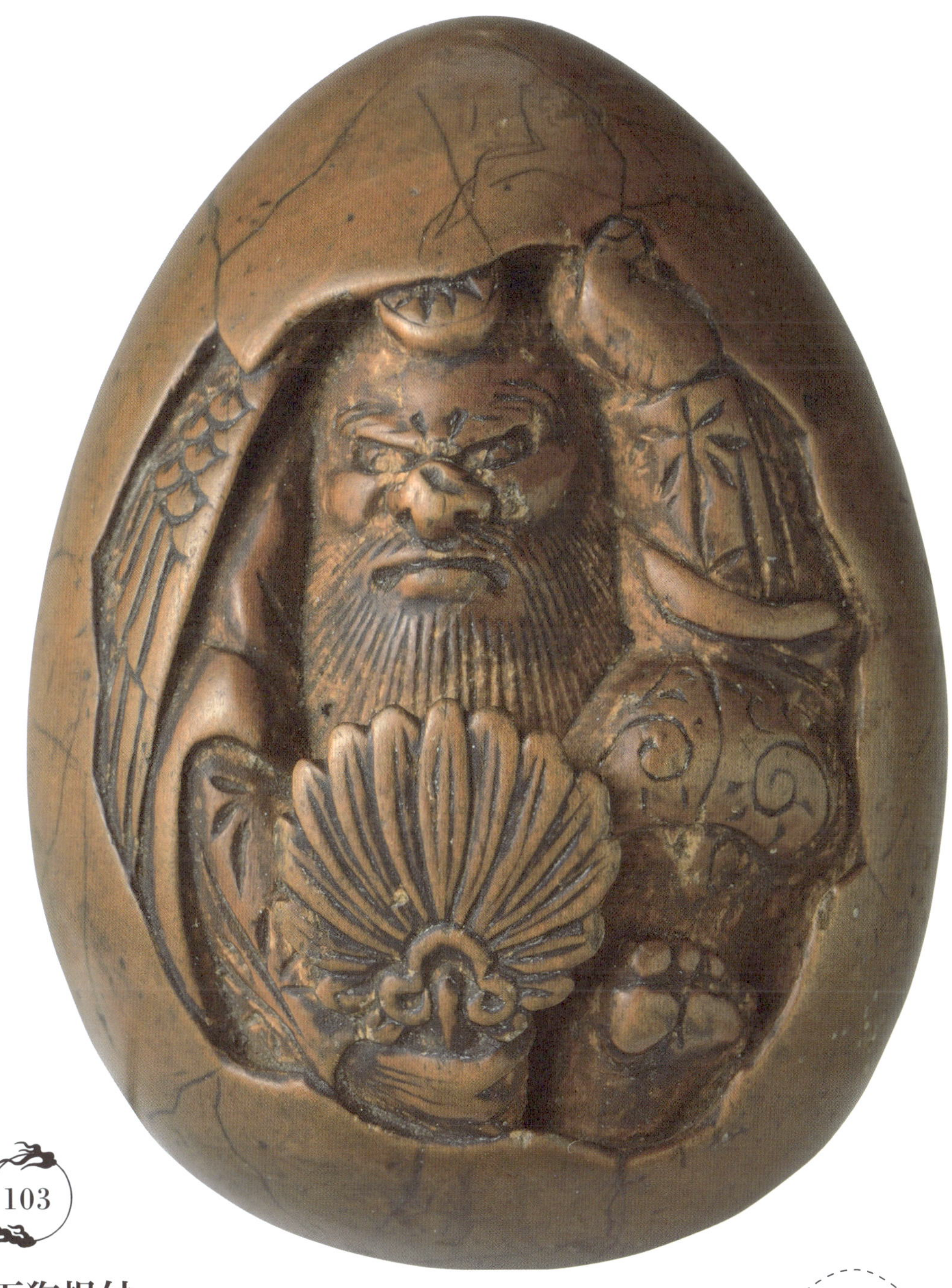

103

天狗根付
てんぐねつけ

Tengu Netsuke

江戸時代　幅 3.5　奥行 3.5　高 4.6　Edo period, Width 3.5, Depth 3.5, Height 4.6

天狗をデザインした根付は多い。とりわけ烏天狗の根付は種々作られたが、卵から産まれて来る場面が多く採用されている。この作品は卵の中にいる天狗といった構図だが、年を取った大天狗のような顔つきで作られており、珍しいタイプの天狗根付だ。

Many *netsuke* use *tengu* designs. Most common are *karasu tengu* (crow goblins), often rendered hatching from eggs. This work shows a *tengu* inside an egg, but the face of the large *tengu* shows its advanced age, which is a rarity.

原寸大
Actual size

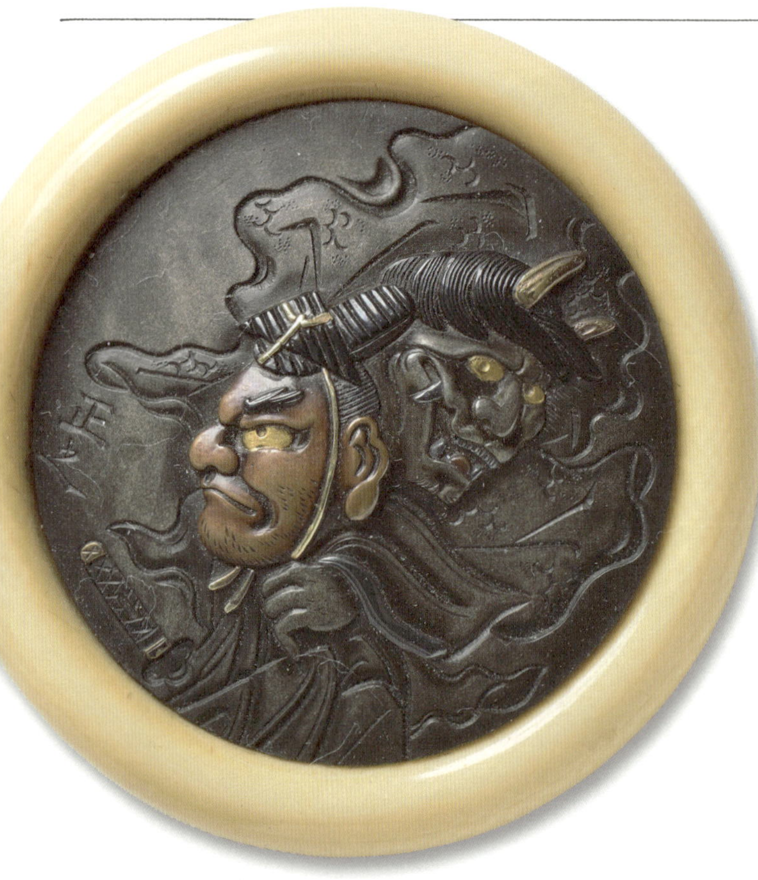

104

大森彦七図鏡蓋根付

おおもりひこしちずかがみぶたねつけ

Ōmori Hikoshichi Mirror-lid Netsuke

江戸時代以降　径 4.7　厚 1.5
Post-Edo period, Diameter 4.7, Thickness 1.5

おぶった美女が鬼に変じて大森彦七を襲おうとして
いる。
The beautiful maiden who Ōmori Hikoshichi agreed to
carry on his shoulders transformed into a monster and
attacked him.

原寸大
Actual size

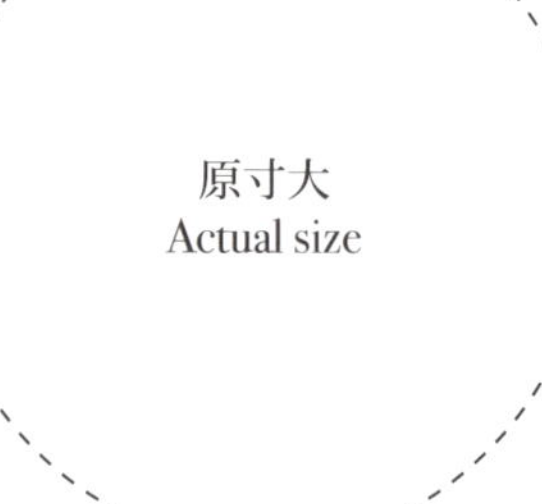

105

河童図鏡蓋根付

かっぱずかがみぶたねつけ

Kappa Mirror-lid Netsuke

江戸時代以降　径 4.5　厚 1.5
Post-Edo period, Diameter 4.5, Thickness 1.5

川辺で釣りをする河童の傍らで遊ぶ小河童。釣りを
そっちのけに心配そうに小河童に目を落としている。
By the river side, a small *kappa* (water imp) plays
alongside a fishing *kappa*. Paying little attention to
fishing, the big *kappa* watches anxiously over the small
one.

原寸大
Actual size

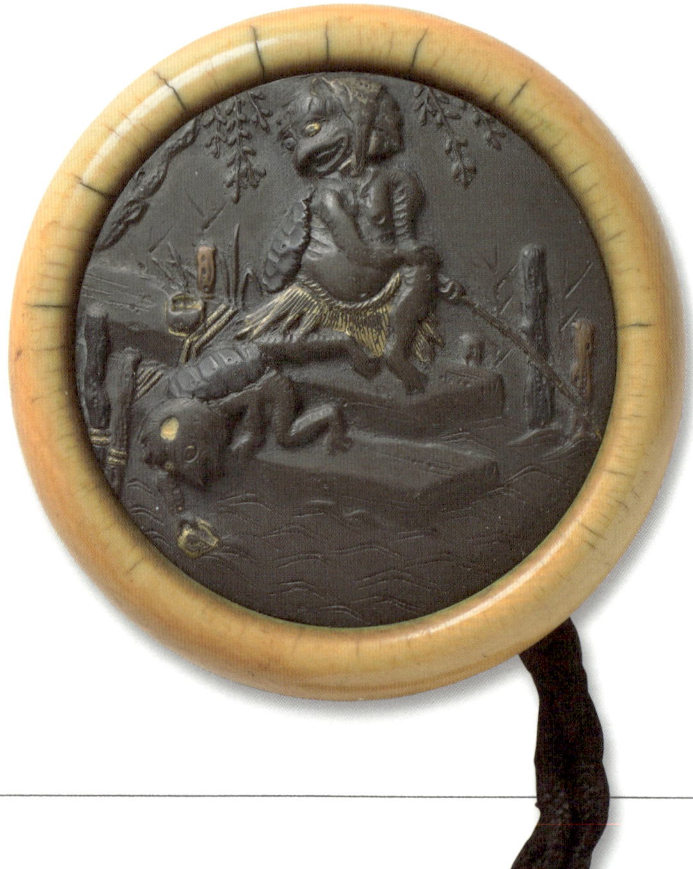

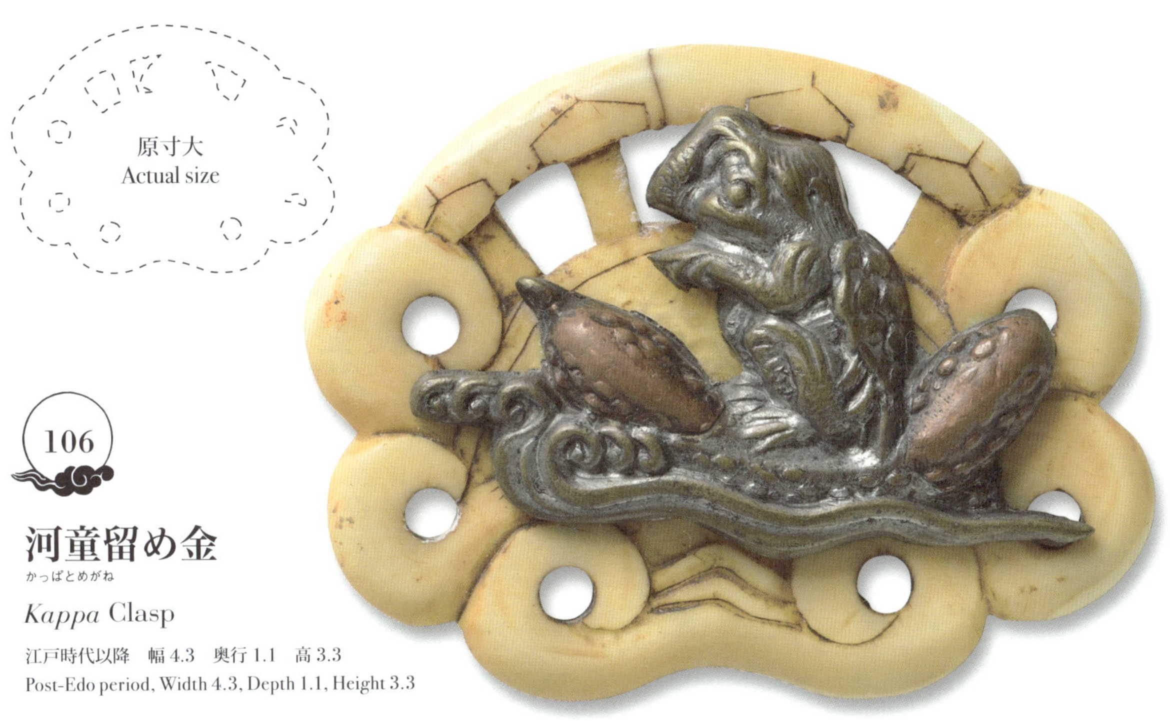

106

河童留め金
かっぱとめがね

Kappa Clasp

江戸時代以降　幅 4.3　奥行 1.1　高 3.3
Post-Edo period, Width 4.3, Depth 1.1, Height 3.3

瓜に乗って水を滑る河童。
A *kappa* riding a cucumber glides on the water.

107

河童根付
かっぱねつけ

Kappa Netsuke

江戸時代以降　縦 1.2　横 9.1　奥行 2.0
Post-Edo period, Height 1.2, Width 9.1, Depth 2.0

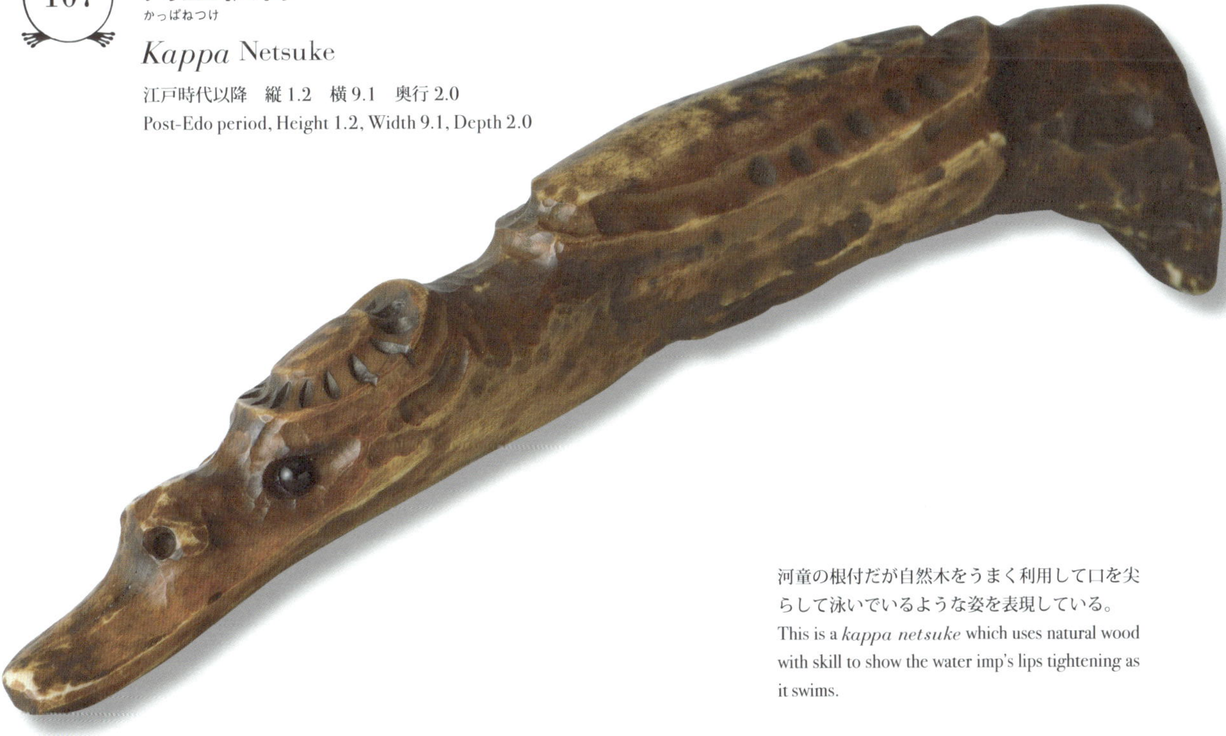

河童の根付だが自然木をうまく利用して口を尖らして泳いでいるような姿を表現している。
This is a *kappa netsuke* which uses natural wood with skill to show the water imp's lips tightening as it swims.

108 人魚根付
にんぎょねつけ

Merperson Netsuke

江戸時代以降　幅 6.5　奥行 1.2　高 1.9
Post-Edo period, Width 6.5, Depth 1.2, Height 1.9

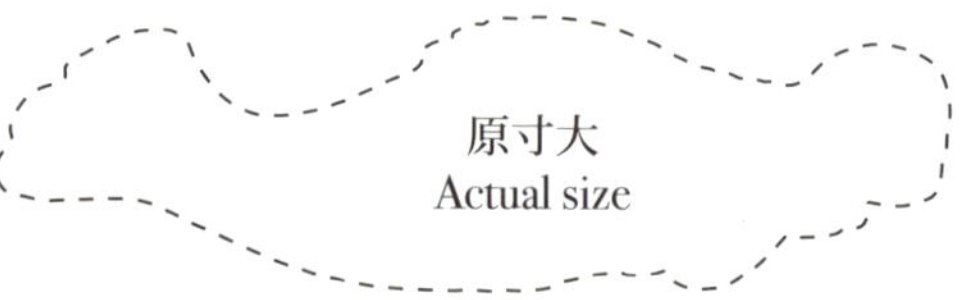

原寸大
Actual size

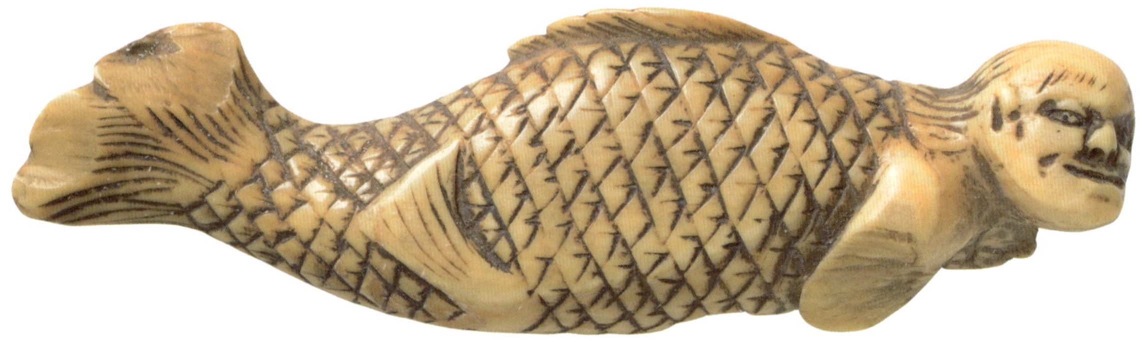

『山海経』などにみられる赤鱬のような姿をしている。
A form like that of the human-faced fish (*sekiju*) of the Classic of Mountains and Seas (*Sengaikyō*).

109

海女房根付
うみにょうぼうねつけ

Wife of the Sea Netsuke
(*Umi Nyōbō Netsuke*)

江戸時代以降　幅 4.4　奥行 3.0
Post-Edo period, Width 4.4, Depth 3.0

亀の上に乗っている海女房。長い
髪で牙を出している。魚をくわえ
た姿などもある。

The wife of the sea rides upon a tur-
tle's back. She has long hair and her
fangs are exposed. Some depictions
place a fish in her mouth.

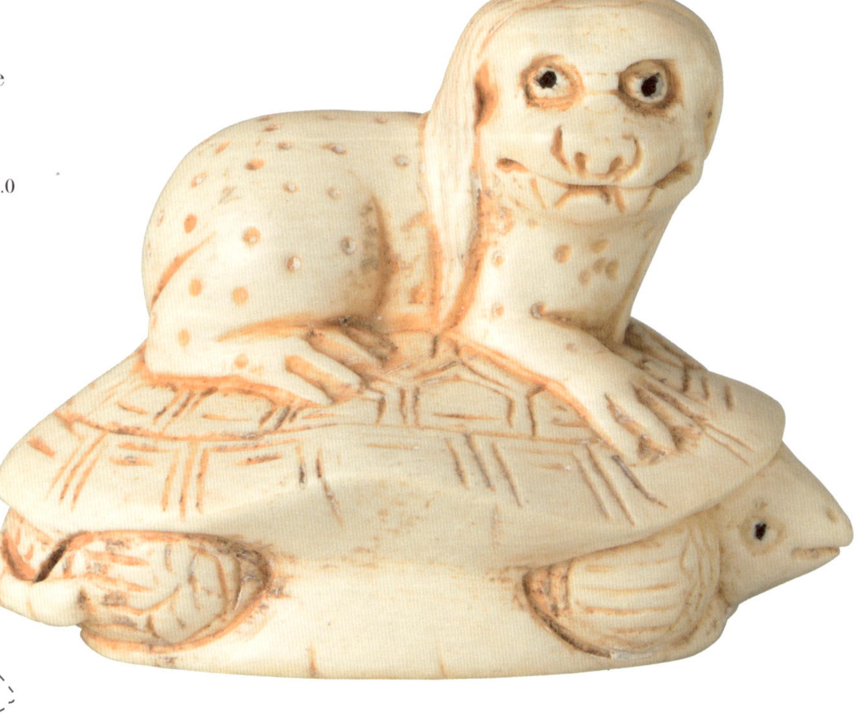

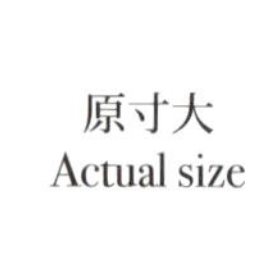

原寸大
Actual size

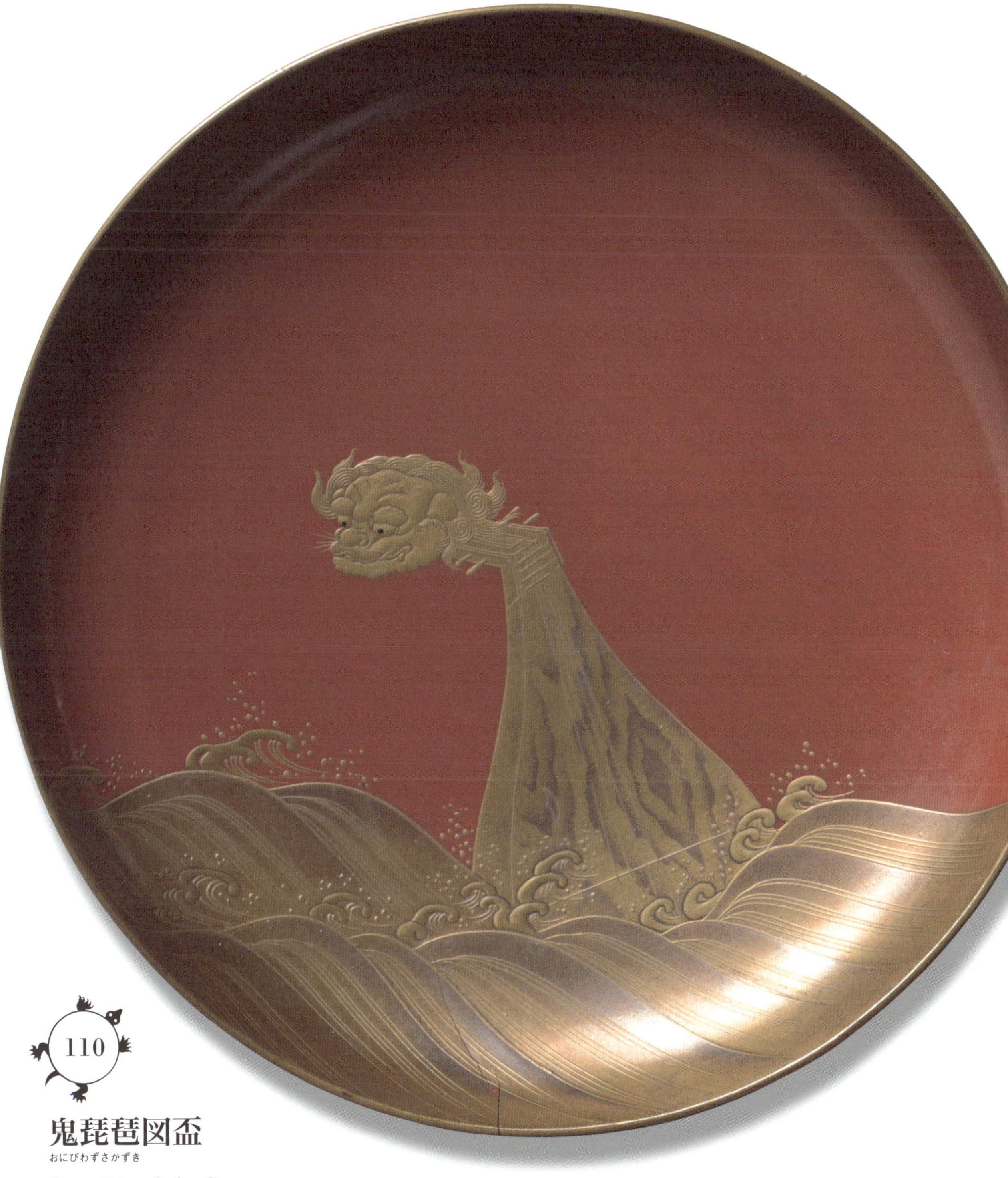

110

鬼琵琶図盃
おにびわずさかずき

Ogre *Biwa* Sake Cup

江戸時代　直径 11.7　厚 2.3　Edo period, Diameter 11.7, Thickness 2.3

先端が鬼の姿の琵琶が波間から出現している場面が朱の漆地にデザインされている。
On a vermilion lacquered background, a *biwa* (Japanese lute) rises from the waves with an ogre on the end of its pegbox.

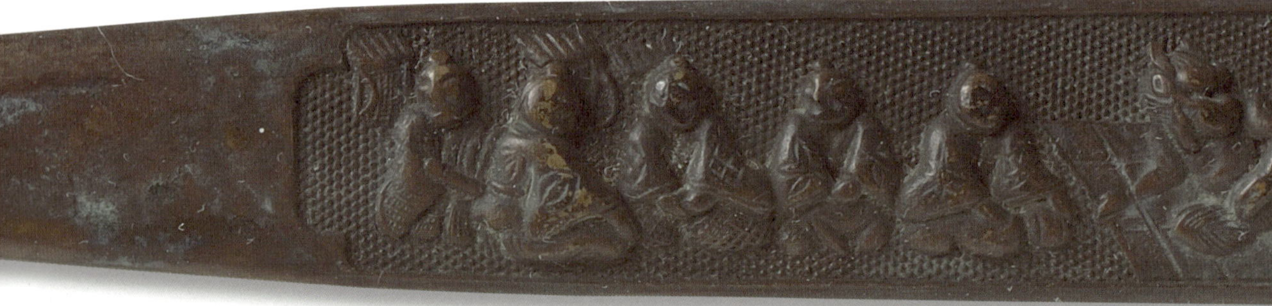

111 鬼図笄
おにずこうがい

Ogre Hairpin (*Kōgai*)

江戸時代以降　横 21.2　幅 1.4　厚 0.4
Post-Edo period, Length 21.2, Width 1.4, Thickness 0.4

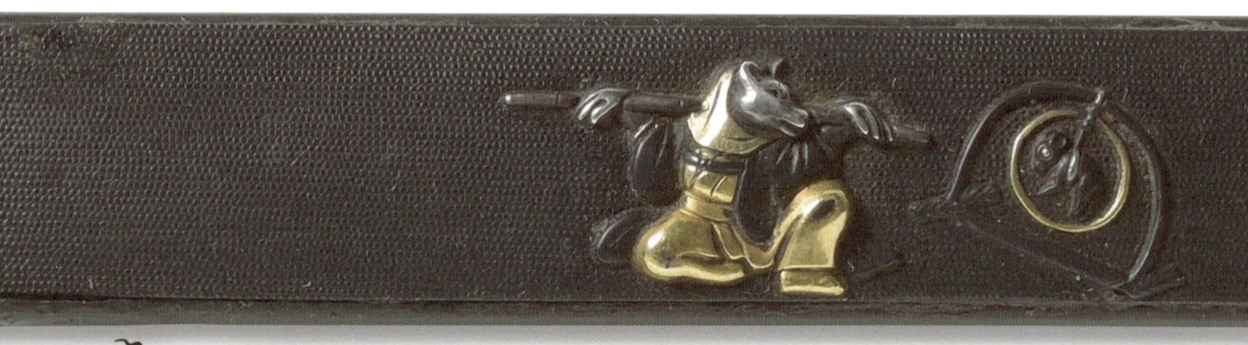

112 釣り狐図小柄
つりぎつねずこづか

Knife (*Kozuka*) with Fox Trapping Design

江戸時代　横 21.0　幅 1.4　厚 0.7
Edo period, Length 21.0, Width 1.4, Thickness 0.7

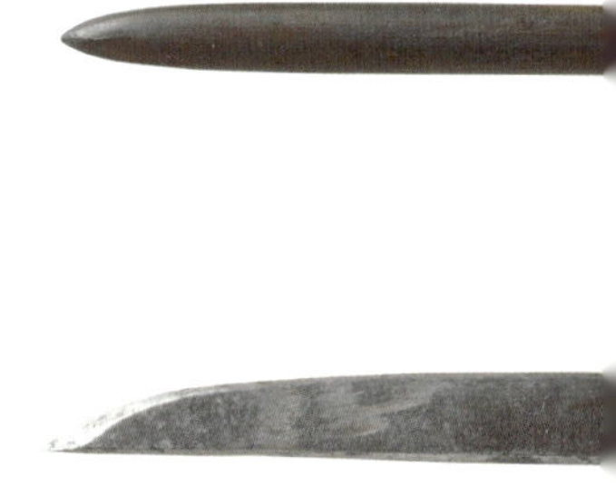

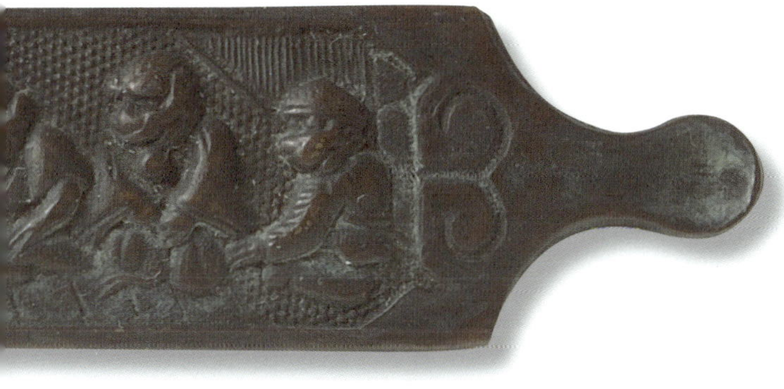

笄は髪をかきあげる道具で、右端の突起は耳かきとして
使うことができる。持つ個所には左に 5 人の武士、右に
は鬼たちがデザインされているので源頼光たちが酒呑童
子を退治するためにその館を訪れた場面だろう。

The *kōgai* (a traditional hair dressing tool) was used for lifting
the hair, and the protrusion on the right end could be used for
ear cleaning. On the haft is a design which may be of Minamoto no Yorimitsu paying a visit to Shuten-dōji's mansion to
vanquish him, as it features five samurai on the left and ogres
on the right.

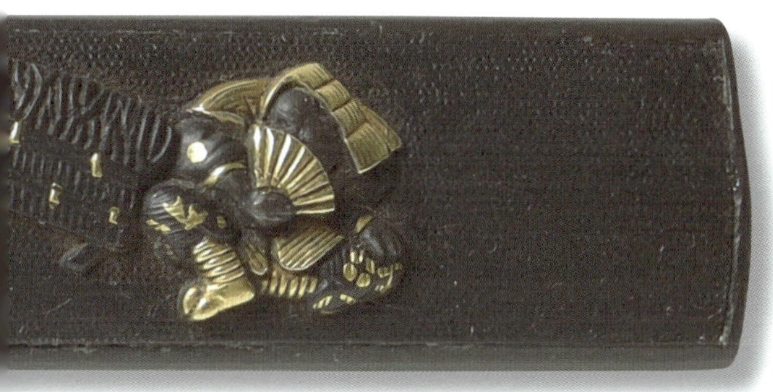

僧に化けた狐が鼠を餌にした罠で正体を現してしまうと
いう有名な話をデザインしている。

The design is of the famous story in which a fox who disguised
itself as a priest was caught in a trap with a mouse as bait,
revealing its true form.

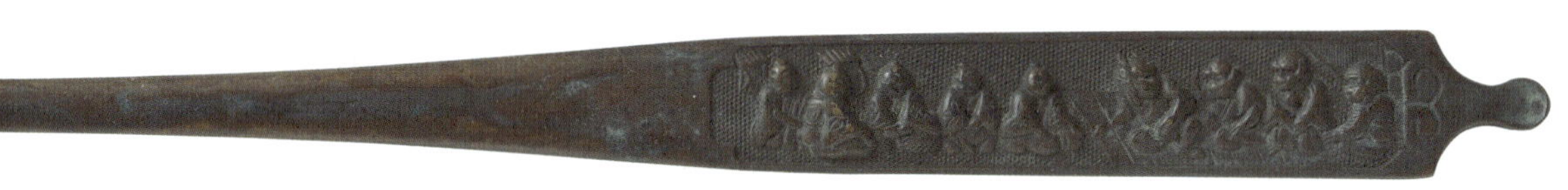

原寸大
Actual size

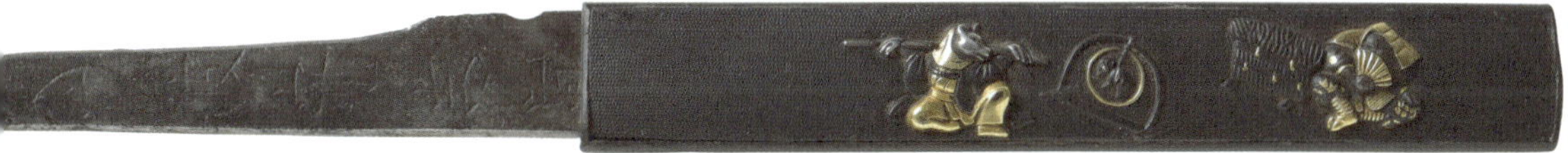

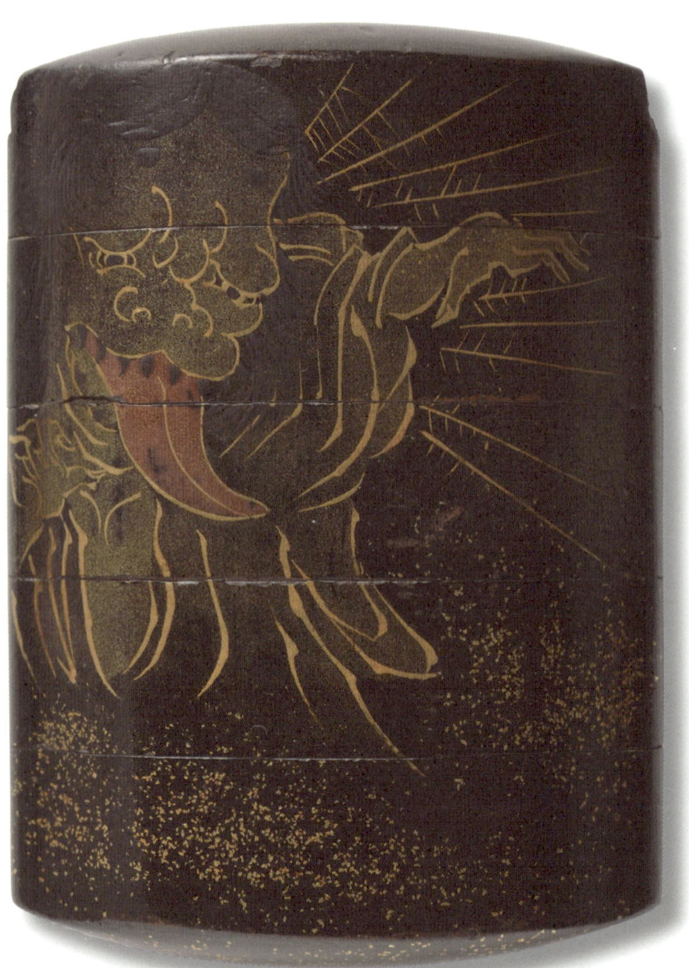

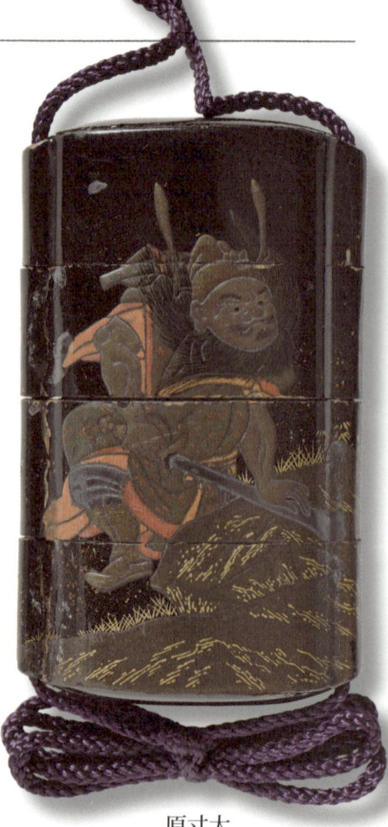

原寸大
Actual size

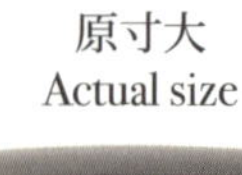

原寸大
Actual size

土蜘蛛図印籠
つちぐもずいんろう

Tsuchigumo Inrō

江戸時代　横 5.5　厚 2.0　高 7.8
Edo period, Width 5.5, Thickness 2.0, Height 7.8

源頼光の館に出現した土蜘蛛。不気味な姿で頼光を襲おうとしている。背面は碁をしながら警護する四天王だが、土蜘蛛の妖術で眠りこけている。

The *tsuchigumo* who appeared in the mansion of Minamoto no Yorimitsu. The fearsome spider is attacking Yorimitsu. On the back is one of Yorimitsu's four retainers who was playing a game of *go* to while away his guard duty, and has been sent to sleep by the *tsuchigumo*'s sorcery.

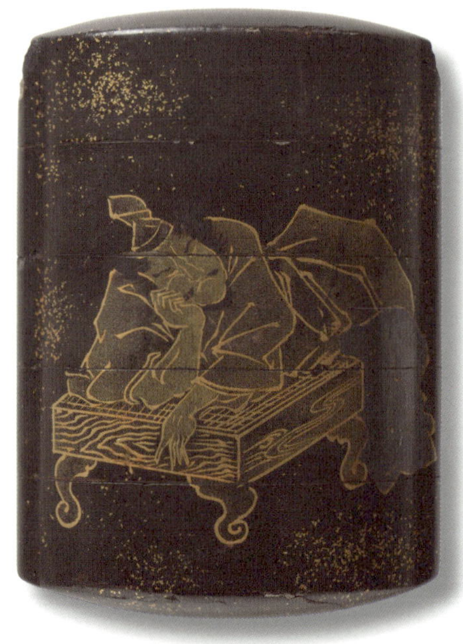

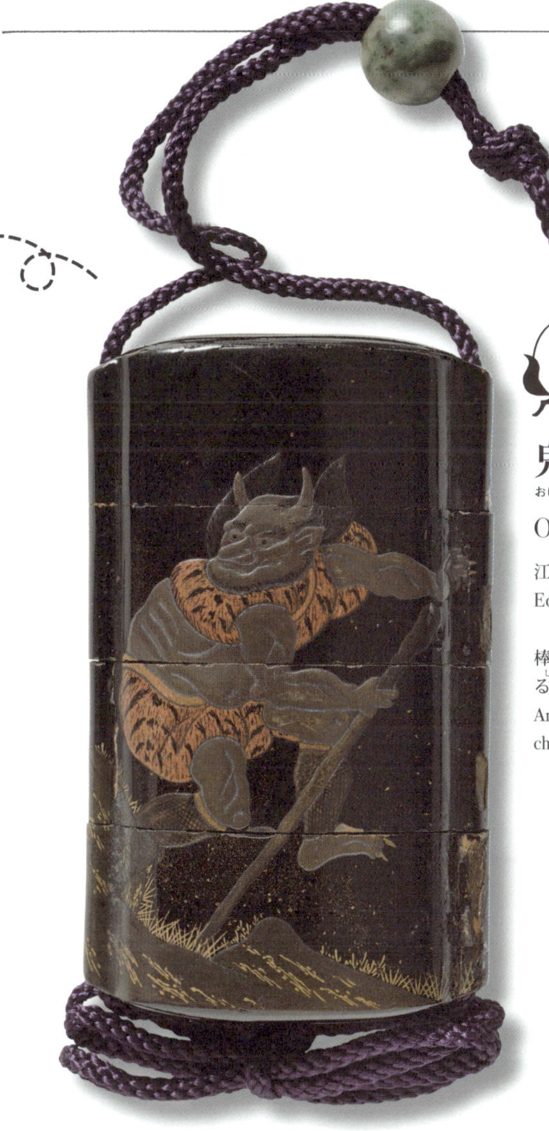

鬼図印籠
おにずいんろう

Ogre *Inrō*

江戸時代　横 4.8　厚 1.3　高 7.8
Edo period, Width 4.8, Thickness 1.3, Height 7.8

棒を握りながら逃げ去る鬼。背面には鬼を追いかけ
る鍾馗がデザインされている。
An ogre flees, gripping a stick. Shōki the demon queller
chasing the ogre is featured on the other side.

幽霊図印籠
ゆうれいずいんろう

Ghost *Inrō*

江戸時代　横 2.6　厚 1.8　高 4.6
Edo period, Width 2.6, Thickness 1.8, Height 4.6

骸骨のような姿の幽霊が出現して燭台を掴もうとし
ているが体は朦朧としている。根付は髑髏。
A skeletal ghost appears, clutching at a lamp, but its
body is insubstantial. The *netsuke* is a skull.

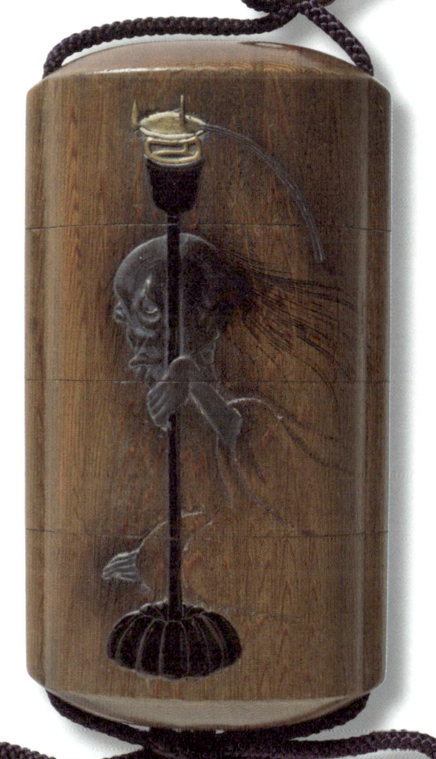

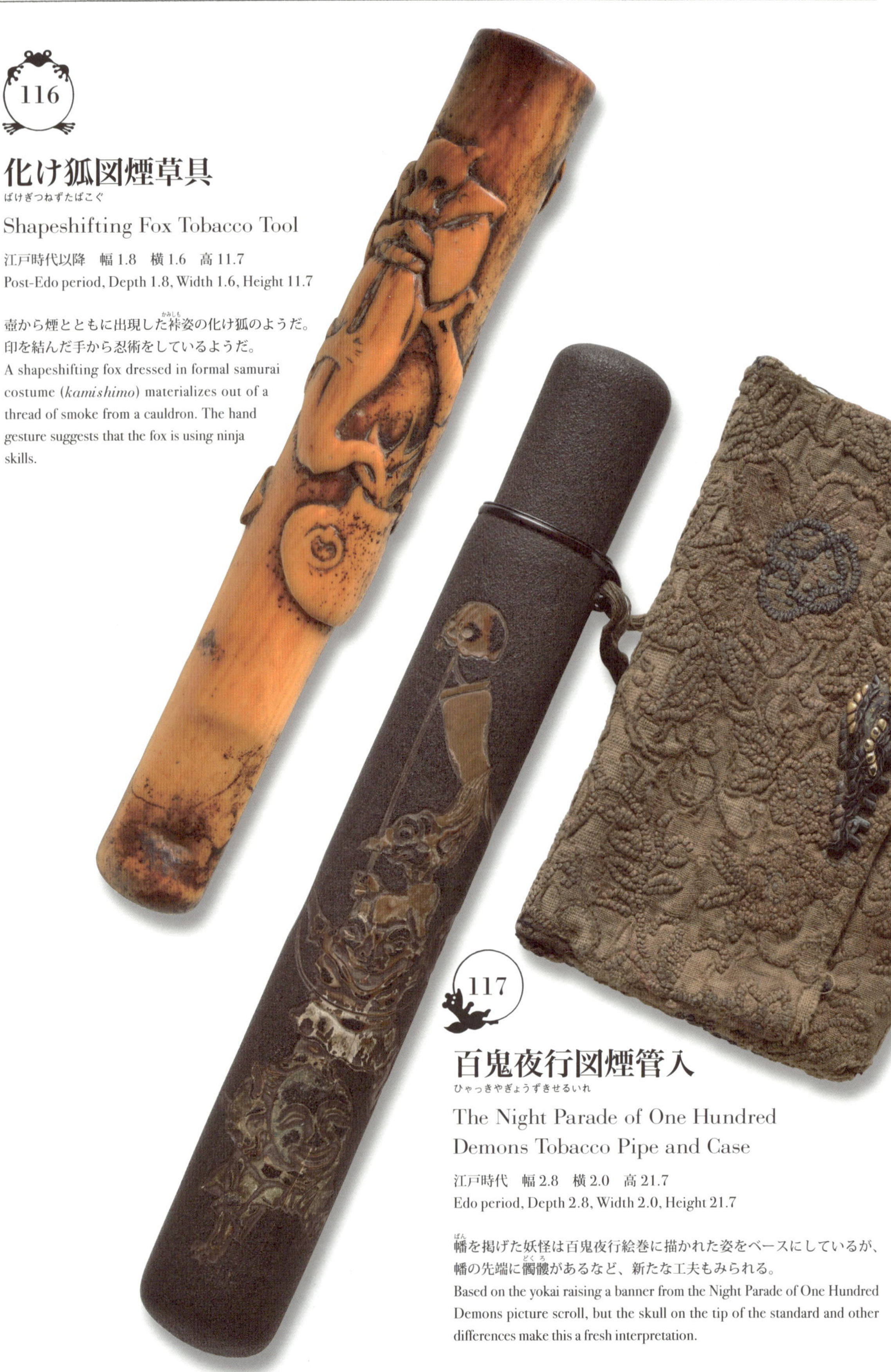

116

化け狐図煙草具

ばけぎつねずたばこぐ

Shapeshifting Fox Tobacco Tool

江戸時代以降　幅 1.8　横 1.6　高 11.7
Post-Edo period, Depth 1.8, Width 1.6, Height 11.7

壺から煙とともに出現した裃姿の化け狐のようだ。
印を結んだ手から忍術をしているようだ。
A shapeshifting fox dressed in formal samurai
costume (*kamishimo*) materializes out of a
thread of smoke from a cauldron. The hand
gesture suggests that the fox is using ninja
skills.

117

百鬼夜行図煙管入

ひゃっきやぎょうずきせるいれ

The Night Parade of One Hundred
Demons Tobacco Pipe and Case

江戸時代　幅 2.8　横 2.0　高 21.7
Edo period, Depth 2.8, Width 2.0, Height 21.7

幡を掲げた妖怪は百鬼夜行絵巻に描かれた姿をベースにしているが、
幡の先端に髑髏があるなど、新たな工夫もみられる。
Based on the yokai raising a banner from the Night Parade of One Hundred
Demons picture scroll, but the skull on the tip of the standard and other
differences make this a fresh interpretation.

118

平維茂鬼女退治図鍔
たいらのこれもちきじょたいじずつば

Taira no Koremochi's Defeat of an Ogress Sword Guard (*Tsuba*)

江戸時代　縦 8.5　横 8.1　厚 0.6
Edo period, Height 8.5, Width 8.1, Thickness 0.6

能の演目「紅葉狩り」などで有名な平維茂の鬼女
退治をデザイン。上から襲いかかる鬼と戦う維茂
の必死な姿が表現されている。
The famous defeat of an ogress by Taira no Koremochi
featured in the Noh play *Autumn Leaf Viewing* among
others. Koremochi's desperation is plain as he struggles
with the monster attacking from above.

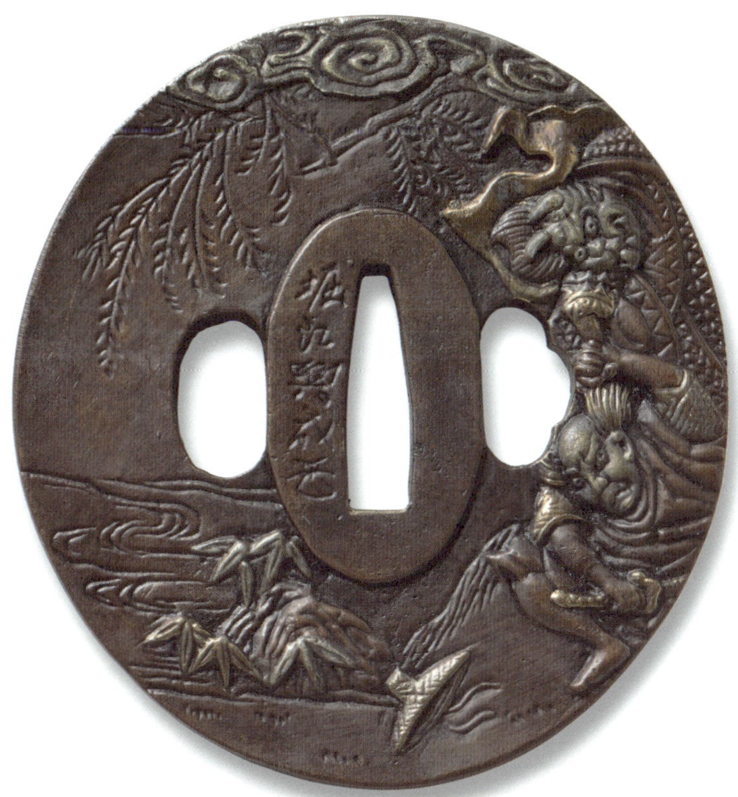

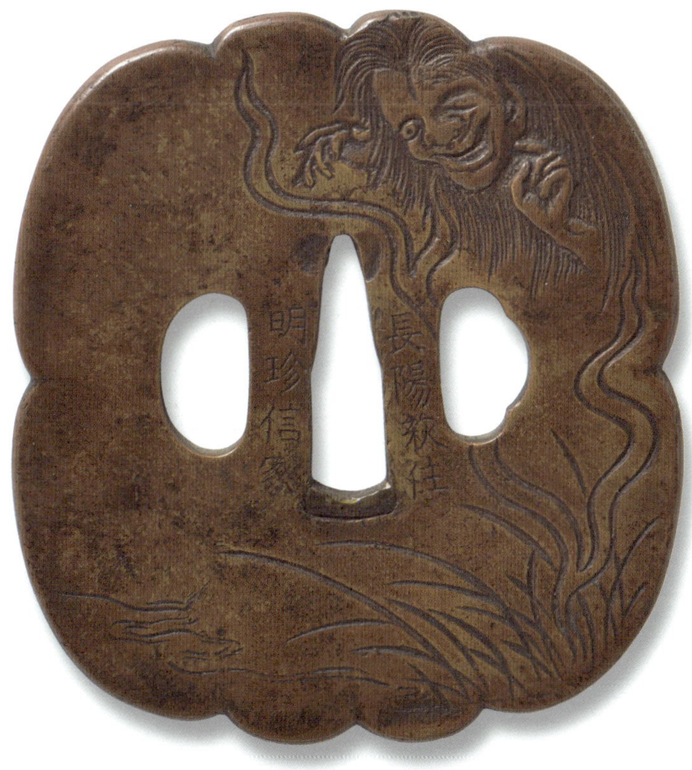

119

幽霊図鍔
ゆうれいずつば

Ghost Sword Guard (*Tsuba*)

江戸時代　縦 8.0　横 7.6　厚 0.3
Edo period, Height 8.0, Width 7.6, Thickness 0.3

草むらから幽霊が現れている。背面には野ざらしの
髑髏がデザインされている。
A ghost emerges from a tuft of grass. On the back is a
skull exposed to the elements.

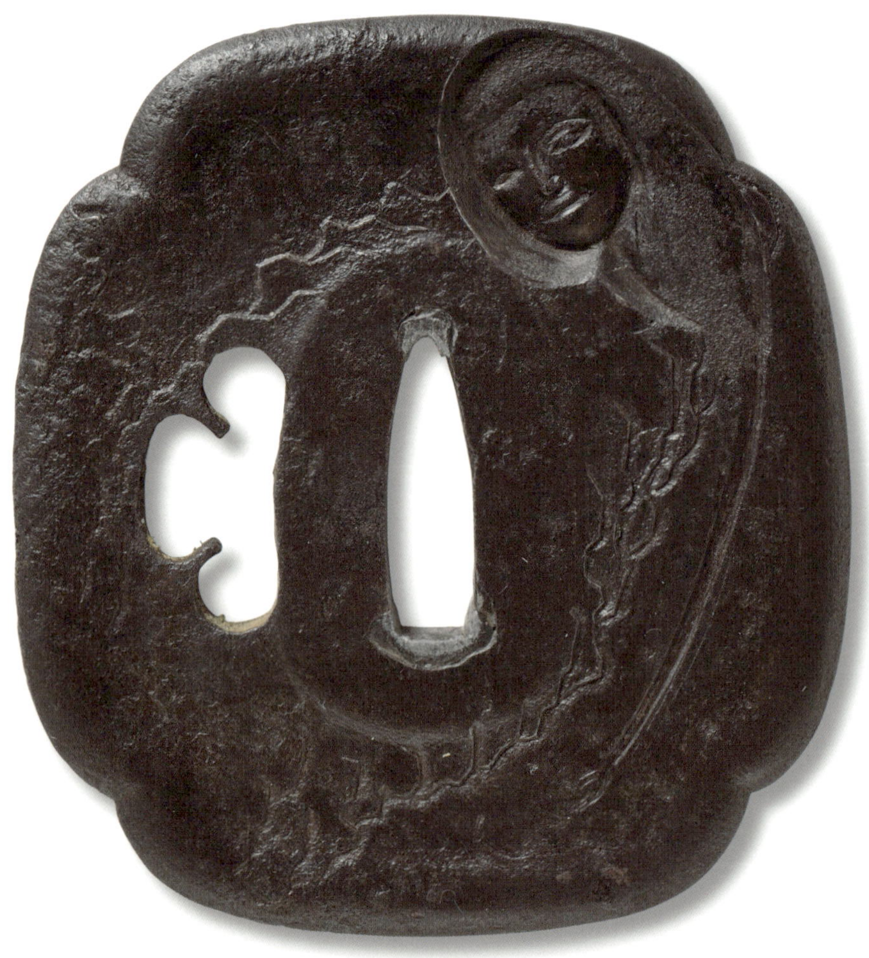

120

幽霊図鍔
ゆうれいずつば

Ghost Sword Guard (*Tsuba*)

江戸時代　縦 8.1　横 7.6　厚 0.3
Edo period, Height 8.1, Width 7.6, Thickness 0.3

右側に煙のように現れた幽霊がデザインされている。顔
ははっきりしているが体は煙のようだ。背面には供養塔
がデザインされている。

On the right side is a ghost which manifests like smoke. The
face is clearly defined but the body is mistily vague. On the
reverse side is a memorial tower.

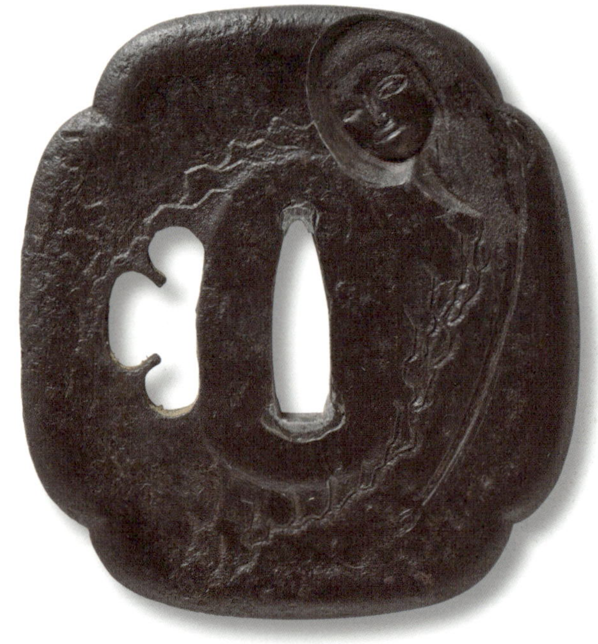

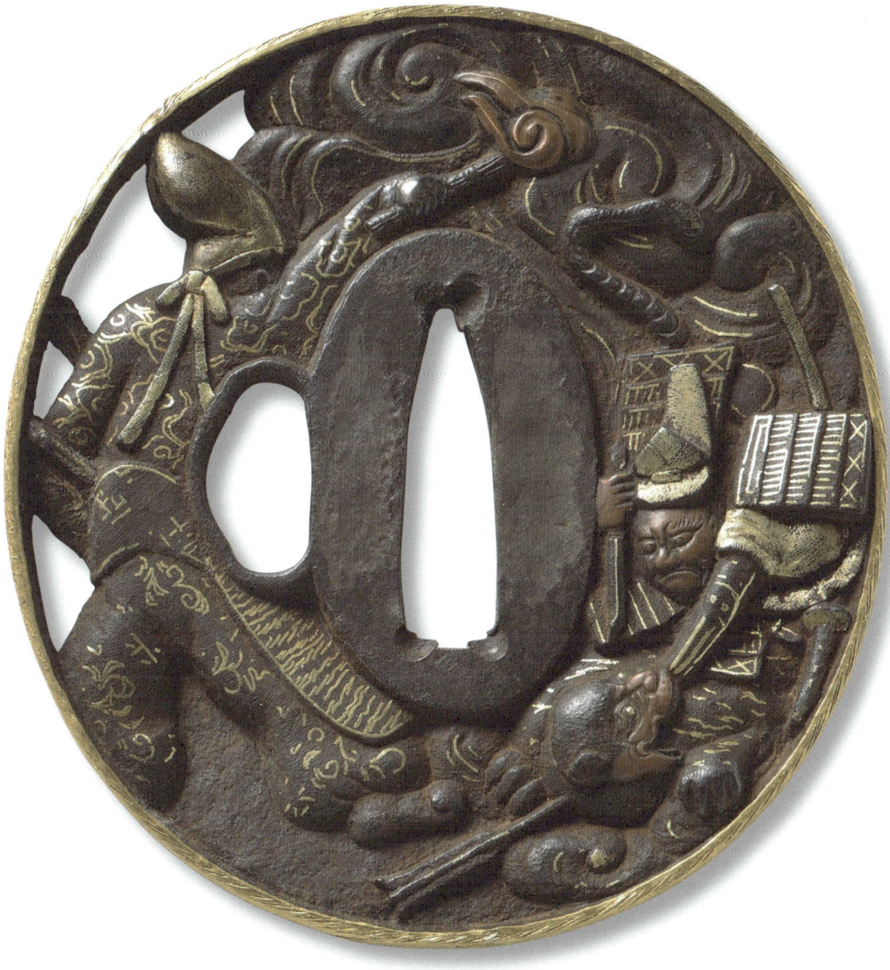

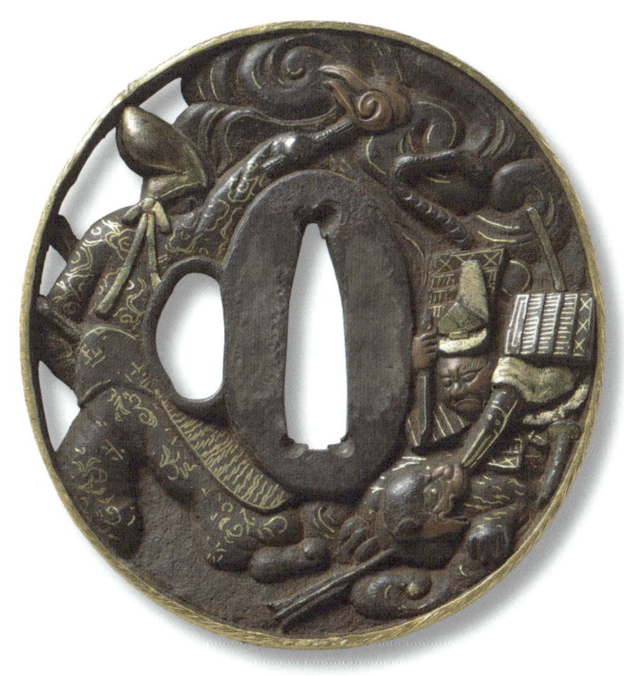

鵺図鍔
ぬえずつば

Nue Sword Guard (*Tsuba*)

江戸時代　Edo period

御所に出現した鵺を源頼政が退治するという話をテーマ
は錦絵をはじめとして種々取り上げられているが、ここ
では鍔という小さなスペースに鵺退治をデザインしてい
る。頼政の弓で空から落ちてきた鵺を退治しているとこ
ろ。

The story of the Nue which appeared in the Imperial Palace
and was defeated by Minamoto no Yorimasa is a popular
theme in various media such as *nishiki-e*, but here the Nue's
defeat is captured within the small space of a sword guard.
This is the moment in which the Nue falls from the sky,
brought down by Yorimasa's bow.

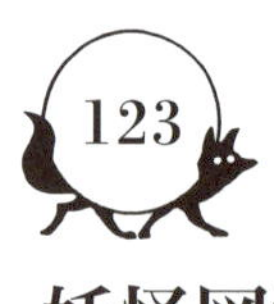

122

妖怪図急須
ようかいずきゅうす

Yokai Teapot

明治時代以降
直径 8.3　高 5.2
Post-Meiji period,
Diameter 8.3,
Height 5.2

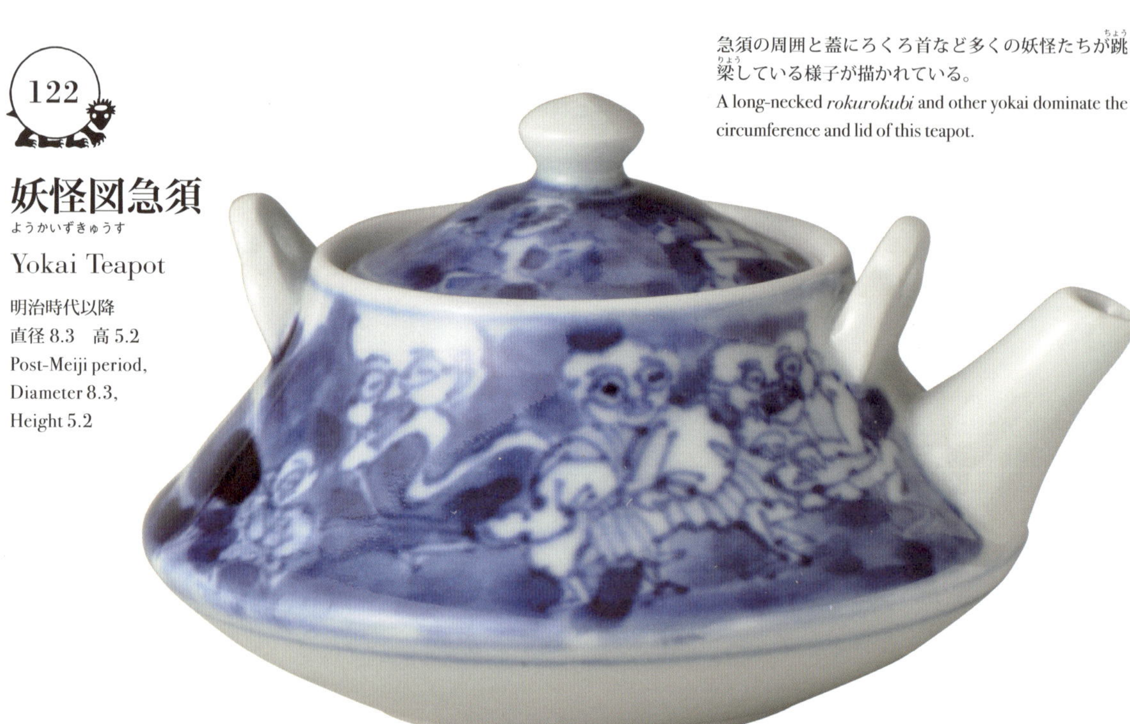

急須の周囲と蓋にろくろ首など多くの妖怪たちが跳
梁している様子が描かれている。
A long-necked *rokurokubi* and other yokai dominate the
circumference and lid of this teapot.

123

妖怪図瓶
ようかいずへい

Yokai Bottle (Early Imari ware)

江戸時代　幅 8.0　奥行 7.1　高 14.1
Edo period, Width 8.0, Depth 7.1, Height 14.1

古伊万里の瓶。髪を振り乱した男の首は長く伸
びている。首は蛇腹のような模様となっている。
A man's head with wild hair stretches out on a long
neck with the pattern of a snake's belly.

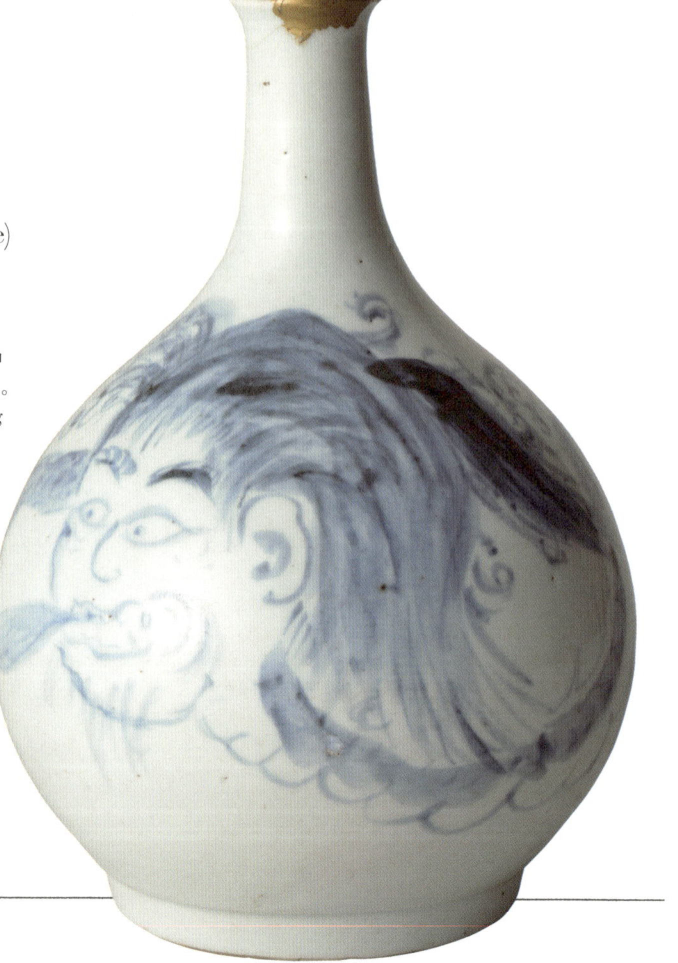

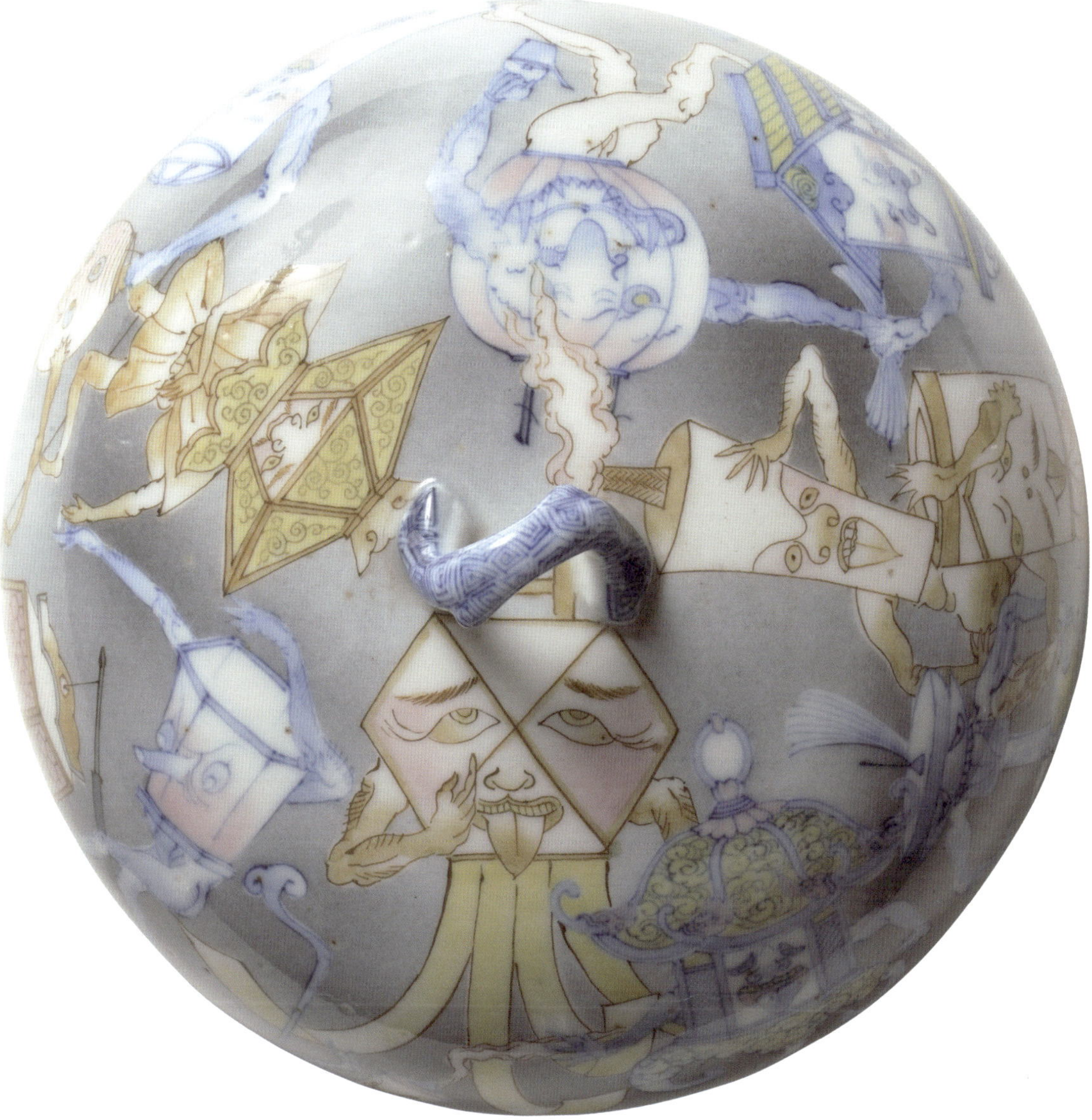

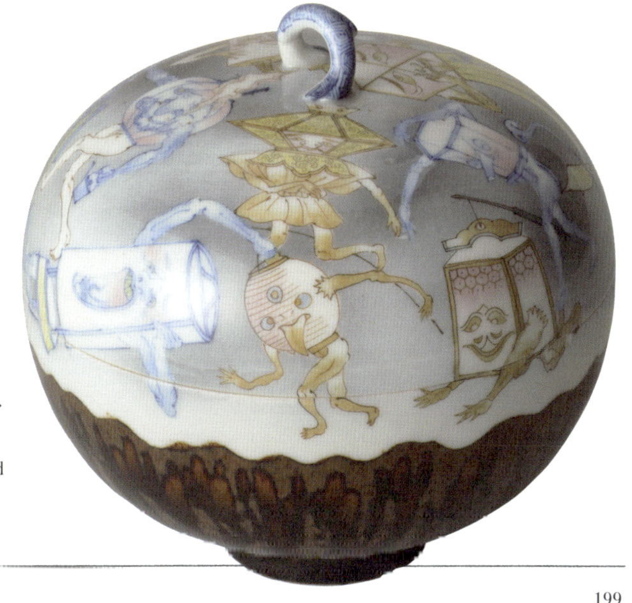

妖怪図菓子入れ

ようかいずかしいれ

Yokai Candy Bowl

明治時代以降　総高 14.6　胴径 14.6
Post-Meiji period, Total height 14.6, Diameter 14.6

蓋を中心に提灯、行灯、蝋燭など照明器物妖怪がデザインされている。丁寧な制作が目立つ作品といえる。
Lighting yokai of lamps, lanterns, and candles are centered around the lid. This work stands out for its careful execution.

ろくろ首水滴
ろくろくびすいてき

Rokurokubi Water Dropper
(*Hirado-yaki* porcelain)

江戸時代以降　直径 14.9　高 21.0
Post-Edo period,
Diameter 14.9, Height 21.0

三味線を弾く芸者のろくろ首をデザインした平戸焼の水滴。首が抜けて水を入れる。首の下部に水を注す穴が開いている。
A water dropper (used for calligraphy) in the shape of a long-necked *rokurokubi* geisha playing a *shamisen*. The neck is removed to fill the dropper with water. At the base of the neck is a hole from which water can be dripped.

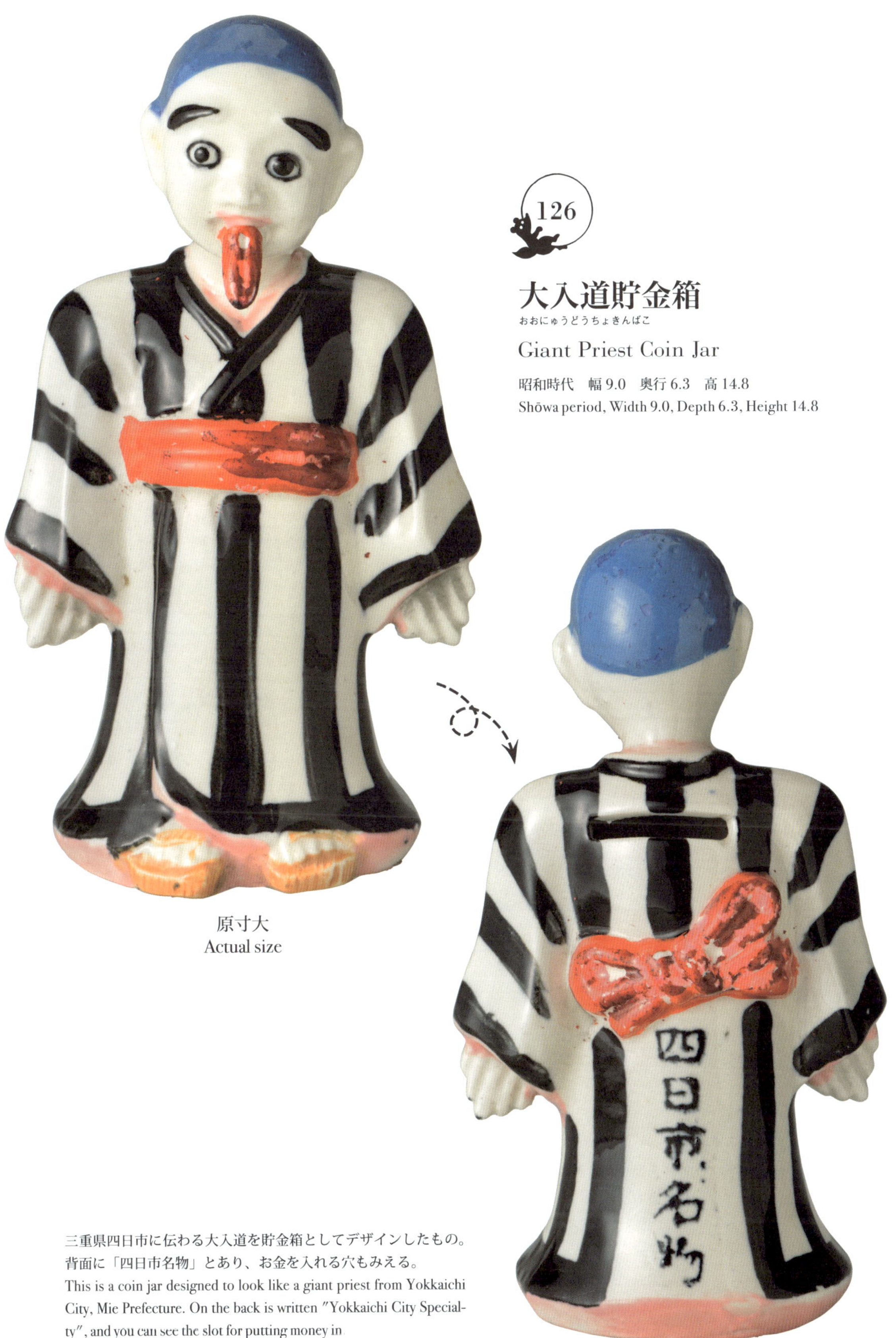

大入道貯金箱
おおにゅうどうちょきんばこ
Giant Priest Coin Jar

昭和時代　幅 9.0　奥行 6.3　高 14.8
Shōwa period, Width 9.0, Depth 6.3, Height 14.8

原寸大
Actual size

三重県四日市に伝わる大入道を貯金箱としてデザインしたもの。
背面に「四日市名物」とあり、お金を入れる穴もみえる。
This is a coin jar designed to look like a giant priest from Yokkaichi
City, Mie Prefecture. On the back is written ″Yokkaichi City Special-
ty″, and you can see the slot for putting money in

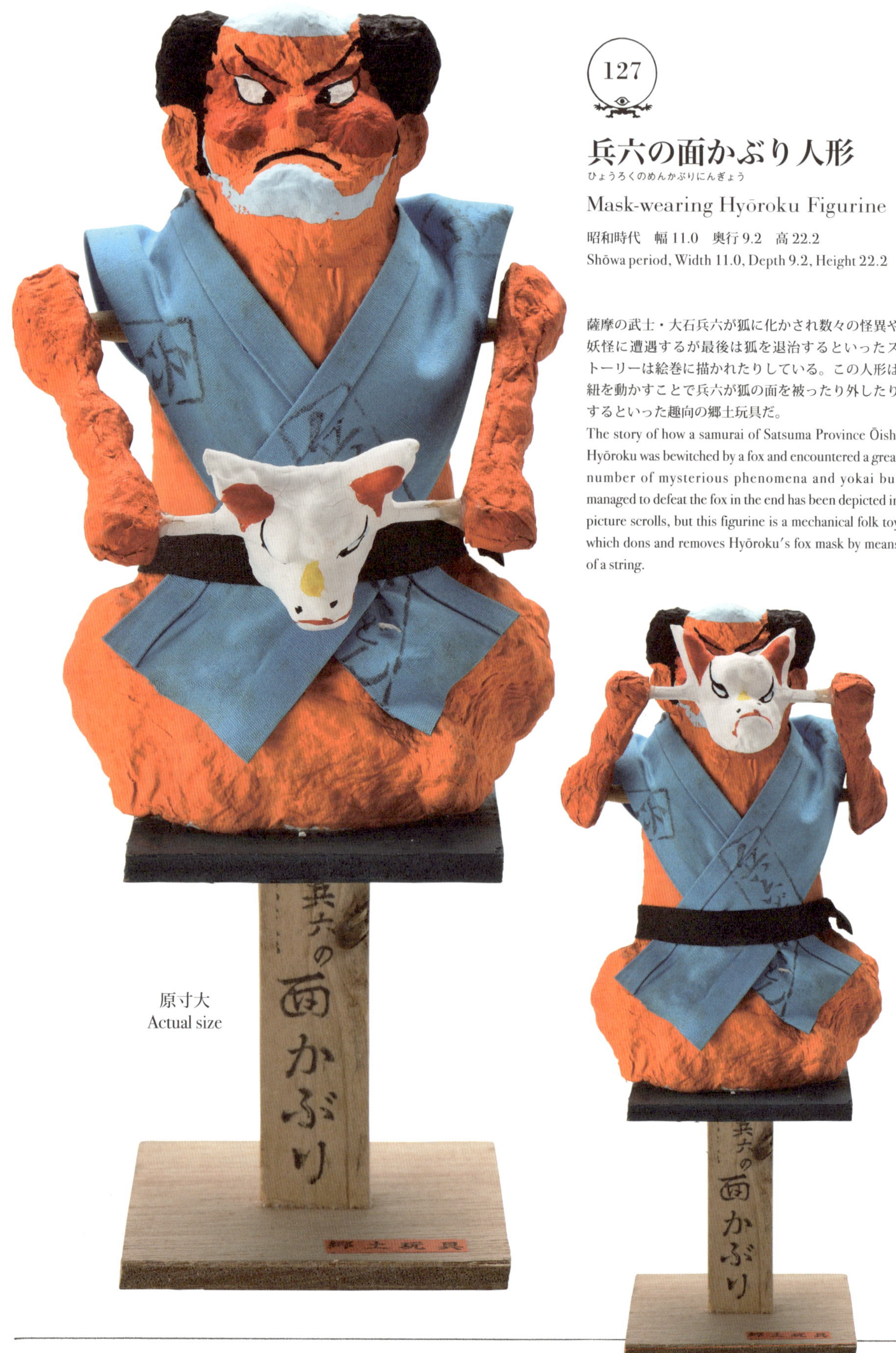

兵六の面かぶり人形
ひょうろくのめんかぶりにんぎょう

Mask-wearing Hyōroku Figurine

昭和時代　幅 11.0　奥行 9.2　高 22.2
Shōwa period, Width 11.0, Depth 9.2, Height 22.2

薩摩の武士・大石兵六が狐に化かされ数々の怪異や妖怪に遭遇するが最後は狐を退治するといったストーリーは絵巻に描かれたりしている。この人形は紐を動かすことで兵六が狐の面を被ったり外したりするといった趣向の郷土玩具だ。

The story of how a samurai of Satsuma Province Ōishi Hyōroku was bewitched by a fox and encountered a great number of mysterious phenomena and yokai but managed to defeat the fox in the end has been depicted in picture scrolls, but this figurine is a mechanical folk toy which dons and removes Hyōroku's fox mask by means of a string.

原寸大
Actual size

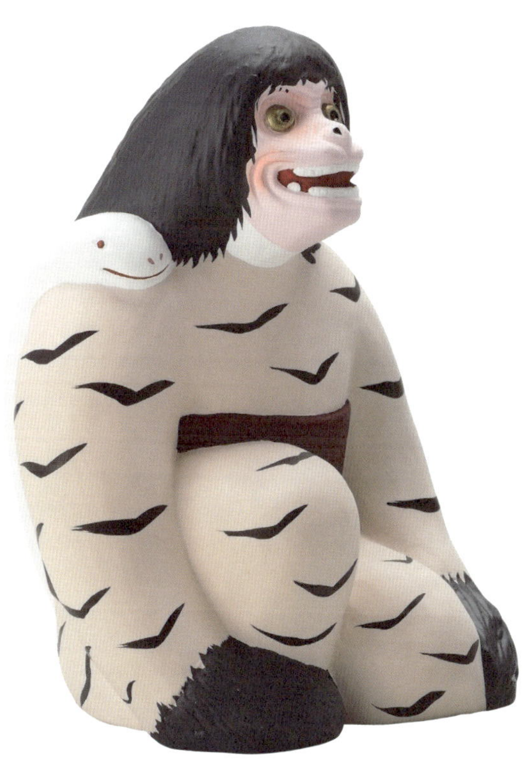
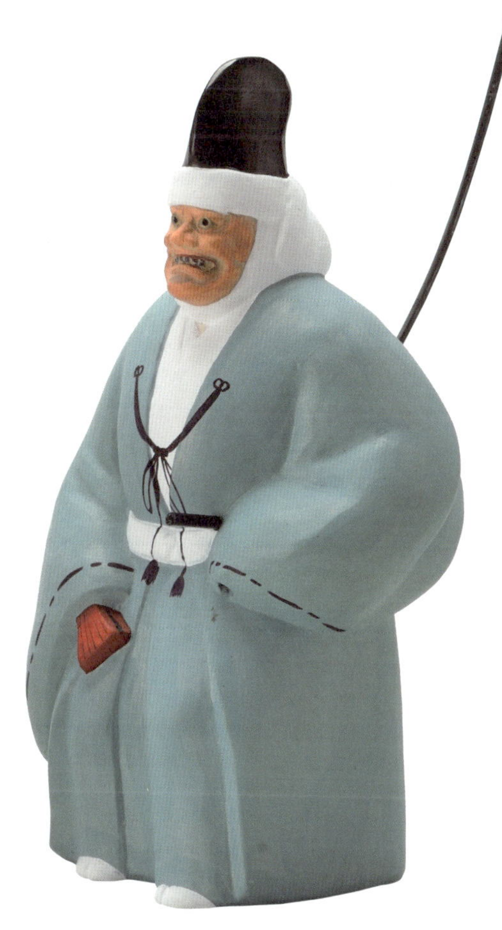

128

鵺と頼政
ぬえとよりまさ

The Nue and Yorimasa
(Mibu Kyōgen figurines)

昭和時代　鵺：幅 10.0　奥行 9.0　高 14.0
頼政：幅 9.9　奥行 7.5　高 16.8
Shōwa period, Nue: Width 10.0, Depth 9.0, Height 14.0,
Yorimasa: Width 9.9, Depth 7.5, Height 16.8

壬生狂言を題材にした京都の郷土人形。右が源頼政、左が鵺。頼政によっ
て鵺が退治されるテーマは錦絵などにも多数描かれている。この作品は頼
政と鵺が別々に扱われているが、実際には 2 体でセットと思われる。デザ
インは錦絵の表現とは異なり、狂言での頼政と鵺の姿だ。

Figurines special to Kyoto derived from *Mibu Kyōgen* theater. On the right is
Minamoto no Yorimasa, on the left is the Nue. Yorimasa's defeat of the Nue is
often used as a theme for *nishiki-e*, but this work separates Yorimasa and the Nue,
although the two figurines are in fact a set. The style of expression differs from that
of *nishiki-e*: these figurines are Yorimasa and the Nue as they appear in *kyōgen*
(traditional short comedic performance art).

129 神戸人形

こうべにんぎょう

Kōbe Figurine

明治時代以降　Post-Meiji period

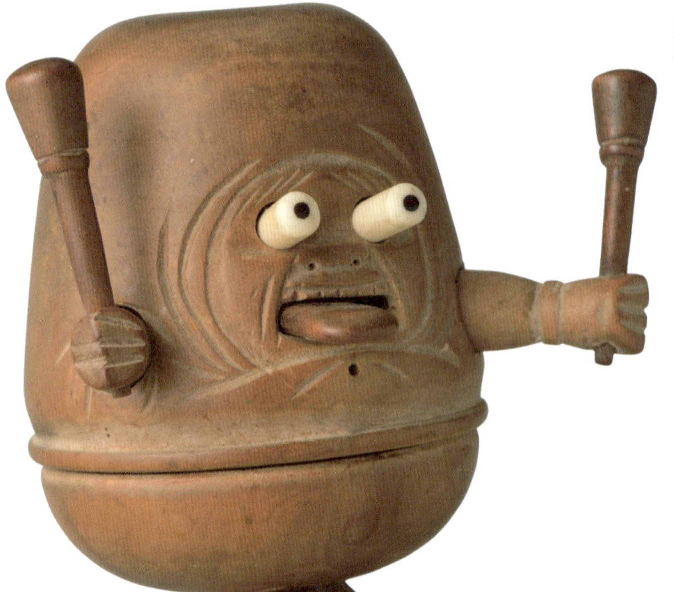

両手に撥を握った大きな顔の妖怪。目と舌が出入りする仕掛けで、腕も動く。

A yokai with a large head, gripping drumsticks in both hands. Constructed so that the eyes and tongue protrude, and the arms move.

幅 4.0　奥行 3.6　高 5.3

Width 4.0, Depth 3.6, Height 5.3

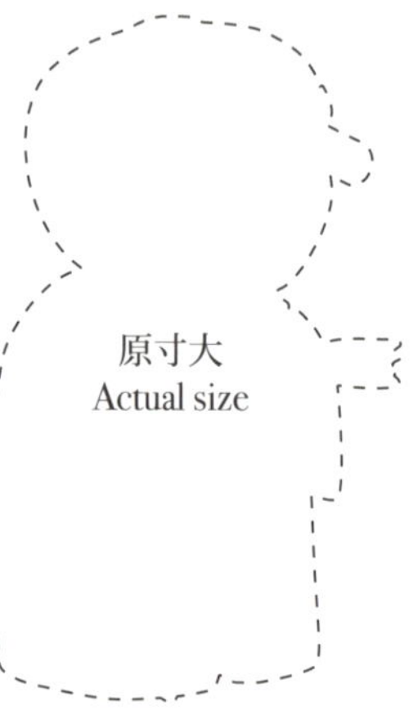

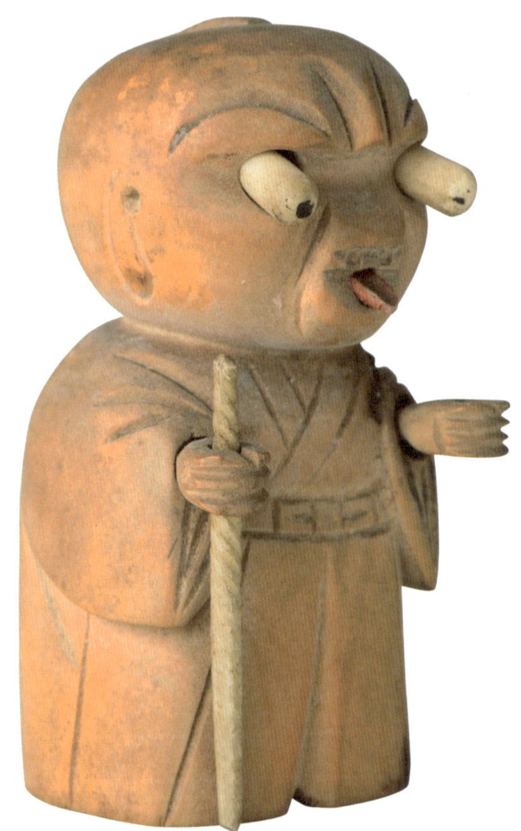

不気味な姿で目と舌が出入りする仕掛けとなっている。

A eerie figure with eyes and tongue poking out.

幅 3.0　奥行 3.6　高 5.6

Width 3.0, Depth 3.6, Height 5.6

130

道成寺
どうじょうじ

Dōjōji Temple (*Kasukabe* papier-mache)

昭和時代以降　幅 12.7　奥行 12.3　高 25.7
Post-Shōwa period, Width 12.7, Depth 12.3, Height 25.7

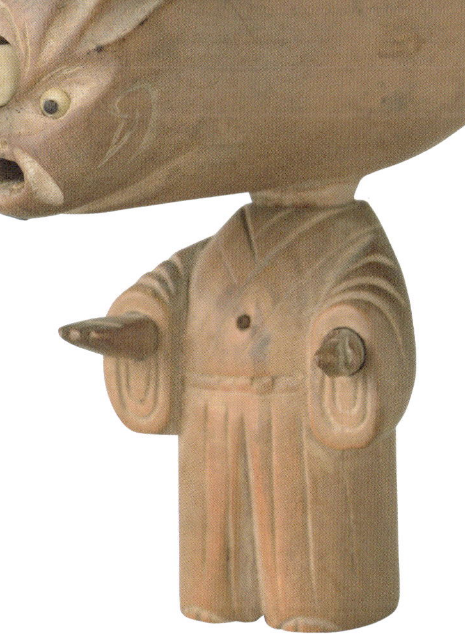

極端に巨大な頭で、三つ目の顔の中央の大きな目は
出入りする仕掛けとなっている。
One large eye sticks out of the middle of its three-eyed
face on an enormous head.
幅 3.0　奥行 7.7　高 7.3
Width 3.0, Depth 7.7, Height 7.3

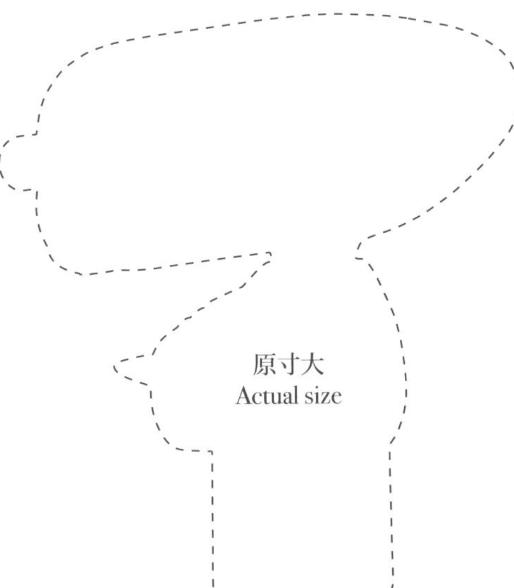

原寸大
Actual size

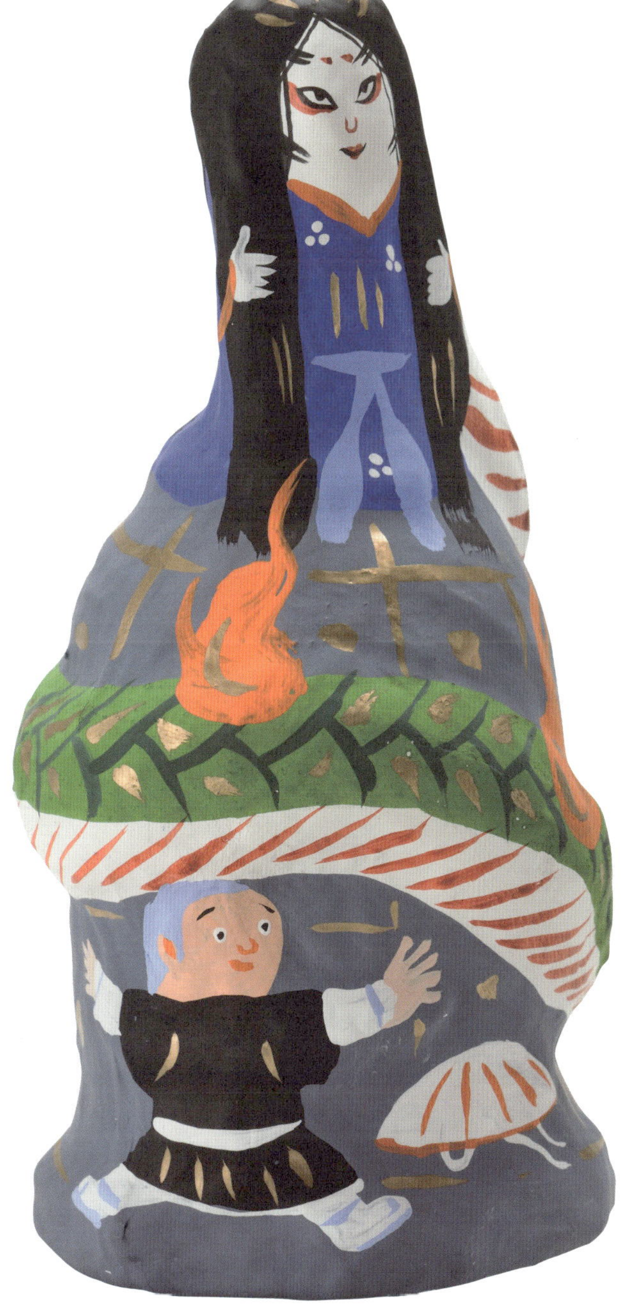

妖怪立像
ようかいりゅうぞう
Standing Statues of Yokai

江戸時代　Edo period

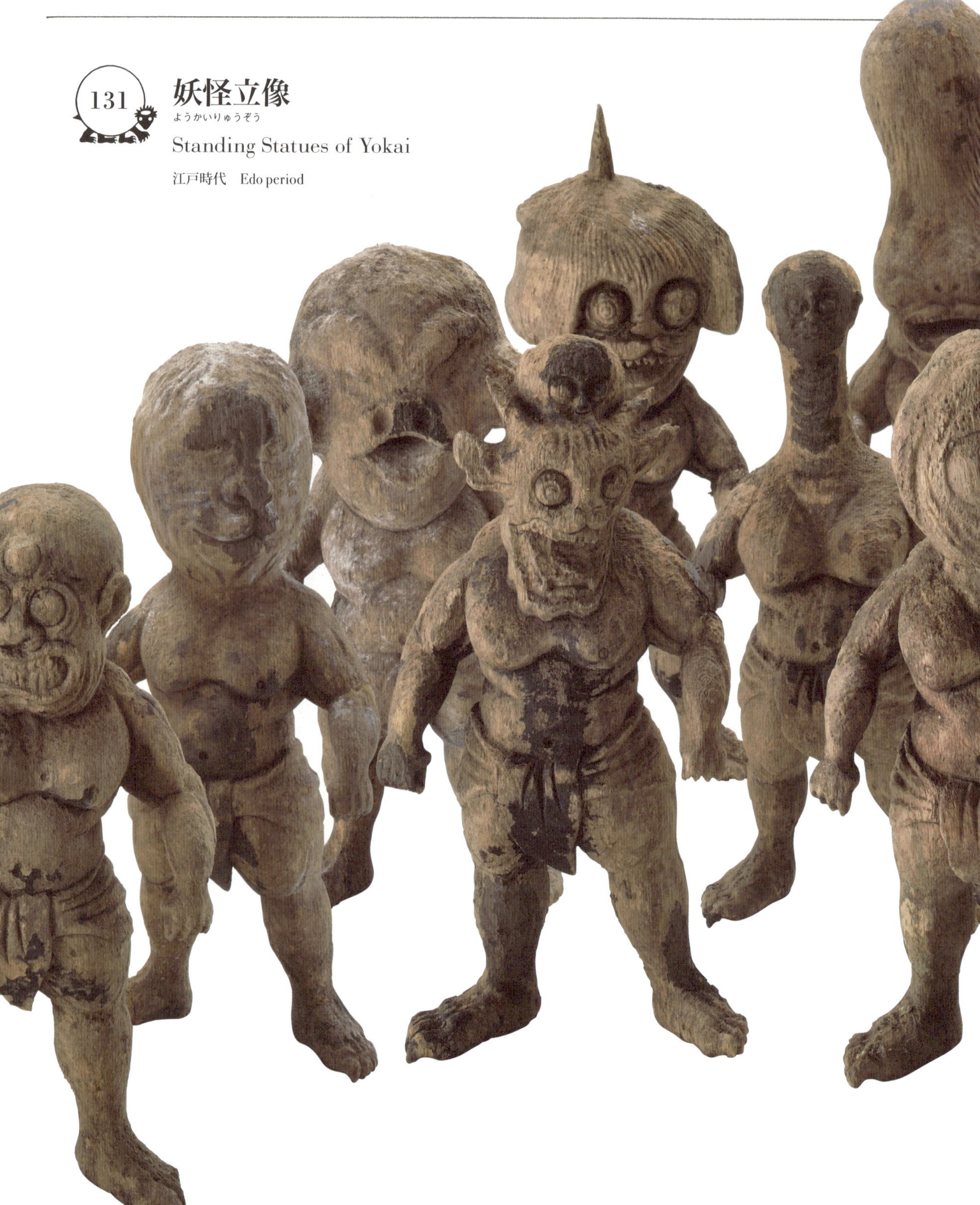

36体の木彫妖怪立像。妖怪はすべて下帯姿で獣、魚、鳥などをイメージしたものや、顔が２つあったり、長い首のものなど多様だ。この妖怪像は福島県いわき市で何箇所かに分散されて伝えられていたものだが、言い伝えによると、いわき市泉町にあった玉光山威徳院にあったものといわれる。威徳院は廃仏毀釈で廃寺となり、この像も地元の人たちが受け継いできたものと思われ、「魔像三十六体」と呼ばれていた。この像が寺にあったときにどのような信仰対象となっていたかは不明だが、妖怪像という稀な資料で今後の研究が俟たれる。

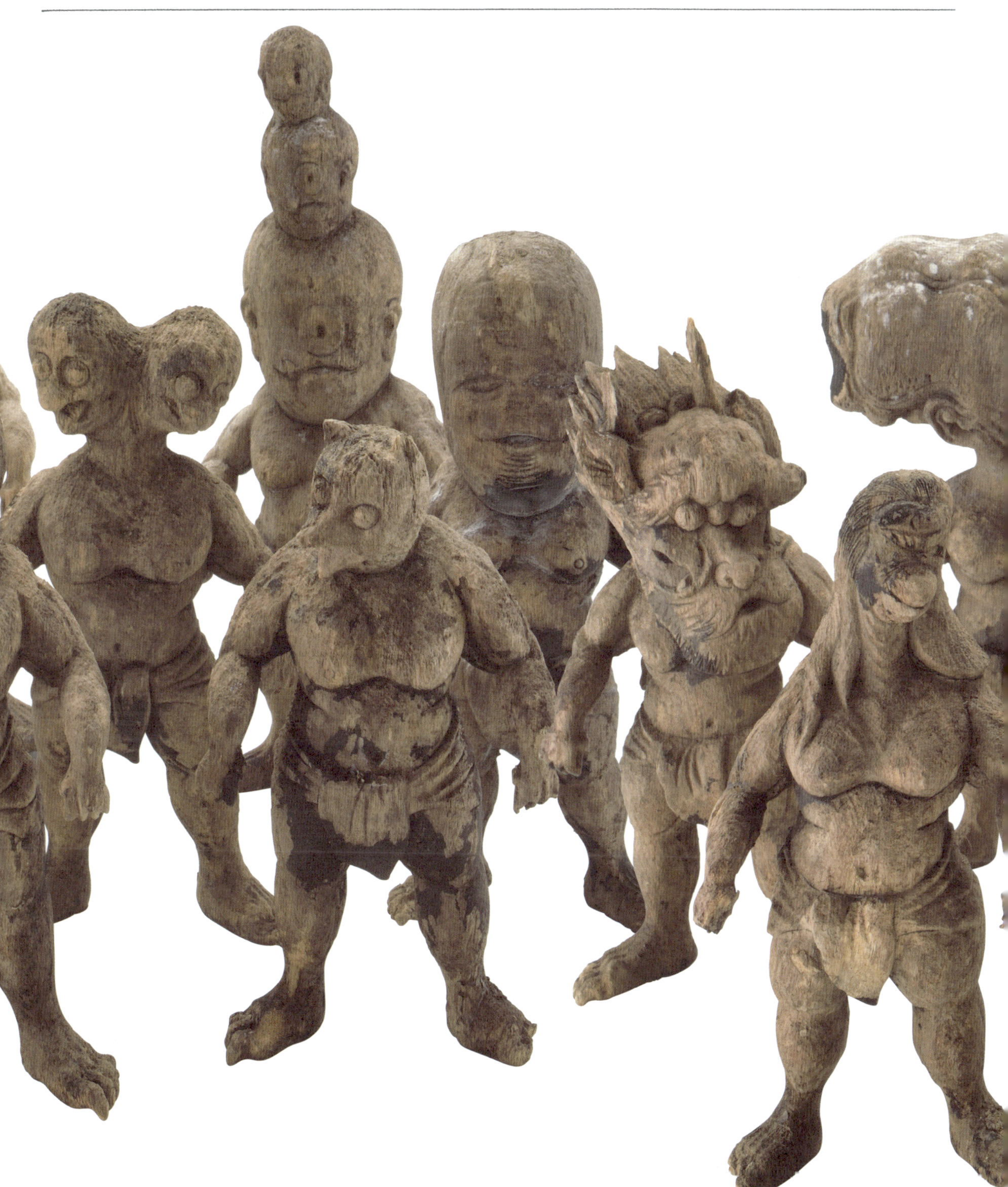

36 standing wooden yokai figurines. The yokai all wear loincloths; beasts, fish and birds are among them, as well as a variety of two-faced and long-necked creatures. These yokai sculptures were made in dozens of locations throughout Iwaki City in Fukushima Prefecture, but legend has it that they all hail from the Gyokugōzan Itokuin temple in Izumi-machi, Iwaki City. When the temple was shut down by the Haibutsu-kishaku movement to abolish Buddhism, these statues known as the '36 Evil Images' are thought to have been inherited by the locals. It is not known what role these statues played during their time at the temple, but as rare yokai figurines they may henceforth be the subjects of research.

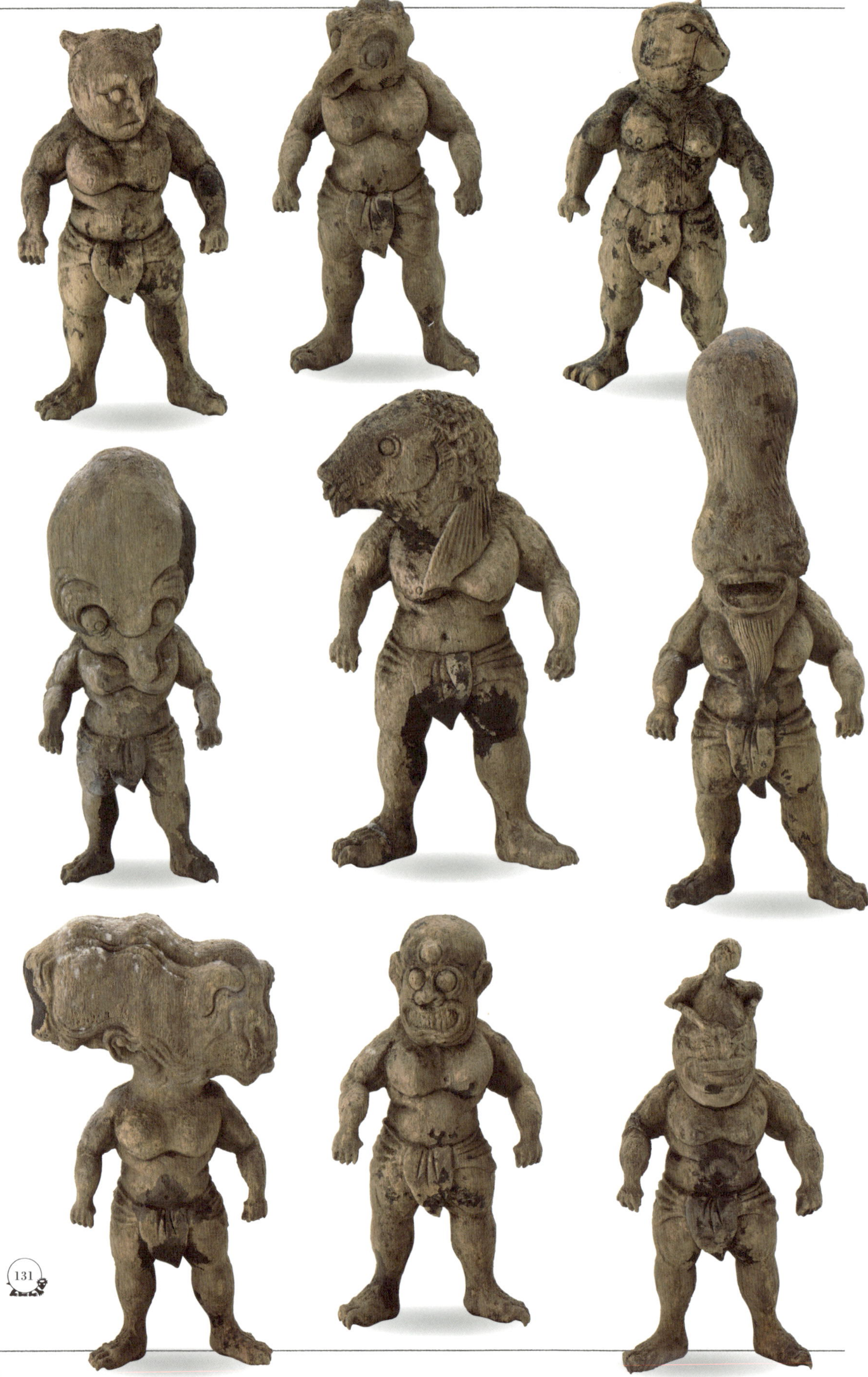

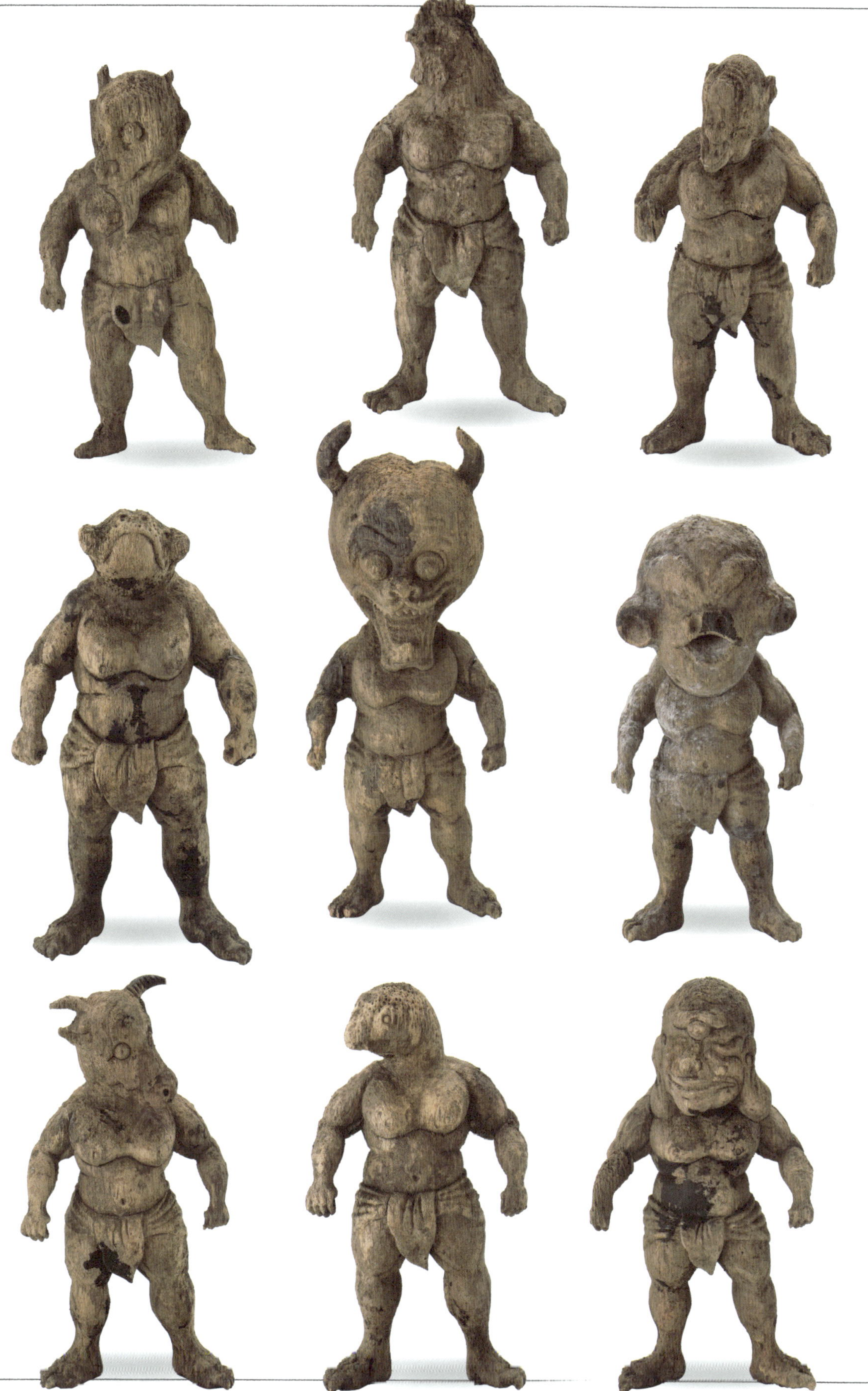

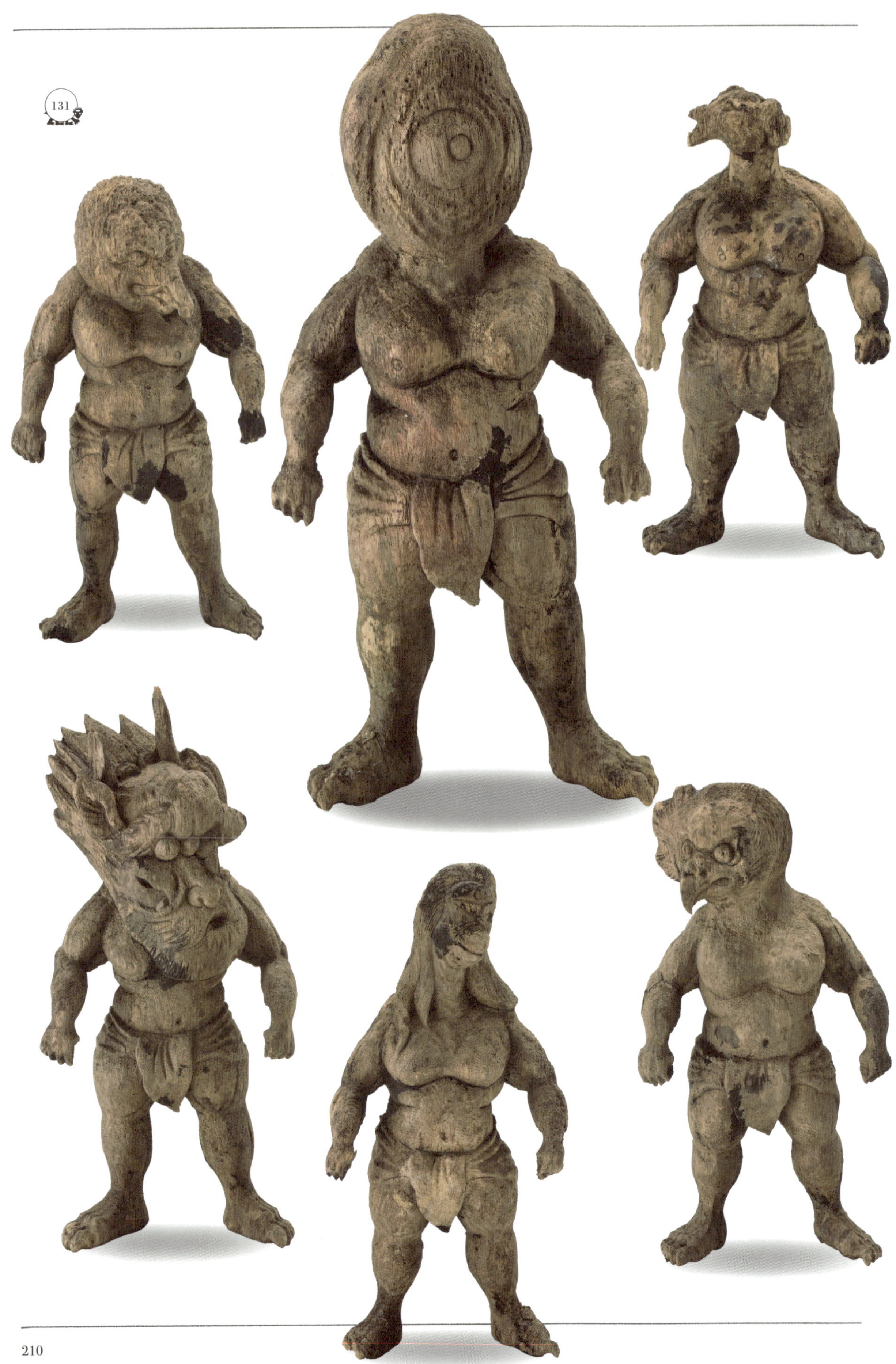

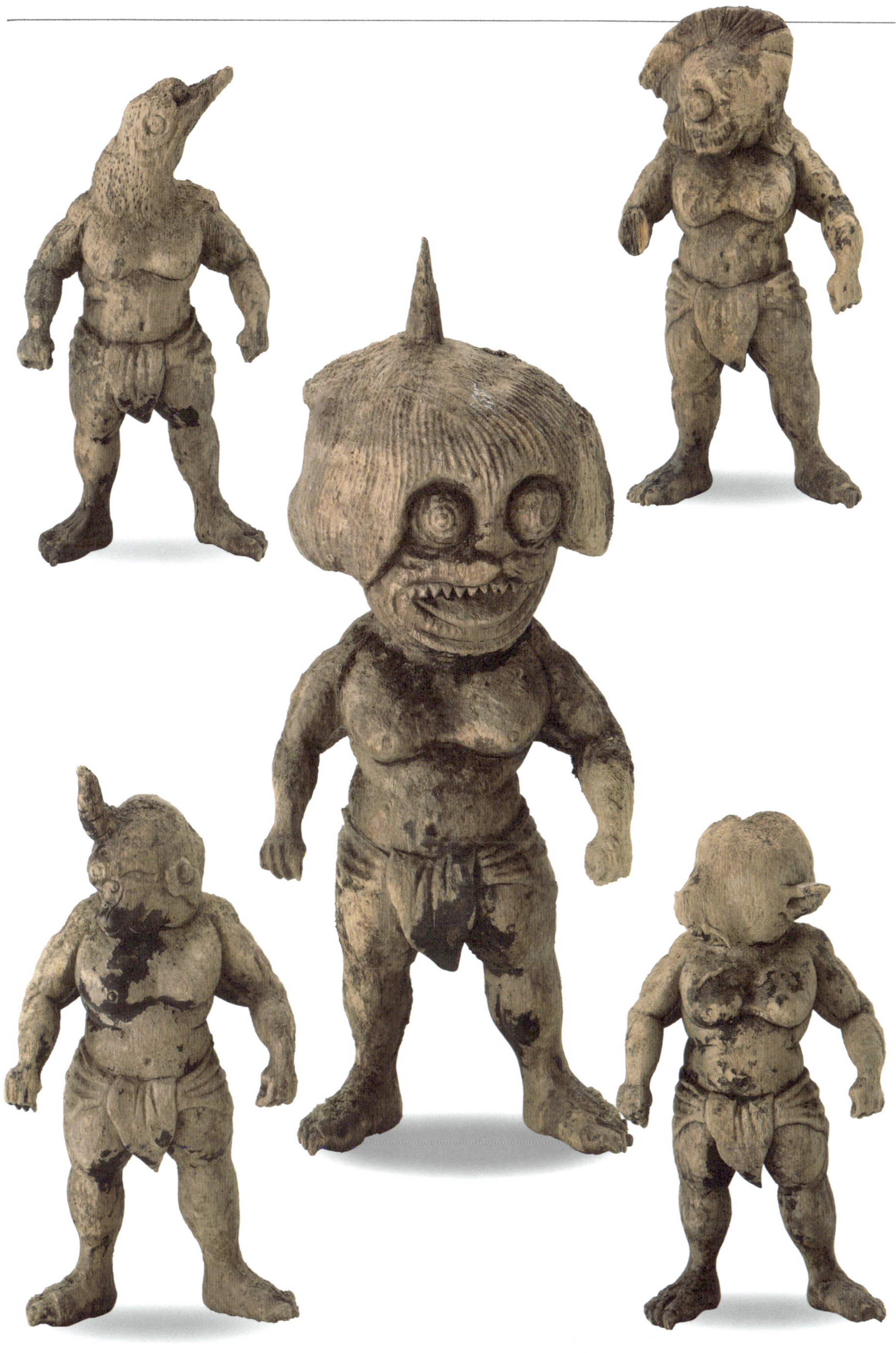

妖怪坐像
ようかいざぞう

Seated Statues of Yokai

江戸時代　Edo period

100 体の木彫妖怪坐像。この像も妖怪立像と同じく威徳
院にあったもので、何箇所かに分散されて伝えられてい
た。立像とは異なり袈裟姿だが、獣、魚、鳥などに加え
て種々の姿の妖怪がみられる。どのような信仰対象だっ
たかなど現状では解明されていない。

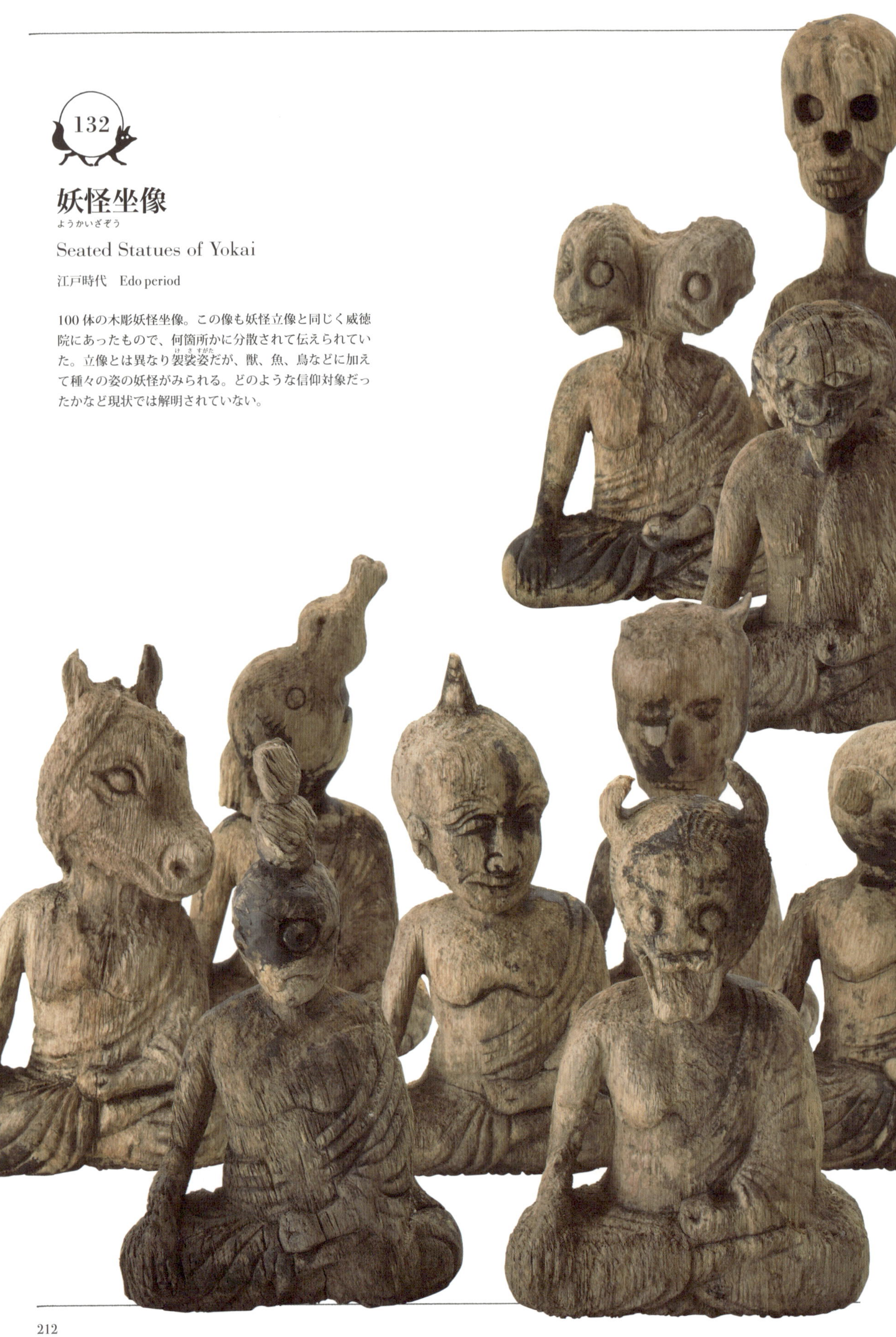

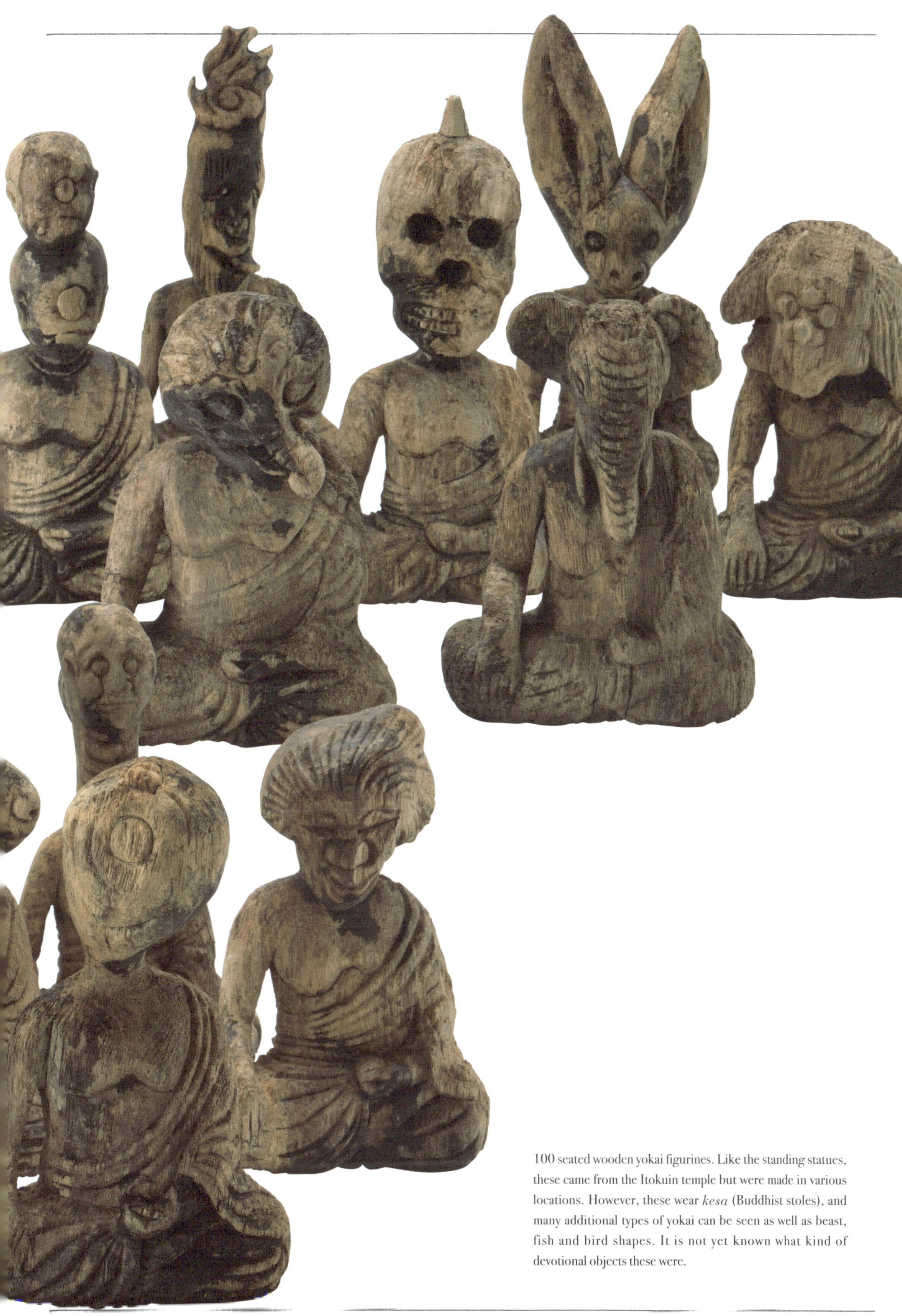

100 seated wooden yokai figurines. Like the standing statues, these came from the Itokuin temple but were made in various locations. However, these wear *kesa* (Buddhist stoles), and many additional types of yokai can be seen as well as beast, fish and bird shapes. It is not yet known what kind of devotional objects these were.

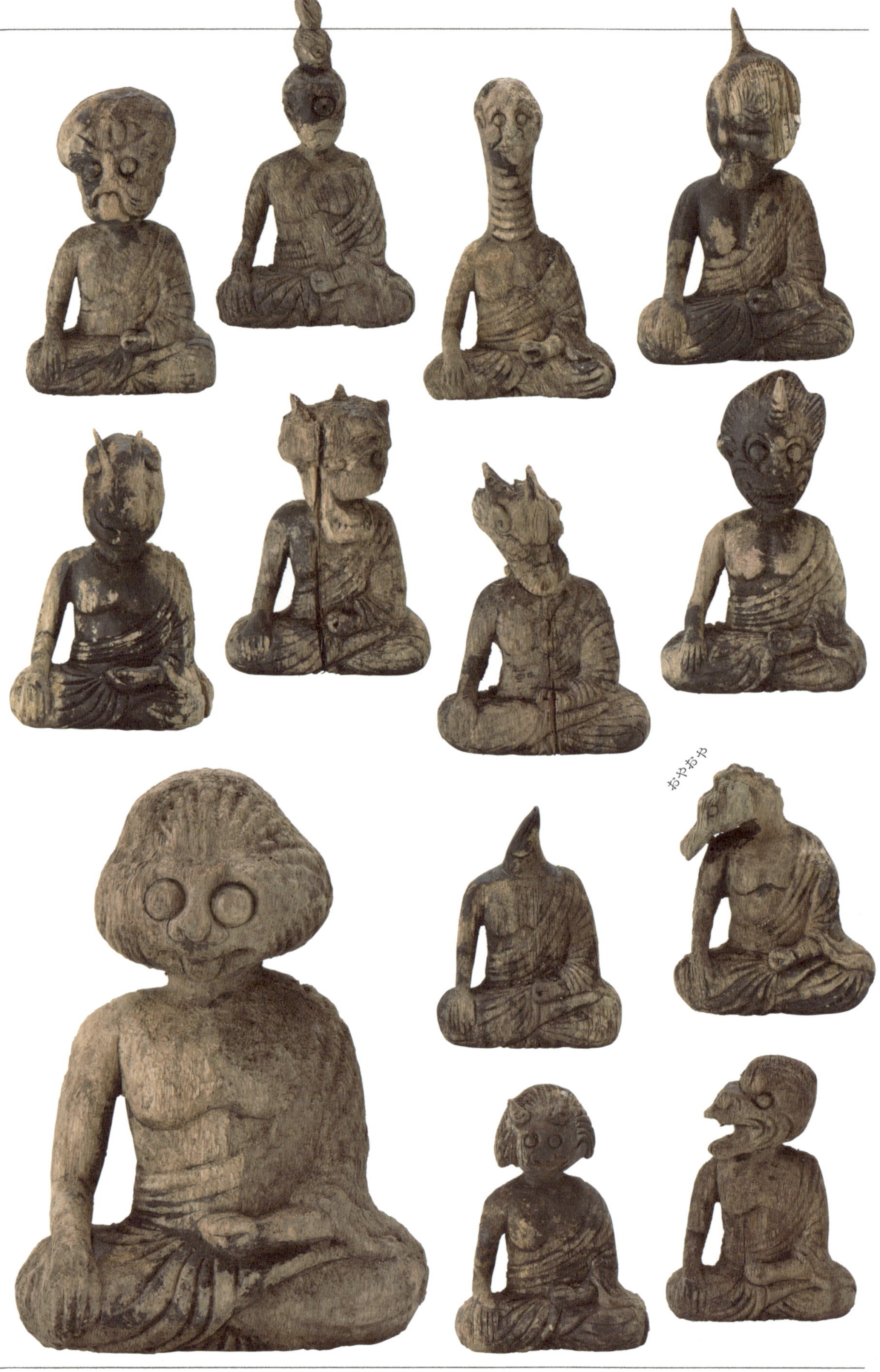
おやおや

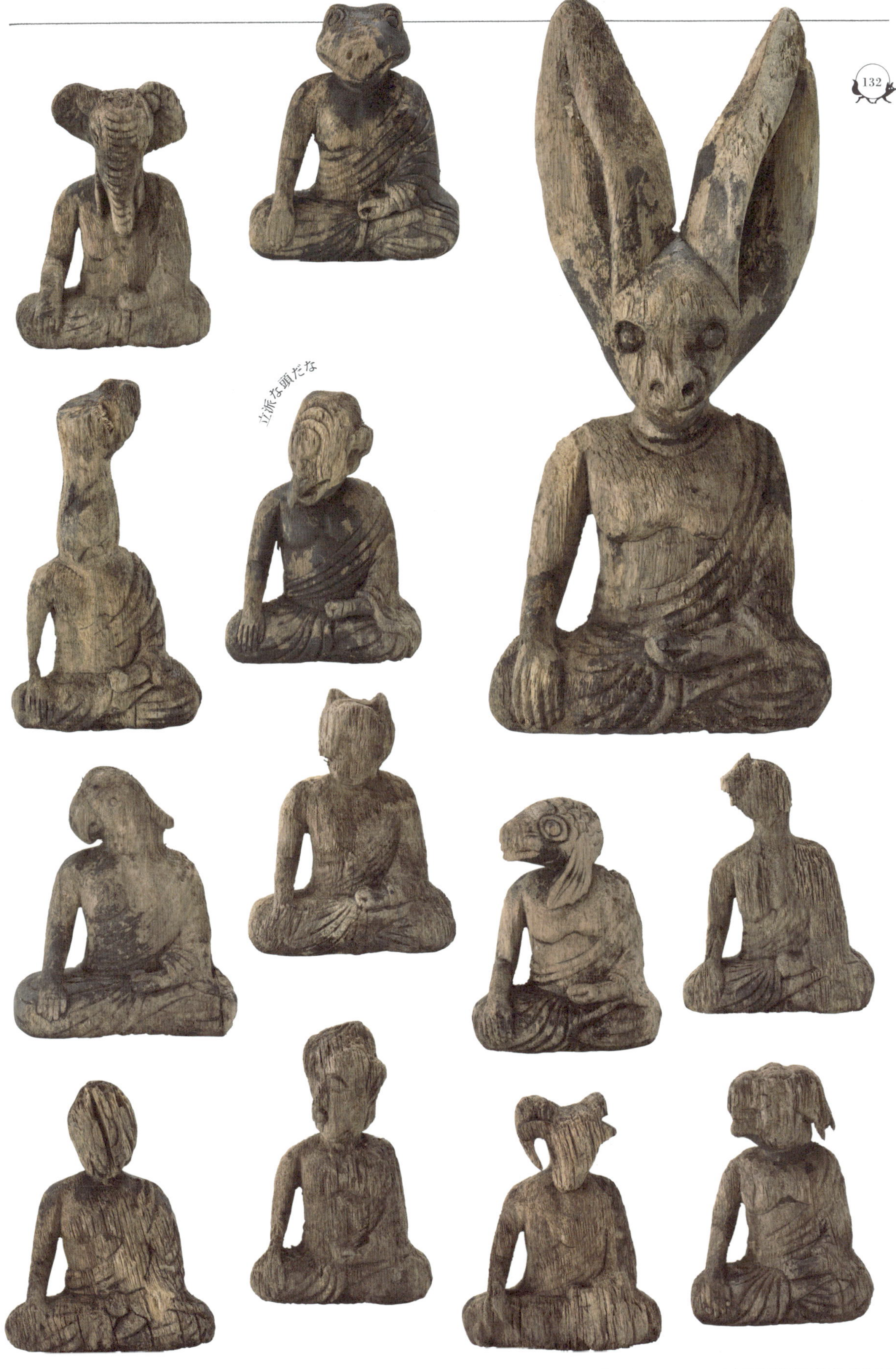
立派な頭だな

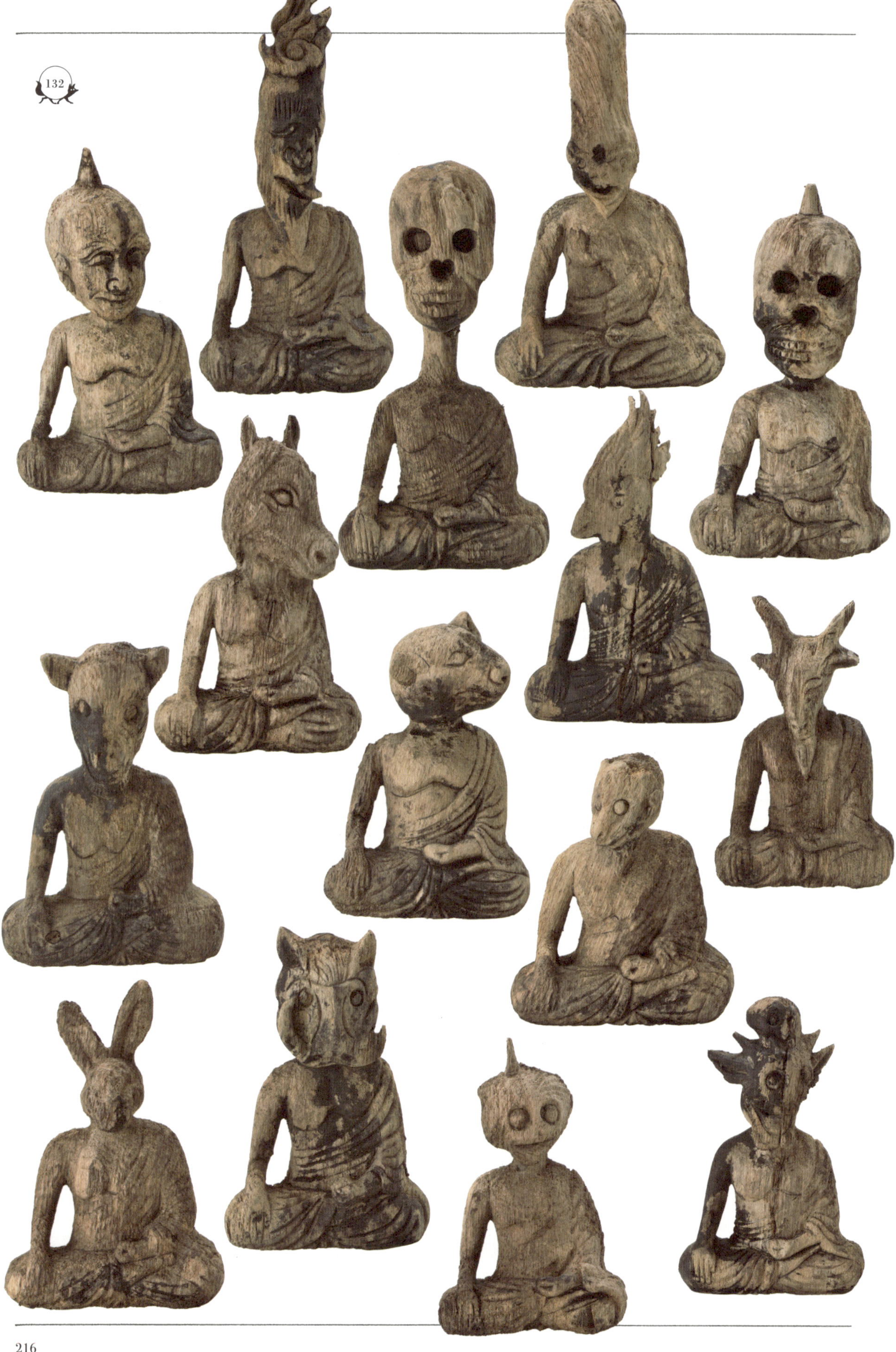

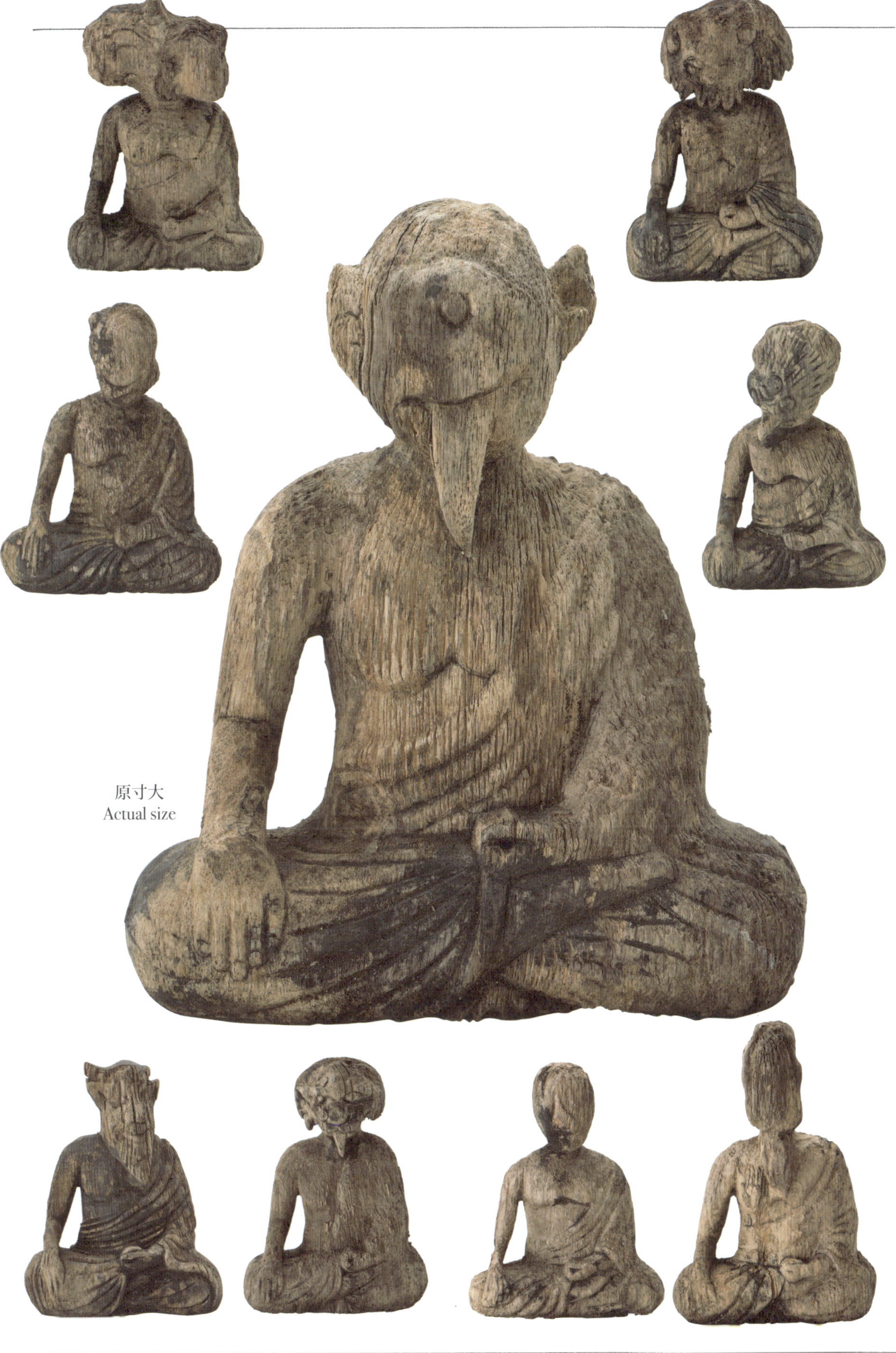

原寸大
Actual size

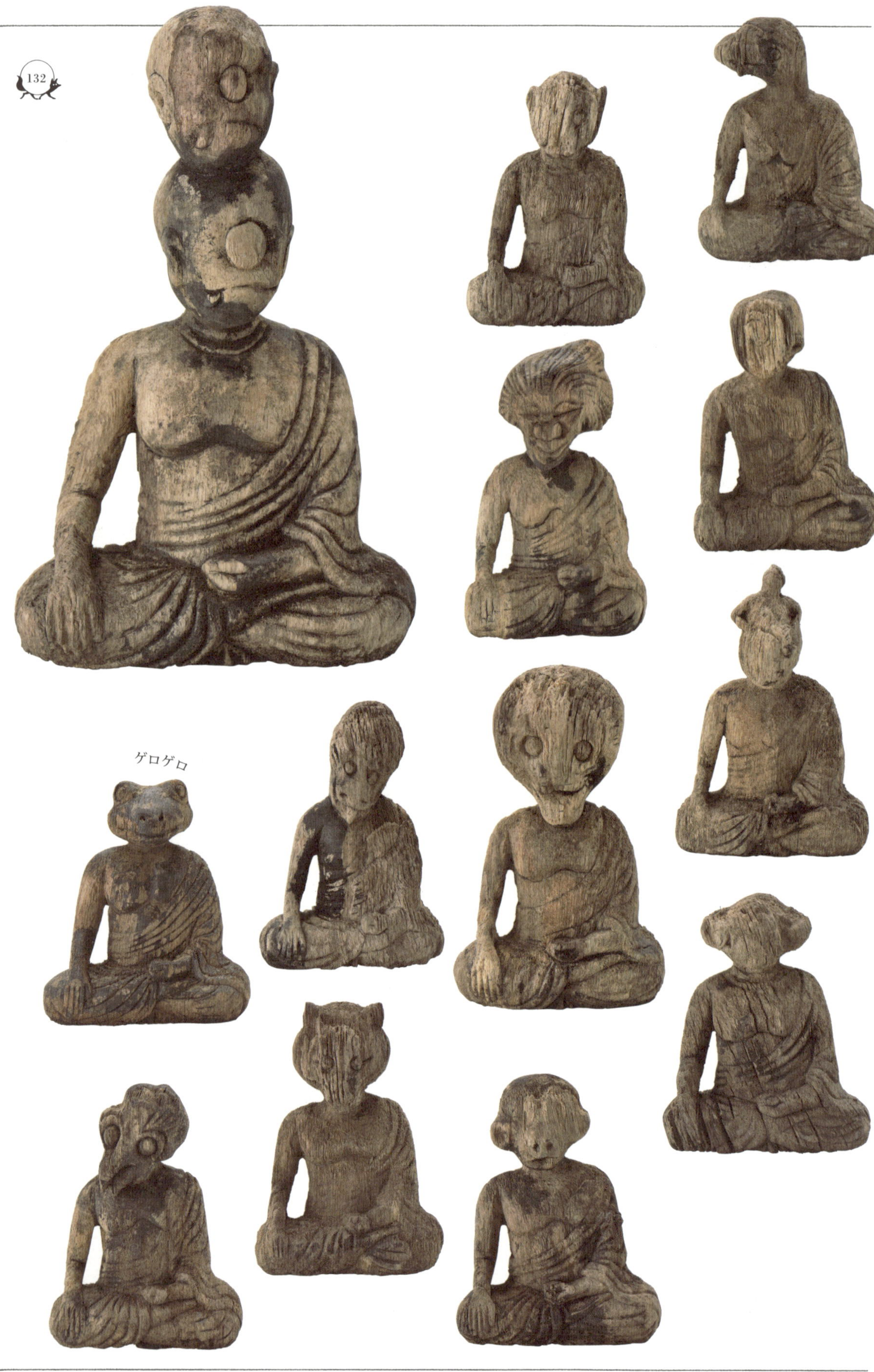
ゲロゲロ

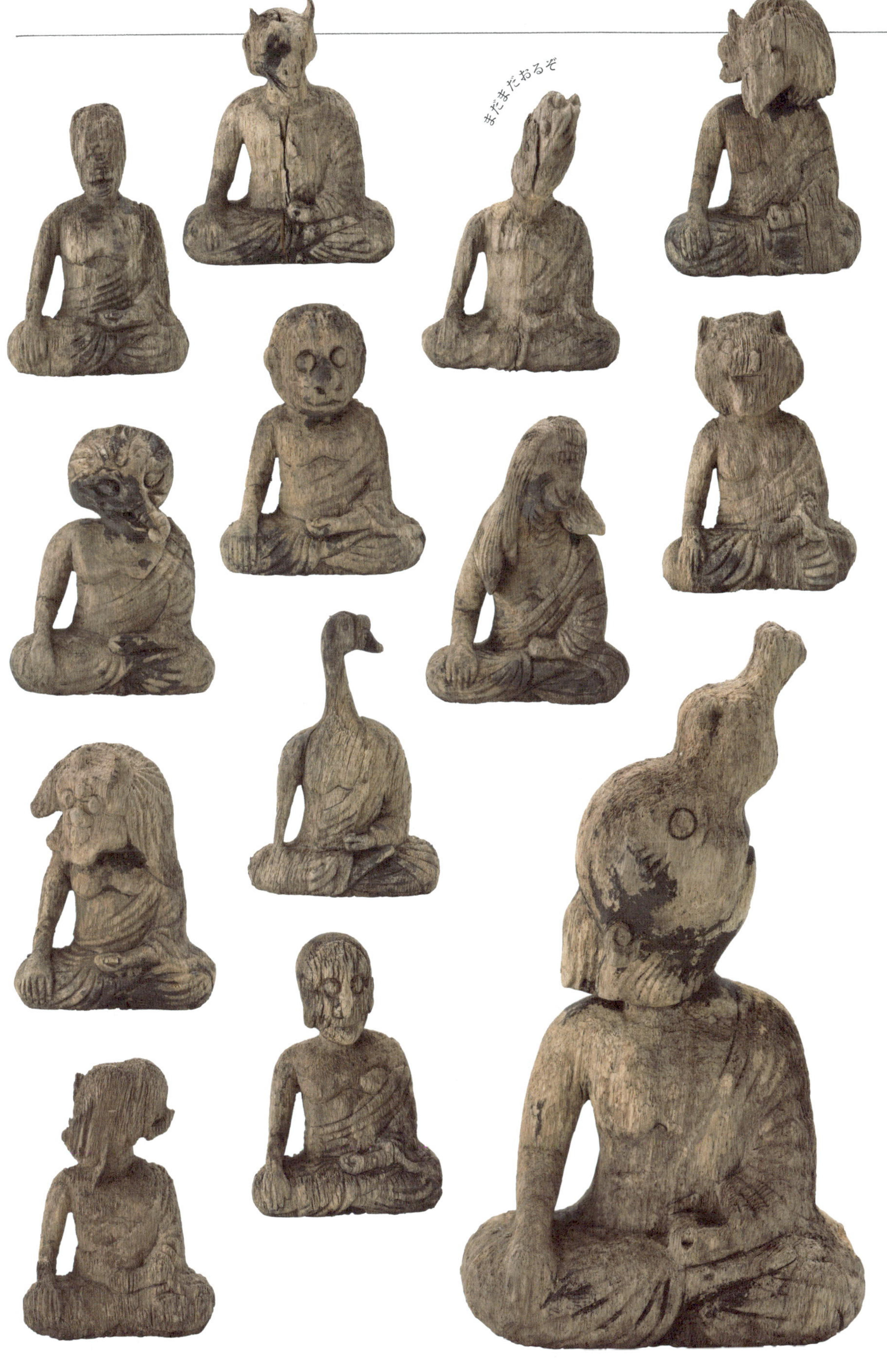
まだまだおるぞ

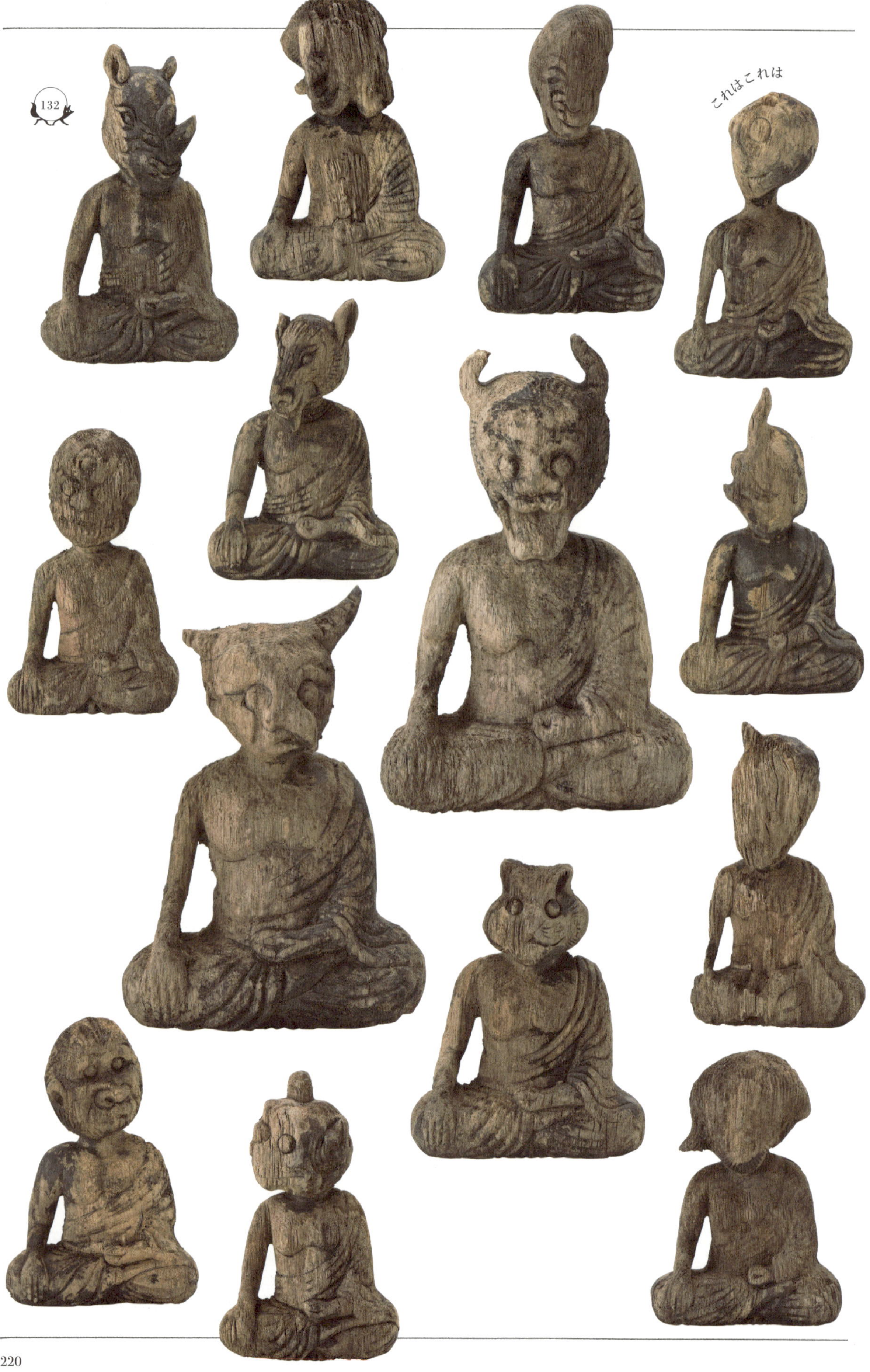
これはこれは

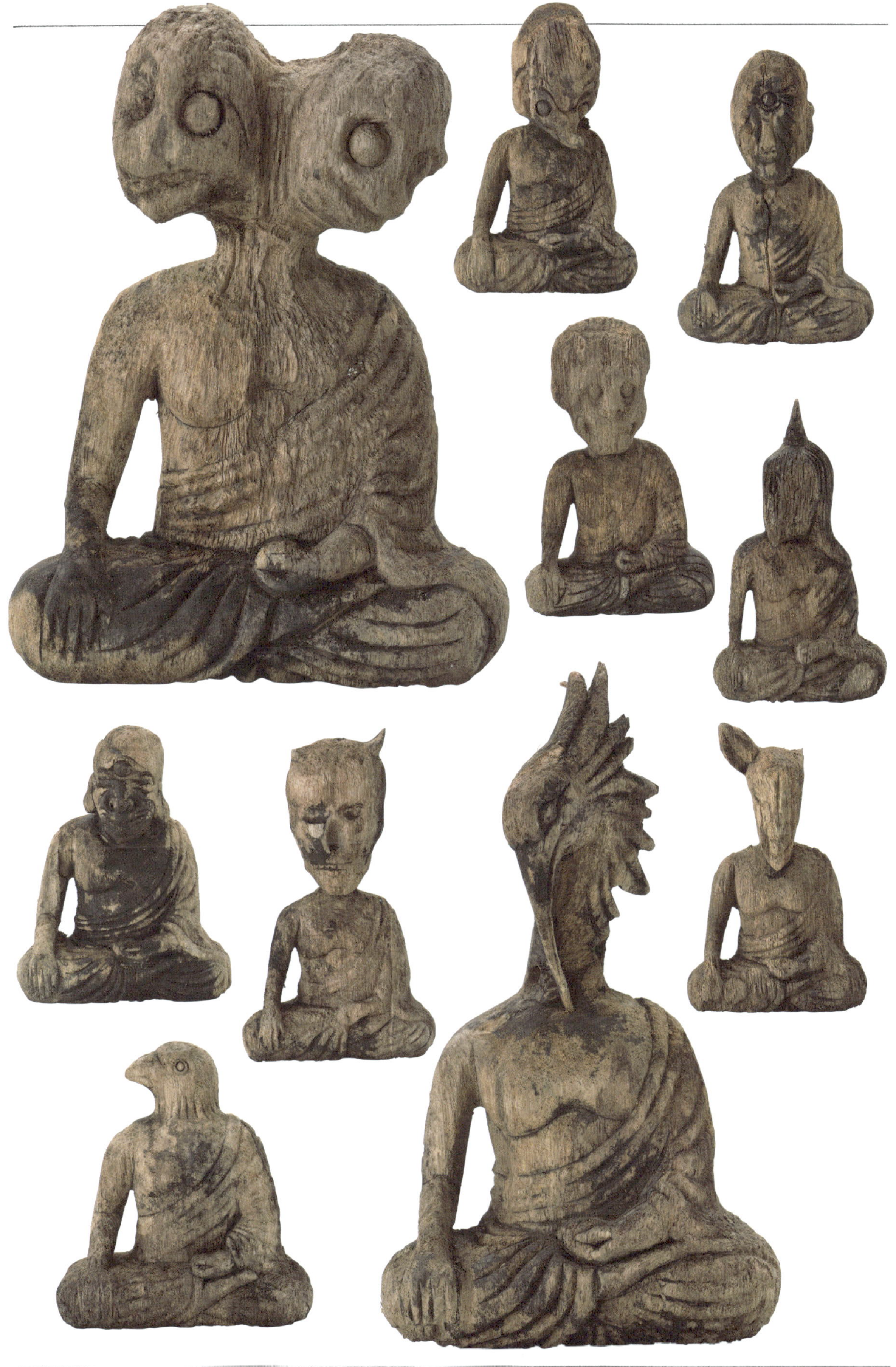

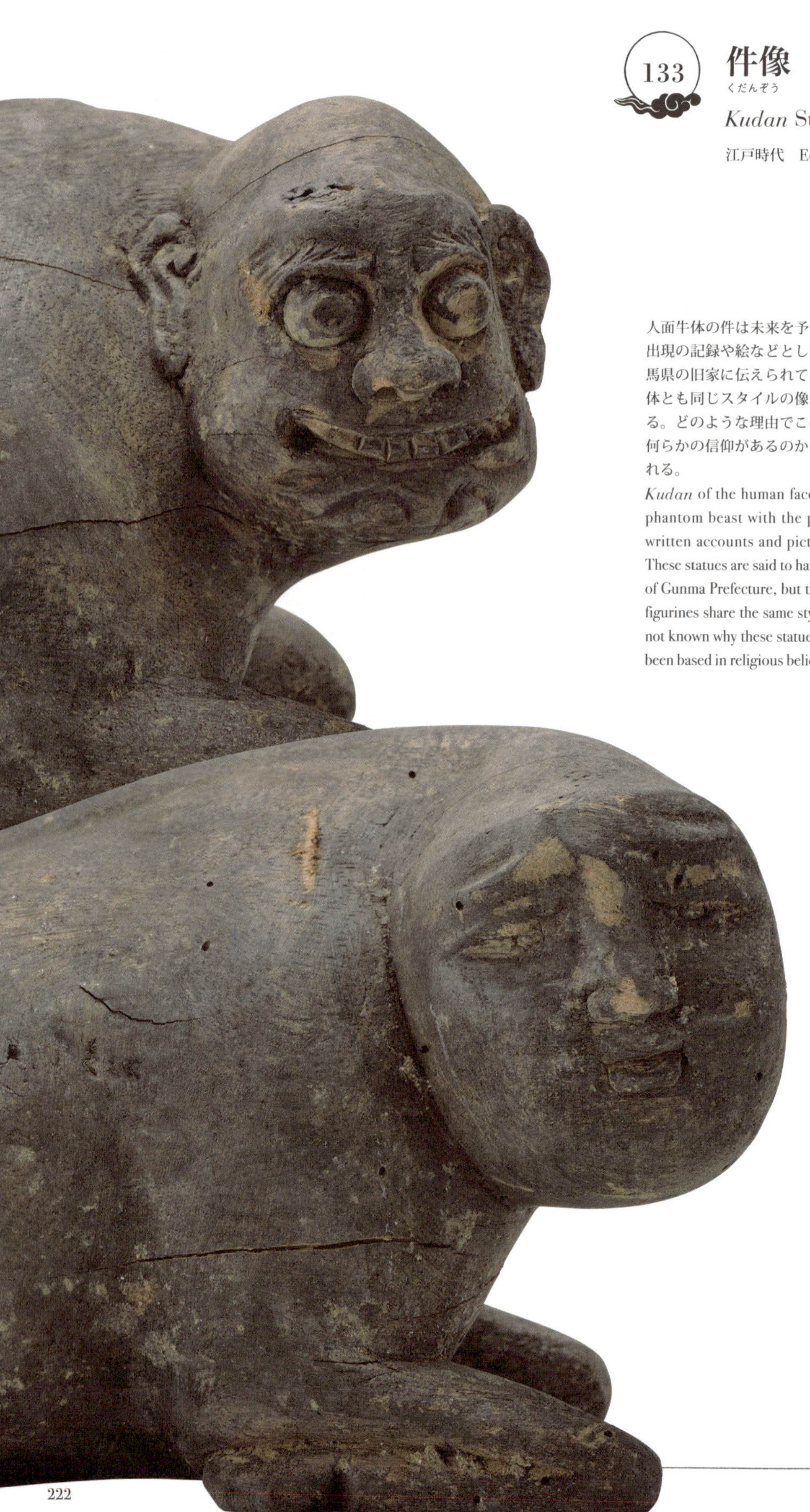

件像
くだんぞう

Kudan Statues

江戸時代　Edo period

人面牛体の件は未来を予言する幻獣として知られており、出現の記録や絵などとしても残されている。この像は群馬県の旧家に伝えられていたというが詳細は不明。２０体とも同じスタイルの像だが、顔はそれぞれ異なっている。どのような理由でこの像が制作されたかは不明だが、何らかの信仰があるのかもしれない。今後の解明が俟たれる。

Kudan of the human face and bovine body is famed as a phantom beast with the power to divine the future, and written accounts and pictures of its appearances remain. These statues are said to have been made for an ancient family of Gunma Prefecture, but the details are unclear. The twenty figurines share the same style, but each face is different. It is not known why these statues were created, but they may have been based in religious belief. We await further research.

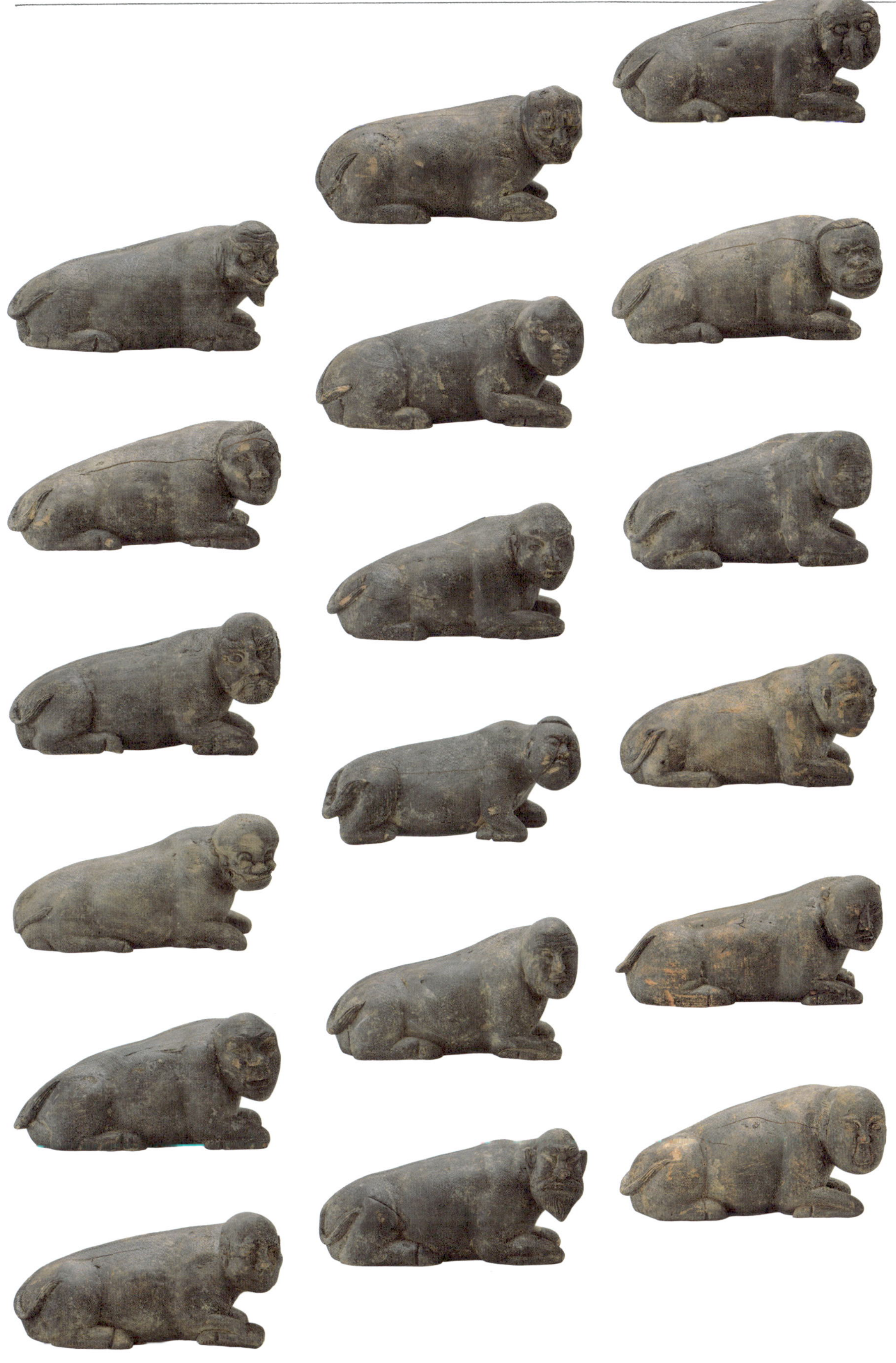

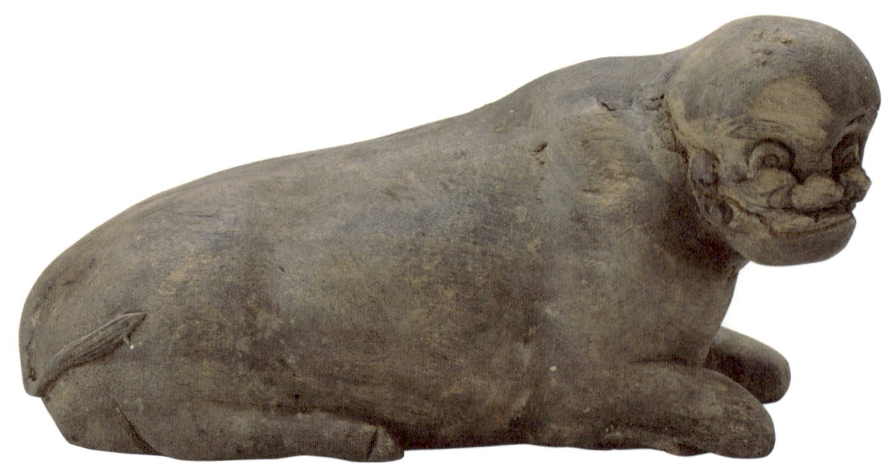
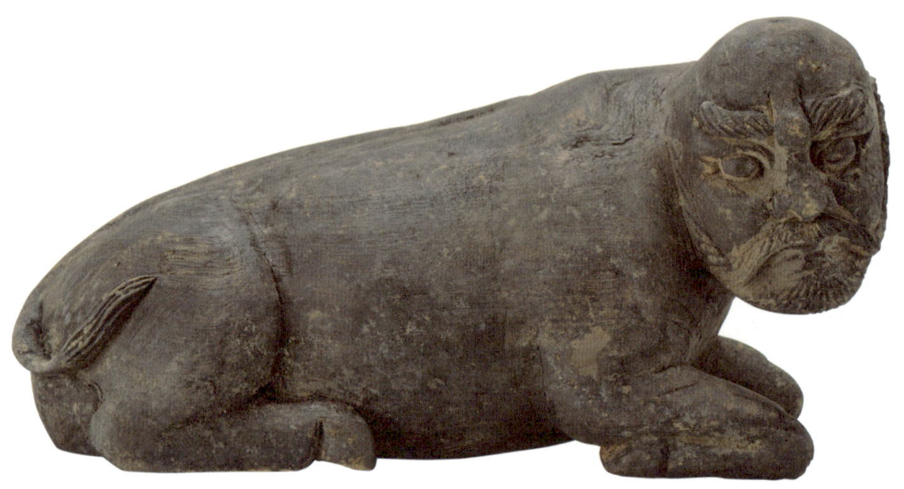
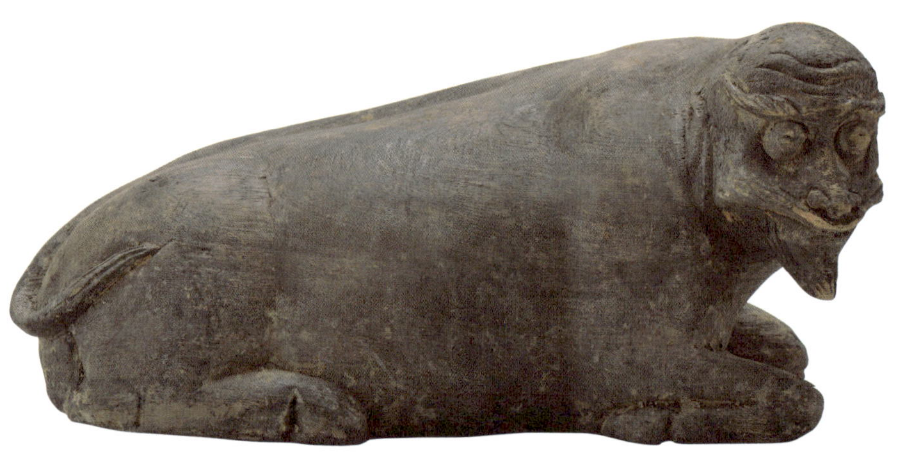

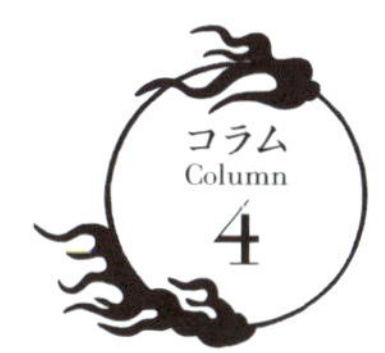

妖怪と親戚？
初公開！ 謎の『人面草紙』

Kindred Spirits?
Debut! The Secret World of
Jinmen Zōshi (*The Book of Faces*)

『人面草紙』の著者といわれる斎藤月岑は天正 10 年（1590）から明治 6 年（1873）までの江戸の市井の出来事を掬いあげた『武江年表』を著した。江戸という大都会での人々の日常の息吹を、年表というスタイルで見事に伝えている。ここに紹介する『人面草紙』も、そんな江戸の庶民の姿を愛情をこめたユニークなタッチで活写した江戸人賛歌なのかもしれない。

Saitō Gesshin, said to be the author of *Jinmen Zōshi*, chronicled the doings of ordinary people from 1590 to 1873 in the *Bukō Nenpyō* (Chronicles of Edo), a chronology which masterfully conveys the living breath of the citizens of the metropolis known as Edo. *Jinmen Zōshi* may be another such celebration of Edo citizens, vividly depicted with a unique touch full of fellow-feeling for the common people of Edo.

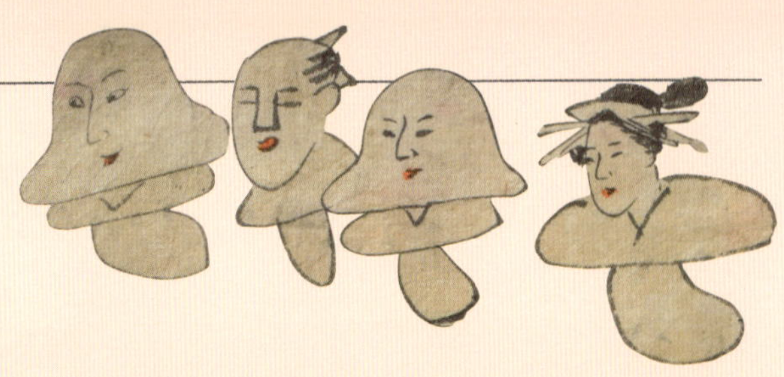

『人面草紙』

じんめんぞうし

江戸時代　縦 23.4 × 横 16.2　42 丁

題簽には「斎藤月岑筆 人面草紙 二ノ内」とある。斎藤月岑は幕末から明治初期にかけての著述家。題簽には斎藤月岑筆とあるが月岑は絵を描かなかったので、「筆」とは絵に添えられた文章の可能性がある。本書の中に「雪堤画」「長谷川雪旦先生 同雪堤子 同雪貢大人」と記された個所がある。月岑が祖父、父の三代にわたって編纂にあたった『江戸名所図会』の絵は雪旦が描き、月岑の著作『東都歳時記』は雪旦、雪堤親子が絵を担当しており、長谷川派との深い関係が窺える。また、題簽には「二ノ内」ともあり、端本なのかもしれないが、孤本のため詳細は不明。内容は異形の人面キャラクターのオンパレードで他に類を見ない。このような想像を絶する絵が登場することも逞しい空想の世界を展開して多種多様な妖怪を生み出した江戸という時代だからこそなのであろう。本書の人面キャラクターはストーリー性のある妖怪おもちゃ絵といっても差し支えないだろう。それらを踏まえて本書に収録した。

Jinmen Zōshi

Edo period, Height 23.4, Width 16.2, 42 folded sheets

The cover reads "By Saitō Gesshin: *Jinmen Zōshi*, one of the two volumes". Saitō Gesshin was a writer active from the latter days of the Tokugawa shogunate to the early Meiji period. Although the cover states "By Saitō Gesshin", Gesshin did not draw the illustrations, so the byline probably refers to the text accompanying the pictures. Inside the book "Settei-ga" ("Picture by Settei") and the names Hasegawa Settan-sensei, Settei-ko, and Sekkō Daijin are recorded in some places. Gesshin's close relationship with the artists of the Hasegawa school is evident in the illustrations which were drawn by Hasegawa Settan for the *Guide to Famous Edo Sites (Edo Meisho Zue)*, a detailed geography which was compiled over three generations by Gesshin, his father and grandfather, and Gesshin's *Record of Annual Events in the Eastern Capital (Tōto Saijiki)* which was illustrated by father-son duo Settan and Settei. The cover also states "one of the two volumes"; this may be one of an incomplete set, but as this is only copy in existence, it is difficult to say. Inside is an exceptional variety of odd-shaped human characters on parade. A world of powerful fantasy is revealed in these wildly imaginative pictures, possibly due to their origin in the period known as the Edo from which countless yokai sprung. The human characters in this book could well be described as yokai *omocha-e* with an element of story. With that in mind, they have been included in this book.

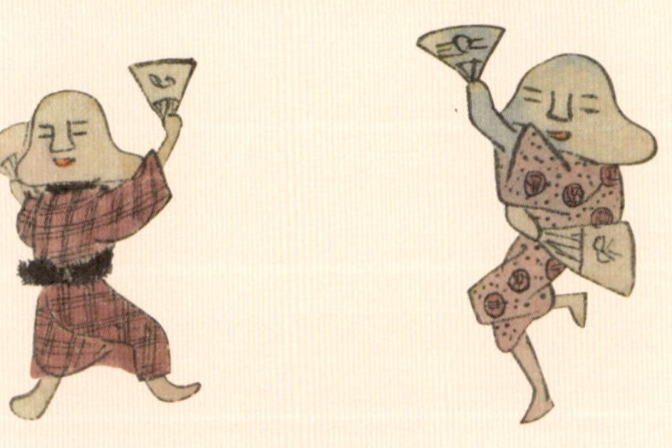

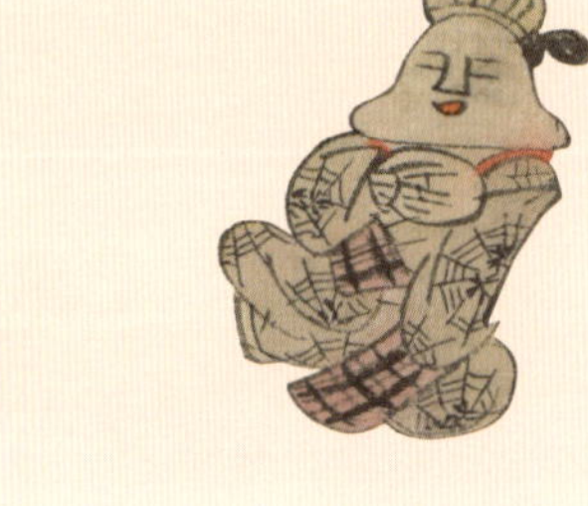

裏表紙内側（表3）に小文が記されている。墨が薄くなって読みづらいが、右横に以前に読んだと思われる箋があり、「前筋（？）に　文政十年歳次丁亥四月十五日金亀山に詣で　同十六日七里浜を過る図あり　市左衛門月岑とあり」とある。ほぼ正確な読みのようだ。
　左下には「此主　岩井里ゆう」とある。

There is some text written on the inside of the back cover. It is difficult to read as the ink has faded, but on the right side is the title previously read, with the text "(illegible) At Mount Kinki on the 15th day of the fourth month of 1827 (Bunsei 10), with illustrations done on the 16th of the same month at Shichirigahama: By Ichizaemon Gesshin". That should be a fairly accurate reading.

　　The name Iwai Ryū is written on the lower left.

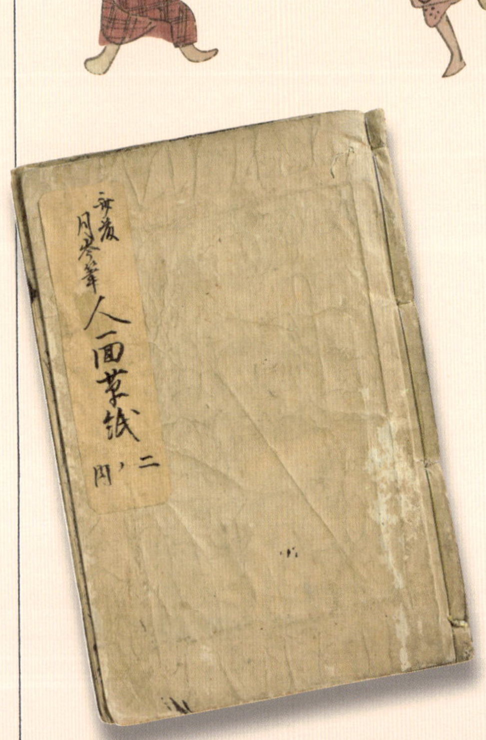

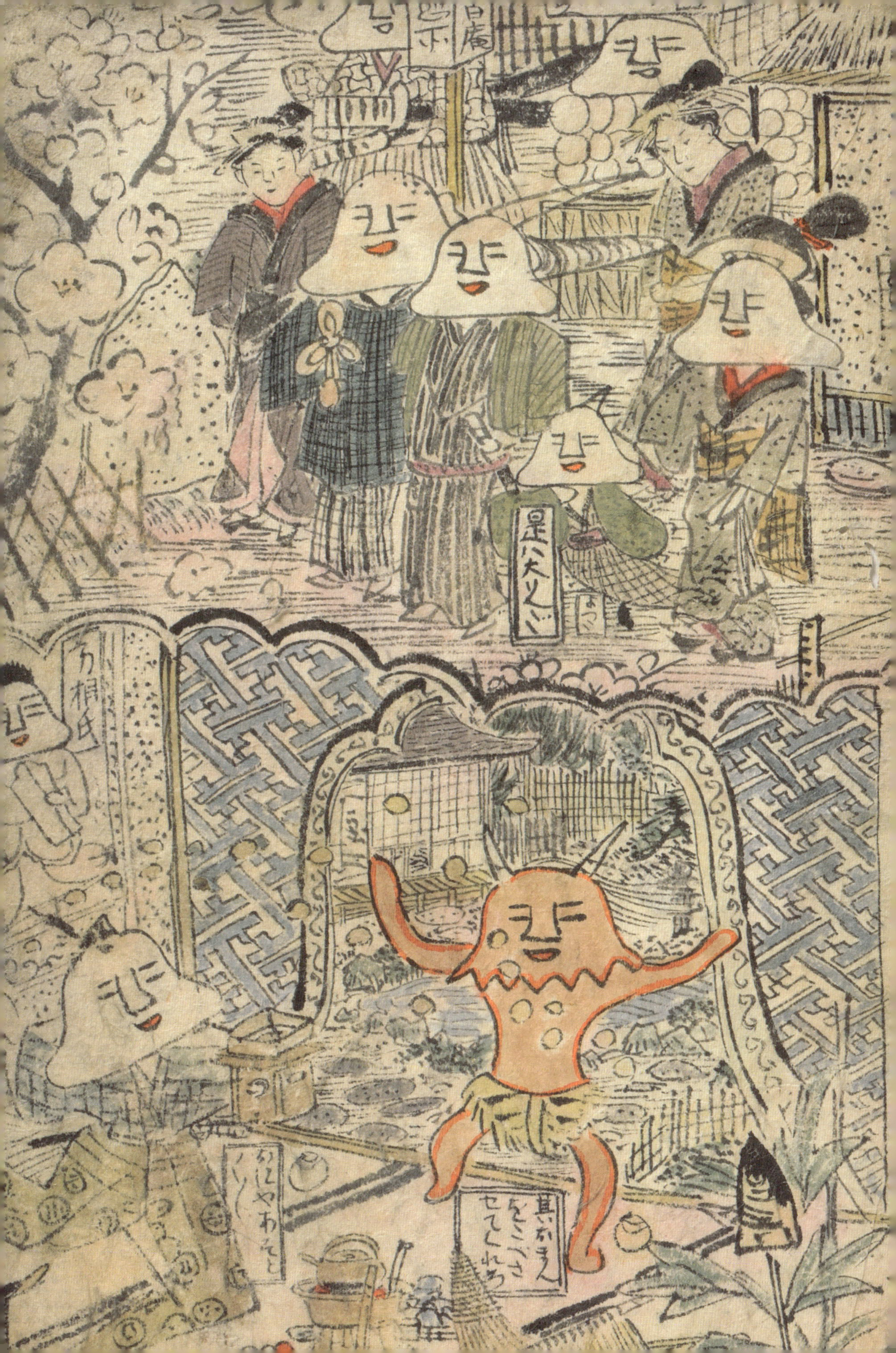

是ハ大いふ
力樹氏
其ほう
をこゝさ
せてくれ
ろ

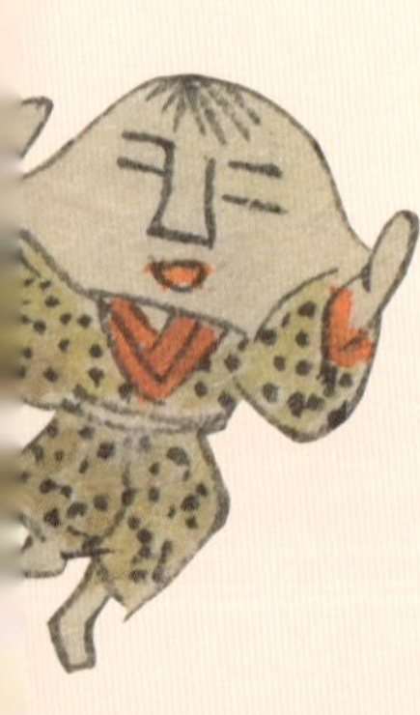

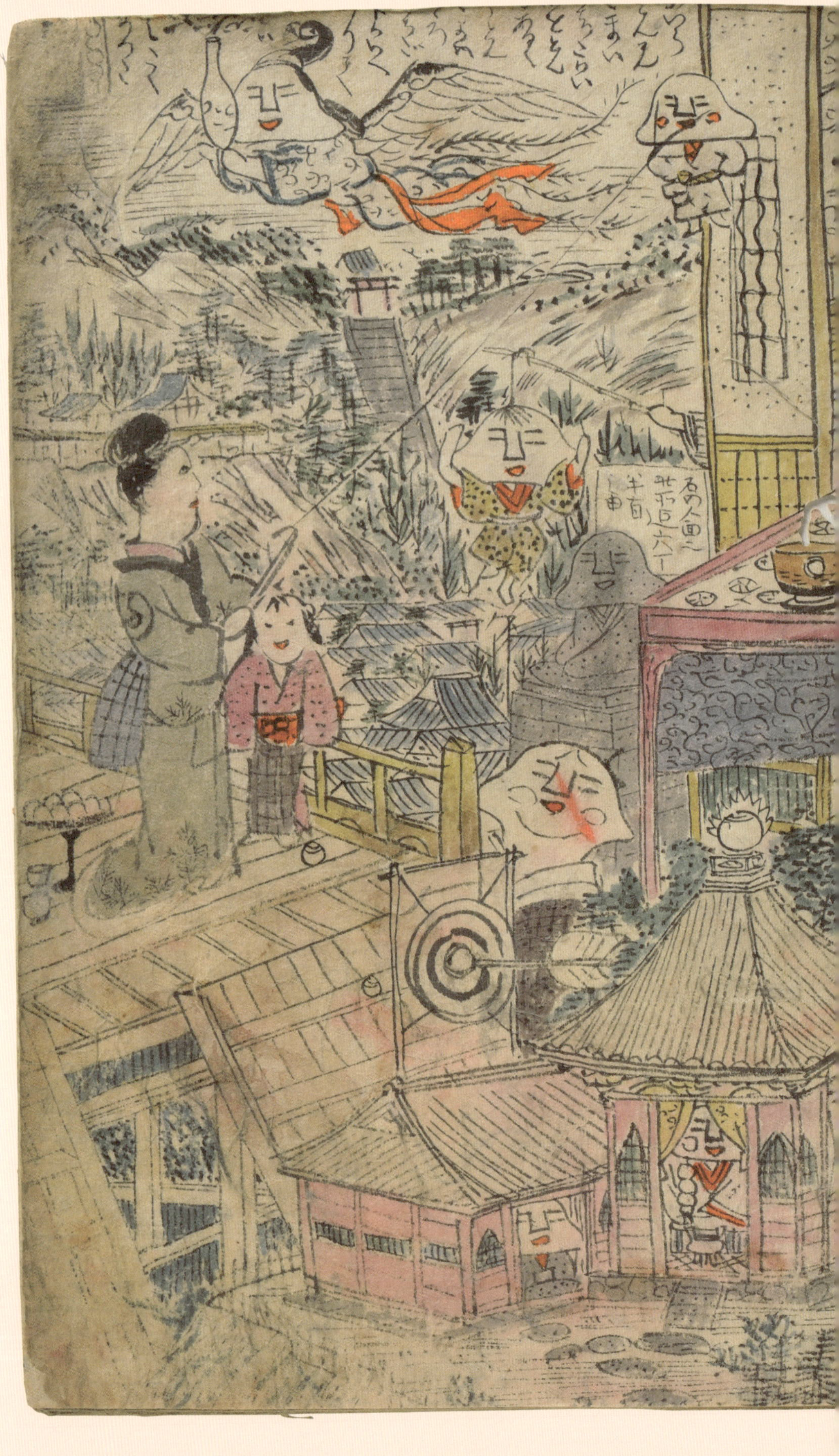

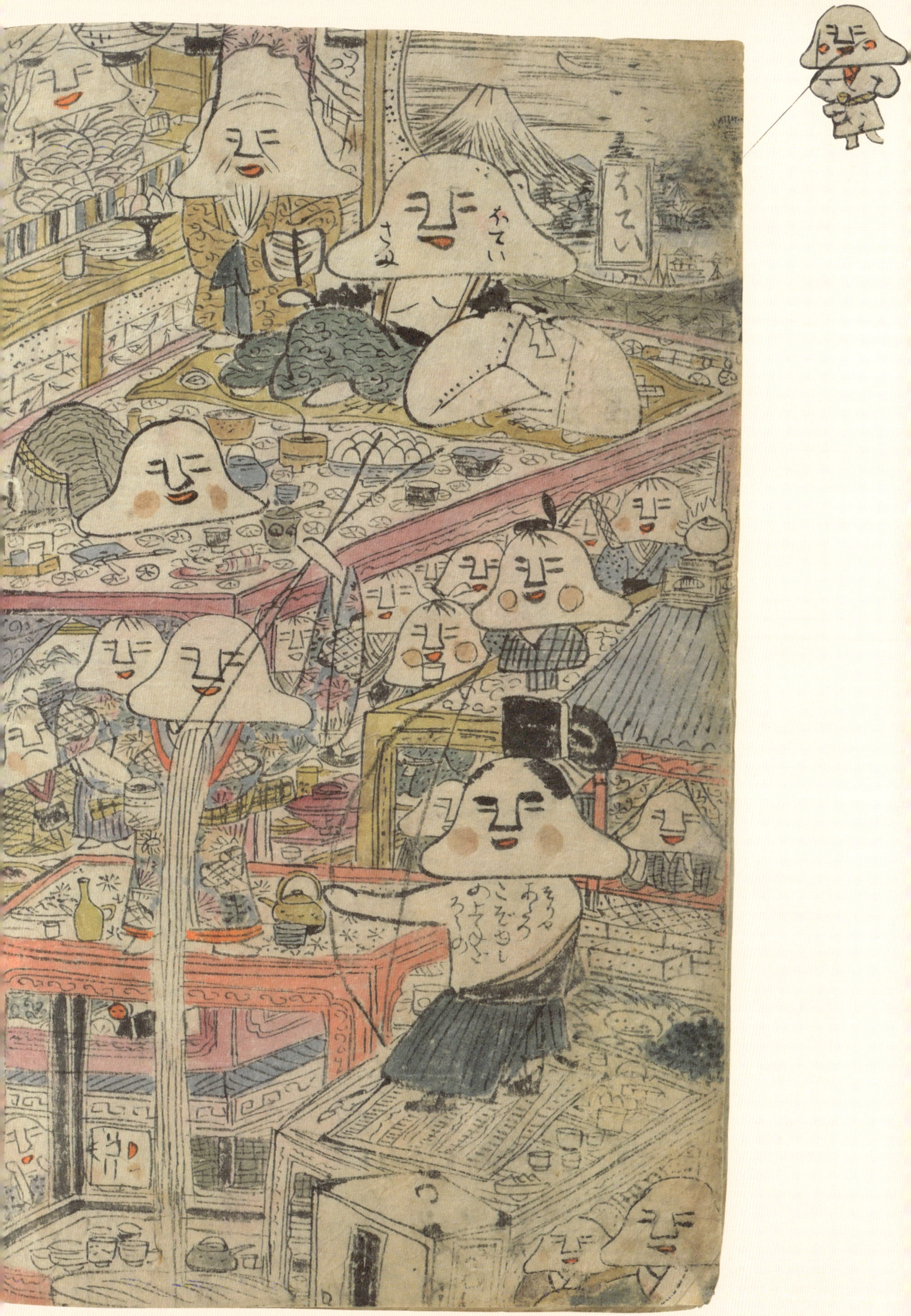

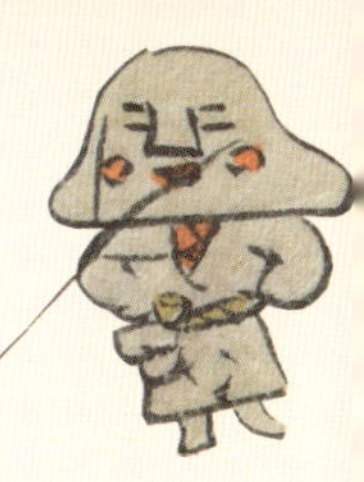

ゑてい
おてい
さる

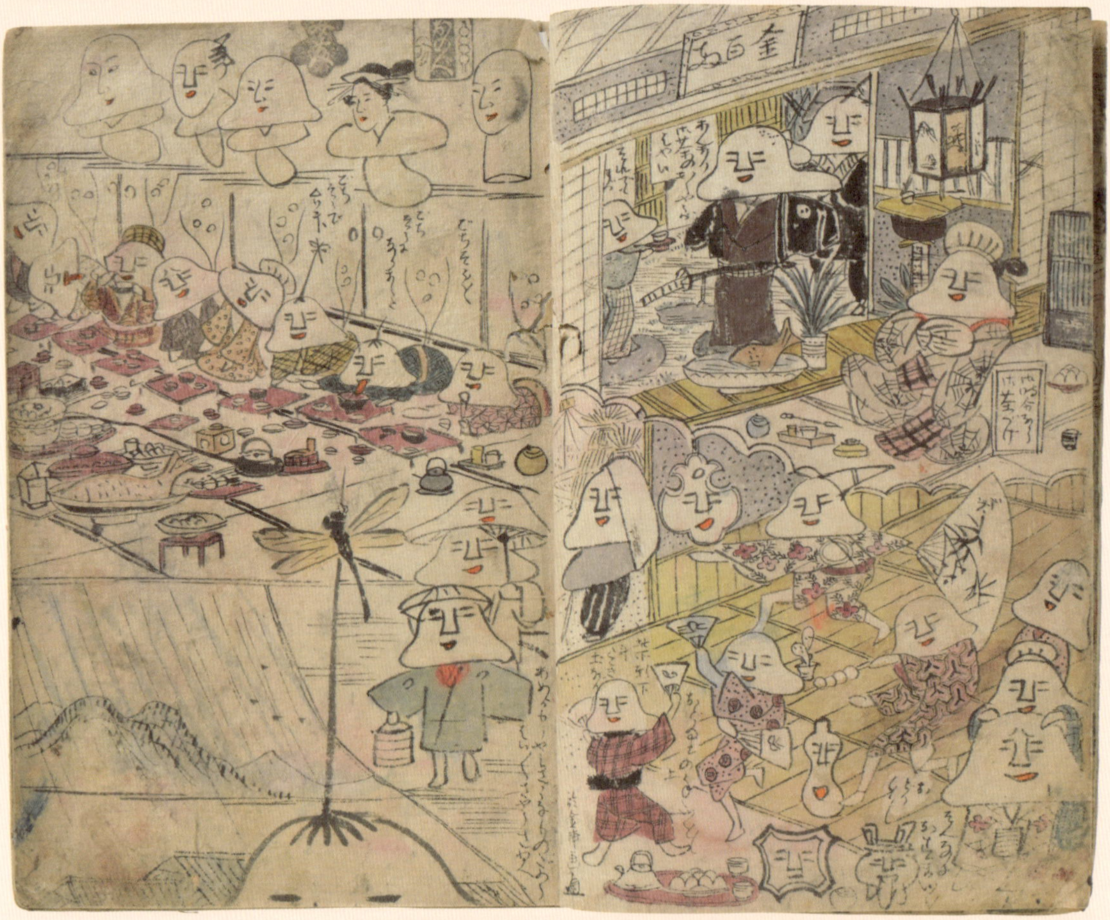

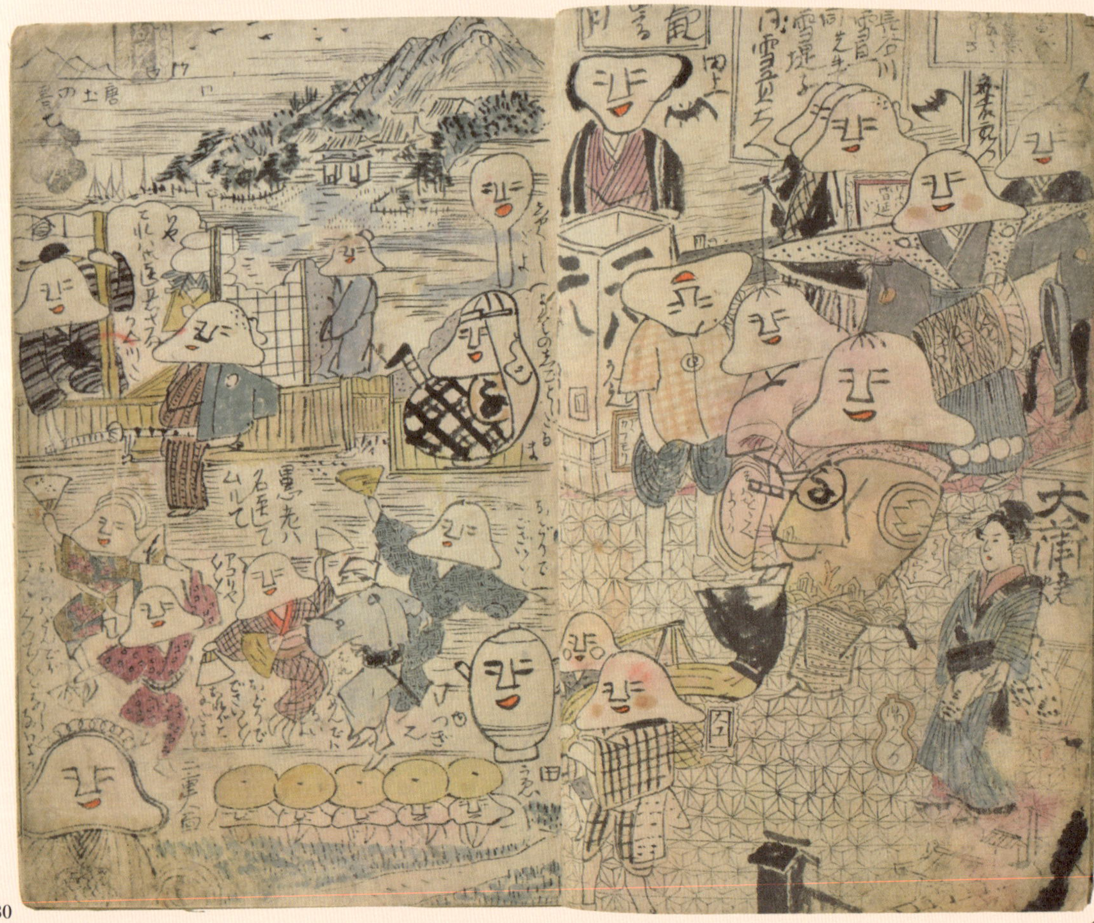

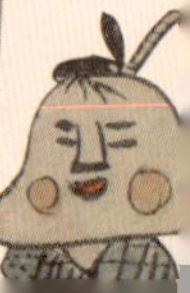

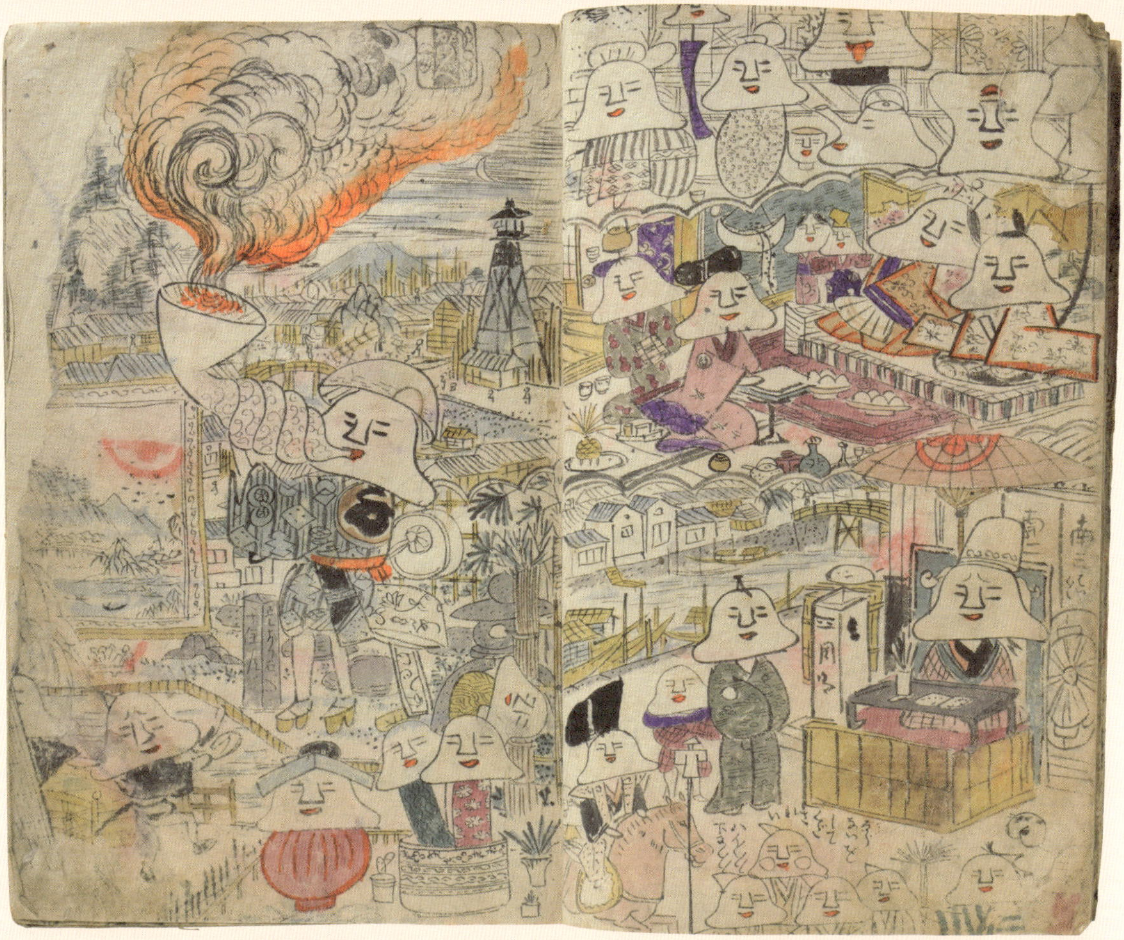

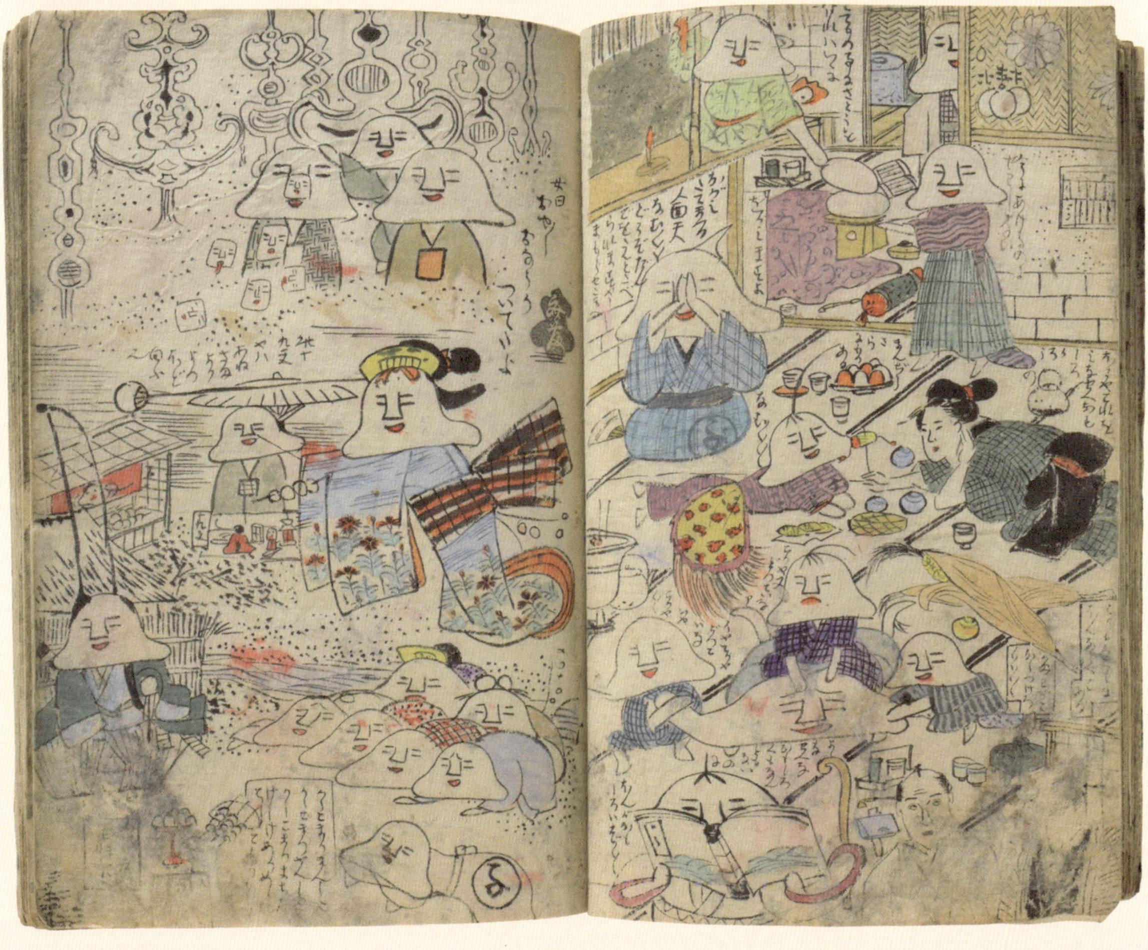

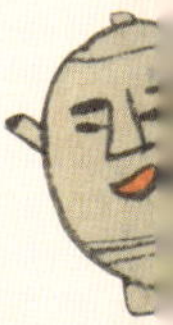

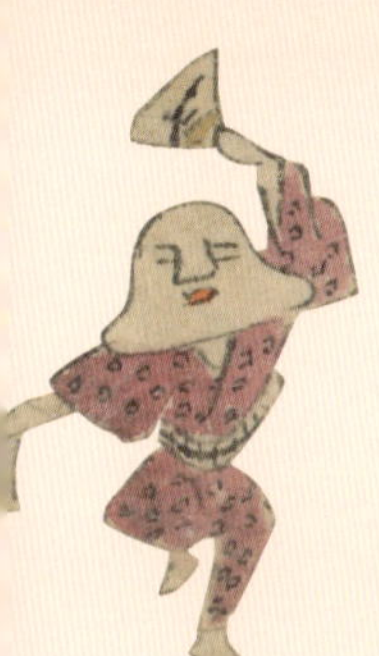

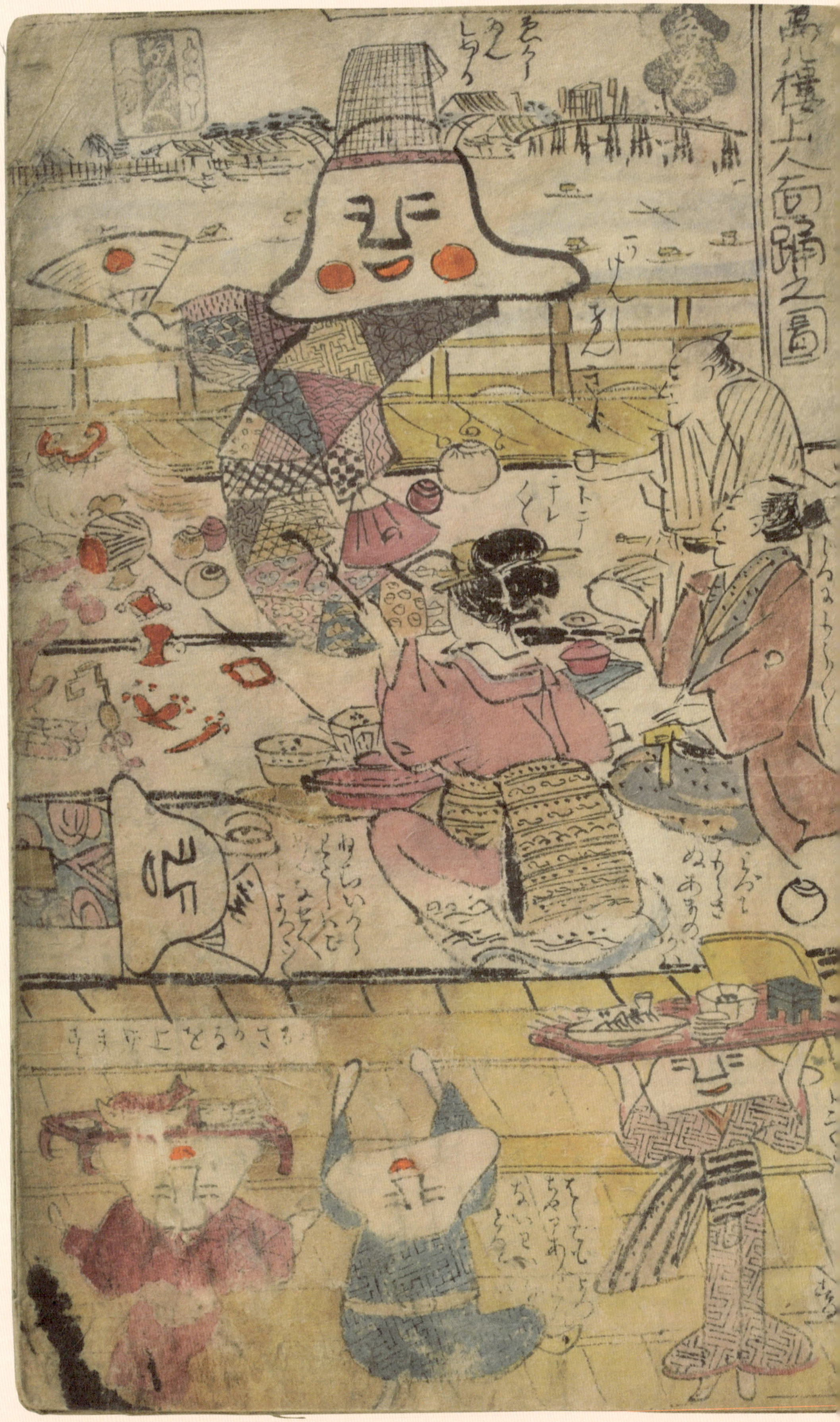

高樓上大面踊之圖

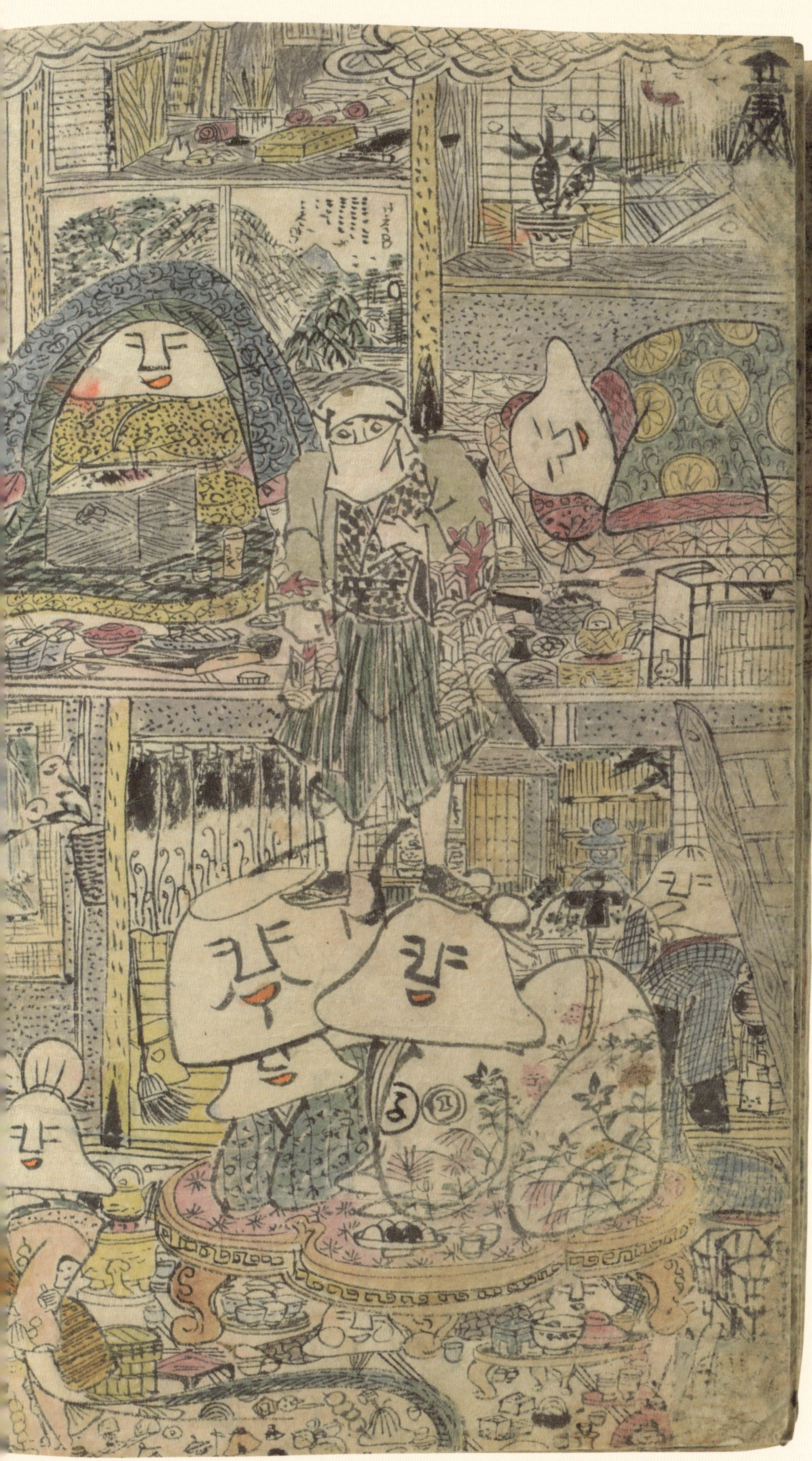

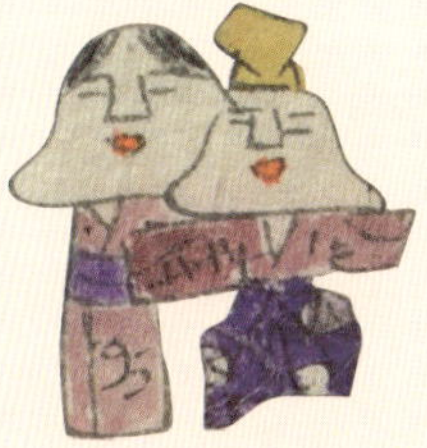

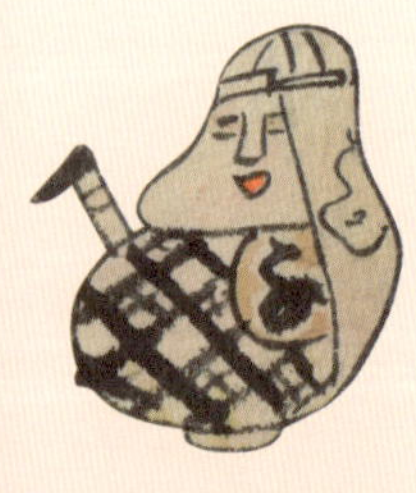

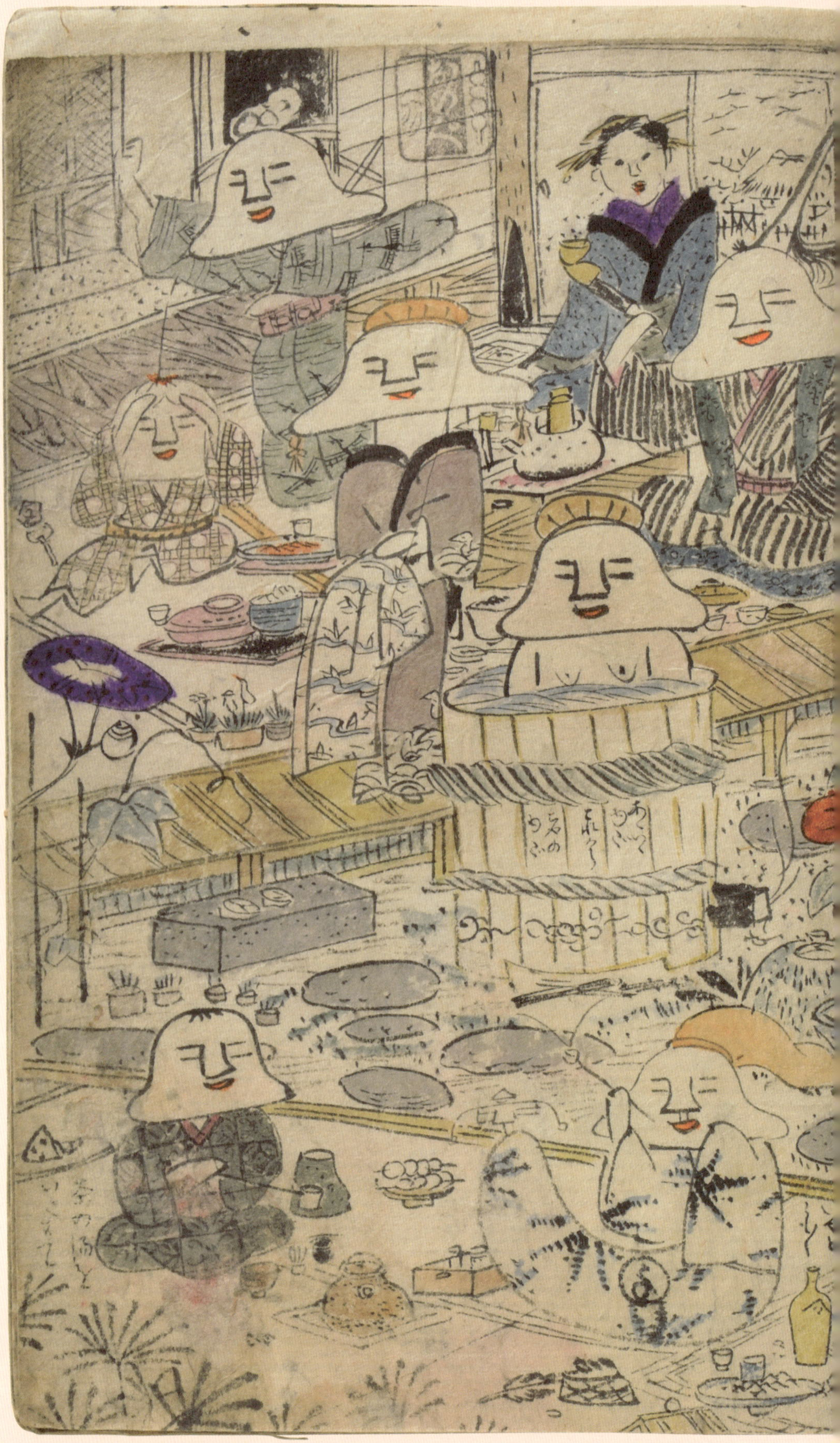

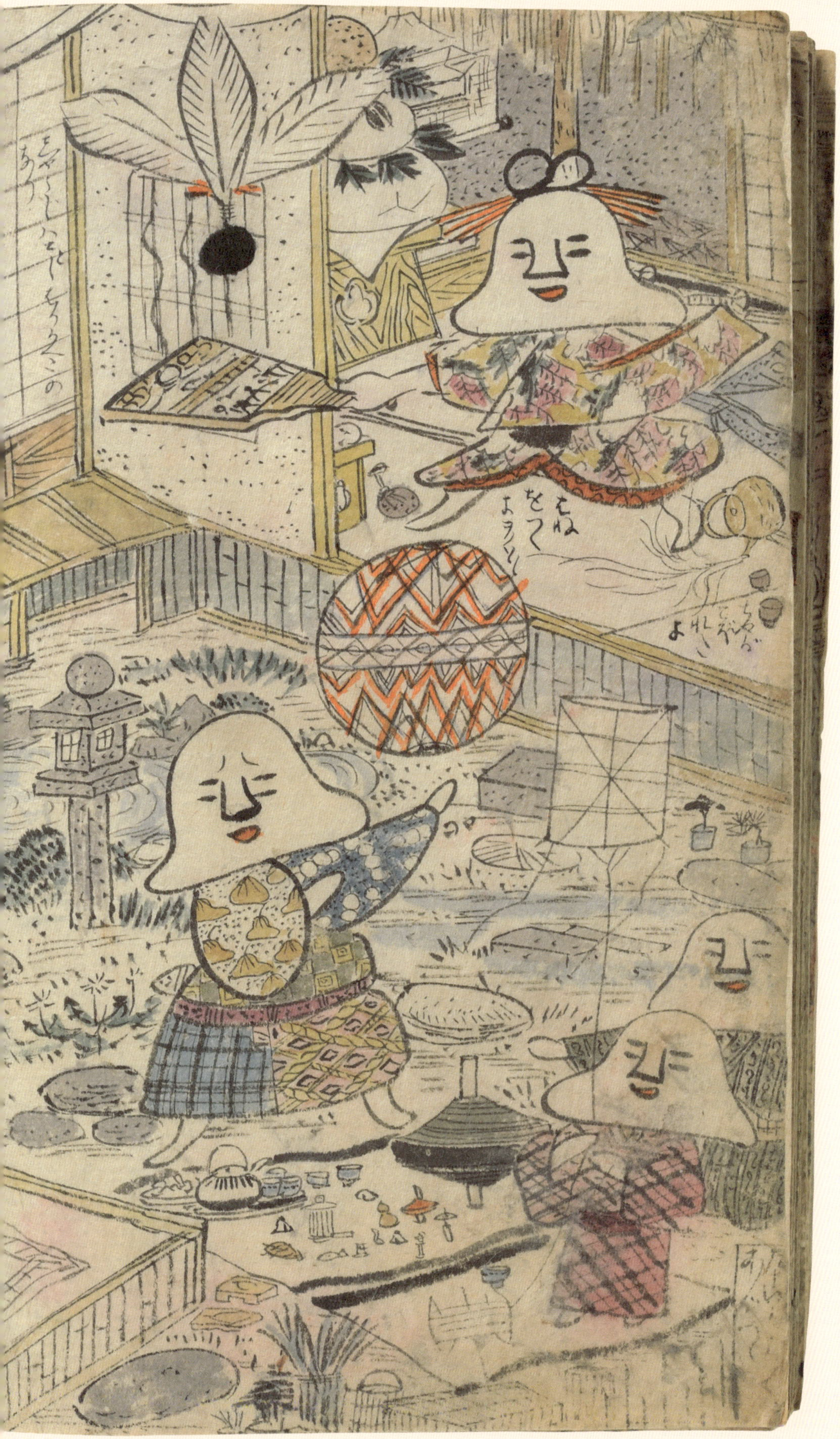

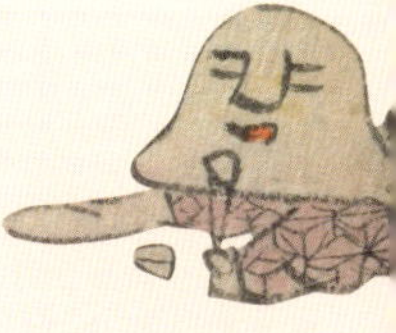

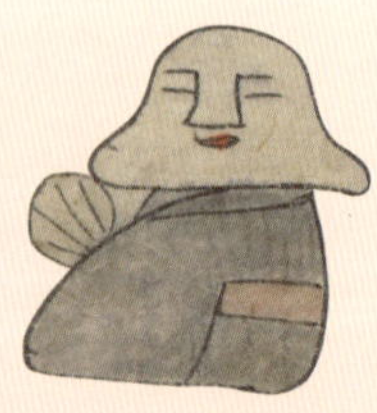

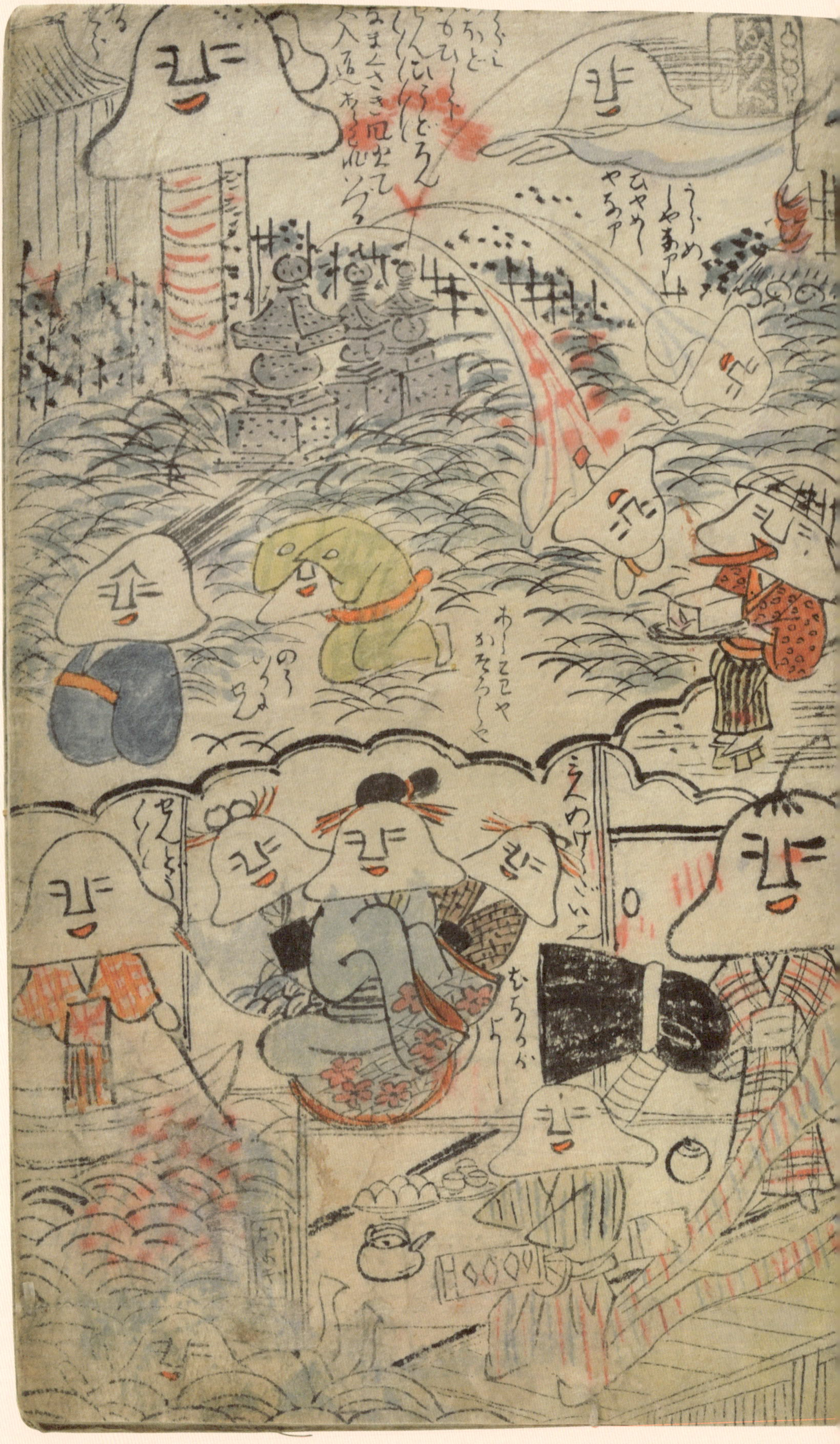

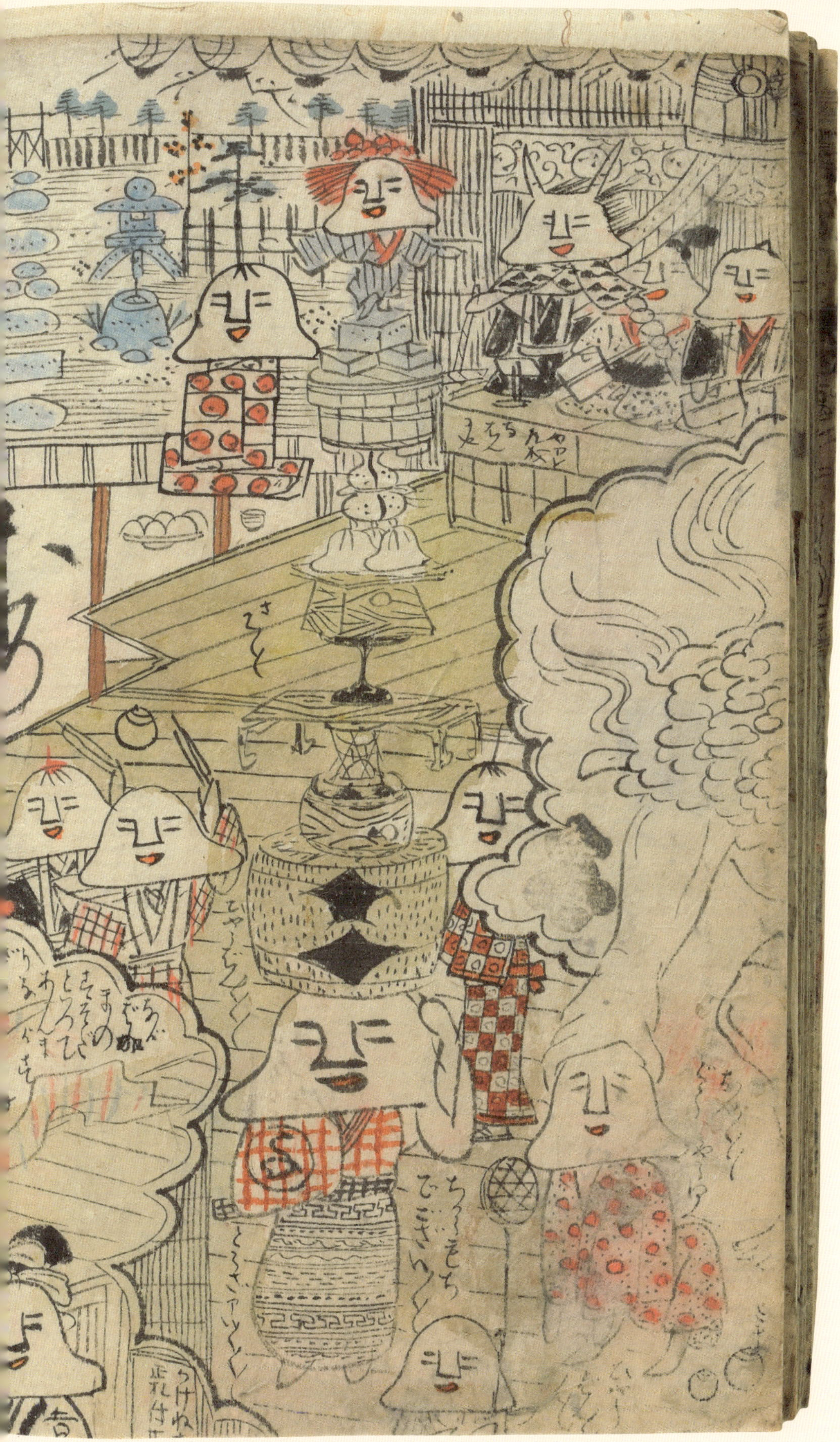

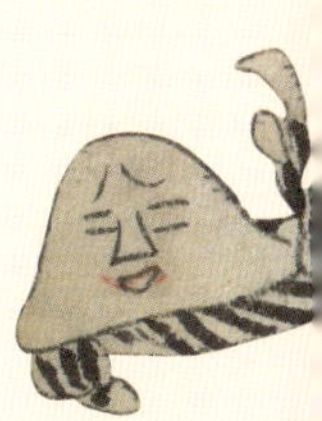

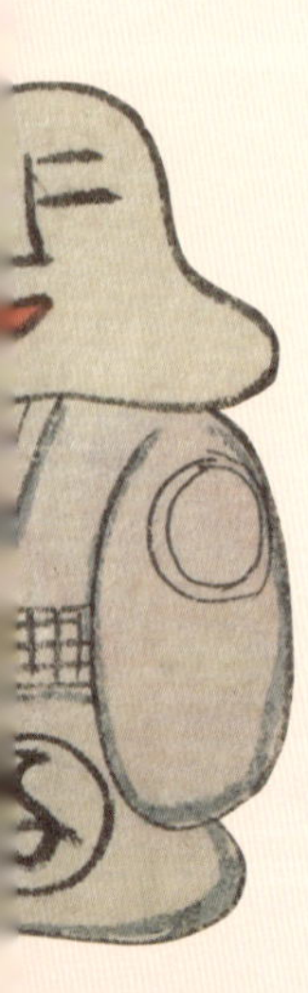

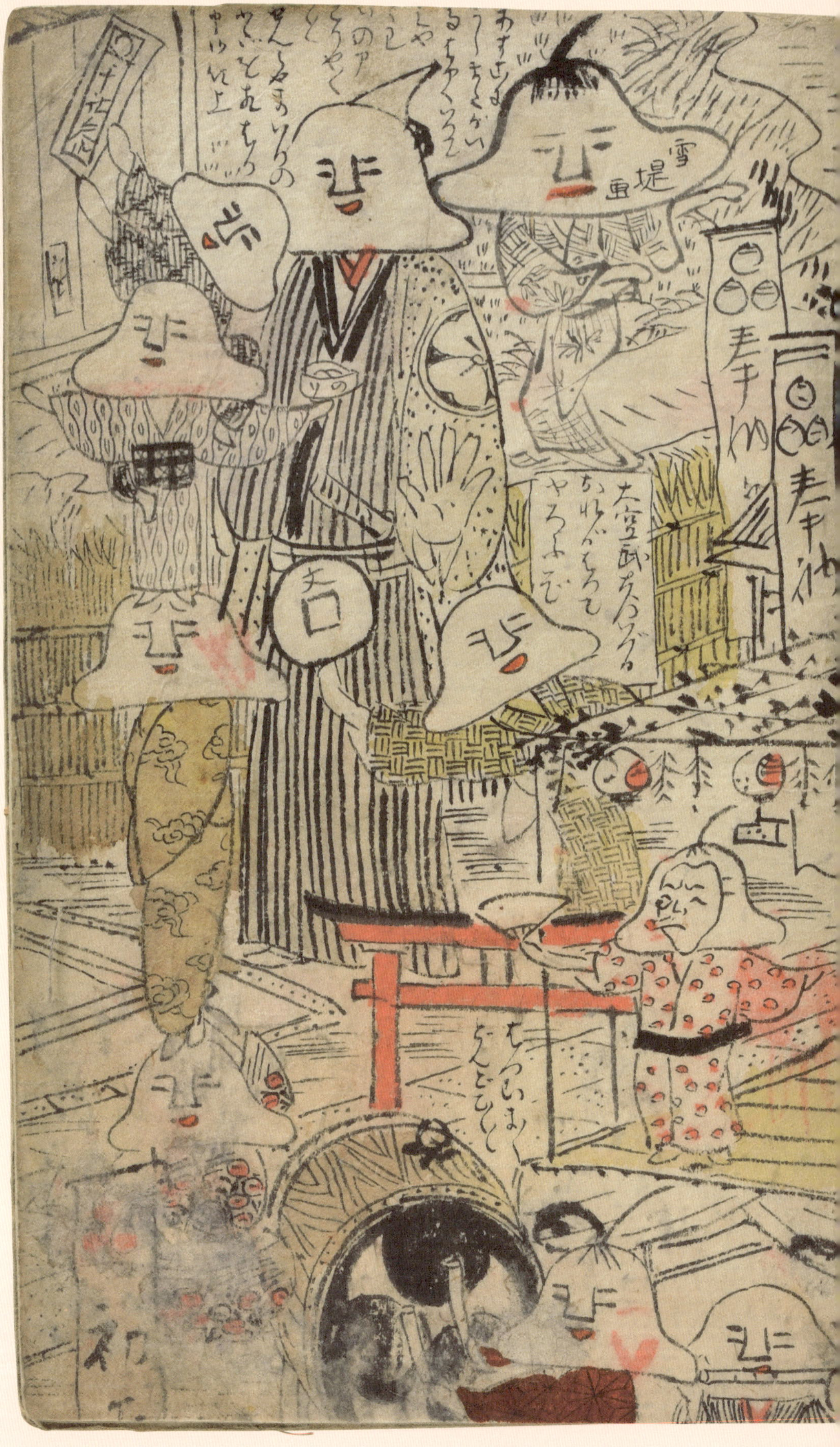

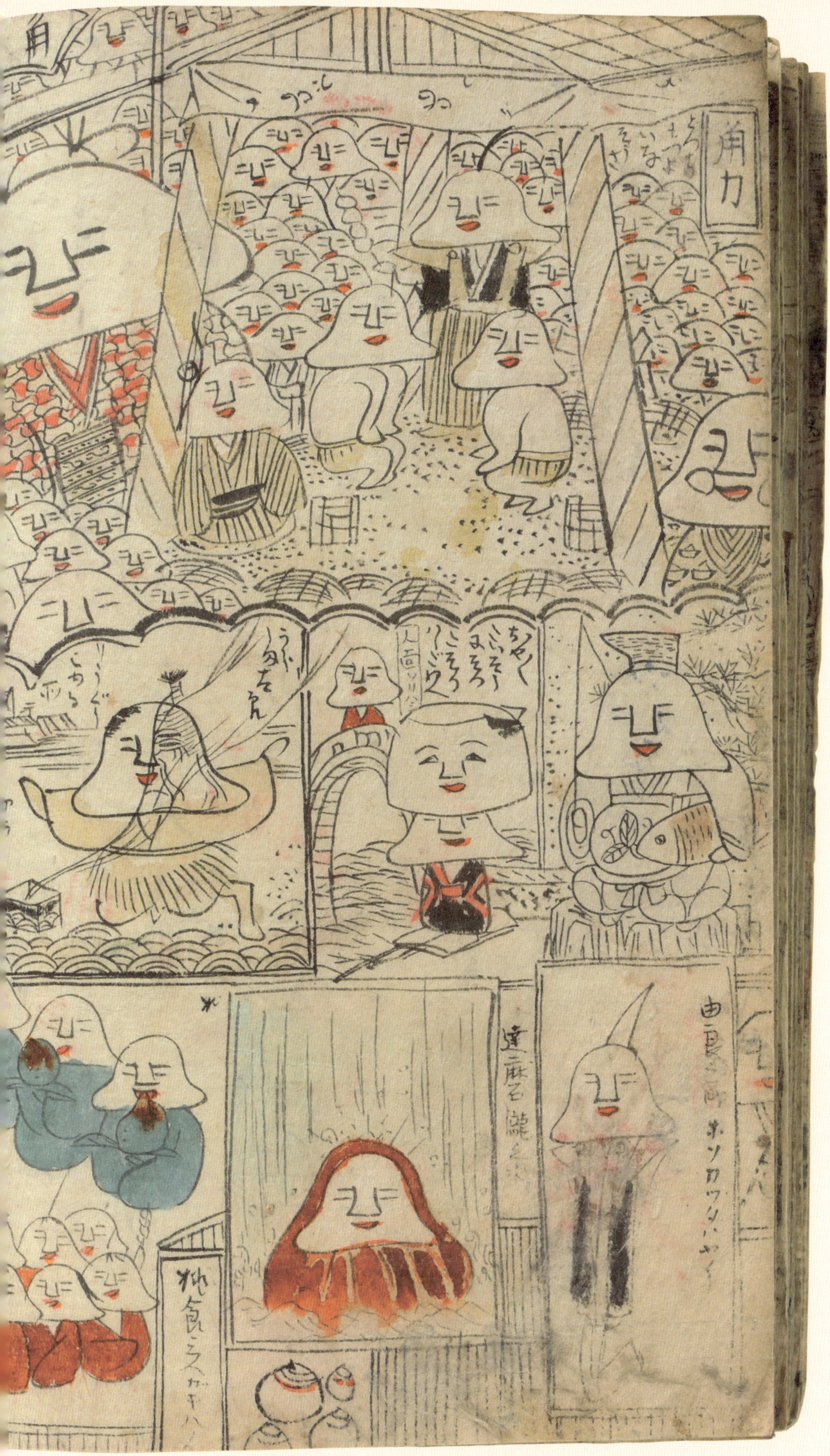

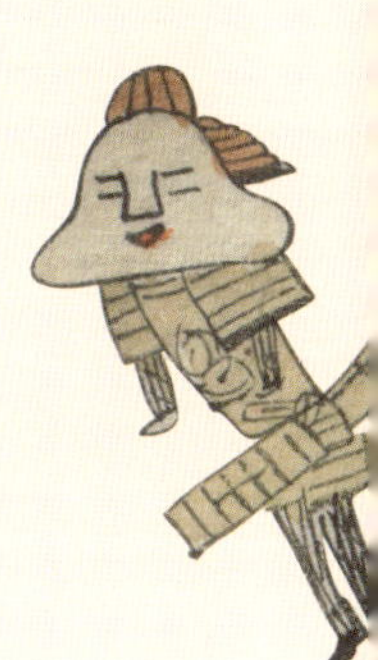

角力

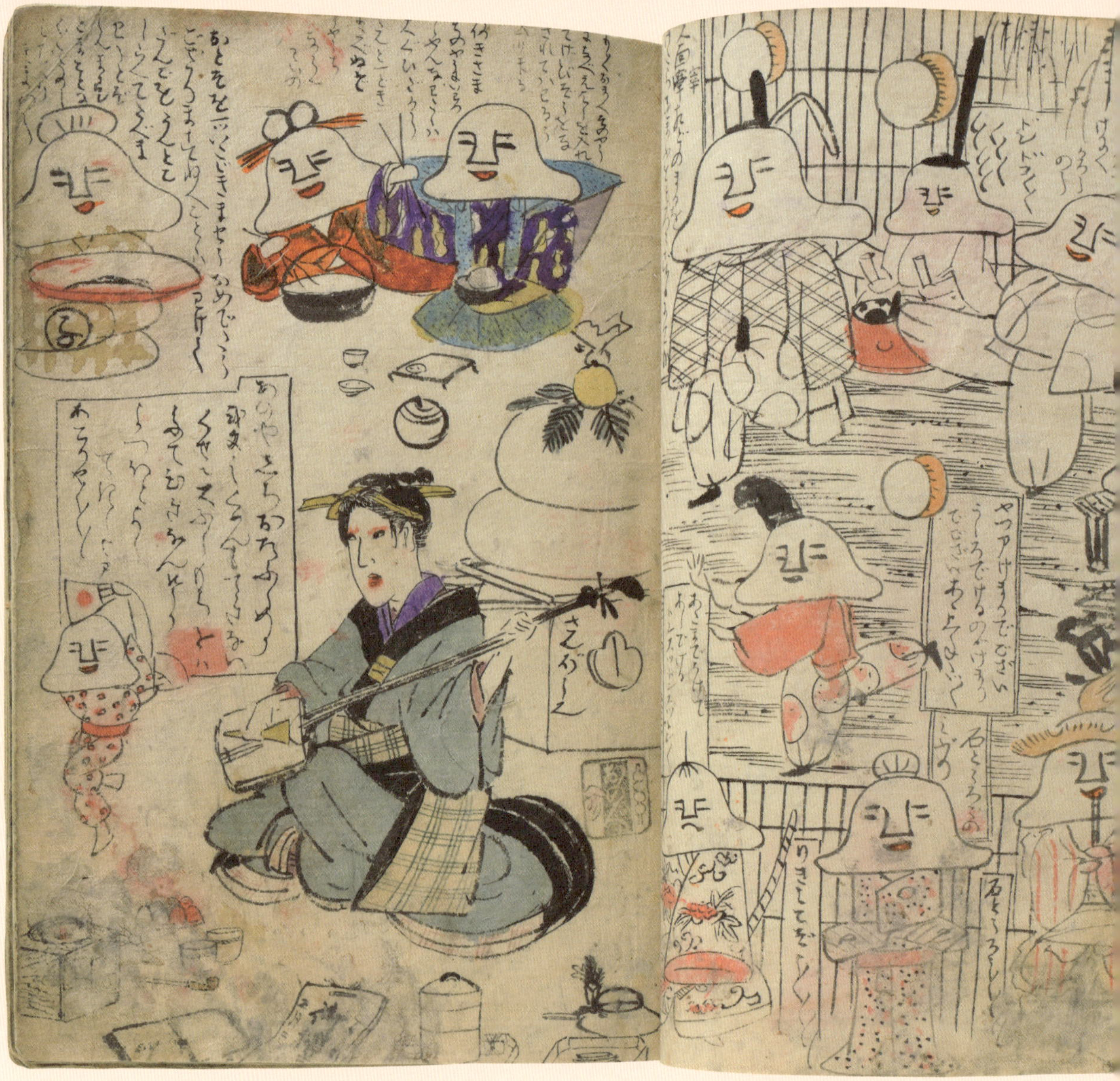

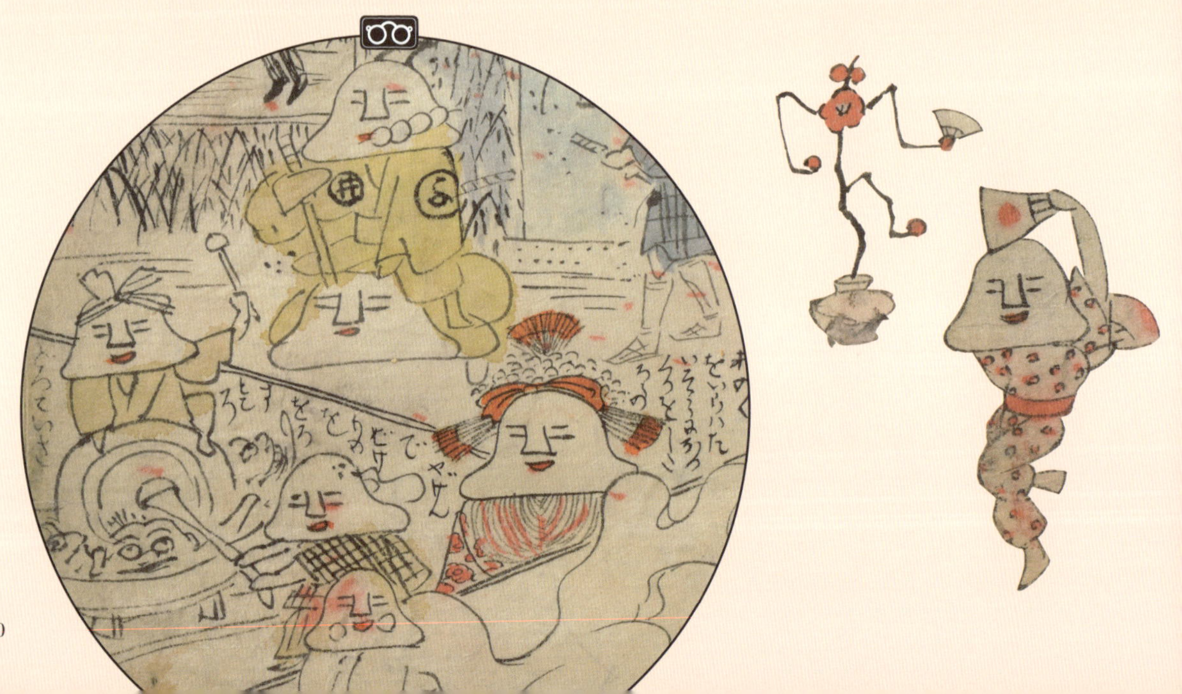

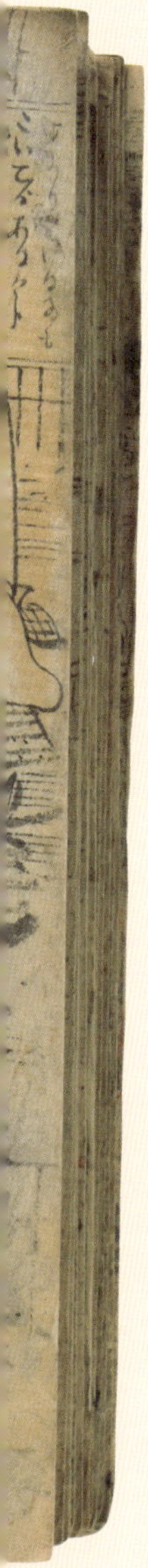

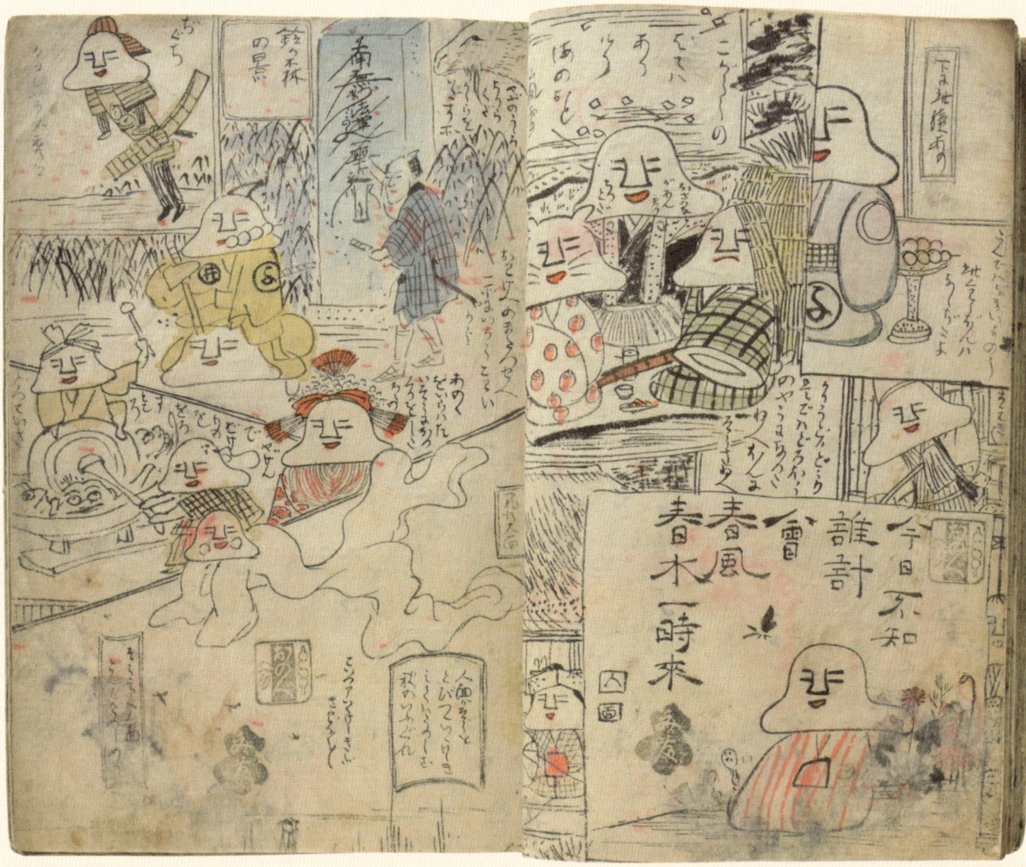

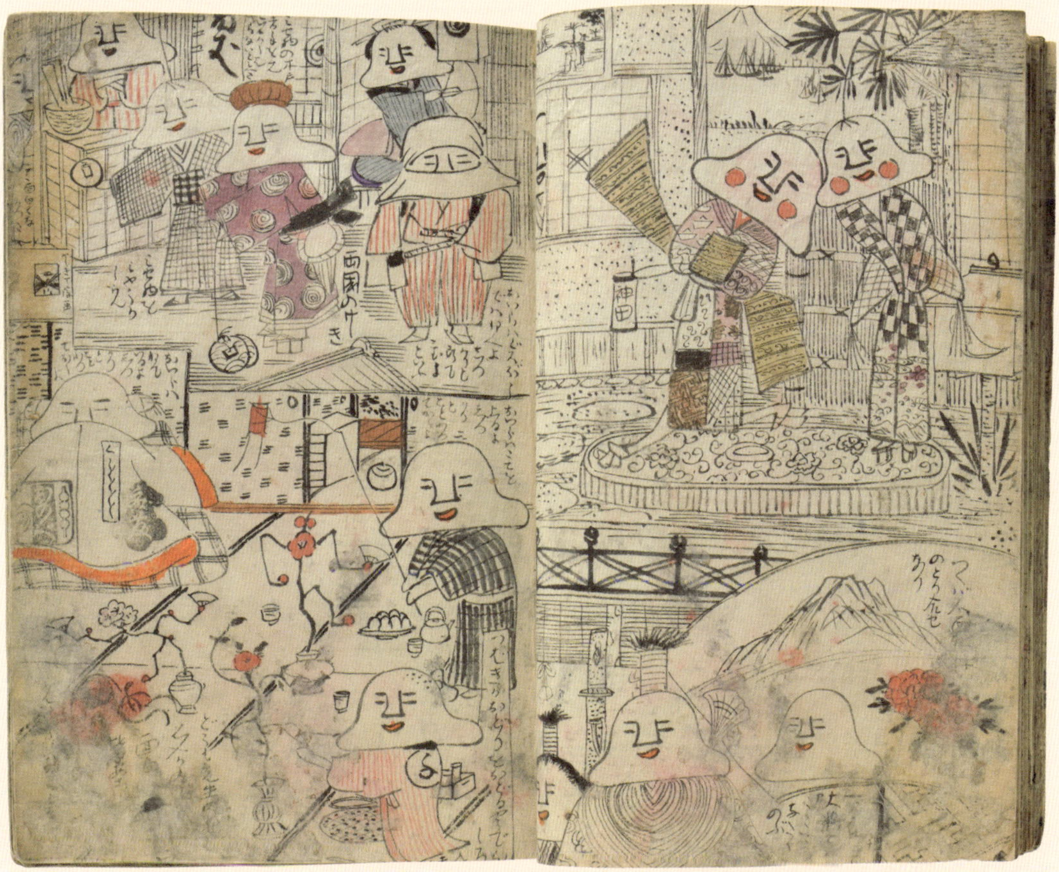

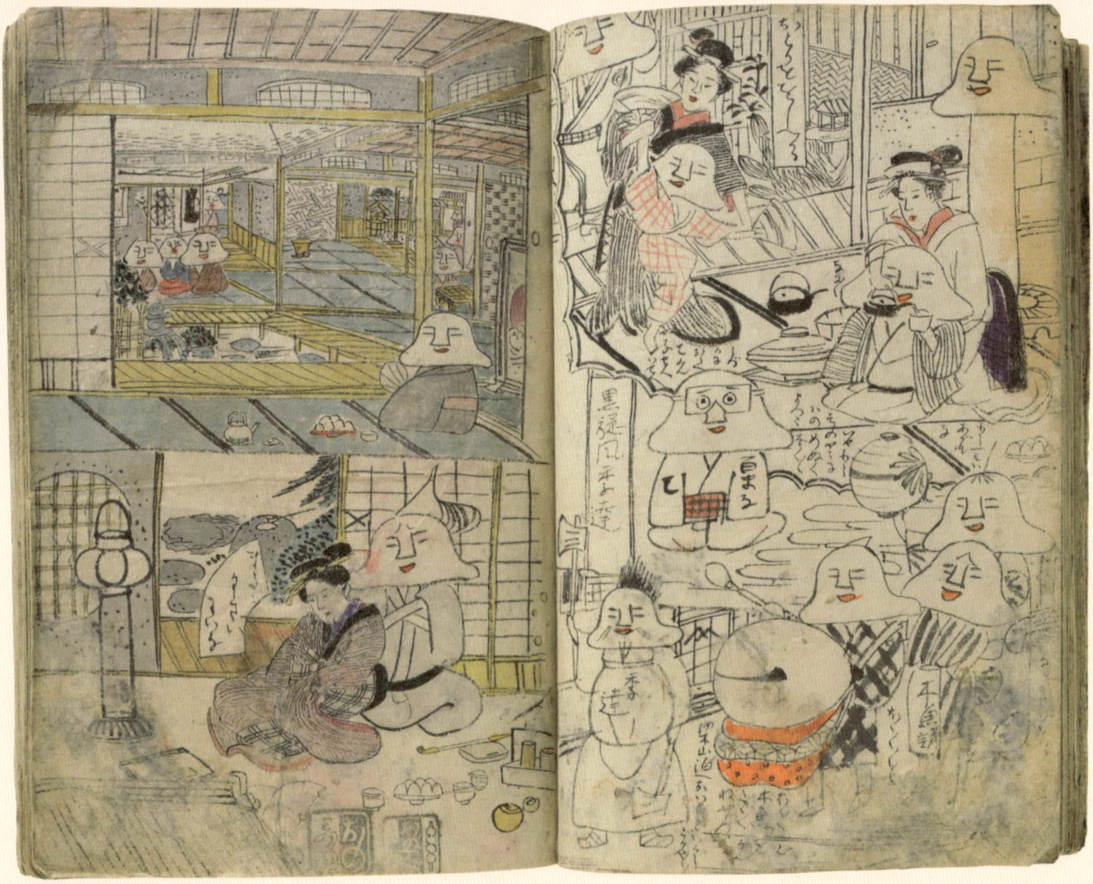

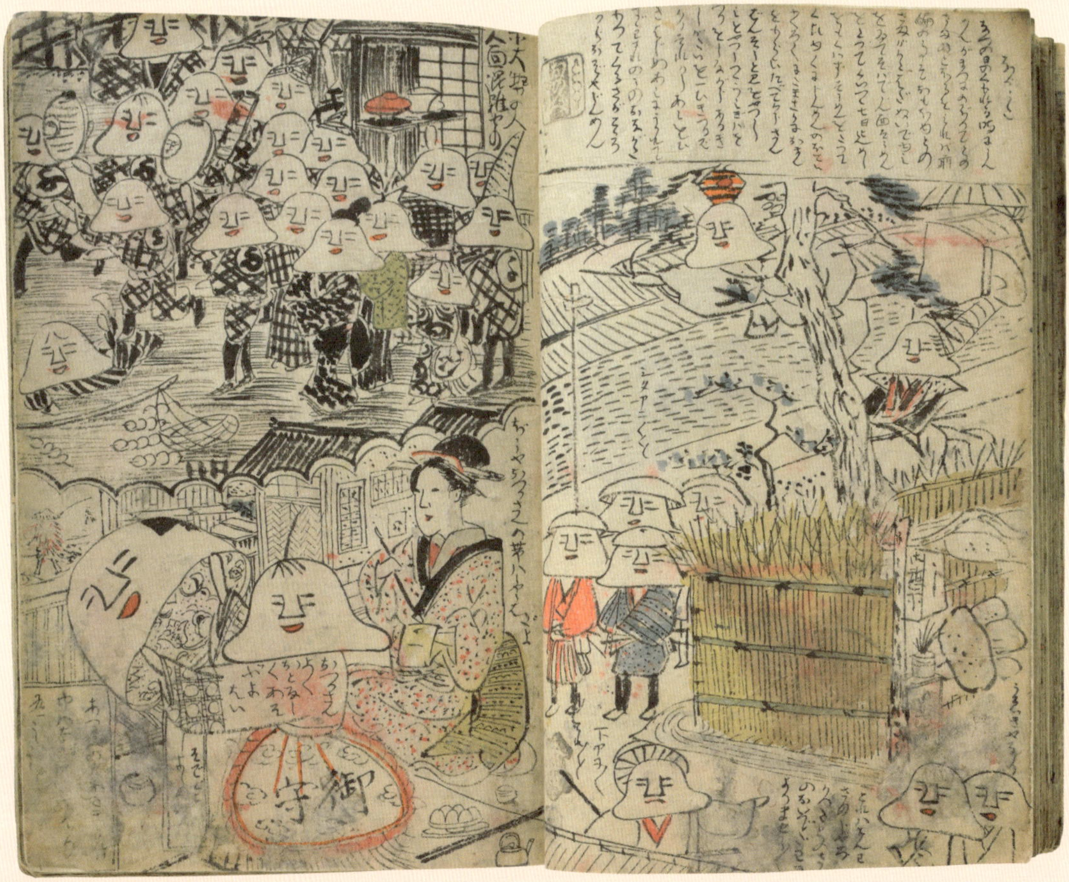

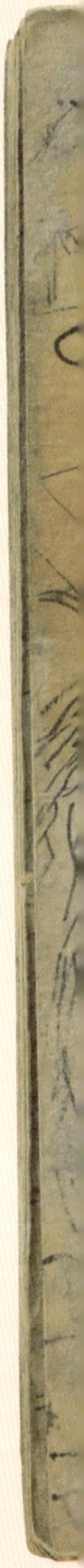

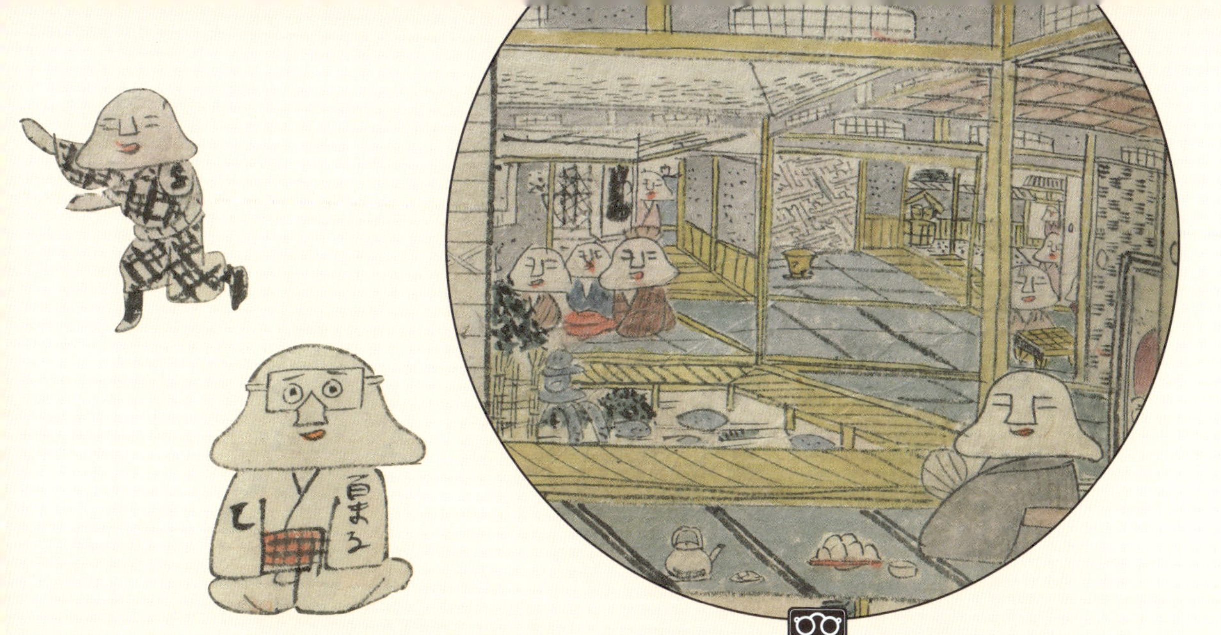

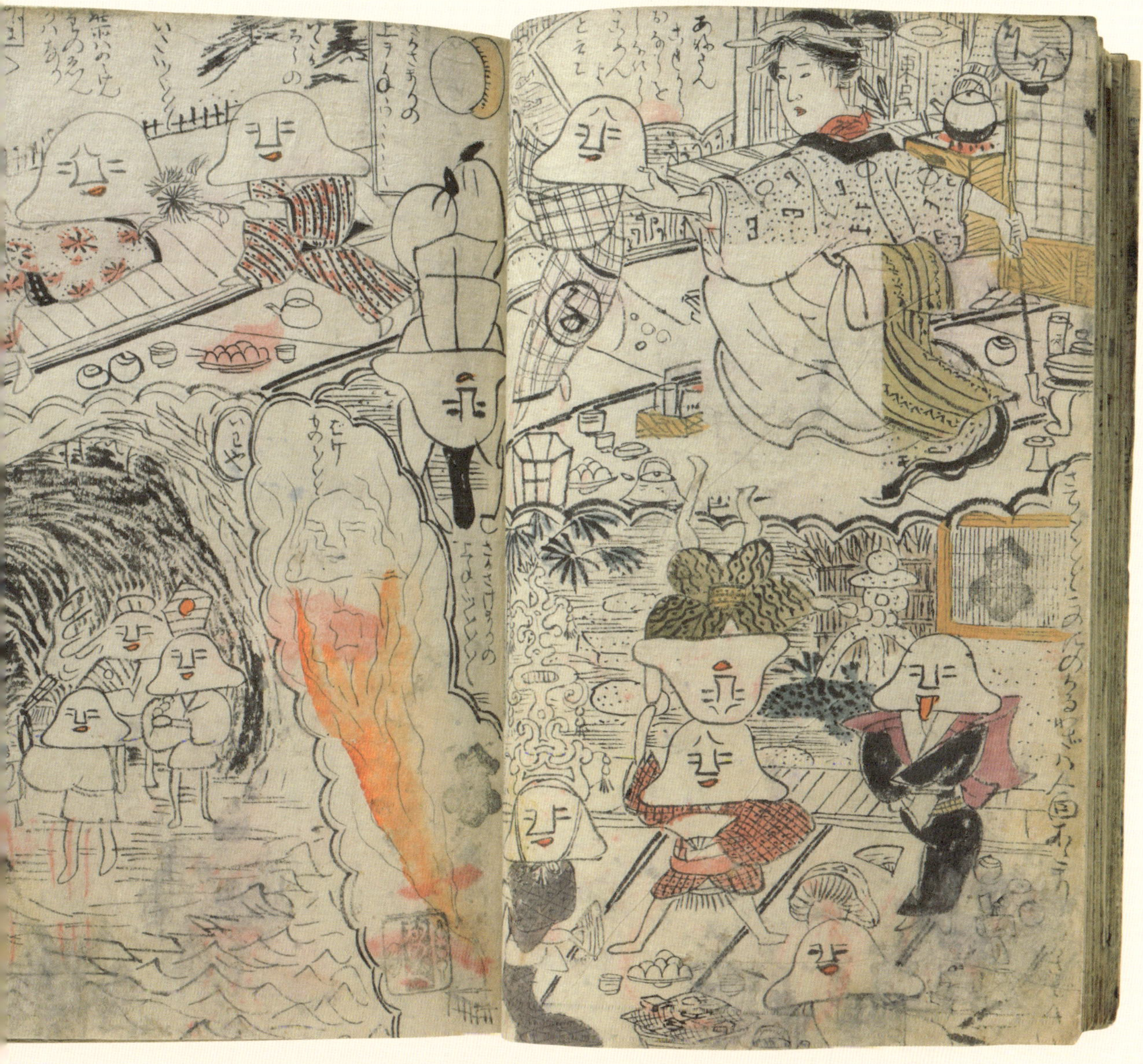

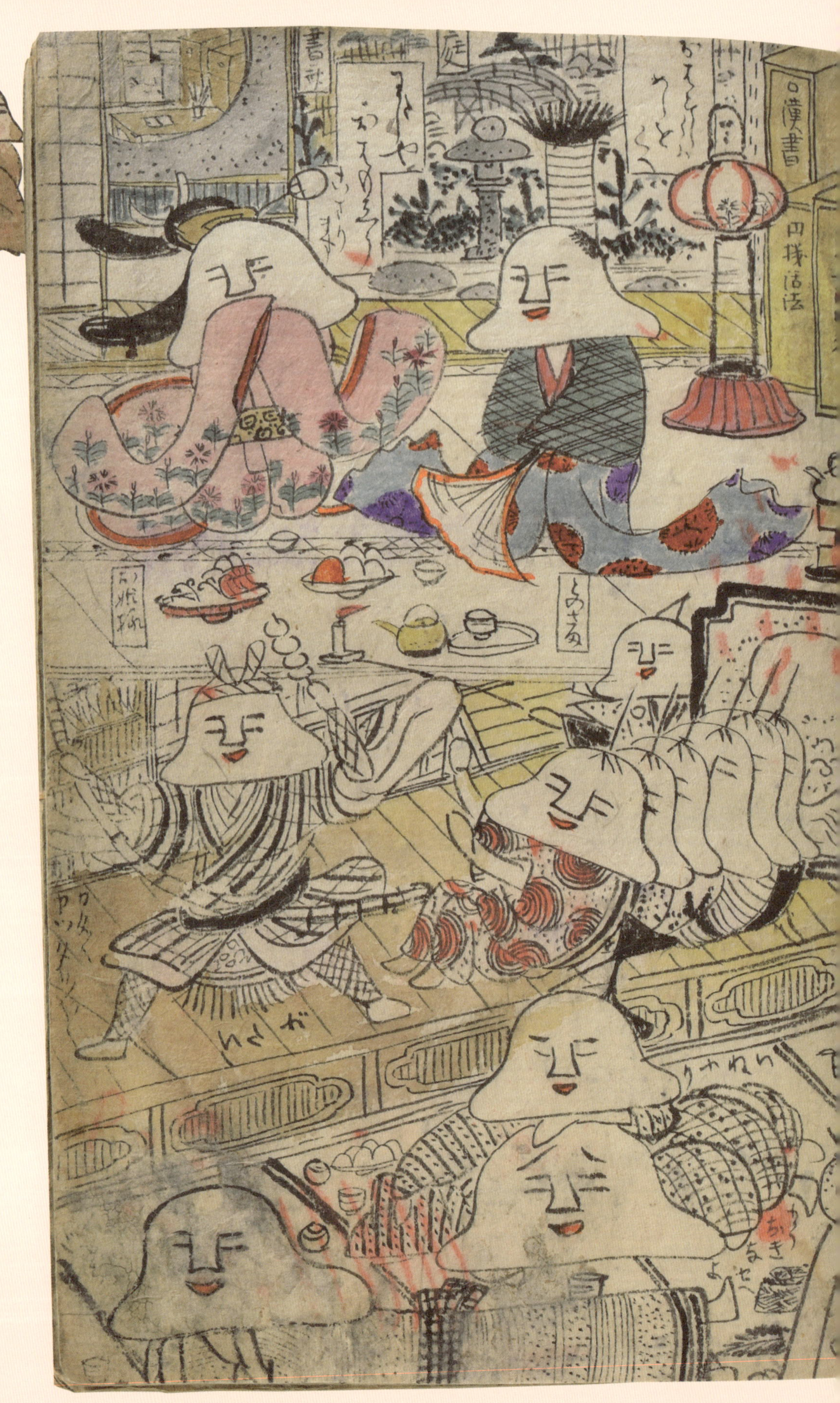

漢書
円珠活法
書画
庭

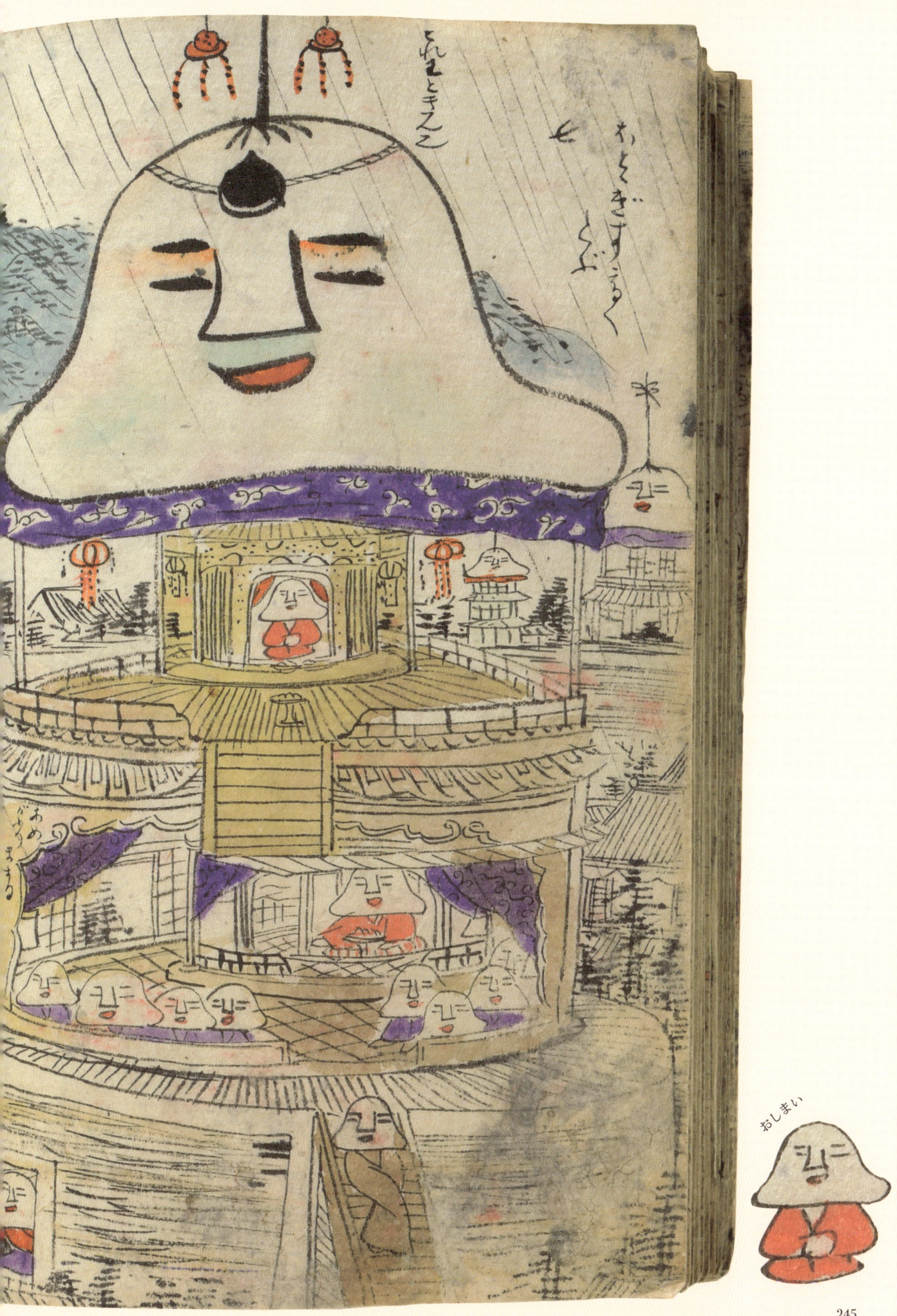
これときこん）
おとゝぎばなし
とぶ
あめがふってくる
おしまい

---

p18

百鬼夜行絵巻
The Night Parade of One Hundred Demons Picture Scroll
器物の妖怪たち中心だが、描かれた内容は類例がないようだ。巻頭は朽ち果てた寺の仏具の妖怪が描かれ、巻末は山の上に上った太陽で終わり、「雲渓」と絵師の名がある。蝦蟇の引く牛車や木馬に跨る妖怪など、本書収録の百鬼夜行絵巻や京都市立芸術大学、東京国立博物館の絵巻をベースにした内容に加えて真珠庵系百鬼夜行絵巻の葛籠の場面などもあるが、全体にはこの絵巻独自の世界を展開している。雲渓は四条派の絵師の可能性があるが、詳細は不明。

This picture scroll mainly features artifact yokai, but the content is highly original. Buddhist altar fittings are pictured in a crumbling temple at the beginning, and the scroll concludes with the sun over a mountain top and the artist's name, Unkei. Some of the content is based on the Night Parade of One Hundred Demons picture scrolls collected in this book and at the Kyoto City University of Arts and Tokyo National Museum, such as the yokai on a wooden horse and the oxcart pulled by a toad, as well as the wicker box scene from the Shinjuan-style Night Parade of One Hundred Demons scroll, but as a whole this scroll develops a unique world. It is possible that Unkei was an artist of the Shijō school, but the details remain unknown.

---

p24

百鬼夜行絵巻
The Night Parade of One Hundred Demons Picture Scroll
巻頭に「百鬼夜行 土佐光信筆写之 嘉永七寅年九月十五日」と書かれた書付けが添付されている。基

本的には真珠庵系を踏襲した妖怪が登場するが巻末が大きく異なっているのがこの絵巻の特徴だ。一般的には大きな火の玉が出現して妖怪たちが逃げ去る場面で終わる。朝日が昇って来て終わるケースも稀に存在するが、人物と対峙した妖怪が驚いて終焉を迎えるというスタイルは知られておらず、この絵巻は百鬼夜行絵巻の研究に一石を投じる資料で、同類の絵巻が存在するのか確認が課題といえよう。書付けの情報がそれなりの信憑性があれば同じタイプのものが発見される可能性も秘めている。

Documentation is attached at the beginning of the scroll which reads "Night Parade of One Hundred Demons: A copy of Tosa Mitsunobu, 15th day of the Ninth month of 1854 (Kaei 7), Year of the Tiger." The yokai are basically Shinjuan-style, however, the distinguishing feature of this scroll is that it ends very differently. Usually the final scene shows yokai fleeing a big fireball. In rare cases scrolls may finish with the sun rising, but a scroll ending in a surprising confrontation with humans was previously unheard of, and caused a paradigm shift in the research on the Night Parade of One Hundred Demons picture scrolls; the challenge is to discover whether there are any others like this one. If this scroll's documentation is accurate it may be the key to discovering another work of the same type.

---

p74

百鬼異形絵巻
One Hundred Demon Forms Picture Scroll
(*Hyakki Igyō Emaki*)
この絵巻はいくつもの妖怪を一つ一つ紹介する妖怪図鑑的絵巻に分類できる。巻頭に目次があり、「百鬼異形之図」として31種類の妖怪を列記しているが、いくつかは欠損している。各妖怪には名が付されていないので、目次で照合するしかない。絵の最後は錦の大きな袋が描かれているが、これは目次には含まれていない。また、巻末には2種類の文書が存在する。一つは跋に相当するもので28行にも及ぶ長文で、元信の百鬼夜行図が伝写されていったこと、この絵巻は押小路公音の第二子・玄長によって描き残されたことなどが記され、

末尾に「正徳癸巳歳孟秋日 棟藜子」とあるが、一部欠損している。この跋の後に、別の筆跡で、「右夜行の図は南窓悦山の蔵する処也 予これを今夜当文政二卯年八月日光において写畢 五岳春仙」とあることから、この絵巻は文政二年現在においては南窓悦山が所有し、それを五岳春仙が写したということのようだ。

This scroll can be classified as a yokai picture scroll which introduces many different yokai individually. At the beginning of the scroll is a table of contents which lists 31 types of yokai as "One Hundred Demon Pictures", but many are missing from the list. The yokai are not labeled with their names, so all one can do is cross-check with the table of contents. The final picture is of a large brocade bag, but this is not included in the list. There are also two different inscriptions at the end of the scroll. One is a long text like an afterword which runs to 28 lines, which records that the scroll was copied from Motonobu's Night Parade of One Hundred Demons, being one of the remaining scrolls by Harunaga, the second child of Oshikōji Kin'oto, and finishes with the words "Early autumn day in 1713 (Year of the *Mizunotomi* (Snake) in the Shōtoku reign): Teizuishi" but one part is missing. Following the afterword in different handwriting is "The pictures of the Night Parade on the right in the possession of Nansō Etsuzan were copied in Nikkō on this night in August 1819 (Bunsei 2), Year of the Hare: Gogaku Shunsen"; it seems that in 1819 this scroll was owned by Nansō Etsuzan, and copied by Gogaku Shunsen.

---

p86

27

妖怪尽くし絵巻
Yokai Zukushi Picture Scroll
いくつもの妖怪を紹介する妖怪図鑑的絵巻は江戸時代を中心に描かれた。そこに収録された妖怪のなかには他の絵巻では未見のものも散見される。このタイプの絵巻は近年になって新しいものもいくつか発見されており、さらなる調査が必要な分野といえよう。この絵巻は昭和時代に描かれたものだ。おもちゃ絵の妖怪尽くしでは明治時代以降にも新たな妖怪が次々と生み出されているが、妖怪図鑑的絵巻においてもこうしたことが行われて

きた。この作品はそうしたことの一端を知ることのできる資料として位置付けることができよう。10種類の妖怪が収録されているが、何れも古くからの伝説などから描き起こしたものではない。絹本絵巻である。

Picture scrolls which were illustrated reference guides introducing numbers of yokai were mainly drawn in the Edo period. Among the collected yokai can be found some that do not appear in other scrolls. In recent years many new picture scrolls of this type have been discovered; this is an area which requires further investigation. This scroll was created in the Shōwa period (mid-twentieth century). After the Meiji period many new yokai were churned out in quick succession in *omocha-e* compendiums of yokai; even this illustrated guide shows just the tip of the iceberg of the activity that was going on. Ten types of yokai are collected, none of which have been passed down through the ages. This is a silk scroll.

---

p88

28

妖怪尽くし絵巻
Yokai Zukushi Picture Scroll
これも新しい妖怪図鑑的絵巻で、10種類が収録された絹本絵巻だ。

This is also a new illustrated guide to yokai, featuring ten types of yokai in a silk scroll.

---

p90

29

おばけおどけ
Supernatural Shenanigans (*Obake Odoke*)
図1右　京都高瀬三喜楼工事中、明治四年四月、大工二階にて休む。大お多福の顔、毎夜出る。
図1左　大阪安重寺町骨屋町東入鈴木裏にて増田タツ方、明治二十五年八月夏夜一時半、便所に行く際、表口に大の坊主が立ち居るを、向こうへ行けば後で寄る、こちらへ来れば傍へ来る、前年より住む古狸。
図2右上　明治七年夏の夜、小谷草原の雪隠を開

けると大きな顔が出る。その人、腰を抜かしたり。

図2右下　明治三年十二月三十一日、心斎橋五龍円の用水の上にずんべらの小人踊りおり。

図2左上　明治十年盆十四日朝四時、谷町地蔵坂松の寺。

此女一生懸命に石碑を拝み居る、いつまでたてど横も向かず。

此男は女の前に回りて顔を見ると目鼻口もなし。

図2左下　此老母の亡霊、増田の前に米屋業なり、一人娘に養子のもらい後に生娘死去し、他より嫁を迎えてまもなく老母は死亡したるに一七日もたたぬまに家をあげ、一度弔いもせず其祟り。

明治二十五年九月、墓の谷中寺町西入増田方にて老母と娘の亡霊出る。

図3右　座摩前古手屋番頭、同家の女中と婦夫約束致し置き、女中は他に奉公忠義、且つすえ婦夫を楽しみ居しに一方番頭はその約束をしながら他に女房を持ち、一方その事を聞き是非の立腹してある夜生霊が婦夫を噛殺したり。その女中は朝、口バタ血に染れり。

図3左　山城長岡のほとり大仙寺の地端に古狸住む。ある夜、酒好きの四人酒呑みたきとて村の無神経の男を酒屋へ凡そ一里もあるところ酒を買いにやるに、いつまで待てども帰り来たらず。故に四人連で一里程の道を尋ね来たるに早や東白み、その阿呆は大仙寺門前に居れる事を訊ねしに余程おもしろい事でありました、いろいろに目をむき七化けを済むとその古狸死したりという。

図4右上　弘化三年十月大和穴虫にて夕方肴売りしもうて帰りがけ、その山の麓に二十歳女一人立ちいるより訪ねて我家に連れ帰り、幸いその魚屋やもめ、すぐ夫婦約束でき睦まじく暮らすうち、ふと友達より変な言を聞き、ある夜寝に就かざるを女房が尻をあげ前に起き上がり見る間に目一つ口は耳まで裂けた姿を現し、永々可愛がってくれたといいち言いて出たり。

わしは此世へ行く出てる魔物である。

図4右下　これこれ、わしらのような目界の見えぬ者、なぶっとくれな。

明治二十八年、東瓦屋町にて九月の夜午後十二時盲按摩に目をむきて出る狸、盲蛇に応ぜず。

図4左上　備前高橋のほとりに光善寺という寺あり。その寺にて芝居かかりの連中十人泊まりおり。ある日芝居休みの夜に肝くらべしようと本堂裏に茶碗を取りに行くを五人目の人が茶碗を取るなり。上の壁に凶相な顔写りその人目を回したり。

図4左下　元土佐堀五丁目運送屋隠居をこの老母

が後に隠居に借り、明くる夜より老母と娘の亡霊が毎夜出で老母は亡霊に向かいて尋ねしに元この家に住居しておるうちにこの二人は死亡して主人は何処とも信じず、弔い一度もしたことなしと言う。すぐ老母は供養をして仏事を営み成仏して亡霊が礼に来たり。

図5右上　天保三年の夏、薩摩堀にヤマ吉と言いし山窩の鉄屋あり。その番頭主人を毒殺して家内や一人子を他に押し込め、後に一子をまた絞め殺し、ある夜更けて奥の宴にて酒を飲み、芸者ひかせて女房としておる内一時過ぎ蔵の窓より主人の亡霊が来てこの番頭を噛み殺し。

図5右下　明治　年、道頓堀竹田芝居興行中に焼けて焼死者二百九十七人あり。この亡霊一家家族四人全部焼死す。この人に弔い頼む。この人これを聞いてすぐ家まで取り調べて供養したり。

図5左上　明治五年六月夜、淡路志筑の沖にて志筑の漁師が網を引くとき海中より大の海坊主が出で。

図5左下　明治□年、生玉正遷宮の察石の鳥居が落ちて死傷者出来、後日にその鳥居を重ねある上に夜更けになるとその時死したる亡霊が上で踊り居りたり。

Fig.1, right. During construction work on the Takase in Kyoto in April 1871 (Meiji 4), the carpenters rested on the upper level. Every night the huge face of an otafuku appeared.

Fig. 1, left. On a summer night at 1.30am in August 1892 (Meiji 25) behind the Suzuki west entrance to Haneyachō, Teramachi, Yasushige in Osaka, on the way to the toilet there was a huge monk standing at the front door, and when one retreated from the monk it followed after, but if one went towards it it approached; an old raccoon dog who had been living there for some years.

Fig. 2, upper right. On a summer night in 1874 (Meiji 7) in a field in Odani, the door to a public toilet was opened and a huge head emerged. The hapless toilet-goer fell over in shock.

Fig. 2, lower left. On December 31 in 1870 (Meiji 3), a stumpy dwarf danced on top of the water tank on the Shinsaibashi Bridge.

Fig. 2, upper left. Jizō-zaka temple in Tanimachi, Osaka, at 4am on July 14 in 1877 (Meiji 10) during the Bon festival.

This woman worshipped a stone monument with all her might, standing upright for all eternity.

A man turned back to look at the woman's face and saw that she had no eyes, nose or mouth.

Fig. 2, lower left. The ghost of this old woman. A former rice dealer of Masuda. After adopting a girl as her only daughter, the girl died, and straight after she married the old woman passed away, and their house was given up before seventeen days had passed without a single prayer said for their souls. The story of their haunting.

The ghosts of the old woman and her daughter emerged from the west entrance to the cemetery (on the Masuda side) in Teramachi, Yanaka (Tokyo), in September 1892 (Meiji 25).

Fig. 3, right. The manager of a used goods store in front of Zama Shrine made a betrothal promise to his maid, who also served others, but while the manager enjoyed living with his maid as man and wife under that promise, he was already married to another, and when the maid found out, she was so infuriated that her vengeful spirit left her body that night and savaged the two of them to death. In the morning, the maid had blood all around her mouth.

Fig. 3, left. An old raccoon dog lived close to Daisen-ji Temple by Nagaoka, Yamashiro. One night, four drunken sake-lovers made the village lout go to buy sake at an *izakaya* more than 1 *ri* (2.5 miles) away, but no matter how long they waited he didn't come back. The four of them made the long journey as day was dawning soon, and found that the fool was in front of the Daisen-ji Temple gate where there were very interesting goings-on, and he had seen many things, but once the old raccoon dog had changed shape seven times, it died.

Fig. 4, upper right. In the early evening in October 1846 (Kōka 3) in Anamushi, Yamato, on the way home from selling snacks, a man met a twenty-year-old woman who was standing alone at the foot of the mountain and brought her back to his home, and fortunately they were soon able to betroth and were living together in harmony, when a friend of his happened to plant the seeds of suspicion, and one night when he had difficulty sleeping, he watched his wife get up before him and her hideous true form was revealed with one eye and a mouth extending out to her ears, upon which she thanked him for loving her for so long and left. She said she was a demon that could go to the other world and back.

Fig. 4, lower right. This here is a person who does not see the visible world as we do; do not mock them. At midnight on a September evening in 1895 (Meiji 28) in east Kawarayamachi, a raccoon dog turned its eyes on a blind masseur, who was totally unfazed.

Fig.4, upper left. There is a temple called Kōzen-ji close to Takahashi in Bizen. At this temple, ten actors lodge. One day, on a night they were not working, the actors decided to see who was the bravest by going to get tea bowls from behind the main hall, and the fifth member went to take one. On the wall was the semblance of an evil face which put him to flight.

Fig. 4, lower left. This old woman owed a debt to a retired carrier in the former Tosabori 5-chōme area; the ghosts of the old woman and her daughter appeared every night, but when he faced them and asked why, the old woman said that the two of them had originally lived in that house and then they died, but the master of the house was an inveterate unbeliever, and so they did not receive even one prayer for their souls. Soon a memorial service was held for the old woman, the Buddhist rites for the dead were done, the spirits went to rest, and the ghosts expressed their gratitude.

Fig. 5, upper right. In the summer of 1832 (Tenpō 3) at Kyomachi Hori, there was a travelling blacksmith family called Yamakichi. Their lord poisoned the blacksmith, imprisoned his wife and son, and later strangled the son, and then one night as it got late, the lord was drinking sake at a party and as he cavorted with geisha, the ghost of the blacksmith came out of the storehouse window after 1am and bit the lord to death.

Fig. 5, lower left. Year unknown in the Meiji period: There was a fire in the middle of a theatrical performance in the Takeda, Dotonbōri, and 297 people burned to death. These ghosts are a family of four who all died in the fire. They are asking this man to pray for them. After hearing their entreaty, he will find their house and hold a memorial service as soon as he can.

Fig.5, upper left. On an evening in June in 1872 (Meiji 5) off the coast of Shizuki, Awaji, a fisherman of Shizuki pulled in his net and from the sea a huge umibōzu (sea bonze) emerged.

Fig.5, lower left. Year unknown in the Meiji period: At Shōsengū, Ikutama, the torii (stone gate) fell, killing and injuring people, and in days following as the night drew late, the ghosts of those who had perished there came to dance on top of the tumbled remains.

---

p94

「大阪妖怪画談」原画
"An Exploration of Osaka Yokai"
(original illustration)
「御堂裏の高入道」原画　「北御堂裏の高入道」と
いう話の挿絵。明治 15 年ころ大阪北御堂裏に現
れる高入道。その正体は古狸で人を誑かしたらし
いという話。
"The Tall Priest Behind the Midō" (original illustration)
Illustration for "The Tall Priest Behind the Midō". In
1882 a tall priest was seen behind the Kitamidō
Temple in Osaka. The story explains that the priest was
really an old raccoon dog who tricked people.

「蒔絵屋の娘の幽霊」原画　　「蒔絵屋の娘の幽霊」
という話。蒔絵屋が生活に困って一人娘が女郎と
なる。その後、店の上り框に娘の顔が現れて忽然
と消えた。半月ほどして早飛脚が来て娘の死を知っ
たが、死んだのは框に顔が現れた時間であったと
いう実話。実際には挿絵として掲載されなかった。
"Ghost of the *Maki-e* Lacquerer's Daughter" (original
illustration)　A story known as "The Ghost of the
Maki-e Lacquerer's Daughter". A *maki-e* lacquerer fell
on hard times and the couple's only daughter became a
prostitute. Following this, her head appeared on the
edge of the entrance to their shop and then suddenly
vanished. A real account of how an express messenger
had informed them of her death half a month ago, but
they saw her head appear. This illustration was not
published.

「塵芥山の大蜥蜴」原画　「塵芥山の大蜥蜴」とい
うタイトルで天満堀川の山のようになった塵芥捨
て場から 6 尺もある大蜥蜴が出現したという話の
挿絵だが、実際には掲載されることがなかった。
"The Giant Lizard of Trash Mountain" (original
illustration)　Entitled "The Giant Lizard of Trash
Mountain", this is an illustration for the story of a six-
foot-long lizard which emerged from a trash heap by
the Tenmabori canal in Osaka which had grown to the
size of a mountain.

「龍田町の古狸」原画　　「龍田町の古狸」という
話の挿絵として描かれたが掲載されなかった。こ
の話は明治 36 年ころに大阪東天満龍田町の老婆
の前に不気味な坊主が現れ、びっくりした老婆が
這いながら家人を呼んだが、その時には坊主の姿
はなく、老婆の菓子も一つ残らずなくなっていた
というもので、古狸の仕業だったろうという内容。
"The Old Raccoon Dog of Tatsuta-cho" (original
illustration)　This was drawn to illustrate the story of
"The Old Raccoon Dog of Tatsuta-cho" but not
published. The story goes that in 1903 a strange priest
appeared in front of an old woman of Tatsuta-cho in
Higashitenma, Osaka, and as she cowered and called
out for her family, the priest disappeared without a
trace along with all the old woman's sweets, which was
blamed on the mischief of an old raccoon dog.

---

p100

源頼光公館土蜘蛛妖怪図
The Yokai of Tsuchigumo at the Mansion of
Minamoto no Yorimitsu (*Minamoto no Yorimitsu Kō
Yakata Tsuchigumo Yōkai Zu*)
源頼光の館に土蜘蛛が出現する話をテーマとした
錦絵は種々出されているが、ほとんどは頼光と土
蜘蛛、四天王に焦点をあてた構図となっている。
いっぽうで、この作品は鳥瞰するスタイルで描か
れ、館の各所に妖怪が跋扈している様子がみてと
れる。左の部屋では碁をしながら警護する傍らに
金棒を持った三つ目の大入道が出現、縁側からは
腰元と思しき妖怪が茶を運び、その後を菓子を持っ
た腰元妖怪も追っている。屋根からは妖怪が中を
窺い、庭では蛙とカタツムリが蛇の行司で相撲を
取ろうとしている。小姓の妖怪がお化け提灯を掲
げて明るくしており、警護の武士はのんびりと煙
草をふかしながら相撲見物だ。その奥には頼光が
刀を握って遠くを睨んでいるが、その視線の先に
は中空に土蜘蛛が不気味な姿をあらわし、館は海
に突き出しているようで、波間からは舟で妖怪た
ちが近づいて来ている。妖怪ワンダーランドのよ
うな場面は見る人を異界に引き込む魅力を発散し
ている。
Many *nishiki-e* have been produced on the theme of

Tsuchigumo's appearance in the mansion of Minamoto no Yorimitsu, but almost all focus on Yorimitsu, his four loyal retainers the Raikō Shitennō, and Tsuchigumo. In contrast, this work is drawn from an overhead viewpoint so that the yokai infesting every area of the mansion can be spotted. In the room on the left, a three-eyed giant priest appears holding a studded war club right next to the guards playing *go*, and a yokai who looks like a female servant is stepping up to the veranda to bring them tea, followed by another bringing sweets. Another creature keeps an eye on the room from above, and in the garden a frog and snail are about to sumo wrestle each other with a snake as referee. A pageboy yokai is dangling a ghost lantern to shed some light on things, and a guard watches the sumo, lazily puffing on his pipe. Behind these is Yorimitsu, gripping his sword and staring into the distance, but his gaze rests on the chilling figure of Tsuchigumo in mid-air; the mansion seems to jut out into the sea, with yokai coming in to land on the waves. Like a yokai wonderland, the scene has an allure which draws the viewer in to an alien world.

---

p103

33

白縫譚
Shiranui Tales (*Shiranui Monogatari*)
「白縫譚」は柳下亭種員、2世柳亭種彦、柳水種清の合作による90編にも及ぶ合巻。菊池氏に滅ぼされた大友宗麟の娘・若菜姫（若那姫）は蜘蛛の精から妖術を授かって男装して白縫大尽と称して菊池氏への仇討ちを謀り、菊池氏の家来鳥山秋作と妖術による戦いを繰り広げるが、やがて心を一にして九州を平定するというストーリーで、歌舞伎でも人気を博した。この作品は嘉永5年に江戸の河原崎座での上演を受けて制作されたのであろう。右に若那姫、左に鳥山秋作を配して妖術合戦の場面を描き、中央には巨大な蜘蛛を登場させている。

Shiranui Monogatari is an epic *gōkan* (a bound-together volume of illustrated books) made up of 90 titles collaboratively written by Ryūkatei Tanekazu, Ryūtei Tanchiko II, and Ryūsui Tanekiyo. The story of Princess Wakanahime, the daughter of Ōtomo Sorin who was destroyed by the Kikuchi family is also popular as a subject for kabuki plays; given sorcery by a spider spirit, the princess disguised herself as a man and took the name Shiranui Daijin to get revenge on the Kikuchis, and fought retainer of the Kikuchi family Toriyama Akisaku with her sorcery, but at long last resolved their differences and conquered Kyūshū. This work was modeled on a performance at the Edo Kawarazaki-za Theater in 1853. The scene is a battle of sorcery, with Princess Wakanahime placed on the right, Toriyama Akisaku on the left, and a huge spider in the center.

「白縫譚」着物下絵
着物や刺子半纏には妖怪柄のものが散見できる。とりわけ刺子半纏の裏地には妖怪柄が種々みられる。これは刺子半纏が火消しの際に身に着け、消火活動が終わると半纏をリバースして妖怪柄で見る人たちをびっくりさせるためともいわれている。この下絵もこうした目的の刺子半纏のデザインの可能性がある。描かれた柄は「白縫譚」の若菜姫（若那姫）が蜘蛛に乗って妖術を使っているところであろう。「白縫譚」は歌舞伎でも上演されて人気を呼んだ物語で、この柄を見れば誰もがその内容を理解したことだろう。右上に「第五」とあり、デザイン画の一つとして描かれたのだろう。こうした妖怪資料は稀で貴重なものといえる。

Shiranui Tales Kimono Sketch
Yokai designs can be found on kimono and quilted *hanten* (short coats). In particular, a variety of yokai designs are found on the inner lining of *hanten*. The reason for this is thought to be that *hanten* were worn for fire fighting and turned inside out when the fire fighting was done to surprise onlookers with designs featuring demonic creatures. This sketch may also have been used for a hanten for this purpose. The pattern sketched out is of Princess Wakanahime of the Shiranui Tales riding a spider and wielding magic. The Shiranui Tales were so popular they were performed as kabuki plays, so anyone who saw this design would have understood the significance of it. On the upper right is written "Number Five", indicating that this was probably one of a set of designs. Yokai materials such as this one are rare and precious.

---

p110

丹波国大江山之図
Mount Ōe of Tanba Province (*Tanba no Kuni Ōe Yama no Zu*)

源頼光の酒呑童子退治は誰でも知っている伝説で能や歌舞伎にもなっているが、絵巻や錦絵においてもポピュラーな画題として描き継がれた。酔いつぶれて正体をあらわし巨大な鬼の姿となった酒呑童子は頼光らに退治されるが、この作品はその前段で、丹波国大江山の酒呑童子の豪壮な館で頼光と四天王たちが鬼とともに酒宴の真っ最中の場面を描いている。手前右では碓氷貞光の大杯に鬼が酒を注いでおり、中央では興に乗った鬼が扇子をかざして踊りまわり、坂田金時、渡辺綱、卜部季武らは酒宴に興じながら虎視眈々と退治する機会を狙っている。奥では多数の侍女を侍らせた酒呑童子を油断させるために平伏して挨拶する頼光の姿もみえる。巨大な館であることは場面からもみてとれるが、その後方にも大広間があり、酒呑童子の想像を絶する力を象徴しているかのようだ。この酒宴のあとでクライマックスの酒呑童子退治が開始される。

Minamoto no Yorimitsu's defeat of Shuten-dōji was a legend known to all which was dramatized in Noh and kabuki plays, and continued to be a popular subject for scrolls and *nishiki-e*. Shuten-dōji was eventually defeated by Yorimitsu and his companions after he fell into an alcohol-induced slumber and revealed his true form as a huge ogre, but this is an earlier scene of the drinking party at Shuten-dōji's luxurious mansion on Mount Ōe in Tanba Province, with Yorimitsu and the Raikō Shitennō as well as ogres in attendance. In the right foreground ogres are pouring sake into Usui no Sadamitsu's vessel, in the center is an ogre who has loosened up enough to dance with a fan, and Sakata no Kintoki, Watanabe no Tsuna and Urabe no Suetake bide their time amongst the revelry, waiting for the right moment to attack. Yorimitsu can be seen offering greetings on his knees to allay the suspicions of Shuten-dōji, who is surrounded by a number of ladies-in-waiting at the back. The sheer size of the room shows that this is a huge mansion, and another vast room opens up beyond it like a metaphor for Shuten-dōji's unimaginable strength. After the drinking party, the climax of his defeat unfolds.

川上演劇歌舞伎座中幕大江山
Middle Act of Kawakami's Mount Ōe at the Kabuki-za (*Kawakami Engeki Kabuki-za Nakamaku Ōe-yama*)

明治期に新派を創始し一大ブームを巻き起こした川上音二郎による演劇「大江山」の歌舞伎座での中幕上演の錦絵。源頼光を音二郎が演じ、他に高田実、藤沢浅次郎、中野信近といった新派草創期を飾った俳優たちや子役の久川竹太郎の名もみえる。壮士芝居で人気を不動のものとし、時事を鋭く捉えた演劇に卓越した才能を発揮した音二郎だったが、こうした作品も演じて「大江山」のような伝統的な出し物にも新派劇という新しいスタイルを持ち込んだといえよう。

Nishiki-e of a performance at the Kabuki-za Theater: the middle act of the play Mount Ōe by Kawakami Otojirō, who created a boom and founded a radical new wave of theater (*Shinpa*) in the Meiji period. Otojirō played Minamoto no Yorimitsu, and alongside him can be seen other actors who pioneered the new school of *Shinpa*: Takada Minoru, Fujisawa Asajirō, Nakano Nobuchika, and famous child actor Hisakawa Taketarō. Political plays (*sōshi shibai*) established Otojirō's popularity, and he excelled in dramas which keenly captured the current events of the day, but this work Mount Ōe brought a fresh *Shinpa* interpretation to a traditional performance.

安倍泰成調伏妖怪図
Abe no Yasunari Exorcises a Yokai (*Abe no Yasunari Yōkai Chōbuku no Zu*)

鳥羽上皇に寵愛された絶世の美女玉藻前は実は妖狐だったという伝説は読本、浄瑠璃、能、歌舞伎などとして広く知られ、錦絵の画題としても種々描かれている。この作品は陰陽師安倍泰成が宝鏡によって玉藻前の正体をあぶり出しているところ。

中央には玉藻前が妖艶な姿をみせているが、泰成の掲げた鏡には狐が映り正体が露わとなっている。鏡から発せられた光のなかには多数の狐が群れをなしている。泰成に見破られた玉藻前は九尾狐となって逃れていったが、上皇の命により泰成が三浦介義純らを伴って退治に赴き那須において征伐、九尾狐は殺生石と化して後の世まで災いをおよぼした。

The incredibly beautiful Tamamo-no-Mae who was the most favored courtesan of the retired Emperor Toba was actually a fox spirit; her legend was popularized through *yomihon*, puppet *jōruri*, Noh and kabuki plays, and portrayed in various incarnations in *nishiki-e*. This work shows the moment when yin-yang master Abe no Yasunari unmasks Tamamo-no-Mae's true form with a magic mirror. Tamamo-no-Mae cuts a seductive figure in the center, but her fox's face is revealed in the mirror held by Yasunari. A skulk of foxes clusters in the light shining from the mirror. Unmasked by Yasunari, Tamamo-no-Mae turns back into a nine-tailed fox and flees, but on the retired Emperor's orders Yasunari and Miura-no-suke Yoshiaki mount a punitive expedition to defeat her at Nasu, and the slain nine-tailed fox changes into the Murder Stone (Sesshō-seki), her evil living on into the afterworld.

---

p115

42

藤原秀郷百足退治図
Fujiwara no Hidesato Battling the Giant Centipede
(*Fujiwara no Hidesato Mukade Taiji no Zu*)
琵琶湖に架かる瀬田の唐橋に大蛇が出没して橋を渡る者はいなくなったが、通りがかった藤原秀郷（俵藤太）は大蛇を恐れることなく踏みつぶして渡っていった。その夜、秀郷のもとに美女があらわれた。話を聞くと美女は大蛇に変じて瀬田の唐橋にいた琵琶湖に棲む龍神で、龍神を悩ます三上山の大百足退治を勇猛な武者である秀郷に頼みに来たのであった。かくて、秀郷は弓と名刀でついに大百足を退治した。瀬田の唐橋で三上山から出現した大百足を退治するという名場面は種々の錦絵に取り上げられたが、この作品もその一つで、中央に大きく大百足を描いて襲って来る迫真を見

事に表現している。

None dared cross the Chinese Bridge of Seta over Lake Biwa which was frequented by a giant serpent, until passerby Fujiwara no Hidesato (Tawara no Tōta) stomped over the bridge undaunted by the monster. That night, a beautiful woman appeared to Hidesato. She told him that she was a dragon deity of Lake Biwa who had taken the form of the serpent on the bridge, and because of his bravery she had come to ask him to defeat the giant centipede of Mount Mikami which had been preying on the dragons. Consequently, at long last Hidesato defeated the giant centipede with his bow and noted sword. The great scene of the battle with the giant centipede from Mount Mikami on the Seta Bridge has been the subject of many *nishiki-e*; this work beautifully captures the scene with a vivid depiction of the giant centipede on the attack in the center.

---

p118

44

応挙之幽霊
Ōkyo's Ghost (*Ōkyo no Yūrei*)
二丁掛の上部に描かれている。円山応挙が幽霊画を得意としていたことはよく知られているが、芳年はそれをテーマとして意表を突く作品として仕上げている。応挙の描いた幽霊があまりにも真に迫り、命を宿して紙から飛び出して描いた応挙も驚愕しているところだ。それくらいに応挙の幽霊画は高い評価を得ていたのであり、戯画的筆致のなかにも芳年の応挙に対するリスペクトの一端が垣間見える作品だ。下半分には雪舟が小坊主のときに絵ばかり描いているので住職に柱に縛られると流した涙で足で鼠を描き、その鼠がまるで生きているようだったという故事を描き、応挙の幽霊と対応させている。

The upper panel of the set of two. Maruyama Ōkyo's special knack for pictures of ghosts was well-known; Yoshitoshi used this fact as a subject for this work with a twist in the tail. The ghost drawn by Ōkyo is so realistic that it comes to life and flies out of the paper, terrifying its creator. So high was the regard for Ōkyo's portrayals of ghosts that even in caricature this work offers a glimpse of Yoshitoshi's deep respect for Ōkyo. To contrast with Ōkyo's ghost, the lower panel depicts the story of how Sesshū as a young monk was tied to a pole by the chief priest as punishment for his idle habit of constantly doodling, and used his feet and flowing tears to draw mice which looked just as real as living creatures.

---

p147

萬国道下尽之内 もうこじん
'The Mongol' from *A Series of Caricatures of Nationalities* (*Bankoku Dōke Tsukushi no Uchi: Mōkojin*)
幕末の開国によって外国の文物や外国人を画題とした錦絵も各種出されるようになったが、この作品は「萬国道下尽」とのタイトルからもわかるように各国人を面白おかしく描いたシリーズで、上と下に別々のテーマで配した二丁掛となっている。このうち、上の蒙古人を描いた絵は吹矢で的に当てるとさまざまな作り物が現れるという遊びだが、ここでは狸の八畳敷が海坊主となって波間から出現したのでびっくりして腰を抜かす蒙古人を描いている。こうした吹矢遊びにも妖怪を登場させて驚かせることも少なからず行われていた。

As Japan ended isolationist foreign policy in the latter days of the Tokugawa shogunate, a great variety of prints depicting foreigners and foreign culture began to appear; as the title A Series of Caricatures of Nationalities suggests, this work is one of a series caricaturing different nationalities, with the upper and lower panels addressing separate themes. The upper panel featuring the Mongol depicts a blowgun game in which fake monsters pop up when a target is hit; an eight-tatami raccoon dog turns into a sea bonze (*umibōzu*) and appears from the waves, scaring the Mongol so badly his legs give way. Yokai popping up to scare people were used in a variety of situations such as this blowgun game.

---

p205

道成寺

Dōjōji Temple (*Kasukabe* papier-mache)
蛇と化して安珍を追ってきた清姫によって鐘のなかに隠れた安珍は焼き殺されたという有名な伝説は絵巻をはじめ数多く描かれ、デザインされてきた。この張子もその一つで、髪を振り乱した清姫の胴体は蛇となり、逃げだす安珍の姿も描かれて火が吹き出しているのも見える。全体は大きな鐘のデザインだ。底に春日部張子のラベルが貼ってあり、埼玉県春日部市で復活された張子人形。

The famous legend of how Princess Kiyohime changed into a snake to pursue Anchin and how he was burnt to death hiding from her inside a bell has been the subject of many picture scrolls and other works. This papier-mache features the upper body of Princess Kiyohime with her hair in disarray changing into a snake; the fleeing figure of Anchin and a burst of flames are also visible. The overall shape is a large bell. On the bottom is a Kasukabe papier-mache label showing that this papier-mache figurine was restored in Kasukabe City, Saitama Prefecture.

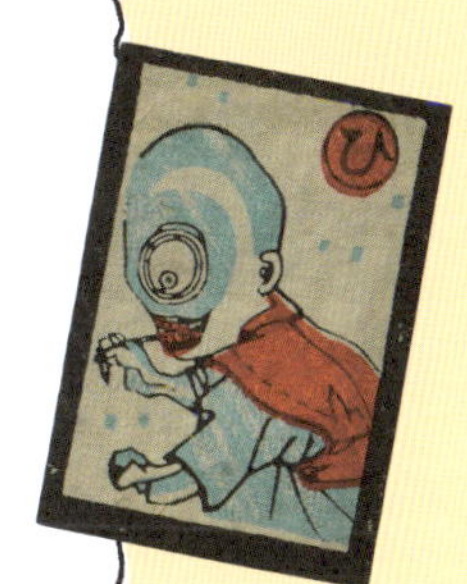

Koichi Yumoto (b. 1950)

Collector and researcher of yokai art. Former
curatorial director of the Kawasaki City Museum.
His first bilingual book on yokai, *Yokai Museum: The
Art of Japanese Supernatural Beings from YUMOTO
Koichi Collection* (PIE International) is a worldwide
seller, and a number of his Japanese-language
titles are well-renowned, such as *Kawaii Yōkai-ga
(Cute Yokai)* and *Japanese Supernatural
Beings* (both published by TOKYO BIJUTSU).

About the YUMOTO Koichi collection

The largest collection of yokai art in Japan: over
5,000 works which range from the Edo period
(16-19th centuries) to the present day. These
include paintings, woodblock prints, scrolls,
ceramics, kimonos, wooden sculptures, magazines,
children's toys, board games, and more. In 2019,
the collection was gifted to the Yumoto Koichi
Memorial Japan Yokai Museum (Miyoshi Mononoke
Museum), Hiroshima.

YOKAI WONDERLAND
More from YUMOTO Koichi Collection:
Supernatural Beings in Japanese Art

Copyright © 2017 Koichi Yumoto / PIE International

All rights reserved. No part of this book may be reproduced in any
form or by any means without written permission from the publisher.

ISBN 978-4-7562-4973-9 (Outside Japan)

Written by Koichi Yumoto
Translated by Sharni Wilson
Designed by Yuko Shoji （karera）
Icon Illustrations by Shinji Abe （karera）
DTP by Emi Kohei
Photographs by Nobuhiro Sakamoto
Edited by Eriko Hara

Printed in Japan

PIE International Inc.
2-32-4 Minami-Otsuka, Toshimaku, Tokyo
170-0005 JAPAN
international@ pie.co.jp

湯本豪一

1950 年生まれ。妖怪研究・蒐集家。元川崎市市民ミュージアム学芸室長。おもな著作に『今昔妖怪大鑑』（パイインターナショナル）、『日本の幻獣図譜：大江戸不思議生物出現録』・『かわいい妖怪画』（ともに東京美術）などがある。

湯本豪一コレクション

約5000 点からなる日本最大の妖怪コレクション。時代は近世から現代まで、ジャンルは絵巻や掛軸などの肉筆画から版本や錦絵などの木版画、着物や金工などの工芸、民芸、玩具まで幅広い。2019年、広島県三次市に開館した「湯本豪一記念 日本妖怪博物館（三次もののけミュージアム）」に寄贈された。

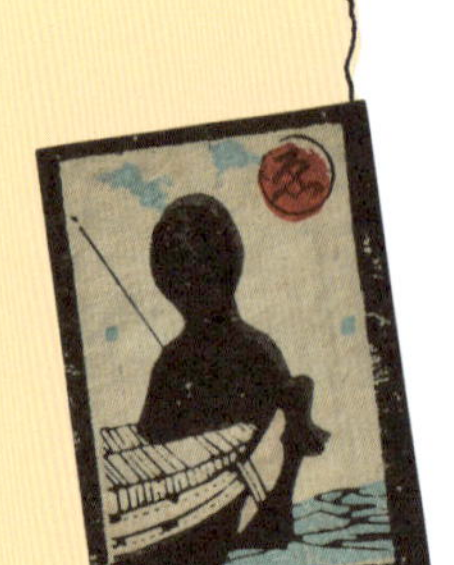

古今妖怪纍纍　湯本豪一コレクション

2017 年 7 月 18 日　初版第 1 刷発行
2022 年 1 月 14 日　　　第 2 刷発行

著者　　湯本豪一
翻訳　　シャーニ・ウィルソン
デザイン　庄子結香（カレラ）
アイコンイラスト　阿部伸二（カレラ）
DTP　　公平恵美
撮影　　坂本敦宏
校正　　株式会社 鷗来堂
編集　　原 瑛莉子

発行人　三芳寛要
発行元　株式会社 パイ インターナショナル
　　　　〒 170-0005　東京都豊島区南大塚 2-32-4
　　　　TEL 03-3944-3981　FAX 03-5395-4830
　　　　sales@pie.co.jp

印刷　　株式会社 広済堂ネクスト

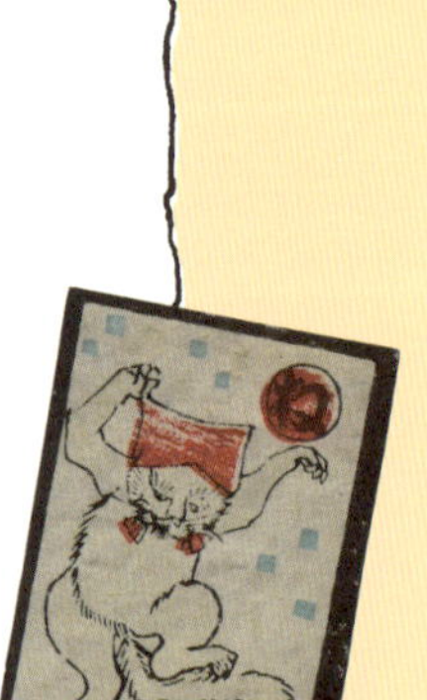